EYEWITNESS TRAVEL

BELGIUM AND LUXEMBOURG

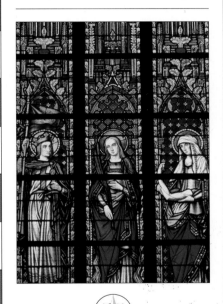

EYEWITNESS TRAVEL

BELGIUM AND LUXEMBOURG

MAIN CONTRIBUTOR: ANTONY MASON

LONDON, NEW YORK,
MELBOURNE, MUNICH AND DELHI
www.dk.com

MANAGING EDITOR Aruna Ghose
SENIOR EDITORIAL MANAGER Savitha Kumar
SENIOR DESIGN MANAGER Priyanka Thakur
PROJECT EDITOR Sandhya Iyer
PROJECT DESIGNER Stuti Tiwari Bhatia
EDITOR Shalini Krishan
DESIGNER Namrata Adhwaryu
SENIOR CARTOGRAPHIC MANAGER Uma Bhattacharya
CARTOGRAPHER Jasneet Arora
DTP DESIGNER Azeem Siddique
SENIOR PICTURE RESEARCH COORDINATOR Taiyaba Khatoon
PICTURE RESEARCHER Shweta Andrews

MAIN CONTRIBUTOR Antony Mason

PHOTOGRAPHERS Lynne McPeake, Paul Tait

ILLUSTRATORS
Surat Kumar, Arun Pottirayil, T. Gautam Trivedi

Printed and bound in Malaysia by Vivar Printing Sdn Bhd

First published in the UK in 2009
by Dorling Kindersley Limited
80 Strand, London, WC2R 0RL, UK

13 14 15 16 10 9 8 7 6 5 4 3 2 1

Reprinted with revisions 2011, 2013

Copyright © 2009, 2013 Dorling Kindersley Limited, London
A Penguin Company

*Front cover main image: Group of people at a sidewalk café,
Grote Market, Veurne, Flanders, Belgium*

MIX
Paper from
responsible sources
FSC™ C018179
www.fsc.org

**The information in this
DK Eyewitness Travel Guide is checked regularly.**
Every effort has been made to ensure that this book is as up-to-date
as possible at the time of going to press. Some details, however,
such as telephone numbers, opening hours, prices, gallery hanging
arrangements and travel information are liable to change. The
publishers cannot accept responsibility for any consequences arising
from the use of this book, nor for any material on third party
websites, and cannot guarantee that any website address in this
book will be a suitable source of travel information. We value the
views and suggestions of our readers very highly. Please write to:
Publisher, DK Eyewitness Travel Guides, Dorling Kindersley,
80 Strand, London, WC2R 0RL, UK, or email: travelguides@dk.com.

◁ The Grand Place, centre of Brussels's Lower Town, at night

CONTENTS

HOW TO USE THIS
GUIDE **6**

Carvings on cathedral door depicting
the Last Judgement, Antwerp

INTRODUCING
BELGIUM AND
LUXEMBOURG

Vibrant, colourful costumes at the
Pageant of the Golden Tree, Bruges

Vineyards stretching across the wine making commune of Remich, along the banks of River Moselle, Luxembourg

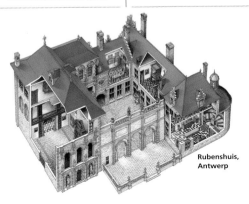

Rubenshuis,
Antwerp

HOW TO USE THIS GUIDE

This guide helps you get the most from your visit to Belgium and Luxembourg. It provides detailed practical information and expert recommendations. *Introducing Belgium and Luxembourg* maps the countries and their regions, sets them in historical and cultural context and describes events through the entire year. *Belgium and Luxembourg Region by Region* is the main sightseeing section. It covers all the important sights, with maps, photographs and illustrations. Information on hotels, restaurants, shops, entertainment and sports is found in *Travellers' Needs*. The *Survival Guide* has advice on everything from travel to medical services, telephones and post offices.

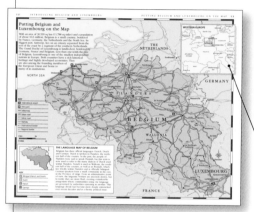

BELGIUM AND LUXEMBOURG ON THE MAP

The orientation map shows the location of Belgium and Luxembourg in relation to their neighbouring countries. Belgium has been divided into six main sightseeing areas, while Luxembourg has been covered as a whole. These seven sections are dealt with in separate chapters in *Belgium and Luxembourg Region by Region*.

A locator map shows where you are in relation to other European countries.

BELGIUM AND LUXEMBOURG REGION BY REGION

Each of the seven regions in this book starts with an introduction and a map. The best places to visit have been numbered on a *Regional Map* at the beginning of each chapter. The key to the map symbols is on the back flap.

1 Brussels
Belgium's capital, dealt with in a separate section, is divided into two sightseeing areas, each with its own chapter. The city centre is shown in detail on the Brussels Street Finder maps on pages 92–7.

All sights are numbered on a map. Detailed information on each sight follows the map's numerical order.

2 Belgium and Luxembourg's Top Sights
These are given two full pages. Historic buildings are dissected to reveal their interiors.

The visitors' checklist provides all the practical information needed to plan your visit.

The list of star features recommends the details that no visitor should miss.

3 Introduction
The landscape, history and character of each region is outlined here, revealing how the area has developed over the centuries and what it offers visitors today.

Each region can be quickly identified by its colour coding. A complete list of colour codes is shown on the inside front cover.

Sights at a Glance lists the chapter's sights by category: Castles, Abbeys, Museums, Historic buildings, Areas of Natural Beauty and so on.

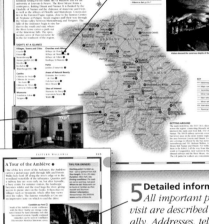

4 Regional Map
This map shows the road network and gives an illustrated overview of the region. All the sights are numbered and there are also useful tips on getting around.

5 Detailed information
All important places to visit are described individually. Addresses, telephone numbers, opening hours and information on admission charges and wheelchair access is also provided.

Driving tours explore areas of exceptional interest in the region.

The information block provides the details needed to visit each sight. Map references locate the sights on the road map on the inside back cover.

6 Street-by-Street Map
This gives a bird's-eye view of the key area in each chapter.

A suggested route for a walk is shown in red.

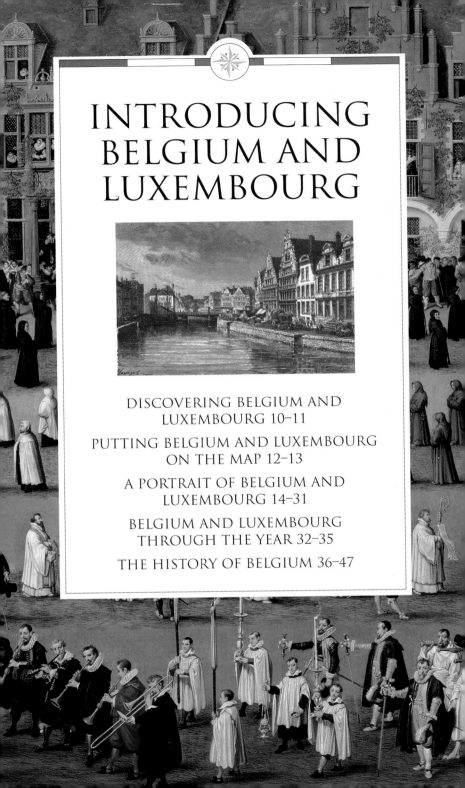

INTRODUCING BELGIUM AND LUXEMBOURG

DISCOVERING BELGIUM AND LUXEMBOURG

Visitors to Belgium and Luxembourg are generally amazed at the kaleidoscope of experiences and attractions on offer. Based on language and culture, Belgium is split into Dutch-speaking Flanders in the north and French-speaking Wallonia in the south. Flanders is famous for its historically great trading cities, such

Quadriga on the Jubelpark arch, Brussels

as Bruges, Ghent and Antwerp, which retain much ornate architecture from their past. Wallonia and Luxembourg have a more rugged landscape, being part of the hilly and forested Ardennes, and both are dotted with cathedrals and châteaux. Museums in these regions explore every subject from lace and paintings to motorcars and chocolate.

Elaborate guildhouses surrounding Brussels's Grand Place

(see p132). In the southern stretches of Western Flanders are the battlefields of World War I and their unremitting cemeteries. In **Ieper** (see p124), the museum called In Flanders Fields recounts the harrowing tales with moving dignity.

BRUSSELS

- Historic centre
- Top museums
- Mould-breaking Art Nouveau

Belgium's debonair capital is best known for its magnificent centrepiece, the beautiful and theatrical **Grand Place** (see pp56–7), which has ornate guildhouses and friendly bar-cafés. Pedestrianized streets, outdoor restaurants and innumerable shopping opportunities add to the pleasure of exploring this area. Beyond this centre are a number of exquisite Art Nouveau buildings, most notably the **Musée Horta** (see p80) and the **Musée des Instruments de Musique** (see p65). Among the city's treasures are the great national art museums, **Musées Royaux des Beaux-Arts** (see pp68–73), which house some of Rubens's finest paintings and many Brueghels as well as the Musée Magritte. A museum much

loved by all ages is the home of Tintin, **Centre Belge de la Bande Dessinée** (see p62).

WESTERN FLANDERS

- Medieval Bruges and Ghent
- The North Sea coast
- World War I battlefields

Nudging the low beaches and nature reserves of the North Sea coast, Western Flanders is most popular for its two great trading cities – **Bruges** (see pp108–117) and **Ghent** (see pp130–35). Bruges is a medieval city in miniature, mirrored in its tranquil canals, but the streets have an upbeat vibrancy. Two outstanding art museums contain classic work by Flemish masters – the **Groeninge Museum** (see pp114–15) and **Memling in Sint-Janshospitaal Museum** (see p113). Ghent is as old, but bigger and with a university and the **St-Baafskathedraal**

CENTRAL AND EASTERN FLANDERS

- Fashion in Antwerp
- Tranquil abbeys
- Rural traditions in Bokrijk

Home to Belgium's most important port-city, **Antwerp** (see pp144–55), Central and Eastern Flanders is characterized by a leisurely pace and open spaces. Wealthy in medieval times, Antwerp flourished again in the age of Rubens, whose restored home, the **Rubenshuis** (see pp150–51), is a monument to the swagger of his era. In recent times, the city has become a sparkling hub of contemporary fashion design, as reflected in its shops. Further east, the venerable university town of **Leuven** (see pp160–61) contains the most beautiful Gothic town hall in Belgium. The Premonstratensian Order of monks was attracted by the tranquillity of this region, founding monasteries at **Tongerlo** (see p157) and **Averbode**

Painting in St-Baafskathedraal

◁ Detail from *The Triumph of the Archduchess Isabella*, painted in 1616 by Denys van Alsloot (1570–1628) (see p162). A major attraction in this part of Belgium is the open-air museum of **Bokrijk Openluchtmuseum** (see p167). Old Flemish farming traditions are preserved here in a collection of historical rural buildings set out in the park.

WESTERN WALLONIA

- **Cathédrale Notre-Dame in Tournai**
- **Rich industrial heritage**
- **Castles and châteaux**

Once the wealthy industrial powerhouse of Belgium, the mining and smelting region around **Charleroi** (see p187) and **Mons** (see p189) have fascinating heritage sites, such as gigantic boat lifts and mining museums. Western Wallonia is also known for its magnificent castles, most notably at **Attre** (see p185), **Seneffe** (see p187) and above all, at **Beloeil** (see p186). The enduring historical importance of this region can be witnessed at one of Belgium's most striking and awe-inspiring cathedrals, the Cathédrale Notre-Dame in **Tournai** (see pp180–84).

CENTRAL WALLONIA

- **River Meuse**
- **Battlefield of Waterloo**
- **Stalactite-filled caves**

Sweeping through the landscape of rolling hills and agricultural land that mark Central Wallonia is the great artery of the south, the **River Meuse** (see p206). Limestone beds and streams cover this part of Belgium, as a result of which, the region is pitted with caves (see pp208–209) dripping extravagantly with stalactites. **Namur** (see p202–203), the capital of Wallonia, contains some of the finest examples of medieval Mosan (literally, of the Meuse) gold, silver and enamel work. In the north, close to Brussels, is the field of **Waterloo** (see pp196–7) with many memorials to its famous battle.

The long colonnaded nave at Tournai's Cathédrale Notre-Dame

EASTERN WALLONIA

- **Great museums in Liège**
- **Beauty of the Ardennes**
- **Memories of the Ardennes Offensive**

Most of Eastern Wallonia is given over to the pristine hills, forests and river valleys of the **Ardennes** (see pp174–5). In the north is **Liège** (see pp216–19), businesslike and full of verve, with two superb museums. The Musée Grand Curtius presents a world-class collection of decorative arts and Musée de la Vie Wallonne is an exemplary museum on local social history, traditions and crafts. For a walk in wild, untamed landscape and even cross-country skiing, the Liègeois head for the high moorland of **Hautes Fagnes** (see p223). Further south, the switchback hills and valleys of the Ardennes were once the scene of the famed Ardennes Offensive of 1944–5, remembered in many museums and monuments, particularly at **Bastogne** (see p230). In the far south, the classic hill-top **Château-Fort de Bouillon** (see 232–3) speaks of the distant age of the crusading knights.

GRAND DUCHY OF LUXEMBOURG

- **Luxembourg City, the astonishing capital**
- **Vineyards of River Moselle**
- **Charming landscape of Little Switzerland**

The jewel in the Grand Duchy's crown is its capital, **Luxembourg City** (see 240–45). Spectacularly perched over a sheer ravine, it was one of the strongest citadels in Europe and retains such mementos of its past as the network of casemates that riddle the cliffs. However, many visitors also come to Luxembourg to explore its unspoilt landscape and nature, particularly in the area known as Petite Suisse (Little Switzerland) near **Echternach** (see p250). In the north are imposing medieval castles. Among them, the château at **Clervaux** (see p252) is notable as the home of Edward Steichen's astounding collection of photographs, The Family of Man. No visit to this country is complete without a pilgrimage to its wine making region around the **River Moselle** (see p249).

River Sûre looping around Esch-sur-Sûre, Grand Duchy of Luxembourg

Putting Belgium and Luxembourg on the Map

With an area of 30,530 sq km (11,788 sq miles) and a population of about 11 million, Belgium is a small country, bordered by France, Germany, the Netherlands and the North Sea. Its biggest port, Antwerp, lies on an estuary separated from the rest of the coast by a segment of the southern Netherlands. The Grand Duchy of Luxembourg is landlocked, bordered by Germany, France and Belgium. Less than one-tenth the size of Belgium, Luxembourg is one of the smallest independent nations in Europe. Both countries have a rich historical heritage and highly developed economies. They are also among the founding members of the European Union and home to many of its institutions.

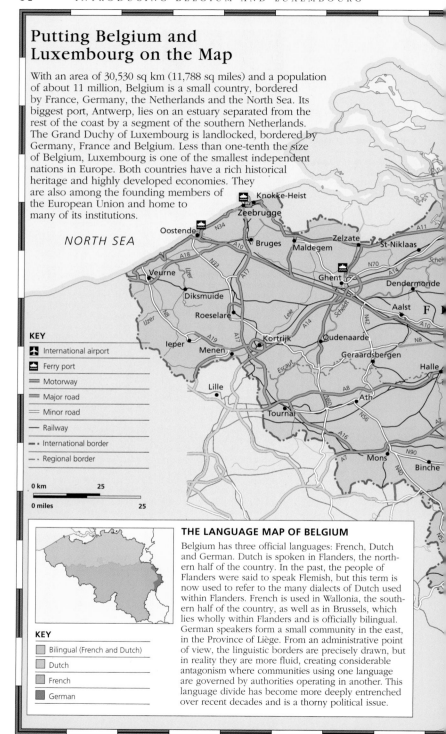

NORTH SEA

Knokke-Heist
Zeebrugge
Oostende
Bruges
Maldegem
Zelzate
St-Niklaas
Ghent
Dendermonde
Aalst
Veurne
Diksmuide
Roeselare
Ieper
Menen
Kortrijk
Oudenaarde
Geraardsbergen
Halle
Lille
Ath
Tournai
Mons
Binche

KEY

✈ International airport
⛴ Ferry port
═══ Motorway
═══ Major road
═══ Minor road
── Railway
──· International border
──· Regional border

0 km   25
0 miles   25

THE LANGUAGE MAP OF BELGIUM

Belgium has three official languages: French, Dutch and German. Dutch is spoken in Flanders, the northern half of the country. In the past, the people of Flanders were said to speak Flemish, but this term is now used to refer to the many dialects of Dutch used within Flanders. French is used in Wallonia, the southern half of the country, as well as in Brussels, which lies wholly within Flanders and is officially bilingual. German speakers form a small community in the east, in the Province of Liège. From an administrative point of view, the linguistic borders are precisely drawn, but in reality they are more fluid, creating considerable antagonism where communities using one language are governed by authorities operating in another. This language divide has become more deeply entrenched over recent decades and is a thorny political issue.

KEY

▢ Bilingual (French and Dutch)
▢ Dutch
▢ French
▢ German

WESTERN EUROPE

THE NETHERLANDS

GERMANY

BELGIUM

WALLONIA

LUXEMBOURG

FRANCE

A PORTRAIT OF BELGIUM AND LUXEMBOURG

Tied together by a shared and complex history, Belgium and Luxembourg are two of the most prosperous countries in western Europe. This is manifest in their rich cultural traditions, the fine art and architecture of the towns, the high quality of cuisine and the genuine warmth with which visitors are welcomed.

Both countries are small. The Kingdom of Belgium, with its capital at Brussels, has a population of some 11 million. More than 90 per cent of the citizens live in urban centres, leaving relatively uninhabited the large areas of farmland in the north as well as the wilder Ardennes in the south. The Ardennes spill over into the Grand Duchy of Luxembourg. This tiny yet independent country has a population of just 512,000. Its capital, Luxembourg City, has about 95,000 inhabitants.

The histories of both countries are closely linked. They are both fairly young nations, in that they became fully independent only in the 1830s.

Belgian lace fan

For centuries before this, they were ruled by a succession of foreign powers: Romans, Franks, French, Spanish, Burgundians, Austrians and the Dutch. They have been fought over ceaselessly, and suffered particularly in the 20th century during the two World Wars.

This bruising history at the hands of their neighbours made Belgium and Luxembourg avid supporters of the European Union (EU) from the start. Today, both Brussels and Luxembourg City play host to many of the EU's major institutions. Along with Strasbourg in France, they are effectively capitals of the EU.

Remnants of medieval walls surrounding the Old Town of Luxembourg City

◁ Revellers at the costumed Ommegang festival in Brussels's Grand Place

The medieval château of Bourscheid, nestling in the remote forests of Luxembourg's Ardennes

LAND AND NATURE

Belgium has the reputation of being a flat country. However, without ever being mountainous, much of the land is, in fact, hilly. This is also the case in Luxembourg, whose capital is perched spectacularly on a rocky escarpment.

Broadly speaking, the landscape of Belgium and Luxembourg can be divided into three distinct zones. The northwest of Belgium is fairly flat and low-lying. However, the land rises in the central band on either side of Brussels. To the west, the area around Oudenaarde is hilly enough to have earned the name, the Flemish Ardennes. To the east of Brussels, productive farmlands cover the hills of the Hageland in Flemish Brabant and the Haspengouw (Hesbaye in French) in southern Limburg. The climate is mild and the land well watered: grapes grown in this area make high-quality Belgian wine.

The third zone is the Ardennes, which covers southeastern Belgium and northern parts of Luxembourg. Once dismissed as remote and underdeveloped, the Ardennes is now a magnet for people who cherish natural beauty. Much of the landscape rests on limestone karst, riddled with spectacular rock formations and caves.

These wilder regions are home to a rich diversity of wildlife that includes eagle owls, black grouse and wild boar. The coastal region of Belgium is on the migratory routes of egrets, spoonbills and storks. Both nations readily appreciate their natural heritage and are wary of the threats posed by uncontrolled development. This sensitivity is reinforced through numerous parks and nature reserves.

PEOPLE AND SOCIETY

Belgium and Luxembourg have three official languages, reflecting their geographical position on the borderlands of three major linguistic groups. Luxembourg has German and French, as well as Lëtzerburgesch, a language of the German family. Many of its people are genuinely trilingual, and switch easily between the three languages.

A flock of gulls shares the beach with walkers along the North Sea coast

Belgium is divided into two main linguistic regions. In the north is Flanders, with 59 per cent of the population. The people, known as the Flemish, speak Dutch. In the south is Wallonia, which holds 31 per cent of the population; people here speak French. Apart from these, there is a small German-speaking community in the border region of the east.

The Dutch-French language divide has existed more or less since Roman and Frankish times, in other words for 1,500 years. In spite of their differences, the Flemish and French-speaking communities have remained in geographical proximity, bonded by their religion, Catholicism. This circumstance is a result of the religious strife of the 16th century, when Protestants moved north to what is today the Netherlands; the Catholics stayed back in modern-day Belgium. Luxembourg is likewise predominantly Catholic.

High-stepping participants in medieval costume enlivening the Pageant of the Golden Tree in Bruges

Religion is still a significant presence: churches are very much a part of the landscape and most traditional rites of passage, including baptisms, weddings and funerals, are conducted through the church. Many of the carnivals, so prevalent in the calendar of events, are religious in origin, and some, such as the Procession of the Penitents at Veurne, are impressive displays of devotion. However, religion does not generally play an overt role, and society is basically secular.

Dutch road signage in Belgium

Across the linguistic divides, Belgians and Luxembourgers share similar goals – to achieve comfortable lifestyles through education, hard work and enterprise. Their prosperity is reflected in international rankings of the total national wealth generated per head of population (Gross Domestic Product per capita): Belgium is 16th on the list while Luxembourg is first. Such wealth has attracted workers from all over the world. Many come from EU countries; some in Belgium have links with its colonial past in Africa, especially the Congo; others come from Muslim countries of the Mediterranean, notably Turkey and Morocco. Luxembourg's immigrants, mainly from Europe, account for 37 per cent of the total population.

Outdoor café culture, enjoyed in every town throughout the region

Modern façade of the European Parliament in Brussels, looming above a statue of industrialist John Cockerill

GOVERNMENT AND POLITICS

Belgium is a constitutional monarchy and King Albert II is the head of state. Politically, Dutch-speaking Flanders and French-speaking Wallonia have each been given their own regional governments, which has, to some degree, satisfied the desire for autonomy. However, it has also reinforced the divisions. There is an overarching federal government, based in Brussels, but intercommunal strains in recent years have resulted in unstable national governments composed of precarious and complex coalitions.

The resentment attached to Belgium's linguistic divide has a long history, dating back to the Middle Ages, when Flanders was ruled by a French-speaking elite. When Belgium began to industrialize, French-speaking Wallonia became the centre of production for coal, steel and manufactured goods. The Flemish fell victim to economic, social and cultural discrimination. This situation has been reversed in recent times. As the economy shifted towards light industries, financial services and international trade, Flanders prospered and Wallonia drifted into the doldrums. Politically, Flanders became more assertive, achieving ever greater degrees of self-rule. However, new resentments grew in these changed circumstances.

Luxembourg is also a constitutional monarchy. The head of state is the grand duke, who has genuine authority over an elected government. The grand ducal family has strong dynastic ties to Belgium – the mother of Grand Duke Henri, the present incumbent, was Princess Joséphine-Charlotte of Belgium, older sister to King Albert II. However, it would be a mistake to think that Luxembourg lives in Belgium's slipstream. Small it may be, but Luxembourg is an utterly independent country with its own distinct culture and identity.

THE ECONOMY

Belgium has a mixed economy of manufacturing, agriculture, trade, financial services and knowledge-based industries such as pharmaceuticals, biotechnology and information and communication technology. Its old traditional industries, such as steel and chemicals, are now mainly in the hands of multinational companies. The prime exports are foodstuffs, textiles, iron and steel, cars and plastics. Antwerp in Flanders is world leader

The old docks at Antwerp, Belgium's most important port-city

Palatial office of the international steel giant Arcelor Mittal in Luxembourg City

in the trade and processing of raw diamonds. Belgium also benefits financially from being the primary centre of EU administration. Tourism is a key sector as well, with its main focus on Brussels and the Flemish cities of Antwerp, Bruges and Ghent.

Luxembourg's largest industry used to be the production of high-quality steel. These days, financial services, banking and insurance, are the main income earners. The country also houses numerous major international Internet companies.

Diamonds from Antwerp

ART AND SPORT

Historically, Belgium is known for having produced some of the finest art and architecture in Europe. This includes the pioneering oil painting of Jan van Eyck and his contemporaries, Rubens's spectacular Baroque canvases, Victor Horta's Art Nouveau style as well as the Surrealism of René Magritte and Paul Delvaux. Like its neighbour, Luxembourg also has an outstanding art scene, boosted by the opening of the prestigious Musée d'Art Modern Grand-Duc Jean (MUDAM) in 2006. Similar dynamism has been shown in ballet and film, and also in fashion, where Antwerp-based designers in particular number

among the industry's most respected names. In the world of books, the Belgian authors Georges Simenon, creator of Inspector Maigret, and Hergé, creator of Tintin, rank among the world's top-selling authors.

Both Belgium and Luxembourg produce talented sportsmen, who acquit themselves well at the Olympics, especially in the fields of judo, high-jump and athletics. Belgium has produced outstanding tennis players in recent years, notably world champions Kim Clijsters and Justine Henin. Both countries excel in professional cycling, with 22 winners of the Tour de France between them. This includes Belgian Eddie Merckx, considered the greatest professional cyclist ever.

Belgium's champion cyclist Eddy Merckx leading the race at Vincennes, 21 July 1974

Landscape and Wildlife

The common heath moth

Belgium has a misleading reputation for being a flat country. This is only true of the northwest, where polders of drained coastal marshes form large expanses of rich green pastures. The central band of the country features undulating farmland, while to the southeast, the terrain rises progressively into the dramatic hills and scenic forests of the Ardennes. The rivers Sambre and Meuse slice through central Belgium, forming a natural northern boundary to the Ardennes. Belgium's wildlife reflects this diversity in landscape with a full cross-section of North European flora and fauna, from deer, wild boar and eagle owls in the Ardennes to the huge flocks of migratory birds that visit the coast.

Limestone caves at Han-sur-Lesse in the Belgian Ardennes

THE COAST

Along Belgium's North Sea shore, sandy beaches slope gently to the sea, creating a long tidal reach. Resorts now line the coast, protected by high dykes, but the old dune landscapes at the eastern and western ends have been preserved as wildlife sanctuaries.

RICH FARMLANDS AND POLDERS

Just inland from the coast, fertile arable land, interspersed with woodland, rises towards a central band. Grain, sugarbeet, vegetables and fruit are grown here. The Pajottenland, Hageland and Haspengouw regions pride themselves on their agricultural produce.

The pink-footed goose (Anser brachyrhynchus) *is among the seasonal visitors to the coast, overwintering to the south of its breeding grounds in the Arctic.*

The red squirrel (Sciurus vulgaris) *is seen around the woodlands, where it nests in conifer trees.*

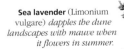

Sea lavender (Limonium vulgare) *dapples the dune landscapes with mauve when it flowers in summer.*

Rosebay willowherb, *or fireweed* (Epilobium angustifolium), *is a tough perennial that lends colour to the fringes of farmland.*

The grey seal (Halichoerus grypus) *lives in the North Sea, and occasionally comes ashore.*

The brown hare (Lepus europaeus) *likes open country, farmland and orchards. Living alone or in pairs, it feeds on grasses and twigs and raises its young above ground.*

DEPLETING WILDLIFE

It is estimated that between a third and a half of Belgium's animal species are threatened with extinction. Twelve mammals are listed as either Endangered, Vulnerable or Near Threatened by the International Union for Conservation of Nature and Natural Resources (IUCN). As ever, the main causes of threat are loss of habitat, climate change, the arrival of exotic predators and pollution or other human activities that cause disturbance. The red squirrel and European otter *(Lutra lutra)* are on the Near Threatened

Bechstein's bat
(Myotis bechsteinii)

The beluga whale
(D. leucas)

list, as is the European beaver *(Castor fiber)*.
The garden dormouse *(Eliomys quercinus)* is listed as Vulnerable, along with four species of bat. But the most threatened are the Cetaceans (whales, porpoises and dolphins) in the North Sea. The harbour porpoise *(Phocoena phocoena)*, sperm whale *(Physeter macrocephalus)* and beluga or white whale *(Delphinapterus leucas)* are all Vulnerable, while the northern right whale *(Eubalaena glacialis)* is Endangered.

FORESTED ARDENNES

The Ardennes cover most of southeastern Belgium and the Oesling area of Luxembourg. Rivers thread through forested hills, with pockets of farmland in the valleys and pastures on open upland. To the south, the land drops away into the rural, wooded Gaume region.

THE MOORS

Much of eastern Belgium is covered by heath and moorland. Large parts of the Kempen (or Campine) region in the north are sandy heathlands of heather and pine woods. The wildest moors are the Hautes Fagnes in the upper Ardennes, east of Liège.

The western honey buzzard
(Pernis apivorus) *arrives in these forests during summer to breed. The bird's name derives from its habit of eating the larvae from wasp and hornet nests.*

Honey mushroom
(Armillaria mellae) *is a forest fungus that lives on the roots of trees.*

Roe deer (Capreolus capreolus) *are shy, solitary deer that live in forests and pasture, eating grasses and shoots. The males grow small antlers each year.*

The European hedgehog
(Erinaceus europaeus) *is an adaptable, mainly nocturnal mammal found in heathland.*

Harebells (Campanula rotundifolia) *are delicate bell-shaped flowers that grow wild on the moors.*

The little bustard
(Tetrax tetrax) *is a migratory bird that breeds on heaths. The male has a flamboyant mating display.*

Belgian Artists

Belgian art rose to the fore when the region came under Burgundian rule in the 15th century. Renaissance painters produced strong works in oil, characterized by intricate detail and lifelike, unidealized portraiture. Trade and artistic links with Italy provided a rich, mutual exchange of painting techniques in the perennial quest to capture visual reality. In contrast, during the 20th century, Belgium's second golden artistic age moved away from these goals, abandoning reality for Surrealism in the work of artists such as René Magritte. Brussels's Musées Royaux des Beaux-Arts *(see pp68–73)*, the Rubenshuis *(see pp150–51)* in Antwerp and the museums around St-Martens-Latem *(see p136)* are fine examples of the respect Belgium shows to its artists' works, homes and contexts.

Portrait of Laurent Froimont by Rogier van der Weyden

THE FLEMISH PRIMITIVES

Art in Brussels and Flanders first attracted European attention at the end of the Middle Ages. **Jan van Eyck** (c.1395–1441) is believed to be responsible for the major revolution in Flemish art. Widely credited as the pioneer of oil painting, van Eyck was the first artist to mix colour pigments for wood and canvas and to use the oil medium to fix longer-lasting glazes. As works could now be rendered more permanent, these innovations spread the Renaissance fashion for panel paintings. However, van Eyck was more than just a practical innovator, and can be seen as the forefather of the Flemish Primitive school, with his lively depictions of

human existence in an animated manner. Van Eyck is also responsible, with his brother, for the striking polyptych altarpiece *Adoration of the Mystic Lamb*, displayed in St-Baafskathedraal *(see pp132)* in Ghent.

The trademarks of the Flemish Primitives are a lifelike vitality, enhanced by realism in portraiture, texture of clothes and furnishings and a clarity of light. A highly expressive interpreter of the style was the town painter of Brussels, **Rogier van der Weyden** (c.1400–64), known in French as Rogier de la Pasture. He combined van Eyck's light and realism in paintings of great religious intensity such as *Lamentation (see p72)*. His work was extremely influential across Europe. **Dirk Bouts** (1415–75) applied the style to his own meticulous, if static, compositions. With his studies of

bustling 15th-century Bruges, **Hans Memling** (c.1430–94) is considered the last Flemish Primitive. Moving into the 16th century, landscape artist **Joachim Patinir** (c.1480–1524) produced the first European industrial scenes.

THE BRUEGHEL DYNASTY

In the early years of the 16th century, Belgian art was strongly influenced by the Italians. Trained in Rome, **Jan Gossaert** (c.1478–1532) brought mythological themes to the art commissioned by the ruling dukes of Brabant. However, it was the prolific Brueghel family who exercised the most influence on Flemish art throughout the 16th and 17th centuries. **Pieter Brueghel the Elder** (c.1525–69), one of the greatest Flemish artists, settled in Brussels in 1563. His earthy rustic landscapes of village life, peopled with comic peasants, are a social study of medieval life and remain his best-known work. **Pieter Brueghel the Younger** (1564–1636) produced religious works such as *The Enrolment of Bethlehem* (1610). In contrast, **Jan Brueghel the Elder** (1568–1625) painted floral still-lifes with such a smooth and detailed technique that he earned the nickname Velvet Brueghel. His son, **Jan Brueghel the Younger** (1601–78) also became a court painter in Brussels and a landscape artist of note.

The Fall of Icarus by Pieter Brueghel the Elder

Self Portrait by Rubens, one of many done by the artist

THE ANTWERP ARTISTS

In the 17th century, the main centre of Belgian art moved from Brussels, the social capital, to Antwerp, in the heart of Flanders. This shift was largely influenced by **Pieter Paul Rubens** (1577–1640), who lived in Antwerp. Rubens was one of the first Flemish artists to become known throughout Europe and in Russia. A court painter, he also served as a roving diplomat abroad. Trained in Italy, he brought a unique dynamism and swagger to painting, which chimed well with the Baroque tastes of the Counter-Reformation.

Chief assistant in Rubens's busy studio was **Anthony van Dyck** (1599–1641), the second Antwerp artist to gain European renown through his court portraiture. Another associate, **Jacob Jordaens** (1593–1678), is best known for his joyous scenes of feasting, while **David Teniers II** (1610–90) found fame with pictures of Flemish life and founded the Royal Academy of Fine Art in Antwerp.

THE EUROPEAN INFLUENCE

The influence of Rubens was so great that little innovation took place in the Flemish art scene over the 18th century. In the early years of the 19th century, Belgian art was largely dominated by the influence of other European schools. The artist **François-Joseph Navez** (1787–1869) introduced Neo-Classicism to Flemish art. Brussels-based **Antoine Wiertz** (1806–65) was considered a Romantic, but is also known for producing melodramatic works, such as the *Inhumation Précipitée* (c.1830). Realism took off with **Constantin Meunier** (1831–1905), a noted sculptor of muscular coal miners and factory workers in bronze. **Fernand Khnopff** (1858–1921) was a leading exponent of Belgian Symbolism, notable for his portraits of menacing and ambiguous women. Also on a journey from Naturalism to Expressionism was **James Ensor** (1860–1949), who often used eerie skeletons in his work, in a manner reminiscent of the 15th-century Netherlandish painter, Hieronymus Bosch. Between 1884 and 1894, the artists' cooperative **Les XX (Les Vingt)** brought together painters, designers and sculptors who reinvigorated the Brussels art scene with exhibitions of famous foreign and avant-garde painters.

Sculpture by Rik Wouters

SURREALISM

The 20th century began with the emergence of Fauvism, as reflected in the charming portraits of **Rik Wouters** (1882–1916), filled with bright counter-intuitive colour.

Surrealism arrived in Brussels in the mid-1920s, dominated from the start by **René Magritte** (1898–1967), who defined his disorientating Surrealism as "[restoring] the familiar to the strange". More ostentatious and emotional, **Paul Delvaux** (1897–1994) produced haunting, dreamlike scenes of skeletons, trams and nudes. In 1948, the **COBRA Movement** promoted abstract art, which gave way in the 1960s to conceptual art, led by installationist **Marcel Broodthaers** (1924–76), who used daily objects, such as a casserole dish of mussels, for his own interpretation.

In recent years, Belgian art has witnessed a resurgence, and a number of artists have made their mark on the international scene, notably **Panamarenko** (b. 1940), **Luc Tuymans** (b.1958) and **Wim Delvoye** (b.1965).

UNDERGROUND ART

Belgian artist Pol Bury, a noted member of the avant-garde COBRA Movement

Some 58 Brussels metro stations have been decorated with a combination of murals, sculptures and architecture by 54 Belgian artists. Only the most devoted visitor to the city is likely to see them all, but there are several notable works worth seeking out. **Annessens** was decorated by the Belgian COBRA artists, Dotremont and Alechinsky. In the **Bourse**, Surrealist Paul Delvaux's *Nos Vieux Trams Bruxellois* is still on show with *Moving Ceiling*, a series of 75 tubes that move in the breeze, by sculptor Pol Bury. At **Horta** station, Art Nouveau wrought-iron work from Victor Horta's now destroyed People's Palace is displayed, and **Stockel** is a tribute to Hergé and his boy hero, Tintin *(see pp24–5).*

Belgian Comic Strip Art

Tintin's dog Snowy

Belgian comic strip art is as much a part of Belgian culture as chocolates and beer. The seeds of this great passion were sown when the US comic strip *Little Nemo* was published in French in 1908 to huge popular acclaim in Belgium. The country's reputation for producing some of the best comic strip art in Europe was established after World War II. Before the war, Europe was awash with American comics, but the Nazis halted the supply. Local artists took over, and found that there was a large audience who preferred homegrown comic heroes. This explosion in comic strip art was led by perhaps the most famous Belgian creation ever, Tintin, who, with his dog Snowy, is as recognizable across Europe as Mickey Mouse.

his work before and during the war, as he expressed a strong sense of justice in stories such as *King Ottakar's Sceptre*, where a fascist army attempts to control a central European state. Hergé took great care in researching his books. For the 1934 *Le Lotus Bleu*, which was set in China, he wrote, "I started… showing a real interest in the people and countries I was sending Tintin off to, concerned by a sense of honesty to my readers."

Cover of the *Spirou*

Hergé, the creator of Tintin

HERGÉ AND TINTIN

Tintin's creator, Hergé, was born Georges Remi in Brussels in 1907. He began using his pen name (a phonetic spelling of his initials in reverse) in 1924. At the age of 15, his drawings were published in the *Boy Scout Journal*. He became the protégé of the priest, Abbot Norbert Wallez – who also managed the Catholic journal *Le XXe Siècle* – and was

made responsible for the children's supplement, *Le petit Vingtième*. Eager to invent an original comic, Hergé came up with the character of Tintin the reporter, who first appeared in *Tintin au Pays des Soviets* on 10 January 1929. Over the next 10 years, the character developed and grew in popularity. Book-length stories began to appear from 1930.

During the Nazi occupation in the 1940s, *Tintin* continued to be published, with political references carefully omitted, in the approved paper, *Le Soir*. This led to Hergé being accused of collaboration at the end of the war. He was called in for questioning but was released the same day without charge. His innocence was amply demonstrated by

Statue of Tintin and Snowy

POST-WAR BOOM

Belgium's oldest comic strip journal, *Spirou*, was launched in April 1938 and, along with the weekly *Journal de Tintin*, which began in 1946, became a hothouse for the artistic talent that was to flourish during the postwar years. Artists such as Morris, Jijé, Peyo and Roba worked on the journal. In 1947, Morris (1923–2001) introduced the cowboy parody *Lucky Luke*, which went on to feature in live-action films and US television cartoons. Marc Sleen, another celebrated Belgian cartoonist, was the creator of the popular character *Nibbs* (or *Nero*).

COMIC STRIP CHARACTERS

Some of the world's most loved comic strip characters originated in Belgium. *Tintin* is the most famous, but *Lucky Luke* the cowboy, *Suske en Wiske* the cheeky children and *The Smurfs* have been published worldwide. Modern artists such as Schuiten continue to break new ground.

Tintin by Hergé

Lucky Luke by Morris

During the 1960s, the idea of the comic strip being the "ninth art" (after the seventh and eighth – film and television) expanded to include adult themes in the form of the comic-strip graphic novel.

PEYO AND THE SMURFS

Best known for *The Smurfs*, Peyo (1928–92) was also a member of the team behind the *Spirou* journal that published his poetic medieval series *Johan et Pirlouit* in 1952. *The Smurfs* appeared as characters here – tiny blue people whose humorous foibles soon eclipsed any interest in the strip's main characters. Reacting to their popularity, Peyo created a strip solely about them. Set in the Smurf village, these stories were infused with satirical social comment. *The Smurfs* went on to become a craze between 1983 and 1985, and were featured in advertizing and merchandizing of every type. They spawned a feature-length film, television cartoons and popular music, and had several hit records.

Modern cover by Marvano

WILLY VANDERSTEEN

While the artists of *Spirou* and *Tintin* filled the French-language journals, Willy Vandersteen (1913–90) dominated the Dutch market. His popular creation, *Suske en Wiske* has been translated into English, appearing as *Bob and Bobette* in the UK and as *Willy and Wanda* in the US. The main characters are a pair of "ordinary" kids between 10 and 14 years of age who have extraordinary adventures all over the world, and also travel back and forth in time. Today, Vandersteen's books sell in their millions.

COMIC STRIP ART TODAY

Comic strips, known as *beeldverhaal* or *bandes dessinées*, continue to be published in Belgium in all their forms. In newspapers, children's comics and graphic novels the "ninth art" remains one of the country's biggest exports. The high standards and imaginative scope of a new generation of artists, such as Schuiten or Marvano, have fed growing consumer demand for comic books. Both French and Dutch

Contemporary comic strip artists at work in their studio

publishers issue over 22 million comic books a year. Belgian cartoons are sold in more than 30 countries.

Larger-than-life cartoon by Frank Pé adorning a Brussels building

STREET ART

There are currently 30 large comic strip images decorating the sides of buildings around Brussels's city centre. This outdoor exhibition is known as the Comic Strip Route and is organized by the Belgian Centre for Comic Strip Art, or the Centre Belge de la Bande Dessineé *(see p62)*, and by the city of Brussels. Begun in 1991 as a tribute to Belgium's talent for comic strip art, this street art project continues to grow. A free map of the route is available from tourist information offices, as well as from the comic museum itself.

Suske en Wiske by Vandersteen

The Smurfs by Peyo   **A contemporary cartoon strip by Schuiten**

Belgian Tapestry and Lace

For over six centuries, Belgian tapestry and lace have been highly prized luxury crafts. Originating in Flanders in the 12th century, tapestry has since been handmade in the centres of Tournai, Brussels, Oudenaarde and Mechelen. The lace trade was prac-

Lace-maker's studio sign

tised from the 16th century onwards in all Belgian provinces. Bruges and Brussels in particular were renowned for their delicate work. The makers of this finery often had aristocratic patrons, as grand tapestries and intricate lace were status symbols of the nobility and staple exports throughout Europe from the 15th to the 18th century. Today, Belgium remains home to the very best tapestry and lace studios in the world.

Tapestry weavers *numbered over 50,000 in Flanders from 1450 to 1550. With the dukes of Burgundy as patrons, hangings grew more elaborate.*

Tapestry designs *involve the weaver and artist working closely together. Painters, including Rubens, produced drawings for sets of six or more tapestries illustrating grand themes.*

The texture of the weave was the finest ever achieved – often 5 threads to a cm (12 per inch).

Weavers working today *in Mechelen and Tournai still use medieval techniques to produce contemporary tapestry, woven to modern designs.*

TAPESTRY

By 1200, the town of Tournai and nearby Arras (now in France) were known as centres of weaving across Europe. Prized by the nobility, tapestries were portable and could be moved with the court as rulers travelled over their estates. As trade grew, techniques were refined. Real gold and silver were threaded into the fine wool, again increasing the value. Blending Italian idealism with Flemish realism, Bernard van Orley (1492–1542) revolutionized tapestry designs, as in *The Battle of Pavia*, the first of a series. Flemish weavers were eventually lured across Europe, and this transfer of skill led to the success of the Gobelins factory in Paris that finally stole Flanders's crown in the late 1700s.

Lace trade *rose to the fore during the early Renaissance. Emperor Charles V decreed that lace-making should be a compulsory skill for girls in convents and béguinages (see p61) throughout Flanders. Lace became fashionable on collars and cuffs for both sexes. Trade reached a peak in the 18th century.*

The Battle of Pavia (1525) is an example of the complex themes that were popular for tapestry series.

Lace-makers, *creating intricate work by hand, are traditionally women. Although their numbers are dwindling, many craftswomen still work in Bruges and Brussels, the centres of bobbin lace.*

The Victorian fashion for lace *triggered a revival of the craft after its decline in the austere Neo-Classical period. Although men no longer wore it, the use of lace as a ladies' accessory and in soft furnishing led to its renewed popularity.*

Belgian lace *is bought today mainly as a souvenir. Despite competition from the machine-made lace of other countries, the quality here still remains as fine as it was in the Renaissance.*

Architecture

Throughout its history, Belgium's international bonds have linked it to the changing trends of European architecture. It was first influenced by Romans, then by the Christian Church and later by styles from across trans-European trade routes. Belgian architecture mirrored trends in Italy and France, moving from Romanesque through Gothic to Baroque and Neo-Classical. However, it always added its own distinctive touches, as seen in the robust muscularity of Scheldt Gothic, in the graceful Brabant Gothic and in the Flamboyant Gothic of town halls. In the 1890s, Belgian architects pioneered the Art Nouveau style.

St-Romboutskathedraal *in Mechelen is a masterpiece of Brabant Gothic. After three centuries, work ceased suddenly in 1546, leaving the tower unfinished.*

St-Niklaaskerk *in Ghent (see pp132–3) was built between the 13th and 15th centuries in the austere and elegant Scheldt (or Scaldian) Gothic.*

1000	1100	1200	1300	1400
ROMANESQUE			GOTHIC	
1000	1100	1200	1300	1400

The Collégiale Ste-Gertrude *(built 1046) at Nivelles is in the Romanesque style called Ottonian, with the high, turreted Westbau (see p199) forming a second transept.*

Cathédrale Sts-Michel-et-Gudule *(see p63) is constructed mainly in the Brabant Gothic style of the 14th and 15th centuries.*

The Stadhuis *in Leuven (see p160) was built between 1439 and 1463 and is the most magnificent example of a secular Flamboyant Gothic building in Belgium. Its façades are encrusted with elaborate stonework of lace-like intricacy, and hundreds of fine statues and carvings.*

Antwerp's Stadhuis *(built 1561–4), shows how Renaissance architecture was adapted with creative swagger to produce a Flemish Renaissance style. This is seen particularly in the crest of its centrepiece, with sculpture and gilding adding flair to the Classical columns and pediment.*

Maison St Cyr *(see p75), a private mansion in Brussels, is an extravagant example of Art Nouveau architecture. Designed by the 25-year-old architect Gustave Strauven and completed in 1903, its swirling ironwork is characteristic of this "new art" that made no reference to any architectural style that had come before it.*

St-Carolus Borromeuskerk in Antwerp was the first Baroque church in Belgium.

The Grand Place *in Brussels (see p56–7) is lined with guildhouses that were rebuilt after 1695 in the Baroque manner. This style was an exuberant elaboration of Renaissance forms.*

1500	1600	1700	1800	1900
RENAISSANCE	BAROQUE	NEO-CLASSICAL	ECLECTIC	ART NOUVEAU
1500	1600	1700	1800	1900

Kasteel Ooidonk, built in 1595 as a grand country residence in Flemish Renaissance style, shows Spanish influence in its bulb-shaped spires.

The St-Servaasbasiliek at Grimbergen, built between 1660 and 1725, is one of the great Baroque churches of Belgium, a bold, triumphant expression of the Counter-Reformation.

The Oude Griffie *in Bruges was built in Renaissance style over 1534–7. Its rectangular windows and Classical columns represented a complete break from the pointed arches of the Gothic style.*

The 14th-century belfry of Tournai, with a carillon of 43 bells

BELFRIES

A symbol of civic pride, the town belfry was used in medieval times to sound an alarm bell as well as to mark the passing of hours. Belfries are built with spiral staircases that lead up through strong rooms where the city charters were kept, and then to the bell lofts and lookout positions. Belgium's belfries are UNESCO World Heritage Sites.

The Théatre Royale de la Monnaie *in Brussels, was built in Neo-Classical style in 1819 and resembles a Greek temple.*

Castles and Châteaux

Belgium has the distinction of having more castles in a given area than any other country in Europe. Luxembourg might come a close second. These castles range from romantic medieval ruins and stern fortresses built for defence, to the 19th-century fantasy palaces of the super-rich. Today, many of the grander châteaux remain in private hands. However, there are plenty that admit visitors on a regular basis, providing a fascinating opportunity to explore the secular architecture of both countries' often tumultuous past from the inside.

Vianden castle *(see p251)* rising above the forested hills of Luxembourg

MEDIEVAL CASTLES

Throughout the medieval period, Viking invasions and constant squabbles between rival duchies made it essential for ruling nobles to protect their interests with robust fortresses. The castles that survived have undergone numerous transformations, but still bear witness to the age of the siege-ladder and catapult.

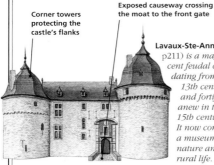

Corner towers protecting the castle's flanks

Exposed causeway crossing the moat to the front gate

Lavaux-Ste-Anne (see p211) *is a magnificent feudal castle, dating from the 13th century and fortified anew in the 15th century. It now contains a museum on nature and rural life.*

Kasteel van Beersel (see p164), *built in the 14th century, has a moat and three towers facing an inner courtyard. It was partly destroyed in 1489, but reconstructed in the 20th century.*

RENAISSANCE CHATEAUX

After the arrival of gunpowder and cannons in the 14th century, medieval fortifications gradually became less effective. During the relatively more stable rule of the Spanish Netherlands in the late 16th century, rich aristrocrats felt confident enough to build grand châteaux with large windows. However, they still kept an eye on the defences.

Château de Jehay (see p220), *another 16th-century fortress, features turrets and a moat. The castle was brought up to date in style during the 18th century, but the interior shows traces of the Renaissance trend towards private, aristocratic life.*

Kasteel Ooidonk (see p137), *dating from the late 16th century, shows influences from the Italian Renaissance. This is overlaid by the distinctive Hispano-Flemish style of the Spanish Netherlands, as seen in the exotic roof.*

17TH-CENTURY FORTRESSES

Armies in this era often adapted medieval castles for defence against powerful artillery. A key figure was the French military architect Marquis de Vauban, who travelled through the Low Countries with Louis XIV's forces. He upgraded the castles of Namur and Bouillon, which had military roles into the 20th century.

Château-Fort de Bouillon (see pp232–3), *on a rock by the River Semois, was the stronghold of the crusader Godefroid de Bouillon. Vauban's work can be seen in the inner courtyards and defensive wall positions.*

The Citadelle de Namur (see p202) *was built on a hilltop site used since Neolithic times. It was fortified by the Romans and rebuilt in succeeding centuries.*

18TH-CENTURY CHATEAUX

Belgium suffered during the wars of the Spanish and Austrian empires, but châteaux reflected less the imperatives of defence and more the status and taste of their owners. The main stylistic influence was French, but only Château Beloeil *(see p186)* begins to match the grandeur of Versailles.

Château d'Attre (see p185), *built 1752, has preserved its original interior, a rare achievement as wars, economic fluctuations and modernization have left few others intact.*

Corner towers reflect military priorities

Large French-style windows

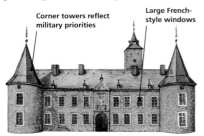

Alden Biesen (see p168) *was owned by the German Order of the Teutonic Knights. The grim exterior expresses their military heritage, while luxurious rooms match their reputation for extravagance.*

Annevoie's famous gardens (see p204), *with their fountains and waterfalls, reflect the 18th-century taste for artistically landscaped nature around grand houses.*

19TH-CENTURY NEO-MEDIEVALISM

Wealthy aristocrats and newly-rich industrialists built fantasy castles, as they sought to combine modern comforts with romanticized notions of past grandeur. Sometimes they converted medieval castles such as Gaasbeek *(see p165)*, often with some of the most lavish interiors.

Romantic roofline of decorative turrets

Large windows with river views

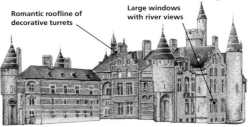

19th-century Kasteel van Bornem *(see p156)*, built in a medieval style

BELGIUM AND LUXEMBOURG THROUGH THE YEAR

Musicians in medieval costume at the Ommegang

Come rain or shine, Belgium has a robust calendar of public events. Some of these are historical parades with centuries of tradition behind them and many are connected to religion, marking saints' days and other Christian festivals. Armies of volunteers turn out in historic costumes and haul vast caricature giants that represent biblical or mythological figures around the streets. New celebrations, particularly music festivals, are also promoted with vigour and become quickly established. The summer months in particular, are thick with outdoor concerts performed on stages erected in town squares. The events are held in the same spirit of public fun that the Flemish artist Brueghel captured in his paintings almost 500 years ago.

SPRING

There may be a chill in the air even as snowdrops and daffodils emerge, and the odd brisk snap can freeze canals, pleasing skaters. Crisp sunny days are ideal for visitors to explore the cities on foot and sample delicious Easter treats.

MARCH

Bal du Rat Mort (*Sat, early Mar*), Oostende. The Dead Rat Ball, a fancy-dress event, named after a Montmartre cabaret in Paris, has been held for over a century.
Mid-Lenten Carnival (*4th Sun of Lent*), Stavelot. The Laetare Procession has the traditional Blancs-Moussis (White-Clad) revellers in hooded robes and long red noses.
Easter (*variable*), nationwide. Children hunt for hidden Easter eggs brought, according to folklore, from Rome by the church bells.

A riot of blossoms welcoming the spring season at Serres Royales

The Holy Blood relic, carried through Bruges by two prelates

APRIL

Serres Royales (*variable*), Laeken. The greenhouses of the royal palace are open to the public for 12 days.
Ronde van Vlaanderen (*early Apr*), Flanders. One of the five Monuments of European professional cycling.
Gentse Floraliën (*late Apr*), Ghent. This vast garden festival fills halls every five years in Ghent, the heart of the horticulture industry.

MAY

Hanswijk Processie (*Sun prior to Ascension Day*), Mechelen. Costumed parades accompany a revered 1,000-year-old statue of the Virgin Mary.
Processie van het Heilig Bloed (*Ascension Day*), Mechelen. An 800-year-old pageant celebrating the Holy Blood relic.
Kattefeest (*2nd Sun, 2012*), Ieper. In the Midde Ages, cats were thrown off the cloth-hall tower. This is re-enacted once in three years with cloth cats.
Kites International (*early May*), Ostend. Demonstrations by kite masters from all over Europe take place at this annual event.
Jazz Marathon (*weekend, late May*), Brussels. Jazz fills the city's squares and cafés.

SUMMER

With longer days and warmer weather, summer has always been the most favourable time for pageants and processions. These months are busy with a variety of excellent outdoor music festivals.

JUNE

Festival van Vlaanderen (*Jun–Dec*), Flanders. The region showcases its high-quality music and dance.

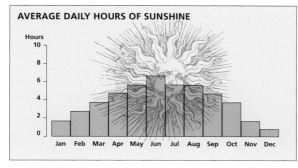

AVERAGE DAILY HOURS OF SUNSHINE

Hours

Climate
Belgium and Luxembourg have a fairly temperate northern European climate. Although not often freezing, winters are chilly and a heavy coat is required. Summers can be pleasantly warm though a jersey might still be needed in the evenings. Rainwear is always a necessity.

Ducasse de Mons *(Trinity Sun)*, Mons. Dating from 1380, it displays the reliquary shrine of St Waudru of Mons in the Procession of the Golden Chariot. It culminates in the Battle of Lumeçon between St George and the Dragon.
Les Journées des Quatre Cortèges *(2nd weekend)*, Tournai. Folkloric giants take to the streets in four traditional parades.
Battle of Waterloo re-enactments *(variable)*, Waterloo. A major re-enactment marks the anniversary of the battle every five years, but smaller events take place around 18 June every year.
Couleur Café Festival *(Jun)* in Brussels offers the best in world music.

JULY

Ommegang *(1st Tue–Thu)*, Brussels. Said to date from 1549, this grand *ommegang* (walk-around) involves 1,400 participants dressed as stilt-walkers, Renaissance nobles, guildsmen, soldiers, flag-throwers, musicians and acrobats. All parade through the Grand Place before the nobility seated on a rostrum.
Rock Werchter *(1st weekend)*, near Leuven. This four-day outdoor rock festival has gained international fame and attracts a line-up of top acts.
Zevenjaarlijkse Kronings-feesten *(early July, 2016)*, Tongeren. The Seven-yearly Crowning Festival has a procession of 4,000 costumed

people, crowning a 15th-century statue of the Virgin.
Guldensporendag *(11 July)*, Flanders. The anniversary of the Battle of the Golden Spurs in 1302 is a Flemish holiday, marked by a variety of events.
Cactusfestival *(2nd weekend)*, Bruges. Minnewater Park's respected rock festival attracts some big names.
Dour Festival *(Thu–Sun, mid-Jul)*, near Mons. A 20-year-old rock festival with an eclectic set of programmes.
Gentsefeesten *(3rd week)*, Ghent. A ten-day party, mixing street theatre and acrobatics with music concerts.

Dynamic performance at the Gentsefeesten

Klinkers *(late Jul–early Aug)*, Bruges. Rock and pop concerts take place in bars, cafés and the two main squares.
Foire du Midi *(mid-Jul–mid-Aug)*, Brussels. Fairground rides and shooting galleries fill the Boulevard du Midi, along with food stands welcoming the shellfish season.

Boetprocessie *(last Sun)*, Veurne. The Procession of the Penitents is a solemn affair, and follows a 450-year-old folkloric tradition *(see p123)*.

AUGUST

Meyboom *(9 Aug)*, Brussels. Giant figures are joyously paraded to witness the planting of a *meyboom* (may tree).
Tapis de Fleurs *(mid-Aug)*, Brussels. In even-numbered years, the Grand Place is carpeted in flowers for four days.
Praalstoet van de Gouden Boom *(late Aug, 2012)*, Bruges. The Pageant of the Golden Tree is held every five years in 15th-century costume evoking the city's golden age.
Reiefeest *(21–31 Aug, 2011)*, Bruges. Theatrical scenes are performed every three years by the River Reie, to celebrate the city's history.
Ducasse *(4th Fri–Mon)*, Ath. This procession has folkloric figures such as Monsieur and Madame Gouyasse (Goliath) and includes Belgium's most celebrated parade of giants.

Millions of flowers in intricate designs at the spectacular Tapis de Fleurs

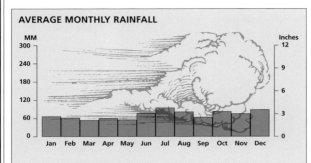

AVERAGE MONTHLY RAINFALL

MM
300
240
180
120
60
0

Inches
12
9
6
3
0

Jan Feb Mar Apr May Jun Jul Aug Sep Oct Nov Dec

Rainfall chart
*On the whole,
Belgium and
Luxembourg are
rather rainy
countries, with
fairly constant low
rainfall throughout
the year. Spring is
the driest season,
but summers can
be damp. In winter,
the rain may turn
into snow and sleet.*

Cars battling for advantage at the Belgian Grand Prix

AUTUMN

September can be pleasantly warm, but with a hint of chill in the air. As the crisp days become shorter, restaurants serve warming game dishes.

SEPTEMBER

Grand Prix of Belgium *(1st Sun)*, Spa-Francorchamps. Formula One racing returned to this popular circuit in 2007 after a gap of four years.
Grande Procession *(2nd Sun)*, Tournai. A costumed procession, first held in 1092 after the passing of a plague, accompanies St Eleutherius's reliquary and other church treasures through the city.
Journées du Patrimoine/Open Monumentendagen *(2nd or 3rd week)*, nationwide. The annual Heritage Days are a rare chance to explore many private historic buildings.
Fêtes de Wallonie *(3rd weekend)*, Namur. Wallonia's role in the 1830 revolution *(see pp44–5)* is celebrated

with events such as a battle of *échasseurs (*stilt-walkers*)* in 17th-century costumes.

OCTOBER

Flanders Film Festival *(variable)*, Ghent. This 12-day international festival is respected for its range of films and focus on film music.

WINTER

The Christmas markets that start in early December bring a glow of good cheer, but carnival parades, the most exuberant public celebrations, are the real showpieces.

NOVEMBER

Toussaint/Allerheiligendag *(1 Nov)*, nationwide. All Saints' Day, or the Day of the Dead, is when family graves are decorated with flowers.
Kaarskensprocessie *(Sun after 1 Nov)*, Scherpenheuvel. A solemn candlelit procession is the culminating point of

the pilgrimage season at the renowned Marian shrine in Scherpenheuvel *(see p162)*.
St Verhaegen Day *(20 Nov)*, Brussels. Students celebrate "Saint" Pierre-Théodore Verhaegen – founder of the original city university – with madcap antics, often on public transport.

DECEMBER

Feast of St Nicholas *(6 Dec)*, nationwide. The 4th-century Bishop of Myra, St Nicholas, parades with Zwarte Peter, or Père Fouettard, who threatens to whip naughty children. It is a day of gift-giving and eating *speculoos*, traditional spiced biscuits.

JANUARY

Driekoningendag/Fête des Rois *(6 Jan)*, nationwide. Epiphany celebrates the visit of the Three Kings to Christ's nativity. The recipient of a trinket baked into an almond cake gets a paper crown.

The traditional Christmas market held in Brussels's Grand Place

AVERAGE MONTHLY TEMPERATURE

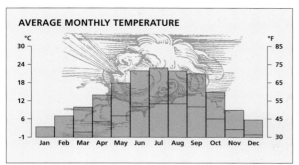

Temperature chart
This chart gives the average maximum and minimum temperatures for Belgium and Luxembourg. Although generally mild, winters can sometimes be bitter, especially on higher ground in the Ardennes and when northeasterly winds blow across the plains.

Ronsense Bommelfeesten *(Sat after 6 Jan),* Ronse. This "festival of fools" centres on a parade of knock-about characters called Bommels.

FEBRUARY

Carnival *(Thu–Shrove Tue),* nationwide. The weekend before Lent is marked by parades in many cities. Eupen celebrates the arrival of His Madness, Prince of Carnival, and Rosenmontag (Rose Monday). Masked folkloric figures called *haguètes* grab onlookers with huge pincers in Malmedy, while Aalst has satirical floats followed by Voil Jeannetten (Dirty Jennies) in male drag. The best-known carnival, at Binche, is a sea of parading *gilles,* or bizarrely costumed jesters *(see p190).*
Krakelingenstoet *(last Sun),* Geraardsbergen. A costumed parade is followed by throwing *krakelingen* (ring-shaped pastries) into the crowd, recalling a 14th-century event.

Participants at the Sprangprëssessioun, Echternach's dancing parade

LUXEMBOURG THROUGH THE YEAR

Liichtmesdag *(2 Feb),* nationwide. In medieval times, the poor asked for food on St Blasius's day. Today, children with lanterns carry on the tradition by begging for treats.
Carnival *(Sun before Shrove Tue),* nationwide. Parades take place in many towns. Diekirch's has donkeys, the town's mascot, while at Remich, *stréimännchen* (straw guys) are set alight and cast into the Moselle.
Buergsonndeg *(Sun after Shrove Tue),* nationwide. In an ancient tradition of *buergbrennen* (bonfire burning), fires are lit on hilltops to drive out winter.
Éimaischen *(Easter Mon),* Nospelt and Luxembourg City. Pottery is a key feature at this folk fair. Visitors take back *péckvillchen,* or bird-shaped cuckoo-whistles.
Octave *(late Apr),* Luxembourg City. Pilgrims parade to the cathedral in honour of a statue of Maria Consolatrix Afflictorum.
Sprangprëssessioun *(Whit Tue),* Echternach. Ranks of dancers spring past the tomb of St Willibrord, the founder of the abbey here.
National Holiday *(23 Jun),* nationwide. Municipal functions and parties mark the birthday of Grand Duchess Charlotte (r.1919–64).
International Festival of Music *(May–Jun),* Echternach. A notable festival of classical and jazz music, drawing top names.
Open-air Festival of Theatre and Music *(weekends in Jul),* Wiltz. This offers a varied programme of opera, music and dance in an outdoor theatre *(see p310).*
Schueberfouer *(Aug/Sep),* Luxembourg City. This modern descendant of a medieval shepherds' market is known for serving traditional food and drink.
Grape and Wine Festival *(2nd weekend in Sep),* Grevenmacher. Held as thanksgiving for the grape harvest, the merrymaking starts with the coronation of the Queen of Grapes and culminates in floats offering free wine.

PUBLIC HOLIDAYS

New Year's Day (1 Jan)
Easter Sunday (variable)
Easter Monday (variable)
Labour Day (1 May)
Ascension Day (variable)
Whit Sunday (variable)
Whit Monday (variable)
Luxembourg's National Day (23 Jun)
Belgian National Day (21 Jul)
Assumption Day (15 Aug)
All Saints' Day (1 Nov)
Armistice Day (11 Nov)
Christmas (25 Dec)

THE HISTORY OF BELGIUM

oth a young country and a very old one, Belgium won independence for the first time in 1830, but owes its name to Gallic tribes who confronted the Romans in 58 BC. Its location on the crossroads of northern Europe made it both a hub of international trade and the battlefield for contending nations. Today, its position has brought new benefits, at the heart of the European Union.

When Julius Caesar set out to conquer the Gauls of western Europe in 58 BC, he encountered a fierce group of tribes there, known as the Belgae. Roman victory in the region led to the establishment of the province of Gallia Belgica. Following the collapse of the Roman Empire in the 5th century, the Germanic Franks came to power here, initially making Tournai, in modern-day Wallonia, their capital. The Frankish ruler Clovis I established the Merovingian dynasty (AD 481–751), whose empire soon encompassed all of Gaul. During this time, Christianity was spread across the land by missionaries such as the French saint Eligius in Flanders. The Merovingians were followed by the Carolingian dynasty (751–987), which produced one of the most important figures of the Middle Ages – Charlemagne, who extended his borders to cover most of western Europe and was crowned by the pope as Emperor of the West. After Charlemagne's death, the empire was divided up among his grandsons, and the province of Belgium was split along the River

Seal of Charles the Bald, King of West Francia

Scheldt. Louis the German, as King of East Francia, took the southern portion called Lotharingia (Lorraine). This included the Walha (later, the Walloons) – Romanized Celts who occupied the Meuse valley. Charles the Bald, King of West Francia, took the western portion, which encompassed a large chunk of Flanders. The French claim to Flanders would haunt the region for the next 600 years.

FLOURISHING TRADE

From about 1100 onwards, a number of fortified trading cities developed on inland waterways. Flanders became the focus of the cloth trade, weaving high-quality wool imported from England into valuable textiles and tapestries. By the late medieval period (14th century), trade routes led to France, Germany and Spain, and over the Alps to Renaissance Italy. Belgian towns such as Brussels, Ghent, Ieper, Antwerp and Bruges became famous for their wealth and luxury. Their elaborate town halls, belfries and market squares were physical symbols of their wealth, pride and sense of independence.

TIMELINE

Charlemagne (768–814)

58–50 BC The Belgae are defeated by Julius Caesar and Roman occupation begins		**860** France makes Baldwin Iron-Arm the first Count of Flanders		**1099** During the First Crusade, Godefroid de Bouillon (see p233) becomes the first ruler of the Kingdom of Jerusalem

	AD 600	700	800	900	1000	1100	1200

AD 460–86 Tournai serves as capital of the Franks, until Clovis I moves it to Paris	**843** Charlemagne's Belgium is divided along the Scheldt: Flanders goes to France and Lotharingia to Louis the German	**979** Official founding of Brussels	*Coat of arms of the Kingdom of Jerusalem*	**1134** A storm creates the Zwin, a tidal inlet, giving Bruges access to the North Sea

◁ **Charles the Bold (1433–77) in *Rules and Ordinances of the Order of the Golden Fleece*, a 15th-century vellum**

The Fight for Independence

Belgium was again occupied by foreign powers between 1794 and 1830 – first, by the French Republican Army at war against Austria, then, after Napoleon's defeat at Waterloo in 1815, by the Dutch. French radical reforms included the abolition of the guild system and fairer taxation laws. Although French rule was unpopular, their liberal ideas were to influence the Belgian drive for independence. In 1815, William I of Orange was appointed King of the Netherlands (which included Belgium) by the Congress of Vienna. His autocratic style, together with a series of anti-Catholic measures, bred discontent, especially in Brussels and among the French-speaking Walloons in the south. The south was also angered when William refused to introduce tariffs to protect their trade – it was the last straw. The uprising of 1830 began in Brussels.

King William I of Orange
William's rule as King of the Netherlands after 1815 was unpopular.

A Cultural Revolution in Brussels
The French drove forward a programme of modernization in Brussels. The 16th-century city walls were demolished and replaced by tree-lined boulevards.

Liberals joined workers already protesting in the square outside. All were prepared to die for the cause.

The Battle of Waterloo
Napoleon's attempt to reconquer Europe ended at Waterloo on 18 June 1815. A Prussian army came to Wellington's aid, and by evening Napoleon faced his final defeat. This led to Dutch rule over Belgium.

Agricultural Workers
Harsh weather in the winter of 1829 caused hardship for both farmers and agricultural labourers, who also joined the protest.

The Revolution in Industry
Taxes, unemployment and social divisions under Dutch rule all contributed to the mood of the rebellion that erupted in 1830.

Le Théâtre de la Monnaie
On 25 August 1830, the patriotic song, L'Amour Sacré de la Patrie, *from French composer Daniel Auber's opera* La Muette de Portici, *goaded the audience into revolt.*

BELGIAN REVOLUTION

The revolution of 1830 was ignited by a radical opera at the Brussels opera house, when the liberal audience rushed out into the street to join a workers' demonstration, raising the Brabant flag. Gustave Wappers (1803–74) brought the drama of Romanticism to his depiction of the Belgian Revolution with the painting, *Day in September 1830.* Troops were sent by William I to quash the rebels, but the Belgian soldiers deserted and the Dutch were able to retake Brussels. Sporadic fighting rumbled on until 1832. William finally accepted the new borders in 1839.

The initial list of demands asked for administrative independence from the Dutch and for freedom of the press.

Late September of 1830 saw days of costly streetfighting in Brussels, as the rebels defended the city against Dutch troops.

King of Belgium, Léopold I
The crowning of German prince, Léopold of Saxe-Coburg, in Brussels in 1831 finally established Belgium's independence.

TIMELINE

William I of Orange

1799 Napoleon Bonaparte rules France

1815 Battle of Waterloo: Napoleon is defeated by an army led by the Duke of Wellington

1830 Rebellion begins at the Théâtre de la Monnaie in Brussels

1800	1810	1820	1830

1792 In the French Revolutionary war against Austria, France invades the Austrian Netherlands

1815 Belgium, allied with Holland under the United Kingdom of the Netherlands, is ruled by William I of Orange; Brussels becomes the second capital

1831 State of Belgium formed on 21 July; Treaty of London grants independence

1835 First continental railway built from Brussels to Mechelen

CONSOLIDATING THE NEW STATE

In Belgium's early days as an independent nation, Brussels was a haven for free-thinkers such as the libertarian poet Baudelaire, and a refuge for exiles such as Karl Marx and Victor Hugo. In 1799, steam power was brought to the textile industry at Verviers, in Eastern Wallonia, and Belgium began following in the tracks of Britain. It was now industrializing fast. Continental Europe's first railway line opened in 1835 between Brussels and Mechelen and by 1870, there were four main railway stations in Brussels that exported goods all over Europe. By this time, the focus of industrial development was Wallonia, with its coal mines and iron industries. This reinforced the age-old supremacy of French-speaking Belgians. Dutch-speaking Flanders remained largely rural, impoverished and increasingly resentful of the imposition of French by the ruling elite – French was the language of administration, education, law and intellectual life.

The long reign of Belgium's second monarch, Léopold II (r.1865–1909), spanned the rapid development of Belgium. He was praised for his vision, but was also associated with the social deprivation that came with industrialization. Equally controversial was his acquisition of the Congo in Africa and the abuses of colonial power that were played out there.

THE GERMAN OCCUPATIONS

Like much of Europe, Belgium was enjoying a *belle époque* before the calamities of the 20th century began to unfold. In the summer of 1914, it was invaded by the German army. Although Belgium had been created as a neutral country, some of the bloodiest battles of World War I were staged on its soil. The front line followed a southward path through the marginally higher land around Ieper. The opposing armies dug in and suffered years of brutal trench warfare in a stalemate that cost nearly a million lives. Today, the peaceful agricultural land on either side of the salient is spattered with military cemeteries filled with the foreign soldiers who came here to contest the Western Front.

While the Belgian army, led by King Albert I (r.1909–34), put up a spirited resistance from their last stronghold in De Panne in the far northwest, most of the rest of the country remained under occupation – often brutal and vindictive – until the last day of the war, 11 November 1918. The 1919 Treaty of Versailles granted Belgium control of Eupen-Malmedy, the German-speaking area in the east.

In 1940, neutral Belgium was invaded again by the Germans under Hitler. Many Belgians took part in

Engraving of the interior of a 19th-century forge near Huy in eastern Belgium

TIMELINE

1847 Opening of continental Europe's first shopping mall, the Galéries St-Hubert, in Brussels

1871 The River Senne in Brussels is covered over, and new suburbs are built to cope with the growing population

1898 The Flemish language is given equal status to French in law

1914–18 World War I; Germany occupies Belgium

1840

1875

1910

The Belgian Congo

1884 Léopold II is granted sovereignty over the Congo

1893–5 Victor Horta builds the first Art Nouveau house in Brussels

1939–44 World War II; Germany again occupies Belgium

German troops raising the flag of the Third Reich at the Royal Castle at Laeken, near Brussels

a courageous resistance movement; the fate of many others was to be forcibly shipped to Germany as labourers. The Nazis also exploited the disaffection of Flemish nationalists, recruiting volunteers to serve their army or operate the notorious concentration camp at Breendonk, near Antwerp. Belgium was liberated by the Allies in September 1944, but the Germans mounted a last-ditch attempt to break the advance by punching a hole through the Ardennes of Luxembourg and southern Belgium in the Battle of the Bulge.

Belgium entered an uneasy peace. King Léopold III (r.1934–51) was at the focus of the contention – he had surrendered in 1940 and was moved to Germany until the end of the war. Rumours, still disputed, that he had collaborated with the Nazis led to his abdication in 1951, in favour of his son, Baudouin (r.1951–93).

INTERNATIONAL STATUS

The latter half of the 20th century has been marked by the ongoing language debate between the Flemish and the French-speaking Walloons. Between 1970 and 1994, the constitution of Belgium was redrawn, creating a federal state with three separate regions – the Flemish north, the Walloon south and bilingual Brussels.

Like most of Europe, Belgium went from economic boom in the 1960s to recession and retrenchment in the 1970s and 80s, and renewed growth in the 1990s. This latter period saw a rapid rise in the prosperity of Flanders, while Wallonia, the old powerhouse of the heavy industries, declined – a reversal of fortune that has reinforced the language divide.

Throughout these decades, Brussels's stature at the heart of Europe was consolidated. In 1958, the city became the headquarters for the European Economic Community (EEC), later the European Union (EU). In 1967, NATO also moved to Brussels. The capital city's international role has helped ease tensions between Flanders and Wallonia, but – as throughout most of its long history – the political future of Belgium remains in the balance.

Flags of the European Union states in front of the EU headquarters in Brussels

1945		1980		2015
1951 Baudouin succeeds Léopold III	**1962** The Belgian Congo is granted independence	**1989** Brussels is officially a bilingual city	**2001** Crown Prince Philippe and Princess Mathilde have a daughter and heir, Elisabeth	
	1967 Brussels is the new NATO headquarters		**2002** The euro becomes legal tender	
	1958 Formation of the EEC, with Belgium as a founder member; Exposition Universelle et Internationale in Brussels, with the Atomium as the star attraction	**1993** King Baudouin dies; Albert II succeeds		

Baudouin

Flag of the European Union

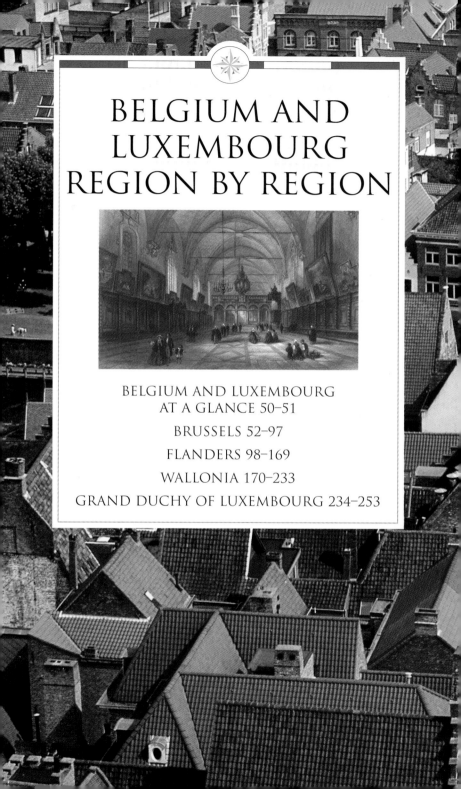

BELGIUM AND LUXEMBOURG REGION BY REGION

Belgium and Luxembourg at a Glance

Essentially, Belgium is divided into two halves – Dutch-speaking Flanders in the north and French-speaking Wallonia in the south. Situated wholly within Flanders is the country's capital Brussels, a separate administrative region with a large French-speaking population. Landlocked but independent, the Grand Duchy of Luxembourg is Belgium's south-eastern neighbour. Most big Belgian cities are located in Flanders and the northern part of Wallonia. The hilly landscape of the Ardennes covers much of the southern and eastern parts of Wallonia as well as Luxembourg. Here the landscape is more sparsely populated, and cherished for its unspoilt natural beauty.

Brussels (see pp52–97) *has a glorious centrepiece in its Grand Place, which is fronted by its ornate Flemish-Renaissance guildhouses.*

WESTERN FLANDERS
(see pp104–139)

BRUSSELS
(see pp52–97)

WESTERN WALLONIA
(see pp176–91)

Oostende (see p122), *clustered around a busy marina and fishing port, is the largest resort-town on the Belgian coast. Home of the maverick late-19th-century artist James Ensor, it also has a notable museum of modern art.*

0 km   25
0 miles   25

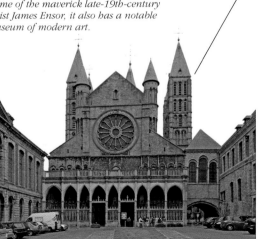

Tournai (see pp180–84) *is the oldest cathedral-city in Belgium. It is justly famous for the splendid Gothic and Romanesque Cathédrale Notre-Dame, originally the seat of the city's first bishop, St Eleutherius, in the 5th century.*

◁ Picturesque townhouses clustering around the narrow canal-side streets of Bruges's historic centre

Antwerp (see pp144–55) *is Belgium's second biggest city, a major European port and an industrial hub. However, its historic centre gives little indication of this. Its primary landmark is the magnificent Gothic Onze-Lieve-Vrouwekathedraal, whose dainty spire soars above the stump of its uncompleted twin.*

The River Semois (see pp228–9) *snakes through the Belgian provinces of Luxembourg and Namur, past a charmed landscape of forested hills. Walkers, canoeists and motorists come to enjoy the tranquillity and the breathtakingly spectacular views.*

CENTRAL AND EASTERN FLANDERS
(see pp140–69)

EASTERN WALLONIA
(see pp212–33)

CENTRAL WALLONIA
(see pp192–211)

GRAND DUCHY OF LUXEMBOURG
(see pp234–53)

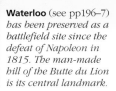

Waterloo (see pp196–7) *has been preserved as a battlefield site since the defeat of Napoleon in 1815. The man-made hill of the Butte du Lion is its central landmark.*

Luxembourg City (see pp240–45) *has a refined elegance befitting the capital of the Grand Duchy. This is exemplified by the large central square named Place Guillaume II, with its equestrian statue of the grand duke of the 1840s, William II.*

BRUSSELS

The capital of Belgium, and effectively the capital of Europe, Brussels has always been a hub of trade and politics. Yet, despite its international prominence, the city retains an intimate, human scale, with a web of medieval streets centring upon the superb Grand Place. Brussels's glorious architecture and gilded spires rise over high-fashion boutiques and quaint, time-warped taverns and cafés.

The origin of Brussels lies in the Frankish settlement known as Bruocsella (Village in the Marshes) and a castle built in AD 977. From these beginnings, it became a massively fortified power base for the ruling dukes of Brabant and Burgundy and evolved into a sophisticated city.

From the 12th century onwards, commerce was the engine of growth. The trading centre around the Grand Place was in the Lower Town. In contrast, the palaces of the dukes and nobles stood aloof on the crest of a hill in the Upper Town – a division between the rulers and the ruled that is still detectable in the architecture today. Because French was the language of the elite classes, it became that of the city, which is a French-speaking bubble surrounded by the Dutch-speaking province of Vlaams-Brabant. Officially, if not in practice, Brussels is a bilingual city and all the street names are in both French and Dutch. The city remained the capital as the Spanish Netherlands gave way to the Neo-Classical era of the Austrian Netherlands. During the 19th century, it underwent rapid expansion as a result of which the elegant Quartier Léopold developed in the Upper Town. Today, this zone of orderly avenues and green spaces is home to institutions of the EU. Punctuated with modern buildings, it busies itself with the governmental bureaucracy so readily attached to Brussels's name.

With an urban area of 160 sq km (60 sq miles) and a population of one million, Brussels juggles its great historical legacy and its role in the modern world by offering the best of both heritage and urban prosperity. And true to a city that has the Manneken-Pis as its mascot, a ripple of good cheer is never far from the surface.

The Palais Royal, seat of the royal family in Brussels and centrepiece of the Upper Town

◁ Café life in the Lower Town, beneath a comic-strip mural and the spire of the Hôtel de Ville

Exploring Brussels

The division of Brussels into Lower Town and Upper Town reflects the lie of the land. With the Grand Place at its focus, the Lower Town is the floodplain of the River Senne, which now runs underground. To the east, the land rises to reach the Place Royale, site of the Musée des Instruments de Musique and Musées Royaux des Beaux Arts. A ridge runs all the way from the Palais de Justice, past Notre-Dame du Sablon and Rue Royal to just north of the Centre Belge de la Bande Dessinée. This shape traces the former line of the 14th-century city walls. Further east, the Upper Town becomes more residential and dedicated to running the businesses of the European Union.

SEE ALSO

- *Street Finder* pp92–7
- *Where to Stay* pp262–3
- *Where to Eat* pp284–6

The triumphal arches at the Parc du Cinquantenaire

SIGHTS AT A GLANCE

Buildings and Monuments
Éditions Jacques Brel ⓯
European Parliament ㉝
Halles St-Géry ❼
Hôtel de Ville ❷
La Bourse ❺
Maison du Roi ❸
Mannekin-Pis ❻
Palais de Charles de Lorraine ㉑
Palais de Justice ㉗
Palais Royal ⓲
Porte de Hal ㉘

Museums, Galleries and Theatres
BELvue Museum and the Coudenberg ⓳
Centre Belge de la Bande Dessinée ⓭
Galeries St-Hubert ⓬
Institut Royal des Sciences Naturelles ㉟
Musée Charlier ㉙

Musée du Costume et de la Dentelle ❶
Musée du Jouet ㉚
Musée des Instruments de Musique ⓴
Musées Royaux des Beaux-Arts de Belgique pp68–73 ㉒
Musée Wiertz ㉞
Théâtre Marionnettes de Toone ❿

Churches
Cathédrale Sts-Michel-et-Gudule ⓮
Église St-Nicholas ❹
Église St-Jacques-sur-Coudenberg ⓱
Église St-Jean-Baptiste-au-Béguinage ❾
Église Ste-Catherine ❽
Notre-Dame de la Chapelle ㉖
Notre-Dame du Sablon ㉔

Parks
Parc du Cinquantenaire pp76–7 ㉛

Streets and Squares
Place du Grand Sablon ㉓
Place du Petit Sablon ㉕
Place Royale ⓰
Quartier Européen ㉜
Rue des Bouchers ⓫

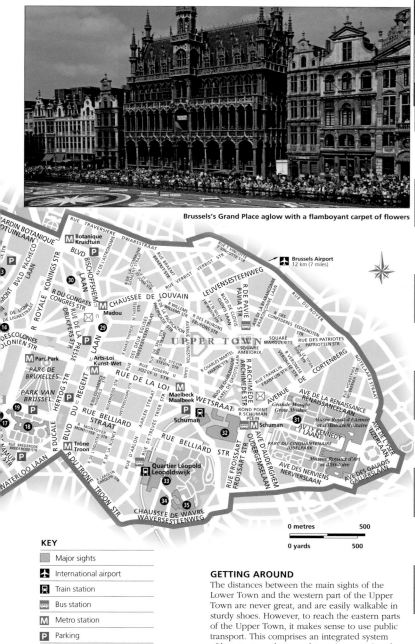

Brussels's Grand Place aglow with a flamboyant carpet of flowers

KEY

	Major sights
✈	International airport
🚆	Train station
🚌	Bus station
M	Metro station
P	Parking
i	Tourist information
✉	Post office
=	Railway

GETTING AROUND

The distances between the main sights of the
Lower Town and the western part of the Upper
Town are never great, and are easily walkable in
sturdy shoes. However, to reach the eastern parts
of the Upper Town, it makes sense to use public
transport. This comprises an integrated system
of bus, tram, underground tram (premetro) and
metro lines. Taxis can be hired from designated
taxi ranks. As Brussels is officially bilingual, the
names of all the streets and stations on this map
are given in both French and Dutch.

The Grand Place

The geographical, historical and commercial heart of the city, the Grand Place is the first port of call for most visitors to Brussels. The square remains the civic centre centuries after its creation, and offers the finest example of Belgium's ornate 17th-century architecture in one area. Open-air markets took place around this site as early as the 11th century, although Brussels's town hall, the Hôtel de Ville, was built only by the end of the 15th century. City traders further added guildhouses in a medley of styles. In 1695, the French destroyed all but the town hall and two guild façades over three days of cannon fire. Urged to rebuild in styles approved by the Town Council, the guilds produced the harmonious unity of Flemish Baroque buildings that is seen here today.

The Grand Place and Baroque guildhalls

The Maison du Roi *was first built in 1536 and redesigned in 1873. Once used to host guests of the monarchy, it now has the Musée de la Ville de Bruxelles, which includes paintings, tapestries and the many tiny outfits of the Manneken-Pis.*

① **NORTHEAST CORNER**

② **MAISON DU ROI**

The Hôtel de Ville (see p58) *occupies the entire southwest side of the square. Still a functioning civic building, Brussels's town hall is the architectural masterpiece of the Grand Place.*

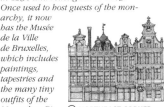

Gilded statue of St Michael killing the devil.

The spire was built by Jan van Ruysbroeck in 1449. It stands 96-m (315-ft) high and is a little crooked.

Everard 't Serclaes *was murdered defending Brussels in 1388. Touching the arm of his statue is said to bring luck.*

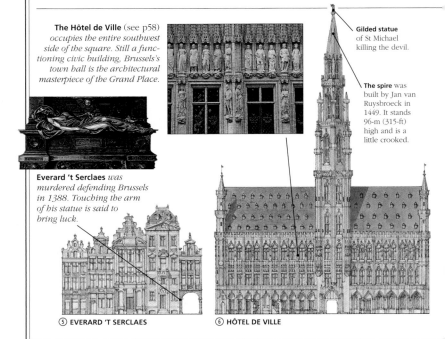

⑤ **EVERARD 'T SERCLAES**

⑥ **HÔTEL DE VILLE**

Le Pigeon *was home to Victor Hugo, the exiled French novelist who chose this house as his Belgian residence in 1852. Some of the most complimentary comments about Brussels emerged later from his pen.*

La Maison des Ducs de Brabant *is a group of six guildhouses. Designed by the Controller of Public Works, Guillaume de Bruyn, the group looks like an Italian Baroque palazzo.*

LOCATOR MAP
See Brussels Street Finder, Map 2

Stone busts of the ducal line along the façade gave this group of houses their name.

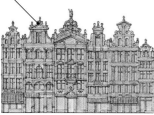

③ **LE PIGEON**

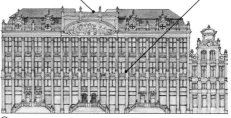

④ **LA MAISON DES DUCS DE BRABANT**

Le Renard *(The Fox) was built in 1699 as the guildhouse of the haberdashers by the Flemish architects Marc de Vos and van Nerum. Façade details show St Nicolas, the patron saint of merchants, and cherubs, playing with ribbons.*

La Maison des Boulangers, *also known as Le Roi d'Espagne, was a showpiece built by the guild of bakers. The 1697 octagonal copper dome is topped by a golden figure blowing a trumpet.*

Le Cornet displays the Italianate Flemish style. This boatmen's guildhouse (1697) is most notable for its gable, which is in the form of a 17th-century frigate's bow.

Le Roi d'Espagne *now houses the Grand Place's finest bar (see p90), with a popular terrace from which to drink in the splendours of the square. The gilt bust over the entrance represents St Aubert, the patron saint of bakers. There is a vast bust of Charles II of Spain on the second level of the façade.*

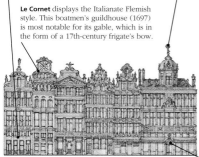

⑦ **LE RENARD, LE CORNET AND LE ROI D'ESPAGNE**

Musée du Costume et de la Dentelle ❶

Rue de la Violette 12, 1000 BRU.
City Map 2 D3. *Tel* (02) 2134450.
🚋 27, 29, 38, 46, 48, 63, 86, 95.
Ⓜ *Bourse, Gare Centrale.* 🚊 3, 4,
31, 32, 33. ◯ 10am–5pm Mon–Sun.
⬤ Wed and public holidays. 🏛 ♿
📷 on request, call (02) 2794355.
www.musees.bruxelles.be

Located within two gabled
18th-century houses is a
museum focusing on one
of Brussels's most successful
exports – lace. The intricate
skill employed by Belgian
lacemakers has played a vital
economic role in the city
since the 17th century, and
the collection explains the
history of this delicate craft.

The second floor houses a
small, carefully stored
collection of antique lace,
demonstrating the various
schools of lacemaking from
France, Flanders and Italy.
The museum also displays
temporary exhibitions
on contemporary textiles
and fashion.

Hôtel de Ville ❷

Grand Place, 1000 BRU. **City Map** 2
D3. *Tel* (02) 2794371. 🚋 27, 29, 38,
46, 48, 63, 86, 95. Ⓜ *Bourse, De
Brouckère, Gare Centrale.* 🚊 3, 4,
31, 32, 33, 55, 81. ⬤ election days.
🏛 📷 Apr–Sep: 3:15pm Tue and
Wed, 10:45am and 12:15pm Sun;
Oct–Mar: 3:15pm Tue and Wed
(English); also offered in French and
Dutch. ♿ **www**.visitbrussels.be

With its delicate spire soaring
to a gilded statue of St Michael
at a height of 96 m (315 ft),
Brussels' town hall is a city

Intricate carving on the towering spire and façade of the Maison du Roi

landmark, and one of the gems
of the Grand Place. It was built
between 1402 and 1455, with
the spire designed by Jan van
Ruysbroeck. During the
French bombardment of 1695
(see p42), most of the building
was demolished, but the spire
survived, in spite of being the
target of French cannons. The
town hall was rebuilt along
Neo-Classical lines and the
grand public rooms are a
mixture of the 18th-century
palatial and 19th-century Neo-
Gothic styles. The exterior,
with its ranks of statues, dates
mainly from the 19th century.

The building is still used as
a town hall and for civic functions. Highlights include the
fine 18th-century tapestries
of the **Alderman's Room**, the
elaborate **Council Chamber**
and the Neo-Gothic **Wedding
Room**. Paintings show the
River Senne flowing sluggishly
through the city, before it was
covered over in the interests
of public health in the 1860s.

Maison du Roi ❸

Grand Place, 1000 BRU. **City
Map** 2 D3. *Tel* (02) 2794350.
🚋 29, 38, 46, 47, 48, 60, 63, 65,
66, 71, 95, 96. Ⓜ *Bourse, De
Brouckère, Gare Centrale.* 🚊 3, 52,
55, 56, 81. ◯ 10am–5pm Tue–Sun.
🏛 📷 **www**.musees.bruxelles.be

Standing on the Grand Place
opposite the Hôtel de Ville,
the Maison du Roi (literally,
King's House, as the site was
once the residence of the
Spanish monarchs) is another
successful venture in the
19th-century Neo-Gothic style.
Built in the 1870s, it was
based on etchings of a 16th-
century predecessor that had
served as the Royal Court of
Assizes. It now houses the
Musée de la Ville de Bruxelles
(Museum of the City of
Brussels), which includes a
fine collection of the historic
crafts made in the city such
as tapestry, retables (intricately
carved and decorated altarpieces), silverware and
porcelain, as well as paintings
and sculptures. There is also
a good section on the history
and development of Brussels,
brought alive by scale
models, paintings and artifacts.
However, this museum's most
famous attraction is the splendid collection of outfits
made for the Manneken-Pis
(see p60). On view is a large
selection of the 815 carefully
tailored costumes – national,
historical, military, tradesmen's clothing and even a

Luxurious furnishings in the Wedding Room at the Hôtel de Ville

For hotels and restaurants in this region see pp262–3 and pp284–6

LUXURIOUS LACE

Lace (*dentelle* in French, *kant* in Dutch) has always been a luxury product, as it is a hugely labour-intensive accessory. Belgian lace has had a high reputation since the bobbin lace technique was introduced from Italy in the 17th century. Patterns are created by manipulating dozens of threads, each attached to a wooden bobbin, around pins embedded in a cushion. Lace has been used for clothes, shawls and church vestments, as well as table and bed linen. Historically, it was made by women of all social classes – by the nobility as a pastime, by nuns and béguines in convents, and by ill-paid cottage workers exploited by unscrupulous middlemen. During the 19th-century love-affair with lace, there were perhaps 50,000 lace-makers in Belgium. Despite competition from machine-made lace, handmade Belgian lace is still produced and carries a certificate of provenance.

A display of delicately patterned lace

La Bourse ❺

Palais de la Bourse, 1000 BRU. **City Map** 1 C2. **Tel** (02) 5091373. 🚌 46, 48, 86, 95. Ⓜ Bourse. 🚊 3, 4, 31, 32, 33. 🚫 No longer open to the public. **Bruxella 1238** (02) 2794355. ⬜ 1st Wed of month; can be visited by appointment at other times. 📷 📷 obligatory, 10:15am (English), 11:15am (French), 2pm (Dutch).

Brussels's Stock Exchange, La Bourse, is one of the city's most impressive buildings, and it dominates the square of the same name. Designed in Palladian style by architect Léon Suys, the building was constructed between 1867 and 1873. Among its most notable features are the ornate carvings on each façade. The great French sculptor, Auguste Rodin (1840–1917), is rumoured to have crafted four caryatids inside, as well as the statues representing Africa and Asia in allegorical groups on the roof. Beneath the colonnade are two beautifully detailed winged figures representing good and evil which were carved by Flemish sculptor Jacques de Haen (1831–1900). Once the scene of frantic trading, La Bourse today houses the offices of Euronext, the owners of the Belgian Stock Exchange, and all financial activity is now via computers.

Allegorical statues crowning the roof line of La Bourse

On its northern side are some archaeological remains from medieval Brussels, exhibited at **Bruxella 1238**. Discovered unexpectedly during road-works in 1998, these include the remains of a 13th-century Franciscan convent, a church and the grave of Duke John I of Brabant who was buried here in 1294.

A small museum has been built on the site, where interested visitors can see the relics of social and religious life in 13th-century Brussels on display. To protect the remains from degradation, the area is accessible only by guided tours, starting from the Musée de la Ville de Bruxelles in the Maison du Roi.

sub-aqua wetsuit – each one donated by a visiting dignitary since the tradition began some three centuries ago.

Église St-Nicolas ❹

Rue au Beurre 1, 1000 BRU. **City Map** 2 D2. **Tel** (02) 5138022. 🚌 29, 38, 46, 47, 63, 65, 66, 71, 86, 88. Ⓜ Bourse, De Brouckère. 🚊 3, 4, 31, 32, 33. ⬜ 8am–6:30pm Mon–Fri, 9am–6pm Sat, 9am–7:30pm Sun and public holidays. 🚫 during services.

A market church was built on this site at the end of the 12th century, but, like much of the Lower Town, it was damaged in the 1695 French bombardment. A cannon ball lodged itself into an interior pillar and in 1714, the bell tower finally collapsed. Several restoration projects were planned but none came to fruition until 1956, when the west side of the building was given a new Gothic-style façade.

Dedicated to St Nicolas, the patron saint of merchants, this low-lit atmospheric church is known for its choir stalls, dating from 1381, which depict the story of St Nicolas on medallions. The unusual angle of the chapel is reportedly to avoid the flow of an old stream.

Simple Gothic shapes on the restored side of the Église St-Nicolas

Manneken-Pis ❻

Corner of Rue de l'Etuve and Rue du
Chêne, 1000 BRU. **City Map** 1 C3.
🚌 27, 29, 38, 46, 48, 63, 86, 95.
Ⓜ Bourse, Gare Centrale. 🚊 3, 4,
31, 32, 33.

An unlikely attraction, this tiny
statue of a young boy, barely
61 cm (2 ft) high, relieving
himself into a small pool is as
much a part of Brussels as the
Trevi Fountain is of Rome.

The current statue of
Mannekin Pis by Jérôme
Duquesnoy the Elder has been
in place since 1619. However,
there is evidence to

suggest that a stone
fountain depicting
the same figure stood
there before it,
possibly as early
as 1451.

The charm of
this famous statue
comes from the
many rumours
and fables

Brussels's iconic behind it. One
Manneken-Pis theory claims
that in the
12th century the son of a duke
was caught urinating against a
tree in the midst of a battle
and was thus commemorated
in bronze as a symbol of
military courage. The inspiration for the statue has been
revealed as Cupid.

In its long history the
statuette has been the victim
of several thefts. A particularly
violent theft in 1965 left the
statue broken in two pieces,
leaving just the ankles and feet
remaining. The missing body
of the statue reappeared a
year later when it was found
in a canal.

In the year 1698 the govenor
of the Netherlands, Maximilian
Emmanuel, brought a gift to
the city in the form of a blue
woollen coat for the statue.
This is a tradition that continues today with visiting heads
of state donating miniature
versions of their national
costume. The little boy has a
collection of over 800 outifts
which are housed in the
Musée de la Ville de Bruxelles,
where 100 are on display at
any one time. Among the collection is a miniature Samurai,
Santa Claus and Elvis suit.

**Busy restaurants and cafés on the
square outside Halles St-Géry**

Halles St-Géry ❼

Place St-Géry 23, 1000 BRU. **City
Map** 1 C2. 🚌 46, 48, 86, 95.
Ⓜ Bourse. 🚊 3, 4, 31, 32, 33.

In many ways, St-Géry can be
considered the birthplace of
Brussels. In the 6th century, a
chapel was built here supposedly by St Géry, the Bishop
of Cambrai at the time. The
chapel was located on an
island in the marshes of the
River Senne, which now
flows underground through
the city. In AD 977, a fortress
took over the site, marking the
real foundation of Brussels.

In 1881, a covered meat
market was built here in the
Neo-Renaissance style. Its glass
and intricate ironwork were
renovated in 1985, and the hall
now serves as a cultural centre
with special focus on the city's
heritage and environment.

Église Ste-
Catherine ❽

Place Ste-Catherine 50, 1000 BRU.
City Map 1 C2. **Tel** (02) 5133481.
🚌 47. Ⓜ Ste-Catherine, De
Brouckère. 🚊 3, 52, 55, 56, 81, 90.
🕙 8am–5:30pm Mon–Sat, 10am–
1:30pm Sun. 🚻 on request.

The first church to occupy
this site was built in the 15th
century. All that remains of
it today is a Baroque tower
dating from 1629. The present
church was redesigned in a
variety of styles between 1854
and 1859 by Joseph Poelaert,
architect of the monumental

Palais de Justice *(see p67)*.
Notable features of the interior include a lovely 14th-
century stone statue of the
Black Madonna as well as
a painted wooden statue
of St Catherine, complete
with the wheel on which
she was martyred. To the
east of the church is the stone
Tour Noire (Black Tower),
a remnant of the city's 12th-
century defensive walls.

Place Ste-Catherine was laid
out as a square in front of
the church in 1870, when the
canal basin originally on this
site was filled in. This used to
be the city's main fish market,
and is still the best spot to
indulge in Brussels's famous
seafood, but prices here are
generally high. Once situated
at the end of the canal link to
the North Sea, the **Quai aux
Briques** (Brick Quay) and **Quai
au Bois à Brûler** (Firewood
Quay) flank the square and
recall the area's trading past.

**Spacious vaulted interior of the
serene Église Ste-Catherine**

Église St-Jean-
Baptiste-au-
Béguinage ❾

Place du Béguinage, 1000 BRU.
City Map 1 C1. **Tel** (02) 2178742.
🚌 47. Ⓜ Ste-Catherine. 🕙 10am–
5pm Tue–Sat, 10am–8pm Sun. 🚻

This stone-clad church was
consecrated in 1676 around
the country's largest béguine
community, which had been
established since 1250. Fields
and orchards around the site
contained cottages and houses

THE BÉGUINE MOVEMENT

The béguine lifestyle swept across western Europe during the 13th century. The order is believed to have begun among widows of the Crusaders who resorted to a pious life of sisterhood on the death of their husbands. Single women opted for a secluded existence devoted to charitable deeds, but not bound by strict religious vows. They were free to leave at any time, for instance to marry. Many béguine convents disappeared during the Protestant Reformation, but begijnhofs

Portrait of a béguine at prayer in a Brussels béguinage

(béguinages) continued to thrive in Flanders. These areas generally consisted of a church, a courtyard, communal rooms and homes for the women. Brussels once had a community of over 1,200 béguines, but the movement dissolved as female emancipation spread during the early 1800s. The sites of a number of béguinages have survived, including those in Bruges *(see p113)*, Ghent *(see p135)*, Leuven *(see p161)* and Aarschot *(see p162)*.

for up to 1,200 béguine women. These were members of a lay religious order who took up charitable work and enclosed living after failed marriages or during widowhood. In medieval times, the

béguines here ran a laundry, hospital and windmill for the people of the city. Still a popular place of worship, the church is notable for its Flemish Baroque details from the 17th century, including

Baroque façade of Église St-Jean-Baptiste-au-Béguinage

the onion-shaped turrets and ornamental walls. The unusually wide aisles give it a light, airy feeling inside. The nave, which is also Baroque, is decorated with ornate cherubs, angels and scrolls, while the confessionals are carved with allegorical figures and saints. The apse contains a striking statue of St John the Baptist, and the 1757 pulpit, a fine example of Baroque woodcarving, depicts St Dominic trampling a heretic underfoot.

Théâtre Marionettes de Toone ⑩

Impasse Ste-Pétronille, 66 Rue du Marché-aux-Herbes, 1000 BRU. **City Map** 2 D2. *Tel* (02) 5117137. 🚏 27, 29, 38, 46, 48, 63, 86, 95. Ⓜ Bourse, Gare Centrale. 🚋 3, 4, 31, 32, 33. ⏰ pub: noon–midnight; theatre: 8:30pm Thu–Sat, 4pm Sat; museum: performance intervals. 🎫 📷 on request, call (02) 2172753. **www.**toone.be

During the period of the Spanish Netherlands *(see pp40–41)*, all theatres were shut down to prevent satirical performances targeting the country's Spanish rulers. This gave rise to a fashion for puppet shows, as the actors' vicious dialogues were more easily forgivable when they came from inanimate dolls.

Harlequin puppet

In 1830, Antoine Toone opened his own puppet theatre and it has been run by Toones ever since – the present owner is the eighth generation Toone. The classics are enacted today by wooden marionettes in the local Bruxellois dialect, and occasionally in French, Dutch, English or German.

The puppet theatre and museum occupy the top two floors of the building, while the ground floor is a popular pub. The museum displays retired marionnettes, some dating to the 19th century.

Rue des Bouchers ⓫

City Map 2 D2. 🚌 27, 29, 38, 46, 47, 48, 63, 66, 71, 86, 88, 95. Ⓜ De Brouckère, Bourse, Gare Centrale. 🚊 3, 4, 31, 32, 33.

Like many streets in this area of the city, Rue des Bouchers retains its medieval name, evoking the time when this meandering, cobblestoned street was home to the butcher's trade. Aware of its historic importance and heeding the concerns of the public, the city council declared this area the **Ilot Sacré** (Sacred Islet) in 1960, restoring surviving buildings and forbidding the further alteration or destruction of architectural façades. Hence, Rue des Bouchers abounds in 17th-century stepped gables and decorated doorways.

Today, this pedestrianized thoroughfare is best known as the "belly of Brussels", a reference to its plethora of cafés and restaurants. Many types of cuisines are on offer here, including Chinese, Greek, Italian and Indian. The most impressive sights are the lavish pavement displays of seafood, piled high on mounds of ice and lit by a romantic amber glow from the lamps.

At the end of the street, at the Impasse de la Fidélité, is a recent acknowledgement of sexual equality. Erected in 1987, **Jeanneke-Pis** is a coy, yet cheeky, female version of her "brother", the more famous Manneken-Pis (see p60).

Soaring domed glass roof of the 19th-century Galéries St-Hubert

Galéries St-Hubert ⓬

Rue des Bouchers, 1000 BRU. City Map 2 D2. 🚊 25, 94. Ⓜ Gare Centrale. ♿

Sixteen years after ascending the throne as the first king of Belgium, Léopold I inaugurated the opening of these grand arcades in 1847. St-Hubert has the distinction of being the first shopping arcade in continental Europe, and one of the most elegant. Designed in Neo-Renaissance style by Belgian architect Jean-Pierre Cluysenaar, its vaulted glass roof covers three sections – Galerie du Roi, Galerie de la Reine and Galerie des Princes – which house a range of luxury shops and cafés. The ornate interior and expensive goods on sale made the galleries a fashionable meeting place for 19th-century society, including the resident literati – Victor Hugo and Alexandre Dumas have attended lectures here. The arcades remain a popular venue, with their shops, a cinema, theatre and restaurants.

Centre Belge de la Bande Dessinée ⓭

20 Rue des Sables, 1000 BRU. City Map 2 E2. Tel (02) 2191980. 🚌 29, 38, 46, 47, 61, 63, 66, 71, 86, 88. Ⓜ Botanique, De Brouckère, Rogier. 🚊 3, 4, 31, 32, 33, 92, 94. 🕐 10am–6pm Tue–Sun. 🎟 ♿ ▯ 🖥 🗎 www.comicscenter.net

Affectionately known by its initials as *cébébédé*, this museum for comic strip art pays tribute to the Belgian passion for *bandes dessinées* (comic strips) and to many internationally acclaimed comic strip artists from both Belgium and abroad.

Arranged over three levels, the collection is housed in a classic Art Nouveau building originally designed in 1903 by Victor Horta (see p80) as Les Magasins Wauquez, an enormous fabric warehouse. Saved from demolition in the 1980s, it reopened in 1989 as an impressive museum and archive centre dedicated to the comic strip, which is often referred to as the "ninth art" (see pp24–5).

One of the most popular permanent exhibitions is a tour of engaging comic strip heroes such as Hergé's *Tintin*, arguably the most well-known Belgian comic character. The tour also includes *The Smurfs*, which first appeared in the *Spirou* journal in 1958 and went on to have its own television show and hit records. Other displays detail the stages of putting together a comic strip, from initial ideas and rough pencil sketches through to final publication. Major exhibitions featuring the work of famous cartoonists and studios are regularly held. The museum also houses some 6,000 original plates, displayed in rotation, as well as an archive of photographs, biographies and other artifacts.

Alfresco dining at the restaurants along Rue des Bouchers

The exquisitely proportioned Cathédrale-Sts-Michel-et-Gudule

Éditions Jacques Brel

Place de la Vieille Halle aux Blés 11, 1000 BRU. **City Map** 1 C3. *Tel (02) 5111020.* 29, 38, 48, 60, 63, 65, 66, 71, 95, 96. M Gare Centrale. 10am–6pm Tue–Fri, noon–6pm Sat & Sun; performances on the hour. www.jacquesbrel.be

Established in 1980 by Jacques Brel's daughter, France Brel, the Éditions Jacques Brel aims to give visitors a sense of the world inhabited by this great singer-songwriter. It achieves this through a changing series of film presentations, which includes footage from his mesmerizing farewell concert at Olympia, Paris, in 1966. Other installations evoke the conditions of his life over the course of nearly 50 years.

The foundation also serves as an archive and research centre. It maintains an impressive collection of articles, manuscripts, slides, playbills and other artifacts associated with Brel's life and work. In addition, it contains several hours of audio and video documentation from some of Brel's public performances.

Cathédrale Sts-Michel-et-Gudule ⑭

Parvis Ste-Gudule, 1000 BRU. **City Map** 2 E2. *Tel (02) 2178345.* 27, 29, 38, 63, 65, 66. M Gare Centrale, Parc. 92, 94. 7am–6pm Mon–Fri, 8:30am–6pm Sat and Sun. to crypt. services throughout the day. on request. **www**.cathedralestmichel.be

Although it is the national church of Belgium, Cathédrale Sts-Michel-et-Gudule was granted cathedral status only in 1962. It was built with a sandy limestone brought from local quarries and is one of the finest surviving examples of Brabant Gothic architecture.

There has been a church on the site of the cathedral since at least the 11th century. Work began on the Gothic cathedral in 1226 under Henry I, Duke of Brabant, and was finally completed 300 years later at the beginning of the 16th century, under the reign of Charles V. It was dedicated to the city's patron saints, archangel Michael and a local 8th-century pious woman, St Gudule.

Owing to ransackings by Protestant iconoclasts in 1579 and thefts by French Revolutionists in 1793, the interior of the cathedral is far less rich than it was in medieval times. It nonetheless contains some fine stained glass, such as the **Last Judgement Window**, dating from 1528, on the west front of the cathedral, facing the altar. The transept windows, designed by Bernard van Orley (c.1490–1541), date from 1538 and represent the region's rulers. Also of particular interest is the beautiful and original Grenzing organ.

The flamboyantly carved **Baroque Pulpit** in the central aisle depicts Adam and Eve's expulsion from Paradise. This pulpit, by the Antwerp-born sculptor Hendrik Verbruggen, was built in 1699, although it was not installed till 1776.

JACQUES BREL

One of the most celebrated and cherished of all Belgians, Jacques Brel (1929–78) rose to stardom in the 1950s, when his evocative, touching and witty songs first came to the attention of the public in Paris. Brel wrote and performed countless songs – about love, ageing, drinking, the risible bourgeoisie, hopeless dreams, Belgium – many of which are still adored and much played today. These include "Ne Me Quitte Pas" and "Le Plats Pays", also known as "Mijn Vlakke Land". Brel performed with total commitment, singing in both French and Dutch. Although his passion is clear in recordings, fans claim that he was even better in live shows, at the end of which he would be famously awash in perspiration. In 1966, Brel announced that he would be giving up performing at concerts and had decided to devote himself to films and to composing music for the stage. This promising future was cut short by lung cancer and Brel was buried in French Polynesia, where he had spent his final years.

Jacques Brel, Belgium's well-loved singer-songwriter, in 1965

Place Royale ⑯

Rue Royale. **City Map** 2 E4. 🚋 *21, 27, 29, 34, 38, 54, 63, 64, 65, 66, 71, 80, 95.* Ⓜ *Trone, Parc.* 🚊 *92, 94.*

The influence of Charles de Lorraine is still keenly felt in the Place Royale. As Governor of the Austrian Netherlands from 1741 to 1780, he redeveloped the site which was then occupied by the ruins of the great, late-medieval **Coudenberg Palace** that had been destroyed by fire in 1731. The ruins of the palace were demolished and the entire site was rebuilt as two squares along Neo-Classical lines reminiscent of Vienna, a city that Charles de Lorraine greatly admired.

In 1995, excavations in the area uncovered ruins of the 15th-century **Aula Magna**, the Great Hall of the former palace. The hall was part of an extension of the palace started under the dukes of Brabant in the early 13th century and further developed by the dukes of Burgundy, in particular by Philip the Good. It was in this room that the Habsburg emperor Charles V abdicated in favour of his son, Philip II. The ruins can now be seen as part of the BELvue Museum.

Although criss-crossed by tramlines and traffic, the Place Royale maintains a feeling of dignity with its tall, elegant, buildings set symmetrically around a cobbled square. The equestrian statue in the centre, erected by King Leopold I in 1848, depicts the 11th-century knight Godefroid de Bouillon, a leader of the First Crusade.

Église St-Jacques-sur-Coudenberg ⑰

Place Royale, 1000 BRU. **City Map** 2 E4. *Tel* (02) 5117836. 🚋 *21, 27, 29, 34, 38, 54, 63, 64, 65, 66, 71, 80, 95.* Ⓜ *Trone, Parc.* 🚊 *92, 94.* ⏰ *1–6pm Tue–Sat, 8:45am–5:45pm Sun.*

Dedicated to the apostle St James, the pretty St-Jacques-sur-Coudenberg is the latest in a series of churches to have occupied this site. There has been a chapel here since the 12th century, when it served pilgrims en route to the saint's shrine at Santiago de Compostela in Spain. When the Coudenberg Palace was built in the 12th century, it became the ducal chapel. The chapel suffered over the years: it was ransacked during the conflict between Catholics and Protestants in 1579, and was so badly damaged in the 1731 fire that it had to be demolished. The present church was built in Neo-Classical style and was consecrated in 1787. During the French Revolution, it served as a Temple of Reason and Law, returning to the Catholic Church in 1802. The interior is elegant, with large paintings by Jan Portaels (1818–95). The church still has royal connections, and the choir has a direct link to the palace.

Glittering chandeliers in the vast Throne Room of the Palais Royal

The 19th-century cupola of Église St-Jacques-sur-Coudenberg

Palais Royal ⑱

Place des Palais, 1000 BRU. **City Map** 2 E4. *Tel* (02) 5512020. 🚋 *21, 27, 29, 34, 38, 54, 63, 64, 65, 66, 71, 80, 95.* Ⓜ *Trone, Gare Centrale, Parc.* 🚊 *92, 94.* ⏰ *mid-July–mid-Sep: 10:30am–5pm Tue–Sat.* 🍴 ♿ 🚫

The official residence of the Belgian monarchy in central Brussels, the Palais Royal is located close to the site of the old Coudenberg Palace. Its construction began in the 1820s, linking two 18th-century side wings. Most of the exterior was completed during the reign of Léopold II (1835–1909) and in the 20th century, the palace underwent interior improvements and restoration of its older sections.

The huge **Throne Room**, decorated in grand style with large pilastered columns and wall-mounted chandeliers, is one of Brussels's original state rooms. Beyond this, the **Long Gallery** displays late 19th-century ceiling paintings representing dawn, day and dusk. The **Small White Room**, a gilt chamber with late 18th-century Rococo furnishings, features rows of 19th-century royal portraits, while the **Pilasters Room** contains the original portrait of King Leopold I made in 1846. The **Hall of Mirrors**, similar in its grand effect to the mirrored chamber at Versailles, features a ceiling that has been decorated in green beetle and wing designs by sculptor Jan Fabre.

BELvue Museum and the Coudenberg ⑲

Place des Palais 7, 1000 BRU. **City Map** 2 E4. **Tel** (070) 220492. 🚌 21, 27, 29, 34, 38, 54, 63, 64, 65, 66, 71, 80, 95. Ⓜ Trone, Parc, Porte de Namur. 🚊 92, 94. ⏰ 10am–5pm Tue–Fri, 10am–6pm Sat & Sun. 🚫 25 Dec, 1 Jan. 📷 ♿ 🍴 🔲 www.belvue.be

With its collection of paintings, documents and other royal memorabilia, the BELvue Museum charts the history of the Belgian monarchy from independence in 1830 to the present day. The museum is housed in the former Hôtel Bellevue, an 18th-century Neo-Classical building.

Belgian history, starting with the 1830 uprising, is displayed here through 1,500 unique historical documents, film fragments, photos and objects. An underground archaeological site and museum, the Coudenberg, is located in the grounds of the BELvue Museum.

The broad and elegant Neo-Classical façade of BELvue Museum

Musée des Instruments de Musique ⑳

Rue Montagne de la Cour 2, 1000 BRU. **City Map** 2 E4. **Tel** (02) 5450130. 🚌 27, 29, 38, 63, 65, 66. Ⓜ Gare Centrale, Parc. 🚊 92, 94. ⏰ 9:30am–4:45pm Tue–Fri, 10am–4:45pm Sat & Sun. 📷 📸 ♿ 🍴 🔲 www.mim.fgov.be

Once a department store, the building known as Old England is a striking showpiece of Art Nouveau architecture. Architect Paul Saintenoy gave full rein to his imagination when he designed these shop premises for the Old England company in 1899. The façade is made entirely of glass and elaborate wrought iron. There is a domed gazebo on the roof, and a turret to one side. Surprisingly, it was only in the 1990s that a listed buildings policy was adopted in Brussels, which has secured treasures such as this. In 2000, it became the new Musée des Instruments de Musique (MIM). Meanwhile, the Old England company is still flourishing, with its premises on the fashionable Avenue Louise.

The collection of the MIM began in the 19th century when the state bought 80 ancient and exotic instruments. The collection was doubled in 1876 when King Léopold II donated a gift of 97 Indian musical instruments presented to him by a maharaja. A museum displaying all of these artifacts opened in 1877, and by 1924 it boasted 3,300 pieces and was recognized as a leader in its field. Today, the collection contains more than 6,000 items and includes many fine examples of wind, string and keyboard instruments from medieval times to the present. Visitors to the museum are provided with headphones which allow them to hear the sounds produced by many of the instruments on display. Among the chief attractions are prototype instruments by Adolphe Sax, Belgian inventor of the saxophone (see p205); mini violins favoured by street musicians; a violin-maker's studio; and a superb group of mechanical instruments, including the componium, a 19th-century barrel organ that composes its own music as it plays. There is also a restaurant (see p285) on the top floor with fine views over Brussels.

Unique marble floor in the state room, Palais de Charles de Lorraine

Palais de Charles de Lorraine ㉑

Place du Musée 1, 1000 BRU. **City Map** 2 D4. **Tel** (02) 5195372. 🚌 27, 29, 38, 63, 65, 66. Ⓜ Gare Centrale, Parc. 🚊 92, 94. ⏰ 1–5pm Wed & Sat. 🚫 last week in Dec. 📸 for details call (02) 5195372.

Set behind a Neo-Classical façade are the few surviving rooms of the palace of Charles de Lorraine, Governor of the Austrian Netherlands and a keen patron of the arts. Few original features remain, as the palace was ransacked by marauding French troops in 1794. The bas-reliefs at the top of the stairway, representing earth, air, fire and water, reflect Charles de Lorraine's interest in alchemy. Most spectacular of all the original features is the 28-point star, set in the floor of the circular state room. Each of the points is made from a different type of Belgian marble, taken from his personal mineral collection. Belgian marble was a much sought-after material used to construct St Peter's Basilica in Rome. The rooms contain a range of 18th-century furnishings and exhibits representing intellectual life during the Enlightenment. The palace also houses the royal library.

The dome of Old England, home to the MIM

Musées Royaux des Beaux-Arts de Belgique ㉒

See pp68–73.

Place du Grand Sablon ㉓

Rue des Sablons, 1000 BRU.
City Map 2 D4. 🚋 27, 29, 38, 63, 65, 66. Ⓜ *Gare Centrale, Louise, Parc.* 🚃 92, 94, 97. 🛍 *Sat and Sun.*

Situated on the slope of the escarpment that divides Brussels in two, the Place du Grand Sablon is like a stepping stone between the upper and lower halves of the city. The square's name derives from the French *sable* (sand), as this old route to the city centre once passed through some sandy marshes.

Today, the picture is very different. This area, roughly triangular in shape, stretches uphill from a 1751 fountain at its base to the Gothic church of Notre-Dame du Sablon. The fountain was a gift from Lord Bruce, an Englishman, in gratitude for the hospitality shown to him while he was exiled here between 1696 and 1741. The square is surrounded by town houses, with some Art Nouveau façades. This is a chic, wealthy and busy part of Brussels, with upmarket antique dealers, fashionable restaurants and trendy bars, which really come into their own in warm weather when people stay drinking outside until the early hours of the

morning. It is a good place in which to soak up the city's atmosphere. **Wittamer**, the well-known chocolate shop and pâtisserie is at No. 12 and has a tearoom on the first floor. The area near the church hosts a lively, if expensive, antiques market every weekend.

Notre-Dame du Sablon ㉔

Rue de la Regence 38, 1000 BRU.
City Map 2 D4. **Tel** (02) 5115741. 🚋 27, 29, 38, 63, 65, 66. Ⓜ *Gare Centrale, Louise, Parc.* 🚃 92, 94, 97. ⏰ *9am–6:30pm daily.* 📷 *on request.* ♿

Along with the Cathédrale Sts-Michel-et-Gudule *(see p63)*, this lovely church is one of the finest surviving examples of Brabant-Gothic architecture in Belgium today.

A church was first erected here when the guild of crossbowmen was granted permission to build a chapel to Our Lady on this sandy hill. Legend has it that a young girl in Antwerp had a vision of the Virgin Mary, who instructed the girl to take her statue to Brussels. The girl carried the statue by boat down the River Senne and gave it to the crossbowmen's chapel in the city. The chapel rapidly became a place of pilgrimage. The statue was was destroyed in 1565 and all

that remains of the incident are two carvings of the original pilgrimage tale, showing the young girl in a boat.

The first attempts to enlarge this church took place around 1400 but, due to lack of funds, the work was not completed until 1550. The interior is simple and beautifully proportioned, with interconnecting side chapels and an impressive pulpit dating from 1697. Of particular interest are the 11 magnificent stained-glass windows, each 14-m (45-ft) high, which dominate the inside of the church. When the building is lit, the windows shine into the night like welcoming beacons. Also of interest is the **Tour et Taxis Family Chapel**, built for a German family that once lived near the Place du Petit Sablon. In 1517, the family commissoned a series of tapestries to commemorate the church's legend. Most of them were stolen in the 1790s by the French Revolutionary Army, but some of the remaining examples are now hanging in the Musées Royaux d'Art et d'Histoire in the Parc du Cinquantenaire *(see pp76–7)*.

Rich stained glass at Notre-Dame du Sablon

Place du Petit Sablon ㉕

Rue de la Regence, 1000 BRU.
City Map 2 D4. 🚋 27, 29, 38, 63, 65, 66. Ⓜ *Gare Centrale, Louise, Parc.* 🚃 92, 94, 97.

These pretty, formal gardens were laid out in 1890 and form a charming spot. On top of the railings that enclose the gardens are 48 bronze statuettes by Art Nouveau designer Paul Hankar (1859–1901). Each of the figures represents a different medieval city guild. Located at the back of the gardens is a fountain built to commemorate the counts Egmont and Hornes, who pleaded against the introduction of the Spanish Inquisition by King Philip II, and were beheaded in 1568. On either

Brussels's famous Wittamer pâtisserie at Place du Grand Sablon

Statues of Count Egmont and Count Hornes at the Place du Petit Sablon

side of the fountain are 12 statues of 15th- and 16th-century figures, including those of Renaissance artist Bernard van Orley and the Flemish map-maker Gerhard Mercator, whose 16th-century projection of the world is the basis of most modern maps.

Notre-Dame de la Chapelle ㉖

Place de la Chapelle 1, 1000 BRU. **City Map** 1 C4. *Tel* (02) 5120737. 🚌 27, 29, 38, 63. Ⓜ Gare Centrale, Anneessens. 🚊 3, 4, 31, 32, 33. 🕐 9am–7pm daily. ✝ 4pm Sat, 8pm Sun. **Flea Market** Place du Jeu de Balle. 🕐 mornings daily.

In 1134, Duke Godefroid I decided to build a chapel outside the city's walls. This quickly became a market church, serving the many craftsmen who lived nearby. By 1210, it had become so popular that it was made the parish church. In 1250, it became truly famous when a donation of five pieces of the True Cross turned the church into a pilgrimage site.

The majority of the original Romanesque church was destroyed by fire in 1405. When rebuilding began in 1421, it was in a Gothic style typical of 15th-century Brabant architecture. The Baroque bell tower was added after the French bombardment in 1695 *(see p42)*. Monstrous gargoyles peer down from the exterior walls, while inside, a chapel and plaque commemorate the 16th-century Belgian artist Pieter Brueghel the Elder *(see p22)* who lived in **Rue Haute** nearby, and is buried here.

Rue Haute leads through the traditionally working-class and independent-minded district known as **Les Marolles**. The area was home to crafts-men and weavers, and street names such as Rue des Brodeurs (Embroiderers' Street) and Rue des Charpentiers (Carpenters' Street) reflect the district's artisanal history.

Today, the area is known for its fine **Flea Market** in the Place du Jeu de Balle, with the biggest and best markets held on Sundays. These sell almost anything from junk to pre-war collector's items.

Palais de Justice ㉗

Place Poelaert 1, 1000 BRU. **City Map** 1 C5. *Tel* (02) 5086578. 🚌 34. Ⓜ Louise. 🚊 91, 92, 93, 94. 🕐 8am–5pm Mon–Fri. ⬤ Jul. 🎦 on request. ♿

Dominating the Brussels skyline, the Palais de Justice can be seen from almost any vantage point in the city. Of all the ambitious projects of King Leopold II, this was perhaps the grandest. It occupies an area larger than St Peter's Basilica in Rome, and was one of the world's most impressive 19th-century buildings. It was built between 1866 and 1883 by Belgian architect Joseph Poelaert who found inspiration for it in the designs of Classical tem-ples built for the Egyptian pharoahs. Unfortunately, Poelaert died in 1879 while it was still under construction. The Palais de Justice is still home to the city's law courts.

Porte de Hal ㉘

Boulevard du Midi, 1000 BRU. **City Map** 1 B5. *Tel* (02) 5341518. 🚌 27, 48. Ⓜ Porte de Hal. 🚊 3, 55, 90. 🕐 9.30am–5pm Tue–Fri, 10am–5pm Sat and Sun. 🎦 ♿ **www**.kmkg-mrah.be

This impressive bastion is the only surviving gate from the 14th-century medieval city walls that once surrounded Brussels, and is a vivid indi-cator of their colossal scale. The walls were pulled down in the 18th century, but their pentagon-shaped path is now occupied by the inner ring road and so is still clearly visible on maps. The Porte de Hal (the gate on the road towards Halle or Hal) survived because it was used as a prison. It was heavily restored in the 1860s when medieval heritage was once again cher-ished. Under the direction of the Musées Royaux d'Art et d'Histoire *(see p77)*, it now presents a permanent collec-tion of armour and weapons, a historical account of the guilds of Brussels and some temporary exhibitions. There is also a walkway on the ram-parts which offers fine views.

The imposing bulk of Porte de Hal, evoking Brussels's medieval past

Musées Royaux des Beaux-Arts de Belgique ㉒
Musée d'Art Ancien

Officially known as the Musées Royaux des Beaux-Arts de Belgique, the Musée d'Art Ancien, Musée Fin de Siècle and Musée Magritte are Brussels's premier art museums. The buildings cover two eras, *ancien* (15th to 18th century) and *moderne* (19th century to present day), as well as René Magritte's works from the early 1900s to 1967. The Musée d'Art Ancien opened in 1887 and has the finest collection of Flemish art in the world. Housed in a Neo-Classical building, designed by fashionable architect Alphonse Balat between 1874 and 1880, the collection was put together in the late 18th century, when it was made up of paintings looted by the French Revolutionary Army. Many more were recovered from France after 1815, and the Musée d'Art Ancien is now the largest of the museums and is famed for holding the finest collection of Flemish art in the world, with Old Masters such as van Dyck and Rubens very well represented.

Façade of Museum
Corinthian columns and busts of Flemish painters adorn the entrance.

Ground level

Main Entrance

Entrance to The Museum Shop

The Census at Bethlehem *(1610)*
Pieter Brueghel the Younger (c.1564–1638) produced a version of this subject, some 40 years after the original by his father. Both works are in the collection, showing the progression to the son's smoother style.

★ The Annunciation *(1406–07)*
The Master of Flémalle, Robert Campin (c.1375–1444) depicted Archangel Gabriel announcing the imminent birth of the Messiah in a contemporary setting. The everyday objects offer a homely contrast to the momentous nature of the event.

STAR PAINTINGS

★ The Assumption of the Virgin

★ The Annunciation

Upper level

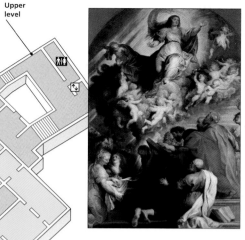

VISITORS' CHECKLIST

Rue de la Régence 3, 1000
BRU. **City Map** 2 D4. **Tel** (02)
5083211. 27, 29, 38, 63, 65,
66. Gare Centrale. 92,
94. 10am–5pm Tue–Sun.
www.fine-arts-museum.be

★ The Assumption of the Virgin *(1610)*
Pieter Paul Rubens (1577–1640) was the leading exponent of Baroque art in Europe, combining Flemish precision with Italian flair. In The Assumption of the Virgin, *he suppressed background colours to emphasize the Virgin's blue robes.*

Madonna with Saint Anne and a Franciscan Donor *(1470)*
Hugo van der Goes (c.1430–82) was commissioned to paint this symbolic work by the monk shown on the right, for his personal devotional use.

To Musée Magrite →

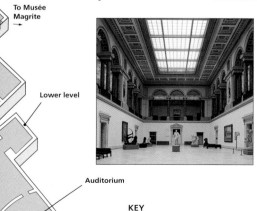

Interior of the Main Hall
Lit from above by a glass roof, the Main Hall provides an impressive gateway to the collections, as well as a generous space to exhibit paintings and a rotating selection of sculptures.

Lower level

Auditorium

KEY

	15th–16th century
	17th–18th century
	Temporary exhibitions
	Non-exhibition space

GALLERY GUIDE
The gallery is divided up into two different eras of art, as shown in the key. Two large auditoriums on the ground and lower levels are used for occasional lectures as well as presentations. Visitors can enter the Musée Magritte and from there, the Musée Fin de Siècle, via the escalator behind the museum's restaurant. Due to ongoing renovation work, gallery layouts may change.

Musées Royaux des Beaux-Arts: Musée Magritte and Musée Fin de Siècle

The Musée Magritte gives unprecedented insight into the life and works of one of Belgium's most celebrated painters, René Magritte, a major exponent of Surrealism. Stretching over five floors, the museum occupies a refurbished Neo-Classical building on the Place Royale. Next to it is the Musée Fin de Siècle, laid out in the 1980s over three storeys and six spiralling levels, all ingeniously sunk into the ground to avoid obscuring the 18th-century Place du Musée. This museum showcases European and international art from the end of the 19th century and the beginning of the 20th century. A D-shaped lightwell allows visitors to view the exhibits by natural light, in spite of the building's location underground.

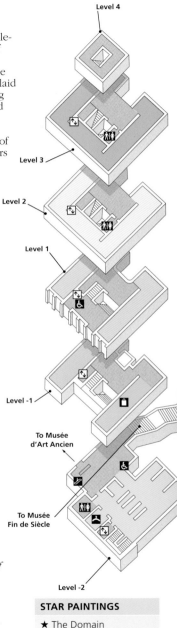

Level 4

Level 3

Level 2

Level 1

Level -1

To Musée d'Art Ancien

To Musée Fin de Siècle

Level -2

Portrait of Baron Francis Delbeke (1917)
Antwerp-born Jules Schmalzigaug (1882–1917) was one of the most original and gifted artists of his generation. He was involved in the Italian Futurist movement in Rome between 1912 and 1914, and his work became increasingly abstract. He moved to the neutral Netherlands at the advent of World War I, where, depressed, he took his own life at the age of 35.

★ **The Domain of Arnheim** (1962)
Magritte's painting of an eagle-mountain rearing over a small bird's nest, precariously perched on a wall, is an unsettling image that teases the viewer for an explanation. The title is from a short story by Edgar Allan Poe (1809–49).

STAR PAINTINGS

★ The Domain of Arnheim

★ Woman in a Blue Dress in Front of a Mirror

La Seine à la Grande-Jatte *(1888)*
It was in this painting that Georges Seurat first applied his pointilism technique on a large scale; colour dots are juxtaposed and optically fuse in the viewer's eye.

KEY

☐	Musée Fin de Siècle: 19th–20th century
☐	Musée Magritte: 1898–1929
☐	Musée Magritte: 1930–1950
☐	Musée Magritte: 1951–1967
☐	Musée Magritte: multimedia area
☐	Temporary exhibitions
☐	Non exhibition space

Level -4

★ **Woman in a Blue Dress in Front of a Mirror** *(1914)*
Brussels-born Rik Wouters (1882–1916) was a sculptor and Fauvist painter whose fascination with the effects of colours led him to experiment with innovative spatula painting and other new techniques.

Level -3

Level -6

Portrait de Marguerite Khnopff *(1887)*
An austere representation of the artist's sister by the famed Symbolist Fernand Khnopff (1858–1921), captures his interest in the mysterious nature of the human soul. Khnopff's sister was a subject of several of his early paintings.

Level -5

Level -8

GALLERY GUIDE

Access to the museums is available through the main ticket hall of Musées Royaux des Beaux-Arts de Belgique. The Musée Magritte is arranged in chronological order. The lowest underground level is a multimedia area, showing Magritte's films. From here, stairs lead down to the uppermost level of the Musée Fin de Siècle, which has been set aside for temporary exhibitions. The area shaded in green is the permanent collection, which displays work from the end of the 19th and start of the 20th century.

Level -7

Exploring the Musées Royaux des Beaux-Arts de Belgique

The several museums that make up the Musées Royaux des Beaux-Arts de Belgique contain works of many artistic styles, from the religious paintings of the 15th-century Flemish Primitives to the Pop Art and Minimalism of the 1960s and 1970s. All are very well set out, guiding the visitor easily through the full collection or directly to a specific art era. Each section is highly accessible, with the two main museums divided into different sections, each relating to the art of a particular century.

Vase of Flowers (1704) by Dutch still-life painter Rachel Ruysch

MUSÉE D'ART ANCIEN

The Musée d'Art Ancien exhibits works dating from the 15th to the 18th centuries. In the first few rooms are works by the renowned school of Flemish Primitives *(see pp102–103).* As is the case with most art from the Middle Ages, the paintings are chiefly religious in nature and depict biblical scenes and details from the lives of saints. Many of these show deeds of horrific torture, martyrdom and violence, attended by the perplexing nonchalance of the elegantly attired bystanders. A typical example is the diptych *The Justice of Emperor Otto III* (c.1460) by Dirk Bouts, which includes a gory beheading (a famous miscarriage of justice in the 12th century) and an execution by burning at the stake. At the same time, the detail is exquisite and provides a fascinating window on the textiles, architecture and faces of the 15th century. Also on display are works such as

Lamentation by Rogier van der Weyden, city painter to Brussels during the mid-15th century, and *The Martyrdom of Saint Sebastian* by the famed Bruges artist Hans Memling (c.1433–94).

Another unique aspect of the section is the extensive collection of paintings by the Brueghels, father and son. Both were renowned for their scenes of peasant life. On display are *The Fall of Icarus* (1558) by Brueghel the Elder and *The Struggle between Carnival and Lent* (c.1559) by his son, Pieter.

In the following rooms are works from the 17th and 18th centuries. A highlight of this section is the world-famous collection of paintings by Baroque artist Pieter Paul Rubens (1557–1640), which affords a fine overview of the artist's work. As well as key examples of his religious works, there are some excellent portraits, such as *Hélène Fourment*, of his young wife. Of special interest are the sketches made in preparation for Rubens's larger works, including *Four Negro*

Heads, for his iconic *Adoration of the Magi* (1624).

Other works of note in this section are the paintings by Old Masters such as van Dyck's *Portrait of a Genoese Lady with her Daughter* from the 1620s and *Three Children with Goatcart* by Frans Hals, the famous portrait painter. Representatives of the later Flemish schools include Jacob Jordaens *(see p103)* and his depiction of myths such as *Pan and Syrinx* (c.1645) and *Satyr and Peasant.* Baroque and Flemish art are all well represented in the museums.

Also on display are some small sculptures that were studies of larger works by Laurent Delvaux, a leading sculptor of the 18th century. Most notably, *Hercules and Erymanthian Boar* is a study for the sculpture by the staircase in the Palais de Charles de Lorraine *(see p65).* Works of the Italian, Spanish and French schools are also represented, notably the Classical landscape painter Claude Le Lorrain's poetic scene of *Aeneas Hunting the Stag on the Coast of Libya* (1672). Other works on show include *Vase of Flowers* (1704) by Dutch artist Rachel Ruysch, who specialized in still-life paintings of flowers and fruits.

MUSÉE FIN DE SIÈCLE

The Musée Fin de Siècle showcases European and international art from the end of the 19th century to the beginning of the 20th century. The collection focuses on the

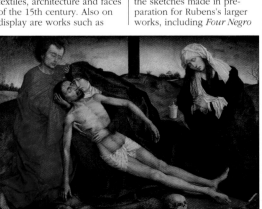

Lamentation (c.1441) by Rogier van der Weyden

combined efforts of various well-established art institutions in Belgium, exploring social topics expressed through decorative arts, literature and music, with influences from Theatre Royal de la Monnaie and the Bibliothèque royale de Belgique.

The collection of work covers 31 different European art academies who, in 1868, collectively created the Société Libre des Beaux-Arts, introducing modernism and the avant-garde to Belgium.

This counterculture art movement pioneered the revolt against materialism and a consequent move towards illustrating landscapes and social ideas as central themes of artwork. The exhibition includes Belgian national literature, the rediscovery of the Primitives, Impressionism, Symbolism and Art Nouveau. Artists in the collection include Khnopff, Seurat, Spilliaert, Gauguin, de Vlaminick and van de Velde, who was also the main founder of the Art Nouveau movement.

There is an excellent range of Symbolist art, including the disturbing classic *Des Caresses* by Fernand Khnopff (1858–1921), which shows an androgynous figure nuzzling a human head on a cheetah's body.

Work by artists such as Henri Evenepoel (1872–99) show a distinctive post-Impressionist style as in *The Orange Market in Blidah* (1898). There are also bizarre paintings by proto-Expressionist James Ensor (1860–1949), including his 1892 work *Singular Masks*.

The highlight of the exhibition and also the main

The Orange Market in Blidah (1898) by Henri Evenepoel

draw to the museum is the extraordinarily vast Gillion Crowet Collection of Art Nouveau paintings and objects, given to the Musées Royaux de Beaux-Arts by the Brussels-Capital Region.

MUSÉE MAGRITTE

The works of the Belgian Surrealist movement have long proved a popular highlight of the Musées Royaux des Beaux-Art's collection. The art of René Magritte in particular has created an extraordinary public fascination since the increase in his popularity in the 1960s. To reflect public demand, and to afford the best possible display, his work is now housed in this separate section of the museum.

Born the son of a wealthy manufacturer in Lessines *(see p185)*, Magritte entered the Brussels Academie des Beaux-Arts in 1916. A former poster and advertisement designer, he created visually striking work, frequently displaying a juxtaposition of

familiar objects in unusual, sometimes unsettling, combinations and contexts. Many of the artist's best-known paintings are shown here in an impressively comprehensive collection of 200 works. These cover everything from large-scale canvases to magazine covers, advertising posters and wallpaper designs, including *L'Empire des Lumières* (1954) and *La Voleuse* (1928). They are also laid out chronologically, so it's possible to see his remarkably rapid development as an artist.

Of particular note are the paintings that date from Magritte's self-titled "Cavernous" period of 1927–30 which reflect both the macabre and the erotic. At this time, while living in Paris, Magritte painted roughly a canvas a day. He then moved back to Brussels, where he lived for the rest of his life. Powerful, arresting paintings on display from this latter period include the eerie *Domain of Arnheim (see p70)* and the melancholic *Saveur des Larmes* (1948).

Des Caresses (1896) by the symbolist artist, Fernand Khnopff.

Musée Charlier, home to one of Brussels's most fascinating collections of art and furnishings

Musée Charlier ㉙

Avenue des Arts 16, 1210 BRU. **City Map** 2 F2. *Tel* (02) 220691. 🚌 22, 65, 66. Ⓜ Madou, Arts-Loi. 🚋 29, 63. ◯ noon–5pm Mon–Thu, 10am–1pm Fri. 📷 🎫 French and Dutch only. **www**.charliermuseum.be

This museum was once home to the wealthy collector and patron of arts, Henri Van Cutsem. In 1890, he asked the young architect Victor Horta *(see p80)* to redesign his house as an exhibition space for his extensive collection. When Van Cutsem passed away, his friend, the sculptor Guillaume Charlier, installed his own art collection in the house.

Charlier commissioned Horta to build another museum to house the Van Cutsem collection – the Musée des Beaux Arts in Tournai *(see p184)*, in western Belgium. After Charlier's death, the house was made into a museum in 1928.

The Musée Charlier contains paintings by several artists, including portraits by Antoine Wiertz, early landscapes by Boulenger, Vogels and Knopff, still lifes by Ensor and other Realist and Impressionist works. The collection holds sculptures by Charlier, as well as glassware, silverware and porcelain. It also has a unique Asian room with Chinese furniture and wallpaper on display. The museum houses tapestries too – some from the Paris studios of Aubusson – set along the staircases and first floor and the elegant

displays of furniture in Louis XV and Louis XVI styles, located on the first floor.

Musée du Jouet ㉚

Rue de l'Association 24, 1000 BRU. **City Map** 2 F2. *Tel* (02) 2196168. 🚌 29, 61, 63, 65, 66. Ⓜ Botanique, Madou. 🚋 92, 93, 94. ◯ 10am–noon and 2–6pm daily. 📷 🖥 🏠 **www**.museedujouet.eu

This well-established toy museum, housed in a 19th-century *maison de maître* (urban mansion), will delight visitors of all ages. It contains some 25,000 artifacts, dating from 1850 onwards. Adults will enjoy the nostalgic thrill of seeing the toys of their youth as well as the lead soldiers, model engines, dolls, rocking horses and wooden jigsaws of earlier generations. Hands-on exhibits have been designed to amuse younger visitors.

Parc du Cinquantenaire ㉛

See pp76–7.

Quartier Européen ㉜

City Map 3 B3. 🚌 12, 21, 22, 27, 36, 59, 60, 64, 79. Ⓜ Maalbeek, Schuman.

The area at the top of the Rue de la Loi and around the Schuman roundabout is

where the main buildings of the European Union's administration are found.

The most recognizable of all the European Union seats is the cross-shaped **Berlaymont** building, a vast four-pointed building that was completed in 1967 and has since become an iconic symbol of the EU's growing power. It is the headquarters of the European Commission, whose workers are, in effect, civil servants of the EU. The Council of Ministers, which comprises representatives of member-states' governments, now meets in the sprawling pink granite block across the

Distinctive Art Nouveau curlicues and flourishes on the Maison St-Cyr

road from the Berlaymont. This building is known as **Justus Lipsius**, after a 16th-century Flemish philosopher.

Further down the road from the Justus Lipsius building is **Résidence Palace**, a luxury 1920s housing complex that boasted a theatre, pool and roof garden. The International Press Centre is currently based in the palace.

This whole area is naturally full of life and bustle during the day, but much quieter in the evenings; it can feel almost deserted on weekends. Pleasant at any time is the proximity of a number of the city's wonderful green spaces, which include the Parc du Cinquantenaire and **Parc Léopold**. The verdant Square Ambiorix, to the north, contains the **Maison St-Cyr** at No. 11 – the most extravagant of all Art Nouveau houses in Brussels, built in 1903 by architect Gustave Strauven.

European Parliament ㉝

Rue Wiertz 43, 1047 BRU. **City Map** 3 A4. 🚌 21, 22, 27, 34, 38, 54, 60, 80, 95, 96. Ⓜ *Maelbeek, Schuman.* 📋 *Book via website: 10am and 3pm Mon–Thu, 10am Fri.* 🔗 **www**.europarl.europa.eu

This vast, modern steel and glass complex, situated just behind the Quartier Léopold train station, is one of the three homes of the European Parliament, the elected body of the European Union. Its permanent seat is located in Strasbourg, France, where the plenary sessions are held once a month. Luxembourg is the administrative centre, and the committee meetings are held in Brussels.

A gleaming state-of-the-art building completed in 1997, it has many admirers, not least the parliamentary workers and Members of the European Parliament (MEPs). However, it also has critics – the huge domed structure containing a hemicycle that seats 700-plus MEPs has been dubbed *le caprice des dieux* – the whim

The European Parliament building behind the trees of Parc Léopold

of the gods – referring both to the shape of the building, which is similar to a cheese of the same name, and to its lofty aspirations. Many also regret that to make room for the new complex, a large part of the Quartier Léopold that stood here has been lost.

Musée Wiertz ㉞

Rue Vautier 62, 1050 BRU. **City Map** 3 A4. **Tel** (02) 6481718. 🚌 12, 21, 22, 27, 34, 36, 38, 44, 54, 59, 60, 71, 79, 80, 95. Ⓜ *Maelbeek, Schuman, Trone.* ◯ *10am–noon and 1–5pm Tue–Fri.* ● *Jul–Aug: Sat and Sun.* **www**.fine-arts-museum.be

The 160 works, including oil paintings, drawings and sculptures that form the main body of Antoine Wiertz's (1806–65) artistic output are housed in Musée Wiertz. The collection fills a studio built for the immensely popular Wiertz by the Belgian state, where he

Awe-inspiring paintings in the huge studio space of the Musée Wiertz

lived and worked from 1850 until his death, when the studio became a museum.

The enormous main room contains Wiertz's largest paintings. Many of them depict biblical and Homeric scenes, some of which are in the style of Rubens, while others bear witness to his macabre imagination. Also on display are his sculptures and death mask. The last of the six rooms contains his more gruesome efforts, with titles as fearsome as their content. These include *Madness, Hunger and Crime* and *Premature Burial.*

Institut Royal des Sciences Naturelles ㉟

Rue Vautier 29, 1000 BRU. **City Map** 3 A4. **Tel** (02) 6274238. 🚌 12, 21, 22, 27, 34, 36, 38, 54, 59, 60, 64, 71, 79, 80, 95. Ⓜ *Maalbeek, Schuman, Trône.* ◯ *9:30am–5pm Tue–Fri, 10am–6pm Sat and Sun.* 🔗 **www**.naturalsciences.be

Established in 1846, the Institut Royal des Sciences Naturelles is best known for its collection of iguanadon skeletons which date from 250 million years ago. Discovered in 1870, at Bernissart near Mons (*see p189*), they were among the first complete dinosaur skeletons to be reassembled – a major contribution to paleontology. The museum contains educational displays on natural history, and a gallery on evolution was added in 2009 to mark the 200th birth anniversary of Charles Darwin.

Parc du Cinquantenaire ❸

The finest of King Leopold II's grand projects, the Parc and Palais du Cinquantenaire were built for the Golden Jubilee celebrations of Belgian independence in 1880. The park was laid out on land used for military training. The palace, at its entrance, was to comprise a triumphal arch and two large exhibition areas, but by the time of the 1880 Art and Industry Expo, only the two side exhibition areas had been completed. Funds were eventually found and work continued for 50 years. Before being converted into museums, the large halls on either side of the archway held trade fairs, the last of which was in 1935. The halls have also been used for horse races and to house homing pigeons. During World War II, the grounds of the park were used to grow vegetables to feed the people of Brussels.

Musée Royal de l'Armée gun

★ **Musée Royal de l'Armée et d'Histoire Militaire**
The museum exhibits cover Belgium's military history with over 200 years of militaria, including historic aircraft.

View of Park with Arch
Originally conceived as a gateway into the city of Brussels, the triumphal arch was completed only in 1905.

The Grand Mosque was built in Arabic style as a folly in 1880. It became a mosque in 1978.

Pavillon Horta

Tree-lined Avenue
Many of the plantations of elms and plane trees that make up the forested walks date from 1880.

STAR SIGHTS

★ Cinquantenaire Museum

★ Musée Royal de l'Armée et d'Histoire Militaire

Underpass

0 metres   100

0 yards   100

Central Archway
The arch is crowned by the sculpture of Brabant Raising the National Flag, *while riding a quadriga.*

VISITORS' CHECKLIST

Ave de Tervuren, 1040 BRU.
City Map 3 C3. 🚌 12, 21, 22, 27, 36, 60, 61, 79, 80, 81, 83.
M *Schuman, Mérode.* 🚻 🏛
Autoworld (02) 7364165. ⏰
Apr–Sep: 10am–6pm Sat & Sun;
Oct–Mar: 10am–5pm Tue–Fri. 🎦
🚻 📷 **Grand Mosque** (02) 735
2173. ⏰ 9am–4pm Mon–Thu.

Autoworld
Set in the south wing of the palace, Autoworld has one of the best collections of automobiles in the world. There are some 300 cars, including an 1886 motor, a 1924 Model-T Ford and American limousines of the 1950s.

The park is popular with Brussels's eurocrats and families at lunchtimes and weekends.

★ Cinquantenaire Museum
Belgian architect Bordiau's plans for these two exhibition halls, later permanent showcases, were partly modelled on London's Victorian museums. The use of iron and glass in their construction was inspired by the Crystal Palace.

Cinquantenaire Museum

Parc du Cinquantenaire 10. **Tel** (02)
7417211. ⏰ 9:30am–5pm Tue–Fri,
10am–5pm Sat, Sun and public holidays. ⏰ 1 May, 1 and 11 Nov. 🎦 🚻
Part of the Musées Royaux d'Art et d'Histoire, the Cinquantenaire Museum has occupied its present site since the early 1900s. It houses four main collections: Antiquity, National Archaeology, European Decorative Arts and Non-European Civilizations, which includes sections on Byzantium, China and the Indian subcontinent, South-East Asia, as well as the pre-Columbian civilizations of the Americas. There are decorative arts from all ages, with silverware, glassware, porcelain and a fine collection of tapestries. Religious sculptures and stained glass are displayed around a courtyard in the style of church cloisters. The use of iron and glass was inspired by the Crystal Palace.

Aircraft display at the Musée Royal de l'Armée et d'Histoire Militaire

Musée Royal de l'Armée et d'Histoire Militaire

Parc du Cinquantenaire 3.
Tel (02) 7377833. ⏰ 9am–noon and 1–4:45pm Tue–Sun. ⏰ 1 May, 1 Nov. 🚻
Together with the section on aviation, the displays cover the Belgian army and its history from the late 1700s onwards, including weapons, uniforms, decorations and paintings. There is a section covering the 1830 struggle for independence (*see pp44–5*). Two other sections showcase the history of the World Wars and the Resistance (*see pp46–7*).

GREATER BRUSSELS

Central Brussels is bound by a heart-shaped ring-road called the Petite Ceinture (Small Belt), which follows the path of the old medieval city walls. Beyond this lie 19 suburbs which form the Bruxelles-Capitale region. Many of these are residential, but a handful contain treasures of Brussels's history. For fans of early 20th-century architecture, the suburbs of St-Gilles and Ixelles offer striking Art Nouveau buildings, such as the Musée Horta. To the west lies the suburb of

Sign at the Erasmus House

Anderlecht and the charming house where the Renaissance humanist Erasmus lived. In Koekelberg is the huge dome of the Basilique Nationale du Sacré-Coeur. To the north, Heysel offers attractions such as the Atomium, originally built in 1958, whose modernity contrasts with the historical city centre. To the east, the Musée Royal de l'Afrique Centrale reflects Belgium's colonial past in the Congo, while Musée du Transport Urbain takes visitors on a journey through Brussels's past.

SIGHTS AT A GLANCE

Buildings and Monuments
The Atomium ⑫
Basilique Nationale du
    Sacré-Coeur ⑨
Begijnhof van Anderlecht ⑧
Erasmus House ⑦

Museums
Musée des Beaux-Arts d'Ixelles ②
Musée Bruxellois de
    la Gueuze ⑥
Musée Constantin Meunier ③
Musée David et Alice
    van Buuren ④
Musée Horta ①
Rene Magritte Museum ⑩

Musée Royal de
    l'Afrique Centrale ⑮
Musée du Transport Urbain
    Bruxellois ⑭

Tours
Art Nouveau Tour ⑤

Parks and Gardens
Bruparck ⑪
Domaine de Laeken ⑬

SEE ALSO

• *Where to Stay* p263

• *Where to Eat* pp286–7

KEY

▪	Brussels city centre
▪	Greater Brussels
✈	International airport
🚉	Train station
═	Motorway
═	Main road
═	Minor road
—	Railway

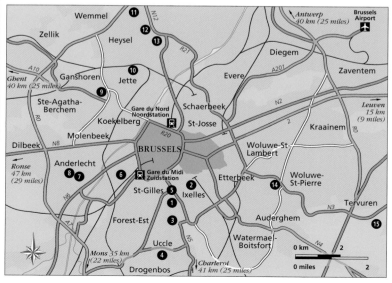

The elegant, light-filled living room showcasing Horta's characteristic style

Musée Horta ❶

Rue Américaine 25, St-Gilles, 1060
BRU. **Road Map** B4. **Tel** (02) 5430
490. 🚌 48, 54. Ⓜ Albert, Louise. 🚊
3, 4, 33, 51, 92, 94, 97. ⬜ 2–5:30pm
Tue–Sun. ♿ **www**.hortamuseum.be

Belgian architect Victor Horta
(1861–1947) is considered by
many to be the father of Art
Nouveau architecture. Horta's
prodigious skill lay not only
in his grand, overall vision
but in his equal talent as an
interior designer. He had a
huge impact on the architecture of Brussels in his day
(see p82), although many of
his buildings no longer exist.
This museum, the most complete exploration of the Art

Nouveau style, is housed in
his restored family home and
studio. These two delightful
buildings were designed by
Horta between 1898 and 1901.
    The airy interior of the house
displays Horta's trademark
architectural style, using iron,
glass and curves, while retaining a functional approach.
The details of his work are
best seen in the living room,
where sculpted bannister ends
and finely made door handles
echo forms found in nature.
The splendid central staircase
is decorated with curved
wrought iron, and the stairs
are enhanced by mirrors,
which bring natural light into
the house. In the dining
room, white enamel tiles line
the walls, rising to an ornate
ceiling decorated with the
scrolled metalwork used in
other rooms. This harmonious
blend of colour and materials
is characteristic of Horta's
work and part of the enduring appeal of Art Nouveau.

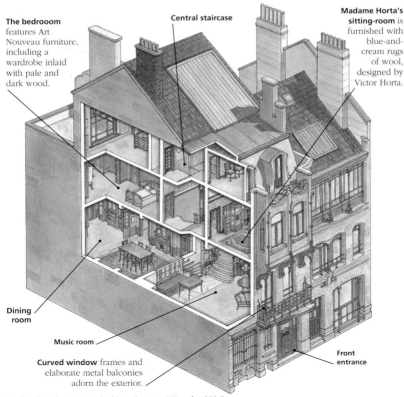

The bedrooom features Art Nouveau furniture, including a wardrobe inlaid with pale and dark wood.

Central staircase

Madame Horta's sitting-room is furnished with blue-and-cream rugs of wool, designed by Victor Horta.

Dining room

Music room

Curved window frames and elaborate metal balconies adorn the exterior.

Front entrance

Wouters's *La Vierge Folle* in the
Musée des Beaux-Arts d'Ixelles

Musée des Beaux-Arts d'Ixelles ❷

Rue Jean van Volsem 71, Ixelles,
1050 BRU. **Road Map** B4. *Tel (02)*
5156422. 🚌 34, 54, 64, 71, 80.
Ⓜ *Porte de Namur.* 🚋 24, 25, 81.
🕙 11:30am–5pm Tue–Sun. ♿ 🏠
www.museedixelles.be

The commune of Ixelles
possesses a remarkably rich
art collection, presented in
this small but highly rewarding gallery. It contains
intriguing but little-known
work by painters such as
Rembrandt, Fragonard and
Picasso and original posters
by Toulouse-Lautrec. There is
a good variety of work by the
Belgian Symbolists Léon
Frédéric and Léon Spilliaert.
Other Belgian artists such as
Magritte and Rik Wouters are
represented with such pieces
as a copy of the latter's
exuberant bronze sculpture
La Vierge Folle (The Mad
Virgin). The museum is also
noted for temporary exhibits.

Musée Constantin Meunier ❸

Rue de l'Abbaye 59, Ixelles, 1050
BRU. **Road Map** B4. *Tel (02)*
6484449. 🚌 38, 60. 🚋 23, 93, 94.
🕙 10am–noon and 1–5pm Tue–Fri.
🏠 www.fine-arts-museum.be

Brussels-born Constantin
Meunier (1831–1905) was
an artist of great distinction,
a realist who painted gritty
industrial scenes in keeping

with his socialist sympathies.
He is best known for bronze
sculptures of factory workers,
such as the *puddleurs* (forge-
workers). These were largely
inspired by his visits to industrial regions around Liège
(see pp216–19) and Charleroi
(see p187) in the 1870s and
1880s. The figures speak
eloquently of that era – bent
by their grim toil and hard-
ships, they nonetheless retain
an air of indomitable dignity.
This museum, a branch
of the Musées Royaux des
Beaux-Arts *(see pp68–73)*,
is located in Meunier's
former home and studio,
built in 1899, where Meunier
lived and worked for the last
five years of his life. In
addition to the sculptures for
which he is famous, the
museum also has a good
cross section of his paintings
and documents, as well as
informative exhibits that
demonstrate some of his
working techniques.

Musée David et Alice van Buuren ❹

Avenue Léo Errera 41, Uccle, 1180
BRU. **Road Map** B4. *Tel (02)*
3434851. 🚌 60, 134. 🚋 3, 23, 24.
🕙 2–5:30pm Wed–Mon. 🖼 🏠
www.museumvanbuuren.com

Set in the prosperous, leafy
suburb of Uccle, this museum
delights on two levels. First,
it is a comfortable, relaxed
villa, originally built and furnished in the late 1920s in a
user-friendly Art Deco style
for the Dutch banker David
van Buuren and his wife.

The iconic *Blacksmith* sculpture on
view at Meunier's former home

Second, since the van Buurens
used their fortune to invest in
their passion for art, the house
contains an outstanding
private collection of artwork.
The art on display includes
a priceless version of *The Fall
of Icarus* by Pieter Brueghel
the Elder, as well as paintings
and sculptures by Vincent van
Gogh, James Ensor and Rik
Wouters. Artists from the St-
Martens-Latem School of Art
(see p136), such as Constant
Permeke and Gustave van
de Woestyne, are also well
represented in the collection.
The van Buurens's quest
for harmonious surroundings
extended to the beautiful
series of gardens outside,
which were carefully
designed according to Art
Deco principles of stylistic
geometry by the noted
landscape architects, René
Pechère and Jules Buyssens.

Charmingly geometric Art Deco style at Musée David et Alice van Buuren

Art Nouveau Tour ⑤

The southern suburbs of Brussels grew rapidly in the late 19th century as wealthy industrialists commissioned grand new town mansions, or *hôtels*, from a new generation of architects. After 1895, Art Nouveau was the most fashionable style in Ixelles and St-Gilles, pioneered by Victor Horta (1861–1947) who built his house here. Much of Brussels's Art Nouveau heritage was lost over the next 60 years, until its revival in the 1960s, making these rare survivors more precious.

Rue Defacqz 71 ③
In 1894, architect Paul Hankar (1859–1901) designed his house in eclectic style, using a variety of models. There are indicators here of the evolving Art Nouveau style.

Rue Faider 83 ⑤
A draughtsman from Horta's studio, Albert Roosenboom (1871–1943) designed this classic Art Nouveau façade in 1906, full of organic, counterintuitive shapes.

Hôtel Ciamberlani ④
Paul Hankar built this house at Rue Defacqz 48 for the Symbolist Albert Ciamberlani in 1897, with murals, ironwork and large round windows.

Hôtel Tassel ⑥
The first Art Nouveau building (1893–5) was designed by Victor Horta for a private client at Rue Paul-Émile Janson 6.

Musée Horta ②
Horta's home and studio *(see p80)* is a masterpiece of Art Nouveau design.

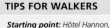

Hôtel Hannon ①
Now a photo gallery, this was built by Jules Brunfaut (1852–1942) for engineer and photographer, Édouard Hannon.

KEY

•••••••• Walk route

TIPS FOR WALKERS

Starting point: *Hôtel Hannon, on the corner of Avenue de la Jonction and Avenue Brugmann.*
Distance: *About 3 km (2 miles).*
Getting there: *Tram 3, 90, 91, 92; Bus 54. Return to the city from Avenue Louise: Tram 93, 94.*
Walking time: *40 minutes, but allow 3 hours for sightseeing.*
Cafés and restaurants: *This is a residential area, but cafés and restaurants are present on the route.*

Hôtel Solvay ⑦
A relatively restrained Horta building at Avenue Louise 224, this was built between 1894 and 1898 for the industrial magnate Ernest Solvay.

Quartier des Étangs ⑧
Around Rue de Vilain XIV, Rue de la Vallée and Rue de Bellevue, there are a number of notable Art Nouveau houses, many designed by Ernest Blérot (1870–1957).

Musée Bruxellois de la Gueuze ❻

Rue Gheude 56, Anderlecht, 1070 BRU. **Road Map** A4. **Tel** (02) 5214928. 🚌 20, 27, 46, 50. Ⓜ *Clemenceau, Gare du Midi.* 🚊 3, 18, 52, 56, 82, 90. ◯ 8:30am–5pm Mon–Fri, 10am–5pm Sat. 🎫 includes tasting. 🖥 🛗 www.cantillon.be

The valley of the River Senne possesses airborne yeasts called *Brettanomyces* that cause beer to ferment spontaneously. This rare phenomenon produces the famous local sour beer known as lambic, which is aged and blended to create gueuze *(see p282).* The beer can only be brewed in winter. At Cantillon – the small family-run brewery museum – the copper cooling vat in the vented roof-top is on display along with the musty cellar full of barrels where beer froths and matures in time-honoured fashion.

Erasmus House ❼

Rue du Chapitre 31, Anderlecht, 1070 BRU. **Road Map** A4. **Tel** (02) 5211383. 🚌 46, 49. Ⓜ *St-Guidon.* 🚊 56. ◯ 10am–6pm Tue–Sun. 🎫 includes the Begijnhof van Anderlecht. ♿ 🛗 www.erasmushouse.museum

The great Dutch scholar and humanist Desiderius Erasmus (c.1469–1536) had a major role in the spread of Renaissance ideas in northern Europe. He travelled widely, was a friend to other humanists such as Thomas More in England, and became advisor to Emperor Charles V. He also unwittingly promoted the ferment of Protestant reforms through his challenging approach to knowledge, and so spent his final years as a refugee from the Catholic church in Germany and Switzerland. After helping found the College of Three Languages at Leuven *(see pp160–61),* Erasmus lived in this pretty red-brick house for five months in 1521. Today, it is a museum with exhibits related to his life and times, including books censored in black ink by the infamous Spanish Inquisition.

The serene Erasmus House, briefly home to the famous philosopher

Begijnhof van Anderlecht ❽

Rue du Chapelain 8, Anderlecht, 1070 BRU. **Road Map** A4. **Tel** (02) 5211383. 🚌 46, 49. Ⓜ *St-Guidon.* 🚊 56. ◯ 10am–noon and 2–5pm Tue–Sun. 🎫 includes Erasmus House. 🛗 www.erasmushouse.museum

Close to the Erasmus House is the charming Begijhof van Anderlecht. Built in the 14th century, this was home to just eight béguines. The buildings are now a museum and one of the best ways to glimpse what these admirable institutions offered, both to the béguines and the public whom they served. The béguinage lies in the shadow of the 15th-century Gothic **Collegiale Kerk van St-Pieter-en-St-Guido**. The latter is a local saint, who was buried here in the 11th century.

🛗 **Collegiale Kerk van St-Pieter-en-St-Guido**
Place de la Vaillance, Anderlecht, 1070 BRU. **Tel** (02) 5230220. ◯ 2–5pm Mon–Fri, Sat on request. ◉ during services. 🛗 📷 Procession of St Guidon (Sep).

Basilique Nationale du Sacré-Coeur ❾

Parvis de la Basilique 1, Koekelberg, 1083 BRU. **Road Map** A3. **Tel** (02) 4258822. 🚌 49, 87. Ⓜ *Simonis.* 🚊 19. ◯ 9am–6pm daily (Dome: Easter–Oct: 9am–5:15pm; Nov–Easter: 10am–4:15pm). 🎫 for dome. 📷 by request.

King Léopold II was keen to build a church which could hold the growing population of early 20th-century Brussels. He commissioned the striking Basilique Nationale du Sacré-Coeur, an Art Deco landmark, in 1904, although it would not be completed until 1970. Originally designed by Pierre Langerock (1859–1923), the final construction of sandstone and terracotta is the less costly version by Flemish architect, Albert van Huffel. The predominant feature of the church, which rises 90 m (295 ft) above the ground, is a vast green copper dome that can be spotted from many places in the city. Very much a 20th-century church, it is dedicated to those who died for Belgium, particularly the thousands of soldiers killed on their own terrain during the two World Wars.

René Magritte Museum ❿

Rue Esseghem 135, Jette, 1090 BRU. **Road Map** A3. **Tel** (02) 4282626. 🚌 49, 53, 89. Ⓜ *Belgica, Bockstael, Pannenhuis.* 🚊 51, 94. ◯ 10am–6pm Wed–Sun. 🎫 🛗 www.magrittemuseum.be

The great Surrealist painter René Magritte *(see p23)* lived here with his wife from 1930 to 1954, during which time he became a widely recognized artist. Their apartment and his studio in the garden, where he produced almost half his total output, have been arranged in an understated and modest manner to look as they did in the artist's time. The museum includes original works, reproductions and material about Magritte and the Surrealists.

Basilique Nationale du Sacré-Coeur, a prominent Brussels landmark

The small-scale model of London's Houses of Parliament, Mini-Europe

Bruparck ⓫

Boulevard du Centenaire, 1020 BRU. **Road Map** A3. **Tel** *(02) 4748383.* 🚌 *84, 88.* Ⓜ *Heysel.* 🚋 *23, 51.* **www**.*bruparck.com* **Mini-Europe Tel** *(02) 4741313.* ◯ *Apr–Jan; see website for details.* **www**.*minieurope.be* **Océade Tel** *(02) 4784320.* ◯ *year-round.* 🎞 **Kinepolis Tel** *(02) 4742600.* 🎞 *for films.* 🚻

Although nowhere near as large or as grand as many of the world's other theme parks, Bruparck is nevertheless a popular family destination. The first and favourite port of call is **Mini-Europe**, where more than 300 miniature reconstructions take visitors around the buildings of the European Union. Built on a scale of 1:25, the collection displays buildings of social or cultural importance, including the Acropolis from Athens, the Brandenburg Gate from Berlin and the Houses of Parliament from London.

For film fans, **Kinepolis** is hard to beat. Popular films from many different countries can be viewed in large auditoriums and on 25 screens. **The Village** is a pedestrianized imitation Flemish village, with plentiful food outlets and children's entertainment.

Another major attraction is **Océade**, a tropically heated water park complete with wave machines, giant slides, bars, cafés and even realistically re-created sandy beaches.

The Atomium ⓬

Atomium Square, 1020 BRU. **Road Map** A3. **Tel** *(02) 4754775.* 🚌 *84, 88.* Ⓜ *Heysel.* 🚋 *23, 51.* ◯ *10am–6pm daily.* 🎫 🚻 **www**.*atomium.be*

Built for the 1958 World Fair, the Atomium is arguably Brussels's most famous landmark structure. Representing an elementary iron crystal magnified 165 billion times, it was designed by the Belgian engineer André Waterkeyn to reflect the new age of science and space travel, as well as to honour the country's all-important metal industry. Although the Atomium was not originally intended to be a permanent structure, it proved to be a very popular attraction. In recent decades, it has undergone several rounds of expensive renovation, and has now been restored to its original gleaming vision.

Each of the nine spheres that make up the crystal is 18 m (60 ft) in diameter. They are linked together by escalators and stairs in the connecting tubes. Five of the spheres, containing exhibition rooms, are open to the public. The uppermost, rising 102 m (335 ft)

above the ground, provides a panaromic view over the cityscape of Brussels, and has a smart restaurant at the top.

Domaine de Laeken ⓭

Laeken, 1020 BRU. **Road Map** A3. 🚌 *53, 84, 89.* Ⓜ *Heysel.* 🚋 *19, 23, 52, 81, 94.* **www**.*tib.be* **Serres Royales** Avenue du Parc Royal, 1020 BRU. **Tel** *(02) 5138940.* ◯ *late Apr–early May.* 🎫 🚻 *reservations required.* 🚻 **www**.*monarchie.be* **Pavillon Chinois** *and* **Tour Japonais** Avenue Van Praet 44, 1020 BRU. **Tel** *(02) 2681608.* ◯ *9:30am–5pm Tue–Fri, 10am–5pm Sat and Sun.* 🎫 🚻 **www**.*kmkg-mrah.be*

The Belgian royal family's second, and preferred, residence is a large palace surrounded by parkland in the northern suburb of Laeken. The 19th-century Château Royal de Laeken is not open to the public. However, the huge and beautiful greenhouses, the **Serres Royales**, built in the 1870s, are open for guided tours in spring. The park provides a pleasant open space for walks and picnics. To the northeast are two

The gigantic Atomium towering above Bruparck

The grand façade of the Musée Royal de l'Afrique Centrale in the suburb of Tervuren

essentially authentic Oriental buildings, commissioned by King Léopold II at the start of the 20th century. These are the only completed pieces of a grandiose scheme to create an architectural world tour in his domain; they are now out-posts of the Musées Royaux d'Art et d'Histoire *(see p77)*. The **Pavillon Chinois** (Chinese Pavilion) contains a fine col-lection of Chinese ceramics, while the **Tour Japonais** (Japanese Tower) is a pagoda decorated in Japanese and Art Nouveau styles, and contains a collection of samurai armour and weapons. An additional museum space is devoted to exhibitions on Japanese art.

Musée du Transport Urbain Bruxellois **⓮**

Avenue de Tervuren 364b, 1150 BRU. **Road Map** B4. *Tel (02) 5153108.* 36, 42. 39, 44. *Apr–Sep: 1–7pm Sat, Sun and public holidays.* includes ride in a vintage tram.
www.trammuseumbrussels.be

The main focus of the Musée du Transport Urbain Bruxellois is the tram, so it is often called the Musée du Tram. Here, lined up in a vast shed, are numerous beautifully res-tored historic vehicles, from the horse-drawn trams of the 1860s to the first electric trams and trolleybuses, through successive phases of modern-ization, each richly redolent of its era. The fees include a 40-minute return journey in

a vintage tram of the 1920s, to the Musée Royal de l'Afrique Centrale or to the Parc du Cinquantenaire *(see pp76–7)*.

Musée Royal de l'Afrique Centrale **⓯**

Leuvensesteenweg 13, 3080 Tervuren. **Road Map** C4. *Tel (02) 7695211.* 44. *10am–5pm Tue–Fri, 10am–6pm Sat and Sun.* **www**.africamuseum.be

In the 19th century, the colony of the Belgian Congo (later Zaire; today, the Democratic Republic of Congo) was Belgium's only territorial

possession. The Musée Royal de l'Afrique Centrale, which opened in 1899, houses a collection gleaned from over 100 years of colonial rule. Its galleries display ceremonial African dresses and masks and exhibits on colonial life. Dugout canoes, religious idols, weapons and stuffed wildlife feature next to rooms on the birds and fish of the region. There is also a collection of giant African insects, much loved by children. Apart from these, the museum contains exhibits relating to the expe-ditions of the famous explorer and journalist, Henry Morton Stanley. The museum hosts temporary exhibitions year-round.

THE BELGIAN CONGO

During the "scramble for Africa" in the 19th century, Belgium was one of several nations that vied for a slice of that continent to colonize and call its own. In 1878, Belgium's King Léopold II commissioned the explorer Henry Morton Stanley (who famously sought and found Dr Livingstone) to map the uncharted Congo Basin. As a result, Belgium laid claim to a vast territory whose rich resources – gold, diamonds, timber, plantation crops – brought great wealth to the

Léopold II (1835–1909), King of Belgium

country. Known as the Congo Free State, this land remained the private fiefdom of Léopold II and eventually became notorious for brutality and exploitation. When this was made public knowledge, the Belgian government was forced to take over, in 1908. In 1960, amidst growing internal unrest, independence was hastily granted. The country's name was changed to Zaire in 1971, during the dictatorial rule of President Mobutu, and since his overthrow in 1997, it has been known as the Democratic Republic of Congo.

SHOPPING IN BRUSSELS

Upmarket stores in Brussels have high-quality goods, elegant wrappings and professional service. International haute couture labels and top-brand chocolate shops radiate a sense of luxury, while the boutiques of up-and-coming designers have an off-hand nonchalance or an edgy intensity.

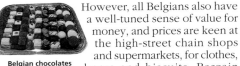

Belgian chocolates

However, all Belgians also have a well-tuned sense of value for money, and prices are keen at the high-street chain shops and supermarkets, for clothes, beers and biscuits. Bargain hunters in search of antiques and bric-a-brac stand a good chance of success, and will certainly enjoy Brussels's vibrant antiques and flea markets.

Window display at a designer fashion boutique on the Rue Neuve

WHERE TO SHOP

Brussels's Grand Place is surrounded by lace vendors, chocolate shops and souvenir outlets. The most impressive collection of shops nearby is Galéries St-Hubert *(see p62)*, an opulent arcade housing upmarket outlets. Northwest of the Grand Place is Rue Antoine Dansaert, centre of the Bruxellois' contemporary fashion scene. For all major high-street chains, there is the pedestrianized Rue Neuve near the Grand Place. Between the Lower and Upper towns is the antiques district of Rue Haute and Rue Blaes. Close by is the Place du Grand Sablon where exquisite chocolate shops can be found alongside high-end florists and antique shops. South of the Palais de Justice lie Boulevard de Waterloo and Avenue Louise, with top boutiques such as Gucci.

DEPARTMENT STORES

City 2, at the northern end of Rue Neuve, is the largest urban shopping centre in Belgium and hosts the department store **Inno**. Further south on the same street lies

Hema, a Dutch low-cost store, selling everything from clothes to kitchen utensils.

MARKETS AND ANTIQUES

On most weekends, visitors will find a *brocante* (a glorified car boot sale combined with street party) somewhere in the city. These are listed in most of the free events magazines, as are the various farmers' markets found across the city. The latter often have some remarkable local breads and cheeses. Cheapest and most extensive of the traditional markets is the **Marché du Midi** (6am–1pm Sundays) that reflects the tastes of the area's North African community. The eclectic **Marolles Marché aux Puces**, a flea market (7am–2pm daily, but best on weekends), dates from 1873 and is the starting point for any antiques hunter. It can take time to sort through the various boxes of items, but there are definitely bargains to be found. For pre-sorted antiques, it is best to head for the more expensive weekend market (9am–6pm Saturday, 9am–2pm Sunday) in front of the Notre-Dame du Sablon.

FASHION

Downtown's Rue Antoine Dansaert is at the heart of Brussels's thriving fashion industry. Its principal outlet **Stijl** has sold the work of fashion graduates from the Antwerp Art Academy since 1984, and still offers the best wares produced by domestic talent. Further down the street are the dresses and womens-wear of **Nicolas Woit** and the beautiful knitwear of **Annemie Verbeke**. In the nearby Rue du Flandre is the shop of **Martin Margiela**, one of Belgium's most talked about designers.

CHOCOLATES

There are 81 chocolatiers listed in the Brussels phone book (not including franchise shops), almost all of high quality. The three biggest chains in Belgium are **Godiva**, **Neuhaus** and **Leonidas**. **Galler** and **Corné Port-Royal** are also excellent. All have numerous outlets throughout the city. The area around the Grand

Shoppers browsing through the wares at the Marolles flea market

Place has many chocolate shops, but true devotees will want to head for the Place du Grand Sablon, location of the **Wittamer** shop and café, which produces some of the finest chocolates and cakes in Brussels. Close by is **Pierre Marcolini**, a more recent star in the chocolate firmament.

BEER

Supermarkets such as Match, GB (which have many outlets) and Delhaize (*see p305*) offer most of the country's finest beers. For rarer finds, as well as appropriate glasses for each beer, gift boxes and other beer paraphernalia, **Beer Mania**, **De Bier Tempel** and **Délices et Caprices** are recommended. Beer glasses can also be found at the Marolles flea market.

COMICS

Brüsel has a vast collection of comics in French, Dutch and English. It also has a gallery of framed original art for sale on the second floor. **Utopia** leans towards American super-hero strips and science fiction, but also has Japanese anime titles. A short walk from the Grand Place, **La Boutique Tintin** offers an interesting variety of Tintin-imprinted knickknacks. The **Centre Belge de la Bande Desinée** (*see p62*) has one of the better stocked comic stores in the city.

BOOKSHOPS

Waterstone's and **Sterling** are the city's best English book-stores, while **Filigranes** also has an excellent English

Brüsel, one of Brussels's numerous well stocked comic-book stores

section. Nestled among the high-fashion boutiques of Rue Antoine Dansaert is **Passa Porta**, which calls itself a trilingual bookstore and an "international house of literature". Besides these, there is the exhaustive French book and CD emporium, **Fnac**.

DIRECTORY

DEPARTMENT STORES

City 2
Rue Neuve 123. **City Map 2** D2. www.city2.be

Hema
Rue Neuve 13. **City Map 2** D2. **Tel** *(02) 2275210.* www.hema.be

Inno
Rue Neuve 111–123. **City Map 2** D2. **Tel** *(02) 2112111.* www.inno.be

MARKETS AND ANTIQUES

Marché du Midi
Gare du Midi. **City Map 1** A5.

Marolles Marché aux Puces
Place du Jeu de Balle. **City Map 1** C5.

FASHION

Annemie Verbeke
Rue Antoine Dansaert 64. **City Map 1** C2. **Tel** *(02) 5112171.* www.annemieverbeke.be

Martin Margiela
Rue de Flandre 114. **City Map 1** B1. **Tel** *(02) 2237520.* www.maisonmartinmargiela.com

Nicolas Woit
Rue Antoine Dansaert 80. **City Map 1** C2. **Tel** *(02) 5034832.* www.nicolaswoit.com

Stijl
Rue Antoine Dansaert 74. **City Map 1** C2. **Tel** *(02) 5120313.*

CHOCOLATES

Corné Port-Royal
Rue de la Madeleine 9. **City Map 2** D3. **Tel** *(02) 5124314.* www.corne-port-royal.be

Galler
Rue au Beurre 44. **City Map 2** D3. **Tel** *(02) 502 0266.* www.galler.com

Godiva
Place du Grand Sablon 47–48. **City Map 2** D4. **Tel** *(02) 5029906.* www.godiva.be

Leonidas
Rue au Beurre 34. **City Map 2** D3. **Tel** *(02) 5128737.* www.leonidas.com

Neuhaus
Galerie de la Reine 25–27. **City Map 2** D3. **Tel** *(02) 5126359.* www.neuhaus.be

Pierre Marcolini
Rue des Minimes 1. **City Map 2** D4. **Tel** *(02) 514 1206.* www.marcolini.be

Wittamer
Place du Grand Sablon 12. **City Map 2** D4. **Tel** *(02) 5123742.* www.wittamer.com

BEER

Beer Mania
Chaussée de Wavre 174–6. **City Map 2** F5. **Tel** *(02) 5121788.* www.beermania.be

De Bier Tempel
Rue Marché aux Herbes 56. **City Map 2** D3. **Tel** *(02) 5021906.*

Délices et Caprices
Rue des Bouchers 68. **City Map 2** D3. **Tel** *(02) 5121451.*

COMICS

Brüsel
Boulevard Anspach 100. **City Map 1** C3. www.brusel.com

Centre Belge de la Bande Desinée
Rue des Sables 20. **City Map 2** E2. **Tel** *(02) 219 1980.* www.comicscenter.net

La Boutique Tintin
Rue de la Colline 13. **City Map 2** E2. **Tel** *(02) 5145152.* www.tintin.boutique.com

Utopia
9th Art Gallery, 26 Quai Aux Huîtres 1300 Wavre. **Tel** *(0475) 817510.* www.9emeartgallery.com

BOOKSHOPS

Filigranes
Ave des Arts 39–40. **City Map 2** F3. **Tel** *(02) 511 9015.* www.filigranes.be

Fnac
City 2, Rue Neuve 123. **City Map 2** D1. **Tel** *(02) 2751111.* www.fnac.be

Passa Porta
Rue Antoine Dansaert 46. **City Map 1** C2. **Tel** *(02) 2260454.* www.passaporta.be

Sterling
Fossé aux Loups 38. **City Map 2** D2. **Tel** *(02) 2236223.* www.sterlingbooks.be

Waterstone's
Boulevard Adolphe Max 71–75. **City Map 2** D1. **Tel** *(02) 2192708.* www.users.skynet.be/waterstones

ENTERTAINMENT IN BRUSSELS

L ying at the crossroads of London, Paris, Amsterdam and Cologne, Brussels enjoys the presence of the best international touring groups. The calendar is full of first-rate opera, jazz, rock and classical and world music, glittering with performers of world renown. The city also generates its own productions of international acclaim, notably in opera and modern dance, while its cosmopolitan culture ensures that the latest films arrive quickly. There is a lively club scene, with venues attracting revellers from all over Europe. Many bars and cafés host live music, providing an easy continuum between traditional taverns and DJ-fuelled dance floors.

Logo for rock venue, Ancienne Belgique

LISTINGS AND TICKETS

Most expatriates in Brussels depend on the weekly English listings guide, **Brussels Unlimited**, and a monthly magazine, **The Bulletin**, which also provides cultural information, weather reports and news online. **Agenda** is a trilingual listings magazine that can be found in boxes outside supermarkets. Its website also has extensive, up-to-date listings in French and Dutch. The Brussels Tourist Office produces useful brochures such as its Brussels Guide and Map and *My Guide to the Night*. Tickets for many events are available from Fnac *(see p87)*.

CLASSICAL MUSIC

The **Théâtre Royal de la Monnaie** is one of Europe's best opera houses. Tickets can be cheap, but many productions sell out in advance. The Victor Horta-designed **Palais des Beaux-Arts** (BOZAR), the country's most notable cultural venue, is home to the Belgian National Orchestra.

DANCE

Belgium is particularly strong in the field of modern dance. Its leading choreographers such as **Michèle Anne de Mey** and **Wim Vandekeybus** have enormous influence internationally. Another important figure, Anne Teresa De Keersmaeker, is currently resident at the Brussels opera, and the director of the world-renowned **Rosas Company**.

JAZZ

Every May, jazz fans from around the world congregate for the **Brussels Jazz Marathon** much of which is free.
  The quintessential Brussels jazz venue is the venerable **L'Archiduc**, an Art Deco gem in the city centre which hosts regular concerts every weekend. **The Music Village** stretches across two 17th-century buildings near the Grand Place and features both local and international names. **Sounds**, in Ixelles, is another popular jazz club boasting a prolific agenda of concerts.

ROCK, REGGAE, FOLK AND WORLD

Brussels is one of the best cities in Europe to catch up-and-coming acts, generally at reasonable ticket prices.
  The **Forêt-National**, lying southeast of the city centre, is Belgium's top arena for big-name acts. Closer to the centre, Brussels's other venues tend to be more intimate, and each have their own favoured genres. **Café Central** leans towards R&B, blues, bossa nova and ambient, while **Cirque Royale** favours indie rock, and has a reputation for booking bands before they become household names. The downtown **Ancienne Belgique** has a similar line-up, but for more established acts.
  The Flemish student venue **Kultuur Kaffee** at the Vrij Universiteit Brussel, the city's Dutch-language university, always has a strong line-up and serves the cheapest beer in the city. **Recyclart** plays avant-garde techno, hardcore, punk and some world music in a refitted train station. The impressive **Halles de Schaerbeek**, formerly a 19th-century market, hosts a range of different groups and other arts events. Reggae concerts are often held at the **VK Club** (Vaartkapoen), while Flemish acts are showcased at the **Beursschouwburg**, the Flemish cultural community centre.

NIGHTLIFE

Brussels's bright young things start the weekend in St Géry, a square in the fashion district of Rue Antoine Dansaert. This area is home to such bars as

Dramatic performance at the prestigious Théâtre Royal de la Monnaie

the latin-flavoured **Mappa Mundo**, popular **Le Roi des Belges** and elegant **Gecko**. The most renowned club in Brussels, **The Fuse**, has earned its reputation for having top-name techno and dance DJs. Once a month, it holds La Demence, a gay night that draws interrnational crowds. **Le You** is another electro-psychedelic dance club with a gay night on Sundays. **Les Jeux d'Hiver** in the Bois de la Cambre woods attracts an affluent crowd. Cuban disco **Havana** is open till 7am on weekends. **Noctis** provides nightlife listings online.

THEATRE

The most important Belgian theatre is the **Théâtre National**, which stages high-quality productions of mainly French classics. Young Belgian playwrights are showcased at the private **Théâtre Le Public**, while French 20th-century and burlesque pieces are staged in the beautifully restored **Théâtre Royal du Parc**. The main Dutch-language company is the **Koninklijke Vlaamse Schouwburg** (KVS) or the Royal Flemish Theatre, which uses several venues clustered in central Brussels.

CINEMA

The massive **Kinepolis Bruxelles** at Laeken boasts 25 screens for the latest blockbusters, always in their original languages. Mainstream cinema can also be enjoyed at the two other central UGC cineplexes. A more intriguing ambience and eclectic line-up of films can be found at the **Arenberg-Galeries**. The **Nova** offers truly independent films, while the **Actors Studio** showcases foreign and art cinema. **Movy Club** screens mainstream films in opulent Art Deco movie-palace surroundings.

DIRECTORY

LISTINGS AND TICKETS

Agenda
www.agenda.be

The Bulletin
www.thebulletin.be

CLASSICAL MUSIC

Palais des Beaux-Arts
Rue Ravenstein 23.
City Map 2 E3. *Tel (02) 5078200.* **www.**bozar.be

Théâtre Royal de la Monnaie
Place de la Monnaie.
City Map 2 D2.
www.lamonnaie.be

DANCE

Michèle Anne de May
www.madm.be

Rosas Company
www.rosas.be

Wim Vandekeybus
www.ultimavez.com

JAZZ

Brussels Jazz Marathon
www.brusselsjazz marathon.be

L'Archiduc
Rue Antoine Dansaert 6.
CIty Map 1 C2.
www.archiduc.net

Sounds
Rue de la Tulipe 28.
www.soundsjazzclub.be

The Music Village
Rue des Pierres 50.
City Map 1 C3.
Tel (02) 5131345. www. themusicvillage.com

ROCK, REGGAE, FOLK AND WORLD

Ancienne Belgique
Boulevard Anspach 110.
City Map 1 C3.
Tel (02) 5482484.
www.abconcerts.be

Beursschouwburg
Auguste Ortsstraat 20–28. **City Map** 1 C2.
Tel (02) 5500350. www. beursschouwburg.be

Café Central
Rue de Borgval 14.
City Map 1 C2.
Tel (02) 5137308.
www.lecafecentral.com

Cirque Royale
Rue de l'Enseignement 81. **City Map** 2 F2.
Tel (02) 2182015.
www.botanique.be

Forêt-National
Avenue Victor Rousseau 208. *Tel (09) 0069500.*
www.forestnational.be

Halles de Schaerbeek
Rue Royale Ste-Marie 22b. *Tel (02) 2182107.*
www.halles.be

Kultuur Kaffee
Blvrd de la Plaine 2.
Tel (02) 6292325.
www.kultuurkaffee.be

Recyclart
Rue des Ursulines 25.
City Map 1 C4.
www.recyclart.be

VK Club
Schoolstraat 76.
Tel (02) 4142907.
www.vkconcerts.be

NIGHTLIFE

Gecko
Place St-Géry 16.
City Map 1 C2.
www.geckococktailbar.be

Havana
Rue de l'Epée 4.
City Map 1 C5. www. havana-brussels.com

Le Roi des Belges
Rue Jules Van Praet 35.
City Map 1 C2. *Tel (02) 5034300.* www.st-gery.be

Le You
Rue Duquesnoy 18. **City Map** 2 D3. *Tel (02) 6391400.* www.leyou.be

Les Jeux d'Hiver
Chemin du Croquet 1.
Tel (02) 6490864.
www.jeuxdhiver.be

Mappa Mundo
Rue du Pont de la Carpe 2. **City Map** 1 C2.
Tel (02) 5143555.

Noctis
www.noctis.com

The Fuse
Rue Blaes 208. **City Map** 1 C5. *Tel (02) 5119789.* www.fuse.be

THEATRE

Koninklijke Vlaamse Schouwburg
Arduinkaai 7. *Tel (02) 2101112.* www.kvs.be

Théâtre Le Public
Rue Braemt 64–70.
City Map 3 1A.
www.theatrelepublic.be

Théâtre National
Boulevard Emile Jacqmain 111–115. **City Map** 2 D1.
www.theatrenational.be

Théâtre Royal du Parc
R de la Loi 3. **City Map** 2 F3. *Tel (02) 5053040.*
www.theatreduparc.be

CINEMA

Actors Studio
Petite Rue des Bouchers 16. **City Map** 2 D2.
Tel (02) 5121696. www. actorsstudio.cinenews.be

Arenberg-Galeries
Galerie de la Reine 26.
City Map 2 D2.
www.arenberg.be

Kinepolis Bruxelles
Bruparck, Boulevard du Centenaire 20.
www.kinepolis.be

Movy Club
Rue des Moines 21.
Tel (02) 5376954.

Nova
Rue d'Arenberg 3.
City Map 2 D2.
Tel (02) 5112477.
www.nova-cinema.com

Brussels's Cafés and Bars

A long history of conviviality lies behind Brussels's countless cafés and bars. Brewing has been a major industry here since medieval times, when the tavern was an important social hub. During the 19th century, the culture of the coffeehouse combined with the time-honoured traditions of the tavern to produce elegant and sophisticated cafés where men and women could meet with decorum and still enjoy a drink in the customary Belgian way. Many contemporary cafés and bars remain delightfully rooted in the past, while others bristle with ultra-modern style, but all are heirs to the same tradition of hospitality.

A glass for every beer

A waiter in a traditional tabard apron at Le Roy d'Espagne

Le Roy d'Espagne *is a huge two-tiered bar occupying the elegant guildhouse of the bakers in the Grand Place. In warmer months, customers spill out from the atmospheric interior, famously decorated with inflated pigs' bladders. It is a fine place to sample the best Trappist beers and traditional tavern food.*

READY FOR ACTION

Bars operate with efficiency when the pressure heats up, and staff work with a dedicated professionalism honed by centuries of experience. Like many bars, Mappa Mundo, in trendy St-Géry, keeps long hours. It may have quiet moments during the day, but will brim over with thirsty customers well into the night.

Café Metropole *is the café-cum-bar of one of Brussels's most prestigious hotels, with an interior lavishly decorated in 18th-century French style. The terrace is the place to see and be seen. Despite its grand air, everyone is made welcome.*

Le Falstaff, *facing the Bourse, is famous for its authentic Art Nouveau decor featuring stained glass, mirrors, lamps and woodwork. This popular bar, café and restaurant seems to have bottled the atmosphere of 1903, the year of its creation.*

À La Mort Subite *is a famous drinking place, given a Classical makeover in 1926. Its unnerving name, meaning Sudden Death, shared also with a brand of beer, in fact refers to a working men's dice game that used to be played here.*

Le Cirio *is a classic traditional café and bar with wall-mirrors, gilding, woodwork and an air of faded grandeur. Founded in 1886 and named after its owner, Le Cirio is famed for its speciality,* half en half – *half white wine, half sparkling wine.*

ON THE MENU

Steak and chips, a bar-food standard, with a garnish of salad and shallots

There is no clear distinction drawn between a café and a bar. Most such establishments offer coffee, tea and hot chocolate, or beer, wine and stronger alcohols. Many of them also serve food of some kind. At its simplest, this will be a plate of rye-bread and cream cheese – traditionally served with beer – or a *croque-monsieur* (grilled cheese and ham on toast). However, many bars and cafés also offer a full menu of substantial bar meals such as steak and chips or mussels, as well as more elaborate dishes.

La Chaloupe d'Or, *the Golden Boat, in the Grand Place, is a long-established café, bar and restaurant of timeless refinement and elegance. This is an excellent place for a light lunch, afternoon wheat beer with a slice of gâteau, or a pre-theatre drink. The staff glide swiftly among the tables, efficiently memorizing orders.*

BRUSSELS STREET FINDER

The map given below shows the area of Brussels covered in the street finder maps. The Lower Town is the area around the Grand Place; the Upper Town includes the Musées Royaux des Beaux Arts, the Palais Royal and the Quartier Européen. Map references for all sights, hotels, restaurants, shopping and entertainment venues given

Nymph in Parc de Bruxelles

in Brussels refer to the maps in this section. The key, set out below, indicates the scales of the maps and shows what other features are marked on them, including transport terminals, emergency services and information centres. Street names are in both French and Dutch. The first figure in the map reference indicates which street finder map to turn to. The letter and number that follow give the grid reference on that map.

KEY

■	Major sight
□	Other sight
□	Other building
M	Metro station
R	Train station
⊞	Tram route
⊞	Bus station
🚕	Taxi rank
P	Parking
i	Tourist information
✚	Hospital
🚓	Police station
🕆	Church
⊠	Post office
=	Railway line
▓	Pedestrian street

SCALE OF MAPS

0 metres   250

0 yards   250

Façade of La Maison des Ducs de Brabant, Grand Place *(see pp56–7)*

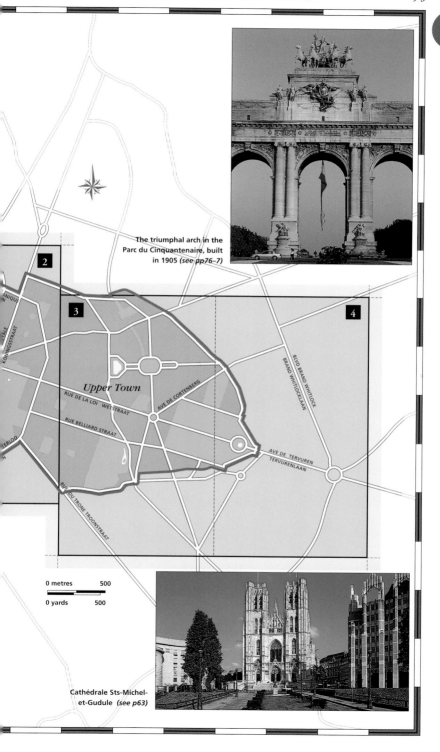

The triumphal arch in the
Parc du Cinquantenaire, built
in 1905 (see pp76–7)

2

3

4

Upper Town

KONINGSSTRAAT

RUE DE LA LOI WETSTRAAT

AVE DE CORTENBERG

RUE BELLIARD STRAAT

BLVD BRAND WHITLOCK
BRAND WHITLOCKLAAN

AVE DE TERVUREN
TERVURENLAAN

RUE DU TRONE TROONSTRAAT

LEERLOO

0 metres   500
0 yards   500

Cathédrale Sts-Michel-
et-Gudule (see p63)

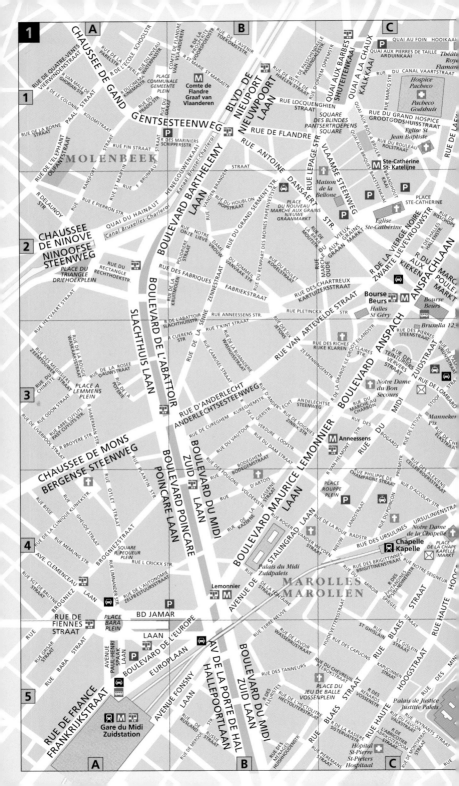

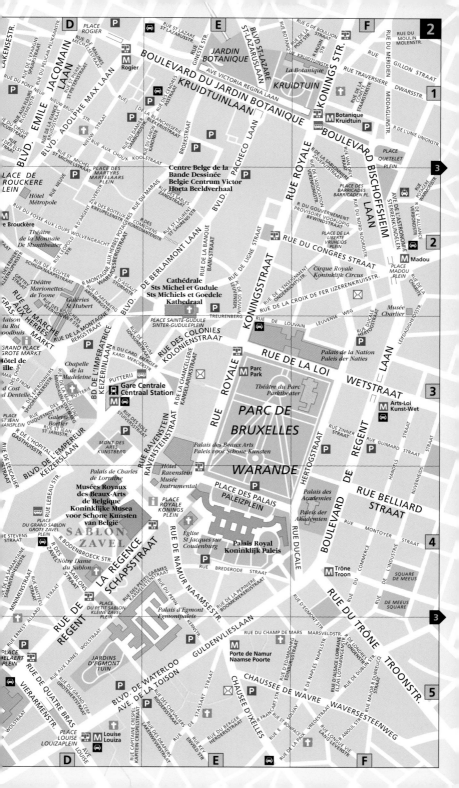

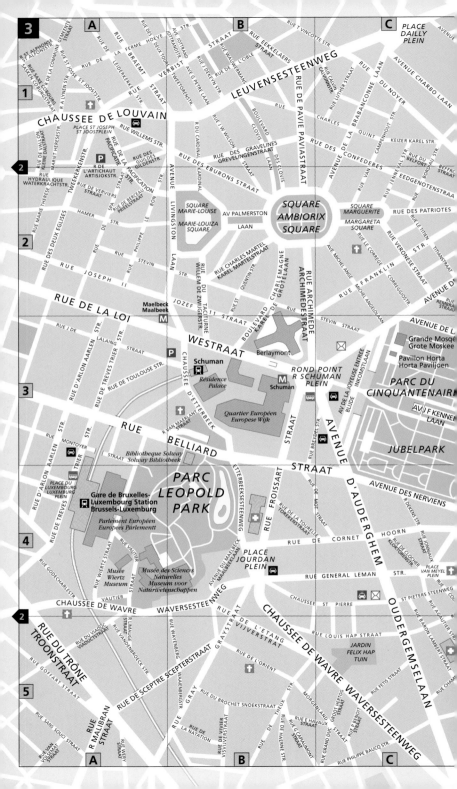

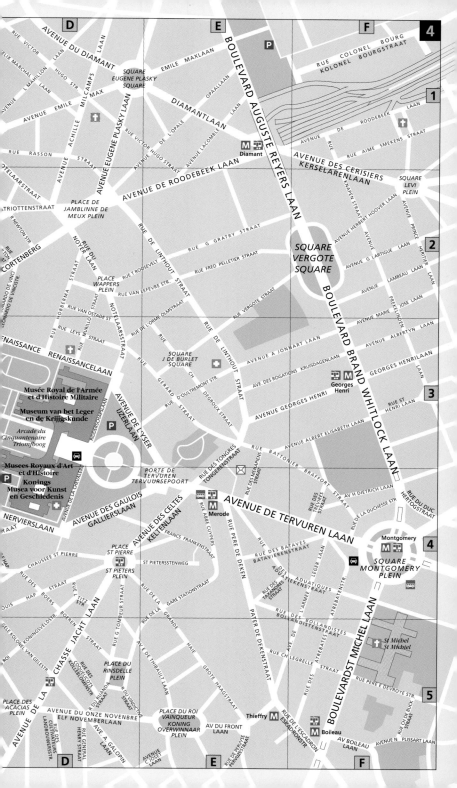

FLANDERS

Flanders at a Glance

Northern Belgium forms the Dutch-speaking region known as Flanders. The language here is spoken in Flemish dialects that vary hugely across the land. The western half of Flanders consists of two provinces – West Vlaanderen, which has a coast on the North Sea, and Oost Vlaanderen. The beautiful cities of Bruges and Ghent are the respective capitals. To the east lie three more provinces: Antwerpen, with its capital in the city of Antwerp; Limburg and Vlaams Brabant. Much of the north is flat, but towards the southern border with Wallonia, the land begins to rise into softly undulating hills.

Ghent *(see pp130–35)*, the capital of Oost Vlaanderen, is most notable for the glorious Gothic architecture that lines the city's picturesque canals and medieval streets.

WESTERN FLANDERS
(see pp104–139)

0 km   25

0 miles   25

The Belgian Coast (see pp118–19) *is a popular destination for family holidays, but sun-lovers may need shelter from the bracing sea breezes. A striking feature here is the investment in contemporary public sculpture, such as the seated figures outside Oostende's railway station.*

Bruges (see pp108–117) *casts a romantic spell with its step-gabled façades and a skyline pricked by medieval towers. The canals that thread through this miniature city were used in the Middle Ages by barges laden with trade goods. The wealth and luxury this trade brought to Bruges is still very evident in the city's monuments and museums.*

◁ Red poppies, a symbol of the war dead, carpeting the battlefields of Flanders

Grimbergen (see p164) – *located just north of Brussels in the Province of Vlaams Brabant – has one of the finest Baroque churches in Belgium. Built between 1660 and 1725, it belongs to an abbey of the Premonstratensian Order, and has given its name to a respected abbey beer.*

Hasselt (see p166), *thriving capital of the Province of Limburg, holds a number of surprises, such as an authentic Japanese Garden, complete with timber pavilions, a stimulating fashion museum and the National Museum of Jenever.*

CENTRAL AND
EASTERN FLANDERS
(see pp140–69)

BRUSSELS
(see pp52–97)

Leuven *(see pp160–61),* the capital of Vlaams Brabant, is the seat of Belgium's oldest university. Founded in 1475, it is wittily symbolized in the Font Sapienza fountain.

Kasteel van Gasbeek (see p165) *sits in the beautiful rural region of Pajottenland, west of Brussels. This great medieval castle was renovated in sumptuous Flemish-Renaissance and Neo-Gothic styles in the late 19th century, creating a stylish aristocratic home, full of fascinating antique furniture, paintings and other* objets d'art.

Flemish Masters

The early Flemish painters had a major impact on the history of European art. Pioneers of oil painting on wooden panels, they created masterpieces in the 15th century, which travelled along trade routes, notably to Italy where artists such as Leonardo da Vinci, stunned by their quality, in turn adopted oil painting. Many Flemish painters subsequently absorbed the advances of the Italian Renaissance, and the peculiarly Flemish qualities of their art softened. Most notably, Pieter Paul Rubens cut his teeth in Italy, then brought back an unprecedented swagger and dynamism, re-establishing Flanders as a European centre for artistic excellence.

Jan van Eyck's realistic portrait of his wife Margareta in 1439

Rogier van der Weyden *is noted for his emotional intensity. A side panel from his triptych* The Seven Sacraments *(1445) depicts ordination, marriage and extreme unction.*

FLEMISH PRIMITIVES

Early Flemish painters such as Jan van Eyck (c.1400–41), Rogier van der Weyden (c.1400–64) and Hans Memling (c.1433–94) are often called the Flemish Primitives. The term comes from Latin *primitivus*, or earliest of its kind, as their art was seen by later historians as a forerunner of the Renaissance. The Flemish Primitives' skills of fine detail and acute observation were based on monastic traditions of manuscript illustration, but used oils instead of water-based paints.

Hans Memling *created several paintings for St-Janshospitaal in Bruges. In* The Mystic Marriage of St Catherine, *from around 1479, the Christ Child places a ring on the saint's finger, attended by the hospital's patrons, St John the Baptist and St John the Evangelist.*

Pieter Brueghel the Elder *(c.1525–69) was the greatest of a family of talented artists. He showed an earthy delight in Flemish rural life and used it as the context for scenes from the Bible or Greek mythology. In his Fall of Icarus (c.1558), the unfortunate pioneer aviator crashes into the sea beside a ship, unnoticed by the nearby ploughman who is concentrating on his work.*

Jan van Eyck demonstrates his exceptional eye for detail, through contemporary touches such as the canon's spectacles, in *Madonna with Canon van der Paele* (1436).

Pieter Paul Rubens *(1577–1640) was known as a master of composition. His* Adoration of the Magi *(1624) brings extraordinary energy to this well worn theme, making the viewer's eye dance around from face to face, although the prime focus always remains the baby Jesus.*

Anthony van Dyck *(1599–1641) worked as Rubens's chief assistant in Antwerp. His gift for portraiture, seen in his self-portrait at the age of 30, later brought him great success at the court of Charles I in England.*

Jacob Jordaens *(1593–1678) worked with Rubens in Antwerp. He is famous for lively paintings such as* The Family Concert *(1638). The matronly central figure watches the others make raucous music, while, unobserved, the dog sniffs the food.*

WESTERN FLANDERS

*C*harming, fascinating and glorying in the treasures of its historic heritage, Western Flanders is home to vibrant cities such as Bruges and Ghent, and smaller towns such as Oudenaarde, Kortrijk and Veurne. Around them lies a tranquil rural landscape of flat or gently hilly farmland, threaded with rivers and canals. To the north, sandy beaches face out on to the bracing North Sea.

Owing to its location at the crossroads of northern Europe, and to its boundary with the North Sea, Western Flanders has often been thrust into the forefront of historical events. Although a Flemish-speaking land, it was ruled during the Middle Ages by French kings *(see pp37–8)* – a cause of much frustration and strife. Despite this, many of the cities, notably Bruges, Ghent, Ieper, Kortrijk and Veurne, were rich from the cloth trade and industrious with crafts meticulously regulated by their proud guilds. The Golden Age followed in the 15th century, when the dukes of Burgundy took possession and made Bruges the glittering capital of their empire.

However, between 1500 and 1945, Western Flanders was in the doldrums. The economy became largely rural, with small cottage industries such as lace-making. The land became a pawn in the big-game politics of Europe, battered by religious struggles in the 16th century as the Spanish Netherlands disintegrated, then fought over by the Austrians, the French and the English in succeeding centuries. The 20th century brought World War I, which scored a line through Western Flanders, creating a wasteland on either side and demolishing Ieper.

All this changed over the latter half of the 20th century with the rise of Flanders as one of Europe's most prosperous regions. The architectural treasures of the old medieval towns, sidelined and ignored for centuries, but preserved untouched, were restored, and the historic heritage of Flanders has now become one of its greatest assets. Furthermore, Western Flanders has done much to encourage visitors, be it in the great cities, the countryside, on the coast, or on the battlefields of the Western Front.

The traditional Flemish way of shrimp fishing from horse-drawn carts, at the Oostduinkerke beach

◁ Tour groups cruising down the scenic Dijver canal through historic Bruges

Exploring Western Flanders

The Belgian coast is a chain of beach resorts terminating in the north with the Zwin nature reserve. A little inland is Bruges, with the beautiful canal landscape around Damme to its northeast. The battlefields of World War I run in a strip from Diksmuide to Ieper and on to Mesen and the hills of Heuvelland. The delightful and historic city of Ghent is the biggest regional centre in Western Flanders, ringed by interesting towns, from Kortrijk and Oudenaarde to Dendermonde and St-Niklaas. All these needed defences, and the green landscape is dotted with castles, such as Beauvoorde, Ooidonk and Laarne. Around Oudenaarde and Geraardsbergen, the landscape becomes quite hilly, inspiring the label the Flemish Ardennes.

Sand yachts with bright sails on the coast near De Panne

SIGHTS AT A GLANCE

Villages, Towns and Cities
Bruges pp108–117 **1**
Damme **2**
Dendermonde **23**
Geraardsbergen **22**
Ghent pp130–35 **16**
Ieper **13**
Knokke-Heist **3**
Koksijde **9**
Kortrijk **15**
Lissewege **6**
Oostende **7**
Oudenaarde **21**
Poperinge **14**
St-Niklaas **24**
Veurne **8**
Zeebrugge **4**

Castles
Kasteel Beauvoorde **10**
Kasteel Ooidonk **18**
Kasteel van Laarne **19**

Museums
IJzertoren **11**
Stoomcentrum
   Maldegem **20**

Tours
A Tour of World War I
   Battlefields pp126–7 **12**
A Tour Around St-Martens-
   Latem p136 **17**

Areas of Natural Beauty
The Zwin **5**

Under the Blinde Ezelstraat bridge on a tour of Bruges

SEE ALSO

- **Where to Stay** pp264–6
- **Where to Eat** pp288–91

Flowering clumps of sea lavender on the flat expanse of marshland at the Zwin nature reserve

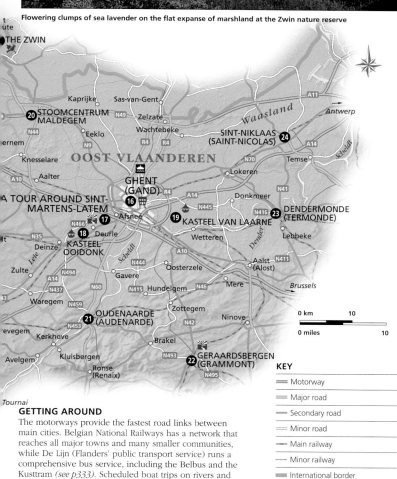

THE ZWIN

STOOMCENTRUM MALDEGEM 20

Kaprijke   Sas-van-Gent

Zelzate   N49

Wachtebeke   Waasland

Antwerp   A11

Eeklo   N44

ernem   N9

Knesselare   OOST VLAANDEREN

SINT-NIKLAAS (SAINT-NICOLAS) 24

Temse   A14

Aalter   A10

R4   R4

N70

Lokeren

GHENT (GAND) 16

A TOUR AROUND SINT-MARTENS-LATEM

Afsnee   A14

Donkmeer   N41

N445

KASTEEL VAN LAARNE 19

KASTEEL VAN LAARNE   N416   DENDERMONDE (TERMONDE) 23

N466   17

Deurle   18

Wetteren   Lebbeke

KASTEEL OOIDONK

Deinze   N35

Scheldt   N444

A10

Aalst (Alost)   N411

Zulte

A14   Gavere   N494

Oosterzele

Brussels

Waregem   N437   N459

N60   N415   Hundelgem   N46   Mere

Zottegem

0 km   10

OUDENAARDE (AUDENARDE) 21

N453

Ninove   N42

0 miles   10

evegem   Kerkhove

Brakel

Avelgem   Kluisbergen

Ronse (Renaix)

GERAARDSBERGEN (GRAMMONT) 22   N493

N495

KEY

Tournai

GETTING AROUND

The motorways provide the fastest road links between main cities. Belgian National Railways has a network that reaches all major towns and many smaller communities, while De Lijn (Flanders' public transport service) runs a comprehensive bus service, including the Belbus and the Kusttram *(see p333)*. Scheduled boat trips on rivers and canals in and around Bruges and Ghent offer a different and more leisurely way of getting around.

▬▬	Motorway
▬▬	Major road
▬▬	Secondary road
═══	Minor road
▬•▬	Main railway
▬▬	Minor railway
▬▬	International border
▬▬	Provincial border

Bruges ●

The city of Bruges originated as a 9th-century fortress built to defend the coast against the Vikings. Dominated by the French and then the dukes of Burgundy, Bruges became one of Europe's most sophisticated cities and an international trading hub, famed for its extravagance and luxury. Today, the city owes its pre-eminent position to the beauty of its historic centre, whose cobbled lanes and meandering canals are lined by medieval buildings. There is a lively cultural scene, embodied in the Concertgebouw, an innovative concert hall built to celebrate Bruges's status as a European City of Culture in 2002.

Bell-maker in the Markt

🏯 The Markt

Bruges's main square, an open space lined with 17th-century houses and overlooked by the Belfort on one side, has held a market since the 10th century. On the eastern side is the Neo-Gothic Provinciaal Hof, built between 1881 and 1921. This denotes Bruges's status as the capital of the Province of West Vlaanderen. In the middle of the square is a statue of Pieter de Coninck and Jan Breydel, two 14th-century guildsmen who led a bloody rebellion known as the Bruges Matins against French troops in 1302. On the northern side lies the Historium Museum, which explores Bruges' Golden Age of 1435.

🏯 The Belfort

Markt. ⏰ *daily.* 🖼
Built between the 13th and 15th centuries, the Belfort is an octagonal bell tower that

The medieval Belfort, towering over the roofs of the city centre

rises to a height of 83 m (272 ft) and dominates the Markt. Inside the tower, 366 steps lead up, past the chamber where the town's rights and privileges were stored, to the roof, which offers delightful views of the

city. The Belfort also contains a famous carillon, with 47 bells that can be played from a keyboard.

🏛 Choco-Story

Wijnzakstraat 2 (St-Jansplein), Bruges. **Tel** *(050) 612237.*
⏰ *10am–5pm daily.* ● *2nd week of Jan.* 🖼 🎦 www.choco-story.be
Set in a 15th-century former wine tavern known as the Huis de Croon, this museum of chocolate shows, through exhibits and tastings, how cocoa is made into chocolate. Choco-Story's artifacts cover the history of chocolate from its origins in Central America to all aspects of its trade.

The same building houses the **Lumina Domestica**, a museum of domestic lighting that displays the private collection of around 6,500 lamps, starting with prehistoric oil lamps.

🏛 Friet Museum

Vlamingstraat 33, Bruges. **Tel** *(050) 340150.* ⏰ *10am–5pm daily.*
● *second week of Jan.* 🖼 🏢 www.frietmuseum.be
Belgian chips or fries (*friet* in Dutch and *frites* in French) are widely acknowledged as the best in the world. The Friet Museum reveals the secrets of this national culinary triumph – the choice of potato, its cut and frying, its history (right back to the ancient Americas) plus everything associated with the Belgian passion for *friet*. Visitors can also taste the product of all this dedicated research. The museum is arranged in the modernized interior of the 14th-century Saaihalle (Serge-weavers' Hall), a building which, until 1516, had served as the Genoese Lodge, the headquarters of traders from the Italian port-city of Genoa.

🏯 The Burg

A pleasant cobbled square near the Markt, the Burg was once the political and religious focus of Bruges. It is also the site of the original fort around which the city grew. Some of the most imposing civic buildings are located here, including the **Stadhuis** and the **Oude Griffie** (Old Recorder's House) with its Renaissance façade. Next

Bruges's medieval buildings flanking the canalized River Reie

door is the **Renaissance Hall**, which houses a massive wood, marble and alabaster chimney designed by the Dutch architect Lanceloot Blondeel. The tree-shaded space on the northern side of the Burg was the site of the Cathedral of St Donation, destroyed by the French in 1799.

🏛 Stadhuis
Burg 12. **Tel** (050) 448711.
🕐 9:30am–5pm daily. 🔴 1 Jan, 25 Dec. 📷 www.brugge.be

The intricately carved façade of the Stadhuis was completed in 1375, but the niche statues are modern effigies of the counts and countesses of Flanders. Much of this building is a triumph of restoration. Inside, a staircase leads up to the Gothic hall, a magnificent parliamentary chamber built around 1400. The ceiling has lavish woodcarvings including 16 beautiful corbels bearing representations of the seasons and the elements. Around the hall is a series of paintings, completed in 1895, portraying key events in the city's history.

Ornate statues decorating the façade of the Basilica of the Holy Blood

🔒 Heilig Bloed Basiliek
Burg 15. **Tel** (050) 336792. 🕐 Apr–Sep: 9:30am–noon & 2–5pm daily; Oct–Mar: 10am–noon & 2–5pm daily. 🔴 Wed pm.

One of Europe's most sacred reliquaries is held at the Heilig Bloed Basiliek (Basilica of the Holy Blood). The basilica is divided into two sections. The lower part is the 12th-century St Basil's chapel and has a plain stone-pillared entrance and arches. The upper chapel was destroyed by the French in the 1790s and rebuilt in the 19th century. Here, brightly coloured decorations surround

a silver tabernacle from 1611 which houses a sacred phial, supposed to contain a few drops of blood and water washed from the body of Christ by Joseph of Arimathea. The phial was brought here from Jerusalem in 1150 and is still the object of great veneration. The church also has a tiny museum.

The Vismarkt
Braambergstraat. 🕐 Tue–Sat am.

From the Burg, an attractive arched path called the Blinde Ezelstraat (Alley of the Blind Donkey) leads to this open-air fish market with its elegant 18th-century colonnades. Fish is still sold here each morning.

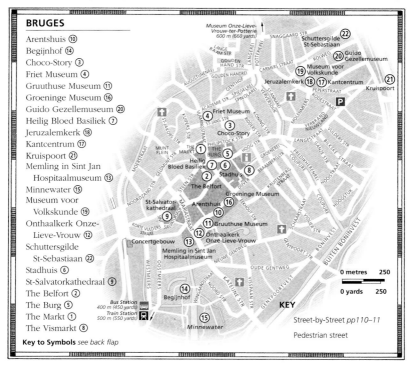

BRUGES

Arentshuis ⑩
Begijnhof ⑭
Choco-Story ③
Friet Museum ④
Gruuthuse Museum ⑪
Groeninge Museum ⑯
Guido Gezellemuseum ⑳
Heilig Bloed Basiliek ⑦
Jeruzalemkerk ⑱
Kantcentrum ⑰
Kruispoort ㉑
Memling in Sint Jan
  Hospitaalmuseum ⑬
Minnewater ⑮
Museum voor
  Volkskunde ⑲
Onthaalkerk Onze-
  Lieve-Vrouw ⑫
Schuttersgilde
  St-Sebastiaan ㉒
Stadhuis ⑥
St-Salvatorkathedraal ⑨
The Belfort ②
The Burg ⑤
The Markt ①
The Vismarkt ⑧

Key to Symbols see back flap

KEY

Street-by-Street pp110–11

Pedestrian street

Street-by-Street: The City Centre

A traditional organ grinder

One of the most popular destinations in Belgium, Bruges is an unspoilt medieval town. The centre of the city is amazingly well preserved, with winding streets that pass by picturesque canals lined with fine buildings. When the River Zwin silted up at the end of the 15th century, the town's trade was badly affected. It was never heavily industrialized and has retained most of its medieval buildings. As a further bonus, Bruges also escaped major damage in both World Wars. Today, the streets are well maintained – there are no billboards or high-rises, and traffic is strictly regulated. All the major attractions are located within the circle of boulevards that marks the line of the old medieval walls.

View of the Rozenhoedkaai
A charming introduction to Bruges is provided by the boat trips along the city's canal network.

Onthaalkerk Onze-Lieve-Vrouw
The massive Welcome Church of Our Lady took 200 years to build and shows many architectural styles.

Memling in Sint-Janshospitaal Museum
Six of the artist's works are shown in the chapel of the 12th-century St Janshospitaal that was functioning as late as 1976.

0 metres   100
0 yards   100

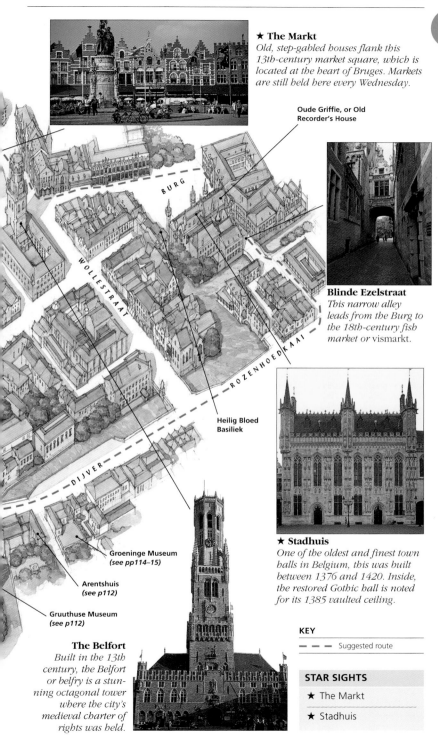

★ **The Markt**
Old, step-gabled houses flank this 13th-century market square, which is located at the heart of Bruges. Markets are still held here every Wednesday.

Oude Griffie, or Old Recorder's House

BURG

WOLLESTRAAT

ROZENHOEDKAAI

Blinde Ezelstraat
This narrow alley leads from the Burg to the 18th-century fish market or vismarkt.

Heilig Bloed Basiliek

DIJVER

Groeninge Museum
(see pp114–15)

Arentshuis
(see p112)

Gruuthuse Museum
(see p112)

★ **Stadhuis**
One of the oldest and finest town halls in Belgium, this was built between 1376 and 1420. Inside, the restored Gothic hall is noted for its 1385 vaulted ceiling.

The Belfort
Built in the 13th century, the Belfort or belfry is a stunning octagonal tower where the city's medieval charter of rights was held.

KEY

– – – Suggested route

STAR SIGHTS

★ The Markt

★ Stadhuis

The stately, pale brick tower of St-Salvatorkathedraal, Bruges

🔒 St-Salvatorskathedraal
St-Salvatorskerkhof 1. *Tel (050) 336188.* ☐ *daily.* 📷

Originally built as a parish church between the 12th and 15th centuries, this brick building became Bruges's cathedral in 1834, following the destruction of the Cathedral of St Donation in the Burg *(see p108)*, by the French army in 1799. The enormous but plain interior of the building is offset by the elaborate Baroque organ, adorned with angels, which was installed in 1682. The choir stalls are decorated with the coats of arms belonging to knights of the Order of the Golden Fleece, dating from a convention held in 1478. The order, founded by Philip the Good in Bruges in 1430, called together many of Europe's rulers and powerbrokers to settle disputes and uphold the ideals of Christianity and chivalry. Above the choir stalls hang handsome Brussels tapestries that date back to the early 18th century and depict scenes from the Bible.

🏛 Arentshuis
Dijver 16. *Tel (050) 448763.* ☐ *9:30am–5pm Tue–Sun.* 📷 www.museabrugge.be

An 18th-century mansion overlooking the Dijver Canal, the Arentshuis is now an annexe of the Groeninge Museum *(see pp114–15)*, which stands nearby. The ground floor is used to house temporary exhibitions. On the first floor are works by Frank Brangwyn (1867–1956), a painter and sculptor born in Bruges of Welsh parents. His father, William Curtis Brangwyn, was an architect

and painter, and one of a number of British residents closely involved in the restoration of Bruges in the 19th century. Most of Frank Brangwyn's life was spent in Britain, but he bequeathed this collection to Bruges, along with his carpets, drawings and furniture. His dark and powerful canvases depicting industrial scenes are particularly striking, and overall this is a surprising and rewarding collection.

🏛 Gruuthuse Museum
Dijver 17. *Tel (050) 448762.* ☐ *9:30am–5pm Tue–Sun (tickets sold until 4:30pm).* 📷

Occupying a large medieval mansion close to the Dijver Canal, the Gruuthuse Museum holds a priceless collection of fine and applied arts. These date from Bruges's heyday as a wealthy trading city, and the subsequent centuries.

In the 15th century, the building was inhabited by the merchant (or lord of the Gruuthuse) who had the exclusive right to levy a tax on *gruut* – an imported mixture of herbs added to barley during the beer-brewing process. The mansion's labyrinthine rooms, with their ancient chimney pieces and wooden beams, have survived intact. Nowadays, they house woodcarvings, musical instruments, weapons, furniture and tapestries. There is even a medical section devoted to cures of everyday ailments such as haemorrhoids. One of the museum's most treasured possessions is the incredibly lifelike wood and terracotta bust of the Habsburg king Charles V carved in

Oak-panelled interior of the chapel at Gruuthuse Museum

1520. This is attributed to the German sculptor Konrad Meit. There are also a number of artifacts recalling the exile of Charles II of England in Bruges. On the second floor is a wooden chapel built in 1472 with a private window into the Onthaalkerk Onze-Lieve-Vrouw next door. The museum is currently undergoing restoration work so some rooms may be closed.

🔒 Onthaalkerk Onze-Lieve-Vrouw
Mariastraat. *Tel (050) 345314.* ☐ *9:30am–5pm Mon–Fri, 9:30am–4:45pm Sat, 1:30–5pm Sun.* ⬤ *for tours during services.* 📷 *choir only.* www.museabrugge.be

The construction of the Onthaalkerk Onze-Lieve-Vrouw (the Welcome Church of Our Lady) began in 1220 and ended 200 years later. In consequence, it incorporates a variety of architectural styles. Its 122-m (400-ft) tall spire is one of the tallest in Belgium. The interior, with its

An elaborate tapestry depicting the "free arts", Gruuthuse Museum

white walls, stark columns and black-and-white tiled floor has a medieval simplicity, while the side chapels and pulpit are lavishly decorated.

One of the church's artistic highlights is Michelangelo's 1505 sculpture, *Madonna and Child*, located at the end of the southern aisle. This marble statue was imported by a Flemish merchant, and was the only one of the artist's works to leave Italy during his lifetime. In the choir, there are fine paintings by Pieter Pourbus (1523–84) including his 1562 *Last Supper* and the carved mausoleums of the Burgundian duke Charles the Bold and his daughter, Mary.

Warm brick tones in an inner courtyard of the St-Janshospitaal

The soaring spire of the eclectic Onthaalkerk Onze-Lieve-Vrouw

🏛 Memling in Sint-Janshospitaal Museum

Mariastraat 38. *Tel (050) 448771.*
🕐 *9:30am–5pm Tue–Sun.* 📷 📱
♿ 📷 www.museabrugge.be
This site has been occupied since the 12th century by the St-Janshospitaal, which closed as a working hospital only in 1976. During Bruges's Burgundian Golden Age in the 15th century, the great German-born painter Hans Memling (c.1433–94) created a number of exquisite paintings, commissioned specially for the hospital chapel in about 1479. The remarkable museum here today therefore has two aspects. First, there are the evocative medieval hospital wards with antique beds, medical instruments, paintings and documentation as well as an old *apotheek*

(pharmacy). Then, in the open-plan site of the old chapel, there is the small but supreme collection of Hans Memling's paintings. This includes the *St Ursula Shrine*, a reliquary painted with scenes from the legend of St Ursula, *The Adoration of the Magi* and the polyptych of *The Mystic Marriage of St Catherine (see p102)*. The martyrdoms of St John the Baptist and St John the Divine (to whom the hospital was dedicated) are illustrated in side-panels.

🏛 Begijnhof

Wijngaardplein 1.
Tel (050) 360140. 🕐 *daily.*
The Bruges begijnhof was founded in 1244 by Margaret of Constantinople, Countess of Flanders. Entered via an 18th-century gatehouse at the end of a bridge that runs over a canal, this is an area of quiet tree-lined paths faced by white, gabled houses and a pleasant green at the centre. It is an enjoyable place for a stroll and visitors can also walk into the small church that was built here in 1602. The nuns who live in these houses today are no longer béguines

(see p61) but Benedictine sisters who moved here in the 1930s. One of the houses is open to visitors and displays simple rustic furniture and artifacts that illustrate the béguines' contemplative lives.

🍀 Minnewater

Just south of the begijnhof, Minnewater is a peaceful park with a lake. The name probably means innerwater, but because *minne* is a Dutch word for love, Minnewater is often referred to as The Lake of Love. Swans have been on this site since 1488 when Maximilian of Austria ordered that they be kept in memory of his councillor, Pierre Lanchals, who was beheaded by the Bruges citizens. The swan appears in the Lanchals coat of arms.

Once a bustling harbour connected to canals and the sea, the Minnewater can today be reached by the barges that take visitors on a tour of Bruges. It is also a popular spot for walkers and picnickers, featuring a pretty 15th-century lock gate, sluicegate house and the 1398 gunpowder tower, Poedertoren.

The sluicegate house on the Southern Bridge at the Minnewater

Bruges: Groeninge Museum

The city's top fine-arts museum, the Groeninge holds a fabulous collection of early Flemish and Dutch masters, featuring artists such as Jan van Eyck (c.1400–41) and Hieronymous Bosch (1450–94), famous for the strange freakish creatures of his moral allegories. Hugo van der Goes (1440–82) is well represented too, as are Gerard David (c.1460–1523) and Hans Memling (c.1433–94). These early works are displayed on the ground floor of the museum along with a collection of later Belgian painters, most notably Paul Delvaux (1897–1994) and René Magritte (1898–1967). Originally built between 1929 and 1930, the museum is small and displays its collection in rotation along with various temporary exhibitions.

Museum Façade
This 1930 gallery was extended in 1994 by architect Joseph Viérin. The old entrance is based on that of a Romanesque convent.

★ **Death of the Virgin** *(1470)*
Hugo van der Goes's treatment of a popular and emotionally charged subject displays his imaginative use of composition. It is also remarkable for its range of carefully observed expressions.

★ **The Moreel Triptych** *(1484)*
Painted by German-born artist Hans Memling, this panel was designed to adorn the altar in a Bruges church. The triptych is said to be one of the earliest portaits of a family group.

STAR PAINTINGS

★ Death of the Virgin

★ The Moreel Triptych

★ Virgin and Child with Canon

★ **Madonna with Canon van der Paele** *(1436)*
Jan van Eyck's richly detailed work is noted for its precision. It shows St George presenting van Eyck's patron, the canon, to St Donatian.

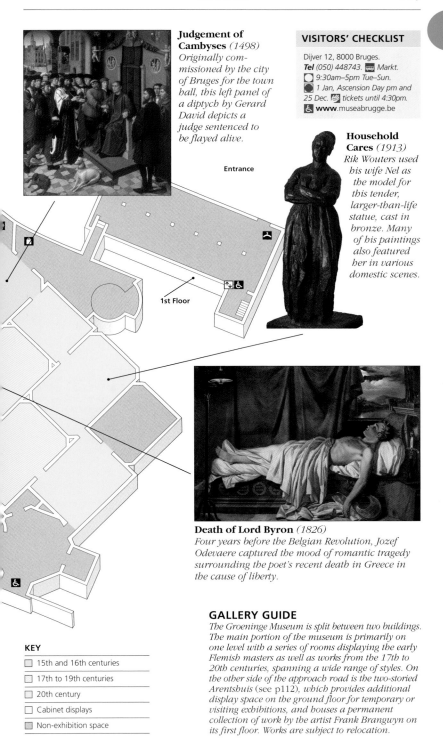

Judgement of Cambyses (1498)
Originally commissioned by the city of Bruges for the town hall, this left panel of a diptych by Gerard David depicts a judge sentenced to be flayed alive.

VISITORS' CHECKLIST

Dijver 12, 8000 Bruges.
Tel (050) 448743. 🚌 *Markt.*
⭕ *9:30am–5pm Tue–Sun.*
⬤ *1 Jan, Ascension Day pm and 25 Dec.* 🎫 *tickets until 4:30pm.*
♿ www.museabrugge.be

Entrance

Household Cares (1913)
Rik Wouters used his wife Nel as the model for this tender, larger-than-life statue, cast in bronze. Many of his paintings also featured her in various domestic scenes.

1st Floor

Death of Lord Byron (1826)
Four years before the Belgian Revolution, Jozef Odevaere captured the mood of romantic tragedy surrounding the poet's recent death in Greece in the cause of liberty.

GALLERY GUIDE

The Groeninge Museum is split between two buildings. The main portion of the museum is primarily on one level with a series of rooms displaying the early Flemish masters as well as works from the 17th to 20th centuries, spanning a wide range of styles. On the other side of the approach road is the two-storied Arentshuis (see p112), which provides additional display space on the ground floor for temporary or visiting exhibitions, and houses a permanent collection of work by the artist Frank Brangwyn on its first floor. Works are subject to relocation.

KEY

☐ 15th and 16th centuries

☐ 17th to 19th centuries

☐ 20th century

☐ Cabinet displays

▨ Non-exhibition space

Exploring Eastern Bruges

Visitors pour into Bruges during the summer, crowding the city centre. Despite this, the narrow cobbled streets and picturesque canals to the east of the Markt remain free of throngs, and this fascinating area continues to be one of the most delightful parts of Bruges. Its avenues of medieval terraced houses are dotted with grand and elegant 18th-century mansions. The best approach to this quarter is via Jan van Eyckplein, which in medieval times was the site of the busy canal-side tollhouse. A short stroll along the Spinolarei and Potterierei streets leads to the handful of intriguing churches and museums in this historic district.

Statue of
Jan van Eyck

The Museum voor Volkskunde, part of a row of 17th-century almshouses

Traditional bobbin-lace techniques demonstrated at the Kantcentrum

🪡 Kantcentrum

Peperstraat 3a. *Tel (050) 330072.*
☐ *10am–5pm Mon–Sat.* 🎫 📷
www.kantcentrum.com

Lace-making skills are kept alive at the Kantcentrum, the Lace Centre, which occupies 14th-century almshouses next to the Jeruzalemkerk in the area east of Potterierei street. This neighbourhood is one of several where, in the past, the city's lace workers plied their craft. Most of the lace makers were women. They worked at home, receiving raw materials from a supplier who also bought the finished product.

The Kantcentrum also includes an exhibition of historic lace, and demonstrations on lace-making are held for visitors every summer afternoon. Finished pieces are sold in the Kantcentrum shop.

⛪ Jeruzalemkerk

Peperstraat. ☐ *10am–noon and 2–6pm Mon–Fri, 10am–noon and 2–5pm Sat.* 🎫

One of Bruges's most unusual churches, the Jeruzalemkerk is based on the design of the

Church of the Holy Sepulchre in Jerusalem. The structure possesses a striking tower with two tiers of wooden, polygon-shaped lanterns, topped by a tin orb. The present building dates from the 15th century, when it was commissioned by Anselmus Adornes and his spouse, members of a rich Italian merchant family, whose black marble tomb can be seen inside the church.

Inside the Jeruzalemkerk, the lower level contains a macabre altarpiece, carved with skulls in imitation of Golgotha, the site of Christ's crucifixion. Behind the altar is a smaller vaulted chapel leading to a narrow tunnel that is guarded by an iron grate. In the tunnel, a lifelike model of Christ in the Tomb can be seen at close quarters.

The distinctive tower of the Jeruzalemkerk

🏛 Museum voor Volkskunde

Balstraat 43. *Tel (050) 448764.*
☐ *9:30am–5pm Tue–Sun, Easter and Whit Mon.* 🎫 www.museabrugge.be

One of the best folk museums in Flanders, the Museum voor Volkskunde occupies an attractive terrace of low brick almshouses located behind an old neighbourhood café called the Zwarte Kat, or Black Cat, which serves as the entrance. Each house is dedicated to a different aspect of traditional Flemish life, with workshops displaying old tools and other relevant artifacts. Several different crafts, such as cobbling and blacksmithing, are represented here, along with a series of typical historical domestic and shop interiors.

🏛 Guido Gezellemuseum

Rolweg 64. *Tel (050) 448711.*
☐ *9:30am–12:30pm and 1:30–5pm Tue–Sun.* 🎫 ♿ www.museabrugge.be

The eldest of five children, the great Flemish poet Guido Gezelle was born and raised in a little red-brick house that is now a museum. With the help of a series of furnished rooms, this place evokes the modest circumstances of his upbringing – his father was a gardener and his mother's family were farmers. Insights into Gezelle's work and life are offered through the museum's exhibits of books and documents. The charm of the building and of the garden outside reflect the character of the man, his piety and his love for nature, which evolved during the course of his childhood spent here.

🚪 Kruispoort

🕐 May–Aug (St-Janshuismolen) and Jul–Aug (Koelwereimolen): 9:30am–12:30pm and 1:30–5pm Tue–Sun. 🖼 www.museabrugge.be

Medieval Bruges was heavily fortified. It was encircled by a city wall that was itself protected by a moat and strengthened by a series of massive gates. Most of the wall was knocked down in the 19th century, but the moat and four of the city gates (*poorten*) have survived. One of these, the Kruispoort, is a monumental structure, dating from 1402, that guards the city's eastern approach. The earthen bank stretching north

The massive Kruispoort, one of the original gates in Bruges's city walls

marks the old city wall, and was once dotted with 20 windmills although only four stand here today. **Bonne Chieremolen**, the first one north of the Kruispoort, was brought here from a Flanders village in 1911. The second, **St-Janshuismolen**, is from the city. This restored structure was originally erected in 1770. **De Nieuwe Papegai**, an oil mill relocated here in 1970, is next, while the fourth, **De Koelweimolen**, is an old flour mill that arrived in the 1990s.

🚪 Schuttersgilde St-Sebastiaan

Carmerssstraat 174. **Tel** (050) 331626. 🕐 May–Sep: 10am–noon Tue–Thu, 2–5pm Sat; Oct–Apr: 2–5pm Tue–Thu and Sat. 🖼

The Longbow Archers' Guild (Schuttersgilde) was one of the most powerful militia guilds. Its 16th- and 17th-century red-brick guildhouse now contains a small museum.

The commercial life of medieval Bruges was dominated by the guilds, each of which represented the interests of a group of tradesmen,

The brick house and tower of the influential Longbow Archers' guild

craftsmen or practitioners of a specific skill. This guild claimed the name of St Sebastian, an early Christian martyr who was sentenced by the Roman Emperor Diocletian to be executed by archers. The bowmen followed their orders, but the saint's wounds healed miraculously. He was ultimately executed by club-wielding assassins.

The guildhouse is notable for its collection of portraits of the guild's leading lights. This includes Charles II of England who caroused here during his exile. It also has a traditional shooting gallery for the still-active archery club.

🏛 Museum Onze-Lieve-Vrouw-ter-Potterie

Potterierei 79. **Tel** (050) 448711. 🕐 9:30am–noon and 1:30–5pm Tue–Sun. 🖼 www.museabrugge.be

Located by the canal in one of the quietest parts of Bruges, the Museum Onze-Lieve-Vrouw-ter-Potterie occupies part of an old hospital that was founded in 1276 to care for elderly women. There is a 14th- and 15th-century cloister, and some of the sick rooms house a selection of intriguing curios and a modest collection of paintings, the best of which are some 17th-and 18th-century portraits of leading aristocrats. The hospital church is a warm, intimate place, decorated with a set of impressive Baroque altarpieces and a number of fine stained-glass windows.

GUIDO GEZELLE

One of Bruges's favourite sons, Guido Gezelle (1830–99) was a much-loved poet, priest and champion of the Flemish language. He is most famous for poetry about nature, which he acutely observed. On this basis, he produced poems that were filled with a sense of religious wonder and subtly drawn spiritual lessons. At the age of 16, Gezelle had finished his schooling in Bruges and began to study for the priesthood at Roeselare, 40 km (25 miles) to the south. Here, he soon began publishing his poetry. In 1853, Gezelle was ordained in Bruges, where he developed close friendships with members of the English community, many of whom were Roman Catholics involved in the restoration of the city. Gezelle went on to become the deputy rector of the Anglo-Belgian Seminary in Bruges, and later, the parish priest of St-Walburgakerk. In 1872, he moved to the Onze-Lieve-Vrouwekerk in Kortrijk, where he would spend the next 27 years. Through his enthusiastic and sometimes controversial promotion of the Dutch language and Flemish dialects, he became a leading figure in the Flemish Movement (*see p125*). In 1899, Gezelle became the Director of the English Convent in Bruges, but passed away shortly afterwards.

Statue of Guido Gezelle in Bruges's centre

The Belgian Coast

The Province of West Vlaanderen meets the North Sea in a 70-km (43-mile) long stretch of coast, whose beaches of soft white sand are rimmed by cheerful seaside resorts. With broad promenades, hotels and high-rise apartment blocks, campsites, seafood restaurants, ice-cream and waffle vendors, bucket-and-spade shops and electronic games arcades, these resorts can get very busy, especially in the high season of the summer months, but there is always an air of leisurely fun. Families return for their summer holidays year after year, generation after generation, relishing the comforts of familiar, time-tested pleasures.

LOCATOR MAP

☐ Belgian Coast

De Panne *is a comfortable, easy-going resort where old-fashioned bathing cabins on wheels line the broad beach, and sand yachts scud on windy days. De Panne is home to the popular Plopsaland theme park for children (see pp316–17), while the nearby Westhoek dunes form a nature reserve with wilder landscapes.*

Oostende *(see p122)* is the largest resort on the coast.

Breder

Middelkerke

Westende-Bad

Nieuwpoort lies at the mouth of the IJzer and is a centre for water sports. A large circular monument overlooks the Ganzenpoot confluence of canals, commemorating the strategic flooding of the polders in World War I.

Nieuwpoort-aan-Zee

Lombardsijde-Bad

A18-E40

Oostduinkerke

St-Idesbald

De Panne

IJzer

Veurne

Koksijde has the Paul Delvaux Museum and the ruins of the Ter Duinen Abbey *(see p123).*

Oostduinkerke *has an interesting folklore museum and a Visserijmuseum (Museum of Fishing). However, the area is most famous for shrimp fishing, which is conducted here on horseback, with heavy draught horses pulling the nets through the shallows.*

Middelkerke *is a typical resort of the Belgian coast, dominated by apartment blocks and far removed from its origins as a 13th-century fishing village. It first developed as a resort in the late 19th century, when it became a link on the coastal tram route, the Kusttram – still the best way to travel from one end of the coast to the other.*

De Haan is cherished as one of the most attractive and agreeable of the resorts, with a good beach, and controlled development that has preserved the handsome, early 20th-century villas. The name, meaning The Cock (Le Coq in French), was given to the town following a legend that fishermen were once led to safety here by a cock crowing on the beach.

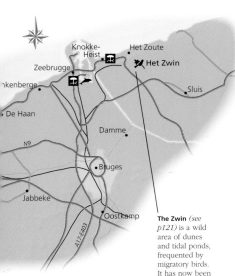

The Zwin *(see p121) is a wild area of dunes and tidal ponds, frequented by migratory birds. It has now been set aside as a nature reserve.*

0 km   5

0 miles   5

Blankenberge *town has a pier, a 2-km (1-mile) long zeedijk (raised promenade), and plenty of holiday entertainment including the National Sealife Marine Park and the Serpentarium. The annual summer Sand Sculpture Festival is currently held here, inspiring breathtakingly ambitious work.*

Zeebrugge (see p120) *is the largest commercial port on this coast and also has a popular beach. A 1960s Soviet submarine and an old lightship are two of the exhibits at Seafront Zeebrugge, the town's main attraction.*

Knokke-Heist (see p120) *is considered the most chic of Belgium's coastal resorts. The tiny Neo-Gothic Fishermen's Chapel in Heist was built in 1892. Today, it is dwarfed by the modern architecture of this western urban end of Knokke-Heist.*

Damme ❷

5 km (3 miles) NE of Bruges.
Road Map B1. 👥 *11,000.* 🚌
🏛 🚶 *Toerisme Damme, Huyse
de Grote Sterre, Jacob van
Maerlantstraat 3; (050) 288610.*
📅 *2nd Sun of every month (books).*
www.toerismedamme.be

This pretty village of historic
red-brick buildings lies amidst
a beautiful polder landscape of
tree-lined canals and pasture.
In the 14th and 15th centuries,
it was a bustling port on the
shores of the Zwin and at the
head of the canal that led into
Bruges. Standing witness to
this golden era are the 15th-
century **Stadhuis** and several
other buildings. These include
the **Huis St-Jan**, once a centre
for the wine trade; the house
where Charles the Bold, Duke
of Burgundy, married Margaret
of York in 1468; and the **St-
Janshospitaal**, which houses a
small museum of artifacts and
church treasures. The **Huyse
de Grote Sterre**, once the
Spanish military
governor's residence,
now has the Visitor
Centre and a
museum devoted to
Tijl Uilenspiegel. Also
of interest are the half
ruined **Onze-Lieve-
Vrouwekerk** and the 19th-
century windmill **Schellemolen**.

🏛 **St-Janshospitaal**
Kerkstraat 33. **Tel** *(050) 461080.*
🕐 *Apr–Sep.* ♿

🏛 **Huyse de Grote Sterre**
Jacob van Maerlantstraat 3.
Tel *(050) 288610.* 🕐 *daily.*
● *noon–2pm.* ♿

🚶 **Schellemolen**
Damse Vaart-West. 🕐 *Easter
and Apr–Sep: Sat, Sun and
public holidays.*

TIJL UILENSPIEGEL

A character that pops up regularly around Bruges
and Damme is Tijl Uilenspiegel, a legendary roguish
trickster. Originally a German creation known as
Till Eulenspiegel, he came to Flanders with the
advent of printing, and was adopted into
the local mythology. The Flemish writer
Charles de Coster (1827–79) revived the
character in a book published in 1867,
and placed him in 16th-century Damme,
fighting for independence from Spain. Tijl, his
fiancée Nele and his sidekick Lamme Goedzak
are remembered in a number of statues, as
well as in the names of several restaurants
and other enterprises.

**Bronze statue of
Tijl Uilenspiegel**

Knokke-Heist ❸

15 km (9 miles) NE of Bruges.
Road Map B1. 👥 *34,000.* 🚗
🚌 🚲 🚶 *Toerisme Knokke-Heist,
Zeedijk-Knokke 660; (050) 630380.*
www.knokke-heist.info

Cited as the smartest seaside
resort on the Belgian coast,
Knokke-Heist is known
for its casino, its streets
of chic boutiques and
art galleries, its ele-
gant villas and
select golf courses.
It is in fact a conur-
bation stretching
some 6 km (4
miles) from Heist
in the west to Het
Zoute in the east, where
development is curtailed by
the dunes of the Zwin nature
reserve. The tale of the Zwin
and the centuries-old fishing
community of Heist – before
tourism transformed the
coast in the late 19th century
– is eloquently told in
Sincfala, the museum of the
Zwin region.
   As a result of the salt sea
water, this natural reserve
has some specific species

**Model of a boat at
the Sincfala museum**

of flora that are rarely
found anywhere else, such
as the exotic sea lavender.
It also houses several species
of migratory as well as native
birds, including woodpeckers
and the tiny egret.

🏛 **Sincfala**
Pannenstraat 140. **Tel** *(050) 630872.*
🕐 *10am–noon and 2–5:30pm daily.*
♿ **www**.sincfala.be

Zeebrugge ❹

Vismijnstraat 7; 15 km (9 miles) NE
of Bruges. **Road Map** A1. 👥 *4,000.*
Tel *(050) 551415.* 🚲 🕐 *Jul–Aug:
10am–7pm daily; Sep–Jun: 10am–
6pm daily.* ● *2nd two weeks of Jan.*
♿ **www**.seafront.be

The deep-water seaport of
Zeebrugge was built at the
start of the 20th century.
Under German occupation
in World War I, it became a
vital strategic port and U-Boat
base, and the target of the
daring Zeebrugge Raid by
British forces in 1918. Today,
Zeebrugge has a rugged
industrial air, with its skyline
dominated by cranes serving
container ships. It is also
Belgium's biggest fishing port.
However, it has a softer side,
with some good beaches and
a sailing marina.
   Close to the town's centre
and occupying the quayside
warehouses of the former fish-
market is **Seafront Zeebrugge**.
This mixed bag of a museum
covers the history of the port
and various maritime themes.
Among the highlights are the
gadget-encrusted chambers of
a large 1960s Soviet submarine.

One of several canals cutting across the polders at Damme

Path leading down from the dyke protecting the Visitor Centre into the wild coastal landscape of the Zwin

The Zwin ⑤

24 km (15 miles) N of Bruges. **Road Map** B1. **Tel** (050) 607086. 📧 13 (Jul and Aug). 🔁 Graaf Léon Lippens-dreef 8, Knokke-Heist. ◯ Easter–Sep: 9am–4:30pm Tue–Sun; Oct–Easter: 9am–4:30pm Tue–Sun. ◉ 1st three weeks Dec. 🦽 🅿 on request. 🖥 www.west-vlaanderen.be

At the far eastern end of the Belgian coast, the border with the Netherlands is delineated by low-lying dunes, salt meadows and tidal inlets. Since 1952 this area has been a nature reserve, the Provinciaal Natuurpark Zwin, famed for its many nesting and migratory birds and its specialized wetland plantlife. There is little here now that speaks of the area's very different past, when the Zwin was a broad, deep channel, running some distance inland. During the medieval period, thousands of trading ships from all over Europe passed through here, bringing goods to Damme, where they were unloaded and transported to Bruges by canal. The navigable inlet was created by a massive storm in 1134 which inundated the coastline. However, it proved to be only temporary. During the 15th century, it began to silt up – partly because of the creation of polders around Damme. This gradually strangled trade, and by the 16th century Bruges's role as one of Europe's most prosperous cities was doomed.

Today, the Zwin is a beautiful stretch of unspoilt tidal coastline, crossed by a number of footpaths. The

Shelducks, the nature park's symbol

main gateway is the Visitor Centre, reached by an inland road, Graaf Léon Lippensdreef, from Het Zoute, the eastern portion of Knokke-Heist. The Visitor Centre forms a triangular area within the reserve, set well back from the sea and protected from inundation by a long, high dyke. Within its large wooded compound are an interpretation centre and a bird park, which has a resident population of storks and various coastal and marshland birds such as owls and herons. The walkway along the dyke offers views over the Zwin, a broad expanse of dunes carpeted with salt-tolerant plants. The lake-like areas of water change with the tides. Simple hides along the dyke offer a good chance of seeing some of the birds that frequent the Zwin. These include geese, ducks, terns, harriers, avocets and egrets. Visitors can also follow paths that lead out from here into the wetland and dunes. Guided tours offer the opportunity to get off the beaten track and into some of the Zwin's more hidden corners.

There are two statues of note at the Zwin. One, near the information centre, is a bronze portrait of the founder of the park, the ornithologist Count Léon Lippens (1911–66). The other stands on the dunes that line the coast – a large, bronze sculpture of a running hare, by the British artist Barry Flanagan (b.1941).

Bird Park at the Zwin, offering a nesting site to a large colony of storks

Brick clocktower of the Onze Lieve Vrouw Bezoekingskerk, Lissewege

Lissewege **6**

8 km (5 miles) N of Bruges. **Road Map** B1. 🏚 *2,500.* 🚉 🚌 **i** *VVV Lissewege-Bezoekerscentrum, Oude Pastoriestraat 5; (050) 552955.* **www**.lissewege.be

The white, flower-bedecked cottages nestling around its church and lining its canal have earned Lissewege a reputation as one of the prettiest villages in Flanders. The handsome church, the **Onze Lieve Vrouw Bezoekingskerk**, was built between 1225 and 1275 in Scheldt Gothic style, using local red brick and blue Tournai stone shipped in via the River Scheldt. Its tower rises to a height of 49 m (162 ft) and offers good views over the village and polders.

In the 12th century, land was donated to Lissewege to the Benedictines. Their Ter Doest abbey – a branch of the Ter Duinen abbey of Koksijde – flourished here until 1571, when it was destroyed by Protestant rebels. Virtually all that remains is the medieval **Abbey Barn**, located 1 km (half a mile) south of the village. This Gothic brick structure supported by oak beams is set in peaceful countryside. The neighbouring 16th-century farm is now the restaurant, Hof Ter Doest (*see p291*).

🏛 **Onze Lieve Vrouw Bezoekingskerk and Abbey Barn**
🕐 *10am–5pm daily.*

Oostende **7**

30 km (18 miles) W of Bruges. **Road Map** A1. 🏚 *69,000.* ✈ 🚉 🚌 🚢 🚌 **i** *Monacoplein 2; (059) 701199.* 🎭 *Bal du Rat Morte (Sat, early Mar).* **www**.toerisme-oostende.be

Set in the middle of the Belgian coast, Oostende is an attractive, modern seaside resort as well as an active fishing and ferry port. It was favoured by royalty and the ruling classes in the late 19th century, and equipped itself with a *kursaal* (casino) and racecourse to complement their elegant villas. Summer holiday-makers arrive for the sand beaches and the seafront promenade, but visitors come all year round for the seafood.

Oostende also has a strong line in art. The **Mu.ZEE** contains a good collection of Belgian art including work by Symbolists such as Léon Spilliaert, Surrealists such as Magritte and Delvaux and by Expressionist artists such as Constant Termeke. The artist most associated with Oostende is James Ensor (*see p23*). His home, the **James Ensorhuis**, with its reconstruction of his aunt's novelty shop explains his influences and vision.

The town's connection with the sea is reflected in the **Mercator Marine Museum**, which is located on the three-masted training ship *Mercator* built in 1932; while what lies under the North Sea is shown at the **Noordseeaquarium**. Oostende's location made it strategically important in war

time. Vivid reminders of this are seen at **Fort Napoleon**, a muscular pentagonal fortress built in 1811 among the dunes to the east of the town. To the west is the **Openluchtmuseum Atlantikwall**, with 2 km (1 mile) of tunnels, trenches and defences that show how the occupying German forces armed the coast against invasion during the World Wars.

Environs
At Jabbeke, 16 km (10 miles) southeast of Oostende, the home and studio of Constant Permeke, one of St-Martens-Latem School of Art's leading figures, has been made the **Provinciaal Museum Constant Permeke**. This exhibits 150 of the artist's paintings, drawings and sculptures.

🏛 **James Ensorhuis**
Vlaanderenstraat 27. **Tel** (059) 508118. 🕐 *Wed–Mon.* 🎟

🏛 **Mercator Marine Museum**
Mercatordok. **Tel** (059) 517010. 🕐 *daily.* 🎟 **www**.zeilschip-mercator.be

🏛 **Mu.ZEE**
Romestraat 11. **Tel** (059) 508118. **www**.muzee.be

🏛 **Noordseeaquarium**
Visserskaai. **Tel** (059) 500876. 🕐 *Apr–Sep: daily; Oct–Mar: Sat, Sun and public holidays.* 🎟 ♿

🏛 **Fort Napoleon**
Vuurtorenweg. **Tel** (059) 320048. 🕐 *Apr–Oct: Tue–Sun; Nov–Mar: Wed–Sun.* 🎟 ♿ 🍴 📷 📷 **www**.fortnapoleon.be

🏛 **Openluchtmuseum Atlantikwall**
Provinciaal Domein Raversijde, Nieuwpoortsesteenweg 636. **Tel** (059) 702285. 🕐 *Apr–Nov.* 🎟 **www**.west-vlaanderen.be

Displays of the North Sea's natural treasures at the Noordseeaquarium

Veurne ❽

25 km (15 miles) SW of Oostende.
Road Map A2. 🎣 *12,000.* 🚃 🚌
ℹ️ *Grote Markt 29; (058) 335531.*
www.veurne.be

The pretty town of Veurne,
sometimes called Little Bruges
owing to its historic charm,
clusters around an attractive
Grote Markt rimmed with 15th-
and 16th-century step-gabled
façades. Its fine Flemish-
Renaissance **Stadhuis**, built
between 1596 and 1612,
has interor walls lined with
embossed Córdoba leather.
This building served as headquarters for the Belgian army
in 1914. Behind it is the
13th-century **St-Walpurgakerk**,
with its soaring nave lit like
a lantern by stained glass.
St Walburga, an 8th-century
missionary nun, is patron saint
of the town. In the Appelmarkt
close by is the 15th-century
St-Niklaaskerk, with three
coolly elegant aisles divided
by sandstone arches. Its
13th-century brick tower is also
a belfry, containing a carillon
installed in 1961 and a small
carillon museum.

On the southern outskirts
is **Bakkerijmuseum**, a museum
of bakery set in 17th-century
almshouses and farm buildings.
It takes visitors on a historic
tour from grain to bread.

🏛️ **Stadhuis**
Grote Markt 27. *Tel (058) 335531.*
⏰ *Apr–mid-Nov.* 🖼️
🏛️ **St-Niklaaskerk**
Appelmarkt. *Tel (058) 335531.*
⏰ *mid-Jun–mid-Sep.* 🖼️ *(tower and carillon museum).*
🏛️ **Bakkerijmuseum**
Albert I-laan 2. *Tel (058) 313897.*
⏰ *Jul–Aug: daily; Sep & Apr–Jun: Sat–Thu; Oct–Mar: Sun–Thu.* 🖼️
📷 ℹ️ **www**.bakkerijmuseum.be

Koksijde ❾

26 km (16 miles) W of Oostende.
Road Map A2. 🎣 *21,000.* 🚌 🚃
ℹ️ *Zeelaan 303; (058) 512 910.*
www.koksijde.be

A popular modern seaside
resort, Koksijde has beach-
fronts at St-Idesbald and
Koksijde-Bad. During the
Middle Ages, the town was

Excavated ruins of the 12th-century Ten Duinen abbey at Koksijde

famed for its influential Abbey
of Our Lady of the Dunes,
called Ten Duinen (or Ter
Duinen) for short. Founded
by the Benedictines in 1107,
it became Cistercian in 1138
and was destroyed by the
Protestant rebels nicknamed
geuzen (sea beggars) in 1566.
The museum **Ten Duinen 1138**
breathes life into the excavated
remains that can be seen in
the adjoining park. Just to the
south is the **Zuid Abdijmolen**,
a wooden windmill dating
from the year 1773.

Located in St-Idesbald is
the impressive **Museum Paul
Delvaux**, containing the largest
single collection of this great
Surrealist's work. Set in a

whitewashed villa built in
traditional style, the museum
was opened by the Paul
Delvaux Foundation in 1982
with the artist's blessing. It
includes a number of drawings, paintings and sculptures
as well as personal possessions
that have a bearing on the
artist's work, as well as a
reconstruction of his studio.

🏛️ **Ten Duinen 1138**
Koninklijke Prinslaan 6, Koksijde.
Tel (058) 533950. ⏰ *Feb–Dec: Tue–Sun.* 🖼️ **www**.tenduinen.be
🏛️ **Museum Paul Delvaux**
Delvauxlaan 42, St-Idesbald. *Tel (058) 521229.* ⏰ *Apr–Sep: Tue–Sun; Oct–Dec: Thu–Sun.* 🖼️ 📷 ℹ️
www.delvauxmuseum.com

PROCESSION OF THE PENITENTS AT VEURNE

Every year on the last Sunday of
July – a day that coincides with
the town's Kermis festival and its
funfair in the Grote Markt – 1,000
citizens of Veurne dress in biblical
costume for the Boetprocessie, the
Procession of Penitence. Making a
circuit of the centre of the town,
successive groups recount the
most famous stories of the Bible.
Among them are 400 *boetelingen*
(penitents) – anonymous men
and women making a genuine
act of religious devotion. Wearing

Veurne's citizens dressed as figures from the Bible

monkish brown robes with masked hoods, and often bare-
foot, they carry large wooden crosses or pull heavy floats
bearing religious statues. After the folkloric early scenes
from Adam and Eve to the Nativity, the mood darkens as
the Crucifixion of Christ approaches, surrounded by increasing numbers of penitents. The crowd looks on in near
silence. The people of Veurne have been re-enacting this
story since the 1640s. In charge is a venerable society
called the Sodaliteit, whose members officiate wearing
17th-century outfits of black velvet robes and red hats.

The controversial IJzertoren with its striking cross-shaped profile

Kasteel Beauvoorde ⑩

Wulveringemstraat 10, Veurne.
Road Map A2. *Tel (058) 299229.*
🚌 ⭕ *Jul–Aug: daily; see website for details.* 🔵 *Nov–Feb.* 🎨 🔂 📷
www.kasteelbeauvoorde.be

With its moat, brick turrets and step gables as well as its parkland setting, Kasteel Beauvoorde is one of the most attractive small castles in Belgium. An earlier castle on the site was destroyed by Protestant rebels in 1584, and this classic Flemish fortified manor was built in its place in the early 17th century. Sympathetically restored in the 19th century, the interior contains furniture, carved wood panelling and ceramics.

Ceramic plate from Kasteel Beauvoorde

IJzertoren ⑪

IJzerdijk 49, Diksmuide; 15 km (9 miles) SE of Veurne. **Road Map** A2.
Tel (051) 500286. 🚆 🚌 ⭕ *daily; see website for details.* 🔵 *3 weeks in Jan.* 🎨 📷 📷 **www**.ijzertoren.org

A vast cross, 84 m (275 ft) tall, rises from the banks of the River IJzer at Diksmuide and towers over the surroundings. This is the IJzertoren (IJzer Tower), a monument to the Flemish dead of World War I, and a physical plea for peace. Remarkably, it contains an impressive museum on 22 floors, leading down from a roof terrace with commanding views over the surrounding flat landscape. The main theme is World War I, evoked through photographs, videos, artifacts, an extensive reconstructed dugout and even the smells of poison gas.

The tower is a controversial monument; not only is it a symbol of world peace but also a mark of Flemish rights. In fact, this is the second tower on the site, completed in 1965. The first, built between 1928 and 1930, was mysteriously blown up in 1946, no doubt because of its powerful symbolic connotations.

Environs
Just 2 km (1 mile) to the north of the IJzertoren is the **Dodengang** (Trench of Death): preserved trenches where, over 1915–18, the Belgian army blocked German troops from advancing across the flooded IJzer. The German military cemetery at **Vladso**, 6 km (4 miles) northeast, contains the heartrending sculptures *Grieving Parents* by celebrated Expressionist artist Käthe Kollwitz (1867–1945). Her 17-year-old son, killed in 1914, is buried here.

🏛 **Dodengang**
IJzerdijk 65, Diksmuide. *Tel (051) 505344.* ⭕ *Apr–Sep: 10am–5pm daily (Oct–mid-Nov: Mon–Fri, mid-Nov–Apr: Tue–Fri).*

A Tour of World War I Battlefields ⑫

See pp126–7.

Ieper ⑬

32 km (20 miles) S of Veurne.
Road Map A2. 🚶 *35,000.* 🚉
🚌 ℹ *Lakenhalle, Grote Markt 34; (057) 239220.* **www**.ieper.be

Ypres in French and "Wipers" to the thousands of British troops who passed this way during World War I, Ieper was once a prosperous medieval cloth town. In 1914, it found itself just to the west of the front line, the Ypres Salient, and was demolished by shelling over the next four years. When peace returned, the citizens reconstructed their town as it had once been. Today, the town acts as a centre for visitors to the battlefields and military cemeteries. Its World War I museum, **In Flanders Fields**, provides a moving background, focussing on the experiences of individuals. To commemorate the dead, the Last Post is played every evening at the Menin Gate, a huge stone arch with the names of 55,000 missing soldiers.

Environs
Located 5 km (3 miles) east of Ieper, **Bellewaerde Park** is a large theme park with an open-air zoo and some 30 other attractions.

🏛 **In Flanders Fields**
Grote Markt 34, Ieper *Tel (057) 239 220.* ⭕ *Apr–mid-Nov: 10am–6pm daily; mid-Nov–end Mar: 10am–5pm Tue–Sun.* 🎨 📷

🍀 **Bellewaerde Park**
E17/A19 Ieper, exit 3 Beselare, Meenseweg 497, Ieper *Tel (057) 468686.* ⭕ *late Mar–Jan.* 🎨 ♿
🎡 🔂 📷

Moving displays at In Flanders Fields, Ieper's Word War I museum

Talbot House chapel, where British soldiers gathered in Poperinge

Poperinge ⑭

12 km (8 miles) W of Ieper. **Road Map** A2. 🚶 20,000. 🚉 🚌
ℹ️ Stadhuis, Grote Markt 1; (057) 334081. 🚋 Fri. **www.**poperinge.be

A cloth town in medieval times, Poperinge became a centre for production of hops (used in beer-making) in the 15th century. Today, this is celebrated in the **Hopmuseum**, an old hop processing plant. The town centres on a Grote Markt with a Neo-Gothic **Stadhuis** built in 1911. Close by is the 15th-century, late-Gothic church, the **Hoofdkerk St-Bertinus**, which contains fine woodcarving in its organ loft and Baroque pulpit. Its tower has an unusual lantern.

Lying some 15 km (8 miles) behind the World War I front line, Poperinge served as a transit point and a recuperation centre for Allied troops. Testimony of this is the **Talbot House**, an 18th-century townhouse that was operated by army chaplain Philip Clayton (1885–1972) as an informal club for British soldiers. The Edwardian-style rooms and the makeshift chapel in the roof are redolent of the era. The grim death cells where deserters awaited the firing squad have been preserved behind the Stadhuis.

🏛️ **Hopmuseum**
Gasthuisstraat 71, Poperinge.
Tel (057) 337922. ⏰ Mar–Nov:
Tue–Sun and public holidays. 📷
🖥️ 🖱️ **www.**hopmuseum.be

🏛️ **Talbot House**
Gasthisstraat 43, Poperinge.
Tel (057) 333228. ⏰ Tue–Sun. 📷
🖱️ **www.**talbothouse.be

Kortrijk ⑮

37 km (23 miles) E of Ieper. **Road Map** B2. 🚶 80,000. 🚉 🚌
ℹ️ Begijnhofpark; (056) 277840.
www.kortrijk.be

A vibrant city with a historic centre, Kortrijk (Courtrai in French) owed its prominence in medieval times to the cloth trade, and textiles still play a key role in its economy. The Battle of the Golden Spurs (*see p38*) was fought near this city, and the museum **Kortrijk 1302** explains the battle and why it is an important Flemish landmark. The captured spurs were triumphantly exhibited in the **Onze-Lieve-Vrouwekerk** until the French recovered them in 1382. Today, this atmospheric church contains two notable treasures – *The Raising of the Cross* (1631), a painting by Anthony van Dyck, and an alabaster statue of St Catherine (1380). The statue stands in the spacious

The sturdy Broeltoren guarding a bridge over the River Leie

14th-century Chapel of the Counts, which is decorated with portraits of the counts of Flanders. Located a short walk from here is the **Begijnhof St Elisabeth**, one of Flanders's most enchanting béguinages.

The town's **Grote Markt** has a fine late-Gothic Stadhuis and a 14th-century brick belfry whose bell is rung by gilded mechanical statues. Close to the medieval Broeltoren – twin towers protecting a bridge over the River Leie – is the **Broelmuseum**, an 18th-century mansion with a collection of paintings that includes work by Kortrijk-born Roelandt Savery (1576–1639).

In a 19th-century flax farm on the southern outskirts is the **Nationaal Vlasmuseum**, which tells how flax and linen played a key role in Kortrijk. River Leie was once called the "golden river" because of all the flax processed in it.

🏛️ **Kortrijk 1302**
Begijnhofpark. **Tel** (056) 277850.
⏰ Tue–Sun. 📷 🖱️ **www.** kortrijk1302.be

⛪ **Onze-Lieve-Vrouwekerk**
⏰ daily.

⛪ **Begijnhof St Elisabeth**
⏰ sunrise–sunset daily.

🏛️ **Broelmuseum**
Broelkaai 6. **Tel** (056) 277780.
⏰ 10am–noon and 2–5pm
Tue–Fri, 11am–5pm Sat–Sun
and public holidays. 📷

🏛️ **Nationaal Vlasmuseum**
Etienne Sabbelaan 4 (relocating 2013). **Tel** (056) 210138. ⏰ Mar–Nov: 9am–12:30pm and 1:30–6pm
Tue–Fri, 2–6pm Sat–Sun. 📷

FLEMISH NATIONALISM IN BELGIUM

The sense of grievance felt by the people of Flanders towards the French-speaking community has a long history, dating back to the 9th century when Flanders was under French rule. The latter's high-handed treatment of successful Flemish cities resulted in an uprising, and a short-lived triumph in 1302 (*see p38*). French, then Burgundian rule favoured French-speakers, a situation that became etched in society and intensified as Wallonia became the economic force of 19th-century industrialization. At the start of World War I, army officers were all French-speaking. King Albert I rallied Flemish troops by promising equality after the war, but this was not fulfilled. The resentment over historic injustice is still palpable at some Flemish museums.

The 1302 Battle of the Golden Spurs

A Tour of World War I Battlefields ⑫

In 1914, the invading German army forced the Belgians to retreat to the far northeast, behind the River IJzer. To impede further German advance, the Belgians opened the sluicegates of the river and flooded the landscape, which formed an effective obstacle as far south as Diksmuide. South of here, the Germans confronted the Allies along a ridge to the east of Ieper (Ypres) called the Ypres Salient. Between 1915 and 1917, this was the front line, where the gruelling stalemate of trench warfare cost more than 500,000 lives. Today, the area around the Salient is a beguilingly pretty landscape dotted with monuments, museums and numerous cemeteries.

Diksmuide and Dodengang ①
The Belgians dug in along the canal of Diksmuide. Some of their trenches have been preserved at Dodengang (*see p124*).

John McCrae Site ②
Bunkers, dressing stations and the Essex Farm Cemetery recall where Canadian medic John McCrae served, and wrote his poem "In Flanders Fields". The poem established the poppy as the symbol of the war dead.

Langemark ③
This haunting German military cemetery has the flat tombstones of some 44,000 soldiers laid out beneath a cloak of trees.

Guynemer Monument ④
A sculpture of a stork at Poelkapelle celebrates the pioneer of military aviation Georges Guynemer, who was lost, presumed dead, near here in 1917.

Canadian Forces Memorial ⑤
At St-Juliaan, the large bust of *The Brooding Soldier* commemorates the 2,000 soldiers who died after the first ever gas attack in 1915.

Tyne Cot Cemetery ⑥
The largest Commonwealth cemetery in the world contains nearly 12,000 graves. The walls bear the names of 35,000 missing soldiers.

Memorial Museum Passchendale ⑦
This 19th-century mansion, located in Zonnebeke, contains numerous World War I artifacts, and includes impressively reconstructed dugouts and trenches.

Menin Gate ⑧
Each evening in Ieper, the Last Post, played by buglers at the Menin Gate, echoes beneath the huge arch which lists the names of 55,000 missing Commonwealth soldiers.

Hill 62, Sanctuary Wood Museum ⑨
A private collection of military jumble leads to a wood where original trenches have been preserved.

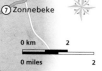

Hill 60, Zillebeke ⑩
A battered, scarred hilltop, the much disputed Hill 60 faced devastating attacks from underground mines.

③ Langemark
④ Poelkapelle
(N313)
⑤
ZONNEBEKE-STRAAT
⑥
(N332)
⑦ Zonnebeke
(N37) (A19)
(N8)
-beekse
er
⑨
Zillebeke
⑩

0 km   2
0 miles   2

Pool of Peace ⑪
Underground mining and a huge explosion beneath German lines in 1917 resulted in the water-filled Lone Tree Crater, which has now been designated the Pool of Peace.

Irish Peace Tower ⑬
This Irish monastic round tower in early medieval style was built in 1998 at Mesen to commemorate the Irish dead, and as a symbol of reconciliation.

French Memorial and Ossuary ⑫
The land rises dramatically in Heuvelland (Hill Country) and around Kemmel. The French fatalities in a battle of 1918 are remembered in a monument on Kemmel Hill, and 5,000 lie nearby in the French Ossuary.

KEY

━━ Tour route
━━ Motorway
═══ Other road
••• Battlefront 1915–17

The Brothers van Eyck sculpted by Geo Verbanck in 1913, outside St Baafskathedraal, Ghent ▷

HUBERTO ET JOHANNI VAN EYCK

Street-by-Street: Ghent ⑯

Bell on display
in the Belfort

As a tourist destination, the Flemish city of Ghent (Gent in Dutch) has long been over-shadowed by its neighbour, Bruges. In part, this reflects their divergent histories. The success of the cloth trade during the Middle Ages was followed by a period of stagnation for Bruges, while Ghent became a major industrial centre in the 19th century. The resulting pollution coated the city's antique buildings in layers of grime from its factories. In the 1980s, Ghent initiated a restoration programme. The city's medieval buildings were cleaned, industrial sites were tidied up and the canals were cleared. Today, the intricately carved stonework of its churches and old buildings, as well as the city's excellent museums and stern, forbidding castle give the centre its character.

Het Gravensteen
Ghent's centre is dominated by the thick stone walls and imposing gatehouse of its ancient Castle of the Counts.

★ The Design Museum Gent
This elegant 19th-century dining room is just one of many charming period rooms in the decorative arts museum. The collection is housed in an 18th-century mansion and covers art and design from the 1600s to the present.

★ Graslei
One of Ghent's most picturesque streets, the Graslei overlooks the River Leie on the site of the city's medieval harbour. It is lined with perfectly preserved guildhouses; some date from the 12th century.

To Ghent St-Piet
Stadsmuseum (S

STAR SIGHTS

★ The Design
   Museum Gent

★ Graslei

★ St-Baafskathedraal

Korenmarkt
This busy street was once the corn market, the commercial centre of the city since the Middle Ages. Today, it is lined with popular cafés.

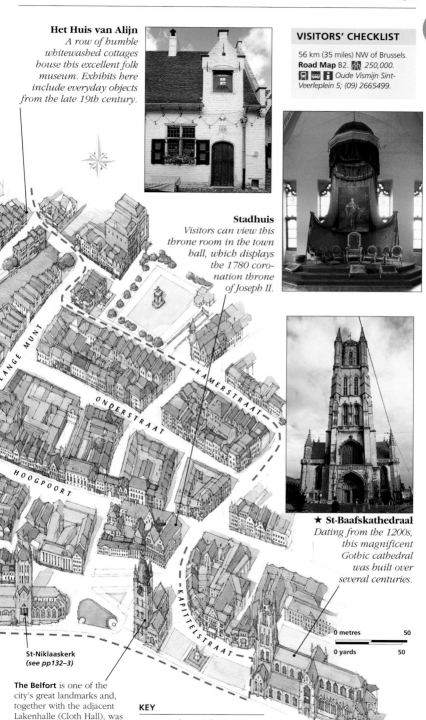

Het Huis van Alijn
A row of humble whitewashed cottages house this excellent folk museum. Exhibits here include everyday objects from the late 19th century.

VISITORS' CHECKLIST

56 km (35 miles) NW of Brussels.
Road Map B2. 250,000.
Oude Vismijn Sint-Veerleplein 5; (09) 2665499.

Stadhuis
Visitors can view this throne room in the town hall, which displays the 1780 coronation throne of Joseph II.

★ **St-Baafskathedraal**
Dating from the 1200s, this magnificent Gothic cathedral was built over several centuries.

LANGE MUNT

ONDERSTRAAT

HOOGPOORT

KAMERSTRAAT

KAPITTELSTRAAT

St-Niklaaskerk
(see pp132–3)

The Belfort is one of the city's great landmarks and, together with the adjacent Lakenhalle (Cloth Hall), was a centre of medieval trade.

0 metres 50
0 yards 50

KEY

– – – Suggested route

Exploring Ghent

In the 9th century, Baldwin Iron-Arm, the first Count of Flanders, laid the foundations of Ghent when he built a castle to protect two abbeys from Viking raids. Ghent's historic centre was originally built during the 13th and 14th centuries, when the city prospered as a result of the cloth trade. Despite the many religious and dynastic conflicts, Ghent flourished throughout the 16th and early 17th centuries. After 1648, the Dutch sealed the Scheldt estuary near Antwerp, closing vital canal links, which led to a decline in the fortunes of both cities. The 19th-century boom in cotton spinning reinvigorated Ghent and led to the building of wide boulevards in the city's south. Today, textiles still feature in Ghent's industry, while its university lends a youthful vibrancy to city life.

Statue overlooking the River Leie

Tiled flooring forming a maze in the Pacification Hall in Ghent's Stadhuis

🔒 St-Baafskathedraal

St-Baafsplein. **Tel** (09) 2251626.
⭘ daily. **Adoration of the Mystic Lamb** ⭘ Apr–Oct: 9:30am–5pm Mon–Sat, 1–5pm Sun; Nov–Mar: 10:30am–4pm Mon–Sat, 1–4pm Sun. 🎟 👤 **www.**
sintbaafskathedraal-gent.be
St Bavo, who was Ghent's own 7th-century saint, left the life of a wealthy degenerate to become first a missionary in Flanders and France and then a hermit. Built in several stages, St-Baafskathedraal represents every phase of Gothic style, from the 13th- and 14th-century chancel to the later cavernous nave that is supported by slender columns. The main attraction here is van Eyck's polyptych *Adoration of the Mystic Lamb*, housed in a side chapel.

🏛 Stadhuis

Botermarkt 1. **Tel** (09) 2665111. 🎟
🎫 May–Oct: 3pm Mon–Thu; tours depart 2:30pm from the tourist office.
The façade of Ghent's town hall displays two distinctly different architectural styles. Overlooking Hoogstraat, the older half dates from the early 16th century and its tracery is in the elaborate Flamboyant Gothic style. The plainer, newer part, which flanks the Botermarkt, is characteristic of post-Reformation architecture. The statues seen in the niches on the exterior were added in the 1890s. Among this group of figures, it is possible to spot the original architect, Rombout Keldermans, who is shown studying his plans.

The building is still the city's administrative centre. Guided tours pass through a series of rooms, the most fascinating of which is the Pacification Hall. This was once the Court of Justice and the site of the signing of the Pacification of Ghent (a treaty between Catholics and Protestants under Habsburg rule) in 1576.

🏛 Belfort

St-Baafsplein. **Tel** (09) 3753161.
⭘ daily. ⬤ 1 Jan, 25 Dec. 🎟
🎫 May–Oct.
Ghent's Belfort (Belfry), a famed landmark rising 91 m (299 ft) high to the gilded-copper dragon on the tip of its spire, is situated between the cathedral and the town hall. Originally built in 1380, the Belfort was restored in the 19th and 20th centuries. Its bells today include a 54-bell carillon, which is used to play tunes to accompany the clock chimes every 15 minutes, and for keyboard concerts every Friday and Sunday at 11:30am. A lift to its parapet at a height of 65 m (213 ft) offers magnificent views over the city.

Below the Belfort is the **Lakenhalle** (Cloth Hall), a fine Flemish-Gothic building from 1425 where the city's cloth-trade was carried out. The building incorporates a small town prison; guided tours are provided on request.

🔒 St-Niklaaskerk

St-Veerleplein. ⭘ 10am–5pm Tue–Sun, 2–5pm Mon.
Built by merchants between the 13th and 15th centuries, this church was dedicated to

Gothic towers of St-Niklaaskerk and the Belfort from St-Michielsbrug

Views of the Graslei and 16th-century guildhouses along the River Leie

guildhouse next door is adorned by bunches of fruit and cartouches. The earliest building in this embankment is the 12th-century **Spijker** (Staple House). This simple Romanesque structure stored the city's grain supply for hundreds of years until a fire destroyed its interior.

Facing the Graslei across the water, the gabled buildings of the Korenlei date from later centuries, but gracefully complement the architecture of the Graslei. The views of the city's iconic buildings from **St-Michielsbrug**, the bridge at the southern end, crossing the River Leie, are among the most beautiful in Ghent.

🏛 Design Museum Gent
Jan Breydelstraat 5. *Tel* (09) 2679999. ◯ 10am–6pm Tue–Sun.
📧 www.designmuseumgent.be
This excellent decorative arts museum occupies an elegant 18th-century townhouse. The displays are arranged in two sections, beginning at the front with a series of lavishly furnished period rooms that feature textiles, furniture and artifacts from the 17th to the 19th centuries. At the back, an airy, modern extension completed in 1992 focusses on 20th-century design ranging from Art Nouveau to contemporary works, and includes furniture by the architects Victor Horta *(see p80)*, Marcel Breuer and Ludwig Mies van der Rohe.

their patron saint, St Nicholas, Bishop of Myra (and model for Santa Claus). The church is a fine example of the distinctive and austere style called Scheldt Gothic. The interior was once filled with guild shrines and chapels, until Protestant church-wreckers destroyed them in 1566. Today, it is remarkable for its pure architectural forms, with soaring columns brightly lit by high windows. The space is punctuated by a massive and extravagantly Baroque altar screen, a clarion call to the Counter-Reformation period; unusually for such latter-day alterations, it harmonizes with the rest of the church's interior to exhilarating effect.

🏛 Graslei and Korenlei
These are two embankments that face each other across the Tusschen Brugghen, once Ghent's main medieval harbour. The Graslei, on the eastern side, possesses a fine set of guildhouses. Among them is the sandstone façade of the guildhouse of the free boatmen, which is decorated with finely detailed nautical scenes. The corn measurers'

THE ADORATION OF THE MYSTIC LAMB

One of the greatest cultural treasures of northern Europe, *The Adoration of the Mystic Lamb* is a monumental, multi-panelled work by the first of the great, early Flemish artists, Jan van Eyck, and his lesser-known brother, Hubrecht. Completed in 1432, it is exquisitely painted with rich glowing colours and meticulously depicted details. It is also an expression of the deepest beliefs of Christianity – that human salvation lies in the sacrifice of Christ, the Lamb of God. What can be seen today in St-Baafskathedraal is almost entirely original; only one panel on the lower left is a modern copy, following the theft of the original in 1934. This is a remarkable achievement, given the painting's tumultuous history. It survived Protestant church-wreckers in 1566; sections of it were taken apart and removed by French soldiers in 1794; and several of the panels were sold in 1816. It even had to be rescued from fire in 1822. Audioguides to the painting (included in the price of the entry ticket) explain the significance of each of the 12 panels, the largest of which depicts the Mystic Lamb.

Central panels of the painting, with the Mystic Lamb as the focal point

♨ Groot Vleeshuis
Groentenmarkt 7. *Tel* (09) 2232324.
🕐 *10am–6pm Tue–Sun.* 🍴 📷
www.grootvleeshuis.be
Literally the Great Meat Hall, the Groot Vleeshuis was built between 1407 and 1419. Its long, low interior space still reflects the area's original purpose as a covered butchers' market, complete with ancient beams and uneven flooring. A large modern glass box has been ingeniously inserted into this to house a centre that promotes local Flemish food. One side is a restaurant that serves good Flemish dishes; the other is a delicatessen.

The original covered butchers' market of the Groot Vleeshuis

♨ Dulle Griet
Groot Kanonplein.
This 5-m (16-ft) long giant cannon, sitting on the embankment of the River Leie, is famous in Ghent folklore. Cast in about 1450 and weighing 16,000 kg (35,300 lb), it could fire stone cannonballs the size of beachballs. It was brought to Ghent in 1578, during an era of the Calvinist government. The name Dulle Griet means Mad Meg, a legendary medieval character who embodied mad, violent frenzy and disorder. The cannon has been repainted in its original red which reflects its other nickname, the Groten Rooden Duyvele (Great Red Devil).

♙ Het Gravensteen
St-Veerleplein. *Tel* (09) 2259306.
🕐 *Apr–Sep: 9am–6pm daily;*
Oct–Mar: 9am–5pm daily. 📷
www.gent.be/gravensteen
Once the seat of the counts of Flanders, the imposing bulk of Het Gravensteen, or the Castle of the Counts, eloquently recalls the unsettled

and violent context of Ghent's early medieval past. Parts of the castle date back to the late 1100s, but most of it comprises later additions. Until the 14th century, the castle, with its massive stone walls, was Ghent's main military stronghold. It was then used as the city's jail until the late 1700s. Later, it became a cotton mill.

From the gatehouse, a long and heavily fortified tunnel leads up to the courtyard, which is overlooked by two large buildings, the count's medieval residence and the earlier keep. Arrows guide visitors around the interiors of both buildings, and in the upper rooms there is a spine-chilling collection of medieval torture instruments.

🏛 Het Huis van Alijn
Kraanlei 65. *Tel* (09) 2692350.
🕐 *11am–5pm Tue–Sat, 10am–5pm Sun.* 📷 📷 **www**.huisvanalijn.be
This is one of Belgium's best folk museums, graphically evoking daily life of the past through a huge collection of fascinating artifacts. This includes dolls and other toys, clothes, games, furniture, kitchenware and funerary mementos as well as complete shops and craftsmen's workshops. The complex also has a puppet theatre that presents plays throughout the

Het Gravensteen, a classic medieval castle

year in Dutch. The museum is set out in a sequence of rooms set in a pretty group of whitewashed almshouses (the House of Alijn) surrounding a grassy courtyard. Although mainly 16th-century, the almshouses were originally founded in 1363 as a children's hospital – not out of philanthropy, but as an act of penance by the Rijm family for the murder of two members of the rival Alijn family.

The surrounding area, known as the **Patershol**, is a grid of quaint little lanes and low brick houses that developed in the 17th century to house the city's weavers. This once down-at-heel area underwent extensive refurbishment in the 1980s and is now one of the trendiest parts of town, but retains a bohemian flair.

Het Huis van Alijn, housed in atmospheric 16th-century almshouses

For hotels and restaurants in this region see pp264–6 and pp288–91

🎭 Vlaamse Opera
Schouwburgstraat 3. *Tel (09) 2681011.* ☐ *for performances.* ♿ 🎥 *3rd Sat of each month.* www.vlaamseopera.be

This classic opera house, built between 1837 and 1840, has now been restored to reclaim its reputation as one of the most spectacular theatres in Europe, with an auditorium and adjoining salons encrusted with gilding, chandeliers, mural paintings and sculptural decorations. The resident company is the much-respected Vlaamse Opera (Flemish Opera), which was formed when the opera companies of Ghent and Antwerp merged.

The opulent, renovated interior of the Vlaamse Opera

🏛 Stadsmuseum Gent (STAM)
Godshuizenlaan 2. *Tel (09) 2671400.* ☐ *10am–6pm Tue–Sun.* 🎥 📷 *on request.* 🔊 ♿ 🍴 www.stamgent.be

This city museum offers a historic view of Ghent through multimedia presentations and a wide variety of artifacts, treasures and documentation. STAM is located in the old **Abdij van de Bijloke**, a rambling set of historic red-brick buildings. This abbey, originally founded in 1204, has over time been a nunnery, a hospital and a museum. The old cloisters, dormitories and refectory (with its 14th-century wall paintings) provide a restful backdrop to the exhibits, which take visitors through all the phases of Ghent's history. This includes its medieval heyday, the rebellion against Charles V in 1539 *(see p40)* and the industrial revolution.

A small courtyard surrounded by step-gabled houses in the Klein Begijnhof

🎭 Klein Begijnhof
Lange Violettestraat 205. ⊘ *closed to the public.*

The prettiest of Ghent's three béguinages, the Klein Begijnhof (Small Béguinage) was founded as a community of single women in 1235 and has been continuously occupied ever since, although the residents are no longer béguines *(see p61)*. The rows of step-gabled whitewashed houses here, most dating from the 17th century, enclose a small park and a Baroque church. Although not open to the public, the structure is a beautiful site to behold.

🏛 Stedelijk Museum voor Actuele Kunst (SMAK)
Citadelpark. *Tel (09) 2407601.* ☐ *10am–6pm Tue–Sun.* 🎥 🍴 📷 www.smak.be.

One of Europe's most dynamic modern art galleries, SMAK is a force in the art world that, over the past two decades, has helped bring the spotlight to the Belgian art scene. Its permanent collection includes works by artists such as Bacon, Beuys, Broodthaers, Long, Muñoz, Nauman, Tuymans, Panamarenko and Warhol. Temporary exhibitions feature international artists at the cutting edge of contemporary art. The airy and attractive building dates from 1949 but was remodelled in the 1990s.

🏛 Museum voor Schone Kunsten
Ferdinand Scribedreef 1, Citadelpark. *Tel (09) 2400700.* ☐ *10am–6pm Tue–Sun.* 🎥 www.mskgent.be

Ghent's impressive collection of pre-modern fine art is displayed in this Neo-Classical building. Medieval paintings include the *Bearing of the Cross* by Hieronymus Bosch as well as work by such artists as Rogier van der Weyden and Hugo van der Goes. Jordaens, Rubens, and van Dyck are also represented here, along with James Ensor, Belgian Symbolists and artists belonging to the St-Martens-Latem School of Art *(see p136)*.

Grand Neo-Classical façade of the Museum voor Schone Kunsten

A Tour Around St-Martens-Latem ⑰

The pretty stretch of countryside along the River Leie just before it reaches Ghent, was famously adopted at the start of the 20th century by a number of Belgian artists who were collectively known as the St-Martens-Latem school. Mostly Symbolists, they included Gustave van de Woestyne, Valerius de Saedeleer, Frits van den Berghe, Albert Servaes, Gustave de Smet and the sculptor Georges Minne. Constant Permeke arrived in 1909, bringing a more radical Expressionistic tone. Many galleries in this part of the Leiestreek (Leie region), display their work.

St-Jan-Baptistkerk ①
The distinctive octagonal tower and spire of the 13th-century Church of St John the Baptist in Afsnee is seen in many paintings.

Gemeentelijk Museum Gevaert-Minne ②
This museum has a major collection of work by the artists of the St-Martens-Latem school.

St-Martens-Latem ③
A short detour along Meerstraat at St-Martens-Latem leads to a curving stretch of the river that makes clear why artists were attracted to this area.

Museum Gustave de Smet ④
Surrounded by trees in a quiet quarter of Deurle, the house where artist Gustave de Smet (1877–1943) lived and worked has been preserved as an art gallery and museum.

Museum van Deinze en de Leiestreek (MuDeL) ⑦
On the eastern outskirts of Deinze, this museum has a fine collection of art, antique furniture and crafts.

Kasteel Ooidonk ⑥
A short detour to this elegant château and its gardens provides an opportunity to see the tranquil farm and woodland areas around the river.

KEY

▬▬	Tour route
▬▬	Motorway
═══	Other road
🛈	Information centre

TIPS FOR DRIVERS

Starting point: Afsnee, just north of the A10 motorway outside Ghent.
Length: About 15 km (10 miles).
Duration: Allow half a day.
Driving conditions: The roads are narrow but good.
Where to eat: Restaurants are at Deinze and St-Martens-Latem.
Visitors' Information:
Deinze: Markt 46, (09) 3804601;
St-Martens-Latem: Dorp 1, (09) 2821700; www.toerisme-leiestreek.be

Museum Dhondt-Dhaenens ⑤
Named after its art-collector founders, this dynamic museum specializes in exhibitions of contemporary art, but also displays selections of its impressive permanent collection.

Corner tower with bulbous spire overlooking the moat at Kasteel Ooidonk

Laarne was remodelled and enlarged in the 17th century to make it a more habitable château. Since 1953, it has been in the hands of the Royal Association of Historic Residences and Gardens. The interior, which can be visited only by a guided tour, holds 17th-century furniture, an exceptional collection of 15th- to 18th-century silver and 16th-century Brussels tapestries depicting domestic and hunting scenes. There is also a well-respected restaurant that occupies the outbuildings.

Kasteel Ooidonk ⑱

Ooidonkdreef 9, Deinze; 24 km (15 miles) SW of Ghent. **Road Map** B2. *Tel* (09) 2823570. ◻ *Apr–mid-Sep: 2–5:30pm Sun and public holidays; Jul–Aug: 2–5pm Sat, Sun and public holidays.* 🖼 🍴 www.ooidonk.be. **Gardens** ◻ *9am–4pm Tue–Sun.*

The impressive castle of Ooidonk sits on a meandering loop of the River Leie, surrounded by **Gardens**, woodland and a moat. It occupies the site of a 13th-century fortress that was wrecked in 1491 by the citizens of Ghent in a revolt against Habsburg ruler Maximilian I. It was then the home of Philip de Montmorency, Count of Hornes, until 1568, when he was executed for opposing the introduction of the Spanish Inquisition. His castle was destroyed by Protestants in 1579. The corner towers are all that remain of this earlier fortress. The rest was rebuilt after 1595 in a mixture of Renaissance and Hispano-Flemish styles, with step-gabled façades and bulb-shaped crests on the towers. The interior was refurbished sensitively in the 19th century to sumptuous standards and has a fitting collection of antique furniture, tapestries, paintings, *objets d'art* and the kind of detail which is seen in a castle that is still lived in by its owners.

Kasteel van Laarne ⑲

Eethoekstraat 5, Laarne; 19 km (12 miles) SE of Ghent. **Road Map** B2. *Tel* (09) 2309155. 🖼 🍴 mandatory; Easter–Sep: 3pm Sun; Jul–Aug: 3pm Thu and Sun. 🍴 www.slotvanlaarne.be

A remarkable castle, Laarne is surrounded by a broad moat and accessed by a long bridge. The castle is artistically set at an angle both to the moat and to the large square forecourt, with corner buildings, that leads up to it. Originally a pentagonal fortress dating from the 12th to 14th centuries, with unusual spires on the towers, it was used by the counts of Flanders, and was the target of repeated sieges.

Stoomcentrum Maldegem ⑳

Stationsplein 8, Maldegem; 32 km (20 miles) from Ghent. **Road Map** B1. *Tel* (050) 716852. ◻ *early May–Sep: 10am–5:30pm Sun; Jul–Aug: noon–5pm Wed and Fri, 10am–5:30pm Sun.* 🍴 Steam Festival (1st weekend of May). www.stoomcentrum.be

The Stoomcentrum (Steam Centre) in Maldegem is the largest collection of steam engines in Flanders. It has agricultural and industrial machines, fire-engines, steamrollers and steam locomotives. The museum is operated by enthusiasts, and visitors can see them working on machines currently under restoration. Steam and diesel trains take visitors for rides on a track to Eeklo 10 km (6 miles) away, and a diesel train runs on a narrow-gauge line to Donk, about 1.5 km (1 mile) away.

Old-fashioned diesel train at Stoomcentrum Maldegem

The Flamboyant Gothic façade of Oudenaarde's elegant Stadhuis

Oudenaarde ㉑

30 km (19 miles) S of Ghent.
Road Map B2. 👥 28,000. 🚍 🚌
🛈 Stadhuis, Markt 1; (055) 317251.
www.oudenaarde.be

Founded as a fortress on the River Scheldt in the 11th century, Oudenaarde (Old Landing Place) has had a long and troubled history, scrapping with the rival city of Ghent in the Middle Ages, and often besieged. Developing as a cloth town, it became celebrated for its tapestries in the 15th century, but fell into decline thereafter.

Oudenaarde has preserved many of its great monuments, chief among which is the outstanding 16th-century **Stadhuis** built in Flamboyant Gothic style. Its interior has carved wood furnishings, a notable silverware collection and work by Adriaen Brouwer (1605– 38), who was born in the town and is famed for his rumbustious paintings of peasants. The nearby **Lakenhalle** (Cloth Hall) contains an exceptional collection of tapestries.

Overlooking the River Scheldt is the grand 16th- to 18th-century mansion **Huis de Lalaing**, now a municipal tapestry workshop where visitors are welcome. A little way up-river, the 13th-century **Onze-Lieve-Vrouwekerk van Pamele** is a classic example of Scheldt Gothic (see p28); Pamele was the name of the twin town that developed on the south bank of the Scheldt. The undulating countryside around Oudenaarde is known as the Vlaamse Ardennen, or the Flemish Ardennes.

🏛 **Stadhuis**
Grote Markt. **Tel** (055) 317251.
◻ Apr–Oct: 11am & 3pm Tue–Sun (guided tours only). 🏷 📷

🏛 **Lakenhalle**
Behind Stadhuis. ◻ Apr–Oct: 9am– 5:30pm Mon–Fri, 10am–5:30pm Sat–Sun and public holidays; Nov– Mar: 9:30am–noon and 1:30–4pm Mon–Fri, 2–5pm Sat. 📷

🏛 **Huis de Lalaing**
Bourgondiestraat 9. ◻ 1:30–4pm Tue–Fri. 🏷

Geraardsbergen ㉒

41 km (25 miles) S of Ghent.
Road Map B2. 👥 31,000. 🚍 🚌
🛈 Stadhuis, Grote Markt; (054) 437289. 🎭 Krakelingenfeest (Feb).
www.geraardsbergen.be

The agreeable town of Geraardsbergen (Grammont in French) is situated in the Vlaamse Ardennen, on the River Dender. The nearby hill of **Oudenberg** rises above the town to a height of 110 m (360 ft), and the steep, cobbled road up it is known to all cycle-race enthusiasts as the Mur de Grammont, a gruelling feature of the Tour of Flanders (see p32). The summit, with its Baroque chapel dating from 1648, is where 8,000 ring-shaped pastries are thrown into the crowd after a costumed parade known as the Krakenlingenstoet (see p35). However, bakers from Geraardsbergen pride themselves more on a sweet cheese tartlet called mattentaart.

The Grote Markt, at the centre of the town, has an impressive **Stadhuis**. The version of the **Manneken-Pis** found outside the Stadhuis was originally installed in 1459, so it predates the one in Brussels by nearly 200 years. The statue's 235 costumes can be admired in a small museum by the tourist office. The 15th-century stone fountain and cross in the square is a town emblem known as the **Marbol**.

Dendermonde ㉓

30 km (19 miles) E of Ghent.
Road Map C2. 👥 43,000. 🚍 🚌
🛈 Stadhuis, Grote Markt; (052) 213956. 🏷 Mon. **www.** dendermonde.be

Its position at the confluence of the Scheldt and Dender has made Dendermonde (literally, Mouth of the River Dender) a strategically important

Dendermonde's picturesque begijnhof overlooking the green

A statue of the benevolent saint outside the Stadhuis at St-Niklaas

location throughout history, even in 1914, when the town was sacked by the Germans. Today, it is a quiet commuter town, famed above all for its celebrated pageant of the steed Bayard, which dates back to the 15th century and is performed every ten years.

Dendermonde's attractive Grote Markt is flanked by the steepled turret and step-gables of its 15th-century **Vleeshuis** (Meat Hall), which now contains a museum. The **Stadhuis** was originally built as a cloth hall in the 14th century. It was wrecked in 1914 and restored in the 1920s. Its belfry has a carillon of 49 bells. The town's **Onze-Lieve-Vrouwekerk**, built between the 13th and 15th centuries, has a remarkable 12th-century carved font made of Tournai stone, and two paintings by Anthony van Dyck – the *Adoration of the Shepherds* (c.1616) and the *Crucifixion* (c.1628).

To the south of the River Dender, in the beguiling **St-Alexiusbegijnhof**, are rows of attractive 17th-century houses lining a triangular green. Located here is a small museum about the béguinage as well as a folk museum.

Environs
Situated 15 km (9 miles) to the west, **Donkmeer** is a lakeland area famed as the place to eat eel dishes such as *paling in't groen (see p278)*. There is also an agreeable nature reserve known as **De Eendenkooi** (The Duck Pen).

Sculpture at Grote Markt, St-Niklaas

St-Niklaas ㉔

39 km (24 miles) NE of Ghent.
Road Map C1. 70,000.
Grote Markt 45; (03) 7609260.
Thu. www.sint-niklaas.be

The sprawling town of St-Niklaas is the commercial centre of Waasland, an area of drained marshes that have become productive farmland. St-Niklaas's Grote Markt is the largest market square in the country. Surrounded by a number of attractive 17th-century buildings and an elegant 19th-century **Stadhuis**, the square really comes alive on market days as well as in early September when scores of hot-air balloons gather for the Vredesfeesten (literally, Peace Festivities). The now revamped **Ste.M** (Stedelijk

Museum) is an intriguing assortment that includes a collection of music recording machines – from musical boxes to early gramophones – historical hairdressing salons (the Barbierama) and recon-structions of life in medieval times based around archaeo-logical finds at the Boudelo Abbey close by.

Set in a Neo-Classical town mansion built over 1928 and 1929, the **Salons voor Schone Kunsten** has elegantly fur-nished rooms and a good collection of paintings by noted 19th-century Belgian artists such as Jan Stobbaerts, Henri de Braekeleer, Henri Evenepoel, James Ensor and Hippolyte Boulenger. The great Renaissance map-maker, Gerardus Mercator (1512–94), creator of the familiar Mercator Projection, was born nearby at Rupelmonde. Dedicated to him, the **Mercatormuseum** explores his contributions to the history of cartography.

Ste.M
Zwijgershoek 14. **Tel** (03) 7603750.
2–5pm Tue–Sat and 11am–5pm Sun.

Salons voor Schone Kunsten
Stationsstraat 85. **Tel** (03) 7781745.
2–5pm Thu–Sat and 11am–5pm Sun.

Mercatormuseum
Zamanstraat 49. **Tel** (03) 7603783.
2–5pm Tue–Sat, 11am–5pm Sun.

THE LEGEND OF THE STEED BAYARD

Set in the times of Charlemagne, the legend of the steed Bayard recounts the derring-do of four knights and a pow-erful horse. The knights were the four sons of Aymon, Lord of Dendermonde, and Aya, Charlemagne's sis-ter. One of them, Reinout, subdued the ferocious steed Bayard. In a quarrel over the horse, Reinout killed Charlemagne's jealous son Lodewijk, after which the brothers, riding the mighty steed, defended themselves from the emperor's wrath. Finally, as a condition of peace, Reinout agreed to kill the steed Bayard. Seeing how Reinout had rejected him, the valiant horse sacrificed himself in the river. Dendermonde's famous pageant today, the Ros Beiaardommegang, centres upon a giant model of the horse ridden by the Aymon brothers in full armour, a role always taken by four real brothers from Dendermonde.

Statue of the steed Bayard with three of the Aymon brothers visible

CENTRAL AND EASTERN FLANDERS

*M*agnificent castles and Gothic churches speak eloquently of this region's rich historic heritage. Central Flanders is the busy axis between Brussels and Antwerp, a hothouse of contemporary culture and fashion. Further east, the beauty and tranquillity of the countryside become the keynotes, in the heaths and woodlands of the Kempen and the sweetly rolling farmlands of the south.

Stretching from River Scheldt in the west to the Province of Limburg in the east, Central and Eastern Flanders is an area of age-old natural and historical beauty, with the straight roads built by the Romans around Tongeren, in eastern Limburg, still in use today.

In AD 843, the lands to the south and east of the River Scheldt were an area called Lotharingia. These followed a trajectory within the Holy Roman Empire, separate from that of the rest of Flanders. Over the next few centuries, the land was further divided between the duchies of Brabant and Limburg, with the prince-bishopric of Liège gaining control of southern Limburg. During this period, the remote forests and woodlands of Eastern Flanders attracted religious communities, most notably the Premonstratensians at Tongerlo and Averbode. In the 15th century, the dukes of Burgundy slowly pulled the region under their control – by marriage, diplomacy or ruthless force. Towns such as Mechelen and Leuven began to flourish, and by the 17th century, the port-city of Antwerp had entered a Golden Age, echoed in the flamboyant paintings of Rubens.

Today, visitors come to admire the many vestiges of this history that are etched into the countryside and the fabric of the towns. They also come to immerse themselves in the natural charm of the landscape, to walk and cycle, and to enjoy the great range of *streekproducten*, the food specialities of the region, particularly from the farmlands and orchards of the Hageland and the Haspengouw.

A flat and tranquil landscape, characteristic of the agricultural regions of Central and Eastern Flanders

◁ Late Gothic façade of the Stadhuis in Leuven's Grote Markt

Exploring Central and Eastern Flanders

The main attractions of Central and Eastern Flanders lie in the west of the region. Antwerp has a clutch of top-quality museums and historic buildings, as well as a celebrated club scene. Leuven and Mechelen are beautiful medieval towns, with outstanding architectural treasures. There are castles at Beersel and Gaasbeek, gardens at Nationale Plantentuin and a World War II concentration camp memorial at Breendonk. More to the east, the beguiling little town of Diest is close to sites such as the pilgrimage shrine at Scherpenheuvel and the Abdij van Averbode. The abbey of Tongerlo is famous for its copy of Leonardo's *Last Supper*, while Hasselt is the place for those who wish to sample *jenever* gin. Roman history is very much in the air in Tongeren. The highlight of the region is Bokrijk's open-air museum, a collection of historic rustic buildings set out in a large park, bringing to life Flanders's rural past.

SIGHTS AT A GLANCE

Villages, Towns and Cities
Aarschot ❾
Antwerp pp144–55 ❶
Diest ❷
Halle ❶❼
Hasselt ❷❷
Leuven pp160–61 ❽
Lier ❻
Maaseik ❷❹
Mechelen ❼
St-Amands ❷
St-Truiden ❷❶
Tienen ❶❹
Tongeren ❷❼
Turnhout ❹
Zoutleeuw ❶❸

Castles
Kasteel van Beersel ❶❽
Kasteel van Gaasbeek ❶❾
Landcommanderij
    Alden Biesen ❷❻

Churches and Abbeys
Abdij van Averbode ❶❶
Abdij Tongerlo ❺
Onze-Lieve-Vrouw van
    Scherpenheuvel ❶❶
St-Servaasbasiliek
    Grimbergen ❶❻

Museums
*Bokrijk Openluchtmuseum
p167* ❷❸
Memorial Breendonk ❸

Parks and Gardens
Nationale Plantentuin ❶❺
Nationaal Park
    Hoge Kempen ❷❺

Areas of
Natural Beauty
Forêt de Soignes ❷❶

The stately 16th-century castle and grounds at Landcommanderij Alden Biesen

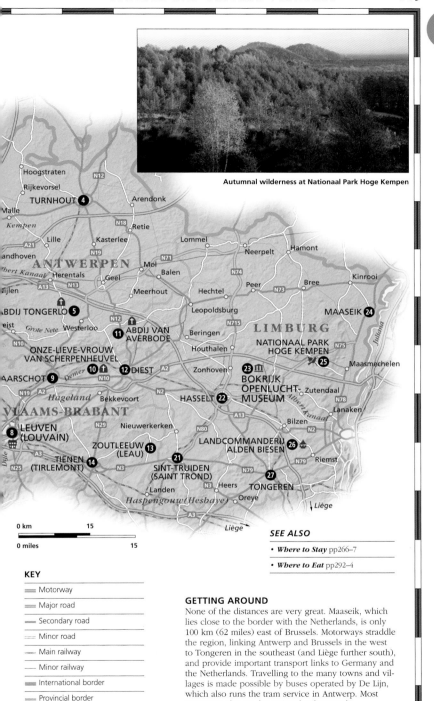

Autumnal wilderness at Nationaal Park Hoge Kempen

Hoogstraten
Rijkevorsel
TURNHOUT **4**
Malle
Arendonk
Kempen
N12
N18
Retie
Lommel
Neerpelt
Hamont
A21
Lille
Kasterlee
andhoven
N19
Mol
N71
bert Kanaal Herentals
ANTWERPEN
Geel
Balen
N74
Peer
Bree
Kinrooi
ijlen
A13
N13
Meerhout
Hechtel
N73
ABDIJ TONGERLO **5**
Leopoldsburg
MAASEIK **24**
eist
Grote Nete Westerloo
N12
N715
Beringen
LIMBURG
ONZE-LIEVE-VROUW
VAN SCHERPENHEUVEL
11 ABDIJ VAN
AVERBODE
Houthalen
NATIONAAL PARK
HOGE KEMPEN
N75
N10
Demer
10
12 DIEST
A2
Zonhoven
23
Maasmechelen
AARSCHOT **9**
N10
BOKRIJK
OPENLUCHT-
MUSEUM
25
N19
A2
Hageland Bekkevoort
N2
HASSELT **22**
Zutendaal
N78
VLAAMS-BRABANT
Nieuwerkerken
A13
Bilzen
Lanaken
Dijle
8 LEUVEN
(LOUVAIN)
N29
N80
LANDCOMMANDERIJ
ALDEN BIESEN
26
N2
A3
ZOUTLEEUW
(LEAU) **13**
21
N79
Riemst
TIENEN **14**
(TIRLEMONT)
N25
N3
SINT-TRUIDEN
(SAINT TROND)
N79
27
TONGEREN
Landen
N3
Heers
Oreye
Haspengouw (Hesbaye)
Liège
A3
Liège

0 km   15

0 miles   15

SEE ALSO

• **Where to Stay** pp266–7

• **Where to Eat** pp292–4

KEY

━━ Motorway

━━ Major road

── Secondary road

┄┄ Minor road

╍╍ Main railway

── Minor railway

▬▬ International border

━━ Provincial border

GETTING AROUND

None of the distances are very great. Maaseik, which lies close to the border with the Netherlands, is only 100 km (62 miles) east of Brussels. Motorways straddle the region, linking Antwerp and Brussels in the west to Tongeren in the southeast (and Liège further south), and provide important transport links to Germany and the Netherlands. Travelling to the many towns and villages is made possible by buses operated by De Lijn, which also runs the tram service in Antwerp. Most towns are also on the national rail network.

Antwerp ❶

The largest city in Flanders and one of Europe's busiest ports, Antwerp is also known as Belgium's second city. Beginning as a settlement on the banks of the Scheldt in the 2nd century AD, Antwerp went on to become part of the Duchy of Brabant, and its main port, in 1106. Over the next 200 years, it was a thriving hub of the European cloth industry. However, its golden age came during the era of Spanish rule *(see p41)*, when it was illuminated by the artistic genius of its most famous son, Pieter Paul Rubens (1577–1640). Today, mirroring this vigorous mercantile and cultural past, Antwerp is undergoing a spirited regeneration, seen in its widespread programme of rebuilding and renovation, and in its reputation as a key European centre of cutting-edge fashion design.

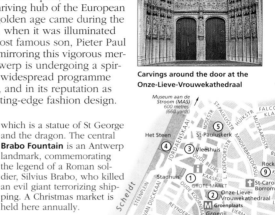

Carvings around the door at the Onze-Lieve-Vrouwekathedraal

Visitors touring Antwerp on a historic horse-drawn bus

which is a statue of St George and the dragon. The central **Brabo Fountain** is an Antwerp landmark, commemorating the legend of a Roman soldier, Silvius Brabo, who killed an evil giant terrorizing shipping. A Christmas market is held here annually.

KEY

Street-by-Street pp146–7

0 metres 400
0 yards 400

Key to Symbols see back flap

🏠 Grote Markt
Tel (03) 2320103.
Antwerp's central square, or Grote Markt, is flanked by the ornately gabled **Stadhuis**, which was completed in 1564 by the architect and sculptor Cornelis Floris. The square's north side has a series of guildhouses, all decorated with gilded figures. The tallest building is the **House of the Crossbowmen**, on top of

Murals depicting the dukes of Brabant in Antwerp's Stadhuis

🏛 Onze-Lieve-Vrouwekathedraal
Handschoenmarkt 1. **Tel** (03) 2139951. ☐ 10am–5pm Mon–Fri, 10am–3pm Sat, 1–4pm Sun.
The building of Antwerp's Onze-Lieve-Vrouwekathedraal (Cathedral of Our Lady) took almost two centuries, from 1352 to 1521. It has a graceful tiered spire that rises to a height of 123 m (404 ft) above the winding streets of the medieval city centre. Inside, the impression of light and

space owes much to the seven-aisled nave and vaulted ceiling. The cathedral's large collection of paintings and sculptures, some on loan from the Koninklijk Museum voor Schone Kunsten (see p152) until 2017, includes three works by Rubens, of which two – *Raising of the Cross* (1610) and *Descent from the Cross* (1612) – are triptychs.

🏛 Vleeshuis

Vleeshouwersstraat 38–40. **Tel** (03) 2926100. ⏰ 10am–5pm Tue–Sun and Easter Mon. 📷 ♿

There has been a Vleeshuis (Meat Hall) on this site since 1250, but the present hall was designed by the architect Herman de Waghemakere and completed in 1504. It

ANTWERP

features slender towers with five hexagonal turrets and rising gables, all built in alternate strips of stone and brick. The Gothic interior holds a museum, City Sounds, which presents artifacts from over 500 years of music in Antwerp.

🏛 Het Steen

Steenplein 1.

Antwerp's castle, Het Steen, was built on the banks of the Scheldt to protect the town and control shipping. Although a castle stood on this site in the 10th century, during the Viking raids, the lower section, which is the oldest part of the present building, dates only from the 13th century. Above that section are vestiges of the rebuilding ordered in 1520 by Charles V. For many centuries, until 1823, Het Steen served as the town's prison. Eventually, the whole edifice underwent a romanticized restoration in the year 1890.

According to legend, the castle was once home to the evil giant Druon Antigoon, who exacted a heavy toll on shipping and cut off the hands of captains who failed to pay him. He was eventually slain by the brave Roman soldier Silvius Brabo, who chopped off the giant's hand in turn and threw it into the River Scheldt. This

The turreted Vleeshuis, formerly the Meat Hall of the butchers' guild

VISITORS' CHECKLIST

47 km (29 miles) N of Brussels.
Road Map C1. 🚶 500,000. ✈
🏠 🚌 🚇 🚆 Grote Markt 13;
(03) 2320103; Centraal Station. 🎭
Grote Markt (Dec); Theaterplein
(Sat and Sun); Kloosterstraat (Sun).

Lange Wapper guarding Het Steen

handwerpen, or hand-throwing, is said by one legend to be the gesture that gave Antwerp its name. The bronze statue dating from 1963 at the base of the entrance ramp depicts another legendary local giant, the jovial rogue Lange Wapper, who could grow taller at will and played alarming tricks on drinkers. Over the main gate is an old sculpture of Semini, Scandinavian god of fertility – the statue was once held to be a talisman for Antwerp's people.

🔒 St-Pauluskerk

St-Paulusstraat 22. **Tel** (03) 2323267. ⏰ Apr–Oct: 2–5pm daily. 📷 3pm Sun and public holidays. ✝

Completed in the early 17th century, this splendid church displays a mix of Gothic and Baroque features. The exterior dates from about 1517, and has an elaborate Baroque gateway, while the interior has intricately carved wooden choir stalls. St-Pauluskerk possesses a series of paintings illustrating the Fifteen Mysteries of the Rosary, one of which, *The Scourging of the Pillar*, is an exquisite canvas by Rubens. There are also paintings by van Dyck and Jordaens.

🏛 Museum aan de Stroom (MAS)

Hanzestedenplaats 19. **Tel** (030) 2060940. ⏰ 10am–5pm Tue–Sun. 📷 ♿ www.mas.be

Set in a spiralling building in the old docks area just north of the historic centre is the Museum aan de Stroom, (Museum on the River). It combines artifacts formerly held in the Maritime, Folklore and Ethnographic museums and the Vleeshuis to present a portrait of Antwerp's historic relationship with the River Scheldt and the world beyond.

Street-by-Street: Around the Grote Markt

Gilt statue on guildhouse

Fanning out from the east bank of the River Scheldt, Antwerp was and is one of the leading trading cities of northern Europe. Today, the city's industries lie away from its medieval core whose narrow streets and fine buildings cluster around the cathedral and the Grote Markt. Packed with evidence of Antwerp's rich history, this is a delightful area to wander in. Most sites of interest are within walking distance of the Grote Markt whose surrounding streets house museums, shops and exuberant cafés and bars.

Het Steen
(see p145)

Vleeshuis
Occupied by the butcher's guild for three centuries, this beautiful 1504 building has striking layers of brick and stone that look like alternating strips of fat and lean meat.

Stadhuis
Flanking Antwerp's spectacular central square is the elegant 16th-century Stadhuis, designed by Flemish architect Cornelis Floris.

KEY

– – – Suggested route

STAR SIGHTS

★ Grote Markt

★ Onze-Lieve-
Vrouwekathedraal

Brabo Fountain
Set in the centre of the Grote Markt, this statue (1887) by Antwerp-born sculptor Jef Lambeaux depicts the Roman soldier Silvius Brabo throwing the hand of the mythical giant Druon Antigoon into the River Scheldt.

St-Pauluskerk
This imposing church was built in 1517, but has a magnificent Baroque gate and spire dating from the late 17th century. Inside, there is a noted collection of paintings, including a particularly fine work by Rubens.

ZIRKSTRAAT

VERSMIDSTRAAT

0 metres   50

0 yards   50

★ **Grote Markt**
Antwerp's golden age of trade in the 16th century is reflected in the square's impressive line-up of elaborate 16th- and 17th-century guildhouses.

★ **Onze-Lieve-Vrouwekathedraal**
The largest Gothic cathedral in Belgium, this building occupies a 1-ha (2.5-acre) site in Antwerp's centre. Work began on the church in 1352 and after two centuries the second spire was left incomplete.

To Rubenshuis and Centraal Station

Groenplaats
The Groenplaats or Green Square is a pleasant open space with trees and a statue of Rubens. Lined with cafés and bars, the square is a popular spot with both locals and visitors for a relaxed stroll or drink.

To Koninklijk Museum voor Schone Kunsten

Exploring Central and Southern Antwerp

Antwerp stretches from its centre out into sprawling suburbs for a distance of 7 km (4 miles). Since it was badly damaged in both World Wars, the city has a broad mix of architecture, ranging from the medieval to the ultramodern. The old city centre is concentrated around the Onze-Lieve-Vrouwekathedraal and the Grote Markt. To the east of the cathedral – beyond Antwerp's pioneering 1930s skyscraper, the Boerentoren – lies the Meir, a premier shopping street. The Zuid (South) district is an area of drained docks. Now rejuvenated, this is a vibrant part of the town, and the old dockland architecture of the streets Waalse Kaai and Vlaamse Kaai now houses a variety of clubs, bars and museums.

Late 16th-century printing press in the Museum Plantin-Moretus

Modernist interior of the reputed Modemuseum

🏛 Modemuseum (MoMu)
Nationalestraat 28. **Tel** (03) 4702770. ◯ 10am–6pm Tue–Sun. 📷 www.momu.be
Following the rise to celebrity in the 1980s of the influential fashion designers called the Antwerp Six, the city has entered the stratosphere of international haute couture, and maintains a glowing reputation for nurturing new

talent. Stars such as Dries van Noten, Ann Demeulemeester, Walter van Bierendonck and Martin Margiela all have a presence in the city.

This museum provides the historical context to Antwerp's rise to glory in the fashion world. Stylish items and accessories are innovatively displayed in changing exhibitions, allowing the museum to serve as a resource for both instruction and inspiration.

🏛 Museum Plantin-Moretus
Vrijdagmarkt 22–23. **Tel** (03) 2211450. ◯ 10am–5pm Tue–Sun and Easter Mon. 📷 free on last Wed of month. www.museumplantin moretus.be
This fascinating museum and World Heritage Site occupies a large 16th-century house that belonged to the printer Christopher Plantin, who moved here in 1576. The house is built around a courtyard with ancient rooms and narrow corridors that resemble the types of interiors painted

by Flemish and Dutch masters. The museum is devoted to the early years of printing, when Plantin and others began to produce books that bore no resemblance to earlier illuminated medieval manuscripts.

Antwerp was a centre for printing in the 15th and 16th centuries, and Plantin was its most successful printer. His legacy was carried on by his son-in-law Jan I Moretus. Today, his workshop displays several historic printing presses, as well as woodcuts and copper plates. Plantin's library is also on show. One of its gems is an edition of the Gutenberg Bible – the first book to be printed using moveable type, a technique that was invented by Johannes Gutenberg in 1455.

⚜ Maagdenhuis
Lange Gasthuisstraat 33. **Tel** (03) 2235620. ◯ 10am–5pm Mon and Wed–Fri, 1–5pm Sat and Sun. 📷
Literally the Maidens' House, this orphanage and foundling hospital for girls was built in two phases during the 16th and 17th centuries, and remained in operation until 1882. It is a delightful historic building with a footnote of tragedy – baby girls were abandoned here by their mothers, often anonymously in a "foundling drawer" set into an outer wall. One half of a playing card was attached to the child, and the mother kept the other half, in the hope that one day they might be reunited. Such cards are among the quirky but intriguing collection of

The charming inner courtyard of the Maagdenhuis

items now on view in a series of rooms that includes furniture, paintings, sculpture, silverware, pottery, needlework and porridge bowls, all belonging to the orphanage, or bequeathed to it. There is also a reproduction of the original foundling drawer that used to be in Rochusstraat.

🏛 Rockoxhuis

Keizerstraat 12. *Tel* (03) 2019250.
⬜ *10am–5pm Tue–Sun.* 🖼
www.rockoxhuis.be

Nicholaas Rockox (1560–1640) was the mayor of Antwerp as well as a humanist, philanthropist and a friend and patron of Rubens. These attributes are reflected in his beautifully renovated home – a series of rooms set around a formal courtyard garden. They hold a fine collection of contemporary furniture and miscellaneous artifacts, all interesting and well chosen. The paintings include work by Pieter Brueghel the Younger, Rubens, Jordaens and van Dyck, as well as by his neighbour, Frans Snyders (1579–1657), who was much admired by Rubens, and painted the fruit and flowers in Rubens's work.

🏛 St-Jacobskerk

Lange Nieuwstraat 73–75, Eikenstraat. *Tel* (03) 2250414.
⬜ *Apr–Oct: 2–5pm Wed–Mon; Nov–Mar: 9am–noon Mon–Sat.* 🖼

Noted as Pieter Paul Rubens's burial place, this sandstone church was built between 1491 and 1656. Rubens's tomb, in his family's chapel

Stained-glass window in St-Jacobskerk

behind the high altar, displays his painting of *Our Lady and the Christ Child Surrounded by Saints*, into which the artist inserted the faces of himself and his family. The rich interior of St-Jacobskerk contains the tombs of several notable Antwerp families, and a fine collection of 17th-century art that includes sculptures by Verbruggen as well as paintings by van Dyck, Otto Venius – who was Rubens's first master – and Jacob Jordaens (see p103).

Fishmarket Antwerp at the Rockoxhuis

🏛 Rubenshuis

See pp150–51.

🏛 Museum Mayer van den Bergh

Lange Gasthuisstraat 19. *Tel* (03) 2324237. ⬜ *10am–5pm Tue–Sun and Easter Mon.* 🖼 http://museum.antwerpen.be/mayervandenbergh

Fritz Mayer van den Bergh (1858–91) was the scion of a wealthy trading family, but

instead of following in his father's footsteps, he devoted himself to collecting works of art. After his death at the young age of 33, his mother created this museum to display his collections. Among the many treasures on display here are tapestries, furniture, ivory carvings, medieval and Renaissance sculpture, stained glass, and a number of excellent paintings. In particular, *Dulle Griet* (Mad Meg) is a powerful image of a chaotic world, painted in 1562 by Pieter Brueghel the Elder (see p103).

🏛 Koninklijk Museum voor Schone Kunsten

See pp152–3.

🏛 Museum van Hedendaagse Kunst Antwerpen (M HKA)

Leuvenstraat 32. *Tel* (03) 2609999.
⬜ *11am–6pm Tue–Sun (until 9pm Thu).* 🖼 🚻 📷 www.muhka.be

This museum fits perfectly into a city famed for its sense of style and design. Once a 1920s dockside grain silo and warehouse, the huge, sculptural building has been transformed into a series of unusual spaces to display works from the front line of international contemporary art. It includes work by many of the artists who helped place Belgium at the forefront of the art scene in recent years, including Luc Tuymans, Panamarenko, Jan Fabre and Wim Delvoye.

🏛 FotoMuseum

Waalse Kaai 47. *Tel* (03) 2429300
⬜ *10am–6pm Tue–Sun.* 📷
www.fotomuseum.be

The city's excellent museum of photography displays a broad variety of historical artifacts and images. The museum has now undergone a complete makeover and has embraced the moving image by incorporating the Antwerp Film Museum. The latter offers regularly scheduled film viewings. In addition to its extensive permanent collection, the museum mounts a series of photography exhibitions that feature both local and international artists.

Choice antique furniture and art in the Museum Mayer van den Bergh

Antwerp: Rubenshuis

Statue in courtyard

Located on Wapper Square, Rubenshuis was Pieter Paul Rubens's home and studio for the last 29 years of his life, from 1611 to 1640. The city bought the premises just before World War II, but by then the house was little more than a ruin, and what can be seen today is the result of careful restoration. It is divided into two sections. To the left of the entrance are the narrow rooms of the artist's living quarters, equipped with period furniture. Behind this is the Kunstkamer, or art gallery, where Rubens exhibited both his own and other artists' work, and entertained his friends and patrons such as the Archduke Albert and Infanta Isabella. To the right of the entrance lies the main studio, a spacious salon where Rubens created – and showed – his works. A signposted route guides visitors through the house.

Façade of Rubenshuis
The older Flemish part of the house sits to the left of the later section, whose elegant early-Baroque exterior was designed by Rubens himself.

Entrance passage

Pavilion and Garden
Rubens was greatly influenced by Italian Renaissance architects such as Alberti. In the 1620s, he added an Italian Baroque pavilion to his house, charmingly set in a small, formally laid-out garden.

★ Rubens's Studio
It is estimated that Rubens produced some 2,500 paintings in this large, high-ceilinged room. In the Renaissance manner, Rubens designed the work, which was usually completed by a team of other artists employed in his studio.

STAR FEATURES

★ Rubens's Studio

★ Kunstkamer

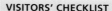

Bedroom
The Rubens family lived in the Flemish section of the house with its small rooms and narrow passages. The furniture in the room, including the bed, is all from Rubens's time.

The Living Room is a cosy sitting room with a pretty tiled floor and view of Wapper Square.

VISITORS' CHECKLIST

Wapper 9–11. *Tel (03)* 2011555. 🚌 9. 🚋 7, 8, 11, 12. ⬜ 10am– 5pm Tue–Sun, Easter Mon, Whit Mon. 📷 **www**.rubenshouse.be

Dining Room
Intricately fashioned leather panels line the walls of this room, which displays a noted still-life by Frans Snyders.

★ Kunstkamer
This art gallery contains a series of painted sketches by Rubens. At the far end is a semicircular dome, modelled on Rome's Pantheon, displaying a number of marble busts.

Chequered mosaic tiled floor

Baroque Portico
One of the few remaining original features, this portico was designed by Rubens and links the older house with the Baroque section. It is adorned with a frieze showing scenes from Greek mythology.

Display in the courtyard of the Museactron in Maaseik

Maaseik ㉔

28 km (17 miles) NE of Genk.
Road Map E1. 🏛 26,000. 🚌
🚉 ℹ *Markt 1; (089) 819290.*
🎭 *Halfvastenstoet (Mar).* **www.**
maaseik.be

Lying close to the River Meuse (Maas in Dutch), which now forms the border between Belgium and the Netherlands, Maaseik developed as a cloth town during the Middle Ages. It is thought to have been the birthplace, in about 1395, of the great pioneer oil painters Jan van Eyck and his brother Hubrecht. A statue of the siblings stands in the tree-lined **Markt**, surrounded by 17th- and 18th-century mansions.

The 19th-century Neo-Classical **St-Catharinakerk**, or St Catherine's Church, has a treasury, containing items from a local abbey, including the 8th-century *Codex Eyckensis*, which is believed to be the oldest book in Belgium. The **Regionaal Archeologisch Museum**, a revamped, inter-active archaeological museum, covers the history of the region starting from the Stone Age. It also provides access to a 17th-century apothecary shop, the Apothekersmuseum, the earliest of its kind in Belgium. Finally, Maaseik's **John Selbach Museum** is housed within a former Ursuline convent. One collection displays more than 400 antique dolls and their accessories, the earliest dating from 1780. The second collection consists of paintings in the Romantic mode from the 16th to the 20th centuries and includes works by notable Belgian artists such as

Ferdinand Braekeleer the Elder (1792–1883).

🏠 **St-Catharinakerk**
Kerkplein. ⬜ *Jan–Jun: Tue–Sun; Jul–Dec: daily.* 🎫

🏛 **Regionaal Archeologisch Museum**
Lekkerstraat 5. **Tel** (089) 566890. ⬜ *Apr–Oct: 10am–5pm Tue–Sun; Nov–Mar: 10am–4pm Tue–Sun.* 🎫 🅿

🏛 **John Selbach Museum**
Boomgaardstraat 20. **Tel** (089) 622008. ⬜ *May–Oct: 11am–5pm Wed–Sat; Nov–Apr: 11am–4pm Wed–Sat.* 🎫

Nationaal Park Hoge Kempen ㉕

Winterslagstraat 87, Genk. **Road Map** E2. **Tel** (089) 322810. 🚌
ℹ *Kattevennen (Genk), Pietersheim (Lanaken), Lieteberg (Zutendaal), Mechelse Heide (Maasmechelen) and Station As (As).* 🖥 **www.** nationaalparkhogekempen.be

The Kempen region of Belgium stretches from the eastern part of the Province of Antwerpen through

Visitors enjoying a nature trail in the Nationaal Park Hoge Kempen

Limburg and across the border into the Netherlands. It has a varied landscape of heath, marsh, woodland and farms. The area is sparsely populated and consequently, cherished by those seeking natural beauty and tranquillity.

A portion of this region between Maaseik and Genk was set aside in 2006 as Belgium's first national park, the Hoge Kempen (High Kempen). It covers 50 sq km (20 sq miles), containing pine-woods and quarry lakes, and features marked walking paths and cycling routes of varying lengths. The land rises to an altitude of 100 m (330 ft) in places, affording fine views.

Environs
South of the Nationaal Park Hoge Kempen, the town of **Maasmechelen** has a large "fashion village", built in an engaging traditional style. With nearly 100 outlets selling both Belgian and international labels at discount prices, plus restaurants and cafés, it attracts shoppers from neighbouring countries such as Germany and the Netherlands.

Maasmechelen
15 km (9 miles) E of Genk.
Tel (089) 774000. ⬜ 10am–6pm daily. ♿ 🍴 **www.**
maasmechelenvillage.com

Landcommanderij Alden Biesen ㉖

Kasteelstraat 6 Bilzen; 20 km (12 miles) S of Nationaal Park Hoge Kempen. **Road Map** E2. **Tel** (089) 519393. 🚌 ⬜ *Easter–Oct: 9am–5pm daily; Nov–Easter: 10am–5pm daily.* ● *mid-Dec–Jan.* 🎫 *for permanent display and garden.* 🍴 🅿
www.alden-biesen.be

A magnificent red-brick castle, Alden Biesen was built between the 16th and 18th centuries with courtyards, turrets, a moat and a large Baroque chapel. It was originally founded in 1220 on land that was given to the German Order of the Teutonic Knights, whose mission was to defend Christendom. By the 16th century, the power of the order rested mainly in

The stately Alden Biesen castle, former headquarters of the German Order of the Teutonic Knights

landholdings. Alden Biesen, as the regional headquarters, or *landcommanderij*, was an expression of this wealth, until the order was evicted in 1795 by the armies of the French Revolution. It then became a private residence.

In 1971, the main part, called the Water Castle, was gutted by fire. Although it has been restored, little of the original interior has survived. Today, the castle is used primarily as a cultural centre by the Flemish community, hosting concerts and exhibitions. The castle complex also offers a permanent display about its history, a formal French garden and beautiful parkland.

Tongeren ㉗

10 km (6 miles) SW of Alden Biesen. **Road Map** E2. 🏘 *32,000.* 🚈 🚌 🛈 *Via Julianus 5; (012) 800070.* 🛍 *Sun.* **www**.tongeren.be

Tournai (*see pp180–84*) and Tongeren both claim to be Belgium's oldest town due to their Roman origins. This heritage is seen in Tongeren's **Gallo-Romeins Museum**, built on the site of a Roman villa. It contains an extensive collection of artifacts and sculptures, extending up to the Middle Ages, from the pre-historic era to the Middle Ages.

Tongeren evolved into a prosperous medieval trading centre, as can be seen in the existing traces of its city walls, such as the **Moerenpoort**, a

14th-century city gate. Today, the **Begijnhof** nearby is a pretty area to wander in. The town is also famous for its huge antiques market.

Another landmark, the **Onze-Lieve-Vrouwebasiliek**, stands on the site of a 4th-century church. The current basilica was built between the 11th and 16th centuries. Its high and elegant Gothic interior is rich in statues and paintings, while the organ loft is a superb example of Baroque extravagance. It is famous for a miraculous statue, in painted wood, of Our Lady of Tongeren. This statue, dating from 1476, is the focal point of the 7-yearly Kroningsfeesten, or Coronation Festival (*see p33*), attended by what is said to be the biggest procession in the

country. The church treasury contains more early wooden sculpture, including a vividly expressive head of Christ, as well as impressively bejewel-led chalices and reliquaries.

The **Haspengouw** region surrounding Tongeren is celebrated for its bountiful farms and orchards and the appealing *hoevetoerisme*, or farmhouse accommodation (*see p252*) that showcases the area's charming rural assets.

🏛 **Gallo-Romeins Museum**
Kielenstraat 15. **Tel** (012) 670330. ◯ *9am–5pm Tue–Fri, 10am–6pm Sat–Sun.* 🈲 🖳 🛍 **www**. galloromeinsmuseum.be

🛆 **Onze-Lieve-Vrouwebasiliek**
Stadhuisplein. ◯ *May–Mar: 9am–5pm daily (basilica); Apr–Sep: 10am–noon and 1:30–5pm Tue–Sun, 1:30–5pm Mon (treasury).*

AMBIORIX AND "THE BRAVEST OF THE GAULS"

The leader of a Belgic tribe called the Eburones, Ambiorix is famous for mounting a fierce cam-paign against the Romans, who had conquered the area in 57 BC. Three years later, they wanted provisions from the Eburones to feed their troops. Ambiorix, who had gained the confidence of the Roman leaders, warned them that a massive army of Germanic tribes was on its way and persuaded them to retreat. As the Romans did so, the Eburones swooped down and massacred them. Julius Caesar decided to reap his revenge personally, and in the resulting campaign he crushed the Belgae

Ambiorix of the Eburones

completely. For his part, Ambiorix vanished along with his troops. These events inspired Caesar to record that "of all the Gauls, the Belgae are the bravest". Today, a 19th-century statue of Ambiorix stands in the Grote Markt of Tongeren.

WALLONIA

Wallonia at a Glance

The southern, French-speaking part of Belgium, Wallonia gets its name from a Romanized Celtic tribe known as the Wala, whose people spoke a French-related language, Walloon. There are five provinces in this region: Hainaut forms Western Wallonia; the provinces of Namur and Brabant Wallon lie in Central Wallonia; and the provinces of Liège and Luxembourg (not to be confused with the independent Grand Duchy of Luxembourg) make up Eastern Wallonia. The largest cities lie in the old industrial heartland that stretches across the north from Charleroi to Liège. Further south, the landscape rises into the Ardennes, with its forested hills and riverside towns and hamlets.

Leuze-en-Hainaut is home to the fascinating Mahymobiles motor museum *(see p185)*.

CENTRAL WALLONIA *(see pp192–2*

WESTERN WALLONIA *(see pp176–91)*

0 km   25

0 miles   25

Mons (see p189) *is the capital of Hainaut. Once a year, during the Ducasse festival, crowds gather in the Grand Place to watch the celebrated Lumeçon battle between St George and the dragon.*

Namur *(see pp202–3), capital of the Province of Namur, lies on the confluence of the rivers Sambre and Meuse. Dominating this busy city is the massive Citadelle, a stronghold reinforced over 2,000 years of military use, which finally ended in 1977.*

◁ **Rural atmosphere characteristic of villages in the undulating Ardennes**

Rochefort (see p211), *in the Province of Namur, is one of many places in the Ardennes to have an extensive cave system (see pp208–9). The Grotte de Lorette-Rochefort has a visitor centre, from where paths lead sharply down for 80 m (262 ft), past encrustations of stalactites and stalagmites, to halls of vast, rugged rock.*

EASTERN WALLONIA
(see pp212–33)

Liège (see pp216–19), *capital of the Province of Liège, has a number of fine churches. This includes the superb Église St-Jacques, which fuses the Romanesque with Flamboyant Gothic.*

Bouillon (see pp230–33), *located in the south of the Ardennes, is famous for its picturesque medieval castle set on a rocky spur near the Semois. Once the home of the 11th-century crusader knight Godefroid de Bouillon, the castle now forms a romantic backdrop to this quiet and elegant little town.*

The Ardennes

The region known as the Ardennes stretches across southern Belgium and into Luxembourg, France and Germany. Located south of the River Meuse, it comprises forested hills and valleys cut by a network of winding, picturesque rivers, notably the Lesse, Semois, Ourthe and Amblève. Namur, Liège and Dinant are the main urban centres, but the Ardennes is predominantly rural and sparsely populated, with river-basin farms and small villages, and areas of upland pasture. The Romans named this forested land after the local Celtic goddess Arduinna. For centuries, it was a backwater, but today its large expanses of unspoilt nature attract numerous visitors who come to walk, cycle, canoe or simply to motor and enjoy the views.

LOCATOR MAP

☐ Ardennes

The River Meuse (see p206) *forms the natural northern boundary to the Ardennes region. This navigable waterway links the cities of Dinant and Namur to Liège. Beyond that, it leads eventually to the North Sea. When Wallonia was the centre of Belgium's old heavy industries, the river was a vital transport artery.*

AN ASTONISHING LANDSCAPE

Beauty and variety of landscape: these are the principal attractions of the Ardennes. In places, the rivers and hills conspire to produce dramatic effects, as seen at the famous Tombeau du Géant (The Giant's Tomb), a strangely regular wooded hill almost encircled by a typically extravagant loop of the River Semois.

Han-sur-Lesse (see p211) *has the best of the many caves that are open to public. Over thousands of years, water has drilled away the limestone rock, creating spectacular tunnels and galleries dripping with stalactites.*

Kayaking (see p313) *is a major holiday pursuit on rivers such as the Semois, Amblève and Ourthe. Often too rocky for larger boats, they provide excellent kayaking conditions as they wind their way through steep, picturesque valleys.*

The Hautes Fagnes (see p223) *is an extensive raised plateau of boggy moorland in the east of the Province of Liège. In winter, and on days of mist and low cloud, these moors can be powerfully gloomy and desolate, but they also have an austere beauty and an abundance of unusual flora and fauna. Here and there, raised walkways have been built to provide access to the marshy interior.*

Walkers *are rewarded by a landscape that is both gently challenging and remarkably varied. The tourist offices have maps of recommended walks, which include a part of the network of Grande Randonnée (GR) long-distance paths.*

Mountain bikers *will find ideal terrain here. There are well-organized, signposted routes for vététistes (from VTT for Vélo Tout Terrain, or All Terrain Bicycle). This includes Grand Raid Godefroy, a 160-km (100-mile) circuit around Bouillon.*

Rock formations, *created where blocks of harder rock have resisted erosion, form major landmarks and are often named after or associated with legends. There are noted rock climbing sites on the River Meuse and in the valley of the River Ourthe.*

WESTERN WALLONIA

Stretching across the Province of Hainaut, Western Wallonia is redolent with the romance of history in such impressive châteaux as Beloeil, Seneffe and Attre, and the intimate medieval centre of Tournai. Hainaut also played a key role in Belgium's industrial development, a past that is now celebrated in several fascinating showpieces of industrial heritage across the region.

Historically a border county, Hainaut has been contested over the centuries between France and the rulers of the rest of central Belgium. The region around Tournai, a city with Roman origins, was the centre of the Frankish empire in the 5th century and remained French until 1513. After a brief English occupation under Henry VIII, it was French again during the time of Louis XIV and through the turmoil that followed the French Revolution (1789–99). This influence is reflected in the local language, Picard, which is distinct from Wallon and shared with Nord-Pas-de-Calais in neighbouring France.

In the 19th century, the green hills of central Hainaut, around the historic cities of Charleroi and Mons were found to contain rich seams of coal. This led to the development of the Région du Centre, around La Louvière, as a powerhouse of industrial development within Belgium. Canals and waterways were built to link the area to Germany, France and the North Sea. The region's affluence grew owing to the mines and factories, but districts around the major cities struggled with growing industrialization and the resultant poverty.

Today, Western Wallonia remains the epitome of Belgium's varied history. The industrial areas across the centre of the region have redefined their collieries and mines as dynamic museums and centres for the arts that draw hundreds of enthusiasts. In addition, the stately châteaux dotting the region bring the splendour of the late medieval period to life for Belgians and visitors alike. The most popular times to visit are when towns across Western Wallonia hold lively carnivals, steeped in pageantry, that attract people from across the world.

Immaculately costumed participants at the bold and sparkling carnival of Binche

◁ **The awe-inspiring altar of St Christopher's Church in Charleroi**

Exploring Western Wallonia

The Province of Hainaut can be divided into three areas. The north is attractive farmland, with châteaux at Beloeil, Attre, Seneffe and Ecaussinnes-Lalaing as well as the impressive cathedral city of Tournai. The central band is the old industrial area running from Mons to Charleroi via La Louvière. This not only has exhilarating industrial constructions, such as the colossal canal lift at Ronquières, but also some exquisite cultural treasures, as at the Musée Royal de Mariemont. In the southern sector, the rural landscape becomes wooded as it rises into the Ardennes hills. The lakes of L'Eau d'Heure are a huge water sports centre.

One of many statues located on the grounds of the Domaine de Mariemont

SIGHTS AT A GLANCE

Villages, Towns and Cities
Ath **3**
Binche **18**
Charleroi **11**
Chimay **22**
Grand Hornu **17**
La Louvière **13**
Mons **16**
Soignies **7**
Tournai pp180–84 **1**
Thuin **19**

Castles
Château d'Attre **5**
Château de Beloeil **6**
Château de Seneffe **10**
Château-Fort
   d'Ecaussinnes-Lalaing **9**

Churches and Abbeys
Abbaye d'Aulne **20**

Museums
Ecomusée Regional
   du Centre **14**
Hôpital Notre-Dame
   à la Rose **4**
Mahymobiles **2**
Musée Royal de Mariemont **12**

Areas of Natural Beauty
Valley de la Sambre **23**

Sites of Interest
Canal du Centre **15**
Lacs de l'Eau d'Heure **21**
Plan Incliné de Ronquières **8**

Dottigniés
(Dottenijs)
Espierres
(Spiere)
Celles
Pecq
Néchin
Frasnes-les
Anvaing
A17
N6
TOURNAI **1**
N7
N508
MAHYMOBI
Antoing
A16
Bla

Terrace cafés lining the Grand Place of Mons, capital of Hainaut

SEE ALSO

- *Where to Stay* pp268–9
- *Where to Eat* pp294–5

KEY

▬▬	Motorway
▬▬	Major road
▬▬	Secondary road
▬▬	Minor road
▬▬	Main railway
—	Minor railway
▬▬	International border
▬▬	Provincial border

Beloeil, home of the princes de Ligne and one of Belgium's most impressive châteaux

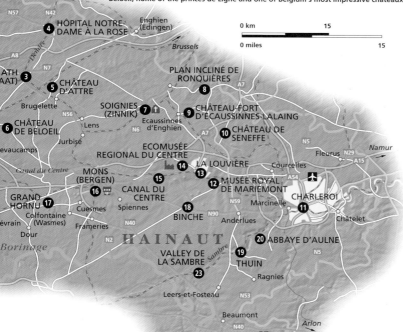

GETTING AROUND
Motorways span northern Hainaut, connecting Tournai, Charleroi and Mons to Brussels and Namur. Trains operated by the national rail company SNCB reach all major towns. Wallonia's public bus service TEC (Transport en Commun) spreads the net further with its two operators, TEC Hainaut (around Mons) and TEC Charleroi. Cyclists use the RAVeL 1 Centre route from Mons to Charleroi and then to Namur. Walkers use the Grande Randonnée (GR) paths 121, 129 and 412-O.

Street-by-Street: Tournai ❶

One of Belgium's oldest urban centres, Tournai has origins dating back to 600 BC. A Roman city, it became the focus of early Christian activity, beginning with St Piat's efforts in the 3rd century AD. Clovis I (AD 465–511), King of the Franks and founder of the Merovingian dynasty and the French royal line, was perhaps born here. The much-venerated St Eleutherius was his first bishop. Although badly damaged by German bombing in World War II, Tournai's long history is written into the city centre. The awe-inspiring Cathédrale Notre-Dame, the soaring belfry and the impressive Grand Place are surrounded by old cobbled streets which provide a constantly changing view of the city skyline.

Église St-Jacques
This 13th-century church was built for pilgrims en route to Santiago di Compostela in Spain.

★ Grand Place
The town square is bounded by numerous 17th-century façades and the cathedral's towers loom in the east. On the western side, the Halle des Draps (Clothmakers' Hall), built in 1610, has a gilded façade. A statue of Christine de Lalaing, local 16th-century heroine, stands in the centre of the square.

RUE DE COURTRA

RUE PIQUET

RUE PERDUE

RUE DE L'YSER

RUE DES ORFÈVR

RUE DES MAUX

KEY

- - - - Suggested route

Église St-Quentin
The grey-stone columns and vaulting give this 12th-century church a tranquil austerity. It was restored in the 1960s, following wartime damage. Its greatest treasure is the silver statue of Notre Dame de la Treille (1724).

STAR SIGHTS

★ Grand Place

★ Cathédrale Notre-Dame

★ The Belfry

★ **Cathédrale Notre-Dame**
The colossal and magnificent cathedral is enriched with a wealth of detail, including tiers of ornate sculpture at the entrance and an elaborately carved 16th-century rood screen inside.

VISITORS' CHECKLIST

89 km (55 miles) SW of Brussels.
Road Map B3. 🏙 69,000.
🚉 🚌 🛈 *Place Paul-Emile Janson; (069) 222045.*
🎭 *Grande Procession (Sep).*
www.tournai.be **Église St-Quentin** Grand Place. ◯ *daily.*
Église St-Jacques Rue du Palais St-Jacques. ◯ *daily.*
Musée de la Tapisserie Place Reine Astrid. **Tel** *(069) 842073.*
◯ *Wed–Mon.* 📷

Cathédrale Notre-Dame's treasury is one of the most precious collections of church treasures in Belgium. It includes the reliquary shrine of St Eleutherius, completed in 1247, which is paraded in the Grande Procession festival.

The River Scheldt
Known here as the Escaut, the river gave Tournai vital, navigable access to the sea, making it a trading hub in the Middle Ages.

RUE DU CURÉ NOTRE-DAME

RUE DE L'HÔPITAL NOTRE-DAME

QUAI DU MARCHÉ AU POISSON

RUE DE LA LANTERNE

RUE DES CHAPELIERS

RUE DE LA WALLONIE

| 0 metre | 50 |
| 0 yards | 50 |

★ **The Belfry**
Begun in the 12th century, but dating mainly from the 14th century, the belfry in Tournai is the oldest in Belgium, and unusual in that it is free-standing. Its carillon of 44 bells sings melodies out over the city centre. The belfry's 257 steps take visitors to the top, where a parapet offers excellent views.

The Musée de la Tapisserie celebrates Tournai's tradition of tapestry weaving.

Tournai: Cathédrale Notre-Dame

One of the great landmarks of Belgium, Cathédrale Notre-Dame has a long history. Tournai's first bishop, St Eleutherius, built a cathedral on this site in the 5th century. The existing church, however, was begun in the 12th century. Construction started at the western end in Romanesque style, and progressed eastwards, becoming Gothic in the 13th-century chancel. The impressive interior was once more elaborate, but much of the decoration was destroyed by Protestant iconoclasts in 1566. Considerable damage was also inflicted by German bombing in 1940. A tornado struck in 1999, highlighting the fragility of the building, and the need to progress with its restoration. In 2000, the cathedral was listed by UNESCO as a World Heritage Site.

The central tower, the oldest, is a "lantern tower", allowing light into the crossing between the nave and the transept.

★ **The Five Towers**
The cluster of pyramid-tipped towers soaring from the transept and crossing, impart a distinctive individuality to the cathedral. Completed in the early 13th century, they reach a height of 83 m (272 ft).

The Romanesque nave has three external tiers of rounded arches. Two flanking aisles help support its high vaulted ceiling.

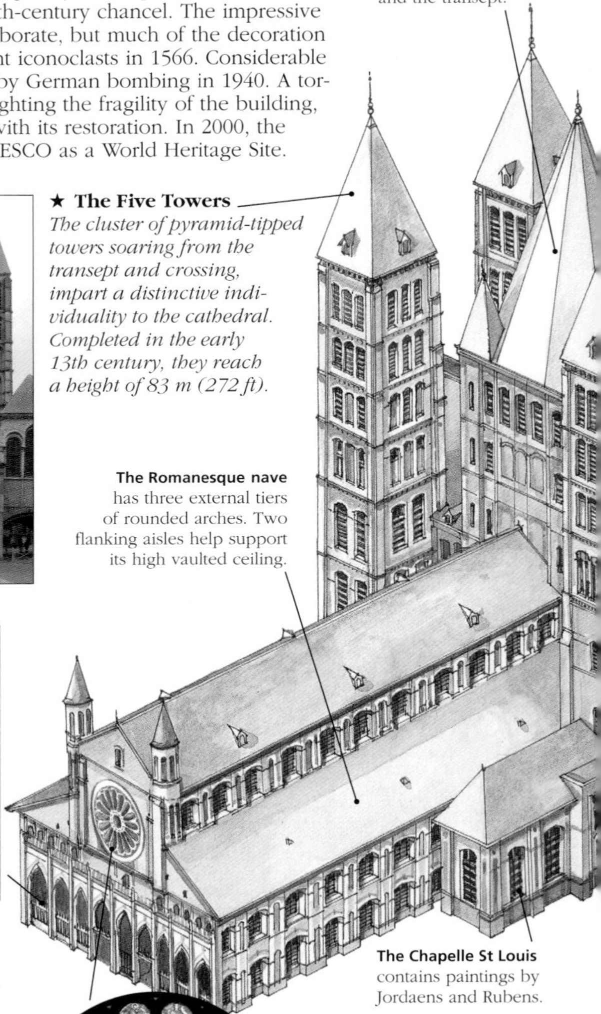

West Porch
The west façade has an arched 14th-century porch decorated with a line of statues dating from between the 14th and 17th centuries.

The Chapelle St Louis contains paintings by Jordaens and Rubens.

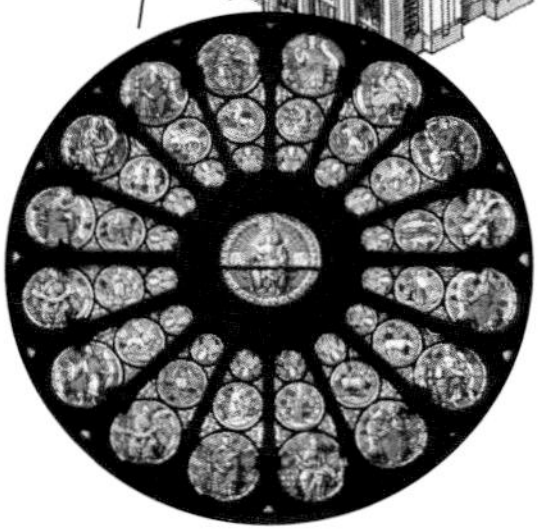

Rose Window
Set in the west façade, the rose window was installed in the 19th century, replacing a Gothic window from 1526. The stained glass depicts Virgin Mary in the centre and the 16 compartments portray the Prophets.

STAR FEATURES

★ The Five Towers

★ Rood Screen

★ Treasury

★ **Rood Screen**
The line between the nave and the choir is marked by an elegant rood screen in polychrome marble. It was designed in Italian-Renaissance style and completed in 1572.

VISITORS' CHECKLIST

Place de l'Evêché 1, Tournai. ▨
◷ Apr–Oct: 9:15am–noon and 2–6pm daily; Nov–Mar: 9:15am–noon and 2–5pm daily. ♿
Treasury ◷ Apr–Oct: 9:30am–noon and 2–6pm Sun–Fri; Nov–Mar: 9:30am–noon and 2–5pm Mon–Fri, 2–5pm Sat, Sun and public holidays. ▨ **www**.cathedrale-tournai.be

The chancel, built between 1243 and 1255, was the first example of the new French Gothic style in Belgium.

High Altar
With the structural weight on external buttresses, the walls of the chancel could be filled with glass, flooding the altar with light. The Gothic pillars and arches are made of the city's famous blue stone.

The transept separates the Romanesque nave from the Gothic choir, both of which, unusually, are almost of equal length.

★ **Treasury**
Rooms in the cathedral contain a wealth of church treasure. Most precious are the large reliquary chests gilded and encrusted with gems. There is also a long tapestry from 1402 depicting St Eleutherius and St Piat, who brought Christianity to Tournai.

Exploring Tournai

A ring of boulevards encircles the centre of Tournai, with the River Escaut slicing through the middle, passing beneath the triple arches of the 13th-century bridge, Pont de Trous. The boulevards follow the path of the 14th-century city walls. The street plan of the centre has remained almost unchanged since the walls were built. From 1187 onwards, Tournai was often under French control; in 1513, it fell to the English, whose 5-year rule is commemorated in the Henry VIII Tower. This is a pleasant place to wander, with the museums clustered to the west of the cathedral.

Exhibit at the Museum of Archeology

🔔 Belfry

Vieux Marché aux Poteries.
Tel (069) 222045. ⬜ *Tue–Sun.*
🌐 www.tournai.be
The city's famous belfry rises to a height of 72 m (236 ft). In 1187, the Tournaisiens wrangled freedom from the count of Flanders and placed themselves under the protection of the king of France. However, they retained a good degree of autonomy – the belfry was a symbol of this, serving as a watchtower, clocktower, place of public announcements, prison and stronghold for town charters. The belfry was revamped after a fire in 1391, and the spires date from between the 16th and 19th centuries. A multimedia show recounts the city's 2,000 years of history.

🏛 Musée du Folklore

Réduit des Sions. *Tel* (069) 224069.
⬜ *Wed–Mon.* 🔵 *Sun mornings.*
🏷️ ♿
Set out in two 17th-century step-gabled houses called La Maison Tournaisienne, this extensive folklore collection is spread over a series of 23 rooms and reconstructions depicting daily life in the past – school and home, the pub, workshops of printers, clog-makers, weavers and coopers, as well as the worlds of the priests, doctors, soldiers, women and children.

🏛 Musée des Beaux-Arts

Enclos St-Martin. *Tel* (069) 332431.
⬜ *Wed–Mon.* 🏷️ ♿
Often referred to as Musée Horta, this art museum was designed by the great Art Nouveau architect Victor Horta *(see p80)* in his later, more sober, Classical style. It opened in 1928. In galleries fanning out from a central polygonal sculpture hall, its impressive collection covers work from the 15th century onwards and includes art by many of the greatest Belgian painters and sculptors. Among them are Rogier van der Weyden, Rubens, Constantin Meunier and James Ensor. International artists such as Watteau, Manet, Monet, Toulouse-Lautrec and van Gogh are also represented.

🏛 Musée de la Tapisserie

Place Reine Astrid. *Tel* (069) 842073.
⬜ *Wed–Mon.* 🔵 *Sun afternoons.*
🏷️
Occupying a grand old Neo-Classical mansion, this museum focusses on the celebrated quality of Tournai's tapestry, notably of the 15th–17th centuries. It has a small but fine collection of historic tapestries, and it is also an active workshop where tapestries are restored and made.

Detail from a tapestry at the Musée de la Tapisserie

🏛 Musée d'Histoire et des Arts Décoratifs

Rue St Martin 50b. *Tel* (069) 332353. ⬜ *Wed–Mon.* 🏷️
The focus of this collection is the porcelain of Tournai, which is noted for the delicacy of its floral decoration. During the 18th and 19th centuries, it was a rival to porcelain from the French town of Sèvres. The museum also displays locally produced wares of gold, silver and pewter, as well as the products of Tournai's mint, which produced coins for France and Spain from the 12th to the 17th century.

🏛 Musée d'Histoire et d'Archéologie

Rue des Carmes 8. *Tel* (069) 221672. ⬜ *Wed–Mon.* 🏷️
Archaeological remains from Tournai's prehistoric, Gallo-Roman and Frankish past are exhibited here. Many of the finds come from recent excavations of graveyards in the city centre, and include sarcophagi, glassware, pottery, weapons and jewellery.

Lavish display of gold and lace furnishings at the Musée du Folklore

For hotels and restaurants in this region see pp268–9 and pp294–5

Mahymobiles

Rue Erna 3, Leuze-en-Hainaut;
16 km (10 miles) E of Tournai. **Road
Map** B3. *Tel* (069) 354545. 🏛
☐ Jul–Aug: 10am–5pm Thu–Mon;
Apr–May and Jun–Sep: 10am–5pm
Sat, Sun and public holidays. 🚲 ♿
💻 www.mahymobiles.be

Some 270 veteran and vintage
vehicles, mainly cars, are on
display at this museum, set in
an old factory. They are chosen from over 1,000 vehicles
assembled since 1944 by the
collector Ghislain Mahy. The
earliest dates from 1890. Also
on show are historic motor-
bikes and bicycles, toy cars
and the paraphernalia of past
decades of motoring.

Ath ❸

42 km (26 miles) E of Tournai.
Road Map B3. 🚶 28,500. 🏛
🚌 🛈 Rue de Pintamont 18; (068)
265170. 🎭 Ducasse (4th weekend
in Aug). www.ath.be

A busy industrial town, Ath
comes alive during its famous
festival Ducasse, when giant
figures are carried through
the streets *(see p33)*. This
Parade of the Giants is celebrated all year round at the
Maison des Géants. Set in the
Château de Cambier, an 18th-
century mansion, it explores
the folkloric background of
the giants, Ducasse itself and
parallel traditions elsewhere
using film and pictures.

🏛 **Maison des Géants**
Rue de Pintamont 18. *Tel* (068)
265170. ☐ Tue–Fri. 💻 🛈 www.
maisondesgeants.be

Ornately decorated interior of the
Hôpital Notre-Dame à la Rose

Hôpital Notre-
Dame à la Rose ❹

Place Alix de Rosoit, Lessines; 10 km
(6 miles) N of Ath. **Road Map** B2.
Tel (068) 332403. 🛈 Rue de
Grammont 2; (068) 333690.
☐ early Apr–late Oct: 2–6:30pm Sat,
Sun & public holidays. 🚲 🗣 3pm
Tue–Sun. 🔔 ♿
www.notredamealarose.com

Founded in 1242 by a French
princess called Alix de Rosoit
as a refuge for the poor, sick
and needy, this establishment
ran as a hospital, and more
recently as an old people's
home, for nearly 750 years,
until 1980. Today, its tranquil
convent buildings, dating from
the 16th to 18th centuries,
serve as a museum, presenting
the work of the institution.
There are wards, beds, medical
instruments and details about
medicines, the pewter dishes
used by patients, Tournai porcelain used by the sisters, a
library of 2,000 antique books,
paintings and sculpture and

precious gold- and silverware.
A cloister, chapel, herb garden and ice house all add to
the picture of this community.
The town of Lessines was
famous for its quarries producing porphyry, a flecked,
deep-red stone used for architectural sculpture. The open
pits can still be visited.

Château d'Attre ❺

Avenue du Château 8, Attre; 5 km
(3 miles) SE of Ath. **Road Map** B3.
Tel (068) 454460. ☐ Jul–Aug: 1–
6pm Sat, Sun and public holidays;
Apr–Jun and Sep–Oct: 2–6pm Sun
and public holidays. 🚲 🏛 www.
chateauxduhainaut.be

This elegant château, built in
1752 in French Neo-Classical
style, still contains its original
decoration, furniture and
furnishings. The suite of
sumptuous rooms evokes the
Rococo tastes of the era. It also
has a large park, crossed by
the River Dender, that includes
a ruined belvedere, dovecote,
Swiss chalet, bathhouse and
the remains of a celebrated
marvel of the 1780s known as
the Rocher (Rock). This is an
artificial mound, with a castle-
like hunting platform on top.

Environs
Pairi Daiza, 5 km (3 miles) to
the southeast, is a large, child-
friendly zoo set in the former
domain of the Château de
Cambron-Casteau.

🦜 **Pairi Daiza**
Domaine de Cambron, Brugelette.
Tel (068) 250850. ☐ late Apr–early
Nov. 🚲 ♿ 🍴 💻 📷
www.pairidaiza.eu

Formal gardens adding to the grandeur of the well-maintained Château d'Attre

Stately avenues leading up to the grand Château de Beloeil, set in green parkland

Château de Beloeil ❻

Rue du Château 11; 10 km (6 miles) SW of Attre. **Road Map** B3. **Tel** (069) 689426. 🚌 ⬜ Easter–Apr: 1–6pm Sat and Sun; May–Sep: 1–6pm daily. 🎫 🐾 **www. chateaudebeloeil.com**

Standing on a site that has been home to the eminent princes de Ligne since the 14th century, Beloeil is a moated château built originally in the 16th century. Until the French Revolutionary Army took over in 1792, it was the domain of Charles-Joseph Lamoral, 7th Prince de Ligne (1735–1814). Field marshal, diplomat and a close confidant of Joseph II of Austria, he was at the courts of France and Russia and inter-acted with many of the leading political figures of his day.

Château de Beloeil was remodelled in the French style during the 17th and 18th centuries with Versailles-like grandeur, but a disastrous fire in 1900 badly damaged the central block. The reconstructed château displays furniture, tapestries, paintings and a 20,000-volume library. An enormous artificial water basin, parklands and formal gardens lie outside.

Soignies ❼

30 km (19 miles) E of Beloeil. **Road Map** C3. 🏛 25,000. 🚉 🚌 ℹ Rue du Lombard 2; (067) 347376.

The agreeable little town of Soignies was once surrounded by woods linked to the Forêt de Soignes (see p165) near Brussels. It later became well known for its blue limestone quarries. Today, its great treas-ure is the robust **Collégiale St-Vincent**, named after St Vincent Madelgaire, Governor of Hainaut, husband of St Waudru of Mons and founder of an abbey built here in AD 650. The church was built between the 10th and 13th centuries, largely in Romanesque style. The pastel interior is impressive for its scale and understated style. It has a polychrome 14th-century statue of the Virgin and Child, in a niche beneath the marble rood loft, as well as carved Renaissance choir stalls dating from 1576.

Coat of arms at Soignies's church

🛈 Collégiale St-Vincent
Grand Place. **Tel** (067) 331210. ⬜ Apr–Sep: 8am–6pm daily; Oct–Mar: 8am–5pm daily.

The control tower rising above the plan incliné at Ronquières

Plan Incliné de Ronquières ❽

Route Baccara 1; 14 km (9 miles) NE of Soignies. **Road Map** C3. **Tel** (078) 059059. ⬜ mid-Mar–Oct: 10am–7pm (last entry 5pm). 🎫 🐾 May–mid-Sep: Sun (boat trips). 🐾 ♿ **http://voiesdeau.hainaut.be**

Modern canal engineering has achieved some impressive feats in the region. One of the most inter-esting structures is on the Brussels–Charleroi canal at Ronquières. Boats weighing up to 1,350 tonnes (1,500 tons) can negotiate a difference in the canal levels of 68 m (221 ft) in a single operation, by using an ingenious transporter lock. Called the *plan incliné* (liter-ally, inclined plane), this is a sloping canal lift almost 1.5 km (1 mile) long. Boats enter one of the two vast water-filled containers at either end of the *plan incliné*. The containers then ride on rollers through the length of the canal lift.

When it was completed in 1968, the lift reduced the time taken by barges to travel between Charleroi and Brussels by some seven hours. To the north, the canal follows a 300-m (984-ft) long aqueduct. A visitors' centre in the soaring control tower explains the system through an audiovisual presentation. Glass footbridges allow a bird's-eye view of the opera-tions of this colossal machine and the landscape. Visitors can also take boat trips through the *plan incliné*.

Château-Fort d'Écaussinnes-Lalaing ⑨

Rue de Seneffe 1, Écaussinnes-Lalaing; 6 km (4 miles) SW of Ronquières. **Road Map** C3. **Tel** (067) 442490. ▦ ☐ Jul–Aug: 10am–noon and 2–6pm Sat–Thu; Apr–Jun and Sep–Oct: Sat, Sun and public holidays. ▨ **www**. chateaufort-ecaussinnes.be

The small, historic village of Écaussinnes-Lalaing is dominated by a gaunt and mighty fortress. Built during the 12th century on a rocky spur, it played a vital strategic role in the Centre Region, a much-disputed border area between France and the Low Countries. During World War I, it served as a German barracks, prison, munitions store and infirmary. Now restored, the echoing interior contains period furniture and armour, as well as a dungeon, a Gothic chapel and a 15th-century kitchen.

Château de Seneffe ⑩

Rue Lucien Plasman 7–9, Seneffe; 10 km (6 miles) SE of Écaussinnes-Lalaing. **Road Map** C3. **Tel** (064) 556913. ☐ 10am–6pm Tue–Sun. ▨ ▯ ▯ **www**.chateaudeseneffe.be

An elegant château, Seneffe was built in the Neo-Classical style during the 1760s as a grand residence for wealthy entrepreneur Julien Depestre. Its interior matches the refined exterior with parquet floors, panelling, stucco work and ornate marble fireplaces. It is now the setting for an important collection of gold and silverware, within a permanent exhibition called The Art of Living in the 18th Century. Outside, there is an extensive garden and park, with an open-air theatre and an orangery. During World War II, the château was the local headquarters and summer residence of General von Falkenhausen, the Nazi military governor of occupied Belgium. The estate subsequently fell into disrepair, but then underwent a prolonged restoration programme that was completed in 1995.

Charleroi ⑪

25 km (16 miles) SE of Seneffe. **Road Map** C3. ▦ 204,000. ▧ ▨ ▦ ▯ Place Charles II; (071) 861414. **www**.charleroi.be

As capital of the Pays Noir (Black Country), surrounded by coal pits and monuments to Belgium's age of booming industrial growth, Charleroi is an important city. Set on the Sambre, it was first called Charnoy, but when it became a military base to fend off the threat of Louis XIV of France in 1666, it was renamed after Charles II, King of Spain and the Spanish Low Countries. Glass has been a key industry here since 1577, but it was the combination of iron and the local abundance of coal

Charleroi's impressive Hôtel de Ville, dominated by its belfry

that turned Charleroi into an industrial powerhouse in the 19th century. The Brussels–Charleroi canal linked the city ultimately to the North Sea, as did the Sambre, contributing to its reputation as a major centre for industrial transport.

The main sight in the city is the massive **Hôtel de Ville** and its belfry, built in a blend of Neo-Classical and Art Deco styles in 1936. The stylish interior includes the **Musée des Beaux-Arts**, on the second floor, which has a good collection of paintings, featuring François-Joseph Navez (1787–1869), pupil of Jacques-Louis David and a leader of the Belgian Neo-Classical movement. It also includes works by the sculptor Constantin Meunier as well as Surrealist artists such as René Magritte and Paul Delvaux.

Environs

The former colliery of **Le Bois du Cazier** at Marcinelle, 3 km (2 miles) to the south, has become an industrial heritage centre with a Musée de Verre (Glass Museum) and a Musée l'Industrie, as well as a memorial exhibition on a historic mining accident that took place here in 1956.

▥ **Musée des Beaux-Arts**
Hôtel de Ville, Place Charles II. **Tel** (071) 861134. ☐ 10am–6pm Tue–Sat. ▨ ♿ **www**.charleroi-museum.org

▥ **Le Bois du Cazier**
Rue du Cazier 80, Marcinelle. **Tel** (071) 880856. ☐ 9am–12:30pm, 1:15–5pm Tue–Fri; 10am–12:30pm, 1:15–6pm Sat & Sun. ▨ ▯ ♿ ▯ ▯ ▯ **www**.leboisducazier.be

Formal lines of the elegant Neo-Classical Château de Seneffe

Pillars and sphinx – ruins of the old castle at Domaine de Mariemont

Musée Royal de Mariemont ⓬

Chaussée de Mariemont 100, Morlanwelz; 24 km (15 miles) W of Charleroi. **Road Map** C3. **Tel** (064) 212193. 🚌 ☐ *Tue–Sun.* 🅿 🚻 **www**.musee-mariemont.be

Built in 1975 in the pleasant **Domaine de Mariemont**, a large park with an arboretum, this uncompromisingly modern museum is home to a major collection of decorative arts. The estate once belonged to a castle built in 1546 by Mary of Hungary. This was destroyed by the French Revolutionary Army in 1794, and its ruins can be seen today. Another mansion, constructed by the Warocqué family of industrialists in the 20th century, was also destroyed, but many of its contents were saved. Today, the museum also has sculpture and artifacts from ancient Egypt, Greece, the Far East and Gallo-Roman times; illuminated manuscripts; lace; and the world's largest collection of Tournai porcelain.

La Louvière ⓭

20 km (12 miles) NW of Charleroi. **Road Map** C3. 🏛 *79,000.* 🚃 🚌 🛈 *Place Mansart 21–22; (064) 261500.* **www**.lalouviere.be

The town of La Louvière was once the hub of the coal and steel enterprise. Industrial heritage is a big theme here, but

the town also has art centres. The **Centre de la Gravure et de l'Image Imprimée** mounts exhibitions of engravings and prints and also has a collection of 5,000 prints. The **Musée Ianchelevici**, in the former law courts, celebrates the life and work of Romanian-born sculptor Idel Ianchelevici, who came to Belgium in his youth.

🏛 **Centre de la Gravure et de l'Image Imprimée**
Rue des Amours 10. **Tel** (064) 278727. ☐ *during exhibitions only: 10:30am–5:30pm Tue–Fri.* 🅿 **www**.centredelagravure.be

🏛 **Musée Ianchelevici**
Place Communale 21. **Tel** (064) 282530. ☐ *2–6pm Tue–Sun.* **www**.ianchelevici.be

Écomusée Regional du Centre ⓮

R St-Patrice 2B, Houdeng-Aimeries; 4 km (3 miles) NW of La Louvière. **Road Map** C3. **Tel** (064) 282000. ☐ *mid-Apr–Oct: daily; Nov–mid-Apr: 9am–5pm Mon–Fri.* 🚌 🅿 🚻 🖥 **www**.ecomuseeboisduluc.be

This industrial heritage site of note has been in existence for over 25 years, recalling the long history of coal mining in Belgium (1685–1973) and at the St Emmanuel mine in particular. It features the paternalistic industrial village that was created here, with its

orderly grid of more than 166 miners' dwellings, plus shops, a church, schools and an infirmary. Offices, workshops and equipment stores cluster around the mine shaft that descends 558 m (1,830 ft) below the surface.

Canal du Centre ⓯

Rue Tout-y-Faut 90, Houdeng-Goegnies; 3 km (2 miles) N of La Louvière. **Road Map** C3. **Tel** (064) 847831. 🛈 *Place Mansart 21; (064) 847831.* 🚢 *Apr–Oct: Tue–Sun (boat trips).* **www**.canalducentre.be

Forged between 1882 and 1917, Canal du Centre was used to transport raw materials and goods to the North Sea, France and Germany. The original canal tackled the 68-m (223-ft) rise in the land with a series of locks and four hydraulic boat lifts spread over 7 km (4 miles) between Thieu and Houdeng-Goegnies. Boats – one going up and the other down – enter a pair of metal counterbalanced containers. As water is pumped, one rises and the other goes down.

After nearly a century, a more efficient system was devised for a new cut of the canal designed to take the 1,350-tonne (1,330-ton) canal boats of the modern era. Here, the rise of 73 m (240 ft) is dealt with by a single huge

The gigantic Ascenseur Funiculaire de Strépy-Thieu at Canal du Centre

For hotels and restaurants in this region see pp268–9 and pp294–5

lift about 2 km (1 mile) to the northeast of the old lift at Thieu. Built from 1982 to 2002, the **Ascenseur Funiculaire de Strépy-Thieu** is a marvel of modern engineering. Raising and lowering boats in two water-filled tanks, it is 110-m (361-ft) high and has fine views from its visitor centre.

The four old boat lifts on the original branch are now UNESCO World Heritage Sites. They still function, but are used only for pleasure crafts. There are 2-hour boat trips between La Cantine des Italiens and Bracquegnies.

🏛 **Ascenseur Funiculaire de Strépy-Thieu**
Tel (064) 671200. ◯ Feb–Nov: daily. **www**.strepy-thieu.be

Mons ⑯

18 km (11 miles) W of La Louvière. **Road Map** C3. 🚶 92,669. 🚗 🚆 ℹ *Grand Place 22; (065) 335580.* **www**.mons.be

Despite its location in the heart of the Borinage mining district, Mons, the vibrant capital of the Province of Hainaut, has considerable charm. On the contours of the hill for which it is named are cobbled streets with 17th- and 18th-century merchant's houses. The city's patron saint, Ste Waudru, built a convent here in AD 650; and the main church, the Brabant Gothic **Collégiale Ste-Waudru** that was built between 1449 and 1686, is dedicated to her. It houses the splendid Car d'Or (Chariot of Gold), built in 1781, which is used to carry the saint's relics in the parade during the annual Ducasse, or Doudou, festivities *(see p33)*.

Mons is particularly proud of its unusual, free-standing, Baroque belfry. Built over 1661–9 and rising to a height of 87 m (285 ft), it contains a carillon of 49 bells. The Gothic **Hôtel de Ville** in the Grand Place dates from 1458, but its distinctive copper-clad, pepperpot tower was added in 1718. Stroking the head of the little cast-iron monkey by the front entrance, the Singe du Grand-Garde, is said to bring good luck. There are three

Brabant Gothic exterior of Collégiale Ste-Waudru, Mons

museums close to the Grand Place. The **Musée du Folklore et de la Vie Montoise** (closed for renovation), housed in the Maison Jean Lescarts, evokes past lifestyles of the people of Mons. The **Musée des Arts Décoratifs François Duesberg** contains an extraordinary collection of elaborate clocks made in Paris in Louis XIV and Empire styles between 1795 and 1815. There are also exquisite decorative arts from the same era. The art museum **Beaux-Arts Mons** focusses on hosting temporary exhibitions.

South of the city centre is the **Maison de van Gogh**, a tiny brick house that was once owned by a miner's family. The artist Vincent van Gogh stayed here while training to be a missionary among the Borinage miners.

Around Mons are a number of cemeteries and monuments that serve as reminders that this region was the scene of fierce battles during both World War I and World War II.

Environs
About 7 km (4 miles) to the southwest is **Parc d'Attractions Scientifiques (PASS)**, a family-oriented, interactive museum demonstrating the concepts of science and technology. At **Spiennes**, 3 km (2 miles) to the southeast, an extensive Neolithic flint mine is now a UNESCO World Heritage Site.

🏛 **Musée du Folklore et de la Vie Montoise**
Rue Neuve 8. *Tel* (065) 314357. ◯ for renovation. 🏷

🏛 **Maison de Van Gogh**
Rue du Pavillon 3, Cuesmes. *Tel* (065) 355611. ◯ Tue–Sun. 🏷

🏛 **Parc d'Attractions Scientifiques (PASS)**
Tel (070) 222252. ◯ Thu–Tue. ● part of Sep. 🏷 **www**.pass.be

Grand Hornu ⑰

R Ste-Louise 82, Hornu; 10 km (6 miles) SW of Mons. **Road Map** B3. *Tel* (065) 652121. ◯ Tue–Sun. 🏷 📷 🖥 **www**.grand-hornu.be

The remains of the large and stylish Neo-Classical buildings of Grand Hornu are the vestiges of a great industrial enterprise. This idealistic colliery complex, built around an oval courtyard with engineering workshops, forges and 440 workers' houses, was created between 1810 and 1830 by French industrialist Henri de Gorge. In 1971, it was made a centre for industrial arts and design. In 2002, new buildings meshing with the old became the home of the **Musée des Arts Contemporaine de la Communauté Française** – a suitable setting for its exhibitions of contemporary art.

Arches in a curved wing around Grand Hornu's large oval courtyard

Posters outside Musée International du Carnaval et du Masque in Binche

Binche ⑱

16 km (10 miles) SE of Mons. **Road Map** C3. 🏘 33,000. 🚌 🚆 ℹ️ Grande Place Binche; (064) 336727. 🎭 Carnival (Feb or Mar). **www.**binche.be

Set amid the old industrial heartlands between Mons and Charleroi, Binche is celebrated for its extraordinary, colourful and elaborate pre-Lenten Carnival, the most famous of Belgium's carnivals. This event takes place mainly in the Grand Place, which is overlooked by a 16th-century Gothic town hall. Those who are unable to visit Binche during the carnival can experience it to an extent at the town's prestigious **Musée International du Carnaval et du Masque**. Occupying an 18th-century building that was formerly an Augustinian college, the museum takes a global look at festivities, masks and carnivals, with special focus on the carnivals of Wallonia and Binche.

The town's long history is underscored by the restored remains of its extensive walls. Built between the 12th and 14th centuries, they stretch continuously across a distance of 2 km (1.5 miles) and include 25 towers.

🏛 **Musée International du Carnaval et du Masque**
Rue St-Moustier 10, Binche. **Tel** (064) 335741. 🕘 9:30am–5pm Tue–Fri, 10:30am–5pm Sat–Sun. 🕘 Ash Wednesday, 1 Nov. 🎟 **www.**museedumasque.be

Thuin ⑲

14 km (9 miles) SE of Binche. **Road Map** C3. 🏘 15,000. 🚌 🚆 ℹ️ Maison du Tourisme Val de Sambre, Place Albert 1; (071) 595454. 🎭 Marche Militaire St Roch (May) **www.**thuin.be

Located close to the French border, Thuin was at the western end of the Principality of Liège, whose ribbon of territory stretched right across the central band of Belgium during the Middle Ages. The upper town was reinforced by Prince-Bishop Notger in the 10th century, but of this work, only the tower, Tour Notger, can be seen today. There are also remnants of 15th-century ramparts – Remparts du Midi.

The military significance of Thuin is further remembered in traditional *spantôle* biscuits, shaped and named after a French cannon captured in 1654. The Place du Chapitre at the town centre has the free-standing 17th-century belfry, **Beffroi de Thuin**. This has an interactive exhibition and also offers enchanting views over the River Sambre, lined with barges.

Environs
At Ragnies, 3 km (2 miles) to the south, is the **Distillerie de Biercée**, famed for flavoured spirits such as Eau de Villée and Poire Williams. At Leers-et-Fosteau, 5 km (3 miles) southwest of Thuin, is the **Château du Fosteau**, which exhibits antique furniture.

🏛 **Beffroi de Thuin**
Place du Chapitre. **Tel** (071) 595454. 🕘 Tue–Sun (Easter holidays, Jul, Aug: daily). 🎟 📷

🏛 **Distillerie de Biercée**
Ferme de la Cour, Rue de la Roquette 36. **Tel** (071) 591106. 🕘 Mar–mid-Dec. 🎟 📷 📷 📷 📷 **www.**distilleriedebiercee.com

🏛 **Château du Fosteau**
Rue du Marquis 1. **Tel** (071) 592344. 🕘 Thu–Mon. 🎟 📷 **www.**chateaufosteau.be

Abbaye d'Aulne ⑳

Rue Vandervelde 275, Thuin. **Road Map** C3. **Tel** (071) 595454. 🚆 🕘 Apr–Oct: Wed–Sun; Jul–Aug: daily. 🎟 📷 📷 📷 **www.**valdesambre.be

The extensive ruins of the Abbey d'Aulne create a picturesque ensemble along the

---

THE CARNIVAL AT BINCHE

Rooted in a long and obscure history, the Carnival at Binche begins as a gradual build-up of festivities over a series of Sundays preceding Lent. This explodes into a frenzy of fancy-dress processions, folk music and street dancing over three days, with the climax on Shrove Tuesday. This is the day of the *gilles* (clowns) – all native men of Binche dressed in the dun-coloured motley of court jesters, heavily padded and rotund, and decorated with heraldic symbols, ribbons and bells. They wear clogs on their feet, and bandaged to their heads are sinister pink masks with moustaches and wire-rimmed green glasses. In the afternoon they put on colossal ostrich-feather headdresses – a reference to Inca costumes at the time of the Spanish conquests during the reign of Emperor Charles V – and parade about tossing oranges at the onlookers. The day ends in dancing and fireworks.

Binche's quirkily costumed *gilles* at the annual Carnival

---

banks of the Sambre. It is said to have been founded in AD 657 by St Landelin in an act of contrition for his former life as a notorious brigand. It rose in wealth and prominence as a Cistercian monastery until it was set ablaze by the French Revolutionary Army in 1794. Dominating the ruins is the 13th-century Gothic abbey church and its contrasting 18th-century Neo-Classical west front. The complex now also includes a brewery, the Brasserie du Val de Sambre.

The opulently furnished theatre at the Château des Princes de Chimay

Lacs de l'Eau d'Heure ㉑

22 km (14 miles) S of Thuin. **Road Map** C3. 🚌 🛈 *Centre d'Acceuil de la Plate Taille; (071) 509292.* ◯ *daily (Barrage de la Plate Taille); Mar–Sep: daily (Relais de Falemprise).* 🅿 **www**.lacsdeleaudheure.be

In the 1970s, the River l'Eau d'Heure was dammed twice to regulate the flow of water in Charleroi canal. The main dams, **Barrage de la Plate Taille** and **Barrage de l'Eau d'Heure**, and a series of subsidiary dams form a set of five lakes – the Lacs de l'Eau d'Heure. These are now a major resort area focussing on water sports. There are also signposted paths for walkers and barbecue sites for picnickers.

Barrage de la Plate Taille, the largest dam in Belgium, has a visitors' centre and a viewing tower 107 m (351 ft) high. Tours in the Crocodile Rouge, an extraordinary bus that also goes on water, begin here. Just 2 km (1 mile) to the east is the **Relais de Falemprise**, a recreational centre that offers a sand beach, pedalos, restaurants, mini-golf, tennis courts, and facilities for beach volleyball and pétanque.

Chimay ㉒

38 km (24 miles) S of Thuin. **Road Map** C4. 🚍 *10,000.* 🚌 🛈 *(060) 211846.* **www**.ville-de-chimay.be

The pretty town of Chimay is the main centre of the Botte du Hainaut, the boot-shaped southern part of the

province. The town's main attraction is the **Château des Princes de Chimay**, a medieval castle that has been the home of the de Croy family and the princes de Chimay since the 15th century. It contains memorabilia of the family, including those of the lively and beautiful Spanish-born Madame Tallien (1773–1835), Princess de Chimay, who escaped the guillotine during the French Revolution and helped engineer the downfall of Robespierre. The castle also has an elaborate 19th-century Rococo theatre.

Chimay's 13th–16th-century **Collégiale des Sts-Pierre-et-Paul** contains tombs of the castle's lords and ladies and a memorial to the medieval chronicler Froissart, who was a canon here. Chimay is also the name of a Trappist beer, brewed under the auspices of monks of the Abbaye Notre-Dame-de-Scourmont, 10 km (6 miles) to the south.

Environs
L'Aquascope Virelles, 3 km (2 miles) to the northeast, is a nature reserve focussing on Belgium's largest natural lake. A popular park and adventure playground, it is linked to Chimay by a train in summer.

🏰 **Château des Princes de Chimay**
Tel (060) 490242. 🅿 📷 *Easter–Oct: 10am, 11am, 3pm and 4pm daily.* **www**.chimaypromotion.be

🅿 **L'Aquascope Virelles**
Rue du Lac 42. **Tel** (060) 211363. ◯ *varies, check website.* 🅿 ♿ 🍴 📷 **www**.aquascope.be

Vallée de la Sambre ㉓

Road Map C3. 🚌 🛈 *Maison du Tourisme Val de Sambre, Place Albert 1; (071) 595454.* **www**.valdesambre-thudinie.be

The River Sambre is a major thoroughfare in Hainaut's old industrial centre, but it has a very pretty, countrified stretch to the west of Charleroi. This makes an attractive excursion. The river passes the Abbaye d'Aulne and Thuin as well as **Lobbes**, which is noted for its fine Romanesque collegiale church, dating in part to about AD 825 and dedicated to St Ursmer (c.644–713). St Ursmer was the influential abbot of the monastery of Lobbes, said to have been founded by his predecessor St Landelin. It was destroyed by the French Revolutionary Army in 1794.

A view of the River Sambre winding through the pretty countryside

CENTRAL WALLONIA

omprising the provinces of Namur and Brabant Wallon, Central Wallonia is characterized primarily by rural landscapes. However, scattered across this expanse are numerous fine castles and abbeys, and some of the most impressive caves of the Ardennes. The city of Namur, capital of Wallonia, sits at its heart, on the broad and busy convergence of the rivers Meuse and Sambre.

The many fortresses of Central Wallonia's provinces bear witness to the military significance of these lands, which have been fending off invaders from the south, east and west for centuries. For instance, the rock on which the formidable Citadelle of Namur was built was once the site of a Roman fortress, and was refortified incessantly over nearly 2,000 years. The dark castles and fortified manor houses are strongly evocative of the region's medieval history. In the southwest are garrison towns dating from the 16th century. One of Europe's most famous battlefields is in the Province of Brabant Wallon – Waterloo, scene of the final defeat of Napoleon in 1815. Central Wallonia also saw much fighting during the World Wars, and Dinant marks the furthest point west reached by the German army during the 1944 Ardennes Offensive.

In parallel with these political and military events, religion left its mark on the land via a number of superb abbeys and cathedrals, such as the Romanesque church in Nivelles. Some buildings, such as the 12th-century Abbaye de Villers, are now no more than spectacular ruins, while others, such as the 19th-century Neo-Gothic Abbaye de Maredsous, are still active monasteries.

While Charleroi to its west and Liège to its east became centres of heavy industry in the 19th century, Central Wallonia remained largely agricultural. Today, its châteaux and abbeys, the picturesque River Meuse and the cities located on its banks are the main draw for visitors. Towards the south, where the Belgian landscape rises to form the Ardennes, limestone caves bristling with stalactites and stalagmites offer an equally appealing attraction.

Fortress city of Dinant, with the onion-domed Collégiale Notre-Dame dominating the banks of River Meuse

◁ The commemorative Butte de Lion providing a lofty vantage point at Waterloo

Exploring Central Wallonia

The fertile, undulating lowlands of Brabant Wallon are the farmland setting for the battle site of Waterloo and for the university at Louvain-la-Neuve. The River Meuse forms a centrepiece, linking Dinant and Namur. It is flanked by the Citadelle of Namur and the châteaux of Annevoie and Freÿr, as well as the abbeys of Floreffe and Maredsous. Couvin nestles in the forested Fagne region, close to the famous Grottes de Neptune at Petigny. Steam engines puff their way through the Viroin valley between Mariembourg and Treignes. The hills of the Ardennes begin to rise further to the south and east, where the River Lesse carves a path out of the limestone hills. The spectacular caves of Han-sur-Lesse lie in the far southeast of the region.

SIGHTS AT A GLANCE

Villages, Towns and Cities
Couvin 20
Dinant 13
Mariembourg 19
Namur pp202–203 8
Nivelles 7
Rochefort 24
Waterloo pp196–7 1

Castles
Château de Freÿr 16
Château de Lavaux
  Ste-Anne 22
Château de Vêves 17
Corroy-le-Château 9

Museums
Fondation Folon 2
Treignes 21

Churches and Abbeys
Abbaye de Floreffe 10
Abbaye de Maredsous 14
Abbaye de Villers 6
Basilique St-Materne 18

Parks
Jardins d'Annevoie 11

Areas of Natural Beauty
Domaine des Grottes
  de Han 23
Folx-les-Caves 5
River Meuse 15

Sites of Interest
Brasserie du Bocq 12
Louvain-la-Neuve 4
Walibi 3

The resplendent interior of De Groesbeeck de Croix museum at Namur

SEE ALSO

- *Where to Stay* pp269–71
- *Where to Eat* pp296–7

Visitors descend the cavernous depths of the grotto at Rochefort

Jodoigne
(idenaken)
A3
Jauche   *Liège*
N91
5 FOLX-LES-CAVES
N29   Ramillies
Mébalgne
ALLON
A4
Éghezée
Bierwart
N91
uzet   A15
mont   N80
Meuse   Andenne
N90
NAMUR   Haillot
8 (NAMEN)
AYE
LOREFFE
Wépion   Gesves   Havelange
Samson
N97
rofondeville **15**
JARDINS   RIVER MEUSE   N A M U R
ANNEVOIE   A4
11   Assesse
N63
Spontin *Bocq*
BAYE DE   Baillonville
REDSOUS   **12** BRASSERIE DU BOCQ
14   Bouvignes   Ciney
Molignée   N4
aën *Valley*   **13** DINANT
Anseremme   Haversin
Celles
Vêves
ÂTEAU **16**   **17** CHÂTEAU DE VÊVES
E FREŸR   Waulsort
Houyet   ROCHEFORT
Agimont   **24**
CHÂTEAU DE   DOMAINE DES
LAVAUX-SAINTE-ANNE   **23** GROTTES DE HAN
Beauraing   **22**
Bois de   Luxembourg
Savry   City
Famenne
Rouille
N95
Gedinne
Houdremont   Bièvre

KEY

▬	Motorway
▬	Major road
—	Secondary road
---	Minor road
—•—	Main railway
—	Minor railway
▬	International border
—	Provincial border

GETTING AROUND

The main motorway, the E411 (A4), slices southwards across the region, connecting Brussels with Luxembourg. It intersects the main east–west link, E42 (A15), just north of Namur. The SNCB railway network covers all major towns, but fewer areas in the more remote regions, for instance, in the area between Couvin and Dinant. A more comprehensive coverage is offered by the bus network of TEC Namur-Luxembourg and TEC Brabant Wallon. Cruises on the River Meuse link Namur and Dinant. For walkers and cyclists, there is the RAVeL 2 all the way from Mariembourg in the south to Hoegaarden, near Leuven in Flanders. It follows disused railways and the River Meuse, via Dinant and Namur. The GR paths for walkers are concentrated in the south.

Namur ⑧

A stately university town, a centre of trade and the capital of Wallonia, Namur straddles the confluence of the rivers Sambre and Meuse. The town's dominant feature is the massive, gaunt Citadelle, mounted on a spur of rock that sits on the Grognon, a dagger-shaped spit of land between the two rivers. The Romans built defences here, and the Citadelle has since seen action in just about every war that has swept across Belgium; the last, World War II, brought widespread damage to the city from air raids. Little remains of the medieval town, the seat of the counts of Namur, but its old residential areas are dotted with elegant 17th- and 18th-century civic buildings and mansions. The suburb to the south of the Meuse, called Jambes, was, until the 15th century, ruled separately by the prince-bishops of Liège.

Namur's mighty Citadelle rising above the banks of the River Meuse

♠ The Citadelle

Route Merveilleuse 64. **Tel** (081) 654500. ☐ Easter–Oct: 11am–5pm. 🈺 🖵 www.citadelle.namur.be

The strategic value of the Champeau hill that rises up from the Grognon has been recognized since prehistoric times. Julius Caesar is said to have laid siege to this rock to oust the Aduatuci Gauls. It has since been fortified and embattled on numerous occasions, most significantly in 1692, when it was seized by the army of French monarch Louis XIV. Louis's great military engineer, Marquis de Vauban, then set his stamp on the fortress with his signature triangular bastions, but it was retaken by William III of Orange three years later. The Citadelle saw action right up to the end of World War II, and was only fully demilitarized in 1977.

The winding road leading up to the top of the Citadelle is called Route Merveilleuse. On the south side, it offers panoramic views over the Sambre and Meuse. The fortress itself is a sprawling complex of robust defensive ramparts, built between the 16th and 20th centuries. Its network of underground passages inspired Napoleon to call it "the termite hill of Europe". There are various exhibits, activities and audiovisual presentations, plus a little train that ferries visitors about. Also on the hill, close to the 17th-century Fort d'Orange, is a small amusement park for children called the Parc d'Attractions Reine-Fabiola.

🏛 Musée Archéologique de Namur

Rue du Pont 21. **Tel** (081) 231631. ☐ 10am–5pm Tue–Fri, 10:30am–5pm Sat and Sun. 🈺 🖵

The impressive 16th-century Halle al'Chair (Meat Hall) is home to a remarkable collection of prehistoric, Gallo-Roman and Meroving-ian artifacts such as statues, pottery, mosaics, jewellery, glassware and weapons. The most celebrated exhibits are the late-Roman treasures of the 4th–5th centuries, excavated from tombs in various local sites. The museum also has a beautiful 17th-century scale model of Namur, made for Louis XIV, which is at the centre of a section on the history and evolution of the city.

🏛 Musée Provincial des Arts Anciens

Rue de Fer 24. **Tel** (081) 776754. ☐ 10am–6pm Tue–Sun. ☐ 14–25 Dec. 🈺 www. museedesartsanciens.be

Home to medieval and Renaissance pieces from Namur, the Musée Provincial des Arts Anciens has a remarkable collection of sculptures, paintings, altarpieces, metalwork, armour, stained glass and embroidery. These are elegantly displayed in a fine 18th-century mansion, the Hôtel de Gaiffier d'Hestroy.

Housed in Musée Provincial des Arts Anciens, Le Trésor d'Oignies has exquisite examples of medieval Mosan (of the Meuse) silver and gold work, ivory carvings, enamelware, glass and mitres. The treasury once belonged to the Priory of Oignies in Hainaut, but was whisked away and hidden from the armies of the French Revolution who destroyed the priory in 1794. The most celebrated pieces are by the 13th-century monk, Hugo d'Oignies, and include bejewelled reliquaries, crosses and ecclesiastical book covers.

Modern galleries at the Musée Provincial des Arts Anciens

The lofty nave and unusual sandstone ceiling at the Église St-Loup

VISITORS' CHECKLIST

59 km (37 miles) SE of Waterloo.
Road Map D3. 🚉 *107,000*.
🚌 🚆 🛈 *Square Léopold,*
Namur; (081) 246449. 🎉 *Fêtes*
de Wallonie (Sep). **www.**
namurtourisme.be

🔒 Église St-Loup

Rue du Collège. **www.**eglise
saintloup.be

One of the great Baroque
churches of Belgium, the
Église St-Loup was built for
the Jesuits between 1621
and 1645. Its striking façade,
adorned by muscular banded
pillars, gives way to an equally
robust interior with banded
pillars of coloured marble
and a contrasting ceiling of
carved sandstone. The French
poet Charles Baudelaire, a
friend of the Namur artist
Félicien Rops (1833–98), suffered a stroke here in 1866,
the year before his death; he
was fascinated by the church,
which he found to be deliciously funereal. It is now
used for concerts.

🏛 Musée Provincial Félicien Rops

Rue Fumal 12. **Tel** *(081) 776755.*
⬚ *Jul–Aug: 10am–6pm daily; Sep–
Jun: 10am–6pm Tue–Sun.* 🖼 🔊
www.museerops.be

A gifted Symbolist artist,
Félicien Rops was born in
Namur. He is known for his
vividly imagined compositions,
often macabre and sacrile-
gious. Rops moved to Paris in
1874, where he led a colourful life among the avant-garde
literary set and became a
successful illustrator of their
work. Set in an 18th-century
townhouse, Musée Provincial
Félicien Rops has a collection
of about 3,000 paintings, prints
and drawings by Rops. It showcases a large selection of the
best, assisted by audio guides
and multimedia presentations.

🏛 De Groesbeeck de Croix Museum

Rue Saintraint 3. **Tel** *(081) 248720.*
⬚ *10am–12:30pm, 1:15–5pm Tue–
Sun.* 🖼

The magnificent 18th-century
Groesbeeck de Croix mansion
has been preserved and restored in Enlightenment and
Louis XV styles to provide a
sympathetic backdrop for an
impressive collection of paintings, sculpture, antique furniture, tapestries, gold and
silverwork, clocks and *objets
d'art.* Outside the mansion
is a pleasant formal garden.

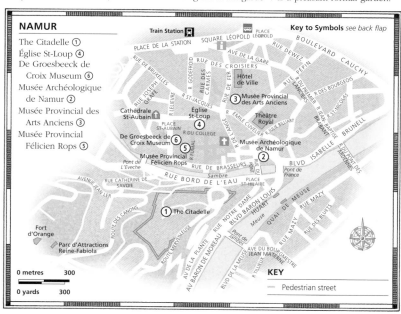

NAMUR

The Citadelle ①
Église St-Loup ④
De Groesbeeck de
 Croix Museum ⑥
Musée Archéologique
 de Namur ②
Musée Provincial des
 Arts Anciens ③
Musée Provincial
 Félicien Rops ⑤

Key to Symbols *see back flap*

KEY

— Pedestrian street

0 metres   300
0 yards   300

Corroy-le-Château ❾

Rue de Corroy-le-Château 4, Gembloux; 20 km (12 miles) NW of Namur. **Road Map** D3. *Tel* (081) 633232. 🛈 *Office du Tourisme de Gembloux, Rue Sigebert 1; (081) 626960.* **www**.corroylechateau.com

Its woodland setting gives this splendid medieval fortress a romantic appeal. The robust 13th-century towers and gateway over the moat lead to an intimate U-shaped courtyard inside. The interiors, however, have been much altered over the centuries and are mainly in the 18th- and 19th-century styles. The castle had been in the same family since 1270, but a protracted succession dispute led to its sale in 2008. Many concerts and special events are held throughout the year, including a medieval fête in late April, with jousting knights on horseback.

Abbaye de Floreffe ❿

Rue du Séminaire 7, Floreffe; 11 km (7 miles) SW of Namur. **Road Map** D3. *Tel* (081) 445303. ⏰ *Jul–Aug: 10:30am–5:30pm; Apr–Jun and Sep–Oct: 1:30–5:30pm.* 📷 📹 🏠 🗓 **www**.abbaye-de-floreffe.be **Moulin-Brasserie** ⏰ *11am–6pm Mon–Fri, 11am–8pm Sat and Sun.*

Occupying a commanding position on a hilltop above River Sambre, the Abbaye de Floreffe exudes a reassuring authority. St Norbert *(see p163)*

The moat and towers at the entrance to Corroy-le-Château

founded a monastery on this site in 1121 and it became one of the region's leading Premonstratensian abbeys. Wrecked many times by military action, it was largely remodelled in the 18th-century in an imposing late-Renaissance style. It was then closed during the French Revolution, but reopened as a seminary in 1830. The church, dating from the 13th century, is an atmospheric potpourri of styles ranging from Neo-Classical to Romanesque. The highlights are the exceptional Baroque choir stalls, masterpieces of the German-born sculptor Peter Enderlin, who devoted 16 years (1632–48) to the intricate carvings.

The abbey is also famous as a producer of beer, cheese and bread, and its products can be sampled at the now restored 13th-century brewery, the **Moulin-Brasserie**.

Jardins d'Annevoie ⓫

Rue des Jardins d'Annevoie 37, Annevoie; 12 km (7 miles) SE of Floreffe. **Road Map** D3. *Tel* (082) 679797. 📷 📹 ⏰ *Apr–Nov: daily.* 📷 ♿ 🏠 🗓 **www**.annevoie.be

The elegant 18th-century **Château d'Annevoie** is famous for its beautiful park packed with water features. Supplied by four springs filling a long basin called the Grand Canal, they include a number of fountains, pools and waterfalls including the strangely hushed corrugated waterfall. Statues, formal gardens, woodland glades and a grotto help create an enchanting environment, all of which was designed in the 18th-century to reflect French and Italian tastes of the period. The château itself has been in the Montpellier family since 1675, and is unfortunately not open to visitors.

Brasserie du Bocq ⓬

Rue de la Brasserie 4, Purnode; 8 km (5 miles) SE of Annevoie-Rouillon. **Road Map** D3. *Tel* (060) 610780. 📹 ⏰ *Jul–Aug: daily; late Mar–Jun and Sep–Oct: Sat and Sun.* 📷 📹 🗓 *2–4pm.* 🏠 **www**.bocq.be

The picturesque, whitewashed Brasserie du Bocq at Purnode was founded by Martin Belot in 1858 and is still run by the family. It makes a wide range of beers, including St Benoît,

Fountains at the extensive and beautiful gardens of the Château d'Annevoie

Triple Moine, Saison Régal and the wheat beer Blanche de Namur. Guided tours show visitors the old copper brewing vessels and the various stages of production, and end with a tasting. Nearby, **Spontin**, also in the Bocq valley, is famous for its mineral water as well as a fairytale medieval château, but this is no longer open to the public.

Dinant ⓭

23 km (14 miles) S of Namur. **Road Map** D3. 🏛 *13,900*. 🚉 🚌 🚢
🛈 *Avenue Cadoux, 8; (082) 222870.* **www**.dinant-tourisme.be

The small town of Dinant has one of the most beguiling and distinctive settings in Belgium. Standing on the east bank of the River Meuse, it clusters around the black onion dome of a Gothic church and under the shadow of a fortress on an escarpment above. Dinant was occupied by the Romans and valued for its commanding position on the navigable River Meuse. It became prosperous in the Middle Ages as a centre for metal-working, earning an international reputation for ornately decorated copper-ware and brassware known as *dinanderie*.

Dominating the town is the church **Collégiale Notre-Dame** whose interior contains two paintings by the Dinant-born, macabre-Romantic painter Antoine Wiertz (1806–65). The Place Reine Astrid, just to the south of the church, is the departure station for the *téléphérique* (cable car) to the **Citadelle**, which is also accessible to walkers via 408 steps. In 1466, Charles the Bold, Duke of Burgundy, sacked the town, after which the Citadelle was rebuilt and reinforced in an effort to prevent such invasions. More changes were made over the centuries and the Citadelle is now primarily 19th-century, and offers glorious views over the Meuse. Its military museum recalls the conflicts that took a heavy toll on Dinant, notably in the two World Wars. About 1 km (half a mile) to the south of the town is the **Rocher Bayard**, a

A river cruise boat passing beneath a bridge on the River Meuse at Dinant

pinnacle of rock, which marks the most westerly point reached by German troops in the Ardennes Offensive *(see p231)*. The name, however, comes from the legend of the rock's creation, supposedly by the hoof of the mighty steed Bayard *(see p139)*.

Dinant is famous for its hard, sculptured honey-based biscuits called *couques de Dinant*, which are used as much for decoration as eating. The town is also the home of the famous abbey beer Leffe. Opposite the old Abbaye de Leffe is its brewery museum, called the **Musée de la Leffe**.

Quays beside the Avenue Winston Churchill are the departure point for cruises on the River Meuse. On its west bank, 500 m (547 yards) west of the bridge, is the **Grotte la Merveilleuse**, one of Belgium's best caves for stalactites.

🏰 Citadelle
Place Reine Astrid 3-5 (cable car and ticket office). **Tel** (082) 223670. ☐ *Apr–Oct: daily; Nov–Dec and Feb–Mar: Sat–Thu; Jan: Sat and Sun.* 🎦 📷 *summer only.* ☐ **www**.citadellededinant.be

🏛 Musée de la Leffe
R du Moulin 18. **Tel** (082) 647583. ☐ *Jul–Aug: Fri–Sun; Apr–Jun and Sep–Oct: Sat and Sun.* 🎦 📷 **www**.breweryvisits.com

🕳 Grotte la Merveilleuse
Route de Philippeville 142. **Tel** (082) 222210. ☐ *Apr–Oct daily; Nov–Mar: school holidays.* 🎦 📷

ADOLPHE SAX

Adolphe Sax, famed Belgian innovator

Dinant was the birthplace of one of the most successful and innovative inventors of musical instruments of all time, Adolphe Sax (1814–94). He followed his father's profession as an instrument maker and musician, moving permanently to Paris in 1841. He is said to have been working on a kind of keyed bugle called the ophicleide when he hit upon the idea of combining this with the single-reed mouthpiece of a clarinet. The saxophone was born, and in 1846, it was patented in seven registers, from contrabass to sopranino. With its conical metal bore and set of keys to operate the valves, it could produce just the kind of volume and expression demanded by opera orchestras, military bands and music halls. It later turned out to be a perfect instrument for jazz. Adolphe Sax did not stop there – he also invented the saxhorn (a family of valved bugles) and a number of other, less successful, instruments, including the saxtuba and saxotromba, and a trombone with seven tubes and bells.

The saxophone, Sax's best-known creation

Cruise boats line up along the tree-lined banks of the River Meuse

Abbaye de Maredsous ⑭

Rue de Maredsous 11, Denée;
12 km (7 miles) NW of Dinant.
Road Map D3. *Tel* (082) 698211.
☐ daily. ♿ ☐ ☐ **www**.
maredsous.com

A vast Neo-Gothic monastery
founded by the Benedictines
in 1872, Abbaye de Maredsous
is set in the tranquil Molignée
valley and built in austere grey
stone. The abbey offers insight
into the lives of the monks and
a chance to sample two of the
institution's famous products –
a soft, orange-rind cheese and
the respected abbey beer. The
grounds have gardens, a playground and walks into the
surrounding countryside.

The soaring and polished chancel
of the Abbaye de Maredsous

There is also a shop selling
regional produce at the
Centre d'Acceuil St-Joseph.

Environs
With **Railbikes of the Molignée**,
visitors can pedal along the
Molignée valley on a four-
person *draisine* (railbike),
on disused railway lines linking Falaën, Maredsous and
Warnant. Falaën, set 4 km (3
miles) southeast of Maredsous,
has the ruins of a mighty 14th-
century castle, **Château-Fort
de Montaigle**, which was destroyed by the French in 1554.

Railbikes of the Molignée
Rue de la Molignée 116, Anhée.
Tel (082) 699079. ☐ daily (Falaën);
Apr–Oct: Tue–Sun (Warnant). ☒
www.draisine.be

🏰 **Château-Fort de Montaigle**
Rue du Marteau 10, Falaën.
Tel (082) 699585. ☐ Jul–Aug: daily;
Apr–Jun and Sep–Oct: Sat and Sun.
☒ www.montaigle.be

River Meuse ⑮

Road Map D3. 🛈 La Compagnie
des Bateaux Touristes de la Meuse,
Rue Daoust 64, Dinant; (082)
222315. www.bateaux-meuse.be

Flowing north out of France,
River Meuse enters Belgium
via the Province of Namur,
coursing past Hastière and the
Château de Freÿr to Dinant
(see p205), and then on to
Namur (see pp202–203). Here,
it is joined by River Sambre
and heads east to Liège. The
prettiest part runs between

Dinant and Namur and many
long-established boat cruises
offer trips along this stretch.
Fully-equipped sightseeing
boats make scheduled excur-
sions up and down the river.
The main departure points
are at Dinant and Namur. The
round-trip between the two
takes about 9 hours, but there
are numerous shorter trips to
points in between. It is necessary, however, to check about
landing possibilities as most
boat trips do not stop at their
destination, but simply turn
round. Landscape, and the
pleasure of being on water,
are the main attractions. The
river banks are dotted with
rocky outcrops and ruined
castles. Points in between
include the pretty towns of
Profondeville and **Wépion**,
the most famous source of
strawberries in Belgium.
    South of Dinant, the stretch
up to Hastière and Waulsort is
also rewarding and includes
the splendid castle at Freÿr.
The main season for river
trips runs between May and
September, with mid-July to
late August being busiest.

Château de Freÿr ⑯

Domaine de Freÿr, Hastière; 5 km
(3 miles) S of Dinant. **Road Map** D3.
Tel (082) 222200. ☒ ☐ Jul–Aug:
Tue–Sun; Apr–Jun and Sep: Sat–Sun;
Oct–Mar: Sun. ☒ 🚗 www.freyr.be

One of the most impressive
châteaux in Belgium stands
right beside the broad River

Meuse. Originally a medieval fortress commanding the river, it was destroyed by the French in 1554, then rebuilt as a palatial residence in fetching Mosan Renaissance style, with touches of French château grandeur, between the 16th and 18th centuries. This was the home of the influential dukes of Beaufort-Spontin. Louis XIV of France stayed here during his siege of Dinant in 1675 and, later that year, signed the Treaty of Frëyr with Charles II of Spain. In the 1770s, the Austrian governor of the Netherlands, Charles of Lorraine, was a visitor.

The château is still owned by the 20th generation of the Beaufort family. Its Italianesque interior is decorated with wood panelling, tapestry, paintings and murals. Outside is a large formal garden in 18th-century French style, with parterres, fountains, pools, an orangery (with 300-year-old orange trees), follies, hedged mazes and an ornate Rococo pavilion overlooking the River Meuse.

The name Frëyr relates to the legend that Freya, the Scandinavian goddess of fertility, stopped to rest here in a cave on the rocky banks of the Meuse, and had to be rescued from a band of naughty Nutons – the elves that play a major role in local mythology.

The medieval frame and conical towers of the Château de Vêves

Château de Vêves ⑰

Noisy 5, Celles-Houyet; 8 km (5 miles) SE of Dinant. **Road Map** D3. **Tel** (082) 666395. ◯ Jul–Aug: 10am–5:30pm daily; Apr–Oct: 10am–5:30pm Tue–Thu, Sat & Sun. 📷 www.chateau-de-veves.be

Perched on a grassy hillock with massive walls, five tall, cone-topped towers and high windows, the 15th-century Château de Vêves resembles a child's drawing of a fantasy castle. Its half-timbered galleries overlook a fully enclosed courtyard. Parts of the interior, such as the huge medieval kitchens, are pleasingly robust, but the private family rooms have been softened by 18th-century refinements. The Seigneurs de Celles, who took

possession of a fortress on this site in the 12th century, came from the Beaufort family, and their descendants still use the castle as a residence, giving it the rare feeling of live-in continuity. The nearby village of **Celles** is considered to be one of the prettiest in Wallonia.

Basilique St-Materne ⑱

Rue de la Basilique 12, Walcourt; 18 km (11 miles) S of Charleroi. **Road Map** C3. **Tel** (071) 611366. 🚆 📖 🛈 Grand Place 25; (071) 612526. ◯ daily. 📷 treasury. www.walcourt.be

A large 13th- to 15th-century church, Basilique St-Materne is distinguished by its turrets and peculiar onion-shaped tips on its spire. Said to be founded by the 4th-century St Maternus of Tongeren, the church became a pilgrimage site focussing on devotion to Notre Dame de Walcourt, a wooden statue dating from the 10th century (with 17th-century silver plating) that now stands in the north transept. This history explains the basilica's size, as well as the richness of its interior, which includes a flamboyant Gothic jubé (rood screen), believed to have been presented by Charles V in 1531. The church's **Treasury** also has many exquisite devotional objects, some of which may be the work of the great 13th-century goldsmith Hugo d'Oignies (see p202).

Environs
Philippeville, 9 km (6 miles) to the southeast, was a fortress town built by Emperor Charles V in 1555 and modernized by the French military architect Vauban in the 17th century. The fortress was demolished in 1860, leaving 10 km (6 miles) of underground passages, called **Les Souterrains**, part of which can be visited by a guided tour.

Les Souterrains
Philippeville. 🛈 Rue des Religieuses 2; (071) 662300. ◯ Jul–Aug: 1:30–3pm daily. www.philippeville.be www.valleesdeseauxvives.be

Stately grandeur of the Mosan Renaissance Château de Frëyr

Caves of the Ardennes

Large areas of the Ardennes consist of karst – areas of soft, porous limestone that, over the centuries, have been gouged out, tunnelled and dissolved by rivers, streams and rain. In numerous places, this has created honeycombs of underground passageways and galleries, some still filled with lakes and rivers and containing fantastical arrays of stalactites and stalagmites. The best of these caves, or *grottes*, have now become major attractions. Visitors are led deep into the landscape, sometimes in boats, to see these extraordinary sculptural formations under dramatic illumination. There is evidence too, that some of these caves were shelters for prehistoric people.

Grottes de Goyet at Gesves, occupied by Neanderthals 40,000 years ago

Grotte la Merveilleuse *in Dinant is celebrated for its "frozen waterfalls": stalactites and stalagmites with the glistening limestone seemingly captured in mid-flow. Guided tours, lasting about 50 minutes, lead visitors through successive chambers via a series of pathways and steps.*

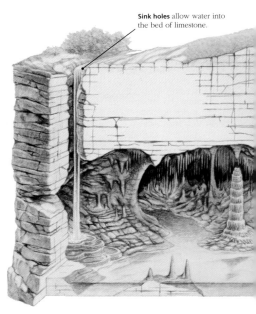

Sink holes allow water into the bed of limestone.

CAVE SYSTEMS

The limestone caves of the Ardennes are celebrated for their astonishing range of concretions of fused stalactite and stalagmite. Streams that are formed by surface water enter cave systems through a sink hole, replenishing the underground rivers. Water dripping through the cave ceiling deposits particles of limestone that slowly build up stalactites, and corresponding stalagmites on the cave floor. The underground river, on a bed of harder rock, continues to carve a path through the softer limestone.

The Grottes de Hotton (see p226) *form a network of deep, underground passages. Narrow paths lead down to a succession of dripping galleries draped with sculptural limestone, noted for its extraordinary range of delicate shapes and colours. The base is flooded by a siphon that marks the modern water table.*

The Grotte de Lorette *at Rochefort (see p211) has been revamped and now has a visitors' centre that delves into the broader realms of geology, including plate tectonics. A man-made corridor cuts through impervious marble to reach the largest of its underground chambers called the Sabbath, the setting for a son-et-lumière presentation.*

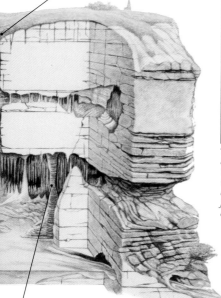

Former sink holes provide water-free entrances to the cave system.

Stalactites and stalagmites line the limestone caves, and over the years, fuse to form a single structure.

The Grottes de Remouchamps (see p225) *have an 8,000-year-old history of human encounter. They opened to visitors in 1912 and were illuminated in 1924. A walkway leads down to a giant chamber called the Cathedral, from where boats follow the underground river, Rubicon, which carved out these caves on its way to the Amblève.*

The Grotte de Han *at Han-sur-Lesse (see p211) is the most famous cave system of the Ardennes. In boats and on foot, visitors can see about 3 km (2 miles) of a huge cave system carved out by the River Lesse. Mirror-still pools reflect the bejewelled ceilings.*

The Grottes de Neptune *near Couvin (see p211) take visitors through three levels of caves and underground rivers, with a boat trip leading to a spectacular son-et-lumière presentation.*

Mariembourg ⓳

34 km (21 miles) SW of Dinant.
Road Map C4. 🏘 3,000. 🚌 🚐
ℹ️ *Marie de Hongrie 1; (060)
311181 (Easter–Oct); (060) 430140
(Couvin).*

The old frontier fortress-town
of Mariembourg was built in
1542 by Holy Roman Emperor
Charles V and his sister, Mary
of Hungary, after whom it was
named. Although supposedly
impregnable, it was captured
by the French in 1554, but
retaken by the Spanish in
1559. Exactly a century later,
it was handed over to Louis
XIV of France by treaty, and
remained French until taken
by the Prussians in 1815. The
fortifications were demolished
in 1855, leaving only the star-
shaped grid of the street plan.
   Mariembourg became an
important railway junction. It is
now the starting point for historic steam trains that journey
through the beautiful Les Trois
Vallées. The **Chemin de Fer des
Trois Vallées** (Railway of the
Three Valleys) takes a 14-km
(8-mile) long route by the
Viroin valley. Mariembourg's
Karting des Fagnes has one of
Europe's longest go-kart tracks.

🏛 **Chemin de Fer des
Trois Vallées**
Chaussée de Givet 49–51 **Tel** (060)
312440. ⬜ Jul–Aug: daily; Mar–Jun
and Sep–Oct: Sat and Sun. ⬜ &
http://cfv3v.in-site-out.com

🎪 **Karting des Fagnes**
Parc Industriel, 13. **Tel** (060)
312670. ⬜ Jul–Aug: daily. ⬤ Thu
during the off season. ⬜ ⬜
www.kartingdesfagnes.com

A historic steam engine running on
the tracks at Mariembourg

Slate-roofed houses of Couvin, a pretty setting for industrial history

Couvin ⓴

5 km (3 miles) S of Mariembourg.
Road Map C4. 🏘 13,500. 🚌 🚐
ℹ️ *Office du Tourisme de Couvin,
Rue de la Falaise 3; (060) 340140.*
www.couvin.be

A fetching little slate-roofed
town set on the River Eau
Noire, Couvin is a popular
centre for exploring the
Fagnes – an unspoilt region
of forests and meadows on a
bed of clay, slate and limestone. Couvin was once an
important iron- and steel-
working centre and vestiges
of its industrial past are still
evident. The town's prettiest
quarter is set on a rocky crag,
formerly the site of a castle
destroyed by the French in
1672. This area was inhabited
by Neanderthals in prehistoric
times, as witnessed in the
caves and museum of the
Cavernes de l'Abîme. A combination ticket includes the
Grottes de Neptune, 3 km
(2 miles) to the northeast.
These are classic limestone
caves of stalactites and stalagmites through which flows
the River Eau Noire.

Environs
Near the historic village of
Nismes, 5 km (3 miles) to the
northeast, is a curious canyon-
like weathered limestone
formation called the **Fondry
des Chiens**. Also of interest
are the wooded hills near
Brûly-de-Pesche, 8 km
(5 miles) southwest of Couvin,
which form the setting of the
**Grand Quartier Général
Allemand 1940** (German

Headquarters 1940). Called
Wolfsschlucht (Wolf's Ravine),
the headquarters include
concrete bunkers from which
Hitler directed his assault on
France in July 1940, plus a
small museum.

🏛 **Cavernes de l'Abîme**
Rue de la Falaise. **Tel** (060) 311954.
⬜ Jul–Aug: daily; Apr–Jun and Sep:
Sat and Sun. ⬜

🏛 **Grottes de Neptune**
Route du l'Adugeoir. **Tel** (060)
311954. ⬜ Apr–Sep: daily; Oct &
Nov: Sat & Sun. ⬜ ⬜

Treignes ㉑

15 km (9 miles) E of Couvin. **Road
Map** D4. 🏘 700. 🚌 ℹ️ *Office du
Tourisme de Viroinval, Rue Vieille
Église 2; (060) 311635.* ⬜ Tue–Sun.
www.treignes.info

Styling itself as the *village des
musées*, Treignes is home to
four museums. Formerly a
key railway hub for trains
crossing into France, the town
now serves as the terminus of
the Chemin de Fer des Trois
Vallées. Treignes's **Musée
du Chemin de Fer à Vapeur**
(Museum of Steam Railways),
is located on the grounds of
the old international railway
station and contains a major
collection of historic trains and
associated memorabilia. The
station itself was bought by the
Université Libre de Bruxelles
in 1972 as a centre for environ-
mental studies. The university
now also runs the **Ecomusée
du Viroin**, lodged in an old
château-ferme (fortified farm),
presenting the traditional crafts

and agricultural heritage of the Viroin valley, as well as its flora and fauna. The **Musée Malgré du Tout et Parc de la Préhistoire** explores the lives of prehistoric hunters and farmers through archaeological finds and reconstructions. Lastly, the **Espace Arthur Masson**, in an old boys' school, celebrates the life and work of local novelist Arthur Masson (1896–1970).

🏛 **Musée du Chemin de Fer à Vapeur**
Plateau de la Gare 1. *Tel (060) 300948.* ⬜ Jul–Aug: daily; Mar–Jun and Sep–Nov: Tue–Sun. 🎫 ▢ ▢ 🎪 Steam Festival (2nd weekend of Sep). **http://**cfv3v.in-site-out.com

🏛 **Ecomusée du Viroin**
Rue Eugène Defraire 63. *Tel (060) 399624.* ⬜ mid-Feb–mid-Dec: Thu–Tue. 🎫 ▢ ▢ **www**.ecomuseeduviroin.be

🏛 **Musée du Malgré Tout**
Rue de la Gare 28. *Tel (060) 390243.* ⬜ Thu–Tue. 🎫 ▢ **www**.museedumalgretout.ne

🏛 **Espace Arthur Masson**
Rue Eugène Defraire 29. *Tel (060) 391500.* ⬜ Mar–Oct: Tue–Sun; Nov–Feb: Sat and Sun. 🎫 🎫 ▢ ▢ **www**.espacemasson.be

Château de Lavaux-Ste-Anne ㉒

Rue du Château 8, Lavaux-Ste-Anne; 44 km (27 miles) E of Couvin. **Road Map** D4. *Tel (084) 388362.* ⬜ daily. 🎫 ▢ ▢ **www**. chateau-lavaux.com

Located on the plains of the Famenne region, part fortress, part château, Lavaux-Ste-Anne is a splendid fusion of power and elegance. Dating originally to 1193, it has round 15th-century corner towers, topped by onion domes, rising from a moat. In contrast, the courtyard inside is flanked by arcaded Renaissance façades in soft-toned brick. The interior has a series of furnished rooms with museums on local wild-life and traditions of Famenne rural life. Visitors can also join tours of the surrounding wetlands landscape.

Environs
Beauraing, 11 km (7 miles) to the west, has numerous sanctuaries that serve pilgrims

Striking corner towers of the sturdy Château de Lavaux-St-Anne

visiting the site where the Virgin Mary appeared to five children in 1932 and 1933.

Domaine des Grottes de Han ㉓

Rue J Lamotte 2, Han-sur-Lesse; 7 km (4 miles) E of Lavaux-Ste-Anne. **Road Map** D4. *Tel (084) 377213.* 🚃 ⬜ Apr–Aug: daily; Sep–Mar: more restricted timetable, see website for details. 🍴 Jan. 🎫 ▢ ▢ **www**.grotte-de-han.be

The most celebrated limestone cave system of the Ardennes, the Grotte de Han is situated in the pretty valley of River Lesse. The river also flows through the cave and has created its impressive water features. Access to the cave entrance is by means of a historic tram from the centre of the village of Han-sur-Lesse. There are impressive galleries of stalactites and stalagmites, but boat rides through the caverns are perhaps the most memorable highlight. Part of

the same complex is **Réserve d'Animaux Sauvages**, a safari-style park featuring animals once native to the Ardennes. These include bears, lynx, bison, wild boar and wolves. Tours of the reserve are conducted in open-sided coaches.

Rochefort ㉔

5 km (3 miles) NE of Han-sur-Lesse. **Road Map** D4. 🏘 12,000. 🚉 ⬜ 🛈 Maison du Tourisme du Val de Lesse, Rue de Behogne 5; (084) 345172. **www**.valdelesse.be

A pleasant town, Rochefort serves as a good base from which to fan out into the wooded hills and valleys of the Ardennes. Rochefort's big attraction is the **Grotte de Lorette**, a limestone cave that is unusual for its towering verticality. There are good views over the town from the **Château Comtal**, set upon a rocky outcrop. The château consists of a Neo-Gothic castle dating from 1906, built next to the ruins of a castle dating from 1155 and demolished in the 1740s. The celebrated Trappist beer called Rochefort is made at the monastery at St Rémy 2 km (1 mile) to the north, but the brewery is not open to the public.

⛰ **Grottes de Lorette**
Drève de Lorette. *Tel (084) 212080.* ⬜ Jul–Aug: 11am–5pm daily; Apr–Jun and Sep–Oct: 10:30am–4:30pm Thu–Tue.

🏰 **Château Comtal**
Rue Jacquet. *Tel (084) 214409.* ⬜ late Mar–Oct: 10am–6pm daily. 🎫

Visitors near a bear enclosure in the Réserve d'Animaux Sauvages

EASTERN WALLONIA

*K*nown above all for its slice of the Ardennes, Eastern Wallonia is a dramatically hilly area of farmland and forests, threaded by fast-flowing rivers and dotted with tranquil towns and villages. Comprising the provinces of Liège and Luxembourg, this once remote region now attracts many visitors, who come to walk or cycle through the beautiful landscape or go kayaking on its swift rivers.

Throughout much of its history, Liège traced a path different from that of the rest of Belgium. Ruled by prince-bishops since the 10th century, it was a principality of the Holy Roman Empire, but was fiercely proud of its autonomous status. Its territory stretched at times right across the central band of Belgium to the French border. Liège retained its prince-bishops until they were over-thrown by rebels during the French Revolution in 1789–94. In 1830, it joined Belgium in the struggle for independence. The Belgian industrial revolution also began near Liège, kick-started by the English entrepreneurs William and John Cockerill, who brought the age of steam to Wallonia's textile industry in the 1800s and set up iron mills just outside the city.

Maps have been repeatedly redrawn in the border areas between Belgium and its neighbours. The Province of Luxembourg formerly belonged to the Duchy of Luxembourg, but under the Treaty of London of 1839, the Duchy was split in two. The eastern part became an independent country, the Grand Duchy of Luxembourg, while the western part was incorporated into Belgium. Similarly, having been intermittently in Belgian possession, Eupen and the German-speaking community in the Cantons de l'Est have been reclaimed into the Province of Liège since the end of World War II.

Over the years, the once sparsely populated region of Eastern Wallonia has become popular with holiday-makers and outdoor enthusiasts. In winter, skiers flock to the highest areas of the Ardennes, around Spa and the Haute Fagnes. Several medieval castles, modern battlefields and museums attract summer visitors.

The immaculately maintained and serene Abbaye d'Orval, a functioning Cistercian monastery

◁ Kayakers on the River Semois, meandering through Eastern Wallonia's green landscape

Exploring Eastern Wallonia

The city of Liège, on the broad River Meuse, remains the main urban centre, surrounded by modern enterprises. Vestiges of the more distant industrial past can be seen at the coal mine at Blégny. Durbuy ranks as one of the prettiest towns in Belgium, while the rural traditions of the Ardennes are presented at Fourneau St-Michel's museums. To the east, the Hautes Fagnes, a wild area of moorland, are the highest part of the Ardennes. Many of the towns in the Province of Luxembourg, notably Bastogne, have monuments and museums that recall the devastation at the end of World War II. Further south, the River Semois runs through wooded hills, passing beneath the dramatic medieval castle of Bouillon, and forming some of the most beautiful landscapes in all Belgium.

The eye-catching Renaissance façade of the Château de Jehay

SIGHTS AT A GLANCE

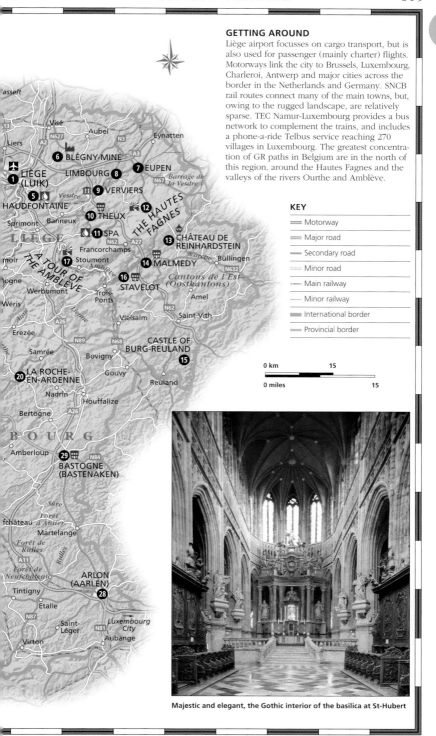

GETTING AROUND

Liège airport focusses on cargo transport, but is also used for passenger (mainly charter) flights. Motorways link the city to Brussels, Luxembourg, Charleroi, Antwerp and major cities across the border in the Netherlands and Germany. SNCB rail routes connect many of the main towns, but, owing to the rugged landscape, are relatively sparse. TEC Namur-Luxembourg provides a bus network to complement the trains, and includes a phone-a-ride Telbus service reaching 270 villages in Luxembourg. The greatest concentration of GR paths in Belgium are in the north of this region, around the Hautes Fagnes and the valleys of the rivers Ourthe and Amblève.

KEY

▬▬	Motorway
▬▬	Major road
▬▬	Secondary road
▬▬	Minor road
▬▬	Main railway
▬▬	Minor railway
▬▬	International border
▬▬	Provincial border

0 km   15

0 miles   15

Majestic and elegant, the Gothic interior of the basilica at St-Hubert

Liège ❶

A busy port-city straddling the River Meuse, Liège has a 20th-century industrial air peppered with medieval and Baroque exuberance. It is known as La Cité Ardent (The Hot-Blooded City), a reference to its fractious history as part of the fiercely independent Principality of Liège. The Coeur Historique (Historic Heart) of the city lies to the north of the River Meuse, around the parallel roads Féronstrée and Rue Hors-Château. Tiny dead-end alleys called Impasses thread north from here, and steps climb up to the old Citadelle, with its panoramic views and interesting hill walks. The Place St-Lambert is the city's main square, overlooked by the Palais des Princes-Évêques. A modern commercial area lies to its southwest, which is served by the Gare du Palais train station.

Display at the Musée des Beaux-Arts de Liège (BAL)

🏛 Place St-Lambert

Junction of Rue Joffre and Rue Léopold. **Palais des Princes-Évêques** ⬜ 10am–6pm Mon–Sun. **Archéoforum Tel** (04) 2509370. ⬜ 9am–5pm Tue–Fri, 10am–5pm Sat & Sun. 📷 ♿ 🚻 www. archeoforumdeliege.be

The vast central square of Liège, Place St-Lambert, is dominated by **Palais des Princes-Évêques**, (Palace of the Prince-Bishops) a mainly 18th-century building in Neo-Classical style. It now houses the Palace of Justice and other government offices, but visitors can explore its 16th-century Renaissance courtyard, which has notable relief sculptures on the columns. The square was the site of the huge Cathédrale St-Lambert, a major pilgrimage centre built in honour of St Lambert of Maastricht, who was murdered here in AD 705. Liégoise revolutionaries destroyed the cathedral between 1794 and 1803, but its foundations, some

Roman remains and a history of the city can be seen at **Archéoforum**, a subterranean museum under the square.

🏛 Le Perron

Hôtel de Ville, Place du Marché 2.

A symbol of civic liberty in the principality, Le Perron is a large stone pillared monument with fountains and balustrades, topped by a single column. The first perrons date from the 11th century, when town guilds bought liberties from their rulers, and laws and judgements were announced in front of them. The association of Le Perron with Liège's independence was so strong that when Charles the Bold suppressed the city's rebellion in 1468, he took the column back to Bruges. It was not restored till his death. The current monument is from the late 17th century, and is crowned by the Three Graces and the symbol of the authority of the

Carving atop Le Perron

prince-bishops, a pine cone and cross. Nearby, the elegant red **Hôtel de Ville** dates from 1718. Its beautiful Italianate entrance hall has a balcony supported by expressive wood sculptures of classical gods.

🏛 Musée de la Vie Wallonne

Cour des Mineurs 1. **Tel** (04) 2379040. ⬜ 9:30am–6pm Tue–Sun. 🎫 1st week in Jan. 📷 ♿ 🚻 www.viewallonne.be

One of the best folklore and local history museums in the country, the Musée de la Vie Wallonne (Museum of Walloon Life) is housed in a former convent, which was recently modernized. The courtyard is in the austere style of late 17th-century Mosan (that is, of the Meuse) architecture, while the interior provides a fascinating tour of daily life in this region until the recent past. The large collection features historic crafts and industries, furniture and domestic wares, religious fetishes and medical equipment, as well as antique posters, old photographs that can be seen through antique stereoscopes, and some splendid oddities such as a real guillotine, which was last used in 1824.

🏛 Musée des Beaux-Arts de Liège (BAL)

Féronstrée 86. **Tel** (04) 2219231. ⬜ 1–6pm Tue–Sat, 11am–6pm Sun. 🎫 1 Jan, 1 May, 1, 2 & 11 Nov, 25 Dec. 📷 ♿ 🚻

Spiralling floors in a 1970s building display the permanent collection of the Musée des Beaux-Arts de Liège, containing more than 3,000 works

The elegant façade behind Hôtel de Ville in Liège's Coeur Historique

of art. It features work by Liège's Renaissance genius Lambert Lombard (1505–66) and by the outstanding 18th-century sculptor Jean Del Cour (1627–1707). There are also paintings by the leading Belgian Neo-Classical artist François-Joseph Navez and a single work by Antoine Wiertz (see p23). Other famed Belgian artists such as Félicien Rops, René Magritte, Alfred Stevens, Henri Evenepoel, Paul Delvaux and Constantin Meunier are also represented.

Also housed within the Musée des Beaux-Arts de Liège is the exquisite collection originally part of the Musée d'Art Moderne et d'Art Contemporain (MAMAC). This collection dates back to the late 19th century and is presented on a rotating basis. It includes

Period furniture at the Museum d'Ansembourg

work by Belgian artists such as Theo van Rysselberghe, Fernand Khnopff, Emile Claus, James Ensor, Constant Permeke and Rik Wouters (see p73), as well as such international luminaries as Pissarro, Signac, Gauguin, Kokoschka, Monet, Picasso and Chagall.

🏛 Musée d'Ansembourg
Féronstrée 114. **Tel** (04) 2219402.
⬜ 1–6pm Tue–Sat, 11am–4:30pm Sun. 🈸 🗖 www.liege.be
Set in the Coeur Historique, this 18th-century banker's mansion contains authentic rooms filled with high-quality 18th-century furniture and furnishings. Many of them were produced locally by the skilled craftsmen of Liège.

🏛 Musée Grand Curtius
Féronstrée 136. **Tel** (04) 221 6817.
⬜ 10am–6pm Wed–Mon. 🈸 🗖 ⚙ 🗖 www.grandcurtiusliege.be
Reopened with great fanfare in 2009, the Musée Grand Curtius brings together the contents of several Liège museums to create one of Europe's best centres for the

decorative arts. The main building is the striped red-brick Maison Curtius, which was the home and headquarters of the wealthy entrepreneur and arms dealer, Jean de Curtius (1551–1628). The current collection of the museum features several archaeological treasures from Ancient Egypt and the Roman and Frankish eras, masterpieces of magnificent medieval Mosan craftsmanship, tapestries, ceramics and many impressive paintings. It also contains world-class collections of fine antique glassware; French clocks dating from 1775 to 1825, in lavish Louis XVI and Empire styles; as well as historic weapons and firearms. It also regularly mounts temporary exhibitions of high international calibre.

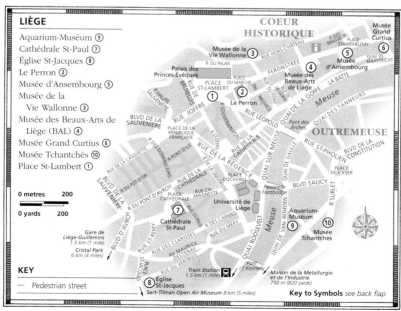

LIÈGE

Aquarium-Muséum ⑨
Cathédrale St-Paul ⑦
Église St-Jacques ⑧
Le Perron ②
Musée d'Ansembourg ⑤
Musée de la Vie Wallonne ③
Musée des Beaux-Arts de Liège (BAL) ④
Musée Grand Curtius ⑥
Musée Tchantchès ⑩
Place St-Lambert ①

0 metres 200
0 yards 200

Gare de Liège-Guillemins 1.5 km (1 mile)
Cristal Park 6 km (4 miles)

KEY

— Pedestrian street

COEUR HISTORIQUE

Musée Grand Curtius

Musée de la Vie Wallonne ③
Palais des Princes-Évêques
Musée d'Ansembourg
Musée des Beaux-Arts de Liège
Le Perron
OUTREMEUSE

Université de Liège
Aquarium-Muséum ⑨
Musée Tchantchès ⑩

Cathédrale St-Paul ⑦

Église St-Jacques ⑧

Train Station 1.5 km (1 mile)
Maison de la Metallurgie et de l'Industrie 750 m (820 yards)
Sart-Tilman Open Air Museum 8 km (5 miles)

Key to Symbols see back flap

Exploring Liège

South of the Coeur Historique, the commercial heart of Liège is clustered around two fine churches, the Cathédrale St-Paul and Église St-Jacques. Further south is the city's prestigous architectural project, the Gare de Liège-Guillemins. Bridges across the River Meuse lead eastwards to the Outremeuse district, which is actually an island formed by a split in the river at its confluence with the River Ourthe. This is an area with its own accent and traditions and was once the haunt of the author Georges Simenon. The annual Festival of the République Libre d'Outremeuse held in August, is an expression of its independent spirit. There are a number of interesting museums on the island and to its east.

Graceful Gothic vaulting spanning the nave of the Cathédrale St-Paul

🔒 Cathédrale St-Paul

Place Cathédrale. **Tel** (04) 2326131.
🕐 8am–5pm daily. 🗷 🔊 🔊
🗎 www.tresordeliege.be
Treasury 🕐 2–5pm Tue–Sun.
This grand though austere church was built over six centuries, beginning in the 13th century. It was promoted to its high status following the destruction of the Cathedral of St Lambert in 1794. Its real attraction is the treasury in the cloister. This contains elaborate pieces of the Mosan school in gold, silver, ivory and enamel. Its supreme treasure is the huge Reliquary of St Lambert – created in about 1512, it is a silver-and-gold bust of the saint and contains his skull. Equally spectacular is the Reliquary of Charles the Bold, which was donated to the city by the duke in 1471. Two statues in gold, silver and enamel depict Charles

holding a relic of St Lambert, with St George standing behind him.

🔒 Église St-Jacques

Place St-Jacques. **Tel** (04) 2221441.
🕐 mid-Jun–mid-Sep: 9am–noon and 2–6pm Mon–Fri, 9am–noon and 2–4:30pm Sat, 9am–noon Sun; mid-Sep–mid-Jun: 9am–noon daily.
The best church in Liège, the Église St-Jacques still has its original Romanesque narthex, or portico, at its western end. The rest of the church is a triumph of Flamboyant Gothic, built between 1514 and 1538, with a wonderful ceiling of interlaced vaulting high above the nave. The 17th-century statues of the saints lining the nave are not of marble, but painted limewood, carved by Liège's most celebrated sculptor Jean Del Cour. The intense clusters of architectural detail, combined with 19th-century Neo-Gothic decoration, create a rich and uplifting impact.

🐟 Aquarium-Muséum

Quai Van-Beneden 22. **Tel** (04) 3665021. 🕐 9am–5pm Mon–Fri, 10:30am–6pm Sat–Sun. 🗷 🔊 🔊
www.aquarium-museum.be
This excellent aquarium has marine and freshwater creatures from all over the world, with 2,500 specimens in 46 tanks. The museum holds a collection of 20,000 stuffed animals and skeletons. Both sets of exhibits belong to the Université de Liège and were founded in the 19th century; hence their location in a 19th-century Neo-Classical building.

🏛 Musée Tchantchès

Rue Surlet 56. **Tel** (04) 3427575.
🕐 Sep–Jun: 2–6pm Tue and Thu; Oct–Apr: 10:30am Sun, 2:30pm Wed (performances). 🗷 www.tchantches.be
The vibrant mascot of Liège, Tchantchès is an irreverent, freedom-loving and courageous lover of *pékèt* (*jenever* gin) who is said to embody the typical characteristics of the Liégeois. He is usually depicted as a puppet dressed in traditional costume. The original legend places him in Charlemagne's era. Born between the paving stones of the Outremeuse in AD 760, he served the emperor valiantly and chaotically, with his large nose as his sole weapon. His love of boasting is habitually crushed by his equally colourful wife, Nanèsse. The small museum devoted to Tchantchès has costumes, puppets and memorabilia, with a theatre for puppet shows.

The puppet theatre and costume display at Musée Tchantchès

🏛 Sart-Tilman Open-air Museum

Université de Liège-Domaine du Sart-Tilman. *Tel* (04) 3662220. 🔄 🅿 🏛 www.museepla.ulg.ac.be

Located on the outskirts of Liège, this museum opened in 1977 as a result of a collaboration between the University of Liège and the Ministry of Culture. A perfect blend of nature and architecture, the museum's permanent collection includes more than 110 pieces. They represent the history of modern open-air sculpture in French-speaking Belgium over the past 40 years. Notable works include *The Mad Virgin* by Rik Wouters, *The Eagle* and *Memory* by André Willequet and *Spring* and *The Prostrate* by George Grard. Charles Leplae's *Young Woman Kneeling* is scheduled to be added to the collection.

The Mad Virgin (1912) by artist Rik Wouters

🚉 Gare de Liège-Guillemins

Place des Guillemins 2. *Tel* (04) 2292610. www.euro-liege-tgv.be

In 1843, a link was forged between Liège and Aachen, in Germany, making the Gare de Liège-Guillemins the world's first international railway station. Opened in 2009, it forms a major hub on the international TGV high-speed train network. To mark the station's significance, Liège commissioned award-winning Spanish-Catalan architect Santiago Calatrava to redesign it as an eye-catching landmark. It is a huge, stunning confection of curving steel and glass, a breathtaking introduction to the city, where visitors immediately get a sense of Liège's newly reinvigorated dynamism.

Historic industrial tools at the Maison de la Métallurgie et de l'Industrie

🏛 Maison de la Métallurgie et de l'Industrie

Boulevard Raymond-Poincaré 17. *Tel* (04) 3426563. ☐ Apr–Oct: 9am–5pm Mon–Fri, 2–6pm Sat–Sun; Nov–Mar: 9am–5pm Mon–Fri. 🔄 🅿 www.mmil.be

Located on the site of an old metalwork factory dating from 1845, this museum is the best place to gauge Liège's history as an industrial centre. Steam power was first used by textile mills in nearby Verviers *(see p222)*, and the iron-and-steel-industry developed at Seraing, outside Liège, where Belgium's first railway engines were built in the 1830s. It displays equipment and machinery spanning four centuries, such as forges, iron-furnaces, steam engines and hydraulic hammers.

🏛 Cristal Park

6 km (4 miles) SW of Liège, Esplanade du Val, Seraing. *Tel* (04) 3303620. ☐ 10am–5pm daily. 🔄 ♿ 🍴 🅿 www.cristalpark.com

The Cristallerie du Val St Lambert, a famous glass-manufacturer established in 1826, has its headquarters at Cristal Park and the Château du Val St-Lambert. There is a glass workshop where visitors can observe glass being blown, cut and engraved, a museum and a showroom displaying glass for sale.

GEORGES SIMENON

Belgium's bestselling author of all time, Georges Simenon (1903–89) was born in Liège, at Rue Léopold 24. When he was two, his family moved across the river to Outremeuse, to a street now renamed Rue Simenon. He trained as a journalist and wrote his first novel in 1919, before heading off to Paris, in 1922, at the age of 19. He went on to write some 350 novels and novellas, translated into many languages; 75 of them feature his most famous creation, the French detective Inspector Maigret, who first appeared in 1931. Maigret reached an even wider audience through the many French feature films based on the novels. After World War II, Simenon lived in the USA and in Switzerland, but Liège continued to occupy his imagination and he set a number of his novels here. The total number of Simenon books printed is thought to be about 550 million. The city's tourist office has a leaflet on the Simenon Trail, which links sites in the Coeur Historique and the Outremeuse districts that are connected to his life.

Georges Simenon, alias The Man with the Pipe

The fawn-and-white patterned Château de Jehay, rising from its moat

Château de Jehay ❷

Rue du Parc 1, Amay; 20 km (12 miles) SW of Liège. **Road Map** E3. **Tel** (085) 824400. ◯ Apr–Nov: 2–6pm Tue–Fri, 11am–6pm Sat, Sun and Easter weekend. ◳ ◔ **www**.chateaujehay.be

With its chequerboard walls of limestone and brown sandstone and its pepperpot towers, this is one of the most delightful castles in Belgium. Although founded in the 11th century, the building dates largely from the 16th century and has a Renaissance feel. In 1698, it was taken over by the van den Steen family. Count Guy van den Steen (1905–99), its most recent owner, was an artist and sculptor who left many works, notably bronze female nudes, in situ when he bequeathed the castle to the Province of Liège. The interior contains tapestries, antique furniture, pottery, silverware, maps and manuscripts, as well as archaeological finds.

Huy ❸

28 km (17 miles) SW of Liège. **Road Map** D3. ⛰ 20,000. ⊞ ⓘ Quai de Namur 1; (085) 212915. **www**.pays-de-huy.be

Founded as a Roman military base, Huy was an important town in the Principality of Liège between AD 985 and 1789. It was renowned in the Middle Ages as a centre for textiles, metal and gold work. Its castle, perched above the town, repeatedly attracted the attention of passing armies,

notably that of Louis XIV of France in the late 17th century; for that reason, the Hutois destroyed it in 1717. Notwithstanding, the Dutch built the massive **Fort de Huy** on the same site in 1818–23. It was used by the Nazis between 1940 and 1944 as a concentration camp – author PG Wodehouse was interned here for a month in 1940. The darker truths of this period are the subject of the **Musée de la Résistance et des Camps de Concentration**. In summer, the fort is accessible by a cable car departing from the left bank of the Meuse.

Huy's main church is the Gothic **Collégiale Notre Dame**, built between 1311 and 1536. Its treasury has fine examples of 12th- to 13th-century Mosan silver and gold work, but the

church is best known for its 15th-century rose window, Li Rondia. This is cited as one of the four wonders of Hutois heritage, the others being Li Tchestia (The Fort), Li Bassinia (the 15th-century fountain in the Grand Place) and Li Pontia (a bridge over the Meuse).

⛨ Fort de Huy
Chaussée Napoléon. **Tel** (085) 212915. ◯ Easter–Sep. ◳

Château de Modave ❹

11 km (7 miles) SE of Huy. **Road Map** E3. **Tel** (085) 411369. ◯ Apr–mid-Nov: 10am–6pm Tue–Sun (Jul–Aug: daily). ◳ ◔ ⓘ **www**.modave-castle.be

Built on a steep rocky spur with views over River Hoyaux, Château de Modave owes its appearance mainly to its over-haul in Flemish Renaissance style by the count of Marchin in 1652–73. The well-furnished rooms are decorated with tapestries, panelling and impressive polychrome stuccowork, and 17th–18th century furniture.

The gardens and fountains of Versailles were fed by a massive hydraulic waterwheel designed by Renkin Sualem (1645–1708), royal engineer to Louis XIV: the 1667 proto-type for it was built at Modave, as an exhibition here explains.

Magnificently furnished interior of the Château de Modave

River Vesdre passing under a flag-decked bridge at Chaudfontaine

Chaudfontaine ❺

8 km (5 miles) SE of Liège. **Road Map** E3. 🏙 *21,000.* 🚃 🛈 *Ave des Thermes 78 bis; (04) 3615630.* **www**.chaudfontaine.be

Sitting prettily on a curve of River Vesdre, Chaudfontaine is the site of the only natural hot springs in Belgium. It first developed its therapeutic activities in 1676, when a local landowner installed rudimentary baths and proclaimed the water's medical benefits. Today, the main treatment centre is the luxurious **Château des Thermes**, a restored 18th-century residence set in a wooded park. At the interactive **Source O Rama** museum, multimedia techniques provide an educational exploration of cold-water and thermal spas.

The tourist train at Blegny's Musée de la Mine

it have been meticulously kept in working order and opened to the public. After an introductory film, visitors don helmets and jackets to go down a shaft in a lift cage. This reaches a depth of 60 m (197 ft) – a mere one-tenth of the full depth of this mine. Guided by a former miner, the tour offers a taste of the noise, danger and harsh working conditions that the so-called *gueules noires* (black faces) had to endure at the coal-face. The **Musée de la Mine** provides more of this history. For a rural contrast, a little tourist road train takes visitors on a 50-minute jaunt through the local orchards and meadows.

🚗 **Château des Thermes**
Rue Hauster 9. **Tel** (04) 3678067.
⏰ *daily.* 🏛 🔥 🛈 🍴
www.chateaudesthermes.be

🏛 **Source O Rama**
Avenue des Thermes 78(b).
Tel (04) 3642020. ⏰ *Sun–Fri; school hols.* 🏛 🔥 🛈
www.sourceorama.com

Blegny-Mine ❻

Rue Lambert Marlet 23, Blegny; 11 km (7 miles) NE of Liège.
Road Map E3. **Tel** (04) 3874333.
🚃 ⏰ *mid-Feb–Easter & mid-Dec: weekends and public hols; Easter– early Sep: daily.* 🏛 🎫 🛈 🔥 🍴
🚗 🛈 **www**.blegnymine.be

The last coal mine in the Province of Liège was forced to close in 1980, but parts of

Eupen ❼

21 km (13 miles) E of Blegny.
Road Map F2. **Tel** (03) 84635082.
🏙 *19,000.* 🚃 🚌 🛈 *Marktplatz 7; (087) 553450.* **www**.eupen-info.be

The capital of Belgium's German-speaking community, Eupen is part of the borderland Cantons de l'Est given to Belgium by the Treaty of Versailles after World War I. From the town's pleasant streets, a massive carnival erupts to mark the start of Lent each year *(see p35).* The **Stadtmuseum** (Town Museum), set in a late 17th-century cloth-merchant's house, tells Eupen's story, alongside local historic craft products such as cloth, pottery, gold work and furniture. On the northern edge of town, the chocolate manufacturers Jacques & Callebaut have a **Musée du Chocolat**, presenting the history of chocolate and how it is made.

🏛 **Stadtmuseum**
Gospert 52. **Tel** (087) 740005.
⏰ *9:30am–noon and 1–4pm Tue– Fri, 1–5pm Sat, 10am–noon and 2–5pm Sun.* ⏰ *during Carnival.* 🏛
www.eupener-stadtmuseum.org

🏛 **Musée du Chocolat**
Rue de l'Industrie 16. **Tel** (087) 592967. ⏰ *9am–5pm Mon–Fri.*
⏰ *during Carnival.* 🏛 🛈
www.chocojacques.be

BELGIAN SPAS

Chaudfontaine is one of two main spa towns of Belgium – the other one being Spa itself *(see p222).* At Chaudfontaine, the water is naturally hot, while at Spa it is cold. It was Spa, however, that first attracted visitors convinced of the medical benefits of mineral-rich waters. They began arriving in 1550 and soon established the town as a destination for nobility and royalty. Waters of both towns are still believed to help sufferers of various maladies, including rheumatism, gout and heart and circulatory disorders. Until the 1860s, visitors tended to drink the waters. Today, the centres offer a full range of treatments, from bathing in pools, saunas and Jacuzzis, to steam rooms, mud baths and beauty therapies. Both towns also produce bottled mineral water bearing their name.

Façade of the Pouhon Pierre-le-Grand spring building at Spa

Limbourg ⑧

27 km (17 miles) E of Liège.
Road Map E2. 🚶 6,000. 🚌 🚐

Set on a rocky spur above a hairpin bend in the River Vesdre, Limbourg developed after 1033 as the fortified capital of the Duchy of Limburg, a historic region between the Meuse and the city of Aachen. As the vestiges of the city walls testify, Limbourg was a military stronghold, besieged on many occasions – notably in 1578 by the Spanish, in 1675 by French king Louis XIV and in 1715 by the Austrians. Today, the upper town – where little has changed since the 18th century – is picturesque, with tree-lined cobbled streets and window boxes full of flowers.

Verviers ⑨

20 km (12 miles) E of Liège.
Road Map E3. 🚶 53,000. 🚌 🚐
🚹 Maison du Tourisme du Pays de Vesdre, Rue Jules Cerexhe 86; (087) 307926. www.verviers.be

Straddling the River Vesdre, which was vital to the textile industry, Verviers is adorned with numerous fountains and water features, and calls itself the Walloon Capital of Water. Belgium's industrial revolution began here in 1799, when the English entrepreneur William Cockerill (1859–1932) established steam-powered woollen textile mills. This history is remembered in the exhibits of **Centre Touristique de la Laine et de la Mode**, set out in a restored Neo-Classical wool factory. The **Musée des Beaux-Arts et de la Céramique** has a major collection of porcelain and art. There is also

the **Musée d'Archéologie et du Folklore**, housed in an 18th-century townhouse, with antique furnishings and a lace collection.

🏛 **Centre Touristique de la Laine et de la Mode**
Rue de la Chapelle 24-30. **Tel** (087) 307920. ◯ 10am–5pm Tue–Sun. 🖼 🏠 🔊 www.aqualaine.be

🏛 **Musée des Beaux-Arts et de la Céramique**
Rue Renier 17. **Tel** (087) 331695. ◯ 2–5pm Mon, Wed and Sat, 3–6pm Sun. 🖼 www.verviers.be

Theux ⑩

20 km (12 miles) SE of Liège. **Road Map** E3. 🚶 11,000. 🚌 🚐 www.theux.be

The attractive town of Theux developed in the shadow of the medieval **Château de Franchimont**. The town was sacked by Charles the Bold, Duke of Burgundy, in 1468, during his conquest of Liège. The castle was reinforced in the 16th century by Erard de la Marck, Prince-Bishop of Liège, but fell into ruin after the 1780s. Theux is also noted for its remarkable **Église Sts-Hermès-et-Alexandre**. A hall-church built from the 9th-century onwards in Gothic and Romanesque styles, its naves have rare, painted, flat ceilings.

Environs
Banneux, 6 km (4 miles) to the west, is a major pilgrimage site, where in 1933 apparitions of the Virgin of the Poor revealed a healing spring to 11-year-old Mariette Beco.

🏛 **Château de Franchimont**
Allée du Château. **Tel** (087) 530489. ◯ Apr–Oct. 🖼 🏠 🖥 www.chateau-franchimont.be

One of many picturesque fountains in the original spa town

Spa ⑪

28 km (17 miles) SE of Liège.
Road Map E3. 🚶 10,500. 🚌 🚐
🚹 Place Royale 41; (087) 795353. www.spa-info.be

The heyday of Spa was in the 18th and 19th centuries, when the well-to-do came here to take the waters, turning the town's name into a generic term for water therapy. Spa retains a leisurely grandeur, with its Neo-Classical **Hôtel de Ville**, the original, now disused baths and the casino. Six springs can still be visited, including the **Pouhon Pierre-le-Grand**, housed in an elegant stone pavilion built in 1880. The modern **Thermes de Spa** (Baths) are at the top of a hill, accessed by cable railway. Spa also has three intriguing museums. Sharing the same location at the **Villa Royale** are Musée de la Ville d'Eaux and Musée Spadois du Cheval: the former has a collection of antique, intricately painted wooden souvenirs (jolités), while the latter is devoted to horse-racing and carriages. The enterprising **Musée de la Lessive** takes a historical look at laundry.

🚿 **Thermes de Spa**
Colline d'Annette et Lubin. **Tel** (087) 772560. ◯ daily. 🖼 🔊 www.thermesdespa.be

🏛 **Villa Royale**
Avenue Reine Astrid 77b. **Tel** (087) 774486. ◯ Sat–Mon. ◯ Dec–Feb. 🖼 🔊

🏛 **Musée de la Lessive**
Waux-Hall, R de la Géronstière 10. **Tel** (087) 771418. ◯ Jul–Aug: 2–6pm daily; Apr–Mar: weekends. 🖼

Moated entrance to the atmospheric ruins of Château de Franchimont

For hotels and restaurants in this region see pp271–3 and pp297–9

The Hautes Fagnes ⓬

A large area of raised, boggy moorland, the Hautes Fagnes (High Fens) extends over much of the eastern part of the Province of Liège. The region straddles the border to form part of a German-Belgian Nature Reserve, and includes some of the German-speaking Belgian areas of the Cantons de l'Est. The centre, around the Signal de Botrange, is a remote and wild bog, admired for its untamed beauty on fine days, but also famous for its desolate, foggy gloom when the weather closes in. At an altitude of 694 m (2,277 ft), this is also the highest point of Belgium.

Bogs of the High Fens
The deep peat bogs, created over 7,500 years, sustain a rich diversity of plant life, including heather and purple moor grass. It is also a haven for rare wild cats and birds.

Trails and Boardwalks
The treacherous bogs have claimed many lives in the past. Today, visitors can admire this unique natural habitat from the safety of walkways.

Barrage de la Gileppe, a dam built between 1867 and 1875, has created a lake surrounded by woodland.

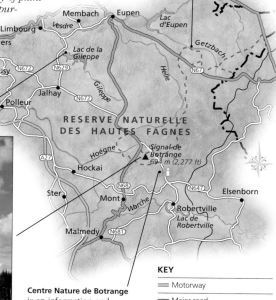

★ Signal de Botrange
A tower, attached to a restaurant, takes visitors 28 m (92 ft) above the highest point in Belgium, and offers views out over the plateau.

Centre Nature de Botrange is an information and exhibition centre. It is also the starting point for guided walks and cross-country skiing.

0 km 5

0 miles 5

KEY

▬▬	Motorway
▬▬	Major road
▬▬	Minor road
—	Railway
– –	Trail
▬•▬	International border
🛈	Information centre

Racing exhibits at the Musée du Circuit de Spa-Francorchamps, Stavelot

Château de Reinhardstein **⑬**

Chemin du Cheneux 50, Ovitat;
17 km (15 miles) SE of Spa. **Road
Map** F3. **Tel** (080) 446868. ⬤ Mon,
Wed, Fri. 📷 📷 11:15am & 2:30pm
daily, 2:30pm (public holidays).
www.reinhardstein.net/blog

The 14th-century fortress
of Reinhardstein was built
by the lords of Waimes and
owned by their descendants,
the German Metternich family.
The château was attacked by
the French Revolutionary Army
in 1795, after which it fell into
ruin. In 1969, historian and
collector Jean Overloop rebuilt
it. Today, tours take visitors
through stone-walled rooms
containing furniture, tapestries,
sculpture and armour.

Malmedy **⑭**

13 km (8 miles) SE of Spa.
Road Map F3. 🎿 11,830. 🚉 🚌
ℹ Place Albert 1er, 29a; (080)
330250. **www**.malmedy.be

The mainly French-speaking
town of Malmedy is one of the
main towns of the Cantons de
l'Est (Oostkantons in Dutch) –
a borderland district that has
been swapped back and forth
with Germany. Until its conquest in 1795 by the French
Revolutionary Army, Malmedy
was ruled by prince-abbots as
part of the twin Principality of
Stavelot-Malmedy, which was
based on two 7th-century
abbeys. The town became rich
through production of cloth,
gunpowder, leather-tanning
and paper. Today, it is a base
for walkers heading to Haute

Fagnes. Its main attraction is
the 18th-century **Cathédrale
Sts-Pierre-Paul-et-Quirinn**, set
in the main square, Place
Albert 1er. Malmedy is most
famous for its 4-day pre-Lenten
carnival, Cwarmê (see p35).

Castle of Burg-Reuland **⑮**

38 km (24 miles) SE of Malmedy.
Road Map F3. **Tel** (080) 420046.
🚌 ◯ 9am–5pm daily. 🏠
www.burg-reuland.be

Located in the south of the
Cantons de l'Est, the pretty
slate-roofed village of Burg-
Reuland is home to one of the
most impressive sets of castle
ruins in Belgium. The Romans
built a fort on this site and the
Franks made it a royal castle:
Charlemagne is said to have
stayed in it. However, the ruins
seen today date from the 10th
to 16th centuries. The round
corner tower and high curtain
walls were built by the counts
of Reuland, vassals of the Holy
Roman Empire. Decline set in

after the castle was sacked by
Louis XIV of France in 1689;
it was dismantled after 1804.

Stavelot **⑯**

10 km (6 miles) SW of Malmedy.
Road Map E3. 🎿 6,670. 🚉 🚌
ℹ Abbaye de Stavelot, Place St
Remacle 32; (080) 862706.
www.stavelot.be

Founded in the 7th century as
an abbey, Stavelot is an attractive town whose old centre is
a cluster of little streets and
squares lined with 17th-century
half-timbered houses. Here,
the **Église St-Sébastien** houses
a masterpiece of Mosan art –
the 13th-century reliquary of
St Remaclus, founder of the
abbey at Stavelot. The striking
deep-red **Abbaye de Stavelot**
dates from the 18th century;
refurbished in 2002, it now
contains three museums. The
**Musée du Circuit de Spa-
Francorchamps**, with its collection of cars, motorcycles
and memorabilia, documents
the history (from 1896) of the
Grand Prix motor-racing track
at Francorchamps, which
lies about 10 km (6 miles) to
the north. There is also the
Musée de la Principauté de
Stavelot-Malmèdy and the
Musée Guillaume Apollinaire,
dedicated to this French poet
(1880–1918) who wrote
eloquently about the Ardennes.
Stavelot is also known for its
carnival, the Laetare (see p35).

🏛 **Abbaye de Stavelot**
◯ 10am–6pm daily. ⬤ Sun and
Mon of carnival weekend. 📷 📷
📷 **www**.abbayedestavelot.be

The village of Burg-Reuland, dominated by the ruins of its lofty castle

A Tour of the Amblève ⑰

One of the key rivers of the Ardennes, the Amblève carves a picturesque path through hills and forests. Walks here lead off along the river's edge or to the woodland waterfalls of the tributaries. Quarries and a railway line are seen early on, but after Aywaille, a busy centre for summer visitors, the landscape becomes wilder and the road hugs the river, giving access to picnic sites on the banks. It then rises to villages such as Stoumont, which offer fine views over the valley. The famous waterfalls at Coo are an impressive note on which to end the drive.

TIPS FOR DRIVERS

Starting point: *Comblain-au-Pont – exit to Sprimont from A26.*
Tour length: *55 km (35 miles).*
Duration: *Allow half a day.*
Driving conditions: *The roads are narrow and busy, but good.*
Where to eat: *Restaurants can be found at Comblain-au-Pont, Aywaille and Stoumont.*
Visitors' information:
Remouchamps: (04) 3843544,
www.ourthe-ambleve.be

Comblain-au-Pont ①
South of the Amblève's scenic confluence with the River Ourthe are strange sculptures formed by hard dolomitic rock that has resisted erosion. Equally sculptural stalactites can be seen in Comblain's Découvertes Mystères limestone caves.

Château d'Amblève ②
A walk across the river from Aywaille ends in a ruined castle linked to the steed Bayard legend *(see p139).*

0 km 3
0 miles 3

Sougné-Remouchamps ③
Visits to the Grottes de Remouchamps include a subterranean boat trip.

Ninglinspo ④
A signposted walk through woodland leads along a stream called Ninglinspo to La Chaudière (The Cauldron), where the stream falls into a basin.

Fonds de Quarreux ⑤
Large quartzite rocks, formed 400 million years ago, lie scattered across the river, which ripples, gurgles and sparkles in the current. Signposts lead to a number of riverside paths.

KEY

▬▬ Tour route
▬▬ Motorway
═══ Other road
──── Railway
🛈 Information centre

Coo ⑥
Belgium's most impressive cascade is a pair of falls roaring down a rocky drop of 15 m (50 ft). Coo is also a resort with the children's theme park, Plopsa Coo *(see p317).*

Durbuy, sheltered by the forested Ardennes, often cited as one of the prettiest towns in Belgium

Durbuy

17 km (11 miles) S of Modave. **Road
Map** E3. 10,700. **Place
aux Foires 25; (086) 212428.**
www.durbuyinfo.be

Established by charter in 1331,
Durbuy is built on an intimate
scale and calls itself the world's
smallest town. Its cobbled
streets of stone houses wind
down to a bridge over the
River Ourthe under the gaze
of an 18th-century château.
The main visitor attraction,
the **Parc des Topiaires**, takes
the art of topiary to surreal
extremes: the box-tree hedges
here have been sculpted into
250 subjects including croco-
diles, birds, a mermaid, and
even the Manneken-Pis.

Environs
Near **Wéris**, 7 km (4 miles) to
the southeast, there are two
dolmens and many menhirs
and megaliths dating back to
the Neolithic era. There is
also a Musée des Mégalithes.

🌿 **Parc des Topiaires**
Rue Haie Himbe 1. **Tel** (086)
219075. Feb–Dec: daily.
www.topiairesdurbuy.be

Grottes de
Hotton

11 km (7 miles) S of Durbuy.
Road Map E3. **Tel** (084) 466046.
Apr–Oct: daily; Nov–Mar:
Sat and Sun.
www. grottesdehotton.be

Located on the River Ourthe,
Hotton has some of the area's
most impressive limestone

caves. Over the millennia, the
river has carved out chasms,
which are draped with stalactites, stalagmites and sculptural
concretions and mineral formations of the utmost delicacy.
Staircases and walkways lead
down through a series of illuminated chambers to Belgium's
largest cave gallery – 200 m
(656 ft) long and 35 m (115 ft)
high. The gardens at the head
of the cave have a path leading to fine views of the area.

La Roche-en-
Ardenne

16 km (10 miles) SE of Hotton. **Road
Map** E3. 4,300. **Place du
Marché 15; (084) 367736.**
www.la-roche-tourisme.com

Set in a deep valley on a loop
of the River Ourthe, La Roche
provides an attractive base for
exploring the Ardennes. The
grim ruins of the imposing
11th–12th-century **Château
Féodal** (Feudal Castle) overlook the town from a rocky

Arrays of stalactites on the ceiling
of Grottes de Hotton

spur known as the Deister.
Destroyed by the Austrians
in the late 18th century, the
château provides a dramatic
backdrop when illuminated
at night during the summer
months. The pottery museum,
Les Grès de la Roche, explains
the history and practicalities
of making traditional blue
stoneware, called grès. It
also covers local culinary
traditions, most notably the
manner of curing hams to
make jambon d'Ardennes.
La Roche was damaged by
bombing during the Battle of
the Bulge (see p231). This
action is remembered in a
collection of uniforms, weapons, vehicles, photographs
and maps in the **Musée de la
Bataille des Ardennes**.

Environs
River Ourthe winds through
one of the most beautiful
valleys in the Ardennes. The
most scenic stretch runs from
Houffalize, 25 km (16 miles)
east of La Roche, to Liège,
95 km (59 miles) north of La
Roche. Kayaking is a popular
pursuit here and equipment
can be rented at La Roche
and other locations.

🏰 **Château Féodal**
Rue du Vieux Château 4. **Tel** (084)
411342. daily (Nov–Mar).
www.chateaudelaroche.be

🏛 **Les Grès de la Roche**
Rue Rompré 28. **Tel** (084) 411878.
Apr–Oct: Tue–Sun; Nov–Mar:
Mon–Fri. **www**.gdlr.be

🏛 **Musée de la Bataille
des Ardennes**
Rue Chamont 5. **Tel** (084) 411725.
Apr–Dec: Wed–Sun; Jan–Mar:
Sat & Sun. **www**.batarden.be

St-Hubert ㉑

25 km (16 miles) SW of La Roche.
Road Map E4. 🚶 5,700. 🚌
ℹ️ *Rue Saint-Gilles 12; (061) 613010.*
📅 *Journées Internationales de la Chasse et de la Nature (1st weekend of Sep).* www.saint-hubert-tourisme.be

Greatly venerated during the Middle Ages, St Hubert was an 8th-century bishop of Tongeren-Maastricht and successor to St Lambert *(see p216)*. According to legend, he was converted to Christianity as a young man after encountering a stag with the image of a crucifix between its antlers. Upon his death, St Hubert became the patron saint of hunting and the stag became his emblem. In the 9th century, the saint's relics were brought to a Benedictine abbey in the present-day Belgian town of St-Hubert. The presence of the relics made it a pilgrimage site for hunters, and the monks here are said to have developed the breed of bloodhound called the St Hubert Hound.

The abbey was rebuilt in 1729, but suppressed in the 1790s. However, its large church, the **Basilique St-Hubert**, remains the centrepiece of the town. Its Baroque façade (1700–02), crested by twin domes, fronts an impressive late-Gothic interior (1526–64). This is a focal point of Journées Internationales de la Chasse et de la Nature, the festival of hunting, which also holds a costumed procession.

The **Centre Pierre-Joseph Redouté** presents a collection of exquisite watercolours by the celebrated flower artist Pierre-Joseph Redouté (1759–1840). The artist was born in St-Hubert but moved to Paris, where he was appointed to the court of Marie-Antoinette.

🕎 **Basilique St-Hubert**
Place de l'Abbaye. *Tel (061) 612388.* ⏰ *daily.* ♿

🏛 **Centre Pierre-Joseph Redouté**
Rue Redouté 11. *Tel (061) 611872.* ⏰ *Jul–Sep: 2–6pm daily.*

The mighty organ of the 16th-century Basilique St-Hubert

Fourneau St-Michel ㉒

8 km (5 miles) N of St-Hubert.
Road Map E4. *Tel (084) 210890.*
🚌 ⏰ *Jul–Aug: daily; late Feb–Jun and Sep–mid-Nov: Tue–Sun.* 📷 🍴
www.fourneausaintmichel.be

The word *fourneau* literally means furnace, and the aptly named community of Fourneau St-Michel was involved in a flourishing iron-smelting business in the 17th and 18th centuries. Scattered in a beautiful forest clearing here are two rewarding museums revealing local life in the past. A rare surviving high furnace from the 18th century and forge workshops, set up by the last abbot of St-Hubert, form the crux of the **Musée du Fer** (Museum of Iron). Close by is the **Musée de la Vie**

Industrial relic at Fourneau St-Michel

Rurale en Wallonie (Museum of Rural Life in Wallonia), also called the Musée Plein Air (Open Air Museum). This has some 50 rural buildings from the 19th century, rescued from all over Wallonia and arranged as nine hamlets. Many of them have been fully restored, with interiors containing authentic furniture and domestic items. A team of animators on site demonstrate rural activities and crafts.

Redu ㉓

17 km (11 miles) W of St-Hubert.
Road Map E4. 🚶 500. 🚌
ℹ️ *Maison du Tourisme du Pays de la Haute-Lesse, Place de l'Esro 63, Redu-Libin.* www.haute-lesse-tourisme.be

Often nicknamed Belgium's Hay-on-Wye, in reference to the town of books that developed in Wales in the 1960s, Redu is above all a book village. It has some 20 book-shops selling new and used books, as well as workshops for papermaking, printing, engraving and other crafts. This tradition was founded in 1984 by Liège-born writer Noël Anselot (b.1924), who was directly inspired by the example of Hay-on-Wye.

Environs
The **Euro Space Center** at Transinne, 6 km (4 miles) to the east, is a family-oriented museum on space exploration.

🏛 **Euro Space Center**
Rue Devant les Hêtres 1, Transinne. *Tel (061) 656465.* ⏰ *mid-Mar–mid-Nov: daily; mid-Nov–mid-Mar: Sat, Sun; Jul & Aug: daily.* 📷 🎥 🍴 🅿
www.eurospacecenter.be

Full-size replica of a shuttle at the Euro Space Center, Transinne

A Drive Along the Semois ㉔

The River Semois flows westwards across the southern parts of the Belgian provinces of Luxembourg and Namur into France, where it joins the River Meuse. Along much of its course, the river cuts an exaggeratedly serpentine path through a dramatic landscape of steep and forested hills. The roads that wind through these valleys have plenty of stop-off points from which to admire the breathtaking scenery and panoramic views.

Jambon de la Semois ①
Signposted from the road, a high viewpoint offers the first glimpse of the river below.

Membre ②
This small resort village is also a gateway to the Parc Naturel de Bohan-Membre.

Vresse-sur-Semois ③
Located close by the river, this attractive village is the main visitors' centre for the Namur sector of the Semois valley.

Rochehaut ④
As its name suggests, Rochehaut (High Rock) provides a fine vantage point. Nestling below, in a curve of the river, is the pretty hamlet of Frahan.

Poupehan ⑤
Marked paths lead up to various spectacular viewpoints, such as the Chaire à Prêcher (Pulpit), where, in medieval times, Peter the Hermit is believed to have called the populace to participate in the First Crusade.

Corbion ⑥
Like many of the villages, Corbion retains the quiet charm of its agricultural past. The buildings are universally roofed in locally-mined slate.

FRANCE

Bouillon ⑦
The largest town at the heart of the valley is dominated by a medieval fortress *(see pp232–3)*.

Tombeau du Géant ⑧
A detour through upland pasture and woodlands leads to a famous viewpoint, just past Botassart. Below, the river sweeps around a forested hillock known as the Giant's Tomb *(see pp174–5)*.

Dohan ⑨

The road crosses the river at Dohan, then provides a series of notable viewpoints. The first of these is near the riverside rocks of the Rocher de Dampiry. Beyond it, the next point lies where the river performs a series of hairpin bends.

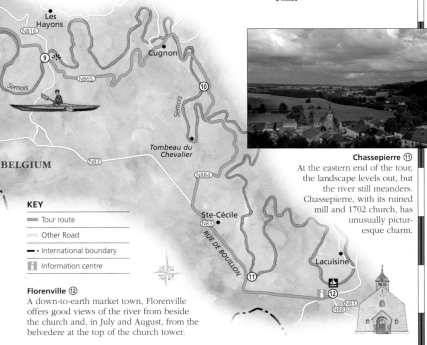

Herbeumont ⑩

A 13th-century castle here commanded a vital strategic position, with extensive views along the river, until it was wrecked by the French in 1657. The castle is under restoration.

TIPS FOR DRIVERS

Starting point: Jambon de la Semois on the N935 is accessed from the A4-E411 Namur–Arlon motorway: from Exit 23 take the N835, then the N952.

Length: About 80 km (50 miles).

Duration of drive: Allow at least a whole day; better to break the journey into two days.

Driving conditions: Roads are small and winding, but wide enough for comfortable driving.

Where to stay and eat: There are restaurants, cafés and accommodation in villages and towns all along the way. Bouillon is the main centre. Many of the viewpoints have picnic tables.

Visitors' Information: Vresse-sur-Semois: Rue Albert Raty 83, (061) 292827; Bouillon: Quai des Saulx 12 and at the château-fort, (061) 466257, www.bouillon-initiative.be; Florenville: Place Albert 1er, (061) 311229, www.semois-tourisme.be

0 km   3

0 miles   3

KEY

▬▬ Tour route

══ Other Road

━•━ International boundary

ℹ️ Information centre

Chassepierre ⑪

At the eastern end of the tour, the landscape levels out, but the river still meanders. Chassepierre, with its ruined mill and 1702 church, has unusually picturesque charm.

Florenville ⑫

A down-to-earth market town, Florenville offers good views of the river from beside the church and, in July and August, from the belvedere at the top of the church tower.

Courtyard of the renowned Cistercian Abbaye d'Orval

Bouillon 🄬

34 km (21 miles) SW of St-Hubert. **Road Map** D4. 🏠 *5,500.* 🚌 🛈 *Quai des Saulx 12; (061) 465211.* **www**.bouillon-initiative.be

The elegant town of Bouillon straddles the River Semois beside the rock on which its famous fortress stands. The town offers activities such as walking, horse riding and kayaking as well as mountain bike circuits. On the castle hill, the **Musée Ducal** has various mementos relating to the history of the castle and town. Housed in a 17th-century convent on the banks of the river, the **Archéoscope Godefroid de Bouillon** presents an innovative multimedia show on this leading knight of the First Crusade.

Environs
At Bertrix, 25 km (15 miles) to the northeast, there is a remarkable underground slate mine and museum called **Au Cœur de l'Ardoise**.

🏛 **Musée Ducal**
Rue du Petit 1–3. **Tel** *(061) 464189.* 🕐 *Easter–Nov.* 🚫 **www**. museeducal.be

🏛 **Archéoscope Godefroid de Bouillon**
Quai des Saulx 14. **Tel** *(061) 468303.* 🕐 *Feb–Dec.* 🚫 🖥 🚫 **www**.archeoscopebouillon.be

🏛 **Au Cœur de l'Ardoise**
Domaine de la Morépire, 1 Rue du Babinay, Bertrix. **Tel** *(061) 414521.* 🕐 *Apr–Nov: Tue–Sun.* 🚫 🚫 **www**.aucoeurdelardoise.be

Château-Fort de Bouillon 🄬

See pp232–3.

Abbaye d'Orval 🄬

Villers-devant-Orval; 25 km (15 miles) SE of Bouillon. **Road Map** E5. **Tel** *(061) 311060.* 🕐 *Mar–May and Oct: 9:30am–6pm daily; Jun–Sep: 9am–6:30pm; Nov–Feb: 10:30am–5:30pm.* 🚫 🚫 🚫 **www**.orval.be

Set in a forested area of the Gaume region, the Cistercian abbey of Notre-Dame d'Orval was one of Europe's most powerful until its destruction in the religious wars and again during the French Revolution in 1793. The abbey became famous for its beer, whose label shows a fish with a ring in its mouth. This recalls the legend of abbey's foundation by Countess Mathilda of Tuscany, in thanksgiving after a trout miraculously recovered her wedding ring from a stream. Today, the public can visit the Romanesque-Gothic ruins of the old 12th- and 13th-century monastery church as well as a museum and a herb garden.

Arlon 🄬

57 km (35 miles) E of Bouillon. **Road Map** E4. 🏠 *26,000.* 🚇 🚌 🛈 *Rue des Faubourgs 2; (063) 216360.* **www**.ot-arlon.be

The capital of the Belgian Province of Luxembourg, Arlon developed as a trading centre called Orolaunum in Roman times, and claims to be one of the oldest towns in Belgium. Many Roman remains have survived, including the **Tour Romaine**, a tower in the Grand Place, and vestiges of

4th-century Roman baths. The town's **Musée Archéologique** contains artifacts from Gallo-Roman times (notably a collection of sculptures) and jewellery and pottery from the Merovingian period. The adjacent **Musée Gaspar** celebrates the Gaspar family of Arlon, including the animal sculptor Jean-Marie Gaspar (1861–1931). Its masterpiece is a 16th-century Fisenne retable.

Arlon's Knipchen hill, site of the Église St-Donat, has views that extend over Belgium, Luxembourg and France.

🏛 **Musée Archéologique**
R des Martyrs 13. **Tel** *(063) 212849.* 🕐 *9:30am–noon and 1:30–5:30pm Tue–Sat, 1:30–5:30pm Sun.* 🚫 🚫 🚫 **www**.ial.be.

🏛 **Musée Gaspar**
R des Martyrs 16. **Tel** *(063) 600654.* 🕐 *9am–noon Tue–Sat, 1:30–5:30pm Sun.* 🚫 **www**.ial.be.

Bastogne 🄬

40 km (25 miles) N of Arlon. **Road Map** E4. 🏠 *14,000.* 🚌 🛈 *Place McAuliffe 60; (061) 212711.* **www**. paysdebastogne.be

Best known as a focal point of the Battle of the Bulge, Bastogne was also a thriving stronghold in medieval times, as witnessed by the Porte de Trèves, the remnant of the 14th-century city walls. Close by, the Église St-Pierre has a 12th-century tower and a 15th-century Flamboyant-Gothic nave with a painted vaulting dating from

Battle monument at Bastogne

1536. The Battle of the Bulge is remembered primarily on Mardasson Hill, 2 km (1 mile) to the northeast of Bastogne, where a star-shaped American Memorial lists the various American units that fought in the battle, and offers extensive panoramic views from the parapet. The site also includes the **Bastogne Historical Center**, a comprehensive museum of the battle.

🏛 **Bastogne Historical Center**
Colline de Mardasson. **Tel** *(061) 211413.* 🕐 *Mar–Dec.* 🚫 🚫 🚫 **www**.bastognehistoricalcenter.be

The Ardennes Offensive

Also known as the Battle of the Bulge, the Ardennes Offensive was a surprise counterattack mounted by the German army during the bitterly cold winter of 1944–5. Allied forces advancing towards Germany had liberated Belgium that September. Beginning on 16 December 1944, German tank divisions led by General von Rundstedt, attempted to punch through the Allied lines across the snow-covered Ardennes in an attempt to reach the Meuse and then advance north to retake Brussels and Antwerp. They managed to push back US and British forces, creating a frontline in the shape of a bulge.

LOCATOR MAP

▢ Battle of the Bulge

COUNTER-OFFENSIVE OF JANUARY 1945

When called upon to surrender in Bastogne, US Brigadier-General McAuliffe defiantly responded, "Nuts!" General Patton's army then rescued Bastogne, and the Allied forces eventually pushed the Germans back by the end of January 1945. It had been the largest land battle of World War II, involving more than a million men and 1,000 tanks.

The battlefront of 16 December, from which the German offensive began, is also called the Siegfried Line!

Dinant and the River Meuse *marked the most westerly point of the German advance. This is commemorated by a monument at the Rocher Bayard, just south of the town.*

0 km   5
0 miles   5

At La Roche-en-Ardenne, *the Musée de la Bataille des Ardennes underlines the human dimension with figures of uniformed combatants from both sides.*

KEY

▢ German army

▢ British army

▢ US army

— Battlefront 16 Dec 1944

– – Battlefront 25 Dec 1944

–·– International border

The Bastogne Historical Center *was inaugurated win 1976. It is built in a star shape, like the American Memorial close by.*

Château-Fort de Bouillon ㉖

Standing on a rocky plinth overlooking a loop in the River Semois, the Château-Fort de Bouillon is of ancient origin and is first mentioned in AD 988. The fortress was a vital stronghold in the borderlands with France, on a route often taken by invaders. It was home of the pious knight Godefroid until he left for the First Crusade (1096–99). Bouillon was still an important bastion in 1676, when it fell into the hands of Louis XIV of France, who commissioned upgrades from his architect Vauban. The castle survived its 15th siege in 1815 and finally ceased its military role in 1853. It is now for the most part unfurnished, but provides a fascinating insight into castle architecture and magnificent views of the valley.

★ **Tour d'Autriche**
Winding stairs lead to the top of the Austria Tower, a key vantage point. Built in 1551, it was named after George of Austria, one of the prince-bishops of Liège.

The clocktower was redesigned by Vauban.

Gun batteries

Vauban's three-slit loopholes gave defenders a broad field of fire.

Bell Tower
Housed in a projecting machicolation, the bell was used to ring out watch-changes and orders. Cast in silver alloy in 1563, it originally came from a chapel and sounds for nearly one minute when struck.

★ **Cour d'Honneur**
The fort's main quadrangle once served as a parade ground. Today, it features owls, eagles and vultures and is also the setting for a spectacular falconry show.

STAR FEATURES

★ Tour d'Autriche

★ Cour d'Honneur

★ Hall of Godefroid de Bouillon

GODEFROID DE BOUILLON

Bouillon castle was once owned by the celebrated crusader knight Godefroid (1060–1100), Duke of Lower Lorraine. In 1095, Peter the Hermit, a French preacher, whipped the local populace into a ferment over Muslim occupation of the Holy Land. Godefroid took up the cause and joined the First Crusade, selling his castle to the prince-bishop of Liège to obtain money for the expedition. In 1099, his troops were the first to enter Jerusalem and Godefroid was offered the crown of the Kingdom of Jerusalem. He refused to accept it on religious grounds, preferring instead to be called Defender of the Holy Sepulchre. He died in Jerusalem a year later.

Godefroid de Bouillon

★ Hall of Godefroid de Bouillon
A large room beneath a massive arch of bare stone, the hall evokes a world of rugged military might. Slots in the floor contain a large and mysterious wooden cross that was discovered in 1962.

A portcullis could be lowered to block the passage beyond.

Drawbridges
The entrance to the castle was protected by three drawbridges. One was made into a stone bridge in 1716. The inscription over the arch is dedicated to King Louis XIV.

The Entrance
There is only one point of access to this fortress – through a narrow arch in the outer castle, flanked by guardrooms. This is now the site of the ticket office, shop and visitors' information office.

GRAND DUCHY
OF LUXEMBOURG

HISTORY OF THE GRAND DUCHY
OF LUXEMBOURG 236–237

Luxembourg City **❶**

Bustling, elegant Luxembourg City is the largest urban centre in the country. Its main draw, La Vieille Ville (The Old Town), is perched high on an escarpment over the rivers Alzette and Pétrusse which flow through verdant ravines below. This historic centre is bound by cliffs that once made the city an easily defensible stronghold. The three Villes Basses (Lower Towns) – Grund, Clausen and Pfaffenthal – hug the eastern side of the Old Town. A munitions explosion in 1554 damaged the town, and the stately web of streets and squares seen here today was built during the 18th and 19th centuries. In 1867, the city was demilitarized and most of its ramparts were demolished. Only the casemates survived – dank gunnery compartments and tunnels carved into the rocks, which are a strange contrast to the charm of the city above.

🏰 Palais Grand-Ducal
Rue du Marché-aux-Herbes 17.
🛈 222809 (tourist office). 🕐 mid-Jul–Aug: Thu–Tue. 🖼 🎫 4pm.
www.monarchie.lu
The official residence of the grand duke of Luxembourg, the Palais Grand-Ducal occupies the site of the old medieval town hall. The earliest part dates from 1573, when it was built as the residence of the governor of Luxembourg. This section includes the Flemish Renaissance façade. The palace was extended in the 18th century, and in 1890 it became the winter residence of the grand dukes. In summer, guided tours take visitors around the sumptuous interior, where the ceremonial rooms are lit by chandeliers and decorated with tapestries, stucco, carved wood panelling and wall paintings. The **Chamber of Deputies** stands to the right of the palace and was built in 1859 in Neo-Gothic style.

Arched doorway leading into the city's Cathédrale Notre-Dame

🔒 Cathédrale Notre-Dame
Rue Notre Dame. 🕐 10am–noon and 2–5:30pm daily. **www.**cathedrale.lu
A curious patchwork of history and styles, Luxembourg's main cathedral, with its dainty 20th-century twin spires, is one of the most eye-catching landmarks of the city. Inside, the nave is early 17th-century and

has an ornate Renaissance gallery beneath the organ loft. A gallery on the left of the nave is reserved for the royal family. This central part was extended in the 1930s in a derivative Art Deco style, and the choir is a Neo-Gothic addition of the same era.

The apse holds the church's most famed treasure – a 17th-century wooden statue of the Madonna and Child known as the **Consolatrix Afflictorum**. Crowned and dressed in elaborate robes, the Madonna is the object of veneration and pilgrimage, and the focus of the Octave festival (*see p.35*).

The crypt contains the vault of the grand ducal family and a 17th-century tomb, depicting the entombment of Christ, with seven attendants, created for the remains of the heroic Jean l'Aveugle (1296–1346), Count of Luxembourg and King of Bohemia. He lost his sight as an adult, but still took to the field with France against the English at the Battle of Crécy, and was killed.

🏰 Casemates de Pétrusse
Place de la Constitution. 🕐 school holidays: 11am–4pm. 🖼 🎫
Located underground, the casemates are a set of dark rooms carved out of the sandstone rockface by the Spanish in the 1640s, to provide gun emplacements overlooking the valley. In 1684, they were developed further by the military engineer Vauban for Louis XIV, and again in the 18th century by the Austrians. Sealed after 1867, they were rediscovered in 1933.

River Alzette wending its way through the Lower Town, a view from the city's medieval ramparts

For hotels and restaurants in this region see pp274–5 and pp300–301

Glass façade of the Musée d'Histoire de la Ville de Luxembourg

🏛 Musée d'Histoire de la Ville de Luxembourg

14 Rue du St-Esprit. **Tel** 47964500. ◯ 10am–6pm Tue–Sun, 10am–8pm Thu. 🎦 ♿ 🛈 www.musee-hist.lu
The history of Luxembourg is revealed in this sleek, ultra-modern museum ingeniously converted from four town-houses dating from the 17th to 19th centuries. Modern interactive display techniques combine with artifacts and informational panels to narrate the story of the city. An added attraction is the view from the huge glass panoramic lift that rises through all six of the museum's levels, gliding past 1,000 years of history.

🏛 Musée National d'Histoire et d'Art

Marché-aux-Poissons. **Tel** 479330-1. ◯ 10am–5pm Tue–Sun, 10am–8pm Thu. 🎦 (free 5–8pm Thu.) 🛗 🛈 www.mnha.lu
A group of elegant townhouses and a monolithic modern block combine to form the intriguing Musée National d'Histoire et d'Art. The historical section of the museum covers the history of Luxembourg from prehistoric to medieval times, and includes numerous Gallo-Roman treasures from archaeological finds: coins, mosaics, sculpture, jewellery and domestic wares. There are also decorative and fine arts, paintings from the Middle Ages to modern times and work by artists from all over Europe, including watercolours of the city by landscape painter JMW Turner (1775–1851).

🏰 The Bock

Montée de Clausen. ◯ Mar–Oct: 10am–5pm daily. 🎦
The city's original castle was built on the Rocher du Bock. In AD 963, it was captured

VISITORS' CHECKLIST

25 km (16 miles) SE of Arlon. **Road Map** F5. 🚶 99,000. ✈ 🚌 🚍 🛈 30 Place Guillaume II; 222809. 🎭 Octave (3rd week after Easter). www.lcto.lu

and reinforced by Siegfried of Lorraine, and became the key stronghold of the city for centuries. Between 1737 and 1746, the Austrians excavated soft sandstone beneath the castle, creating a network of galleries, staircases and tunnels over a distance of 23 km (14 miles). These casemates included gun emplacements for 50 canons, munitions stores, workshops, stables and kitchens: sufficient for a garrison of 1,200 men. They were part of a programme of reinforcements that made the city almost impregnable – or what French military engineer Lazare Carnot (1753–1823) termed the Gilbraltar of the North. The casements were also used as bomb shelters for 35,000 people during World War II. Tours take visitors around a small portion of the tunnels. The **Archaeological Crypt** presents the excavated remains of the Bock castle.

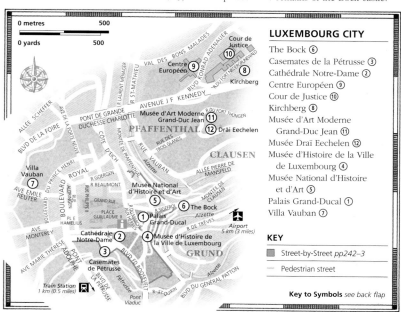

0 metres	500
0 yards	500

LUXEMBOURG CITY

The Bock ⑥
Casemates de la Pétrusse ③
Cathédrale Notre-Dame ②
Centre Européen ⑨
Cour de Justice ⑩
Kirchberg ⑧
Musée d'Art Moderne
    Grand-Duc Jean ⑪
Musée Draï Eechelen ⑫
Musée d'Histoire de la Ville
    de Luxembourg ④
Musée National d'Histoire
    et d'Art ⑤
Palais Grand-Ducal ①
Villa Vauban ⑦

KEY

▨ Street-by-Street pp242–3

— Pedestrian street

Key to Symbols see back flap

Street-by-Street: The Old Town

With its cliffs and deep river valleys, La Vieille Ville (The Old Town) has one of the most remarkable locations in any capital city. Although vestiges remain of the mighty military fortifications, which once defended the city in concentric rings, it is the refined elegance of 18th- and 19th-century urban building that predominates, with the Palais Grand-Ducal as the centrepiece. Two of the city's best museums are also found here. But the highlights of the area are the spectacular views, notably from the Place de la Constitution, the Plateau du St-Esprit and the Chemin de la Corniche.

Place Guillaume II
The city's largest square is named after Grand Duke William II (r.1840–49), whose equestrian statue stands in the centre. The 19th-century Neo-Classical Hôtel de Ville lines the entire southern side of the square, which is also known as the Knuedler.

Gëlle Fra
The Monument of Remembrance, in the Place de la Constitution, is a statue on a tall granite obelisk. It commemorates soldiers who served in World War I.

Cathédrale Notre-Dame
Central to the public life of the nation, Cathédrale Notre-Dame was originally a Jesuit church, consecrated in 1621. It became a cathedral when the Grand Duchy was awarded its own bishopric in 1870. The ornately carved gallery forming the organ loft dates from the 17th century.

STAR SIGHTS

★ Palais Grand-Ducal

★ Casemates du Bock

The Plateau du St-Esprit is a spur of rock fortified in the 1680s. After sensitive modernization, it became the site of the Cité Judiciaire, headquarters of the country's justice system.

RUE CHIMAY

PLACE D'ARM

BOULEVARD F D ROOSEVELT

RUE DE LA CO

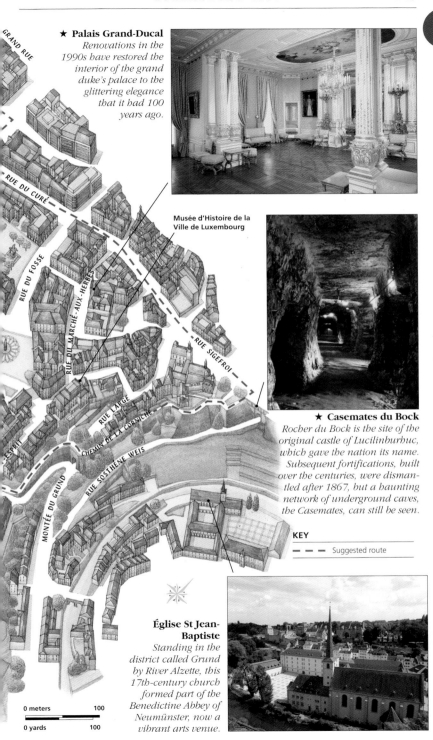

GRAND RUE

RUE DU CURÉ

RUE DU FOSSE

RUE DU MARCHÉ-AUX-HERBES

RUE SIGEFROI

RUE LARGE

CHEMIN DE LA CORNICHE

RUE SOSTHÈNE WEIS

MONTÉE DU GRUND

L'ESPRIT

★ **Palais Grand-Ducal**
Renovations in the 1990s have restored the interior of the grand duke's palace to the glittering elegance that it had 100 years ago.

Musée d'Histoire de la Ville de Luxembourg

★ **Casemates du Bock**
Rocher du Bock is the site of the original castle of Lucilinburhuc, which gave the nation its name. Subsequent fortifications, built over the centuries, were dismantled after 1867, but a haunting network of underground caves, the Casemates, can still be seen.

KEY

– – – Suggested route

Église St Jean-Baptiste
Standing in the district called Grund by River Alzette, this 17th-century church formed part of the Benedictine Abbey of Neumünster, now a vibrant arts venue.

0 meters   100

0 yards   100

Exploring Luxembourg City

Northeast of the city centre lies the hill of Kirchberg where modern tower blocks house many of the major European institutions that make Luxembourg the third capital of the European Union. There is much here to interest enthusiasts of modern architecture, and some cultural treasures as well. This includes Luxembourg's prestigious modern art museum, set in a sensational cluster of glass prisms and sweeping curves. Just below it, facing the Old Town, is an evocative fortress called Dräi Eechelen, one of many that once ringed the city. Another, the Villa Vauban, stood westwards. Now the home of a fine municipal art collection, its military past is remembered only in its name.

The elegant Villa Vauban set in the calm environs of the city park

🏛 Villa Vauban

Avenue Émile Reuter 18.
Tel 47964552. ◯ 10am–6pm Wed–Mon, 10am–9pm Fri. 🖼
www.villavauban.lu

In the 1680s, the great French military engineer Vauban built a set of outlying fortresses to protect the approaches to Luxembourg City. One of these was located on the western side of the Old Town. Today, this site is occupied by the 19th-century Villa Vauban. A grand residence built between 1871 and 1873, the villa once belonged to the family of the politician, entrepreneur and philanthropist Jean-Pierre Pescatore (1793–1855). For many years it housed a public art museum displaying his impressive collection as well as other bequests to the city. After a 5-year programme of renovations and extension, the museum is now known as Villa Vauban – Musée d'Art de la Ville de Luxembourg. Its collection of some 300 paintings consists mainly of Dutch, Flemish, French, German and Italian art dating from between the 17th and 19th centuries. It includes work by Jan Steen, Anthony van Dyck, Canaletto, Eugène Delacroix and Gustave Courbet. The museum's setting is also a pleasure – it has its own gardens and is surrounded by an extensive municipal park.

Kirchberg

Marché-aux-Poissons. **Tel** 479330-1. ◯ 10am–6pm Tue–Sun. 🖼 🔲 🔲
At the eastern end of the Pont Grande Duchesse Charlotte (built 1966) lies the raised plateau of Kirchberg where a host of administrative, financial and cultural buildings are concentrated into a strip some 3 km (2 miles) long. Kirchberg was developed as the centre for Luxembourg's European institutions. In recent years, however, a broader vision has overtaken these bureaucratic beginnings and the area has become the focus of a number of exciting architectural projects for financial institutions and the arts. These include the dramatically futuristic MUDAM building and the impressive concert hall of the **Philharmonie Luxembourg**, a delicately columned drum designed by the award-winning French architect Christian de Portzamparc.

Kirchberg's eastern end, with its concentration of international banks, includes strikingly innovative architecture, such as the **HypoVereinsbank Luxembourg**, designed by the American architect Richard Meier, and has his signature white cladding. Kirchberg is also remarkable for its **Central Park**, which contains the largest sports arena in the country. Dotted around this district are public sculptures by international artists such as Henry Moore, Jean Dubuffet, Frank Stella and Richard Serra.

🚇 Centre Européen

Montée de Clausen. **www**.lcto.lu
A number of major European institutions stand at the western end of Kirchberg. These include the Court of Justice of the European Union (Cour de Justice) and the **European Court of Auditors**. There are also the **European Investment Bank**, designed by Denys Lasdun, architect of the National Theatre in London, and the **Secretariat of the European Parliament**, which operates from the towers, designed by Spanish architect Ricardo Bofill, on either side of Avenue John F Kennedy. The tallest of these structures is the **Alcide de Gasperi Building** or Tower Building, which is part of the European

View of the European Union's Cour de Justice on the Kirchberg plateau

The futuristic glass forms of the Musée d'Art Moderne Grand-Duc Jean

Parliament's Congress and Conference Centre. The **National Library**, to the west of the Philharmonie, was founded in the late 18th century and will take up residence in a new purpose-built home in the Kirschberg area in 2014. To the south is the curious, cantilevered **Hemicycle**. Completed in 1979, it was used for plenary sessions of the European Parliament and now serves as a conference centre.

🎗 Cour de Justice
Boulevard Konrad Adenauer.
www.perraultarchitecte.com
One of the most impressive buildings in Kirschberg has always been the Cour de Justice – Court of Justice of the European Union. This classically proportioned, yet uncompromisingly modern structure of dark-brown steel is raised on a broad plinth, suggesting the full force of orderly law. Designed by a Belgian-Luxembourg partnership, it was completed in 1970. The Court has the task of ensuring that EU law is correctly interpreted and applied across all the member states – a huge task that has become even greater with the recent enlargement of the EU to 27 member states.
The original building has been renovated and extended to create an even more impressive effect. Following designs by French architect Dominique Perrault (b.1953), it has been completely surrounded by a giant square frame on pillars, complemented by two additional towers, and all covered in bronzed sheeting.

🏛 Musée d'Art Moderne Grand-Duc Jean (MUDAM)
Park Draï Eechelen, Kirchberg.
Tel 453785-1. ⬤ 11am–8pm Wed–Fri, 11am–6pm Sat–Mon. 🖼 🔗 🖥
📷 **www**.mudam.lu
Abbreviated to MUDAM, this modern art museum is the country's most prized architectural statement: a stunning glass and sandstone edifice designed by Ieoh Ming Pei, the Chinese-American architect best known for his ingenious glass pyramids at the Louvre in Paris. MUDAM first opened its doors in 2006. The exhilarating spaces on three levels inside, are used for temporary exhibitions, where artists are invited to interact with the unique opportunities offered by the varying shapes and light provided by the architecture. MUDAM's growing permanent collection of paintings, photography, film, video art and installations, is also exhibited in rotation at the museum. It includes work by well-known names such as Gilbert & George, Richard Long, Cy Twombly, and Grayson Perry.

🏛 Draï Eechelen
Park Draï Eechelen 5, Kirchberg. **Tel** 264335. 🖼
www.visitluxembourg.lu
The Three Acorns (Draï Eechelen in Lëtzebuergesch, Trois Glands in French) is the nickname given to Fort Thüngen, because of the acorn symbols that crown each of its three round towers. Although it looks more like a Renaissance fortress, this curious bastion, with its arrow-shaped ground plan, was built by the Austrians in 1732–3; a century later, it was upgraded by the Prussians. After the destruction of the city's fortifications in 1867, the fort was all but buried and forgotten. However, its historic and architectural value was reassessed and it has now been restored and turned into the fortress museum of military and national history, with particular focus on Vauban's contribution to Luxembourg City's fortifications. The fort forms part of the **Vauban Circuit**, a 4-km (3-mile) long walk that loops between Kirchberg and the eastern side of the Old Town.

Stalwart towers of the Draï Eechelen, defending the approaches to the city

Deep tranquillity of the Luxembourg Ardennes surrounding Esch-sur-Sûre ▷

Fond-de-Gras ❷

Administration, Place du Marché 1,
Pétange; 20 km (12 mile) SW of
Luxembourg City. **Road Map** E5.
Tel 26504124. 🖪 ◻ *May–Sep:
12:30–7pm Sun and public holidays.*
🖾 🖳 www.fond-de-gras.lu

Known as Le Pays des Terres
Rouges (The Red Lands),
the southwestern part of the
Grand Duchy forms the old
industrial heartlands, centre
of the iron-and-steel manufacturing. Located here, close to
the borders with Belgium and
France, is the **Parc Industriel
et Ferroviaire du Fond-de-Gras**
(Industrial and Railway Park
of Fond-de-Gras), a collection
of industrial heritage attractions
that provides a fascinating
insight into bygone days.

Fond-de-Gras is based
around an old railway depot.
Steam and diesel trains make
a 20-minute journey from
here to Pétange under the
title Train 1900. There is an
industry-themed **Musée de
Plein Air** (Open Air Museum),
with miners' houses, workshops and heavy industrial
equipment. A narrow-gauge
mine train, *minièresbunn*,
travels underground through
a disused iron-ore mine to
Lasauvage, a preserved iron-
founding and mining village.
Also of interest here is a
nature reserve located in
a former open-cast pit.

Musée National
des Mines de Fer ❸

Carreau de la Mine Walert,
Rumelange; 17 km (11 miles) S of
Luxembourg City. **Road Map** F5.
Tel 565688. 🖪 ◻ *Apr–Jun & Sep:
2–6pm Thu–Sun; Jul & Aug: 2–6pm
Tue–Sun.* 🖾 🖋 🖢 www.mnm.lu

This museum takes visitors
underground into the galleries
from which ore was extracted
for iron-smelting for nearly
200 years, until the 1980s.
Guided tours travel into the
mine by train. Visitors are
then free to wander the galleries and see the collection
of massive mining machines.
Exhibits reveal the arduous
nature of mining, and how
this evolved over time.

The soaring façade of the Église
St-Michel at Mondorf-les-Bains

Environs
Bettembourg, 8 km (5 miles)
to the north, has an activity
park and zoo for children.
Parc Merveilleux offers moving
models of classic fairytales, as
well as a mini-train, mini-cars,
mini-golf and playgrounds.

🎪 **Parc Merveilleux**
Route de Mondorf. *Tel* 5110481.
◻ *late Mar–mid-Oct.* 🖾 🖢 🍴
www.parc-merveilleux.lu

Mondorf-les-
Bains ❹

15 km (9 miles) SE of Luxembourg
City. **Road Map** F5. 🏘 3,500. 🚌
🅸 *Avenue des Bains 26-28;
23667575.* www.mondorf.info

A pretty town on the border,
Mondorf-les-Bains is the
Grand Duchy's only spa centre. Supplied with naturally
hot waters that emerge from
the ground at 24ºC (75ºF),
Mondorf has been attracting
visitors since the 1820s. The

mineral-rich water is said to
benefit those suffering from
liver and digestive complaints
and rheumatism. The spa
installations in the park setting of the **Domaine Thermal**
include open-air and indoor
pools, saunas, Turkish baths,
a fitness centre, massage and
a variety of special treatments.
Mondorf also has a gambling
centre, **Casino 2000**, established in 1983. The town's
most interesting church is the
pink **Église St-Michel** (built
1764–66), whose interior has
stucco work, *trompe-l'oeil*
paintings in the apse and a
lavish polychrome pulpit.

🅾 **Domaine Thermal**
Avenue des Bains. *Tel* 236660.
◻ *daily.* 🖾 🖢 🍴 🖳
www.montdorf.lu

Luxembourg's
Moselle Valley ❺

Road Map F5. 🚉 **Remich** 🅸
Esplanade; 236984. **Grevenmacher**
🅸 Route du Vin 10; 758275.
Wellenstein 🅸 Heenegässel;
23699858. www.moselle-tourist.lu

The broad River Moselle
forms the southeastern border
of Luxembourg with Germany.
Flowing north from its source
in Alsace in France, it enters
Luxembourg at the village of
Schengen, then runs for a distance of 42 km (26 miles) to
Wasserbillig before turning
east into Germany and joining
the River Rhine at Koblenz. In
Luxembourg, the Moselle valley is known above all for its
vineyards, producing mainly
white wine. Various vineyards

Extensive vineyards of the Moselle Luxembourgeoise, Grevenmacher

The market town of Larochette, huddled in a verdant glen formed by the River Ernz Blanche

and producers on the Route du Vin (Wine Road) along the river offer wine tastings and tours, for instance at **Remich**, Wormeldange, **Grevenmacher** and the wine cooperatives of **Wellenstein**. Just north of Wellenstein, among the winerys of Bech-Kleinmacher, is a charming wine and folklore museum, the **Musée A Possen**. This has furnished rooms in a set of 400-year-old winemaking buildings and includes wine tasting among its draws. The town of Ehnen, in the commune of Wormeldange, is the site of the **Musée National du Vin**, which explains winemaking processes, again with tastings.

The wine-growing village of Schengen is where the Schengen Agreement was signed in 1985 by European ministers, loosening the border controls between participating countries.

Cruises offer an agreeable way to see the extensive Moselle Luxembourgeoise. The cruise-boat **Princesse Marie-Astrid** runs a daily schedule between varying destinations – with return trips by coach – from late March to late September. Details are available from the Grevenmacher tourist office.

🏛 **Musée A Possen**
Keeseschgaessel 2, Bech-Kleinmacher. *Tel* 23697353.
⭘ Easter–Oct: 11am–7pm Tue–Sun.
www.musee-possen.lu

🏛 **Musée National du Vin**
Route du Vin 115, Ehnen.
Tel 760026. ⭘ Apr–Oct: Tue–Sun.

Larochette ❻

20 km (12 miles) N of Luxembourg City. **Road Map** F4. 🏠 *1,500*. 🚌 *Chemin J.A. Zinnen 33; 837038.* **www**.larochette.lu.

A pleasant market town in the valley of River Ernz Blanche, Larochette has more than 800 years of history, centring upon its castle set on a rocky sandstone crag that dominates the town. This location gave the town its name: Larochette is French for The Small Rock. In German, the town is Fels (Rock). Extensive ruins of the 11th–16th-century **Château de Larochette**, destroyed by fire

in 1565, cover the top of the crag. Located here is Palais des Hombourg, the medieval palace of two noble sisters who married brothers from the House of Homburg in 1338–45. Restoration of the castle has begun with the now complete Maison de Créhange, an impressive evocation of a 14th-century fortified residence named after a family that inhabited this part of the castle. Looping out from the town are some 30 km (18 miles) of walking paths.

🏰 **Château de Larochette**
Tel 837497. ⭘ Easter–Oct: 10am–6pm daily.

THE WINES OF LUXEMBOURG

Appreciated by wine enthusiasts for their dry, fresh flavours, Luxembourg wines have little of the cloying fruitiness sometimes associated with northern white wines. The Romans are said to have brought wine grapes to the Moselle valley, and the local grape variety Elbling may date right back to that era. The vines grow in a string of 28 town and villages lining the left bank of the river between Schengen and Wasserbillig. Slopes here are sunny and the climate is cool, favouring white wine grapes. The main varieties are Rivaner, Auxerrois Blanc, Elbling, Riesling, Pinot Blanc and Pinot Gris. Chardonnay and Gewürztraminer also make an appearance. Pinot Noir is grown to make rosé and a small amount of red wine. A sizeable proportion of the harvest is used to make the sparkling wine Crémant Luxembourgeois, and there are three types of sweet wines: *vin de glace, vin de paille* and *vendanges tardives*. Some 80 per cent of the total white wine production is consumed in Belgium, and much of the rest is sent to Germany to be made into *sekt* (sparkling wine).

Barrels stacked in a wine cellar of the Moselle valley

A Tour of Petite Suisse Luxembourgeoise ➐

Aptly called Petite Suisse (Little Switzerland), this segment of the Germano-Luxembourg Nature Park has steep, twisting valleys made intimate by woodlands, rushing streams and dramatic rock formations. Tours take a scenic route to Beaufort castle and to the Ernz Noire valley via Müllerthal village. Müllerthal is also used to refer to Petite Suisse Luxembourgeoise as a whole. Stop-off points along the way give access to signposted paths that go deeper into the landscape.

Gorge du Loup ➁
A walk close to Echternach leads to this Wolf Gorge, with its cleft between two towering walls of rock. Steps lead up to a spectacular viewpoint.

Berdorf ➂
A centre for rock-climbing, the area around Berdorf village has numerous marked paths for walkers. Rising above a plateau, the spire-cum-watertower of Berdorf's church is a noted landmark.

Predigstuhl ➃
Named for its shape, the Predigstuhl (Pulpit) is one of many strange rock formations in the region.

Echternach ➀
This old abbey town is the main urban centre in the region, as well as a hub for activity holidays.

Werschrumschluff ➄
Close to the Predigstuhl, the Werschrumschluff is an immense rock crevice, just wide enough for a walker to pass through.

Beaufort ➅
Extensive ruins of a 12th–16th-century castle, in a wooded valley, stand ready to be explored. The village of Beaufort is noted for its blackcurrant liqueur, Cassero.

KEY

▬▬▬ Tour route

═══ Other Road

TIPS FOR DRIVERS

Starting point: Echternach.
Length: About 35 km (22 miles).
Duration of drive: Allow half a day, but a whole day if on foot.
Driving conditions: Roads are narrow and winding, but have good surfaces and signposts.
Where to stay and eat: Echternach is the main centre, but there are options at Berdorf, Beaufort and Müllerthal.
Visitors' information:
www.mullerthal.lu
www.echternach.lu
www.berdorf-tourist.lu
www.visitluxembourg.lu

Müllerthal ➆
The Schiessentümpel bridge and its triple waterfall are set amid woodland. This is a famous beauty spot in the valley of Ernz Noire, which is often referred to as the Müllerthal.

Echternach ⑧

35 km (22 miles) NE of Luxembourg City. **Road Map** F4. 🏛 *5,000.* 🚌
ℹ *Parvis de la Basilique 9–10; 720230.* 🎻 *International Classical Music Festival (May–Jun and Sep).* **www**.echternach-tourist.lu

Capital of Luxembourg's Little Switzerland, Echternach is also the country's oldest town. An abbey was founded here in AD 698 by St Willibrord, a Yorkshire missionary monk who was said to cure chorea (or St Vitus's Dance), a disease of the nervous system. This is believed to be the reason for the curious motion of the participants in Echternach's dance parade, the Sprangprëzessioun *(see p35).* The town is dominated by the massive abbey, which dates mainly from its makeover in austere Classical style in 1727–31. Until its closure in 1794 by the French Revolutionary Army, it was a Benedictine monastery of great influence, noted for its illuminated manuscripts produced during the Middle Ages. These can be seen at the **Musée de l'Abbaye**, laid out in the cellars of the old Abbot's Palace. The crypt of the accompanying **Basilique St-Willibrord** contains the sarcophagus of the saint, as well as 11th-century frescoes. The town's centrepiece, the **Place du Marché**, is an ensemble of traditional buildings, some old, some reconstructed, including the Gothic 15th-century law courts, the **Dënzelt**.

🏛 **Musée de l'Abbaye**
Parvis de la Basilique 11.
Tel *727472.* ◻ *daily.* ■ *Nov–Feb.*
🖼 **www**.willibrord.lu

Diekirch ⑨

21 km (13 miles) NW of Echternach.
Road Map F4. 🏛 *6,405.* 🚆 🚌
ℹ *Place de la Libération 3; 803023.* http://tourisme.diekirch.lu

Located on the River Sûre, Diekirch is an attractive base from which to explore the surrounding area. The town was badly damaged during the Ardennes Offensive *(see p231),* a subject that is

Echternach's Place du Marché, with cobbled streets and old buildings

covered by the **National Museum of Military History**, through photographs and film, various artifacts and life-size dioramas. The museum also covers the history of Luxembourg's army. The **Conservatoire National de Véhicules Historiques**, a veteran car museum, displays changing exhibits mounted by collectors and includes bikes, fire engines – even children's cars. It shares premises with the **Museum of the Diekirch Brewery**; Diekirch is a famous brand of beer. Also of note is Église St-Laurent, a Gothic and Romanesque church built over the site of a Roman villa and containing Roman and early medieval sarcophagi.

🏛 **National Museum of Military History**
Bamertal 10. **Tel** *808908.* ◻ *daily.* 🖼 **www**.mnhm.lu

🏛 **Conservatoire National de Véhicules Historiques**
Rue de Stavelot 20-22. **Tel** *2680 0468.* ◻ *10am–6pm Tue–Sun.* **www**.cnvh.lu

Vianden ⑩

22 km (14 miles) NW of Echternach.
Road Map F4. 🏛 *1,600.* 🚌
ℹ *Rue du Vieux Marché 1A; 834257-1.* **www**.tourist-info-vianden.lu

This little town of Vianden, on the River Our, is famous for the large medieval **Château de Vianden** that is perched over the town on a rocky outcrop. This château was the seat of the counts of Vianden and the Orange-Nassau family, until it was given to the state by Grand Duke Jean in 1977. The building dates mainly from the 12th and 13th centuries and has Romanesque and Gothic structures.

Vianden also has a charming **Musée d'Art Rustique**, with rustic furniture, domestic artifacts, clothing and dolls. The Gothic abbey church, **Église des Trinitaires**, dating mainly from 1250, has a double nave with Baroque flourishes and a tranquil cloister. Also of interest is **Maison de Victor Hugo**, which recalls the author's stay here in 1871. Luxembourg's only *télésiège* (chairlift) rises 220 m (720 ft) from Rue du Sanitorium and offers views over the town and castle.

⛵ **Château de Vianden**
◻ *daily.* 🖼 **www**.castle-vianden.lu

🏛 **Musée d'Art Rustique**
96-98 Grande-rue. **Tel** *834591.*
◻ *Easter–Oct: 11am–5pm Tue–Sun.* 🖼

The Château de Vianden towering over the eponymous riverside town

For hotels and restaurants in this region see pp274–5 and pp300–301

Château de Bourscheid **⓫**

11 km (7 miles) W of Vianden. **Road Map** F4. 🚌 ℹ️ *Buurschtermillen, Bourscheid-Moulin; (621) 237960.* 🕐 *Apr–Oct: 9:30am–6pm daily; Nov–Mar: 11am–4pm daily.* 📷 🐾 🏠 *www.bourscheid.lu*

Now largely reconstructed from ruins, the Château de Bourscheid is an evocative example of a medieval walled fortress. Building began in about AD 1000, and it was then ruled by the lords of Bourscheid for more than 400 years, from 1095 to 1512. Set 150 m (492 ft) above a dramatic loop of the River Sûre, the castle offers fine views from the ramparts. The current ring wall, with its eight towers, was built between 1350 and 1384, along with the step-gabled **Stolzemburger House** in the lower part of the castle. This now contains a small museum of archaeological finds. The gateway giving access to the upper and lower castle was completed in 1477. Decline set in after 1512, following the death of the last Bourscheid – the ruins were bought by the state in 1972.

Environs
The N27 follows a scenic route along the River Sûre. The **Upper Valley** runs from Ettelbruck, via Bourscheid, for some 70 km (43 miles) almost to the Belgian border.

The sturdy towers and ramparts of Château de Bourscheid

Clervaux **⓬**

16 km (10 miles) N of Bourscheid. **Road Map** F4. 🚶 *1,800.* 🚉 🚌 ℹ️ *Grand Rue 11; 920072.* *www.tourisme-clervaux.lu*

Located on a loop in the River Clerve in the Germano-Luxembourg Nature Reserve, Clervaux lies at the heart of the forested Ardennes region known as Oesling in northern Luxembourg. At the centre of the town is a whitewashed château of medieval origins, which has been much altered over the centuries. It contains three permanent exhibitions. The first is a collection of photographs known as **The Family of Man**. Then there are the **Musée de la Maquette**, with models of 22 castles in Luxembourg, and **Musée de la**

Guerre or Battle of the Bulge Museum. The tower of the Neo-Romanesque church of the **Abbaye Bénédictine de St-Maurice et de St-Maur**, founded in 1910, crests a hill outside the town. The austere interior of the church is bathed in light from fine stained glass and contains an exhibition on monastic life. The abbey is internationally famed for its choir, which specializes in Gregorian chant.

🏛️ **The Family of Man**
Château de Clervaux. **Tel** 929657. 🕐 *Mar–Dec: 10am–6pm Tue–Sun.* 📷 ♿ 🚻 *www.family-of-man. public.lu*

🏛️ **Musée de la Maquette** and **Musée de la Guerre** Château de Clervaux. **Tel** 9210481. 🕐 *Mar–Dec.*

Wiltz **⓭**

11 km (7 miles) NW of Bourscheid. **Road Map** E4. 🚶 *4,500.* 🚉 🚌 ℹ️ *Château; 957444.* 🎭 *Open-air Festival of Theatre and Music (Jul).* *www.wiltz.lu*

This town is a good base for touring the local Ardennes. The lower part of the town runs along both banks of the River Wiltz, while the upper town shares higher ground with an impressive château. This former residence of the counts of Wiltz is in the Renaissance style. Its stables contain the agreeable **Musée National d'Art Brassicole et de la Tannerie**, which is devoted to beer-brewing, with a small

---

THE FAMILY OF MAN PROJECT
The American photographer Edward Steichen (1879–1973) was born in Luxembourg. He became famous during the 1920s, and after World War II was Director of Photography at the Museum of Modern Art in New York. In 1951, he invited submissions for a collection of photographs that would record the unique and universal qualities of mankind. From some two million submissions, he chose 503, by 273 photographers from 68 countries, and assembled them under 37 themes – work, family, birth, war, faith and so on. The Family of Man was first exhibited in 1955 and toured the world to great acclaim. In 1964, the US government gave it to the Grand Duchy of Luxembourg in accordance with Steichen's wishes. Since 1994, the collection has been at the Château de Clervaux, and it is now listed by UNESCO on its Memory of the World register.

Edward Steichen, pictured in 1955

section on leather-tanning. Both trades are historically associated with Wiltz. The museum also has its own micro-brewery and a traditional-style bar and *bistrot* called **Café Jhang Primus**. Wiltz is also well known for its Open-air Festival of Theatre and Music *(see p35)*.

🏛 **Musée National d'Art Brassicole et de la Tannerie**
Château de Wiltz. **Tel** 957444.
🕐 *Jul–Aug: 10am–6pm daily; Jan–Jun and Sep–Dec: 9am–noon and 2–5pm Mon–Fri, 10am–noon Sat.* 📷 🕍 🍴

Esch-sur-Sûre ⑭

10 km (6 miles) S of Wiltz. **Road Map** E4. 🚌 🏨 *Rue de l'Eglise 14; 26889541.* **www**.esch-sur-sure.lu

This village is famous above all for its spectacular setting, on an oxbow loop of the River Sûre that virtually performs a complete circle around it. Concentric rings of streets and slate-roofed houses cluster at the foot of a jagged outcrop of rock and the ruins of the castle that line the ridge. The castle dates back to AD 927 and remained in use until the French Revolutionary Army destroyed it in 1795. West of Esch-sur-Sûre, the river is dammed, creating a serpentine lake that is popular for water sports. There are many marked footpaths for walkers.

Fairytale flourishes on the handsome castle of Schoenfels

Rindschleiden ⑮

8 km (5 miles) S of Esch-sur-Sûre. **Road Map** E4. 🏨 *889358.* **www**.wahl.lu

The village of Rindschleiden is best known for a little white-washed church built originally as a chapel in Romanesque style in the 10th century, and later extended. During the 15th and 16th centuries, 170 sq metres (1,830 sq ft) of the vaults and walls inside were painted with delicate murals depicting saints. The church was dedicated in the 16th century to Willibrord, saint of Echternach *(see p251)*. Close by is a spring which the saint is said to have divined with his rod – this is the focus of an annual Whitsunday pilgrimage.

Vallée des Sept Châteaux ⑯

20 km (12 miles) SE of Rindschleiden. **Road Map** F4.
🏨 *Hôtel de Ville; 3250231.* **www**.septchateaux.lu

From Mersch, the River Eisch can be followed westwards for 37 km (23 miles), on the CR 105, to Gaichel, on the Belgian border. This stretch is the Vallée des Sept Châteaux (Valley of the Seven Castles). A footpath, the **Sentier des Sept Châteaux**, also follows the valley. The restored medieval castle at Mersch is now the site of the town hall and tourist office. The second castle is at **Schoenfels**, on CR 102, by the River Mamer. This is a tall medieval keep revamped in the 19th century. **Ansembourg** has two castles. The one above the village is of 12th-century origin, and has been home of the counts Marchant d'Ansembourg since the 17th century. The other, in the valley, is a fine 17th-century Renaissance château with numerous cone-roofed turrets. The medieval-looking **Château de Hollenfels** dates mainly from the 18th-century and serves as a youth hostel. **Septfontaines** sits beneath the impressive ruin of a 13th–15th century castle, and **Koerich**, lying south of the route, has another imposing ruin of a medieval castle, as well as a fine Baroque church.

Rustic beauty of the riverside landscape at Esch-sur-Sûre

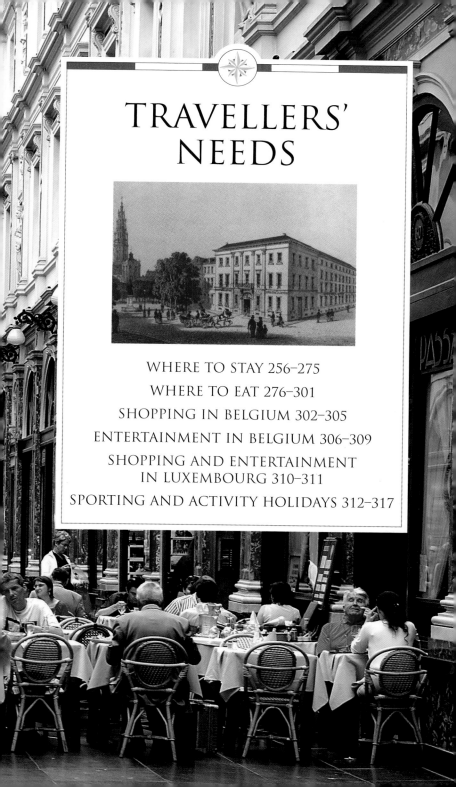

TRAVELLERS' NEEDS

WHERE TO STAY

The hotel and accommodation industry in Belgium and Luxembourg is extremely well organized. High professional standards run right through the industry, from the top five-star and boutique hotels to budget hotels and bed-and-breakfast stays. A full range of accommodation is available, so it is worthwhile exploring all the different options to find one

Métropole porter

that suits individual tastes. There are competitively-priced, efficient business hotels, where location is more important than style; there are small, luxurious, family-run townhouse hotels, designed to pamper guests; and there is a growing set of delightful, rural bed-and-breakfasts, full of rustic charm. With a little research, most travellers will find that they are spoilt for choice.

Hallway in the Hotel Métropole on Place de Brouckère, Brussels

HOTELS

There are hotels to satisfy every taste, from highly individual historic homes to sleek, top-notch international establishments, with every facility imaginable and prices to match. Hotels are closely regulated to meet high industry standards. At the upper end, there are a number of familiar chains such as **NH Hotels**, **Conrad-Hilton**, **Marriott** and **Radisson**. Many good, midrange hotels are affiliated to the **Best-Western** group. The group **Logis de France**, specializing in comfortable country hotels, crosses the border with its selection of Logis in Belgium and Luxembourg. The **Accor Group** has hotels at every price level, from the basic Formule 1 chain (offering out-of-centre rooms with shared bathroom facilities), to Etap, Ibis, Mercure, Novotel and the very chic Sofitel chain at the top. All are efficient,

clean and offer good value for money. The **Intercontinental** hotels group, similarly, has the brands Express, Crowne Plaza and Holiday Inn. There are also numerous individual hotels, often taking pride in being family-run, and paying particular attention to service.

HOTEL GRADINGS

Hotels in Luxembourg and Belgium are judged according to Benelux standards, and the regional licensing authority issues a blue permit shield bearing the number of stars (one to five) that a hotel has been awarded. The star system rates hotels according to their facilities, the quality of their welcome and helpfulness of the staff, the decor, the tranquillity of the rooms and even the price. It guarantees certain standards of quality and the provision of such items as lifts, fire doors and a desk in the room. However, membership to this scheme is voluntary and there may be high-quality hotels that are not graded. In general, one- and two-star hotels are basic.

ROOM RATES

Hotels at the top end of the scale offer high standards of comfort and convenience and their prices reflect this – rates in excess of €350 per night for a double room are not unusual. In larger cities, they are designed primarily for corporate clients, which means that during weekends and holiday periods, rates can be attractive. Moderately priced hotels charge between

€80 and €130 per night, while bed-and-breakfast prices are usually between 40 and 90 euros. Rates vary according to the season, but not by much in busy holiday or business centres. Discounts may be available for Internet bookings.

In general, the low season is from November to March, with exceptions at Easter, Christmas and New Year, and other holiday weekends. The high season is over the summer holidays, from early July to the end of August.

TAXES AND CHARGES

Room taxes and sales taxes are usually included in the cost of a room, so the price quoted should be the total. Full room rates are posted on the back of room doors: this is an opportunity to check what kind of discount was given at the time of booking. In the centre of busy cities, there may be a charge for using the hotel car park.

Elegant 19th-century façade of the luxurious hotel, Conrad Brussels

◁ Galéris St-Hubert, a premier shopping destination in Brussels

The Hotel Ter Brughe, next to one of Bruges's many canals

HOW TO BOOK

For those in a hurry to secure a reservation, a telephone call may be the best method: most hotels have receptionists who speak English. Alternatively, hotels can be contacted through their websites. The independent hotel reservation service **Resotel** specializes in Belgium and Luxembourg. The **Visit Brussels** tourist office and website also offers reservation service, as does the **Luxembourg City Tourist Office**. Likewise, many local tourist offices will reserve accommodation for visitors; this is a good way of securing rooms when arriving in a town or city without a prior booking. A credit card number is usually required for making reservations, to serve as a deposit against cancellation or failure to show up.

HOTEL FACILITIES

Most hotels above the budget or one-star category will have rooms with en-suite bathroom facilities. A television comes with virtually every room right across the range. These usually have a vast range of European channels provided by a cable link. Phone calls using the landlines in hotel rooms can be extremely expensive – many guests prefer to use their own mobile phones. Many hotels have tea- and coffee-making facilities in the rooms. They may also have minibars, with a range of alcoholic drinks, mixers, fruit juice and mineral water, and some Belgian beer;

prices should be supplied and are not always exorbitant. Many of the top city hotels, and some leading country hotels, have fitness and spa facilities, including saunas and gymnasiums, but only a handful have swimming pools.

The attractive entrance of the Sporthotel Leweck in Luxembourg

BREAKFAST

It is important to establish whether breakfast is included in the price of the room:

where it is not, guests may find that breakfast comes as an expensive additional cost. That said, many hotels do include breakfast in the price. This may vary from a simple Continental breakfast (croissants and other pastries, bread rolls, jam and butter, tea or coffee), to a full and magnificent buffet with cereals, cold meats, sliced cheese, boiled eggs, yoghurt, fruit juices, fresh fruit and more.

Some gourmet-focussed hotel-restaurants, and some rural bed-and-breakfasts, take special care to present local produce, plus home-made jams, breads and pastries.

INTERNET INFORMATION

Increasingly, hotels, and even bed-and-breakfast accommodation, have Wi-Fi Internet connections, available either free of charge or for a modest fee. All major hotels, many of the smaller ones, and some bed-and-breakfast establishments, have their own websites. There is also a website for **Hotels in Brussels**. These give guests varying amounts of information, ranging from basic details, room rates and email contact, to virtual tours of the rooms and facilities. Usually, these sites can be used to make a reservation.

Independent advice and recommendations are available on online reviews submitted by travellers to travel websites such as **TripAdvisor** – but these reviews should, of course, be treated with some caution.

Artistically-designed interior of the elegant Hotel Bloom

Porter attending to luggage at
the hotel, Conrad Brussels

ACCOMMODATION FOR
DISABLED TRAVELLERS

Hotels in Luxembourg and
Belgium take the needs of
disabled travellers seriously.
Most have rooms designed for
wheelchair-bound guests. It is
worth remembering, however,
that many hotels are in historic
buildings and may not be suitable. Most hotels allow the
visually handicapped to bring
a guide-dog on the premises.
It is essential to ask in advance
about the facilities available.
Bruxelles Pour Tous and the
Access-able Travel Source
have some listings.

TRAVELLING
WITH CHILDREN

Children are welcome in just
about all hotels in Belgium
and Luxembourg. Indeed,
many hotels make a concerted
effort to cater to the needs of
those travelling with children.
Most allow one or two children under the age of 12 to
stay in their parents' room
without extra charge, or to
stay for a small supplement.
Some hotels extend this to
travellers under the age of 16,
or even under 18. When travelling with children, it is worth
booking in advance, so that
the hotel can reserve the room
best suited to their needs.

BED-AND-BREAKFASTS

A pleasant alternative to
staying in a small hotel, B&Bs
are essentially rooms in private
houses and the style of accommodation varies considerably,
from the mundane to the truly

special. For instance, some
B&Bs may be in historic
homes, close to a city centre
or set in the countryside, with
antique furniture and high
standards of comfort. Many
are run more like mini-hotels,
with owners who are careful
to provide a high level of
professional service in such
details as the quality of linen
and breakfast. This type of
accommodation best suits the
kind of traveller who enjoys
personal contact with the
owners, who are often excep-
tionally welcoming and a fount
of local knowledge. That said,
some B&Bs are simply rented
rooms in private houses, and
the owners may not live on the
premises at all. **Bed & Brussels**
specializes in B&Bs for
Brussels; **Taxistop** has listings
for all Belgium. In addition,
tourist offices can supply lists
of B&B accommodation.

HOEVETOERISME AND
CHAMBRES D'HOTES

There is little to distinguish
chambres d'hôtes (guest
rooms) from B&Bs, but usually
the former denotes something
a little more special – perhaps
a warm welcome in a beautiful farmhouse, a manor house
or a historic building. In the
Flanders region, many farm
B&Bs belong to the movement
known as *hoevetoerisme* (farmstead tourism), under the
umbrella federation **Vlaamse
Federatie voor Hoeve- en
Plattelandstoerisme**. Its equivalent in Wallonia is **Fédération
des Gîtes de Wallonie**, which,
like its Flemish counterpart,
also covers self-catering holiday
cottages, or *gîtes*.

APARTMENT-HOTELS

A number of city hotels offer
apartments rather than rooms.
For instance, the Citadines
company has two "apart-
hotels" in Brussels *(see p262).*
The rooms may be suites, with
a sitting area and kitchen facilities, or the hotel may also
have a breakfast room for
guests. The reception services
can be as minimal as collecting
the key, registering and
paying. Apartment-hotels are
designed for guests staying a
number of days, if not weeks,
but some are happy to offer
accommodation for one night
only. They can be very useful
for families on a longer visit.

YOUTH AND BUDGET
ACCOMMODATION

There are youth hostels in
most major towns and cities:
more than 30 in Belgium and
about 10 in Luxembourg.
These tend to have excellent
modern facilities, reasonably
priced food and the chance of
more privacy than is usually
associated with hostel stays.
Accommodation may be in
double or single rooms, or
in dormitories. Although
called youth hostels, there is
in fact no age limit for guests.
Flanders, **Wallonia** and
Luxembourg each have their
own youth hotel association.
Members of **Hostelling
International**, or an equivalent
approved national organization,
will find the rates less expensive than non-members.

There are also numerous
hostel-like budget hotels, particularly in the popular tourist
cities such as Brussels and

Stylish bedroom in the contemporary Hotel Les Nuits in Antwerp

Bruges. Called *logements pour jeunes* or *jeugdlogies*, they are specially geared and styled for young people, and may offer a more characterful (not to say hit-and-miss) experience than official hostels.

GAY AND LESBIAN ACCOMMODATION

There are no specifically gay or lesbian hotels, but same-sex couples should have few problems finding welcoming accommodation. **Tels Quels** is a good source of information for Brussels, and there are websites for **Antwerp** and **Bruges**. The **Flandern Gay-Guide** (in German) has comprehensive listings for Flanders, including gay-friendly hotels. The **Rosa**

Grand lobby at Le Méridien, one of the top hotels in central Brussels

Lëtzebuerg organization in Luxembourg provides a similar service. The **Navigaytor** website includes Belgium in its worldwide listings.

SELF-CATERING AND GITES

Belgium and Luxembourg also have a range of self-catering properties for rent. Many of these are located in the countryside and follow a pattern similar to that of the French *gîtes* – self-catering holiday cottages.

Local tourist offices usually provide detailed information for their areas. Vlaamse Federatie voor Hoeve-en Platterlandstoerisme and the Fédération des Gîtes de Wallonie have listings. **Ardennes-Étape** has more than 500 holiday homes to let; and the company **Maisons de Vacances** has chalets in the Hautes Fagnes region.

DIRECTORY

HOTELS

Accor Group
www.accorhotels.com

Best-Western
www.bestwestern.be

Conrad-Hilton
www.conradhotels1.hilton.com

Intercontinental
www.ichotelsgroup.com

Logis de France
www.logis.be

Marriott
www.marriott.com

NH Hotels
www.nh-hotels.com

Radisson
www.radissonblu.com

HOW TO BOOK

Luxembourg City Tourist Office
30 Place Guillaume II, Luxembourg City.
Tel 222809. www.lcto.lu

Resotel
Ave E Van Nieuwenhuyse 6, 1160 BRU. *Tel (02) 779 3939.* www.resotel.be

Visit Brussels
Rue Royale 2-4 and Hôtel de Ville, 1000 BRU.
Tel (02) 5138940. www.visitbrussels.be

INTERNET INFORMATION

Hotels in Brussels
www.brussels-hotels.com

TripAdvisor
www.tripadvisor.com

ACCOMMODATION FOR DISABLED TRAVELLERS

Access-able Travel Source
www.access-able.com

Bruxelles Pour Tous
www.bruxellespourtous.be

BED-AND-BREAKFASTS

Bed & Brussels
Rue Kindermans 9, 1050 BRU. *Tel (02) 6460737.* www.bnb-brussels.be

HOEVETOERISME AND CHAMBRES D'HÔTES

Fédération des Gîtes de Wallonie
Ave Prince de Liège 1/21, Jambes (Namur).
Tel (081) 311800.
www.gitesdewallonie.be

Vlaamse Federatie voor Hoeve- en Platterlandstoerisme
Diestsevest 40, Leuven.
Tel (016) 286035. www.hoevetoerisme.be

YOUTH AND BUDGET ACCOMMODATION

Flanders
Vlaamse JeugdHerbergen, Van Stralenstraat 40, Antwerp. *Tel (03) 232 7218.* www.vjh.be

Luxembourg
Centrale des Auberges de Jeunesse Luxembourgeoises, Rue du Fort Olisy 2, Luxembourg City.
Tel 26276640.
www.youthhostels.lu

Hostelling International
2nd Floor, Gate House, Fretherne Road, Welwyn Garden City, Herts, AL8 6RD, England.
Tel (01707) 324170 (UK).
www.hihostels.com

Wallonia
Les Auberges de Jeunesse de Wallonie, Rue de la Sablonnière 28, 1000 BRU. *Tel (02) 2195676.* www.lesaubergesdejeunesse.be

GAY AND LESBIAN ACCOMMODATION

Antwerp
www.gay-antwerp.com

Bruges
www.j-h.be

Flandern Gay-Guide
www.gaybelgium.be

Navigaytor
www.navigaytor.net

Rosa Lëtzebuerg
Rue des Romains 60, Luxembourg City.
Tel 26190018.
www.gay.lu

Tels Quels
Rue du Marché au Charbon 81, 1000 BRU.
Tel (02) 5124587.
www.telsquels.be

SELF-CATERING AND GITES

Ardennes-Étape
Ster 3b, Stavelot.
Tel (080) 292400.
www.ardennes-etape.com

Maisons de Vacances
Chemin du Raideu 21, Xhoffraix-Malmedy.
Tel (080) 799016.
www.maisons-de-vacances.be

Camping and Chalet Parks

Outdoor life is the principal attraction for a number of visitors to Belgium and Luxembourg. They spend summer vacations at the seaside or take hiking, kayaking or cycling trips among the forested hills and rivers of the Ardennes. Camping and caravanning also offer a chance to live close to nature and are remarkably economic ways of holidaying. To meet these needs, both countries offer a great number of campsites – there are more than 500 in Belgium and 120 in Luxembourg.

TYPES OF CAMPSITES

In both countries, campsites vary from rural farm sites, where simplicity is a virtue, to large holiday camps with swimming pools, sports facilities, bicycles for hire, fishing rights and archery. The latter also offer restaurants, cafés, shops, games arcades and evening entertainment. Some campsites have chalets, caravans and pre-installed tents for hire, so all visitors need to do is pitch up and enjoy.

Campsites in Belgium and Luxembourg are ranked into five categories, from one star to five star. One star indicates minimum facilities: drinking water, cold showers, flush toilets and power points. Three stars indicate hot showers, sports facilities and a shop. The five-star camps will in addition have a restaurant, children's playground and a wider range of facilities. Most campsites are ranked as one or two star. Often, it is not a question of facilities, but of the location. Websites offer good, sometimes visual, information on campsites. In a one- or two-star site, a family of four with a tent or caravan can expect to pay about €15–25 per night. There are also a few naturist campsites.

CAMPING ORGANIZATIONS

In Belgium, there are two camping authorities – the **Flanders Camping Federation**, and a parallel organization in Wallonia called **Walcamp**. In Luxembourg, the organization is named **Camprilux**. These embrace all forms of camping, from tents to caravans and motorhomes (or camping cars). Their websites provide detailed information. Listings of campsites are also available through the various regional tourist offices *(see p323)* and the local ones. A useful and comprehensive list of campsites is available on the Eurocampings website. This includes a database on campsites that cater to disabled people. The main umbrella organization is the **FICC** (Féderation Internationale de Camping et de Caravanning), based in Brussels. This also covers motorhomes. The FICC issues the **Camping Card International** (CCI), which bestows a number of club advantages on its holders, including discounts of up to 25 per cent at certain listed campsites.

BOOKING AND ARRIVING

Campsites in popular areas, such as on the Belgian coast, may be booked up months in advance for the high season of July and August. It is therefore necessary to phone or email ahead to reserve a site. In general, campers can arrive any time after 2pm and are expected to vacate the site and check out by midday.

INDEPENDENT CAMPING

Wild or free camping is the term used for pitching a tent wherever a camper chooses. When practised outside official commercial campsites, this activity is frowned upon in Belgium and Luxembourg. The argument is that there are plenty of cheap campsites, so there is no excuse to fail to use these and threaten to despoil and pollute the countryside.

Campers by the River Sûre in the forested Ardennes of Luxembourg

A slice of Switzerland, Durbuy Adventure's welcoming Chalet Suisse

However, there is nothing to stop travellers from camping on private land with the permission of the landowner. Wild camping or wilding for motorhomes and camper vans faces official disapproval for similar reasons: most campsites accept motorhomes and there are also dedicated *aires* (parks), some with basic facilities, which allow overnight stays for a small fee. Police may fine motorhome owners who halt overnight illegally.

TREKKERS' HUTS

Many campsites across the region offer what are known as trekkers' huts or hikers' huts. These are designed especially for walkers using long-distance paths and for cyclists. Such accommodation permits them to travel without carrying camping equipment. In Flanders, these huts are called *trekkershutten*, while in Wallonia, they are known as *cabanes des randonneurs* or *cabanes pour routards* and in Luxembourg, *Wanderhütten*. The huts can be reserved in advance. In Flanders, this is done via **Reservieringscentrale Trekkershutten Vlaanderen**. In Wallonia, campsite listings show fixed accommodation (chalets, bunglows, tents, caravans) for rent, which can be used for a similar purpose. In Luxembourg, individual camps across the country are listed by **Wanderhütten Luxemburg**.

CARAVAN AND MOTORHOME SITES

The majority of campsites also accept caravans and motorhomes. Any campsite with one star or more will have electrical hook-ups. Listings will show the degree to which each campsite is geared towards caravans and motorhomes, as opposed to tents. A few sites are reserved exclusively for motorhomes.

CHALET PARKS AND ADVENTURE CAMPS

Some campsites offer small chalets, also called bungalows or cottages. This is particularly the case in Luxembourg, which has **Europacamping Nommerlayen** near Larochette. There are also a few fully-fledged holiday resorts based around chalet accommodation, set in the countryside. These offer a range of sporting and outdoor facilities, including swimming pools, cycle paths, tennis courts, fitness centres and sauna suites, as well as restaurants and entertainment. The best known of these belong to **CenterParcs**, which has parks across northern Europe. Belgium has two: De Vossemeren and Erperheide, both in the Province of Limburg. Also in Limburg is the chalet park **Molenheide**. There are other centres that focus on more rugged outdoor challenges, such as pot-holing, quadbiking, rock-climbing, and kayak rafting. **Durbuy Adventure** in the Ardennes offers its guests Indian tepees, wooden tree-cabins, igloo tents and residential caravans.

DIRECTORY

CAMPING ORGANIZATIONS

Camping Card International
www.campingcard international.com

Camprilux
p/a Camping Auf Kengert, 7633, Medernach.
www.camping.lu

Eurocampings
www.eurocampings.net

FICC
Rue des Colonies 18-24, 1000 BRU. *Tel (02) 5138782.* www.ficc.org

Flanders Camping Federation
www.camping.be

Walcamp
Rue du Monty 5, Florenville. *Tel (061) 321611.* www. campingbelgique.be

TREKKERS' HUTS

Reservieringscentrale Trekkershutten Vlaanderen
Grote Markt 44, Turnhout. *Tel (014) 408262.* www.vlaanderen-vakantieland.be

Wanderhütten Luxemburg
www.wanderhutten.lu

CHALET PARKS AND ADVENTURE CAMPS

CenterParcs
Tel (070) 224900. www.centerparcs.be

De Vossemeren:
Elzen 145, Lommel.
Tel (011) 548200.

Erperheide:
Erperheidestraat 2, Peer. *Tel (011) 616263.*

Durbuy Adventure
Rue de Rome 1, Durbuy.
Tel (086) 212815. www. durbuyadventure.be

Europacamping Nommerlayen
Rue Nommerlayen, Nommern, Luxembourg.
Tel 878078. www. nommerlayen-ec.lu

Molenheide
Molenheidestraat 7, Houthalen-Helchteren.
Tel (011) 521044. www.molenheide.be

Choosing a Hotel

The hotels and lodgings in this guide have been selected across a wide price range for their good value, facilities and location. The prices listed are those charged by the hotel, although discounts may be available at off-peak times and through agencies. The hotels are listed by area. For map references in Brussels, see pages 92–7.

PRICE CATEGORIES
The following price ranges are for a standard double room and taxes per night during the high season. Breakfast is not included, unless specified.

€ Under €80
€€ €80–€130
€€€ €130–€180
€€€€ €180–€260
€€€€€ Over €260

BRUSSELS

CENTRAL BRUSSELS Sleep Well Youth Hotel
€

Rue du Damier 23, 1000 BRU **Tel** *(02) 2185050* **Fax** *(02) 2181313* **Rooms** *93*   **City Map** *2 D1*

Centrally located, this good-value, clean and cheery hotel has dormitory rooms for up to 8 people and plenty of smaller, private rooms. There is no curfew, but there is a lock-out in the middle of the day. An annexe called the Sleep Well Star operates less like a youth hostel. Continental breakfast included in the price. **www.sleepwell.be**

CENTRAL BRUSSELS Brussels Welcome Hotel
€€

Quai au Bois-à-Brûler 23, 1000 BRU **Tel** *(02) 2199546* **Fax** *(02) 2171887* **Rooms** *17*   **City Map** *1 C1*

Bali, Tibet, Egypt, Zanzibar, the Silk Road – all rooms in this delightful hotel have been individually decorated to evoke travellers' dreams. There are good fish restaurants at hand. Also near are the Grand Place and the fashion street Rue Antoine Dansaert. Price includes breakfast in the Art Deco buffet bar. **www.brusselswelcomehotel.be**

CENTRAL BRUSSELS Café du Vaudeville
€€

Galérie de la Reine 11, 1000 BRU **Tel** *(02) 5112345* **Fax** *(02) 5124077* **Rooms** *4*   **City Map** *2 D3*

This bed-and-breakfast has four luxuriously stylish rooms in the elegant 19th-century shopping arcade Galéries St-Hubert. Breakfast, included in the price, is brought to the room. All rooms have private bathrooms. The restaurant below is attached to a restored Vaudeville theatre. **www.chambresdhotesduvaudeville.be**

CENTRAL BRUSSELS Manhattan
€€

Boulevard Adolphe Max 132-40, 1000 BRU **Tel** *(02) 2291619* **Fax** *(02) 2232599* **Rooms** *62*   **City Map** *2 D1*

With its location close to the Gare du Nord, the Manhattan is well positioned for accessing the city centre and the shops on Rue Neuve. The hotel is a bit basic but the rooms are clean and comfortable and there are plenty of restaurants within easy walking distance. Room price includes a Continental breakfast. **www.hotelmanhattan.be**

CENTRAL BRUSSELS Noga
€€

Rue du Béguinage 38, 1000 BRU **Tel** *(02) 2186763* **Fax** *(02) 2181603* **Rooms** *19*   **City Map** *1 C1*

A well-established favourite with many regular vistors, Noga is small and comfortably decorated in a mixture of modern and antique styles. Located in a tranquil district, it is conveniently near the city centre. Its snooker room converts into a business meeting room. Breakfast is included in the price. **www.nogahotel.com**

CENTRAL BRUSSELS Atlas
€€€

Rue du Vieux-Marché-aux-Grains 30, 1000 BRU **Tel** *(02) 5026006* **Fax** *(02) 5026935* **Rooms** *88*   **City Map** *1 C2*

This well-presented, well-run, modern hotel not far from the Grand Place caters to a business clientele during the week, so a lower price range often applies at weekends and during the summer holidays. Price includes a Continental breakfast. There are plenty of good restaurant options nearby. **www.atlas-hotel.be**

CENTRAL BRUSSELS Citadines Ste Catherine Apart' Hotel
€€€

Quai au Bois-à-Brûler 51, 1000 BRU **Tel** *(02) 2211411* **Fax** *(02) 2211599* **Rooms** *169*   **City Map** *1 C1*

Just north of the Grand Place, this modern apartment-hotel offers studio flats or larger apartments on a self-catering or bed-and-breakfast basis. Apartments have kitchen facilities and sitting areas. A good choice for visitors, especially families, making short stays of a week or even just a night. **www.citadines.com**

CENTRAL BRUSSELS Floris Arlequin Grand Place
€€€

Rue de la Fourche 17-19, 1000 BRU **Tel** *(02) 5141615* **Fax** *(02) 5142202* **Rooms** *92*   **City Map** *2 D2*

A modern, three-star hotel located at the heart of the historic centre. Long established, it is now a part of the Floris chain. Some of the guest rooms boast great views over the city – guests can enquire about these when booking. Breakfast is included in the price. There are plenty of restaurants in the vicinity. **www.florishotels.com**

CENTRAL BRUSSELS Le Dixseptième
€€€€

Rue de la Madeleine 25, 1000 BRU **Tel** *(02) 5171717* **Fax** *(02) 5026424* **Rooms** *24*   **City Map** *2 D3*

One of Brussels's most charming hotels, Le Dixseptième is set in the old residence of the Spanish ambassador, built in the late 17th century. Suites are elegantly furnished with a mixture of antique charm and modern flair and are named after Belgian artists. Breakfast is included in the price. **www.ledixseptieme.be**

Key to Symbols *see back cover flap*

CENTRAL BRUSSELS NH Atlanta   🚫 P 🍴 📺 📶 📋   €€€€
Boulevard Adolphe Max 7, 1000 BRU **Tel** *(02) 2170120* **Fax** *(02) 2173758* **Rooms** *241*   **City Map** 2 D1

A large and busy hotel with the polished professionalism of the international NH group. The comfortable rooms have an intimate charm. Located close to shopping on the Rue Neuve, within easy walking distance of the Grand Place. A buffet breakfast – included in the price – is served in the rooftop breakfast room. **www.nh-hotels.com**

CENTRAL BRUSSELS Amigo   P 🍴 📺 📶 📋   €€€€€
Rue de l'Amigo 23-27, 1000 BRU **Tel** *(02) 5474747* **Fax** *(02) 5135277* **Rooms** *173*   **City Map** 1 C3

Named after L'Amigo, the prison on this site in the era of the Spanish Netherlands, this hotel belongs to the Rocco Forte group and guarantees comfort and elegance. The spacious rooms are individually styled with all modern conveniences and marbled bathrooms. Superbly located, right by the Grand Place. **www.hotelamigo.com**

CENTRAL BRUSSELS Hotel Bloom   🚫 P 🍴 📺 📶 📋   €€€€
Rue Royale 250, 1210 BRU **Tel** *(02) 2206611* **Fax** *(02) 2178444* **Rooms** *305*   **City Map** 2 D2

Located near the botanical gardens, this well-connected contemporary hotel offers rooms which are clean, stylish and individually styled with hand-painted frescoes. Other amenities offered here include a restaurant serving cocktail desserts such as the mohito dessert and a trendy bar area. **www.hotelbloom.com**

CENTRAL BRUSSELS Le Méridien   🚫 P 🍴 📺 📶 📋   €€€€
Carrefour de la Europe 3, 1000 BRU **Tel** *(02) 5484211* **Fax** *(02) 5484080* **Rooms** *224*   **City Map** 1 C2

A modern luxury hotel between the Gare Centrale and Grand Place, Le Meridien is designed to fulfil the needs of both vacationers and business clients. On offer are all the facilities that come with a five-star rating. Rooms and suites are designed in a comfortable modern style, with touches of personality. **www.starwoodhotels.com**

CENTRAL BRUSSELS Métropole   🚫 P 🍴 📺 📶 📋   €€€€€
Place du Brouckère 31, 1000 BRU **Tel** *(02) 2172300* **Fax** *(02) 2180220* **Rooms** *300*   **City Map** 2 D2

This is the most celebrated of the grand hotels in Brussels, glittering with *belle époque* charm, but updated to top modern standards. Centrally located, close to the Place St-Catherine, the hotel also has a splendid bar and café with a pavement terrace. Breakfast is included in the room price. **www.metropolehotel.com**

CENTRAL BRUSSELS Radisson Blu Royal Hotel   P 🍴 📺 📶 📋   €€€€€
Rue du Fossé-aux-Loups 47, 1000 BRU **Tel** *(02) 2192828* **Fax** *(02) 2196262* **Rooms** *281*   **City Map** 2 D2

The Radisson SAS chain offers comfort and efficiency with style. Guests are welcomed in a towering atrium with fountains and plants, and glass lifts to all floors. The hotel also has one of Brussels's most celebrated fish restaurants, the Sea Grill. **www.radissonblu.com/royalhotelbrussels**

CENTRAL BRUSSELS Renaissance Brussels   🚫 P 🍴 🏊 📺 📶 📋   €€€€€
Rue de Parnasse 19, 1050 BRU (Ixelles) **Tel** *(02) 5052929* **Fax** *(02) 5052555* **Rooms** *262*   **City Map** 3 A4

Part of the Marriott chain, this sleek hotel is located close to the European Parliament. Weekends are often quiet and result in bargain rates. Although out of the centre, the hotel is not far from Palais Royal and top museums such as the Musée Wiertz. Also, a rare Brussels hotel with a swimming pool. **www.marriott.com**

GREATER BRUSSELS Les Bluets   €
Rue Berckmans 124, 1060 BRU (St-Gilles) **Tel** *(02) 5343983* **Fax** *(02) 5430970* **Rooms** *8*   **Road Map** B5

A charming, family-run hotel in a 19th-century townhouse. The rooms are decorated with a laidback mixture of antique furniture, *objets d'art* and modern facilities. The name means The Cornflowers, and the plant theme is echoed in the small conservatory. A Continental breakfast is included in the price. **www.bluets.be**

GREATER BRUSSELS Résidence Rembrandt   €
Rue de la Concorde 42, 1050 BRU (Ixelles) **Tel** *(02) 5127139* **Fax** *(02) 5117136* **Rooms** *12*   **Road Map** B5

More like a bed-and-breakfast, this small and friendly guesthouse is decorated with old photographs and Old Masters. Good value, given its position near the Art Nouveau district and the shops of Avenue Louise. Only six of the rooms have full en-suite bathrooms. Breakfast is included in the price. **www.hotelrembrandt.be**

GREATER BRUSSELS Monty Small Design Hotel   📶   €€€
Boulevard Brand Whitlock 101, 1200 BRU **Tel** *(02) 7345636* **Fax** *(02) 7345005* **Rooms** *18*   **Road Map** B5

Located just east of the Parc du Cinquantenaire, this hotel is a restored 1930s *maison de maître* (townhouse). The rooms are decorated to high standards, with furniture by local designers. On offer are a communal lounge, a bar and a private garden. Room price includes a Continental breakfast. **www.monty-hotel.be**

GREATER BRUSSELS Conrad Brussels   🚫 P 🍴 🏊 📺 📶 📋   €€€€€
Avenue Louise 71, 1050 BRU (Ixelles) **Tel** *(02) 5424242* **Fax** *(02) 5424200* **Rooms** *266*   **Road Map** A5

Much favoured by travellers in this particular price bracket, this modern and super-luxurious hotel is a 20-minute walk from the Grand Place. Facilities include a spa with swimming pool (not included in the room price) and a health club. The rooms are spacious and comfortable with hints of classic tradition. **www.conradhotels1.hilton.com**

GREATER BRUSSELS Le Châtelain   🚫 P 🍴 📺 📶 📋   €€€€€
Rue du Châtelain 17, 1000 BRU **Tel** *(02) 6460055* **Fax** *(02) 6460088* **Rooms** *107*   **Road Map** B5

A five-star hotel specializing in suites and maintaining a high standard of luxury. Its location is in an agreeable and tranquil part of Ixelles, well south of Avenue Louise, and close to Musée Horta and the Art Nouveau district. There are good public transport links to the city centre. **www.le-chatelain.com**

WESTERN FLANDERS

BRUGES Charlie Rockets
P 🍴 **€**

Hoogstraat 19, 8000 Bruges **Tel** *(050) 330660* **Rooms** *19*
Road Map *B1*

Set just east of the Burg, this engaging youth hostel occupies a converted cinema and is fronted by a big, raucous and atmospheric café-bar serving nachos and burgers to the beat of rock – a lively atmosphere of international exchange. The rooms, sleeping two, four or six people, are basic but keenly priced. **www.charlierockets.com**

BRUGES Alegria
P **€€**

St-Jakobsstraat 34, 8000 Bruges **Tel** *(050) 330937* **Fax** *(050) 347686* **Rooms** *6*
Road Map *B1*

Utterly charming, family-run guesthouse close to the Markt. Each of the well-equipped rooms has been thematically styled; some overlook the garden to the rear. A good breakfast, included in the room price, is served in the garden room. The owners provide excellent advice about Bruges's attractions and restaurants. **www.alegria-hotel.com**

BRUGES Ter Brughe
P **€€**

Oost-Gistelhof 2, 8000 Bruges **Tel** *(050) 340324* **Fax** *(050) 338873* **Rooms** *46*
Road Map *B1*

This charming hotel in a converted 16th-century family home has luxury rooms, antique furnishings, great canal views and a large outdoor patio. Even the standard rooms have wooden-beamed ceilings. There is a large outdoor patio to relax in. A buffet breakfast is included and served in the medieval basement. **www.hotelterbrughe.com**

BRUGES Coté Canal
€€€

Hertsbergestraat 8-10, 8000 Bruges **Tel** *0475 457707* **Rooms** *4*
Road Map *B1*

An excellent bed-and-breakfast set in an 18th-century townhouse beside one of central Bruges's most picturesque canals, the Groene Rei. There are two suites, styled with simple, antique-oriented elegance and modern facilities. Breakfast, included in the price, may be served at the water's edge. **www.bruges-bedandbreakfast.be**

BRUGES De Castillion
♿ P 🍴 📺 🖨 **€€€**

Heilige-Geeststraat 1, 8000 Bruges **Tel** *(050) 343001* **Fax** *(050) 339475* **Rooms** *20*
Road Map *B1*

This sumptuous hotel occupies a 17th-century mansion, once home to Jean-Baptiste-Louis de Castillion, Bishop of Bruges. Rooms are comfortably decorated and have modern facilities. The price includes a buffet breakfast. The hotel also has an equally sumptuous restaurant, Le Manoir Quatre Saisons. **www.castillion.be**

BRUGES Kempinski Hotel Duke's Palace
♿ P 🍴 🏊 📺 🛏 🖨 🔲 🍸 **€€€€**

Prinsenhof 8, 8000 Bruges **Tel** *(050) 447888* **Fax** *(050) 447880* **Rooms** *93*
Road Map *B1*

The Prinsenhof was once the location of the palace of the dukes of Burgundy. A Neo-Gothic nunnery built on the site in the 19th-century now serves as a five-star hotel – Bruges's first – established by the Kempinski group. The generous sense of space extends into a huge sculpture garden at the back. **www.kempinski-bruges.com**

BRUGES Martin's Orangerie
♿ P 🖨 **€€€€**

Kartuizerinnenstraat 10, 8000 Bruges **Tel** *(050) 341649* **Fax** *(050) 333016* **Rooms** *20*
Road Map *B1*

Elegantly decorated in traditional style, this delightful establishment belongs to the Martin chain of intriguing hotels, which specializes in interesting buildings and a warm welcome. The hotel occupies a converted 15th-century convent overlooking the Dijver canal. Breakfast served by the water's edge. **www.hotelorangerie.com**

BRUGES Oud Huis de Peellaert
♿ P 🍴 🛏 🖨 **€€€€**

Hoogstraat 20, 8000 Bruges **Tel** *(050) 337889* **Fax** *(050) 330816* **Rooms** *50*
Road Map *B1*

There is charm and grandeur in equal measure in this large and restored 19th-century mansion located just east of the Markt, the heart of the city. The 16th-century cellars have been converted into a fitness suite and sauna. A generous buffet breakfast, included in the price, is served in a garden room. **www.depeellaert.com**

BRUGES Relais Oud Huis Amsterdam
P 🍴 🛏 🖨 **€€€€**

Genthof 4a, 8000 Bruges **Tel** *(050) 341810* **Fax** *(050) 338891* **Rooms** *44*
Road Map *B1*

A group of 17th-century mansion houses lining the beautiful Spiegelrei canal is the setting for one of Bruges's best-loved hotels. Rooms have handsome antiques, but are styled with a casual elegance. The hotel has a relaxed charm, which is reflected in the management style. The price includes a buffet breakfast. **www.oha.be**

BRUGES Walburg
P 🍴 🛏 **€€€€**

Boomsgaardstraat 13-15, 8000 Bruges **Tel** *(050) 349414* **Fax** *(050) 336884* **Rooms** *19*
Road Map *B1*

A grand 19th-century mansion, stylishly restored to a state of cool and spacious elegance. Some of the rooms overlook the garden at the back. A buffet breakfast is included in the price. The location is in an interesting area to the east of the Markt, close to canal walks along St-Annarei and Spinolarei. **www.hotelwalburg.be**

DAMME Hoeve de Steenoven
🖨 ♿ P **€**

Damse Vaart Zuid 24, 8340 Oostkerke Damme **Tel** *(050) 501362* **Rooms** *4*
Road Map *B1*

Set in the tranquil countryside of pasture and canals near Damme, this is an excellent example of *hoevetoerisme* bed-and-breakfasts. Rooms have a simple rustic style with flagstones, exposed beams, wood and wicker. Breakfast is a buffet that includes fresh home-made cookies, jams and freshly laid farm eggs. **www.hoevedesteenoven.be**

Key to Price Guide *see p262* **Key to Symbols** *see back cover flap*

DE HAAN Romantik Manoir Carpe Diem
P ⛱ ♿ · €€€

Prins Karellaan 12, 8421 De Haan **Tel** *(059) 233220* **Fax** *(059) 233396* **Rooms** *15* **Road Map** *A1*

This hotel is a villa standing on raised ground in the centre of the seaside resort. Whitewashed walls, the inscription, gables and red-tiled roofs are reminiscent of the architecture of the tranquil béguinages. Rooms offer elegant comfort and there is a heated pool. A generous breakfast is included in the price. **www.manoircarpediem.com**

DENDERMONDE Cosy Cottage
P · €€

Oude Eegene 38, 9200 Dendermonde **Tel** *(052) 428443* **Rooms** *6* **Road Map** *C2*

Situated 5 km (3 miles) outside Dendermonde, next to the River Scheldt, Cosy Cottage is a B&B that would rank as a four-star hotel. Rooms are decorated to a high level of comfort. The garden runs down to the bicycle path along the riverbank. The complimentary breakfast is superb and there is a reliable restaurant nearby. **www.cosycottage.be**

GHENT Erasmus
♿ · €€

Poel 25, 9000 Ghent **Tel** *(09) 2242195* **Fax** *(09) 2257591* **Rooms** *11* **Road Map** *B2*

A late 16th-century patrician's house, this small hotel retains many original features as well as a fine collection of antique furniture. The owners are welcoming and the atmosphere is relaxed. The hotel is located just west of the city centre, close to the Graslei, shops and a good range of restaurants. **www.erasmushotel.be**

GHENT Monasterium PoortAckere
P ♟ ♿ · €€

Oude Houtlei 56, 9000 Ghent **Tel** *(09) 2692210* **Fax** *(09) 2692230* **Rooms** *54* **Road Map** *B2*

Located in a largely 19th-century converted convent, this hotel has an air of deep tranquillity. There is still an ecclesiastical feel to some of the public rooms and the simply furnished bedrooms. A special place, enhanced by a relaxed atmosphere, and the convenient location just west of the city centre. **www.poortackere.com**

GHENT NH Gent Belfort
♿ P ♟ ▦ ♿ ▤ · €€

Hoogpoort 63, 9000 Ghent **Tel** *(09) 2333331* **Rooms** *175* **Road Map** *B2*

Now run by the NH chain, the Belfort offers stylish comfort to international standards, yet with an appreciation for the need for individuality. It is centrally located, close to the belfry, and is perfectly positioned for wandering the medieval streets. The hotel has its own restaurant, plus a garden and a fitness centre. **www.nh-hotels.com**

GHENT Sandton Grand Hotel Reylof
▤ ♿ P ♟ ⛱ ▦ ▤ · €€

Hoogstraat 36, 9000 Ghent **Tel** *(09) 2354070* **Fax** *(09) 2354079* **Rooms** *158* **Road Map** *B2*

Situated in the historical centre of Ghent, this luxury hotel boasts an imposing structure, the oldest part of which is an 18th-century hotel or townhouse built in Louis XIV style. Wellness facilities offered here are gym, solarium, steam bath and sauna. Other features include a restaurant, cocktail bar, patios and classical enclosed gardens. **www.sandton.eu/gent**

IEPER La Porte Cocherel
▤ P · €€

Patersstraat 22, 8900 Ieper **Tel** *(047) 7379505* **Rooms** *3* **Road Map** *A2*

Built in authentic French style, this aristocratic house is located in the heart of Ieper and within walking distance from all major attractions. The rooms are spacious, beautifully decorated and provide suitable modern conveniences. Breakfast is included in the room price. **www.laportecochere.com**

KEMMEL Hostellerie Kemmelberg
P ♟ ♿ · €

Kemmelbergweg 34, 8950 Kemmel **Tel** *(057) 452160* **Fax** *(057) 444089* **Rooms** *16* **Road Map** *A2*

For visitors to the World War I battlefields and cemeteries, this place is balm – a modern hotel-restaurant sitting on top of the Kemmel hill, the highest point in Flanders. Some of the comfortable, well-furnished rooms have balconies to profit from the splendid views. Breakfast is included in the room price. **www.kemmelberg.be**

KNOKKE-HEIST Manoir du Dragon
♿ P ♿ · €€€€€

Albertlaan 73, 8300 Knokke **Tel** *(050) 630580* **Fax** *(050) 630590* **Rooms** *16* **Road Map** *B1*

A small hotel by the golf course, this comfortable 20th-century manor has all the ease and elegance of a premier seaside resort in Belgium. Many of the rooms are spacious suites, with windows looking out onto the extensive gardens. A gastronomic breakfast is included in the room price. **www.manoirdudragon.be**

KORTRIJK Broel
♟ ⛱ ♿ · €€€

Broelkaai 8, 8500 Kotrijk **Tel** *(056) 218351* **Fax** *(056) 200302* **Rooms** *70* **Road Map** *B2*

Standing by the River Leie and the medieval Broeltoren bridge, this engaging, spacious and comfortable hotel was once a tobacco factory. The interior has now been been remodelled on a medieval theme and is geared up as a conference centre, with all modern conveniences, a bistro and a swimming pool. **www.sandton.eu/kortrijk**

OOSTENDE Andromeda
♿ P ♟ ⛱ ▦ ♿ · €€€

Kursaal Westhelling 5, 8400 Oostende **Tel** *(059) 806611* **Fax** *(059) 806629* **Rooms** *94* **Road Map** *A1*

A modern high-rise hotel with straightforward comfortable rooms and balconies overlooking the town's best beach and the evening sun. There is an indoor pool for less clement days and a thalassotherapy centre offering sauna and massage, plus a brasserie and a respected seafood reataurant. **www.andromedahotel.be**

OUDENAARDE De Rantere
P ♟ ♿ · €€

Jan Zonder Vreeslaan 8 **Tel** *(055) 318988* **Rooms** *28* **Road Map** *B2*

A comfortable, efficiently-run business hotel overlooking the River Scheldt, just south of the Markt. Comfortable if rudimentary rooms, with modern conveniences. The well-respected restaurant has a garden terrace. Breakfast is included. The hotel also has an apartment-hotel 3 km (2 miles) outside the town. **www.derantere.be**

POPERINGE Manoir Ogygia   ⌖ � 🍴   €€

Veurnestraat 108, 8970 Poperinge **Tel** *(057) 338838* **Fax** *(057) 332911* **Rooms** *9*   **Road Map** *A2*

Listed as a Historic Hotel of Europe, this elegant step-gabled brick manor dates from 1879 and stands in a shaded park close to the town centre. The rooms have a simple, classical elegance. There is also a wellness centre with sauna, Jacuzzi and massage. Breakfast, included in the price, is served in the garden in summer. **www.ogygia.be**

POPERINGE L'Hôtel Recour   ⌖ P 🍴 ⏲   €€€

Guido Gezellestraat 7, 8970 Poperinge **Tel** *(057) 335725* **Fax** *(057) 335425* **Rooms** *19*   **Road Map** *A2*

A comfortable hotel with a garden, close to the main square of Poperinge. The decor is grand, with gilt frames and chandeliers, and yet, in some rooms, fetchingly rustic, with exposed beams and brickwork. It is famous for its restaurant, Pegasus, and has a sauna, Jacuzzi and Turkish bath with an ice shower. **www.pegasusrecour.be**

VEURNE 't Kasteel en 't Koetshuys   🍴 ⏲   €€

Lindedreef 5-7, 8630 Veurne **Tel** *(058) 315372* **Rooms** *12*   **Road Map** *A2*

This grand old mansion has been turned into a small, family-run hotel. The big, airy rooms are decorated with antique furniture and curios. In summer, breakfast (included in the price) is served in the garden. The hotel also has a wellness centre, with sauna, Turkish bath and massage. **www.kasteelenkoetshuys.be**

CENTRAL AND EASTERN FLANDERS

AARSCHOT Hotel Geerts   ⌖ P 🍴 ⏲ 🖥   €€€

Grote Markt 50, 2260 Westerlo **Tel** *(014) 544017* **Fax** *(014) 541880* **Rooms** *18*   **Road Map** *D2*

Some 12 km (7 miles) north of Aarschot and Diest, this agreeable hotel lies in the centre of the small town of Westerlo. Rooms are comfortable and spacious. A substantial buffet breakfast is included. There is also a gourmet restaurant and the excellent Bistro Orangerie, which spills out on to the garden in summer. **www.hotelgeerts.be**

ANTWERP International Zeemanshuis   ⌖ P 🍴 ⏲   €

Falconrui 21, 2000 Antwerp **Tel** *(03) 2275433* **Fax** *(03) 2342603* **Rooms** *114*   **Road Map** *C1*

A 1950s modernist high-rise block, International Zeemanshuis was once a seamans' hostel, but is now open to all. Rooms are simple, but have en-suite bathrooms. Hotel and restaurant are good value, given the location in the trendy, if somewhat shabby, area between the Grote Markt and the old docks. **www.zeemanshuis.be**

ANTWERP Rubens Grote Markt   P ⏲ 🖥   €€

Oude Beurs 29, 2000 Antwerp **Tel** *(03) 2224848* **Fax** *(03) 2251940* **Rooms** *36*   **Road Map** *C1*

This quietly situated four-star hotel offers deluxe accommodation, including spacious double rooms and a romantic junior suite with private terrace. Breakfast is included in the price. The rear courtyard has a rare surviving example of the many medieval lookout towers that used to prick Antwerp's skyline. **www.hotelrubensantwerp.be**

ANTWERP Firean   🍴   €€€

Karel Oomsstraat 6, 2018 Antwerp **Tel** *(03) 2370260* **Fax** *(03) 2381168* **Rooms** *11*   **Road Map** *C1*

A welcoming hotel in a 1929 Art Deco mansion, close to the main art museums. With stained-glass doors, crystal chandeliers in the lounge, antique furnishings in the rooms and a secluded garden, the hotel offers its own brand of stylish luxury. The restaurant is well respected and breakfast is included in the price. **www.hotelfirean.com**

ANTWERP Julien   P 🖥   €€€

Korte Nieuwstrrat 24, 2000 Antwerp **Tel** *(03) 2290600* **Fax** *(03) 2333570* **Rooms** *11*   **Road Map** *C1*

A *hôtel de charme* in the pretty medieval area just east of the cathedral and close to the shopping streets. The two renovated 16th-century townhouses contain 11 rooms, each individually styled, fusing the old and the new with pared-down elegance and exposed wooden beams. Tranquil courtyard garden. **www.hotel-julien.com**

ANTWERP Linnen Hotel   🖥   €€€

Lijnwaadmarkt 9, 2000 Antwerp **Tel** *(04) 75763074* **Rooms** *3*   **Road Map** *C1*

Set in a traditional house, this B&B sits adjacent to the cathedral in the heart of Antwerp. All rooms are decorated in pure white Belgian linen. They are spacious and contemporary in design and offer free Wi-Fi. The cocktail bar on the first floor is an added bonus. **www.sleepingatlinnen.be**

ANTWERP Radisson Blu Park Lane Hotel   P 🍴 ≋ 📺 ⏲ 🖥   €€€

Van Eycklei 34, 2018 Antwerp **Tel** *(03) 2858585* **Fax** *(03) 2858586* **Rooms** *174*   **Road Map** *C1*

A smart, modern luxury hotel opposite the Stadspark (City Park), close to the diamond district and within 2 km (1 mile) of the historic city centre. It has a reasonably priced restaurant serving French and Belgian cuisine. There is also a swimming pool and fitness room suite. **www.radissonblu.com/parklanehotel-antwerp**

ANTWERP De Witte Lelie   P 🖥   €€€€

Keizerstraat 16-18, 2000 Antwerp **Tel** *(03) 2261966* **Fax** *(03) 2340019* **Rooms** *11*   **Road Map** *C1*

A five-star B&B in Antwerp's historical centre, the whitewashed De Witte Lelie (The White Lily) is constructed out of three converted 17th-century canal houses. Rooms are decorated in a mix of white-linen sofas, antique furnishings and up-to-date facilities. Relaxed, gracious and stylish. **www.dewittelelie.be**

Key to Price Guide *see p262* **Key to Symbols** *see back cover flap*

ANTWERP Les Nuits
P | €€€€

Lauge Gasthuisstraat 12, 2000 Antwerp **Tel** *(047) 214101* **Rooms** *24* **Road Map** *C1*

Located in the city centre of Antwerp, this hotel lies close to the cathedral, museums and theatres. Each room offers Auping Boxspring beds with high quality linen, walk-in shower, flat screen TV and free Wi-Fi. The hotel's restaurant boasts a sunny terrace area and a trendy bar. **www.hotellesnuits.com**

ANTWERP 't Sandt
P | €€€€

Zand 13-19, 2000 Antwerp **Tel** *(03) 2329390* **Fax** *(03) 2325613* **Rooms** *29* **Road Map** *C1*

A cosy four-star hotel in Antwerp's historical centre, 't Sandt occupies a protected mid-19th century building. The stylish decor is aptly called Louis-Philippe Neo-Rococo. Suites are set around a courtyard garden. The Cathedral Penthouse has one of the city's best views. Breakfast is included in the price. **www.hotel-sandt.be**

DIEST De Fransche Croon
P | €€

Leuvensestraat 26, 3290 Diest **Tel** *(013) 314540* **Fax** *(013) 333159* **Rooms** *28* **Road Map** *D2*

A whitewashed 19th-century coaching inn has been adapted into this agreeable, unpretentious hotel. It is within walking distance of all the sights, shops, restaurants and bars. Six of the rooms have been given a modern makeover; the rest are more traditional, but all are comfortable. Breakfast is included. **www.defranschecroon.be**

HALLE Warandehof
P | €€

Warandestraat 34, 1755 Oetingen **Tel** *((054) 566104* **Rooms** *7* **Road Map** *C2*

Just 12 km (7 miles) from Halle, this hospitable *hoevetoerisme* hotel, set out in a modernized farmhouse and stable blocks, caters to families and business clients. Buffet breakfast is part of the price. There is a help-yourself bar and open fire in the communal dining area. **www.warandehof.be**

HASSELT Radisson Blu Hotel
P | €€

Torenplein 8, 3500 Hasselt **Tel** *(011) 770007* **Fax** *(011) 770099* **Rooms** *126* **Road Map** *E2*

A 1970s towerblock in the town centre has been turned into a sleek modern hotel. Views from the upper floors are exhilarating. The rooms radiate high international standards, and have Jan van Eyck artwork. The Koper restaurant provides Flemish cuisine with a modern touch. **www.radissonblu.com**

LEUVEN Martin's Klooster
P | €€€€

Predikherenstraat 22, 3000 Leuven **Tel** *(016) 213141* **Fax** *(016) 223100* **Rooms** *103* **Road Map** *D2*

A beautifully renovated 16th-century monastery provides spacious suites and rooms, each with plenty of character, without forgoing a sense of monastic purity. Peace and calm pervade the stylish public rooms. Lying just west of the Grote Markt, the hotel is within easy reach of all the sights. **www.martins-hotels.com**

LIER Hof van Aragon
€€

Aragonstraat 6, 2500 Lier **Tel** *(03) 4910800* **Fax** *(03) 4910810* **Rooms** *20* **Road Map** *C1*

Occupying a renovated building in a quiet canal-side street, this small hotel offers simple well-presented rooms, with en-suite bathrooms. Buffet breakfast included. It is also possible to make half-board arrangements with a fixed menu at a very reasonable price. Walled garden for summer relaxation. **www.hofvanaragon.be**

MAASEIK Hotel Aldeneikerhof
€€

Hamontweg 103, 3680 Maaseik **Tel** *(089) 566777* **Fax** *(089) 566778* **Rooms** *8* **Road Map** *E1*

A solid, four-storey 19th-century residence just east of the town has been prettily renovated to make a charming guesthouse with garden. Breakfast included. Gastronomic dinner and half-board available by arrangement. Also on offer are 2- to 4-night cycling holidays, with packed lunch. **www.aldeneikerhof.be**

MAASEIK Kasteel Wurfeld
P | €€€

Kapelweg 60, 3680 Maaseik **Tel** *(089) 568136* **Fax** *(089) 568789* **Rooms** *33* **Road Map** *E1*

A vast country mansion dating from the 19th century, surrounded by 2.5 hectares (6 acres) of park. Some of the rooms are in a separate wing, but all offer spacious comfort. It is also possible to book half-board accommodation to take advantage of the excellent veranda-restaurant. Breakfast is included. **www.kasteelwurfeld.be**

MECHELEN Hotel Vé
P | €€€€

Vismarkt 14, 2800 Mechelen **Tel** *(015) 200755* **Fax** *(015) 200 760* **Rooms** *36* **Road Map** *C2*

A 1920s fish-smoking factory in the old fish market has been imaginatively converted into a stylish hotel, where minimalism meets comfort – a refreshing contrast to all the medieval wonders outside. The warm welcome is extended equally to visitors and business travellers. A buffet breakfast is included in the price. **www.hotelve.com**

TONGEREN Ambiotel
P | €€

Veemarkt 2, 3700 Tongeren **Tel** *(012) 262950* **Fax** *(012) 261542* **Rooms** *22* **Road Map** *E2*

A modern hotel in the middle of one of Belgium's oldest cities and a good base from which to explore sights on foot. Rooms are straightforward, but spacious and well presented. Breakfast included in the price. Lunch and dinner available at the brasserie Den Ambi – a reference to Ambiorix, the Gallic chieftain. **www.ambiotel.be**

TONGEREN De Tornaco
P | €€

Romeinse Kassei 5, 3840 Voort-Borgloon **Tel** *(012) 672600* **Rooms** *6* **Road Map** *E2*

A rambling collection of farm buildings stands on the site of an old Roman inn, 8 km (5 miles) from Tongeren. This has been made into a quiet and delightful *hoevetoerisme* B&B, with emphasis on horse riding and country produce. Spacious rooms with boutique-hotel standards. Restaurants in nearby Borloon. **www.detornaco.be**

TURNHOUT Priorij Corsendonk   🅿️ 🍴 🛁   €€
Corsendonk 5, 2360 Oud-Turnhout **Tel** *(014) 462800* **Fax** *(014) 390260* **Rooms** *78*   **Road Map** *E2*

A 17th-century priory, 15 km (9 miles) from Turnhout, converted into a comfortable hotel surrounded by gardens. There is a monastic air to the rooms, which are spread over several annexes. Although geared up for events, the hotel welcomes individual guests. Restaurant open subject to sufficient reservations on weekends. **www.priorij-corsendonk.be**

WESTERN WALLONIA

ATH Le Parc   🍴 🛁 📧   €€
Rue de l'Esplanade 13, 7800 Ath **Tel** *(068) 285485* **Fax** *(068) 285763* **Rooms** *11*   **Road Map** *B3*

A small family hotel located in a townhouse opposite a park and close to the centre of Ath. The somewhat basic rooms are quiet and comfortable and have en suite bathrooms and Wi-Fi. The on-site restaurant serves gourmet cuisine. **www.hotelduparcath.be**

CHARLEROI Leonardo Hotel Charleroi City   🅰️ 🅿️ 🍴 🛁 📧   €€
Boulevard Tirou 96, 6000 Charleroi **Tel** *(071) 319811* **Fax** *(071) 301596* **Rooms** *67*   **Road Map** *C3*

An efficient business hotel, with comfortable rooms. Services include a Sleep & Fly package with free airport transfers. Part of the Israeli Leonardo group. There is another Best Western Leonardo at Boulevard Pierre Mayence 1A – formerly simply called the Business Hotel. **www.leonardo-hotels.com**

CHARLEROI Le Mayence   🅿️ 🍴 🛁   €€
Rue du Parc 53, 6000 Charleroi **Tel** *(071) 201000* **Fax** *(071) 201009* **Rooms** *6*   **Road Map** *C3*

This apartment-hotel, in an attractively converted townhouse to the southeast of the centre, is just 10 minutes away from the Charleroi airport. It is attached to a restaurant (with terrace) of some standing. The beautifully presented rooms have their own kitchenettes. **www.le-mayence.be**

CHIMAY Hostellerie du Gahy   🅿️ 🍴 ♨️ 🛁   €€
Rue du Gahy 2, 6590 Momignies **Tel** *(060) 511093* **Fax** *(060) 513005* **Rooms** *6*   **Road Map** *C4*

Momignies is 11 km (7 miles) west of Chimay and close to the French border. The large stone farmhouse lies in the countryside, just north of the village, in a deeply tranquil setting. Unusually, it has a large indoor swimming pool. There is also a well-respected restaurant specializing in local cuisine. Breakfast is included in the room price.

CHIMAY Le Franc Bois   🅿️   €€
Rue Courtil aux Martias 18, 6463 Lompret **Tel** *(060) 214475* **Fax** *(060) 215140* **Rooms** *8*   **Road Map** *C4*

Lying 6 km (4 miles) east of Chimay, this delightful country hotel in a rough stone building has well-appointed, comfortable rooms with en suite bathrooms. A buffet breakfast is included in the price. A restaurant in the village serves regional specialities and Chimay beer. Walks lead along the River Eau Blanche. **www.hoteldefrancbois.be**

CHIMAY Le Petit Chapitre   €€
Place du Chapitre 5, 6460 Chimay **Tel** *(060) 211042* **Rooms** *5*   **Road Map** *C4*

Centrally located B&B in a red-brick and stone building that was formerly a religious house for canons, then nuns. After undergoing sympathetic renovations, it now gives guests the impression of being in "old Chimay". Equal attention has been lavished on the bedrooms. **http://users.skynet.be/bs938209/lepetitchapitre**

ÉCAUSSINNES-LALAING Le Manoir du Capitaine   🅰️ 🅿️ 🛁   €€
Chemin Boulouffe 1, 7181 Feluy **Tel** *(067) 874540* **Fax** *(067) 874550* **Rooms** *30*   **Road Map** *C3*

A brewery in the 19th century, then a stud farm, this attractive collection of red-brick buildings has been turned into an elegant apartment-hotel. It is primarily designed for seminars, but overnight guests are welcome. Feluy is 3 km (2 miles) from the fortress of Écaussinnes-Lalaing. **www.manoirducapitaine.com**

LA LOUVIÈRE Hôtel Tristar   🅰️ 🅿️ 🍴 🛁 📧   €
Place Maugrétout 5, 7100 La Louvière **Tel** *(064) 236260* **Fax** *(064) 261423* **Rooms** *29*   **Road Map** *C3*

An efficient business hotel in the middle of La Louvière, offering a full set of services to business clients, but also welcoming those travelling for pleasure. Gastronomic restaurant, plus the more modest La Dolce Vita next door, reflecting the influence of the large Italian community in this area. Breakfast is included. **www.hoteltristar.be**

MARIEMONT La Villa d'Este   🅿️ 🍴 🛁   €
Rue de la Déportation 63, 7100 Haine-St-Paul **Tel** *(064) 228160* **Fax** *(064) 261646* **Rooms** *8*   **Road Map** *C3*

Located 5 km (3 miles) west of Musée Royal de Mariemont, this hotel-restaurant occupies a large and handsome Renaissance-style building. The rooms are comfortable. Among the attractions are a gastronomic restaurant and a shaded garden. Breakfast is included. **www.lavilladeste.be**

MONS Infotel   🅰️ 🅿️ 🛁   €
Rue d'Havré 32, 7000 Mons **Tel** *(065) 401830* **Fax** *(065) 356224* **Rooms** *35*   **Road Map** *C3*

Despite its name, this is an attractive and welcoming hotel occupying part of a renovated 18th-century house, within walking distance of the Grand Place. The rooms are quiet, overlooking a central courtyard. A car-parking space is included in the price. There are plenty of restaurant choices in the vicinity. **www.hotelinfotel.be**

Key to Price Guide *see p262* **Key to Symbols** *see back cover flap*

MONS Best Western Hôtel Lido
🛗 P 📺   €€

Rue des Arbalestriers 112, 7000 Mons **Tel** *(065) 327800* **Fax** *(065) 843722* **Rooms** *72*   **Road Map** *C3*

This attractive hotel is in an uncompromisingly modern style that might even be called post-modern. Lido refers to the Jacuzzi and sauna suite, which form part of the fitness facilities available here. A reliable level of comfort and services, as suggested by the Best Western brand. Breakfast is included. **www.lido.be**

MONS St James
🛗 P 🚲   €€

Place de Flandre 8, 7000 Mons **Tel** *(065) 724824* **Fax** *(065) 724811* **Rooms** *21*   **Road Map** *C3*

Located east of the city centre, the St James occupies an attractive 18th-century building of stone and red-brick renovated to high standards. The rooms have been stylishly decorated in a near-minimalist contemporary style, with high-quality fittings. The centre of Mons is a 10-minutes' walk away. **www.hotelstjames.be**

THUIN Manon de la Source
📑 P   €€

Rue du Jeu de Balle 8 , 6560 Hantes Wihéries **Tel** *(071) 555170* **Fax** *(071) 558708* **Rooms** *4*   **Road Map** *C3*

A short distance away from Thuin, this B&B is set in the heart of the tranquil village of Hantes Wihéries. Visitors can choose from four beautifully decorated rooms, ideal for a romantic, relaxing stay. Guests can enjoy the outdoor spa or make use of the free bicycles provided. **www.manondelasource.be**

TOURNAI Hôtel Alcantara
P 🚲   €€

Rue des Bouchers St-Jacques 2, 7500 Tournai **Tel** *(069) 212648* **Fax** *(069) 212824* **Rooms** *24*   **Road Map** *B3*

A family-run hotel comprising the 17th-century mansion of a Spanish nobleman and an 18th-century bank building, close to Église St-Jacques. Rooms are furnished in a simple, elegant style, with historical touches. A buffet breakfast included. The hotel also has an apartment for longer stays. **www.hotelalcantara.be**

TOURNAI Hôtel Cathédrale
🛗 P 🍴 🚲   €€

Place St-Pierre 2, 7500 Tournai **Tel** *(069) 250000* **Fax** *(069) 250001* **Rooms** *59*   **Road Map** *B3*

A traditionally styled, modern hotel in a pleasant quarter east of the cathedral, conveniently near all the sights. Rooms are spacious and comfortable. There is a general orientation towards business conferences and events. The hotel has its own restaurant, and there are many other options in the locality. **www.hotelcathedrale.be**

CENTRAL WALLONIA

ANNEVOIE Le Moulin des Ramiers
P 🍴 🚲   €€€

Rue Basse 32, 5332 Crupet **Tel** *(083) 690240* **Fax** *(083) 699868* **Rooms** *6*   **Road Map** *D3*

A hotel-restaurant in a beautifully converted millhouse complex, 8 km (5 miles) east of Annevoie. The rooms are elegantly decorated, with antique touches, stone walls and other original features. There is an atmosphere of rural tranquillity. **www.moulindesramiers.be**

COUVIN Au Sanglier des Ardennes
🛗 P 🍴 🚲 ▤   €€

Rue JB Periquet 4, 5670 Oignies-en-Thiérache **Tel** *(060) 399089* **Fax** *(060) 390283* **Rooms** *8*   **Road Map** *D4*

A hotel-restaurant in an isolated Ardennes village close to the French border, 15 km (9 miles) southeast of Couvin. Surrounded by nature and also hunting grounds – game plays a major part in the cuisine. Simple rooms in a handsome stone building, with hospitality redolent of solid Belgian traditions. **www.ausanglierdesardennes.be**

DINANT Hotel Ibis Dinant
🛗 🚲 ▤   €

Rempart d'Albeau 16, 5500 Dinant **Tel** *(082) 211500* **Fax** *(082) 211579* **Rooms** *59*   **Road Map** *D3*

The reliable, Ibis chain of modern, no-frills and competitively priced hotels offers perhaps the best accommodation in town. Hotel Ibis Dinant stands on the river's edge, close to the town centre. Snack food is available at the hotel, but there are some good restaurants close by. Public parking 50 m (160 ft) away. **www.ibishotel.com**

DINANT Auberge-Grill Le Freÿr
P 🍴   €€

Chaussée des Alpinistes 22, 5500 Anseremme **Tel** *(082) 222575* **Rooms** *9*   **Road Map** *D3*

Agreeably straightforward hotel-restaurant 7 km (4 miles) south of Dinant, in a modern chalet-style building. The decor is unfussy and family-oriented. Rooms occupy a stable-like extension overlooking the garden. Prices are for half-board. The restaurant prides itself on traditional cooking and seasonal ingredients. **www.lefreyr.be**

DINANT Best Western Castel de Pont-à-Lesse
🛗 P 🍴 🏊 🚲 ▤   €€€

Pont-à-Lesse 31, 5500 Anseremme **Tel** *(082) 222844* **Fax** *(082) 226303* **Rooms** *91*   **Road Map** *D3*

This establishment offers all the polished comforts that attract both business and tourist clientele. Occupying an 1810 manor house, with its restaurant and swimming pool in a modern glass extension, the hotel lies 10 km (6 miles) south of Dinant. **www.casteldepontalesse.be**

FLOREFFE Le Castel
P 🍴 🏊   €

Rue du Chapitre 10, 5070 Fosses-la-Ville **Tel** *(071) 711812* **Fax** *(071) 712396* **Rooms** *10*   **Road Map** *D3*

A 19th-century mansion located 9 km (6 miles) southwest of Floreffe. The rooms are modern and stylish. The outdoor heated swimming pool can be used between June and September. Fine restaurant specializing in modern adpatations of traditional dishes. Breakfast, served in the garden in summer, is included. **www.lecastel.be**

HAN-SUR-LESSE Grenier des Grottes   €€

Rue des Chasseurs Ardennais 1, 5580 Han-sur-Lesse **Tel** *(084) 377237* **Fax** *(084) 378050* **Rooms** *41* **Road Map** *D4*

Part of a small chain called Cocoon Hotels, this medium-sized establishment is ideally located in front of the departure point for the caves of Han-sur-Lesse. The spacious rooms offer all comforts. There is also a restaurant, garden and a health centre with sauna, hammam and Jacuzzi. Breakfast is included. **www.cocoonhotels.com**

HAN-SUR-LESSE Hôtel du Vieux Moulin   €€

Rue de l'Aujoule 51, 5580 Éprave **Tel** *(084) 377318* **Rooms** *9*   **Road Map** *D4*

Éprave lies 3 km (2 miles) north of Han-sur-Lesse in the heart of the cave region. This small "design hotel" in the village has been renovated to a high standard, with a clean-cut, minimalist style, making a virtue of natural materials. Fine dining at the attached Auberge du Vieux Moulin, run by the same owners. **www.eprave.com**

LAVAUX-STE-ANNE Beau Séjour   €€

Rue des Platanes 16, 5580 Villers-sur-Lesse **Tel** *(084) 377115* **Fax** *(084) 378134* **Rooms** *13*   **Road Map** *D4*

A rural village setting for charming accommodation, with a noted restaurant. The building is a fully renovated farmhouse. The rooms are individually styled, with views out on to the garden and an old royal hunting lodge. An unusual feature is the bathing pond. **www.beausejour.be**

LAVAUX-STE-ANNE Lemonnier   €€

Rue Baronne Lemonnier 82, 5580 Lavaux-Ste-Anne **Tel** *(084) 388883* **Fax** *(084) 388895* **Rooms** *9*   **Road Map** *D4*

A celebrated restaurant in a tranquil, countrified setting. Rooms are very comfortable and stylishly decorated. This is a good base from which to explore the region, with Dinant, Bouillon, St Hubert and Fourneau St-Michel all falling in a 40-km (25-mile) radius. Tables are set out in the garden during summer. **www.lemonnier.be**

LOUVAIN-LA-NEUVE Hôtel Mercure   €€

Blvd de Lauzelle 61, 1348 Louvain-la-Neuve **Tel** *(010) 450751* **Fax** *(010) 450911* **Rooms** *77*   **Road Map** *D2*

The Mercure chain of efficient, attractively priced business hotels offers a reliable choice of accommodation. This large, modern complex, geared up for seminars, is set in parkland close to the university. Rooms are comfortable and of international style. An on-site restaurant serves delicious food. **www.mercure.com**

NAMUR Grand Hôtel de Flandre   €

Place de la Station 14, 5000 Namur **Tel** *(081) 231868* **Fax** *(081) 228060* **Rooms** *33*   **Road Map** *D3*

A neat, modernized hotel handy for visitors arriving by train, this hotel is 10-minutes' walk from the city centre and is close to the museums. It is set in a classic 19th-century hotel building, but the rooms have been updated in an attractive style. There is pay-parking close by at a very reasonable day-rate. **www.hotelflandre.be**

NAMUR Beauregard   €€

Avenue Baron de Moreau 1, 5000 Namur **Tel** *(081) 230028* **Fax** *(081) 241209* **Rooms** *47*   **Road Map** *D3*

Aptly named Beauregard (Fine View), this hotel overlooks the River Meuse. Rooms are modern and spacious; those in the front have balconies. The hotel is part of the Casino of Namur and so is well placed for sightseeing and a flutter at the gaming tables. There is also a restaurant with river views. **www.hotelbeauregard.be**

NAMUR Les Tanneurs   €€

Rue des Tanneries 13B, 5000 Namur **Tel** *(081) 240024* **Fax** *(081) 240025* **Rooms** *32*   **Road Map** *D3*

Set in the city centre, with its own parking, this hotel-restaurant occupies a handsome 17th-century building, sensitively modernized to stress its architectural heritage. Rooms vary in size and price, but all are smart, modern and comfortable. There are two restaurants – the Grill and the much revered L'Espièglerie. **www.tanneurs.com**

NAMUR Château de Namur   €€€

Avenue de l'Ermitage 1, 5000 Namur **Tel** *(081) 729900* **Fax** *(081) 729999* **Rooms** *29*   **Road Map** *D3*

This grand hotel-restaurant, close to the Citadelle, is a huge early 20th-century red-brick château, with views of the Meuse valley from the front and of parkland at the back. Pastel-painted, modern rooms offer complete tranquillity. L'Ermitage restaurant has attractive set menus. **www.chateaudenamur.com**

NIVELLES Ferme de Grambais   €

Chaussée de Braine-le-Comte 102, 1400 Nivelles **Tel** *(067) 874420* **Fax** *(067) 841307* **Rooms** *10*   **Road Map** *C3*

An old, red-brick farmhouse has been converted into a hotel-restaurant, sympathetically reflecting its rural roots. Rooms are spacious and decorated in an unpretentious style. The family oriented restaurant serves traditional Belgian cuisine beneath the parasols on the terrace in summer. **www.fermedegrambais.be**

PHILIPPEVILLE Hôtel-Restaurant La Côte d'Or   €€

Rue de la Gendarmerie 1, 5600 Philippeville **Tel** *(071) 668145* **Fax** *(071) 666797* **Rooms** *8*   **Road Map** *C3*

A family-run hotel-restaurant respected for its well-priced, high-quality cooking, making half-board a good option. Set in a large house close to the heart of Philippeville, it has a rear extension overlooking a large garden. The rooms are straightforward, but have all the usual facilities. **www.lacotedor.com**

ROCHEFORT La Martinette   €

Rue Louis Banneux 65, 5580 Rochefort **Tel** *(084) 752243* **Rooms** *5*   **Road Map** *D4*

A B&B in a huge *belle époque* mansion, set on a hill with fine views over the River Lomme, surrounded by 3 hectares (7 acres) of woodland. All the bedrooms have en-suite bathrooms. Breakfast is included. There is also a *gîte*, and seminar facilities for personal development courses. **www.martinette.be**

Key to Price Guide *see p262* **Key to Symbols** *see back cover flap*

ROCHEFORT Lafayette
Rue Jacquet 87, 5580 Rochefort **Tel** *(084) 214273* **Fax** *(084) 221163* **Rooms** *8*　　　　　**Road Map** *D4*

Named after the French hero of the American Revolution who was arrested in Rochefort in 1792, this hotel-restaurant has a pretty, whitewashed street-front close to the the Château Comptal. Rooms are simple, but nicely presented. The restaurant serves traditional French-Belgian dishes at a reasonable price. **www.hotellafayette.be**

ROCHEFORT Le Vieux Logis
Rue Jacquet 71, 5580 Rochefort **Tel** *(084) 211024* **Fax** *(084) 221230* **Rooms** *10*　　　　　**Road Map** *D4*

A grand 17th-century residence has been turned into a comfortable and attractive hotel. The interior is ornamented with rustic antique furniture and furnishings. The rooms have been decorated in a similar style. Breakfast is included in the price and can be taken in the garden during summer. **www.levieuxlogis.be**

ROCHEFORT La Malle Poste
Rue de Behogne 46, 5580 Rochefort **Tel** *(084) 210986* **Fax** *(084) 221113* **Rooms** *24*　　　　　**Road Map** *D4*

A beautiful 17th-century posthouse and coaching inn is now a sumptuous hotel-restaurant. Suites have beamed ceilings, flagstone floors and linen-draped fourposter beds. The double bedrooms are almost as special. There is an indoor swimming pool, sauna and hammam and a large garden. Breakfast is included. **www.malleposte.be**

ROCHEFORT Château de Hassonville
Route d'Hassonville 105, 6900 Aye **Tel** *(084) 311025* **Fax** *(084) 316027* **Rooms** *20*　　　　　**Road Map** *D4*

Located 10 km (6 miles) northeast of Rochefort, this turretted castle was built for the French king Louis XIV and is now a luxury hotel. Rooms are individually styled with old-fashioned touches; some have views over the large park. The much-garlanded restaurant is located in a modern extension and serves gastronomic French cuisine. **www.hassonville.be**

EASTERN WALLONIA

ARLON Château du Pont d'Oye
Rue du Pont d'Oye 1, 6720 Habay-La-Neuve **Tel** *(063) 420130* **Fax** *(063) 420136* **Rooms** *18*　　　　　**Road Map** *E4*

A beautiful red-brick château, dating from 1652, set among beech forests. The suites are lordly; some doubles are more like servants' quarters, yet attractive enough. There is a respected gourmet restaurant and breakfast is included in the price. The hotel is about 12 km (7 miles) west of Arlon. **www.chateaudupontdoye.be**

BASTOGNE Hôtel Collin
Place McAuliffe 8-9, 6600 Bastogne **Tel** *(061) 214358* **Fax** *(061) 218083* **Rooms** *16*　　　　　**Road Map** *E4*

Located in the town centre, this hotel dates from 2000 and was developed by the owners of the restaurant Le 1900, Claudine and Philippe Collin. The rooms, all with en suite bathrooms, are modern and functional. A buffet breakfast is included in the room price. A good base for exploring Bastogne. **www.hotel-collin.com**

BASTOGNE Château de Strainchamps
Strainchamps 12, 6637 Fauvilliers **Tel** *(063) 600812* **Fax** *(063) 601228* **Rooms** *8*　　　　　**Road Map** *E4*

Situated 15 km (9 miles) south of Bastogne, this grand country residence dates from the18th and 19th centuries and has been a hotel-restaurant since 1990. The rooms are simple and comfortable. Breakfast is included. The restaurant is much respected, making half-board arrangements attractive. **www.chateaudestrainchamps.com**

BOUILLON Hôtel de la Poste
Place St-Arnould 1, 6830 Bouillon **Tel** *(061) 465151* **Fax** *(061) 465165* **Rooms** *60*　　　　　**Road Map** *D4*

A historic four-star hotel in the middle of the town, this establishment was founded in about 1730 and took on its present form in the 19th century. It retains a quality honed from centuries of hospitality. Rooms and suites are of varying sizes, some with river views. Breakfast is included in the room price. **www.hotelposte.be**

BOUILLON La Ferronnière
Voie Jocquée 44, 6830 Bouillon **Tel** *(061) 230750* **Fax** *(061) 464318* **Rooms** *12*　　　　　**Road Map** *D4*

On a hillside above the town, a hunting lodge-style half-timbered mansion with Art Nouveau touches has become a hotel-restaurant. Rooms are stylish and comfortable; some have views of the castle of Bouillon. Wellness facilities include sauna, hammam, Jacuzzi and Ayurvedic massage. Breakfast is included in the price. **www.laferronniere.be**

BOUILLON Panorama Hôtel
Rue au-dessus de la Ville 25, 6830 Bouillon **Tel** *(061) 466138* **Fax** *(061) 468122* **Rooms** *23*　　　　　**Road Map** *D4*

As the name suggests, this family-run hotel-restaurant, perched on a hillside, has wonderful views over Bouillon and its castle. The rooms are spacious and well-presented. The excellent restaurant serves French and Belgian dishes, notably game. Breakfast is included in the room price. **www.panoramahotel.be**

BOUILLON Auberge du Moulin Hideux
Route de Dohan 1, 6831 Noirefontaine **Tel** *(061) 467015* **Fax** *(061) 467281* **Rooms** *12*　　　　　**Road Map** *D4*

Part of the distinguished Relais et Château group, this beautifully converted 18th-century mill offers great comfort and elegance. It has a tennis court and indoor swimming pool as well as a gastronomic restaurant. The hotel is about 7 km (4 miles) east of Bouillon. **www.moulinhideux.be**

CHAUDFONTAINE Château des Thermes

Rue Hauster 9, 4050 Chaudfontaine **Tel** *(04) 3678067* **Fax** *(04) 3678069* **Rooms** *47*   **Road Map** *E3*

The main hotel of this spa town is a grand 18th-century residence, restored to modern magnificence and set in a pleasing wooded park. There is pampered luxury at every turn. The price includes breakfast as well as access to the spa centre. Fine dining in the restaurant. **www.chateaudesthermes.be**

DURBUY Clos de Récollets

Rue de la Prévôté 9-13, 6940 Durbuy **Tel** *(086) 212969* **Fax** *(086) 213685* **Rooms** *8*   **Road Map** *E3*

A charming hotel-restaurant in a 17th-century house, part stone, part half-timbered brick. The interior has been lovingly restored and imaginatively decorated to evoke a warm welcome and sense of comfort. Some of the rooms are small, but that is in the nature of the building. The restaurant is first rate. **www.closdesrecollets.be**

DURBUY Hébergerie de Petite Enneille

Petite Enneille 31, 6940 Durbuy **Tel** *(0473) 422574* **Fax** *(086) 387154* **Rooms** *4*   **Road Map** *E3*

An exquisite B&B in an old farmhouse filled with antique furniture. Outside is a terrace and garden, with views of the River Ourthe valley. On Fridays and Saturdays, only half-board two-night bookings are available. One-night stays are possible during the week. Evening meals can be pre-booked. **www.hebergerie-de-petite-enneille.be**

DURBUY Hôtel Victoria

Rue des Récollectines 4, 6940 Durbuy **Tel** *(086) 212300* **Fax** *(086) 212784* **Rooms** *15*   **Road Map** *E3*

A hotel-restaurant-grill in a grand townhouse. The interior has been refurbished in a relaxed Post-Modern style. Bedrooms are elegantly brushed with antique touches, in the exposed beams and furnishings. There is a family room in the roof space, as well as a large terraced garden for alfresco dining in summer. **www.hotel-victoria.be**

DURBUY Tropical Hôtel

Rue des Comtes de Luxembourg 41, 6940 Durbuy **Tel** *(086) 213995* **Fax** *(086) 213993* **Rooms** *34* **Road Map** *E3*

A large heated indoor swimming pool surrounded by deckchairs and tropical plants forms the centrepiece in this modern hotel complex. The main building and bungalows are set around a large Japanese water garden. Modern bedrooms and suites are available in all sizes. Good for family and activity-based holidays. **www.tropical-hotel.be**

FLORENVILLE La Ferme du Charmois

Rue du Charmois Moyen-Izel, 6810 Chiny-Jamoigne **Tel** *(0475) 782078* **Fax** *(052) 376067* **Rooms** *9*   **Road Map** *E4*

A beautifully restored 19th-century farmhouse, surrounded by softly undulating countryside and woodland, offers comfortable B&B rooms. Two-night bookings only. Le Charmois is about 5 km (3 miles) northeast of Florenville as the crow flies. **www.lecharmois.be**

HUY Hôtel du Fort et Sa Réserve

Chaussée Napoléon 5-9, 4500 Huy **Tel** *(085) 212403* **Fax** *(085) 231842* **Rooms** *28*   **Road Map** *D3*

The renovated Hôtel du Fort is a straightforward modern hotel by the River Meuse, and, as the name suggests, close to the Fort de Huy. This is a 5-minutes' walk from the centre. The hotel has been run by the same family since 1957. The restaurant serves traditional French-Belgian dishes at very reasonable prices. **www.hoteldufort.be**

HUY Château de Vierset

Rue la Coulée 1, 4577 Vierset-Barse **Tel** *(085) 410170* **Fax** *(085) 410150* **Rooms** *5*   **Road Map** *D3*

About 7 km (4 miles) south of Huy is a beautiful 18th-century, Renaissance-style château of brick and stone, with a moat and park. Sensitively restored, it is used for exhibitions, seminars, banquets and concerts, but also has simply and elegantly furnished *chambres d'hôte* rooms in the courtyard. **www.chateaudevierset.be**

LIÈGE Best Western Univers Hotel

Rue des Guillemins 116, 4000 Liège **Tel** *(04) 2545555* **Fax** *(04) 2545500* **Rooms** *51*   **Road Map** *E2*

Conveniently close to the prestigious Liège-Guillemins station, the Univers Hotel is only 2 km (1 mile) from major sights in the heart of the city. It has all the usual, reliable comforts and facilities offered by a Best Western establishment. There are plenty of restaurants within walking distance. **www.univershotel.be**

LIÈGE Cygne d'Argent

Rue Beeckmann 49, 4000 Liège **Tel** *(04) 2237001* **Fax** *(04) 2224966* **Rooms** *20*   **Road Map** *E2*

This agreeable small hotel occupies a modernized townhouse in a quiet street within walking distance of the Liège-Guillemins station and the Coeur Historique. The rooms are straightforward, modern and unfussy. The human touch is in the quality of service, a matter of pride for the hotel management. **www.cygnedargent.be**

LIÈGE Hors Château

Rue Hors Château 62, 4000 Liège **Tel** *(04) 2506068* **Fax** *(04) 2505631* **Rooms** *9*   **Road Map** *E2*

In the centre of the Coeur Historique, this small, modern hotel is perfectly placed for seeing the best of Liège. The rooms are small but stylish. This is a fascinating part of town to wander in, with plenty of bars and restaurants. Also nearby are the city's foremost museums and the La Batte Sunday market. **www.hors-chateau.be**

LIÈGE Ibis Liège Centre Opéra

Place de la République Française 41, 4000 Liège **Tel** *(04) 2303333* **Fax** *(04) 2230481* **Rooms** *78*   **Road Map** *E2*

A hotel of the Ibis chain with a central location, beside Place St-Lambert, the Centre Opéra offers easy access to all the sights, shops, bars and restaurants and the opera. The rooms are international in style, well-presented and "functional", as the hotel puts it. Pay-parking is available close by. **www.ibishotel.com**

Key to Price Guide *see p262* **Key to Symbols** *see back cover flap*

LIÈGE Château de Limont
Rue du Château 34, 4357 Limont-Donceel **Tel** (019) 544000 **Fax** (019) 545757 **Rooms** 23   **Road Map** D2

A handsome, modernized 18th-century château-farm, 15 km (9 miles) southwest of Liège, set on a quiet estate. Rooms are simply but comfortably furnished. The hotel specializes in hosting seminars and events; restaurant available on reservation. Also on offer: table tennis, pool table, pétanque, bicycles and Jacuzzi. **www.chateaulimont.be**

LIÈGE Ramada Plaza Liège City Centre
Quai St Léonard 36, 4000 Liège **Tel** (04) 2288111 **Fax** (04) 2274575 **Rooms** 149   **Road Map** E2

The Bedford, the old prestige hotel of Liège, has been taken over by the Ramada group and now has all the comforts and high standards associated with that chain. Overlooking the Meuse, it lies near the Musée Grand Curtius. The restaurant is in the oldest part of the complex, a former convent. **www.ramadaplaza-liege.com**

MALMEDY La Forge
Rue Devant les Religieuses 31, 4960 Malmedy **Tel** (080) 799591 **Fax** (080) 799598 **Rooms** 15   **Road Map** F3

This holiday hotel in the centre of town justifiably describes itself as "sympa" (friendly and agreeable). The rooms are simple but comfortable; family rooms are available. The café-bar, specializing in local beers, spills out onto a terrace in the summer. Book in advance for the races at Francorchamps. **www.hotel-la-forge.be**

MALMEDY Hotel Saint Géréon
7-8 Place Saint Géréon, 4960 Malmedy **Tel** (080) 330677 **Fax** (080) 339746 **Rooms** 10   **Road Map** F3

Situated on a quiet square in the centre of Malmedy, this hotel is a welcoming, family-run establishment with bright, comfortable and well-equipped rooms. The exterior is attractive and rustic in style, while the inside is modern and functional. Breakfast is included in the price, as well as free Wi-Fi. **www.saintgereon.be**

MALMEDY L'Esprit Sain
Chemin Rue 46, 4960 Malmedy **Tel** (080) 330314 **Fax** (080) 770338 **Rooms** 11   **Road Map** F3

A quiet, renovated hotel-restaurant with comfortable, modern rooms. The restaurant is celebrated for its down-to-earth traditional French cuisine. Breakfast is included in the room price. The hotel is close to a number of walks, cycle paths and horse-riding trails into the surrounding countryside. **www.espritsain.be**

SPA La Vigie
Avenue Professeur Henrijean 129, 4900 Spa **Tel** (087) 773497 **Rooms** 5   **Road Map** E3

Located 2 km (1 mile) from the town centre, this stone and half-timbered Ardennes house, built in 1902, is now a super-comfortable B&B set by a tranquil park. The rooms are beautifully presented, all details carefully thought through, with a strong emphasis on white linen. On weekends, two nights minimum stay. **www.lavigie.be**

SPA Villa des Fleurs
Rue Albin Body 31, 4900 Spa **Tel** (087) 795050 **Fax** (087) 795060 **Rooms** 12   **Road Map** E3

A small and charming hotel of the Best Western Group, in an elegant late 19th-century hôtel de maître (townhouse). Breakfast is included and in summer can be taken on a terrace overlooking the garden. Rooms vary in size, but all are decorated to a high standard. **www.villadesfleurs.be**

SPA Radisson Blu Balmoral
Avenue Léopold II, 40, 4900 Spa **Tel** (087) 792141 **Fax** (087) 792151 **Rooms** 106   **Road Map** E3

Set in woodlands just north of the town, close to the spa facilities, this hotel has the qualities of a four-star hotel plus its own indoor swimming pool, fitness centre and treatment options. Rooms are simply but comfortably furnished. Breakfast is included. These is also the Radisson Blu Palace Hotel in the centre of Spa. **www.radissonblu.com**

SPA Manoir de Lébioles
Domaine de Lébioles, 4900 Spa **Tel** (087) 791900 **Fax** (087) 791999 **Rooms** 16   **Road Map** E3

An impressive manor and park at Creppe is the setting for one of the town's most lavish hotels – a prestigious location for seminars, complete with heliport. Built in Flemish Renaissance style in 1905–12, it was briefly owned by a Belgian princess. The suites are luxurious, with a restaurant to match. **www.manoirdelebioles.com**

STAVELOT Hôtel Dufays
Rue Neuve 115, 4970 Stavelot **Tel** (080) 548008 **Rooms** 6   **Road Map** E3

Occupying an 18th-century maison de maître is this immensely stylish boutique hotel. Each room has been subtly decorated to a named theme – African, Chinese, 1001 Nights, 1930s and so forth. Breakfast is included. Prices rise for the Belgian Grand Prix at Francorchamps in late August–early September. **www.bbb-dufays.be**

STAVELOT Hotellerie "La Maison"
Place St-Remacle 19, 4970 Stavelot **Tel** (080) 880891 **Fax** (080) 600201 **Rooms** 19   **Road Map** E3

An elegant 18th-century mansion on the central marketplace houses this hostellerie-restaurant of classic charm. The spacious rooms have been refurbished, but retain an old-world dignity, mixing antique furnishing with all modern conveniences. Breakfast is included in the room price. **www.classic-hotels.be**

STAVELOT Le Val d'Amblève
Route de Malmedy 7, B-4970 Stavelot **Tel** (080) 281440 **Fax** (080) 281459 **Rooms** 18   **Road Map** E3

Located in the heart of the Liège Ardennes, Le Val d'Amblève is an architectural delight. Blending modern and traditional styles, this hotel ensures a comfortable stay, especially for families. Wellness facilities include sauna and hammam. Visitors can hire classic cars to explore the area. Price includes breakfast. **www.levaldambleve.be**

GRAND DUCHY OF LUXEMBOURG

BERDORF Le Bisdorff
Rue Heisbich 39, 6551 Berdorf **Tel** *790208* **Fax** *790629* **Rooms** *25*   **Road Map** *F4*

An utterly charming hotel-restaurant surrounded by a shaded garden. The pretty buildings have an old-fashioned air, with handsome rooms. Breakfast is included. Celebrated chef Sylvie Bisdorff runs the restaurant, specializing in traditional Luxembourgeois cuisine. Indoor heated swimming pool and sauna available. **www.hotel-bisdorff.lu**

BOURSCHEID Hôtel du Moulin
Buurschtermillen 1, 9164 Bourscheid-Moulin **Tel** *990015* **Fax** *990740* **Rooms** *14*   **Road Map** *F4*

Occupying a large milllhouse dating from 1714, this delightful hotel-restaurant stands at the foot of the castle of Bourscheid, close to the River Sûre, surrounded by wooded countryside. There is a restaurant, plus an indoor heated swimming pool and sauna. Minimum two nights' stay. A buffet breakfast is included. **www.moulin.lu**

BOURSCHEID Sporthotel Leweck
Route de Clervaux, 9378 Lipperscheid **Tel** *990022* **Fax** *990677* **Rooms** *51*   **Road Map** *F4*

Built in an impressive, vaguely château-like style, this very comfortable modern hotel sits in a large park and focusses on sport, well-being and gastronomy. Heated outdoor and indoor pools available. The restaurant plus brasserie serves Luxembourgeois dishes. A buffet breakfast is included in the price. **www.sporthotel.lu**

CLERVAUX Hôtel-Restaurant Koener
Grand-Rue 14, 9701 Clervaux **Tel** *921002* **Fax** *920826* **Rooms** *48*   **Road Map** *F4*

An elegant hotel, modern but with traditional standards, in the pedestrianized heart of Clervaux. Its wellness centre includes a sauna, hammam and covered swimming pool. A buffet breakfast is included. Restaurant, plus a brasserie with tables on the terrace out front. Rates are much reduced on weekdays. **www.koenerclervaux.lu**

ECHTERNACH Le Petit Poète
Place du Marché 13, 6460 Echternach **Tel** *7200721* **Fax** *727483* **Rooms** *12*   **Road Map** *F4*

A reasonably priced small hotel-restaurant in the town centre. Rooms are somewhat spartan, but have all modern necessities, plus views over the square. The restaurant, serving French-style cuisine, has a large terrace at the front for outdoor dining in the summer. Price includes a Continental breakfast. **www.lepetitpoete.lu**

ECHTERNACH Hostellerie de la Basilique
Place du Marché 7-8, 6460 Echternach **Tel** *729483* **Fax** *728890* **Rooms** *14*   **Road Map** *F4*

This traditional-style, family-run Hostellerie de la Basilique is the most luxurious in the town centre. Rooms are spacious and elegantly furnished. A buffet breakfast is included. There is a restaurant, as well as a brasserie with a shaded outdoor terrace for seating in the warmer months. **www.hotel-basilique.lu**

ECHTERNACH Eden au Lac
Oam Nonnesees, 6474 Echternach **Tel** *728283* **Fax** *728144* **Rooms** *60*   **Road Map** *F4*

A modern five-star hotel geared up to activity holidays and families. Set in parkland, with views over a lake and the valley of Echternach, it offers swimming pools, a wellness centre, gym, tennis and squash courts and bike hire. There are two restaurants, and a buffet breakfast is included in the price. **www.edenaulac.lu**

EISCHEN Hôtel de la Gaichel
Maison 5, 8469 Gaichel-Eischen **Tel** *390129* **Fax** *390037* **Rooms** *12*   **Map** *E4*

Close to the Belgian border, this delightful hotel-restaurant is surrounded by its own park. Operating since 1852, it offers exquisitely designed rooms and a plush restaurant celebrated for its first-rate French cuisine. A larger La Gaichel Auberge-Brasserie, with 17 rooms, shares the same park and tennis court. Price includes breakfast. **www.lagaichel.lu**

ESCH-SUR-SÛRE Hôtel de la Sûre
Rue du Pont 1, 9650 Esch-sur-Sûre **Tel** *839110* **Fax** *899101* **Rooms** *30*   **Road Map** *E4*

This well-established, family-run hotel-restaurant stands beneath the castle ruins. The rooms are simple in style and vary in size, but are comfortable. A buffet breakfast is included in the price. The focus is on activity holidays such as walking and cycling. There is also a fitness centre with sauna, Jacuzzi and hammam. **www.hotel-de-la-sure.lu**

LUXEMBOURG CITY Studio Hotel Belappart
Rue du Fort Neipperg 69, 2230 Luxembourg **Tel** *2360451* **Fax** *23664803* **Rooms** *9*   **Road Map** *F5*

A small, modern apartment-hotel, located near the railway station, within walking distance of the Old Town. Ideal for short as well as long stays, with one- and two-bedroom options. The apartments have kitchen facilities, but there are plenty of restaurants and bars in the area. Public car parking facilities close by. **www.belappart.lu**

LUXEMBOURG CITY Mercure Grand Hotel Alfa Luxembourg
Place de la Gare 16, 1616 Luxembourg **Tel** *4900111* **Fax** *490009* **Rooms** *141*   **Road Map** *F5*

This large, efficient and comfortable business hotel stands opposite the station, close by the Old Town, and is well placed for travel, sightseeing and shopping. It has a brasserie and bar, but there are numerous other dining options in the vicinity. The hotel also has its own shuttle service to the airport. **www.mercure.com**

Key to Price Guide *see p262* **Key to Symbols** *see back cover flap*

LUXEMBOURG CITY Hotel-Restaurant Français

Place d'Armes 14, 1136 Luxembourg **Tel** *474534* **Fax** *464274* **Rooms** *24* **Road Map** *F5*

An attractive hotel on one of the main squares of the Old Town. Modern, but with a traditional approach to management. Rooms are neat and well presented. The hotel has the popular brasserie-restaurant Café Français, with a terrace on the square. A buffet breakfast is included. Public car parks close by. **www.hotelfrancais.lu**

LUXEMBOURG CITY Rix

Boulevard Royal 20, 2449 Luxembourg **Tel** *471666* **Fax** *227535* **Rooms** *21* **Road Map** *F5*

An elegant small, modern hotel in the high-rise banking district just west of the Old Town. The decor of the public rooms sets the scene, with gilt mirrors and chandeliers. The rooms are simply furnished but comfortable and stylish. Free parking is an advantage here. The hotel also has bicycles for hire. **www.hotelrix.lu**

LUXEMBOURG CITY Grand Hôtel Cravat

Boulevard Roosevelt 29, 2450 Luxembourg **Tel** *221975* **Fax** *226711* **Rooms** *60* **Road Map** *F5*

An atmospheric hotel close to the city centre, between the Place de la Constitution and the cathedral. The decor inside is smart but nostalgic, with 1950s-style furniture, wall paintings and chandeliers. Rooms are equally individual, but have all the four-star necessities. A buffet breakfast is included in the price. **www.hotelcravat.lu**

LUXEMBOURG CITY Le Royal

Boulevard Royal 12, 2449 Luxembourg **Tel** *2416161* **Fax** *225948* **Rooms** *210* **Road Map** *F5*

One of the grand hotels of Luxembourg – polished, up-to-date five-star luxury from top to bottom – conveniently situated near the Old Town. The hotel has two restaurants, including the much-garlanded Pomme Cannelle. The health club has a heated swimming pool, exercise room and beauty salon. **www.leroyal.lu**

LUXEMBOURG CITY Sofitel Luxembourg Europe

Rue du Fort Niedergrünewald 4, 2015 Luxembourg **Tel** *437761* **Fax** *425091* **Rooms** *109* **Road Map** *F5*

The only five-star hotel on the Kirchberg, this is a fabulous-looking hotel fronted by a soaring glass atrium. It has a noted Italian restaurant, as well as Le Stübli offering upmarket Luxembourgeois and regional fare. Sofitel also owns the equally-starred Hotel Grand Ducal Luxembourg, just south of the Old Town. **www.sofitel.com**

MONDORF-LES-BAINS Mondorf Parc Hôtel

Avenue des Bains 52, 5601 Monforf-les-Bains **Tel** *236660* **Fax** *23661093* **Rooms** *134* **Road Map** *F5*

This is a modern spa hotel – spacious, airy, relaxed and surrounded by a park. It has direct access to the spa at the Domaine Thermale, which offers thermal baths, fitness pavilions and heated outdoor and indoor swimming pools. In the hotel complex are two restaurants and a bistro. A buffet breakfast is included. **www.mondorf.lu**

REMICH Hôtel des Vignes

Rue de Montdorf 29, 5552 Remich **Tel** *23699149* **Rooms** *24* **Road Map** *F5*

Paradise for wine enthusiasts, this fine hotel-restaurant is set amidst vineyards, with views of the River Moselle. Rooms are modern and comfortable; the best have terraces. The Restaurant Du Pressoir specializes in French and Luxembourgeois cuisine, and fine local wines. A buffet breakfast is included in the price. **www.hotel-vignes.lu**

REMICH Hôtel St-Nicolas

Esplanade 31, 5533 Remich **Tel** *26663* **Fax** *26663666* **Rooms** *40* **Road Map** *F5*

This medium-sized hotel has all the comforts that go with a well-managed and welcoming four-star hotel, including a pool and spa complex. Its restaurant, the Lohengrin, has earned a good reputation for its French-Mediterranean food. Dining in the open air in summer. A buffet breakfast is included. **www.saint-nicolas.lu**

VIANDEN Auberge du Château

Grand-Rue 74-80, 9401 Vianden **Tel** *834574* **Fax** *834720* **Rooms** *42* **Road Map** *F4*

This well-established, family-run hotel, occupies a handsome, flower-decked townhouse that has beautifully presented and comfortable rooms. The restaurant serves regional specialities. Mountain bikers and hikers are made especially welcome. **www.auberge-du-chateau.lu**

VIANDEN Oranienburg

Grand-Rue 126, 9411 Vianden **Tel** *8341531* **Fax** *834333* **Rooms** *25* **Road Map** *F4*

A traditional hotel run by the family with a hands-on approach. The hotel's kitchen prepares regional cuisine for its restaurant Le Châtelain. Breakfast is included in the price, but the hotel also offers advantageous half-board arrangements. A brasserie-terrace out front offers views of the castle. **www.hoteloranienburg.com**

WILTZ Hôtel du Vieux-Château

Grand-Rue 1-3, 9530 Wiltz **Tel** *958018* **Fax** *957755* **Rooms** *8* **Road Map** *E4*

Set in a large town mansion, this small hotel-restaurant has elegant, subtly coloured rooms equipped to four-star standards. High-quality French cuisine is the primary focus of the restaurant. Cycling is a passion of the owner, who can advise on local routes. **www.hotelvchateau.com**

WILTZ Hôtel-Restaurant aux Anciennes Tanneries

Rue Joseph Simon 42a, 9550 Wiltz **Tel** *957599* **Fax** *957595* **Rooms** *18* **Road Map** *E4*

An old leather tannery in a tranquil location by the River Wiltz has been smartly converted into a stylish hotel complex. The bedrooms are individually designed, with a decor sympathetic to the historic nature of the building. The restaurant takes pride in its French cuisine. **www.auxanciennestanneries.com**

WHERE TO EAT

Belgium has some of the best food in Europe served by restaurants of all price brackets. Food that is all presentation and no substance is rarely tolerated as Belgians pride themselves on delicious cuisine that is carefully prepared with fresh local and seasonal produce. Restaurants that do not satisy these criteria are simply not

Thai chef in Brussels

frequented. Visitors will find that it is best to be wary of eateries that openly court tourists rather than cater to the local clientéle. Luxembourg's cuisine exhibits all the skill of French cooking but also has its own range of robust dishes. As in Belgium, establishments that cook and serve fine food are treated with respect and win loyal custom.

Enjoying drinks, snacks and sunshine on a pavement terrace

WHAT TO EAT WHERE

It is possible to eat just about any kind of food anywhere in Belgium and Luxembourg. Each region, however, has its local specialities (*produits du terroir* or *streekproducten*), which change with the season. The coast, for instance, is the best place to eat seafood, while game is a speciality of the Ardennes, particularly in winter, and hop shoots are a spring-time treat in Western Flanders. Eels are best at Donkmeer, near Ghent, while Ghent itself is the true home of the creamy chicken or fish *waterzooi*. The most delicious strawberries are found at Wépion, on the River Meuse. Geraardsbergen is the place for *mattentaart* pastries and Dinant for *flamiche* leek tarts. When in Arlon, visitors should drink a *maitrank* apéritif, but *jenever* in Hasselt or *pékèt* gin in Liège. Luxembourg has its famed Moselle wines (*see p249*), but excellent wines are also produced in the Hageland region of Vlaams Brabant.

Beers too are brewed to high standards in all quarters. Locally-produced brews, such as Boeteling, which celebrates Veurne's annual Procession of the Penitents, are also highly recommended. Some restaurants, such as Den Dyver in Bruges (*see p288*), specialize in dishes cooked with beer.

HOW TO CHOOSE A RESTAURANT

Hotels and tourist offices will often willingly suggest good local restaurants. Most eateries display menus outside, and visitors can ascertain the bill of fare and price beforehand. It is best to avoid tourist-trap places where waiters win customers by importuning them on the street, or where menus are posted in six languages by the door. Good restaurants will be full of people eating happily, not waiting to be served.

It is also possible to eat well in brasseries and cafés. Here, it is often best to choose mainstream fare such as *steak-frites* or *moules*, rather than more elaborate dishes that might

tax the establishment's equipment and personnel. Meals can range from 10–20 euros for a simple brasserie meal to more than 70 euros for a full three-course dinner.

CUISINES ON THE MENU

The food of Belgium and Luxembourg is solidly North European and an expression of what the land produces. Should the palate tire of this, there are other options. North African cuisine is available in the outlying districts of the larger cities, and the well cooked tagines, couscous and pastry-based briks are good value. Food from the Congo, Rwanda and Senegal is a speciality of the Matonge district in Ixelles. Italian and Chinese restaurants are fairly ubiquitous and there are also some Portuguese, Spanish, Greek, Turkish, South American, Thai and Indonesian establishments. Indian restaurants are often upmarket and relatively rare. Japanese food also tends to be expensive but is generally of a high quality.

Art Nouveau decor in Brussels's highly praised Comme Chez Soi

Fast food outlets at Place Guillaume II in Luxembourg City

There was a time, not long ago, when French was the standard language of food acoss the region. In Flanders, now, it is more usual to see menus in Dutch, sometimes with a French translation. Many restaurants also provide English translations or even separate English menus. Staff can usually explain, or failing that, the menu reader *(see p281)* and phrase book *(see pp348–52)* will be useful.

VEGETARIANS

Despite a marked increase in vegetarian eating, Belgium and Luxembourg are not generally oriented towards vegetarians and restaurants dedicated to them are rare. Many menus will, however, include at least one vegetarian dish for each course, or allow a vegetarian starter (or two) as the main course. Vegans might have a harder time. Some health-food shops have cafés and staff that may be able to advise about local vegetarian and vegan-friendly restaurants. Those whose diet extends to fish will have no problems finding excellent food throughout the region.

EATING ON A BUDGET

Good, reasonably-priced food can be found at many cafés. There are also plenty of fast-food outlets, such as the burger chain Quick. Many delicatessens offer a sand-wich-making service plus a range of sophisticated cold foods (with plastic forks), that are good for picnics. The

Belgian chain, Le Pain Quotidien (Het Dagelijks Brood in Dutch) serves upmarket sandwiches and salads to eat at shared pine tables. The special lunch menus offered by many of the best restaurants can be a real bargain.

The classic Belgian street food is a cornet of freshly fried *frites* or *frieten* (chips) from one of the many street-side vans or shed-like outlets called variously as *friteries* or *kots à frites* (*frituurs* or *frietkoten* in Dutch). They will also provide mayonnaise (the tra-ditional accompaniment), plus a range of extra foods that includes meatballs, fishcakes, *carbonnades* (beef stewed in beer) and *fricadelles* (sau-sages in batter), all at very reasonable prices. The chips, however, are an inexpensive meal in themselves, and can be second to none.

Street food, Belgian style

TIPPING AND TAXES

Prices shown on restaurant menus usually include both a Value Added Tax charge of 21 per cent and service charges (usually 16 per cent). It is therefore not necessary to add a tip, unless service has been exceptional. In that case, a small cash tip of perhaps 2–5 euros is acceptable.

CHILDREN

Restaurants in Belgium and Luxembourg are usually willing to receive children, although some upmarket establishments may be too formal for the very young. It is acceptable for chil-dren to bring their comics, colouring books and games along to entertain them-selves during long meals. Many restaurants have children's menus that offer reduced-price dishes that are likely to appeal to younger palates. In addition, high chairs are generally available on request in most establishments.

SMOKING

Establishments in Belgium and Luxembourg strictly forbid smoking inside the premises where food is served. This rule is not enforced on terrace areas. However, visitors averse to cigarette smoke should mention this when making reservations or taking their seats so that adequate arrangements can be made.

Dining on the river at Lier's De Fortuin restaurant

The Flavours of Belgium

Most Belgians are passionate about food and standards are very high. The many first-class bakers, greengrocers, fishmongers, butchers and *pâtissiers*, including Belgium's noted chocolatiers, are held in high public esteem, alongside the top chefs and restaurateurs. Restaurant cooking in Wallonia and Flanders is, respectively, French and Dutch in character. Belgian diners appreciate hearty traditional fare, which depends on good ingredients cooked well. Moroccan, Italian, Spanish, Chinese and Indian restaurants add variety to the mix.

Belgian chocolates

Bunches of white asparagus, a seasonal early-summer treat

THE NORTH SEA

No place in Belgium is more than a three-hour drive from the coast, and consequently, fresh seafood plays a central role in Belgian cuisine. On the coast, as well as in the fish restaurants of the major cities, a wide variety of the best fish – sole, cod, turbot, skate, hake and monkfish – is always on the menu, either simply grilled, fried in butter or swathed in a well-judged sauce. Huge platters of *fruits de mer*, or mixed seafood, are also widely available in restaurants all over Belgium.

A uniquely Belgian fish dish that is well worth seeking out is *anguilles au vert* (*paling in 't groen* in Dutch), which consists of large chunks of eel cooked with a mass of finely chopped, fresh green herbs.

PASTURE AND WOODLAND

Northern Belgium and the hills of the south are home to herds of cattle. The Herve Region produces most of Belgium's mostly French-style soft, or semi-soft, cows-milk cheeses. Quality beef is the stock-in-trade of any Belgian butcher, and *steak-frites* (steak and chips) is a classic dish on bistro menus.

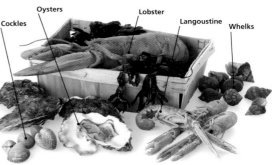

Oysters   Lobster   Langoustine   Whelks
Cockles

A selection of fine quality North Sea seafood

LOCAL DISHES AND SPECIALITIES

Although Belgian chefs produce some of the world's most complex and sophisticated cooking, many of Belgium's greatest classic dishes are relatively simple, striking a healthy balance between nourishment and pleasure. Fine examples include steaming platefuls of *moules-frites* and warming stews such as *carbonnades flamandes* and *waterzooi*, which is made with either fish or chicken. These dishes might be labelled comfort food; however, the quality of the ingredients and the skill put into cooking such dishes in Belgium invariably turns such homely fare into a feast. An unusual conserve to look out for at the breakfast, or cheese, table is *sirop de Liège*, a soft spreading fruit paste made of concentrated pears, apples, plums and apricots.

Fruit used in *sirop de Liège*

Moules-frites *are mussels steamed with onion and white wine, and served with chips (fries) and mayonnaise.*

Fish restaurant in the elegant Galéries St-Hubert in Brussels

Belgians are so confident about their beef that they are happy to eat it raw, either in *steak américaine* (steak tartare) or on toast as the snack, *toast cannibale*.

Pork products include the noted Ardennes ham, patés and sausages. In autumn and winter, game such as wild boar, pheasant and venison is served, often in a rich fruity sauce. Quail, guinea fowl, pigeon and rabbit are also popular.

THE VEGETABLE PATCH

Not long ago, most Belgian householders filled their gardens with tightly-packed rows of top-class vegetables such as beans, leeks, carrots, lettuces, asparagus, potatoes and onions. This tradition may be waning, but the same quest for quality lives on in commercial market-gardens. In the 1840s, Belgian farmers created *chicon* (*witloof* in Dutch) by forcing the roots of the chicorée lettuce. It is now one of Belgium's most widely used vegetables. The most popular vegetable must

Freshly made waffles at a street stall, a familiar sight in Belgium

be the potato, in the form of chips (French fries). These *frites* (*friet* in Dutch), served with a dollop of mayonnaise, are a favourite street food.

THE PATISSIER

No Belgian community is without a pâtisserie selling superlative tarts, cakes and biscuits, and many *pâtissiers* double-up as chocolatiers. *Gaufres* (waffles) are also a a great sweet treat, sold at specialist shops and street stalls or made at home on festive occasions. Belgian bakers also make a range of dry, buttery biscuits, such as the spicy *speculoos*, which are associated with Christmas.

BELGIAN CHEESE

Bouquet des Moines Mild and gooey, with a white rind, this cheese is from Herve.

Chimay Made by the Trappist Abbey here, this is a semi-soft cheese with an orange rind.

Herve and Limburger These are both soft, pungent cheeses with washed rinds.

Maredsous This is a family of St-Paulin-style, semi-soft abbey cheeses.

Passendale This light, semi-soft cheese with tiny holes is from Western Flanders.

Remoudou A strong-smelling Herve cheese, this has a red-brown washed rind.

Carbonnades flamandes *combines beef cooked in Belgian beer with a touch of sugar in a hearty casserole.*

Waterzooi *is a classic stew from Ghent with either fish or chicken and vegetables, poached in a creamy broth.*

Flamiche aux poireaux *is leeks fried in butter, whisked with cream and eggs and baked in a pastry shell.*

The Flavours of Luxembourg

The traditional food of Luxembourg is a blend of French and German influences, but more recently it has also absorbed elements of the cuisines of Portuguese and Italian immigrants. As elsewhere in Europe, young chefs are experimenting with innovative takes on traditional dishes, as well as introducing new ingredients and flavours from around the world. As a result, you may have to make a conscious effort to experience genuine Lëtzebuergesch cooking – but it is still out there, in pubs and country bistros, at roadside snack bars, and at all the big annual festivals.

Plums

HONEST FARE

It has been said that the food of Luxembourg is "French cuisine in German quantities". This is sometimes viewed as rather dismissive, but, for diners, it is simply the best of both worlds. Local produce is of excellent quality, and the standard of restaurant cooking very high, as might be expected from a land with one of the world's highest per capita incomes.

Grocer's shop selling a range of fresh local and international produce

Pork, cured and preserved in a variety of hams and sausages

Rather like their Belgian neighbours, Luxembourgers have scant regard for over-fussy cuisine. They enjoy familiar, family cooking, which more clearly reveals Germanic influences, such as robust platters of roast pork or sausage with *sauerkraut*, followed by a plum tart. When out and about, they might snack on a sausage and roll – particularly a small, spicy *Thüringer* or a *Lëtzebuerger Grillwurscht* – from a street vendor.

FISH CUISINE

Despite being landlocked, Luxembourg is only 150 km (93 miles) from the sea, and fish plays a major role on menus, with mussels being especially popular. However, freshwater fish such as trout and pike abound in rivers and lakes, and are traditional favourites. Crayfish are also part of the national diet, but demand has now outstripped local supply, so they may very well be imported.

LUXEMBOURG DISHES AND SPECIALITIES

Luxembourg's signature dishes are grounded in traditional produce. The landscape and climate favour robust farming – grains, root crops and pig-rearing – as well as fruit orchards. There are numerous potato-based dishes, including *Gromperenzopp* (potato and leek soup) and *Gromperekichelcher* (potato cakes). Pork is made into countless types of cured ham and sausage. Buckwheat dumplings, or *Stäerzelen*, are eaten with cream and bacon. In winter, rich game dishes are popular, while in spring, the favourite is *Brennesselszopp*, a delicate soup made with young nettle tips. Moselle vineyards serve dishes cooked with wine, such as *Frell am Reisleck*, trout in Riesling sauce. Another speciality is *friture de la Moselle* – small freshwater fish, deep-fried in a light batter.

Buckwheat

Judd mat Gaardebounen, *a smoked collar of pork served with broad beans in cream sauce, is the national dish.*

Reading the Menu

It is worth avoiding tourist restaurants that display menus in English, but many of the best eateries supply translations of their dishes, or have staff on hand who can translate for customers. Belgian cooking is modelled on French cuisine, so those who are familiar with common culinary terms will have little problem with menus in Brussels and Wallonia, or even in Luxembourg. In Flanders, menus are often in Dutch, but someone can usually provide an explanation. The list below covers dishes typical of both countries, as well as words commonly seen on menus.

North Sea mussels

Signage offering a fixed-price menu, often very good value

FRENCH/WALLONIA

Anguilles au vert Eel in a thick green sauce of fresh herbs, particularly chervil.
Asperges à la flamande Boiled white asparagus with chopped hard-boiled egg.
Carbonnades flamandes Rich beef stew with beer.
Chicon Belgian endive (chicory). *Chicons au gratin* are wrapped in ham and cooked in cheese sauce.
Coucou de Malines Mechelen cuckoo. A type of chicken, often braised with beer and *chicons*.
Crevettes grises Tiny but tasty North Sea shrimps.
Croque monsieur Toasted cheese and ham sandwich.
Escavèche Fish cooked in a herb-flavoured stock.
Faisan à la brabançonne Pheasant baked with chicon.
Flamiche au poireaux Quiche-like leek tart.
Frites Chips/fries.
Jets d'houblon Hop shoots in a creamy sauce.
Moules Mussels.

Plateau de fruits de mer Platter of mixed seafood.
Salade liègeoise Warm potato, bacon, and green bean or frisée lettuce salad.
Steak à l'américaine Minced raw steak (tartare).

DUTCH/FLANDERS

Aardappelen Potatoes.
Asperges op vlaamse wijze see *Asperges à la flamande*.
Boterham Sandwich.
Friet/frietjes Chips/fries.
Garnaalkroketten Deep-fried shrimp croquettes.
Gentse hutsepot Meat stew with winter vegetables.
Karbonaden see *Carbonnades flamandes*.
Konijn Rabbit.
Kreeft Lobster.
Mechelse koekkoek see *Coucou de Malines*.
Noordsee vissoep Thick soup of North Sea fish.
Op zijn Brussels In Brussels style: with *chicons* or beer.
Paling in't groen see *Anguilles au vert*.
Pannekoek Pancake.
Sint-Jacobsoesters/ schelpen Scallops.
Stoemp Potato mashed with

chopped vegetables or meat.
Tonijn Tuna.
Vlaamse stoverij see *Carbonnades flamandes*.
Waterzooi Chicken or fish poached in a creamy broth.
Wild Game.
Witloof see *Chicon*.
Zalm Salmon.

LUXEMBOURG

Brennesselszopp Soup made with nettle tips.
F'rell am Reisleck Trout in Riesling wine sauce.
Friture de la Moselle Deep-fried freshwater fish.
Gromperekichelcher Deep-fried potato cake, with onions and parsley.
Gromperenzopp Potato soup with leeks.
Judd mat Gaardebounen see *opposite page*.
Kriibsen crayfish.
Lëtzebuerger Grillwurscht Small spicy sausage, also known as *Thüringer*.
Quetscheflued Plum tart.
Sauerkraut Shredded, pickled cabbage.
Stäerzelen Buckwheat dumplings.

Dining outside at a fish restaurant near the Grand Place in Brussels

Belgian Beer

Belgium makes more beers, and in a greater mix of styles and flavours, than any other country in the world. The nation's breweries produce over 400 different beers, and even small bars will stock at least 20 varieties. The Belgian citizen drinks on average 100 litres (200 pints) a year. Even the cheerful peasants in Brueghel the Elder's 16th-century medieval village scenes would have been drinking beer from the local brewery, as most small towns and communities have produced their own beer since the 11th century. By 1900, there were some 3,000 private breweries throughout Belgium. Today, more than 100 still operate, with experts agreeing that even large industrial concerns produce beer of a fine quality.

Gambrinus, the legendary Beer King

Detail from *The Wedding Dance* by Pieter Brueghel the Elder

TRAPPIST BEERS

Chimay label with authentic Trappist mark

Label for Westmalle Trappist beer

The most revered of refreshments, Belgium's Trappist beers have been highly rated since the Middle Ages when monks began brewing them. The drink originated in Roman times when Belgium was Gallia Belgica, a province of Gaul. Beer was a private domestic product until the monasteries took over and introduced hops to the process. Today's production is still controlled solely by the five Trappist monasteries, although the brewers are mostly laymen. Trappist beers are characterized by their rich, yeasty flavour. They are very strong, ranging from 6.2 to 11 per cent in alcohol content by volume. Perhaps the most famous of the five brands is Chimay, brewed in Belgium's largest monastic brewery in Hainaut. This delicate but potent bottled beer has three different strengths, and is best kept for many years before drinking. The strongest Trappist beer is Westvleteren, from Ieper.

Chimay served in its correct glass

LAMBIC BEERS

The unique family of lambic beers has been made for centuries in the Senne valley around Brussels. The beers are brewed by allowing the yeasts present in the air to ferment the beer, rather than by adding yeasts separately to the water and grain mix. Containers of unfermented wort (water, wheat and barley) are left under a half-open roof in the brewery and fermented by airborne yeasts that are specific to this region of Belgium. Unlike the sterility of many breweries, lambic cellars are officially exempt from EU hygiene regulations, and deliberately left dusty and uncleaned in order for the necessary fungi to thrive. Matured in untreated wooden casks for up to five years, the lambic is deliciously sour to drink, with a strength of 5 per cent alcohol.

Young and old lambic beers are blended to produce the variant gueuze. A tiny bead, distinctive champagne mousse and a toasty, slightly acidic flavour are its characteristics. Bars and restaurants lay down their gueuze for up to two years before it is drunk.

Lambic cherry beer

Brewer sampling beer from the vat at a brewery in Anderlecht, a suburb of Brussels

SPECIALITY BELGIAN BEERS

Duvel

Chimay

Brugse Tripel

De Verboden Vrucht

Kwak

Speciality beers are common in Belgium, where the huge variety of brands includes unusual tastes and flavours. For a characterful amber ale, Kwak is a good choice. Fruit beers are a Brussels speciality but are available throughout the country. The most popular, kriek, is traditionally made with bitter cherries grown in the Brussels suburb of Schaerbeek. Picked annually, these cherries are added to the lambic and allowed to macerate, or steep. The distinctive almond tang comes from the cherry stone. Raspberries are used to make a framboise beer, or frambozen.

Strong beers are also extremely popular. These include the pilseners De Verboden Frucht (The Forbidden Fruit) and Duvel (Devil). Leffe Radieuse holds 8.2 per cent alcohol by volume, while at 10.5 per cent, Hainaut's Bush beer ranks among the strongest. The bestsellers, Jupiler and Stella Artois, are also good-quality beers.

Fruit beer mat of Chapeau brewery

The façade of a beer emporium in Brussels

BLANCHE BEERS

Hoegaarden

Belgium's refreshing wheat beers are known as blanche, or white beers, because of the cloudy sediment that forms when they ferment. Sour, crisp and light, they are relatively low in alcohol at 5 per cent. Blanche is produced in the Brabant town of of Hoegaarden, after which the best-known blanche brand is named. Many people now serve them with a slice of lemon to add to the refreshing taste, especially on warm summer evenings.

HOW TO DRINK BELGIAN BEER

There are no snobbish distinctions made in Belgium between bottled and casked beer. Some of the most prestigious brews are served in bottles, and, as with casks, bottles are often laid down to mature. However, the choice of drinking glass, is a vital part of the beer-drinking ritual. Many beers must be drunk in a particular glass, which the barman will usually supply. These range from goblets to long thin drinking tubes. Beers are often served with a complementary snack – cream cheese on rye bread and radishes are a popular accompaniment.

The traditional drinkers' snack of *fromage blanc* on rye bread

Restaurants, Cafés and Bars

The restaurants given here have been selected for their good value, food and location. Also listed are the best and most colourful cafés and bars. Cafés serve alcoholic drinks and soft drinks, while bars offer coffee in addition to alcohol. Snacks and larger meals can be found at both. For map references in Central Brussels, see pages 92–7.

PRICE CATEGORIES
The following price categories are for a three-course evening meal for one, including a half-bottle of house wine, tax and service.
€ Under €25
€€ €25–€37
€€€ €37–€50
€€€€ €50–€62
€€€€€ Over €62

BRUSSELS

CENTRAL BRUSSELS À la Mort Subite €
Rue Montagne aux Herbes Potagères 7, 1000 BRU **Tel** *(02) 5131318*   *City Map 2 D2*

Opened in 1928, À la Mort Subite (Sudden Death) gets its name from a game of dice. The original owner, Théophile Vossen, also used this name for his brand of gueuze beers. Now run by the fourth generation of Vossens, the establishment serves a full range of Brussels beers, other drinks and traditional salads, omelettes and snacks.

CENTRAL BRUSSELS La Fleur en Papier Doré €
Rue des Alexiens 56, 1000 BRU **Tel** *(02) 5111659*   *City Map 1 C3*

A traditional *estaminet* (tavern) that was the haunt of the Surrealists, Magritte included, who left suitably bizarre mementos and poems that now decorate the series of small rooms. A lovely time-capsule in which to enjoy fine Belgian beers and a platter of tasty food such as cold meats, smoked salmon, pasta, salads and traditional Belgian dishes.

CENTRAL BRUSSELS Le Cirio €
Rue de la Bourse 18, 1000 BRU **Tel** *(02) 5121395*   *City Map 1 C2*

Francesco Cirio, 19th-century Italian pioneer in food canning, set up one of his prestige outlets by the Bourse. When it became a café-bar, the name was retained. It is now a well-known landmark, cherished for its splendidly old-fashioned interior and its famous tipple, the *half-en-half* (half sparkling wine, half still). Traditional bar food.

CENTRAL BRUSSELS Le Pain Quotidien €
Rue Antoine Dansaert 16, 1000 BRU **Tel** *(02) 5022361*   *City Map 2 D4*

This was the first branch of the chain Le Pain Quotidien. Lovely bread with delicious fillings, salads and pastries. The formula has since become an international hit, with 25 branches in Belgium alone, 10 of which are in Brussels. Brilliant for lunch, but also good for breakfast and early evening (closes between 6 and 7pm).

CENTRAL BRUSSELS Mappa Mundo €
Rue du Pont de la Carpe 2-6, 1000 **Tel** *(02) 5135116*   *City Map 1 C2*

One of the most popular bars in the trendy St-Géry area. It has many of the attributes of a traditional Bruxellois bar, but the clientèle is young and cosmopolitan, and the theme lightly South American. Bars upstairs too, and a street terrace. Open from 11am to 2am on weekdays, and to 4am Fridays and Saturdays. Closed Sundays.

CENTRAL BRUSSELS Restaurant 't Kelderke €€
Grand Place 15, 1000 BRU **Tel** *(02) 5137344*   *City Map 1 D3*

This 17th-century cellar restaurant has a decidedly genuine feel and is generally busy. Here, the Bruxellois will rub shoulders with visitors to their city. The food is entirely Bruxellois – *carbonnades flamandes*, *stoemp*, *bloedpens* (blood sausage), rabbit cooked in kriek (*see p283*) and, of course, *moules-frites* (mussels and fries).

CENTRAL BRUSSELS Aux Armes de Bruxelles €€€
Rue des Bouchers 13, 1000 BRU **Tel** *(02) 5115550*   *City Map 2 D2*

In an area notorious for substandard tourist restaurants, the Aux Armes de Bruxelles is a shining exception – a classic restaurant serving first-class Belgian cuisine, fish in particular. An excellent place to try such dishes as *croquettes de crevettes* (shrimp croquettes), *waterzooi* or *anguilles au vert*. Jacques Brel ate here.

CENTRAL BRUSSELS Brigittines Aux Marches de la Chapelle €€€
Place de la Chapelle 5, 1000 BRU **Tel** *(02) 5126891*   *City Map 1 C4*

An elegant Art Nouveau-style restaurant with a soothing decor and deep green, wood pannelling; an open fire burns in winter. The assured service is equally welcoming – a good backdrop for fine, market-fresh Franco-Belgian cooking, which has won many devotees. Closed for Saturday lunch and on Sundays.

CENTRAL BRUSSELS Clef des Champs €€€
Rue de Rollebeek 23, 1000 BRU **Tel** *(02) 5122193*   *City Map 2 D4*

Set in a pretty little street, this highly respected restaurant is run by a husband-and-wife team. It serves regional French cuisine in a setting of warm Provençale colours. Dishes of the day are written on a blackboard. Look out for their bargain fixed-price offers at lunch time (Tuesday–Friday). Closed Sunday evenings and Mondays.

Key to Symbols *see back cover flap*

CENTRAL BRUSSELS In 't Spinnekopke

Place du Jardin aux Fleurs 1, 1000 BRU **Tel** *(02) 5118695*   **City Map** *1 B2*

A rare surviving *estaminet* dating back to 1762 and still delightfully atmospheric. In 't Spinnekopke (At the Sign of the Spider's Head) specializes in good traditional Bruxellois and Belgian dishes – seafood, steak, *waterzooi* and dishes cooked in beer. Friendly service and a lovely terrace. Closed Saturday lunch, Sunday.

CENTRAL BRUSSELS La Chaloupe d'Or

Grand Place 24-25, 1000 BRU **Tel** *(02) 5114161*   **City Map** *1 D3*

Occupying the beautiful Baroque-style guildhouse of the tailors, this is an elegant and sophisticated restaurant and café. A good place to soak up the busy atmosphere of the city centre while sipping a beer or coffee, or eating a slice of pâtisserie at tea time. Lunch is offered from a menu of well-prepared dishes. Popular among locals.

CENTRAL BRUSSELS La Villette

Rue du Vieux Marché aux Grains 3, 1000 BRU **Tel** *(02) 5127550*   **City Map** *1 C2*

A charming little tavern-style restaurant with wood panelling and gingham tablecloths. It specializes in Belgian dishes – tomatoes filled with little grey shrimps from Oostende, cod with Belgian endives, salmon cooked in wheat beer, mussels and *steak-frites*. Meals are concluded with a *jenever* gin. Closed Saturday lunchtime and Sundays.

CENTRAL BRUSSELS Le Falstaff

Rue Henri Maus 19, 1000 BRU **Tel** *(02) 5118789*   **City Map** *1 C2*

This celebrated bar and brasserie-restaurant is famed for its Art Nouveau decor, but also has a robust, tavern-like atmosphere in keeping with its Shakespearean name. A good place for a drink and bar snack. The restaurant, spilling out on to a heated terrace, offers full meals, mainly of Belgian and Bruxellois inspiration.

CENTRAL BRUSSELS Le Roy d'Espagne

Grand Place 1, 1000 BRU **Tel** *(02) 5130807*   **City Map** *1 D3*

With its premier position in the old bakers' guildhouse on the Grand Place, and with its sunny, south-facing terrace, this is justifiably one of the city's most celebrated watering holes. The waiters' tabard aprons and the Breughelesque decor of the interior add a medieval air. Food ranges from snacks to substantial dishes.

CENTRAL BRUSSELS Restaurant MIM

Rue Montagne de la Cour 2, 1000 BRU **Tel** *(02) 5029508*   **City Map** *2 E4*

The restaurant atop the splendid Art Nouveau building that houses the Musée des Instruments de Musique is open during museum hours (10am–4:30pm Tuesday–Sunday). Its main draw is the fabulous view over Brussels. The well-prepared food includes salads and open sandwiches, plus typical brasserie dishes such as fish and steaks.

CENTRAL BRUSSELS La Belga Queen

Rue Fossé aux Loups 32, 1000 BRU **Tel** *(02) 2172187*   **City Map** *2 D2*

This splendidly theatrical restaurant, created by maestro eatery-architect Antoine Pinto, is located in an imaginatively transformed 19th-century bank, all marble columns and high arches. The refined cuisine has a determinedly Belgian slant. There is also an oyster bar, beer bar and cigar lounge.

CENTRAL BRUSSELS La Roue d'Or

Rue des Chapeliers 26, 1000 BRU **Tel** *(02) 5142554*   **City Map** *1 D3*

A fine brasserie richly evoking early 20th-century Brussels with its dark-wood panelling, brass fittings, mirrors and Magritte-inspired murals. It is a spell-binding setting for a broad range of high-quality brasserie food, with plenty of good Belgian classics such as *croquettes de crevettes* and *waterzooi*. Closed for four weeks over July–August.

CENTRAL BRUSSELS Vincent

Rue des Dominicains 8-10, 1000 BRU **Tel** *(02) 5112607*   **City Map** *2 D3*

Entering past the steaming kitchen, guests will find a room decorated with tiles illustrating maritime themes. Fish and oysters are on the menu, but there is also a strong emphasis on meat. There's a true Bruxellois feel to this place: a family-run enterprise founded in 1905 where visitors can tuck into good wholesome fare.

CENTRAL BRUSSELS Comme Chez Soi

Place Rouppe 23, 1000 BRU **Tel** *(02) 5122921*   **City Map** *1 C4*

Widely regarded as the city's best restaurant, Comme Chez Soi is the domain of the Wynants family, with the highly respected chef Lionel Rigolet. Exquisitely presented dishes of lobster and game. Closed Sundays, Mondays, Wednesday lunch and mid-Jul to mid-Aug. Only 40 seats, so booking ahead is a good idea.

CENTRAL BRUSSELS L'Écailler du Palais Royal

Rue Bodenbroeck 18, 1000 BRU **Tel** *(02) 5128751*   **City Map** *2 D4*

An *écailler* is a professional shellfish seller and opener: a clue to the orientation of this splendidly traditional and august fish and seafood Michelin-starred restaurant. Set in a 17th-century townhouse, the decor is plush, the service and cuisine absolutely as they should be: classic, but with inventive flair. Closed August, Sundays and public holidays.

CENTRAL BRUSSELS La Belle Marâichère

Place Ste-Catherine 11, 1000 BRU **Tel** *(02) 5129759*   **City Map** *1 C2*

The former site of the fish market, Place Ste-Catherine is still the place to eat fish in Brussels. Founded in1973, the family-run La Belle Marâichère (The Pretty Market Gardener) is one of the best-loved fish restaurants. Classic dishes, including the very Belgian fish *waterzooi*. Meat dishes are also served. Closed Wednesdays and Thursdays.

CENTRAL BRUSSELS MuseumBrasserie
🍽 V 🏷   €€€€€

Rue de la Regence 3, 1000 BRU **Tel** *(02) 5083580*   **City Map** 2 D4

The Musées Royaux des Beaux Arts de Belgique have raised their game on the culinary front with the MuseumCafé within the museum and this separate brasserie. Designed with panache by Antoine Pinto, it offers excellent Belgian dishes refined by top chef Peter Goossens. The place also to try first-rate Belgian wines. Closed Sunday evenings and Mondays.

CENTRAL BRUSSELS Sea Grill
🍴 🍽 📶 V 🏷   €€€€€

Rue du Fossé-aux-Loups 47, 1000 BRU **Tel** *(02) 2179225*   **City Map** 2 D2

An impressive entrance – the great glass atrium of the Radisson Blu hotel – leads to one of the greatest fish restaurants of Europe (it has two Michelin stars). Fêted chef Marc Yves Mattagne has been in charge of the kitchen since 1989. Absolutely first-rate service, in a classically elegant decor, with seashell motifs. Closed mid-July to mid-August.

GREATER BRUSSELS Café Belga
🍽 📶 V   €

Place Eugène Flagey, 1050 BRU (Ixelles) **Tel** *(02) 6403508*   **Road Map** B5

The 1930s Art Deco Flagey radio building – known as the *paquebot* (steamship) for its shape – is now home to a super-trendy café that draws a young and artistic crowd. On offer are beers, cocktails and sophisticated *petite restauration* (light meals) of seasonal dishes, soup and sandwiches (9am–4pm). It is also a music and events venue.

GREATER BRUSSELS Chez Moeder Lambic
📄   €

Rue de Savoie 68, 1060 BRU (St-Gilles) **Tel** *(02) 5441699*   **Road Map** A5

This is a famous address on the beer-pilgrimage route – a welcoming pub with some 450 kinds of beer listed in its printed menu. Guests who need advice will find that the staff are helpful, informative and able to skilfully diagnose individual needs. Simple but wholesome bar food is available. Open 4pm–3am daily.

GREATER BRUSSELS Colmar
🍴 🍽 V   €

Boulevard de la Woluwe 71, 1200 BRU (Woluwe-St-Lambert) **Tel** *(02) 7629855*   **Road Map** B5

This outpost of the Colmar chain of eateries is an excellent-value stop-off in the east of the city. Set in a converted 16th-century building that was once a Spanish prison, it is a buffet-style restaurant and grill. Various fixed-price formulae offer a self-service buffet for starters and desserts, plus a main course, with wine or other drinks included.

GREATER BRUSSELS Maison Antoine
♿ 📄 📶 V   €

Place Jourdon 1, 1040 BRU **Tel** *(02) 2305456*   **Road Map** B5

Founded in 1948, this is the best loved friterie in Brussels. The delicious double-fried frites that Maison Antoine serves can be devoured along with a choice of over 20 sauces and other toppings. Burgers, sandwiches and croquettes are also served here. It remains open till 1am on Fridays and 2am on Saturdays.

GREATER BRUSSELS Au Vieux Bruxelles
♿ V 🏷   €€

Rue St-Boniface 35, 1050 BRU (Ixelles) **Tel** *(02) 5033111*   **Road Map** B5

Located just a short distance away from the Louise area, this restaurant is popular for its classic mussel dishes. Also on the menu are excellent Belgian specialities such as *waterzooi* chicken with vegetables and *stoemp*. It has a small seating area, so make sure you get there early.

GREATER BRUSSELS Chez Oki
🍴 🍽   €€

Rue Lesbroussart 62, 1050 BRU (Ixelles) **Tel** *(02) 6444576*   **Road Map** B5

Japanese and French fusion is the formula for this highly rated restaurant. The inventive cuisine by Oki Haruki is sensationally presented and includes dishes such as sushi with *foie gras* and soy sauce, and beef steak cooked with acacia honey. Minimalist Japanese decor. Closed on Saturdays and Mondays during lunch, and on Sundays.

GREATER BRUSSELS La Porteuse d'Eau
€€

Avenue Jean Volders 48a, 1060 BRU (Ixelles) **Tel** *(02) 5376646*   **Road Map** A5

Located at the smarter end of St Gilles, this is one of the most visually stunning cafés in Brussels. Its ornate, refurbished Art Nouveau interior is dazzling, with swirling organic lines, spiralling staircases and, to top it all, friezes of the delicate water bearers who give the café its name. The food is decent; try the *chicons au gratin* or simply have a coffee or beer.

GREATER BRUSSELS La Canne en Ville
🍴 🍽 📷   €€€

Rue de la Réforme 22, 1050 BRU (Ixelles) **Tel** *(02) 3472926*   **Road Map** B5

Useful when visting the Art Nouveau district, La Canne en Ville is a delightful restaurant in a delicately converted butcher's shop, complete with the original tiled walls. The welcome is friendly and the cooking French-based, full of imagination and first rate. Attractive south-facing terrace in summer. Closed Saturday lunch and Sundays and weekends in July and August.

GREATER BRUSSELS La Mirabelle
🍴 🍽 📷 V   €€€

Chaussée de Boondael 459, 1050 BRU (Ixelles) **Tel** *(02) 6495173*   **Road Map** B5

Close to the Université Libre de Bruxelles, this airy restaurant offers a European brasserie menu with inventive touches – beef *carpaccio stoemp*, gaut *waterzooi* mussels. There is a covered terrace, but on fine days, the large garden really comes into its own.

GREATER BRUSSELS La Terrasse
🍴 📷   €€€

Avenue des Celtes 1, 1040 BRU (Etterbeek) **Tel** *(02) 7322851*   **Road Map** B5

A classic Brussels brasserie, La Terrasse is known for its eponymous shaded front terrace and cosy interior, with wooden benches and booths. Here, you can rub shoulders with MEPs from the nearby EU institutions over plates of hearty Belgian food and an eclectic mix of international cuisine. Look out for the Beer of the Month.

Key to Price Guide *see p284* **Key to Symbols** *see back cover flap*

GREATER BRUSSELS Le Délire Parisien   📋 🖼 Ⅴ   €€€

Rue Jourdan 16, 1060 BRU (St-Gilles) **Tel** *(02) 5370694*   **Road Map** *A5*

An agreeable restaurant with a modern feel, warmly decorated with candles, paintings and plants. The location on a pedestrianized street makes the pavement terrace all the more inviting. As the name suggests, the menu is primarily French, but with a handful of tasty Belgian standards for good measure. Closed Sundays and public holidays.

GREATER BRUSSELS Les Dames Tartines   ⑪ 🖺   €€€

Chaussée de Haecht 58, 1210 BRU (St-Josse-ten-Noode) **Tel** *(02) 2184549*   **Road Map** *B4*

Just north of the Jardin Botanique, this charming restaurant is decorated like the dining room of a private house, with linen tablecloths and old photos on the walls. The French-style cooking, using seasonal produce, is of a high standard; the subtle use of truffles is a speciality. Extensive wine list. Closed Sundays and Mondays.

GREATER BRUSSELS Tsampa   🖼 Ⅴ   €€€

Rue de Livourne 109, 1050 BRU (Ixelles) **Tel** *(02) 6470367*   **Road Map** *B5*

Attached to a whole-foods shop, this is widely held to be the best vegetarian (but not vegan) restaurant in Brussels. Garden and veranda seating in summer. On offer are salads, tarts, terrines and bakes, many Asian-inspired. These are also available as take-away. Open noon–7:30pm. Closed Saturdays and Sundays.

GREATER BRUSSELS Belgium Taste   ⑪ ⑪ 🖾   €€€€

Square de l'Atomium 1, 1020 BRU (Laeken) **Tel** *(02) 4795850*   **Road Map** *A4*

Belgium Taste is an engineering triumph, one of the great wonders of Belgium. The uppermost orb has a stunning 360-degree panorama and also houses a restaurant serving a broad range of Belgian dishes and Belgian wines, based on fixed-price menus. Evenings offer views over the glittering, illuminated city.

GREATER BRUSSELS La Brouette   ⑪ 📋 🖺   €€€

Boulevard Prince de Liège 61, 1070 BRU (Anderlecht) **Tel** *(02) 5225169*   **Road Map** *A4*

Translating as The Wheelbarrow, La Brouette is a modest name for one of Anderlecht's best restaurants. The smart interior complements top-class French-style cuisine. Dishes are based on local, seasonal produce and are exquisitely presented. Closed Saturday lunch, Sunday evening and Monday.

GREATER BRUSSELS Rouge Tomate   🖼 Ⅴ 🖺   €€€€

Avenue Louise 190, 1050 BRU (Ixelles) **Tel** *(02) 6477044*   **Road Map** *B5*

Set in a large townhouse dating from 1883, this is a strongly design-oriented restaurant. The decor is a sleek modern confection of soothing white and reds, with plenty of airy space and an emphasis on natural materials. The menu is very much in the same vein: fresh, seasonal and local, but sophisticated. Saturday and Sunday dinner only.

GREATER BRUSSELS Ventre St Gris   ⑪ 📋 🖼 Ⅴ 🖺   €€€€

Rue Basse 10, 1180 BRU (Uccle) **Tel** *(02) 3752755*   **Road Map** *B5*

A much respected restaurant that has been renovated in an elegantly cool minimalist style, the Ventre St Gris offers fine French cuisine. An admirable *rapport qualité-prix* (price-quality ratio) applies particularly to the fixed-price menus. Garden seating available in the summer. Closed Mondays.

GREATER BRUSSELS Bon-Bon   ⑪ 🖼 🖺   €€€€€

Rue des Carmélites 93, 1180 BRU (Uccle) **Tel** *(02) 3466615*   **Road Map** *B5*

A charming place with simple modern decor. Subtitling itself Salon Artisan-Cuisinier, the restaurant serves French-style cuisine from a menu that changes daily. Top produce inspirationally prepared makes this Michelin-starred restaurant a Brussels favourite. Closed on Saturday, Sunday and Monday lunch.

GREATER BRUSSELS Bruneau   ⑪ 📋 🖼 🖺   €€€€€

Avenue Broustin 73-5, 1083 BRU (Ganshoren) **Tel** *(02) 4217070*   **Road Map** *A4*

Since 1979, Jean-Pierre Bruneau's restaurant, close to the Basilique Nationale du Sacré Coeur, has been a beacon of shining excellence. The inventive French-style cuisine, attentive service and elegantly understated decor have earned one Michelin star. Closed Tuesdays, Wednesdays, mid-June to mid-July and first week of January.

GREATER BRUSSELS La Quincaillerie   ⑪ 📋 🖼 ⑪ Ⅴ 🖺   €€€€€

Rue du Page 45, 1050 BRU (Ixelles) **Tel** *(02) 5339833*   **Road Map** *B5*

A wonderfully stylish restaurant in the midst of the Art Nouveau district. Installed in an astonishing, preserved and converted hardware store, La Quincaillerie put designer Antoine Pinto on the map in 1988. The high-quality brasserie-style food and shellfish bar match the surroundings. Closed for Sunday lunch.

GREATER BRUSSELS Le Stelle   ⑪ 📋 🖼 Ⅴ 🖺   €€€€€

Avenue Louis Bertrand 53-7, 1030 BRU (Schaerbeek) **Tel** *(02) 2450359*   **Road Map** *B4*

Perhaps the capital's best Italian restaurant, Le Stelle occupies a handsomely decorated house with a shaded garden for summer eating. There is also a smaller, neighbouring branch, the Osteria delle Stelle, an Art Nouveau-style bistro with similar fare and marginally cheaper. Closed on Sundays.

GREATER BRUSSELS Villa Lorraine   ⑪ 🖼 ⑪ 🖺   €€€€€

Avenue du Vivier d'Oie 75, 1000 BRU (Uccle) **Tel** *(02) 3743163*   **Road Map** *B5*

One of the best restaurants in Belgium, on the edge of the Bois de la Cambre. The main dining room is a winter garden, a covered veranda overlooking the garden, where tables are placed under the trees in summer. On the menu is top-quality French cuisine. Formal attire is requested. Closed on Sundays and for two weeks in July.

WESTERN FLANDERS

BLANKENBERGE Oesterput
€€€

Westduinse Steenweg 16, 8370 Blankenberge **Tel** *(050) 411035*   **Road Map** *A1*

A full-on fish restaurant by the harbour entrance, in a canteen-style, fish-market environment, complete with live lobster tanks. *Plateaux de fruits de mer* are a speciality. Also available are fish soups, smoked eel, shrimps and fish dishes of all kinds. Highly rated for its price-quality ratio. Large outdoor terrace for fine weather. Closed Tuesdays.

BRUGES 't Brugs Beertje
€

Kemelstraat 5, 8000 Bruges **Tel** *(050) 339616*   **Road Map** *B1*

One of the great beer pubs, renowned for its friendly atmosphere. Its shrine-like status is underscored by the beer memorablia that plaster the walls. There are 300 different Belgian beers to choose from, including guest beers on tap. Traditional snacks, such as ryebread and cheese, keep hunger at bay. Closed on Wednesdays.

BRUGES De Republiek
€

St Jakobsstraat 36, 8000 Bruges **Tel** *(050) 340229*   **Road Map** *B1*

A large and animated café, popular with students, artists and the youth in general, De Republiek is part of a cinema and theatre complex. Beer and cocktails on offer; snacks and "world food" dishes at student prices. In warm weather, the doors open on to a large courtyard garden.

BRUGES Het Dagelijks Brood
€

Philipstockstraat 21, 8000 Bruges **Tel** *(050) 336050*   **Road Map** *B1*

A branch of the super-successful chain Le Pain Quotidien, under the Dutch version of its name. Wholesome fare based around fine crusty bread, plus pâtisserie and other snacks, in an attractive rustic setting. A useful refueling stop in the middle of town for hungry sightseers. Open 8am–6pm; last sitting 5:30pm.

BRUGES Est Wijnbar
€€

Braambergstraat 7, 8000 Bruges **Tel** *(050) 333839*   **Road Map** *B1*

This friendly wine bar occupies a small tavern, dating from 1637, called De Kogge (a medieval sailing ship). It has an excellent selection of wine, including delicious Belgian wines, plus a very good range of tavern food. A narrow staircase leads to a second floor, where live music is played on Sunday nights. Closed Mondays and Tuesdays.

BRUGES Gran Kaffee de Passage
€€

Dweersstraat 26, 8000 Bruges **Tel** *(050) 340232*   **Road Map** *B1*

Housed in an elegant 18th-century mansion, Passage is also a budget hostel-hotel. The interior – part caravanserai, part Edwardian salon with Art Deco touches – provides a cosy setting to sample some good Belgian beer. The traditional Belgian dishes are well cooked and good value. Open in the evenings only. Closed on Sundays 4pm onwards.

BRUGES Bistro De Eetkamer
€€€

Eeekhoutstraat 6, 8000 Bruges **Tel** *(050) 337886*   **Road Map** *B1*

A coolly elegant restaurant, just south of the city centre, where the emphasis is on *eerlijk* (honest) food, prepared with flair to perfection. The focus is on local and seasonal produce, with a changing daily menu. The restaurant is well supported by locals, who see it as good value for money. Closed Tuesday evenings, Wednesdays and Thursdays.

BRUGES De Schaar
€€€

Hooistraat 2, 8000 Bruges **Tel** *(050) 335979*   **Road Map** *B1*

This welcoming and attractive restaurant is on a canal called the Coupure (the Cut). On offer is good-quality, honest fare: this is the kind of owner-operated restaurant patronized by locals. It specializes in fish and meats grilled over an open wood fire. The menu is refreshed twice a month. Closed Thursdays; and Wednesdays in winter.

BRUGES Kok au Vin
€€€

Ezelstraat 19-21, 8000 Bruges **Tel** *(050) 339521*   **Road Map** *B1*

A delightful little restaurant run by a young couple whose enthusiasm for their vocation shines through the warm welcome and excellent cooking. Dishes of the day are posted on the board and include inventive concoctions of seafood, meat, game and new interpretations of Flemish classics. Closed Sunday and Monday.

BRUGES Den Dyver
€€€€

Dijver 5, 8000 Bruges **Tel** *(050) 336069*   **Road Map** *B1*

This elegant, family-run restaurant is famous for its focus on beer cookery – many of the dishes are cooked with Belgian beer. Each dish can be accompanied by a different beer, revealing an astounding range of flavours. There is also plenty on the menu for non-beer drinkers. Closed on Wednesdays and Thursdays.

BRUGES Aneth
€€€€€

Maria Van Bourgondiëlaan 1, 8000 Bruges **Tel** *(050) 311189*   **Road Map** *B1*

Tranquilly located, Aneth is a much-garlanded restaurant focussing mainly on fish preparations. It is already in possession of one Michelin star. There are just seven tables, set in a beautifully renovated *maison de maître*. Paul Hendrickx is the chef with the magic touch. Closed for Saturday lunch, and on Sundays and Mondays.

Key to Price Guide *see p284* **Key to Symbols** *see back cover flap*

BRUGES De Karmeliet
Langestraat 19, 8000 Bruges **Tel** *(050) 338259*   **Road Map** *B1*

One of the two restauraunts in Belgium that have three Michelin stars. On offer are lobster, langoustine, caviar, oysters, quail, top market-produce – all processed by the alchemy of chef Geert Van Hecke and his team into divine dishes, beautifully presented. Polished modern decor and a lovely garden. Book in advance. Closed Sundays and Mondays.

BRUGES Patrick Devos
Zilverstraat 41, 8000 Bruges **Tel** *(050) 335566*   **Road Map** *B1*

One of Bruges's most respected restaurants, cherished for Patrick Devos's creative and light touch in the kitchen, producing French-style gourmet cuisine. The setting is a polished and elegant *belle époque* interior in De Zilveren Pauw (The Silver Peacock), a house dating back to the 13th century. Closed for Saturday lunch and on Sundays.

DAMME Siphon
Damse Vaart-Oost 1, 8340 Oostkerke **Tel** *(050) 620202*   **Road Map** *B1*

A charming restaurant set among the tree-lined canals between Bruges and Damme, Siphon has been run by the same family for three generations and serves Flemish food. Fish is prominent – *paling in 't groen*, peeled shrimps, lobster – plus game dishes in winter. Tearoom and terrace for afternoon pancakes. Closed Thursdays and Fridays.

DE PANNE Hostellerie Le Fox
Walckierstraat 2, 8660 De Panne **Tel** *(058) 412855*   **Road Map** *B1*

This is the place to eat in the Westhoek area, a hotel-restaurant with classic wood-panelled elegance, folded linen, silver, fresh flowers and two Michelin stars. The focus is on seafood – canneloni of sole and langoustine, with black truffles and the like. Closed Mondays and Tuesdays (but open on Tuesday evenings over mid-July–mid-August).

DENDERMONDE 't Truffeltje
Bogaerdstraat 20, 9200 Dendermonde **Tel** *(052) 224590*   **Road Map** *C2*

An old mansion has been modernized to create this spacious restaurant, which has a Michelin star. French-style cuisine, with Belgian and Asian influences, is applied to a broad range of ingredients, including, truffles. Courtyard terrace for summer. Closed Saturday lunch, Sunday evenings, Mondays, Tuesdays and for four weeks in July–August.

DONKMEER Palingrestaurant De Nieuwe Pluim
Brielstraat 9, 9290 Berlare-Overmere **Tel** *(09) 3678070*   **Road Map** *C2*

Donkmeer, a set of lakes near Berlare, is the place to eat eels. Occupying a chalet-like house with an outdoor terrace, this restaurant is one of several overlooking the lake. Cosy and well presented, it specializes in eel dishes – *paling in 't groen* in particular – but offers alternatives. Closed on Mondays and Tuesdays.

GERAARDSBERGEN 't Grof Zout
Gasthuisstraat 20, 9500 Geraardsbergen **Tel** *(054) 423546*   **Road Map** *B2*

An elegant old building that was once a mirror factory has been converted into this charming restaurant. The chef-patron uses interesting ingredients – guinea fowl, pigeon, sea bass, fennel, bulgar wheat – to conjure up French-Belgian dishes. A terrace offers seating in summer. Closed Saturday lunch, Sunday evenings and Mondays.

GHENT 't Dreupelkot
Groentenmarkt 12, 9000 Ghent **Tel** *(09) 2242120*   **Road Map** *B2*

A lovely little old bar on the waterfront, 't Dreupelkot serves only *jenever* and is a classic place to sample this gin in all its flavours: fruit, vanilla, chocolate and pure. Those who need guidance can ask the barman, Pol, a Ghent institution. Open from 4pm daily (6pm in summer). Next door is a famous pub, Het Waterhuis aan de Bierkant.

GHENT Dulle Griet
Vrijdagmarkt 50, 9000 Ghent **Tel** *(09) 2242455*   **Road Map** *B2*

With a choice of 250 beers, this is one of the celebrated "beer academies" of Belgium, with encrustations of beer memorabilia and bric-a-brac on its walls and ceilings. This includes a basket, hoisted to the roof, in which guests must deposit a shoe as security when drinking The Max, a beer served in a large and particularly cherished glass.

GHENT Frituur Jozef
Vrijdagmarkt, 9000 Ghent   **Road Map** *B2*

In the middle of the market square, beneath the grand façade of Ons Huis (headquarters of the Socialist Workers' Union) stands an increasingly rare example of a traditional *fritkot*, a stall (established 1898) selling perfect fries. Sitting on a bench, guests can have a whole meal here, with sausages, meatballs or *stoofvlees* (beef stewed in beer).

GHENT Groot Vleeshuis
Groentenmarkt 7, 9000 Ghent **Tel** *(09) 2232324*   **Road Map** *B2*

Occupying a large, modern glass box set in a sensational medieval butchers' hall spanned by ancient exposed beams, Groot Vleeshuis promotes Flemish food. The small restaurant serves interesting and good-value Flemish dishes and is an unforgettable lunch stop. Kitchen open 10am–3pm; delicatessen until 6pm. Closed Mondays.

GHENT Gruut City Brewery
Grote Huidevettershoek 10, 9000 Ghent **Tel** *(09) 2690269*   **Road Map** *B2*

Located in the heart of Ghent, this one-of-a-kind city brewery serves 5 different varieties of beer made in-house with a unique blend of spices. The menu includes traditional meat stew or *stoofvlees*, prepared using Belgian beef and beer. Reservations should be made in advance for tours of the brewery.

GHENT Belga Queen
🍽🗒🖼📺Ⓥ   €€€
Graslei 10, 9000 Ghent **Tel** *(09) 2800100*   **Road Map** *B2*

Belga Queen was designed by Antoine Pinto, famous for his spectacular restaurants. His trademark panache is seen in the interior of this 12th-century building overlooking the Graslei. Franco-Belgian cooking in high-end brasserie style. Good-value fixed-price menus. Lunch is served daily using fresh Belgian produce.

GHENT Brasserie Pakhuis
🗒🖼   €€€
Schuurkenstraat 4, 9000 Ghent **Tel** *(09) 223555*   **Road Map** *B2*

Another of Antoine Pinto's designs, the Pakhuis is a converted 19th-century warehouse, full of fancy ironwork, balconies, cunning lighting and above all pizzazz – an invigorating place to eat. Well-prepared food to suit all appetites and tastes. The eatery is big, but very popular, so it is best to make reservations. Closed Sundays.

GHENT Coeur d'Artichaut
🍽🖼   €€€
Onderbergen 6, 9000 Ghent **Tel** *(09) 2253318*   **Road Map** *B2*

A handsome *maison de maître* has been stylishly renovated with pared-down elegance to create a highly respected restaurant, famed for its light wholesome food, particularly salads. There is a pretty patio area at the rear for summer dining. Located just south of the Korenlei and Graslei. Closed Sundays and Mondays.

GHENT Keizershof
🖼   €€€
Vrijdagmarkt 47, 9000 Ghent **Tel** *(09) 2234446*   **Road Map** *B2*

Once a traditional tavern, the Keizershof has been revamped in an upbeat modern style, opening up the floors and beams of this 17th-century building. However, it still maintains its tradition of serving good Belgian dishes, such as *garnaalkroketten* (shrimp coquettes) and *Gentse stoverij* (a beef stew). Closed Sundays and Mondays.

GHENT Bij den Wijzen en den Zot
€€€€
Hertogstraat 42, 9000 Ghent **Tel** *(09) 2234230*   **Road Map** *B2*

Located in the folksy Patershol area is this beautiful 16th-century, step-gabled guildhouse of the leatherworkers with three dining rooms. The food is traditional Flemish cuisine; home cooking with flair. This is the place to try Ghent's signature dish, *waterzooi*, made with either chicken or fish. Closed on Sundays and Mondays.

IEPER Pacific Eiland
🍽♿🖼📺Ⓥ   €€€
Island 2, 8900 Ieper **Tel** *(057) 200528*   **Road Map** *A2*

A short walk from the city centre and Ieper train station, this eatery boasts an idyllic setting on a small island that can be reached via a bridge. Modern and spacious, it serves inventive French and Belgian cuisine prepared using local seasonal produce. Boats are available on hire during summer. Closed Monday evenings and Tuesdays.

IEPER Hostellerie St-Nicolas
🍽🗒🖼   €€€€€
Veurnseweg 532, 8906 Elverdinge **Tel** *(057) 200622*   **Road Map** *A2*

Elverdinge is 5 km (3 miles) northwest of Ieper, and worth the trip for this first class restaurant that boasts two Michelin stars. Exquisite Franco-Belgian cooking by chef Franky Vanderhaeghe at prices that could be more extreme for this calibre. Lovely garden terrace in summer. Closed on Sundays and Mondays.

KEMMEL In de Wulf
🍽📺Ⓥ   €€€
Wulvestraat 1, 8950 Heuvelland-Dranouter **Tel** *(057) 445567*   **Road Map** *A2*

This delightful guesthouse and restaurant in rural Dranouter, 5 km (3 miles) southwest of Kemmel, occupies an old farmhouse. Dishes are prepared using natural, seasonal ingredients from both sea and land. A restorative retreat for visitors to the battlefields. Lovely garden terrace. Closed Mondays and Tuesdays and for lunch on Wednesdays and Saturdays.

KNOKKE-HEIST À l'Improviste
🍽🖼   €€€
Zeedijk 245, 8301 Knokke-Heist **Tel** *(050) 515111*   **Road Map** *B1*

A stylish, modern fish restaurant with wood flooring, ceiling fans and handwritten suggestions posted on blackboards. On offer are traditional fish recipes, with *croquettes de crevettes* and oven-baked cod, fish and seasonal dishes including asparagus. An attractive fixed-price lunch menu, to be enjoyed on the terrace overlooking the sea.

KNOKKE-HEIST Bartholomeus
🍽🗒🖼   €€€€€
Zeedijk 267, 8301 Knokke-Heist **Tel** *(050) 517576*   **Road Map** *B1*

Set on the sea dyke of Heist, the focus of this Michelin-starred restaurant is, of course, seafood. The decor is modern and fresh; the cooking inventive and carefully judged to extract the best flavours through a wide palette, including Asian (wasabi, ginger, curry). Meat dishes are also available. Closed on Tuesdays, Wednesdays and Thursdays.

KNOKKE-HEIST Sel Gris
🗒🖼   €€€€€
Zeedijk 314, 8301 Duinbergen **Tel** *(050) 514937*   **Road Map** *B1*

The seafront restaurant of one of the new stars of Belgian cookery, Frederik Deceuninck, who was awarded his first Michelin star in 2008. Turbot, sole, plaice, mackerel, skate, scallops, lobster and other North Sea treasures are turned into exquisitely judged dishes prepared using seasonal ingredients. Closed on Wednesdays and Thursdays.

KORTRIJK Saint-Christophe
🍽🗒🖼🖼   €€€€€
Minister Tacklaan 5, 8500 Kortrijk **Tel** *(056) 200337*   **Road Map** *B2*

Close to the station, this very elegant restaurant is in an old *maison de maître*. The cuisine is classic French, scrupulously realized. The fixed-price menus are good value for this kind of culinary treat. Garden terrace for summer dining. Closed Sunday and Tuesday evenings, all day Mondays and two weeks in early August.

LAARNE Restaurant Kasteel van Laarne

Eekhoekstraat 7, 9270 Laarne **Tel** *(09) 2307178*

Road Map B2

Located in a set of pretty outbuildings at the wonderful medieval castle of Laarne, this prestigious restaurant offers a French-Belgian menu that is a gastronomic tour de force. The fixed-price lunch menu can be particularly good value. Lovely stone terrace with views over the moat and castle in summer. Closed Mondays, Tuesdays and Sunday evenings.

LISSEWEGE Hof Ter Doest

Ter Doeststraat 4, 8380 Lissewege **Tel** *(050) 544082*

Road Map B1

A large 17th-century farmhouse, whitewashed and red tiled, stands on the tranquil green opposite the medieval barn of Ter Doest. Inside it are exposed oak beams and, in winter, an open fire. This rural setting forms the back-drop for refined dishes prepared along traditional lines, based on local seafood and meat from Ter Doest's farm.

OOSTENDE Fort Napoléon

Vuurtorenweg, 8400 Oostende **Tel** *(059) 332160*

Road Map A1

Built in 1811, the old Napoleonic fortress provides an unusual setting for high-class French and Belgian cuisine. The indoor seating is under the impressively massive arches of the fortification, but there is also a large terrace for sunny days, with fine views. A *bistrot* section serves lighter meals. Closed Monday lunch.

OOSTENDE Le Grillon

Visserskaai 31, 8400 Oostende **Tel** *(059) 706063*

Road Map A1

This classic Belgian restaurant offers first-class cooking without pretension, but with the confidence of skill honed since the establishment opened in 1969. It overlooks the old fishing harbour and seafood takes precedence – Oostende shrimps are a must – but there is meat too. Closed on Wednesday evenings and Thursdays.

OOSTENDE Ostend Queen

Monacoplein, 8400 Oostende **Tel** *(059) 445610*

Road Map A1

Another project by star designer Antoine Pinto, this large and stunning restaurant on the top floor of the seafront *kursaal* (casino) uses top quality fish and seafood and seasonal produce to create inventive dishes, such as seabass marinated in beetroot and herring caviar. Closed Sundays and Mondays.

OUDENAARDE Bistro 't Veer

Berchemweg 191, 9700 Oudenaarde **Tel** *(055) 302588*

Road Map B2

Located outside the town, just south of the River Scheldt, this well-established, family-friendly restaurant has an attractive, modern and elegantly simple decor. Bistro 't Veer prides itself on providing good and ample food at easy prices. The cuisine comprises straightforward Belgian classics prepared with care. Closed Thursdays.

OUDENAARDE Hof van Cleve

Riemegemstraat 1, 9770 Kruishoutem **Tel** *(09) 3835848*

Road Map B2

About 7 km (4 miles) northwest of Oudenaarde lies Hof van Cleve. A pretty collection of farm buildings, surrounded by tranquil countryside, it is an ideal setting for Peter Goossens's three-star Michelin restaurant, with all the cooking perfection and polished hospitality that this entails. Closed Sundays and Mondays and for Tuesday lunch.

POPERINGE 't Hommelhof

Watouplein 17, 8978 Watou **Tel** *(057) 388024*

Road Map A2

Lying close to the French border, 6 km (4 miles) west of Poperinge, this friendly hostelry focusses on beer cookery where dishes are prepared using local beer. Open daily between July and August; otherwise closed in the evenings on Mondays, Tuesdays and Thursdays, and all day on Wednesdays.

ST-MARTENS-LATEM Nenuphar

Afsneedorp 28, 9051 Afsnee **Tel** *(09) 2224586*

Road Map B2

Set on the River Leie in the pretty village of Afsnee, this is a good place to visit on a summer's day, when tables are set out on a shaded terrace right beside the river. There is also a pretty dining room inside, decorated with a mural by Gustave de Smet. Elegant and carefully considered dishes. Closed Sunday evenings, Tuesdays and Thursdays.

ST-MARTENS-LATEM Orangerie

Pontstraat 41, 9830 Deurle **Tel** *(09) 2823144*

Road Map B2

The Michelin-starred restaurant of Auberge du Pêcheur, a hotel beautifully set on the banks of River Leie. High-quality French cuisine is served in an elegant dining room. In summer, tables are set on the terrace. There is also a cheaper brasserie and summer afternoon tearoom. Closed Saturday lunch, Mondays and Sundays from October to March.

ST-NIKLAAS Kok O Vin

Heidebaan 46, 9100 Sint Niklaas **Tel** *(03) 7668661*

Road Map C1

A sleek and modern restaurant in a restored suburban villa to the east of the town. It offers a French-Belgian menu founded on old-fashioned traditions of quality, seasonal ingredients and value-for-money. *Coq-au-vin* is of course on the menu; there is even a recipe on the wall. Closed Tuesdays, Wednesdays and for Saturday lunch.

VEURNE Brasserie Christophe

Grote Markt 24, 8630 Veurne **Tel** *(058) 314022*

Road Map A2

Located in the main square, this brasserie-style restaurant serves authentic Belgian cuisine and is good value for money. When in season, the moules frites are the most popular choice with locals and visitors alike. Closed Thursday evenings and Fridays.

VEURNE Orangerie

Noordstraat 9, 8630 Veurne **Tel** *(058) 313128*   **Road Map** *A2*

Part of the family-run hotel-restaurant Croonhof Hostellerie, the restaurant, Orangerie, is considered the best in town. The gastronomic dishes are founded on a classic Franco-Belgian base, with Italian touches, featuring local produce from sea and land. The decor is classically elegant. Closed on Sundays and Mondays.

CENTRAL AND EASTERN FLANDERS

ALDEN BIESEN Het Vlierhof

Hasseltsestraat 57A, 3740 Bilzen **Tel** *(089) 414418*   **Road Map** *E2*

A charming restaurant in a rustic setting, 5 km (3 miles) north of Alden Biesen. The chef is a dedicated plantsman and creates good Flemish dishes using produce from the restaurant's gardens and orchards, plus fresh, seasonal produce from the Haspengouw region and beyond. Closed Saturday lunch, Monday evenings and Wednesdays.

ANTWERP Den Engel

Grote Markt 3, 2000 Antwerp **Tel** *(03) 2331252*   **Road Map** *C1*

A friendly pub evincing traditons of centuries of hospitality, Den Engel (The Angel) is a typical Belgian *bruine kroeg* or brown pub – brown with the patina of age. With mirrors and marble-topped tables, the atmosphere is ideal for trying a *bolleke* (chalice-like glass) of De Koninck, Antwerp's own brew. Traditional light snacks are available.

ANTWERP Het Elfde Gebod

Torfbrug 10, 2000 Antwerp **Tel** *(03) 2893466*   **Road Map** *C1*

Facing the cathedral, Het Elfde Gebod (The Eleventh Commandment) is a popular haunt for the liberal minded who enjoy the jokey and eye-catching mass-display of religious statuary and symbols. The reaction to it is clear-cut: visitors either love it or hate it. The beer is fine and there is plenty of good-value Flemish bar food.

ANTWERP Kulminator

Vleminckveld 32, 2000 Antwerp **Tel** *(03) 2324538*   **Road Map** *C1*

This beer-drinker's shrine is a traditional-style pub with over 800 beers listed in a thick menu, plus guest draught beers. The staff are knowledgeable guides. Light snacks of cheese, sausages and salami help to ward off hunger. Located in a quiet street just south of the cathedral. Opens at 4pm daily, from 8pm on Mondays. Closed on Sundays.

ANTWERP Patine

Leopold De Waelplaats 1, 2000 Antwerp **Tel** *(03) 2570919*   **Road Map** *C1*

A wonderfully individual establishment, this folksy bare wood restaurant calls itself a wine bistro, but is open for breakfast from 9am. For lunch and dinner, it serves soup, pasta, quiches, salads and light Flemish dishes. It also holds live music nights, and futhermore has bed-and-breakfast accommodation.

ANTWERP De Cuisinier

Tavernierkaai 1, 2000 Antwerp **Tel** *(03) 2253637*   **Road Map** *C1*

Originally the sluicegate master's house, the Bassin stands alone, overlooking the river and the Bonapartedok. It has been converted into a smart brasserie with retro touches, serving traditional fare and a selection of meat and fish. It has a congenial environment and something to suit all appetites. Closed Saturday lunch.

ANTWERP Dock's Café

Jordaenskaai 7, 2000 Antwerpen **Tel** *(03) 2266330*   **Road Map** *C1*

Antoine Pinto is the designer behind the wonderfully inventive interior of the Dock's Café. Dating from 1995, the café is built on two levels in a building that overlooks the River Scheldt. The decor creates a sense of pizzazz among diners, as does the food – excellent brasserie dishes, stylishly prepared and presented. Closed Sundays.

ANTWERP Grand Café Horta

Hopland 2, 2000 Antwerp **Tel** *(03) 2322815*   **Road Map** *C1*

A large, ultra-stylish café-bar-brasserie close to the Rubenshuis. Its dynamic space has been created around salvaged metal struts from Victor Horta's Art Nouveau Volkshuis in Brussels which was demolished in 1965. On offer are upmarket brasserie food and service that is polished and professional. Open daily from 9am to 10pm, to 11:30pm on Fridays.

ANTWERP Zuiderterras

Ernest van Dijckkaai 37, 2000 Antwerp **Tel** *(03) 2341275*   **Road Map** *C1*

Architect Bob Van Reeth set out to turn Antwerp's eyes to the River Scheldt with this landmark edifice built over the water. Guests are the main beneficiaries of the unparalleled views from a dining room of cruise-liner elegance and first-class brasserie-style cooking. Also open for very reasonably priced breakfast from 9am to noon.

ANTWERP Bernardin

St-Jacobsstraat 17, 2000 Antwerp **Tel** *(03) 2130700*   **Road Map** *C1*

A 17th-century mansion by St-Jacobskerk with a coolly elegant white, grey and black interior provides the backdrop for chef Bernard Lescrinier's exquisitely artistic dishes – French-Belgian classics revisited. The weekday fixed-price lunch menu can be a bargain. Large summer terrace. Closed for Saturday lunch and on Sundays and Mondays.

Key to Price Guide *see p284* **Key to Symbols** *see back cover flap*

ANTWERP Het Pomphuis
Droogdok, Siberiastraat 7, 2030 Antwerp **Tel** *(03) 7708625* **Road Map** *C1*

In keeping with the city's passion for industrial retro-bar conversions, the docklands' dry-dock pumphouse, built in grand Neo-Classical style, was converted into a restaurant retaining much of the original hydraulic machinery. The food is creative and wide-ranging; French-Belgian in style with an injection of Asian tastes.

ANTWERP Huis de Colvenier
St-Antoniusstraat 8, 2000 Antwerp **Tel** *0477 232650* **Road Map** *C1*

An old town mansion is the setting for this friendly, sophisticated restaurant. An open kitchen reveals the high attention to detail that goes into its classic French cuisine. Guests may visit the extensive wine cellar. Dining spaces include a winter garden and a summer terrace. Closed on Sundays and Mondays.

ANTWERP Mise en Place
Door Verstraeteplaats 4, 2018 Antwerp (Zurenborg) **Tel** *(03) 2947877* **Road Map** *C1*

Just north of the fantasy architecture of Cogels-Osylei, Mise en Place is a delightful *belle époque*-style restaurant in an elegantly renovated town mansion. It serves a limited menu of first-rate Belgian cuisine. The fixed-price menus can be attractively priced, especially at lunch. Closed for Saturday lunch, and on Sundays and Mondays.

DIEST De Groene Munt
Veermarkt 2, 3290 Diest **Tel** *(013) 666833* **Road Map** *D2*

Located in the heart of Diest, this intimate and comfortable eatery has classic English decor and serves French gastronomic cuisine, prepared using freshly caught fish and seasonal produce. A tasting menu recommended by the chef himself is an added attraction. Reservations are recommended. Closed for lunch on Saturdays.

DIEST De Proosdij
Cleyneartstraat 14, 3290 Diest **Tel** *(013) 312010* **Road Map** *D2*

This beautiful 17th-century house, close to the St-Sulpitiuskerk, was formerly the home of the provost. Luxuriously and elegantly refurbished, it is now the domain of the celebrated chef Anny Smets, an expert in classic French cuisine. Aperitif and coffee served in a stunning garden. Closed for Saturday lunch, and on Sunday evenings, Mondays and Tuesdays.

HALLE Les Éleveurs
Suikerkaai 1A, 1500 Halle **Tel** *(02) 3611340* **Road Map** *C2*

The original purpose of these attractive buildings by the Brussels-Charleroi canal was to breed Brabantine draught horses. They are now the location of a hotel-restaurant famed for high-quality Franco-Belgian food by chef Sofie Dumont. Elegant dining room and pretty bricked terrace. Closed Saturday lunch, Sundays and Mondays.

HASSELT De Kwizien
Jeneverplein, 3500 Hasselt **Tel** *(011) 242344* **Road Map** *E2*

With its striking glasshouse extension on the tranquil square dedicated to Hasselt's famous gin, De Kwizien has caused something of a stir. The innovative cuisine for which the restaurant is named is produced with flourish in the open kitchen. Relaxed, fun and engaging atmosphere. Closed Tuesdays, Wednesdays and for Saturday lunch.

HASSELT 't Kleine Genoegen
Raamstraat 3, 3500 Hasselt **Tel** *(011) 225703* **Road Map** *E2*

The traditional cuisine of Limbourg, with modern gourmet twists, is celebrated in this popular family-run restaurant. Seasonal *streekproducten* (regional produce) such as rhubarb, cherries and rabbit, form the basis of the menu. The setting is a 17th-century building, utterly modernized inside. Closed Sundays and Mondays.

HASSELT 't Claeverblat
Lombaardstraat 34, 3500 Hasselt **Tel** *(011) 222404* **Road Map** *E2*

Experienced chef Peter Piakowski creates superb modern French-style cuisine at this restaurant. In a townhouse close to the centre, the dining rooms are intimate and classical, the perfect canvas for the beautifully presented dishes. Closed on Thursdays, Sundays and lunch on Saturdays.

LEUVEN Café De Blaue Schuit
Vismarkt 16, 3000 Leuven **Tel** *(016) 220570* **Road Map** *D2*

Established for over 30 years, De Blaue Schuit (The Blue Barge) is a popular café-style pub in a 19th-century building decorated with disparate memorabilia, and with a tree-shaded terrace. The kitchen is open 11am–10pm and offers pastas, salads, chilli con carne and daily specials.

LEUVEN Domus
Tiensestraat 8, 3000 Leuven **Tel** *(016) 201449* **Road Map** *D2*

A unique Belgian institution, this pub is supplied by its own brewery next door (founded in 1985) and the Domus beer is pumped directly into the taps of the agreeable, traditional-style tavern. Snacks, including breakfast and pub food – pasta, salads, steaks, spare ribs, pancakes – are served throughout the day. Closed Mondays.

LEUVEN De Blauwe Maan
Mechelsestraat 22, 3000 Leuven **Tel** *(016) 299747* **Road Map** *D2*

There is a buzz to De Blauwe Maan (The Blue Moon), a modern eatery whose changing daily dishes and fixed-price lunch menus are particularly good value. Snack or feast – all appetites are welcome. The cooking is mainly French-Belgian-Italian, a solid base with gastronomic flourishes. Closed on Sundays and Mondays.

LIER Numerus Clausus

Keldermansstraat 2, 2500 Lier **Tel** *(03) 4805162*

Road Map *C1*

This romantic restaurant is located near the St Gummarus church and faces the house of Felix Timmermans. It offers refined French cuisine inspired by the creativity of chef Steven Persyn and prepared using local seasonal ingredients. Reservations are recommended. Closed Saturday lunch, Sundays and Mondays.

MECHELEN D'Hoogh

Grote Markt 19, 2800 Mechelen **Tel** *(015) 217553*

Road Map *C2*

This is the grand restaurant of Mechelen, a gilded 17th-century mansion filled with elegant, antique charm. The cooking is equally aristocratic, founded on all the best Belgian principles of being true to the natural qualities of top seasonal ingredients. Closed for Saturday lunch, and on Sunday evenings, Mondays and Tuesdays.

MECHELEN Folliez

Korenmarkt 19, 2800 Mechelen **Tel** *(015) 420302*

Road Map *C2*

Restaurant Folliez's motto, "obsessed by flavour, with an eye for detail", encapsulates the classic but modern cooking of this eatery. Fish and meat dishes prepared with creative imagination; divine desserts. Smart and relaxed decor of wine-red walls and contemporary photographs. Closed on Saturdays and Sundays.

ST-TRUIDEN Sud et Sol

Plankstraat 2, 3800 St-Truiden **Tel** *(011) 686660*

Road Map *D2*

This delightful restaurant glows with Mediterranean warmth, both in the decor and the cooking. The chef applies his southern Italian roots to pasta, seafood, chicken and veal, with some southern French and Spanish flourishes. The fixed-price lunch menus are particularly good value. Closed on Mondays and for Thursday lunch.

ST-TRUIDEN Aan de Kerck van Melveren

St-Godfriedstraat 15-21, 3800 St-Truiden **Tel** *(011) 683965*

Road Map *D2*

A 16th-century farmhouse of warm red brick is now the lovely setting for this first-rate restaurant, 3 km (2 miles) northeast of St-Truiden. The garden is particularly beautiful. Classic French cuisine on offer, with special attention to exquisite presentation. Closed for Saturday lunch, Sunday dinner and all day Mondays and Tuesdays.

ST-TRUIDEN De Fakkels

Hasseltsesteenweg 61, 3800 St-Truiden **Tel** *(011) 687634*

Road Map *D2*

Set in an elegantly furnished 1930s mansion just northeast of St-Truiden, De Fakkels sources the highest quality ingredients from the Haspengouw region – famous for its farm produce – for its elaborate French cuisine. Wonderful garden in summer. Closed on Mon and Tue. Open for lunch on Sun, Wed, Thu and Fri and for dinner on Sat.

TIENEN De Refugie

Kapucijnenstraat 75, 3300 Tienen **Tel** *(016) 824532*

Road Map *D2*

A charming restaurant run with a very hands-on approach by its owner-chef. The dining room is modern, but panelling and antique touches give it an atmosphere of intimacy. Garden terrace for summer dining. The cuisine is French and Belgian with a special focus on seafood. Closed Tuesdays, Wednesdays and for Saturday lunch.

TONGEREN De Pelgrim

Brouwersstraat 9, 3700 Tongeren **Tel** *(012) 238322*

Road Map *E2*

In a town steeped in history, De Pelgrim is located ideally on the cobbled Brouwersstraat (Brewers' Street), in the pretty begijnhof quarter. This fine old pub occupies a red-brick, step-gabled building from 1642. A traditional interior of exposed beams, wooden furniture. Excellent beer, and a range of pub food from snacks to spare ribs.

TONGEREN Magis

Hemelingenstraat 23, 3700 Tongeren **Tel** *(012) 743464*

Road Map *E2*

A grand old mansion, once owned by the Teutonic knights of Alden Biesen, has been given a modern makeover to create the Magis. It serves Michelin-star rated gastronomic French cuisine, with special emphasis on artistic presentation. There is also a large garden, with an ornamental pool, for summer dining. Closed on Tuesdays and Wednesdays.

TURNHOUT Cucinamarangon

Patersstraat 9, 2300 Turnhout **Tel** *(014) 424381*

Road Map *D1*

In a beautifully converted patrician home, Fabio and Liana Marangon have created a theatrical setting for their refined northern Italian cuisine. Seafood is a speciality as are *carpaccio*, risotto, pasta and classic Italian main dishes with a twist. Good-value fixed-price menus. Closed on Mondays and for lunch on Wednesdays and Saturdays.

WESTERN WALLONIA

ATH Viandes etc

Place du Maché aux Toiles 5-7, 7800 Ath **Tel** *(068) 445977*

Road Map *B3*

The name Viandes etc (Meats etc) sets the scene for dedicated non-vegetarian cooking that adheres to local produce and is inventive and good value. The simple decor that includes the exposed wall of a medieval tower. The plain tables are covered with red-checked cloths. Located near the Grand Place. Closed Tuesday evenings and Wednesdays.

Key to Price Guide *see p284* **Key to Symbols** *see back cover flap*

ATTRE Le Vieux Chaudron
Avenue du Château 14, 7941 Attre **Tel** *(068) 454279*   **Road Map** *B3*

This long-established family-run restaurant is in a charming 14th-century stone-and-brick house. It is primarily a lunch spot, opening in the evening only on Saturdays; closed all day Wednesdays. Well-prepared Belgian and French cooking, with traditional dishes created from seasonal produce. Log-fire in winter, pretty garden in summer.

BINCHE Le Bercha
Route de Mons 763, 7130 Bray **Tel** *(064) 369107*   **Road Map** *C3*

A highly creative chef controls the kitchen at this wayside restaurant 5 km (3 miles) west of Binche, winning many plaudits and a loyal following. The French-style cooking is *du terroir* (based on local produce and traditions). Family-run and family-friendly, with outdoor terrace and playground. Closed Sunday evenings, Mondays and Tuesdays.

CHARLEROI La Bruxelloise
Place Émile Buisset 9, 6000 Charleroi **Tel** *(071) 322969*   **Road Map** *C3*

A good, well-presented restaurant popular with locals, with well-made dishes based on seasonal ingredients. On offer are mussels, steaks (with a choice of eight sauces), *waterzooi* of fish and game in winter. Lobster is a speciality. Not exactly cheap, but certainly good value relative to quality. Located close to the River Sambre.

CHARLEROI La Mirabelle
Rue de Marcinelle 7, 6000 Charleroi **Tel** *(071) 333988*   **Road Map** *C3*

This is a popular little upstairs restaurant, in the south of the city centre. The owner-chef is in charge of the kitchen, creating savoury French cuisine. Good-value, all-inclusive fixed-price menus. Serves delicious cuisine during lunch hours. Closed on Wednesdays and for dinner on Fridays and Saturdays.

CHARLEROI Les 3 P'Tits Bouchons
Avenue Paul Pastur 378, 6032 Charleroi **Tel** *(071) 325519*   **Road Map** *C3*

Located on the outskirts of Charleroi, this restaurant was co-founded by sommelier Roland Kempinaire and chef Yoshida Shunshuke. It serves contemporary cuisine prepared using fresh produce and boasts an impressive wine list to choose from. Closed on Saturdays and Sundays.

CHIMAY Chez Edgard et Madeleine
Rue du Lac 35, 6460 Chimay **Tel** *(060) 211071*   **Road Map** *C4*

Set beside the Lac de Virelles, 3 km (2 miles) east of Chimay, this restaurant dates back to 1910. Wood-panelling and crisp white linen reflect the cooking, which is *à l'ancienne* (old style), with lake trout and seafood, plus seasonal game (hare, venison, partridge). Good wine list and, of course, Chimay beers. Closed Sunday evenings and Mondays.

LA LOUVIÈRE Les Gourmands Disent
Rue Sylvain Guyaux 8, 7100 La Louvière **Tel** *(064) 284095*   **Road Map** *C3*

Located in the heart of La Louvière, Olivier Bayet's modern and contemporary restaurant serves gastronomic cuisine with an emphasis on fresh market produce. Menu varies according to the season and market produce. Reservations are recommended. Closed Mondays and Tuesdays.

LESSINES Le Tramasure
Porte d'Ogy 3, 7860 Lessines **Tel** *(068) 335082*   **Road Map** *B2*

The exposed brick walls and oak rafters of a former herbalist's shop create an old-world setting for this restaurant specializing in *cuisine du terroir* – cooking based on local produce and traditions. Snails, duck, rabbit, tripe sausages, Belgian endives, plus seafood. Closed Mondays, and evenings on Sundays and Tuesdays to Fridays.

MONS Les Enfants Gâtés
Rue de Bertaimant 40, 7000 Mons **Tel** *(065) 723973*   **Road Map** *C3*

Considered by many to be the best restaurant in Mons. In a tavern-like setting, the first-rate gourmet cooking is southern French in style with Mediterranean touches. The menu has dishes such as swordfish *carpaccio*, langoustine with truffles, pigeon with *foie gras*. Closed for Saturday lunch, and evenings on Sundays and Mondays.

THUIN Au Bief du Moulin
Rue Vandervelde 290, 6534 Gozée **Tel** *(071) 516074*   **Road Map** *C3*

A modern restaurant on the banks of the River Sambre. *Bief* means watercourse, and the *moulin* was the old abbey mill. The cooking is *familiale*: good-quality home cooking, and the prices, notably the set menus, are very reasonable. Outdoor eating and a children's playground. Closed Mondays and Tuesdays.

TOURNAI L'Écurie d'Ennetières
Ruelle d'Ennetières 7, 7500 Tournai **Tel** *(069) 215689*   **Road Map** *B3*

A refreshingly traditional and unpretentious brasserie serving good reasonably priced Belgian fare. On offer are scampi, *filet américain*, *façon tartare*, steak, *jambonneau* (knuckle of ham), *crème brûlée* and so on. Good-value fixed-price menus. The building, formerly a stable for a coaching inn, has been modernized with a light touch.

TOURNAI Le Giverny
6 Dock Fish Market, 7500 Tournai **Tel** *(069) 224464*   **Road Map** *B3*

Located on the banks of a river, this eatery has an elegant setting and provides spectacular views. It serves French cuisine with an emphasis on flavour and fresh produce. Reservations are recommended. Closed on Mondays, Tuesday and Sunday dinner and Saturday lunch.

CENTRAL WALLONIA

ANNEVOIE Jardin d'en Bas   €€€
Rue d'en Bas 1, 5537 Annevoie **Tel** (082) 613706   **Road Map** D3

Set in a lovely 17th-century house decorated in historical style, this family-run restaurant offers "home-cooked" Belgian cuisine. The traditional fare is met with a close attachment to local produce – smoked duck, trout, *terrine de foie gras*, snails, rabbit. Located 2 km (1 mile) south of Annevoie. Closed Tuesdays and Wednesdays.

DINANT La Broche   €€€€
Rue Grande 22, 5500 Dinant **Tel** (082) 228281   **Road Map** D3

A handsome 19th-century shopfront of stone and red brick in the high street is the preface to an attractive and welcoming restaurant. The cooking is grounded in French cuisine, but with some Asian touches. A comfortable modern dining room decorated with old portrait photographs. Closed on Tuesdays, and for Wednesday lunch.

DINANT Jardin de Fiorine   €€€€€
Rue Georges Cousot 3, 5500 Dinant **Tel** (082) 227474   **Road Map** D3

A large *maison de maître* of 1885, gently modernized, is the setting for light French gourmet cooking and *cuisine de terroir*. There is a specially designed menu for children called An Introduction to Gastronomy. Summer dining in a large garden by the River Meuse. Closed on Sunday evenings, Wednesdays and Thursdays.

FLOREFFE Mas des Cigales   €€€
Rue du Moncia 9, 5150 Floriffoux **Tel** (081) 444847   **Road Map** D3

Located 2 km (1 mile) east of Floreffe, Mas des Cigales (Farmstead of the Cicadas) is a southern French reference which shines through the excellent cooking. The decor of the dining rooms is similarly Provençale – sunny yellows and warm reds. Lunch is the main focus: open for the evening only on Fridays and Saturdays; closed Wednesdays.

LA HULPE Côté Jardin   €€
Rue de Genval 14, 1310 La Hulpe **Tel** (02) 6530113   **Road Map** C2

A small, family-run restaurant with tables put out in the garden during summer. On offer are salads with shrimp or smoked duck, scampi salad and steaks, all at very reasonable prices. The decor is simple and modern. Open 8:30am–3pm Monday–Saturday, and till late on Friday evenings. Closed Sundays.

LOUVAIN-LA-NEUVE La Baïta   €€€
Drève du Golf 3, 1348 Louvain-la-neuve **Tel** (010) 451165   **Road Map** D2

A large wooden chalet at the edge of a forest, 3 km (2 miles) north of the university town. This has been the tranquil scene for fine Italian and French cooking since 1992. The classic dishes include pasta, *carpaccio*, seafood, veal and chicken. Very reasonably priced *plats du jour*. Shaded terrace in the summer. Closed Mondays.

MAREDSOUS La Fermette   €€€€
Rue du Château-Ferme 30, 5522 Falaën **Tel** (082) 688668   **Road Map** D2

Located 4 km (2 miles) southeast of Maredsous in one of Wallonia's prettiest villages is La Fermette – a farmhouse restaurant serving first-class French cuisine to its many dedicated fans. Meals can be finished with a platter of Falaën cheeses. Lovely rural garden. Closed on Wednesdays. Jun–Aug: closed Wednesday and Thursday.

NAMUR La Mère Gourmandin   €
Rue du Président 13, 5000 Namur **Tel** (081) 227208   **Road Map** D3

A charming restaurant with a courtyard garden, that serves meals of home-cooked pasta, savoury crêpes, quiches and salads. Open all day. The companion restaurant Le Père Gourmandin is open for lunch only, serving organic sandwiches, stuffed baked potatoes, pasta and quiches. Both are closed on evenings from Mondays to Thursdays and Sundays.

NAMUR Cuisinémoi   €€€€
Rue Notre Dame 44, 5000 Namur **Tel** (081) 229181   **Road Map** D3

This small, Michelin-starred restaurant at the foot of Namur's Citadelle has a narrow, bright and modern dining room, and a kitchen on a brickwork balcony. The inventive French-style cuisine includes seafood and meat dishes that are presented in magical combinations of flavours. Closed for Saturday lunch, and on Sundays and Mondays.

NAMUR La Petite Fugue   €€€€
Place Chanoine Descamps 5, 5000 Namur **Tel** (081) 231320   **Road Map** D3

A thoroughly seductive, ultramodern restaurant. The shell is 17th-century, but dining spaces are decorated in cream and chocolate with bare wood floors and soft lighting. The cooking is imaginative, springing off a solid French foundation. The fixed-price lunch menu is a bargain. Tables also on the terrace at the front.

NAMUR La Plage d'Amée   €€€€
Rue des Peupliers 2, 5100 Jambes **Tel** (081) 309339   **Road Map** D3

On the east bank of the River Meuse, 5 km (3 mile) from central Namur, is this modern restaurant with a balcony overhanging the river. The interior is spacious, airy and relaxed. In the kitchen is a team eager to impress with their first-class French-style cooking. Fish and seafood are high on the agenda. Closed on Sunday evenings and Mondays.

Key to Price Guide see p284 **Key to Symbols** see back cover flap

NIVELLES Le Champenois ❙❙❙ €€€€
Rue des Brasseurs 14, 1400 Nivelles Tel (067) 213500 **Road Map** C3

A first-class gastronomic restaurant in a picturesque old quarter of the town. The service is impeccable and the decor drenched with comforting reds. The French-style cuisine is sumptuous: classic yet inventive and beautifully presented. Enticing *menu dégustation* (tasting menu). Closed Saturday lunch, Sunday evenings and Wednesdays.

ROCHEFORT Restaurant La Couleur Basilic ❙❙❙ V €€€
Rue de Behogne 43, 5580 Rochefort Tel (084) 468536 **Road Map** D4

A small restaurant in elegant rustic-kitchen style and featuring the green colour of basil. It serves a full range of classic dishes such as lobster and quail, but also pasta and *pissaladière* (southern French pizza). Menu of the month tracks the changing seasons. Good-value fixed-price lunch menus. Closed on Tuesdays and Wednesdays.

WALCOURT Hostellerie Dispa ❙❙❙ €€€€
Rue du Jardinet 5-7, 5650 Walcourt Tel (071) 611423 **Road Map** C3

Both a hotel and a highly respected restaurant, the Hostellerie Dispa occupies a grand mansion dating from around 1900. There is an Art Nouveau dining room, with a modern veranda extension. The kitchen produces elaborate French cuisine. Closed on Wednesdays and Tuesday and Sunday (except July and August) evenings.

WATERLOO Chez Lucien ❙❙❙ €€€€
Chaussée de Bruxelles 178, 1410 Waterloo Tel (02) 3530724 **Road Map** C2

Just north of the centre of Waterloo town is a charming restaurant where the patron-chef creates first-class dishes using seasonal produce. The intimate dining room is designed to make diners feel *comme à la maison* (at home). Summer dining in the garden. Good-value two-course lunch. Closed for Saturday lunch and on Mondays.

WAVRE La Table des Templiers ❙❙❙ €€€€
Chemin du Temple 10, 1300 Wavre Tel (010) 881350 **Road Map** D2

A classic 17th-century Brabant courtyard farm, once owned by the Knights Templar, with whitewashed walls and shutters: this has become a first-class restaurant with a broad, gastronomic menu based on seasonal produce. Fixed-price lunch menu is also available here. Outdoor dining available in summer. Closed on Saturdays and Sundays.

EASTERN WALLONIA

ARLON L'Eau à la Bouche ❙❙❙ €€€€
Route de Luxembourg 317, 6700 Arlon Tel (063) 233705 **Road Map** E4

A delightful, spacious and elegant restaurant in a grand, comfortable villa run by a husband-and-wife team. Pastel colours and wooden flooring. The cooking is elaborate French haute cuisine. Superb garden terrace for summer dining. Closed for Saturday lunch, Sunday and Tuesday evenings and all day on Wednesday.

AYWAILLE Le Prieuré Saint-Pierre ❙❙❙ V €€€
Rue St-Pierre 10, 4920 Aywaille Tel (04) 3847640 **Road Map** E3

A former farmhouse has been restored in rustic style – exposed brickwork, stone and beams, plus a giant chandelier – to create this family-friendly restaurant in the Amblève valley. Varied menu of good French cuisine, regularly adjusted to the seasons. Garden dining in summer. Closed Mondays and for lunch on Tuesdays.

BASTOGNE Wagon-Restaurant Léo ❙❙❙ €€€
Rue du Vivier 6, 6600 Bastogne Tel (061) 211441 **Road Map** E4

The origin of this restaurant in 1946 was a simple *friterie* – an old Brussels tram wagon that offered chips. Today, it is a glitzy and fun 250-seat brasserie with retro decor, still with a wagon-frontage, run by a third generation. The broad-ranging menu comprises traditonal Belgian fare from meatballs and chips to lobster. Closed Mondays.

BOUILLON La Vieille Ardenne €€
Grande-Rue 9, 6830 Bouillon Tel (061) 466277 **Road Map** D4

A long-established restaurant in a 16th-century house in the heart of the town. The interior is rustic in style, unpretentious and traditional. The same can be said of the excellent cooking: good *cuisine du terroir*, adhering to local products and traditions, such as trout, and game in the season. Closed Wednesdays out of season.

CHAUDFONTAINE Le Long du Bief ❙❙❙ V €€€
Le Long du Bief, Rue Hauster 5, 4051 Chaudfontaine Tel (04) 3679127 **Road Map** E3

Set along a tranquil river, this family-run restaurant is located at the entrance of Parc Hanster de Chaudfontaine. The atmosphere is warm, friendly and peaceful. Specialities include grilled meat, beef, duck and other seasonal produce. Access to the open terrace in summer. Reservations are recommended.

DURBUY Le Fou du Roy ❙❙❙ €€€
Rue Comte d'Ursel 4, 6940 Durbuy Tel (086) 210868 **Road Map** E3

An intimate little restaurant, Le Fou du Roy (The King's Fool) is packed with curios and bric-a-brac. The food, however, is seriously good French cuisine with Mediterranean touches. Lovely garden terrace. Closed on Mondays and Tuesdays out of season, but on those evenings the sister restaurant La Cannette remains open.

DURBUY La Gargouille 🍴●📶 ©©©©

Rue Rowé de Remouleu 20, 6941 Heyd **Tel** *(086) 499210*   **Road Map** *E3*

Some 9 km (6 miles) east of Durbuy, this 19th-century farmhouse has been given a rustic fairytale makeover. The cooking here is based on local, seasonal produce prepared with flair and imagination by the *patronne-chef* Brigitte Mairesse. Open only in the evenings from Fridays to Mondays; on Sundays, it is open for brunch and lunch as well.

EUPEN Brasserie Delcoeur 🍴●📶📶 ©©©

Gospertstrasse 22-24, 4700 Eupen **Tel** *(087) 561666*   **Road Map** *F2*

This is a cheering, relaxed and family-friendly brasserie serving anything from blood sausage with apple sauce to steak and lobster. The modern decor has a pampered elegance: soft pinks and crisp white linen. There is also a tiny gourmet restaurant attached, with just five tables. Lovely terrace. Closed for Saturday lunch and on Thursdays.

FOURNEAU ST-MICHEL Auberge du Prévost 🍴●📶Ⅴ ©©©

Fourneau St-Michel, 6870 St-Hubert **Tel** *(084) 210915*   **Road Map** *E4*

A half-timbered 18th-century tavern, part of the Musée de la Vie Rurale en Wallonie, provides a rustic setting for a full menu of fine, traditional Belgian cuisine. There are *jambon d'Ardenne*, dishes cooked in beer and good-value fixed-price meals. Closed Mondays, Wednesdays and Thursday evenings, and all day Tuesday.

FRAHAN Les Croisettes 🍴●📶 ©©©©

Les Croisettes 1, 6830 Bouillon-Frahan **Tel** *(061) 467439*   **Road Map** *D4*

Set along one of the most beautiful sections of the River Semois, this agreeable little inn, dating originally from 1920, offers well-priced meals. The menu swings between local regional dishes (wild boar and pheasant, home-produced *foie gras*) and Catalan cuisine. There is also a lighter brasserie menu. The terrace has views of the valley.

HOTTON Les Pieds dans le Plat 🍴●📶Ⅴ📶 ©©©©

Rue du Centre 3, 6990 Marenne **Tel** *(084) 321792*   **Road Map** *E3*

An atmospheric restaurant located at Bourdon, halfway between Hotton and Marche-en-Famenne. The old village school here has been imaginatively transformed into a set of rustic dining rooms, with a veranda and garden, for succulent and seasonal French cuisine. Closed Wednesday and Thursday evenings, and on Mondays and Tuesdays.

HUY Li Cwerneu 🍴●📶📶 ©©©©©

Grand Place 2, 4500 Huy **Tel** *(085) 255555*   **Road Map** *D3*

The guiding spirit behind this small, charming restaurant is Michelin-starred chef, Arabelle Meirlaen. Her imaginative "feminine" cuisine adheres to local produce and even includes use of wild herbs. Open in the evenings only. Closed Mondays and Sundays.

LIÈGE Le Paris-Brest ©©

Rue des Anglais 18, 4000 Liège **Tel** *(04) 2234711*   **Road Map** *E2*

This agreeable little restaurant has a loyal following: lawyers, executives and arts students. They come for dishes of well-made regional cuisine, including *boulets à la liégeoise* (meatballs sweetened with currants and a sauce using *sirop de Liège*), as well as more exotic and adventurous fusion cuisine. Closed Saturdays and Sundays.

LIÈGE Restaurant-Café Lequet 📶 ©©

Quai sur Meuse 17, 4000 Liège **Tel** *(04) 2222134*   **Road Map** *E2*

This is a well-known, classic and folksy Liège brasserie, 1900 in style, set by the River Meuse, near the cathedral and the La Batte Sunday market. It is famous for its *boulets à la liégeoise*, served with thick *frites* and salad. Other good-value traditional dishes are also available. Closed on Tuesdays between April and October.

LIÈGE Frédéric Maquin 🍴●📶 ©©©

Rue des Guillemins 47, 4000 Liège **Tel** *(04) 2534184*   **Road Map** *E2*

This sleek, modern restaurant, close to Guillemins station, was established in 2002. Since then, the owner-chef Frédéric Maquin has built up a formidable reputation for his high-end gastronomic French cuisine. Dishes are prepared with fresh seasonal ingedients. Closed Saturday lunch, Monday evenings and Tuesdays.

LIÈGE Petits Plats Canailles du Beurre Blanc 📶 ©©©

Rue du Pont 5, 4000 Liège **Tel** *(04) 2212265*   **Road Map** *E2*

Run by a husband-and-wife team who have more than 30 years of experience in creating atmospheric restaurants. *Canaille* (mischievous) signals their inventiveness. Classic French cuisine, with changing menus that follow the market. The modern dining room includes a preserved 14th-century façade. Closed Wednesdays and Sundays.

LIÈGE Bar à Gouts 🍴●📶Ⅴ ©©©

Rue St-Rémy 19, 4000 Liège **Tel** *(04) 2232238*   **Road Map** *E2*

This modern restaurant in the the city centre has an open kitchen where the chefs conjure up cosmopolitan fare – sushi, seafood risotto, wok food and meat dishes scented with curry. With the Menu Mixed, diners allow the chef to cook what takes his fancy that day. Good-value, good quality. Closed Saturday lunch and Sundays.

LIÈGE Tentation 🍴●📶⑪📶📶 ©©©©©

Boulevard d'Avroy 180, 4000 Liège **Tel** *(04) 2500220*   **Road Map** *E2*

In the southern part of the city centre, this stylish modern restaurant offers only menus based on a *formule découverte*: diners choose a meal of 3, 5, 7 or 10 courses (2 at lunchtime), and the chef produces what he has devised for that day in his fusion-style *haute cuisine*. Closed Saturday lunch, Sundays and Mondays.

Key to Price Guide *see p284* **Key to Symbols** *see back cover flap*

LIMBOURG Le Casino

Avenue Reine Astrid 7, 4831 Limbourg **Tel** (087) 762374   **Road Map** E2

Located in the heart of the medieval town of Limbourg, this family-run restaurant offers French cuisine prepared using fresh market produce carefully selected by the chef himself. The open terrace is an ideal place to relax in summer. Reservations are recommended.

MALMEDY Cyrano

Rue Chanteraine 11, 4950 Waimes **Tel** (080) 679989   **Road Map** F3

This modern hotel-restaurant specializes in inventive cuisine prepared from recipes inspired by the French region of Périgord (Dordogne) – truffles, *foie gras*, *confit* of duck, goat cheese. *Patron-chef* Gerty Linnertz also runs Chez Gerty, a brasserie offering light meals and *cuisine du terroir*. Closed for Saturday lunch and on Mondays..

MODAVE La Roseraie

Route de Limet 80, 4577 Modave **Tel** (085) 411360   **Road Map** E3

First-rate *cuisine française* has been served since 1982 in this handsome, tranquil and beautifully presented villa. Menus reflect the changing seasons. Open fire in the winter; in summer, apéritifs can be taken in the garden. Closed Mondays and Tuesdays. There are also four *chambres d'hôtes* for overnight stays.

REDU La Gourmandine

Rue de St-Hubert 16, 6890 Redu **Tel** (061) 656390   **Road Map** D4

A restored 19th-century farm in the heart of this village, La Gourmandine has perserved much of its authentic decor and charm. The restaurant offers classic French dishes and traditional regional fare, such as *jambonneau* (knuckle of ham), plus lighter meals such as goats-cheese salad omelettes. It also has *chambres d'hôtes* for overnight stays.

SPA Source de Barisart

Route de Barisart 295, 4900 Spa **Tel** (087) 770988   **Road Map** E3

This is a large, modern chalet-like restaurant in a woodland setting, 2 km (1 mile) south of the centre. Good-value fixed-price menus, including *fondue bourguignonne* (beef fondue). *Petite restauration* includes salads, sandwiches and pasta. There is also a tearoom for waffles and crêpes. Closed on Monday evenings and Wednesdays.

SPA Art de Vivre

Avenue Reine Astrid 53, 4900 Spa **Tel** (087) 770444   **Road Map** E3

A grand old 19th-century mansion offers lessons in the art of living through its inspired cooking. The menu is inspired by the restaurant's inventive *patron-chef*: quinoa, macadamia nuts, quince and seaweed feature. Modern decor with teak decking around a fountain for summer dining. Closed for Monday lunch and on Wednesdays and Thursdays.

STAVELOT Val d'Amblève

Route de Malmedy 7, 4970 Stavelot **Tel** (080) 281440   **Road Map** E3

A hotel-restaurant in a building dating from the 1930s with its own wooded park. The restaurant has a large conservatory-style *jardin hiver* (winter garden) and serves French cuisine, created by the Dutch owner-chef who, with his wife, has been running the establishment since the 1980s. Garden dining in the summer. Closed Mondays.

ST-HUBERT Le Cor de Chasse

Avenue Nestor Martin 3, 6870 St-Hubert **Tel** (061) 611644   **Road Map** E4

Hunting is the big theme of St-Hubert and this hotel-restaurant is good place to eat game during the hunting season. Good preparations of quail, rabbit and trout throughout the year, and well-made traditional Belgian dishes of all kinds, including seafood. Comfortable and straightforward hotel decor, with a garden terrrace.

ST-HUBERT Auberge du Grandgousier

Rue du Staplisse 6, 6870 Mirwart **Tel** (084) 366293   **Road Map** E4

A typical Ardennes, half-timbered hostelry which has kept its rustic charm while providing all the comforts of a good hotel-restaurant. An elegant professionalism is evident in the dining room, beneath the exposed beams. High-quality French cooking. Closed Tuesdays and Wednesdays. Mirwart is 10 km (6 miles) northwest of St Hubert.

THEUX L'Aubergine

Chaussée de Spa 87, 4910 Theux **Tel** (087) 53 0259   **Road Map** E3

Renovated to create a sublimely light and airy interior – with whites softened by exposed brick and wood – this restaurant serves much admired French cuisine. Husband Marc is in the kitchen and Cécile out front. Truffle cuisine is a speciality. The three-course lunch menu is very well priced. Closed Tuesdays and Wednesdays.

VERVIERS Au Clair Obscur

Place Albert 1er 5, 4800 Verviers **Tel** (087) 232221   **Road Map** E3

A fine Neo-Classical mansion houses this elegant restaurant with an open kitchen, run by a husband-and-wife team. The restaurant specializes in creative cuisine prepared using local, seasonal ingredients. On sunny days, the parasols come out on a tranquil terrace. Some comfortable rooms are also available. Closed Saturday lunch and Sundays and Mondays.

VERVIERS Château Peltzer

Rue Grétry 1, 4800 Verviers **Tel** (087) 230970   **Road Map** E3

The Neo-Gothic mansion of a wool tycoon, complete with turrets and surrounded by a park, is now a top-ranking restaurant run by a husband-and-wife team. *Haute cuisine française* in the *restaurant gourmand*, but there is also a less expensive Club des Tisserands serving soups, salads, and light dishes. Closed Sundays and Mondays.

GRAND DUCHY OF LUXEMBOURG

AHN-WORMELDANGE Mathes
Route du Vin 37, 5401 Ahn-Wormeldange **Tel** *760106*
Road Map *F5*

The Moselle Luxembourgeoise has a famous fish dish called *friture de la Moselle* – small river fish deep-fried in batter. Mathes is the place to eat it, along with other local specialities, and good-quality *cuisine française* of all sorts. Set in a mansion by the river, with a large garden and children's play area. Closed Mondays and Tuesdays.

CLERVAUX Les Écuries du Parc
Rue du Parc 4, 9708 Clervaux **Tel** *920364*
Road Map *F4*

Stables once belonging to the counts of Clervaux have been beautifully converted into a rustic restaurant. The speciality is meat – horse steak, cooked ham, veal and beef brochette. Pizzas are also served here, but there are more elaborate dishes on the menu. Lunch or dinner outdoors in the summer. Closed Mondays.

CLERVAUX Restaurant-Brasserie K
Rue de Stavelot 2, 9964 Huldange **Tel** *979056-1*
Road Map *F4*

This enterprise is in Burrigplatz, the highest point in Luxembourg. It has a wood panelled restaurant for contemporary French-style cuisine and a lower-priced modern brasserie serving traditional fare including scampi and casseroles. Outdoor terraces and children's play area. Closed on Mondays and Tuesdays and also Wednesday and Thursday evenings.

ECHTERNACH Au Vieux Moulin
Lauterborn 6, 6562 Echternach-Lauterborn **Tel** *720068-1*
Road Map *F4*

On the site of a former millhouse 3 km (2 miles) southwest of Echternach, this pretty hotel-restaurant has been built in a wooded setting. The restaurant, in comfortable Classical-modern style, serves elegantly presented French cuisine, organized around seasonal fixed-price menus. Closed Tuesday lunch and Mondays.

ESCH-SUR-ALZETTE Favaro
Rue des Remparts 19, 4303 Esch-sur-Alzette **Tel** *542723*
Road Map *F5*

Haute cuisine Italienne draws customers to Favaro and has won it a Michelin star. Behind the restaurant's striking brick-red façade, Renato Favaro applies well-judged invention to carpaccio, gnocchi, pasta, risotto and fish and meat dishes. Closed for Saturday lunch as well as on Sunday evenings and Mondays.

LAROCHETTE La Distillerie
Rue du Château 8, 6162 Bourglinster **Tel** *7878781*
Road Map *F4*

Some 12 km (8 miles) south of La Rochette, the castle of Bourglinster has been given a new lease of life as a culinary centre. It has a gourmet restaurant called La Distillerie, and also a more down-to-earth but high-quality brasserie called Coté Cour. Both are made special by their magical setting. Closed on Mondays, Tuesdays and Sunday evenings.

LUXEMBOURG CITY Um Dierfgen
Côte d'Eich 6, 1450 Luxembourg City **Tel** *226141*
Road Map *F5*

A traditional-style inn with wooden tables and paper place mats. Specializes in *cuisine luxembourgeoise*. Plenty of hearty pork dishes and other grilled meats (including horse steaks), sausages and sauerkraut. Good-value *plat du jour* (dish of the day). Also showcases Luxembourg beers. Closed for evening on Sundays and Mondays.

LUXEMBOURG CITY Come Prima
Rue de l'Eau, 1449 Luxembourg City **Tel** *241724*
Road Map *F5*

One of the Espaces Saveurs group, Come Prima specializes in Italian food. The mood is more Sienna than Naples: bare brick walls, exposed beams and soft lighting. The antipasto buffet offers a selection of some 30 dishes; then there is pasta, lamb with rosemary, *saltimbocca* and other classics. Closed for Saturday lunch and on Sundays.

LUXEMBOURG CITY Il Cherubino
Rue de Turi, 3378 Livange **Tel** *26522626*
Road Map *F5*

The cuisine and wine of Apulia, Italy, is the main culinary thrust of this excellent restaurant. The decor is classic Italian, with crisp linen, sideboard displays of bottles. Pasta, skewer-grilled meat, veal escalopes, *tiramisu* and *panna cotta* and a range of pizza – plenty to suit all tastes and appetites. Closed Sundays.

LUXEMBOURG CITY L'Annexe
Rue du St-Esprit 7, 1475 Luxembourg City **Tel** *26262507*
Road Map *F5*

A classic-style brasserie devised by the owners of Clairefontaine, a much-garlanded restaurant close by. Brown wood, potted plants and chalked menu boards. The food is all-embracing brasserie-style: tortillas, pasta, salads, tagines, *tartare de boeuf*, steaks and ice cream. Good-value *plats du jour*. Closed Saturdays, Sundays and last two weeks of August.

LUXEMBOURG CITY La Médina
Rue de la Loge 2, 1945 Luxembourg City **Tel** *26270909*
Road Map *F5*

Another restaurant of the Espaces Saveurs group, offering good value for money. The interior is designed with muted lights and warm colours. The focus is on North African dishes, with tagines, couscous, and *bricks* (savoury-filled crispy pastry). Hanging lamps, carpets and antique woodwork cast the spell. Closed Sundays and Mondays.

Key to Price Guide *see p284* **Key to Symbols** *see back cover flap*

LUXEMBOURG CITY Maison des Brasseurs
€€€ Road Map F5

Grand Rue 48, 1660 Luxembourg City Tel 471371

A restaurant serving generous portions of typical Luxembourg dishes such as *Judd mat Gaardebounen*, chicken cooked in Moselle Riesling and *Träipen* (fried blood sausage). Favoured by local clientèle. The decor is smart, but retro, evoking the 1930s. Kitchen open from 11am to 10pm. Closed Saturday evenings and Sundays.

LUXEMBOURG CITY Mousel's Cantine
€€€ Road Map F5

Montée de Clausen 46, 1343 Luxembourg City Tel 470198

A warm and welcoming brasserie, Mousel's Cantine is linked to the Mousel brewery that has been making beer in Clausen since 1825. The place to sample Luxembourg dishes such as *Judd mat Gaardebounen* and grilled pork knuckle, as well as French-style brasserie dishes such as scampi and omelettes. Closed Saturday lunch and Sundays.

LUXEMBOURG CITY Apoteca
€€€€ Road Map F5

Rue de la Boucherie 12, 1247 Luxembourg City Tel 267377-1

A medieval building, with cellars perhaps 1,000 years old, has been given a contemporary revamp to create an attractive restaurant, but still respecting its history. The cooking is French with strong Asian and Italian inputs. Also upmarket burgers and bar food. Unusually, vegetarians are given due consideration. Closed Saturday lunch and Sundays.

LUXEMBOURG CITY Wengé
€€€€ Road Map F5

Rue Louvigny 15, 1946 Luxembourg City Tel 26201058

Just south of the Place des Armes, Wengé has a street-front outlet for its upmarket take-away savoury snacks, pâtisserie, chocolates and tea. Behind and upstairs is a sleek modern restaurant of Zen-inspired equilibrium, serving inventive, beautifully presented French cuisine. Open lunch only, Mondays to Saturdays. The tearoom is open in the afternoon.

LUXEMBOURG CITY Bouquet Garni
€€€€€ Road Map F5

Rue de l'Eau 32, 1449 Luxembourg City Tel 26200620

Smart and sophisticated, Bouquet Garni occupies an 18th-century building refurbished in period style, beneath exposed beams. The Michelin-starred French cuisine is underpinned by adherence to what is fresh in the market. Impeccable service adds to the pleasure. The wine list includes Luxembourg's finest. Closed Saturday lunch and Sundays.

LUXEMBOURG CITY Mosconi
€€€€€ Road Map F5

Rue Münster 13, 2160 Luxembourg City Tel 546994

An Italian restaurant considered to be the best in the city; has earned two Michelin stars. It has all the associated polish, plus Ilario Mosconi's genius for raising Italian cuisine to exquisite gastronomic levels. Divine pastas, plenty of truffles. Lovely south-facing terrace overlooking the Alzette. Closed Saturday lunch, Sundays and Mondays.

MERTERT Joël Schaeffer
€€€€€ Road Map F4

Rue Haute 1, 6680 Mertert Tel 26714080

At the northern end of the Moselle Luxembourgeoise, a historic building has been given a relaxed contemporary interior. Young chef Joël Schaeffer creates beautifuly presented French cuisine, influenced by local traditions, but also with some exotic touches. Bargain fixed-price lunch menu. Closed Mondays, Tuesdays and all August.

MONDORF-LES-BAINS De Jangeli
€€€ Road Map F5

Rue du Dr E Feltgen, 5601 Mondorf-les-Bains Tel 23666525

This is the main restaurant of the Domaine des Thermes, the town's primary spa centre. The French-inspired cuisine is healthy, but elaborate and appetizing. The menu provides wine suggestions for each dish, many of them from Luxembourg. Modern decor, crisp linen.

MONDORF-LES-BAINS Léa Linster
€€€€€ Road Map F5

Route de Luxembourg 17, 5752 Frisange Tel 23668411

Named after the celebrated chef who has built a huge reputation for fine dining at this Michelin-starred restaurant, 8 km (5 miles) west of Mondorf-les-Bains. Superlative French cuisine. Peaceful rural setting and a coolly modern dining room, suffused with whites. Closed Mondays, Tuesdays and for lunch between Wednesdays and Fridays.

PÉTANGE Lëtzebuerger Kaschthaus
€€€ Road Map E5

Route Rue de Bettembourg 4, 3333 Hellange Tel 516573

Owned by Luxembourg's star chef Lea Linster, this is a more casual, less expensive option than her flagship restaurant in nearby Frisange. It has the look of a rustic tavern, with a delightful rear terrace, but the traditional Luxembourg cuisine is first-rate and in keeping with Linster's attention to culinary detail. Closed Tuesdays and Wednesdays.

PETITE SUISSE LUXEMBOURGEOISE Parmentier
€€€€ Road Map F4

Rue de la Gare 7, 6117 Junglinster Tel 787168

A family-friendly hotel-restaurant, dating from 1904, at the southern gateway to Petite Suisse Luxembourgeoise. It serves good-quality bistrot-style food. The two-course lunchtime *plats du jour* are very attractively priced. There is also a sleek wine bar, specializing in Luxembourg wines. Restaurant closed on Tuesdays and Wednesdays.

VIANDEN Auberge Aal Veinen"Beim Hunn"
€€€ Road Map F4

Grand-Rue 114, 9411 Vianden Tel 834368

This popular village inn beneath Vianden's castle serves traditional food, notably steaks grilled over an open fire. With its rustic decor of exposed beams, stone arches and wood furniture, it has a folkloric charm. The building dates from 1683 and was once a smithy. Restaurant closed on Tuesdays. There are also eight bedrooms.

SHOPPING IN BELGIUM

Belgians love to shop. They use the French term for window shopping with good reason: *lécher les vitrines* literally means licking the windows. This urge is satisfied by a host of excellent shops in every town and city, ranging from highly competitive supermarkets to the most exclusive boutiques. High streets remain vibrant as Belgians enjoy the choice, service and expertise of individual traders. Merchandise of all kinds is available and although it is not cheap, wise shoppers will find it can be good value for money.

Chic clothes on display

Rue Neuve, the longest pedestrian shopping street in Brussels

OPENING HOURS

Shops are open between 10am and 6pm from Monday to Saturday. Many open at 9am and some stay open until 7 or 8pm, especially if they close for an hour at lunchtime. Food shops and supermarkets have longer hours, from 9am to 8pm. Most supermarkets and shops close on Sundays, although many pâtisseries are open on Sunday mornings.

WHERE TO SHOP

Most towns are built around a central square – the Grand Place or Grote Markt – which used to be the focus of trade, guilds and the town administration in medieval times. Today, these squares have weekly markets and many of the best shops. Larger towns and cities have pedestrianized shopping streets or covered malls at their centre. Large supermarkets selling clothes, electrical goods, hardware and CDs tend to be on the outskirts, where they can provide parking. **Delhaize**, **Carrefour** (which now also owns the

GB brand), **Cora**, **Colruyt** and **Champion** are the big supermarket chains. Roads leading into towns may be lined with large-scale commercial enterprises – car showrooms, hardware superstores, garden centres and fashion outlets. The Maasmechelen "fashion village" (*see p168*) is a purpose-built, discount-driven shoppers' paradise.

MARKETS

Towns usually host markets once or twice a week, often in the main square. They sell fruit, vegetables, meat, cheese and local food products as well as clothes, textiles, shoes, household goods, flowers and craft products. The largest market, La Batte, is a sprawling, mixed, Sunday market along the northern bank of the River Meuse in Liège. Many towns also have regular or occasional antique or flea markets (the distinction is often blurred). The largest of these is held on Sunday mornings in Tongeren (*see p169*). Christmas markets, decorated with lights and selling all sorts of festive fare, are held in December, from before the Feast of St Nicolas on 6 December to 24 December.

Shoppers thronging a display of fresh wares at a town market

HOW TO PAY

Cash is the most readily accepted means of payment. Most market stalls will only accept cash. However, smaller enterprises are not keen on the large-denomination notes, which include the 200-euro and the 500-euro notes. Most high-street shops accept payment by credit or debit card.

VAT REFUNDS

Those who live outside the EU can reclaim the Value Added Tax (TVA in French, BTW in Dutch) for any single transaction to the value of over 125 euros. VAT stands at 21 per cent of the purchase price. Shops that have a Tax-free Shopping logo can provide a Tax-free Shopping Cheque on request (customers will need to show their passport). The purchased items and the documentation are stamped at the airport customs before check in, after which the refund can be collected at the Europe Tax-free Shopping desk. Detailed information is available from the main VAT refund agents **Global Refund** and **Premier Tax Free**.

CLOTHES SIZES

The EU is in the process of introducing a new set of standardized clothes sizes. At present, however, there are different sizing systems in operation. Some manufacturers even use "vanity sizes", marking larger clothes with smaller sizes to flatter customers. The best advice is for customers to get themselves measured, and certainly to try all clothes on in the shop.

Chocolate and Chocolatiers

High-quality Belgian chocolate is famous all over the world for three reasons. Firstly, Belgian chocolatiers insist on top-quality ingredients, starting with the chocolate itself. This has a high density of cocoa-solids and cocoa-butter, which evaporates on the tongue, giving the flavour a cool and silky lift. Secondly, the Belgians

White chocolate with dark icing

(Jean Neuhaus, in 1912, to be precise) pioneered filled chocolates or pralines. These are made with a variety of fillings including hazelnut cream, fresh cream, marzipan, liqueur and assorted fruit pastes. Lastly, Belgian chocolatiers invented the famous white chocolate, a luxury confection of cocoa-butter and milk.

Large-scale manufacturers *for leading brands strictly maintain high standards, and their products are exported all over the world.*

Filled chocolates or pralines *were originally named for their combination of chocolate and hazelnut cream known as* praliné.

CHOCOLATE MANUFACTURERS

The best-known brands are Corné Port-Royal, Neuhaus, Leonidas and Godiva. They have numerous outlets and sell slabs of chocolates as well as pre-packed boxes of pralines. In Belgium, such boxes are remarkably good value, given their very high quality. A large 750-g (26-oz) box will typically cost about 10–30 euros. Cream-filled chocolates have a limited shelf-life, but will keep fresh for three weeks in cool conditions.

SPECIALIST CHOCOLATIERS

There are many small, specialist chocolatiers creating their own products, especially in the cities and popular towns. A number of *pâtissiers* run a sideline in handmade chocolates as well. There are also some other good, large-scale manufacturers, whose products reach the supermarkets. These include Guylian, who make pralines in the shape of sea creatures; and Galler, famous for their Langues de Chat brand with artwork by the comic-strip artist Philippe Geluck. Côte d'Or is a brand that produces delicious mini-bars called Mignonnette.

A shop displaying assorted Belgian chocolates

Customers can make their selection *from the cabinet, and individual chocolates are picked out by the white-gloved shop assistants, placed in a box, weighed and beautifully wrapped in paper and ribbon.*

Displays of chocolate *in shops radiate an atmosphere of opulence. They are also incomparable for the sheer variety of shapes and choice of flavours.*

Brands of Belgian beer on sale at a specialist beer shop, Bruges

FASHION

Belgian fashion has become a force to be reckoned with since the 1980s, when a group of designers, the Antwerp Six, rose to fame. Among them were Dries van Noten, **Ann Demeulemeester** and **Walter van Beirendonck**. Although each is very different, they all developed a novel urban look, which was sometimes anarchic and controversial, and sometimes demurely chic.

Led by the famous school of fashion at the Royal Academy of Fine Arts, Antwerp is a key player in international fashion and a good place to shop. Dries van Noten has an outlet at **Het Modepaleis**. The shop called **Louis** carries the work of many top designers including Raf Simons and Martin Margiela. Likewise, **Verso** has Kris Van Assche and Dirk Schönberger, as well as international brands. Boutiques are also seen in Kammenstraat, Nationalestraat, Kloosterstraat and Schuttershofstraat. **Coccodrillo** is best for shoes.

Leading designers also have shops in other cities, most notably in Brussels (see p86). **Annemie Verbeke** has an outlet in Brussels as well as in Antwerp. **Olivier Strelli** has branches in 11 towns and cities in Belgium.

CHILDREN'S CLOTHES

Belgians produce some very attractive clothes for children. These are available from specialist high-street shops, such as **Filou & Friends**, as well as department stores such as **Inno** (which has branches in 11 towns and cities) and even the major supermarkets.

DIAMONDS

Antwerp is the global capital for diamonds – the Jewish Quarter near Centraal Station, is where 70 per cent of the world's diamonds are cut and polished. Retail outlets at Pelikaanstraat and neighbouring streets offer diamonds at prices that are 15–30 per cent lower than prices in the high streets of other European cities. A good place to start is the Diamond Museum (see p154) or **Diamondland**, the largest diamond shop in the city. Bruges claims to have been a pioneer in diamond cutting and polishing in the 15th century, a story celebrated in the city's **Diamantmuseum**, which also has a shop.

BELGIAN LACE

Lace (see pp26–7) has been a traditional product of Belgium since the 16th century. Handmade lace is expensive. It is available at specialist outlets such as **Manufacture Belge de Dentelles** in Brussels as well as **The Little Lace Shop** and **Kantcentrum** (see p116) in Bruges – both cities long associated with lace-making. The tradition of handmade lace has been dramatically undercut by machine-made lace, particularly from the Far East, and is also available for sale in outlets in Belgium. It is therefore important to insist on a certificate of authenticity.

BEER

It is well worth bringing home some bottles of Belgian beer (see pp282–3). There are at least 400 different beers to choose from, and a huge number of brands. Specialist beer shops such as **The Bottle Shop** and the **Brugse Bierpaleis** in Bruges, and a number of others in Brussels (see pp87) offer the best. Supermarkets carry a large stock of many top brands, at the best prices.

JENEVER

Belgium produces more than 270 types of this high-quality gin (see p166), including fruit-flavoured *jenever*, Liège *pékèt*, straight *jenever* and associated spirits such as *brandewijn* and *corenwijn*. Some are still sold in traditional ceramic bottles that make intriguing gifts for aficionados of fine spirits. Belgian *jenever* is a gin to be drunk pure and on its own, not with a mixer or even as a chaser. To taste the full range before buying, it is best to go to an authentic specialist bar such as **De Vagant** in Antwerp or **'t Dreupelkot** in Ghent.

BISCUITS AND PATISSERIE

Belgium has simply fabulous pâtisseries. Every town has several top-class specialist pâtissiers producing sumptuous chocolate cakes, glazed fruit tarts and a range of simpler tarts based on almonds and *crème pâtissière*. Turnover is high and competition fierce. Therefore, tarts and cakes are remarkably good value for money. Belgium also has a

Clothes, purses and tablecloths trimmed with fine Belgian lace

fine tradition of butter-based biscuits such as crumbly *sablés*, delicately thin and crispy *pain d'amandes* (or *amandelbroodje*) and spicy *speculoos*. The most famous specialist biscuit-maker of Brussels is **Dandoy**. A good, distinctively packaged brand that is available in supermarkets is **Jules Destrooper**.

COMIC BOOKS

Brussels with the comic-strip museum, the Centre Belge de la Bande Dessinée *(see p62)*, cites itself as the comic book capital. However, many cities in Belgium claim this title and specialist comic strip bookshops, with a range of titles, are found in all urban centres.

Browsers at the display window of The Tintin Shop in Bruges

TINTIN MERCHANDISE

Apart from the books, Tintin merchandise includes games, figurines, clothes, key rings and mugs. The brand is very carefully protected and official merchandise is tasteful

and made to high standards. There is an official **The Tintin Shop** in Bruges, another in Brussels *(see p87)* and plenty of outlets that sell Tintin items among other stock.

GLASS AND LEATHER

The **Cristallerie du Val Saint Lambert** at Seraing, near Liège, has been making fine glass since 1826. Its products, mainly blown, cut and engraved clear and coloured glass, are highly sought after. The factory is now open to public during demonstrations. The best high-quality leather handbags and suitcases are found at shops of **Delvaux**, a Brussels-based firm with branches in major cities.

DIRECTORY

WHERE TO SHOP

Carrefour
www.carrefourbelgium.be

Champion
www.champion.be

Colruyt
www.colruyt.be

Cora
www.cora.be

Delhaize
www.delhaize.be

VAT REFUNDS

Global Refund
www.globalrefund.com

Premier Tax Free
www.premiertaxfree.com

CHOCOLATE AND CHOCOLATIERS

Corné Port-Royal
www.corneportroyal.be

Côte d'Or
www.cotedor.com

Galler
www.galler.com

Godiva
www.godiva.be

Guylian
www.guylian.be

Leonidas
www.leonidas.com

Neuhaus
www.neuhaus.be

FASHION

Ann Demeulemeester
Leopold de Waelplaats, Antwerp. **www.**anndemeulemeester.be

Annemie Verbeke
Rue A. Dansaertstreet 64, 1000 BRU. www.annemieverbeke.be

Coccodrillo
Schuttershofstraat 9, Antwerp. **www.**coccodrillo.be

Het Modepaleis
Nationalestraat 16, Antwerp. **www.**driesvannoten.be

Labels Inc
Aalmoezenierstraat 4, Antwerp. *Tel (03) 2326056.* **www.**labelsinc.be

Louis
Lombardenvest 2, Antwerp. *Tel (03) 2329872.*

Olivier Strelli
www.strelli.be

Verso
Lange Gasthuisstraat 11, Antwerp. *Tel (03) 2269292.* **www.**verso.be

Walter van Beirendonck
St-Antoniusstraat 12, Antwerp. **www.**walter vanbeirendonck.com

CHILDREN'S CLOTHES

Filou & Friends
www.filoufriends.com

Inno
www.inno.be

DIAMONDS

Diamondland
Appelmansstraat 33a, Antwerp. *Tel (03) 2292990.*

Diamantmuseum
Katelijnestraat 43, Bruges. *Tel (050) 342056.* **www.**diamondmuseum.be

BELGIAN LACE

Manufacture Belge de Dentelles
6-8 Galerie de la Reine, 1000 BRU. *Tel (02) 5114477.* **www.**mbd.be

The Little Lace Shop
Market 11, Bruges. **www.**muylle.com

Kantcentrum
www.kantcentrum.com

BEER

The Bottle Shop
Wollestraat 13, Bruges. *Tel (050) 349980.*

Brugse Bierpaleis
Katelijnestraat 25, Bruges. *Tel (050) 343161.*

JENEVER

De Vagant
Reyndersstraat 25, Antwerp. *Tel (03) 2331538.* www.devagant.be

't Dreupelkot
Groentenmarkt 12, Ghent. *Tel (09) 2242120.*

BISCUITS AND PATISSERIE

Dandoy
R au Beurre 31, 1000 BRU. *Tel (02) 5110326.* **www.**biscuiterie dandoy.be

Jules Destrooper
Gravestraats 8647, Ghent. **www.**destrooper.com

TINTIN MERCHANDISE

The Tintin Shop
Steenstraat 3, Bruges. *Tel (050) 334292.* **www.**tintinshopbrugge.be

GLASS AND LEATHER

Cristallerie du Val Saint Lambert
Rue du Val 245, Seraing. *Tel (04) 3303800.* **www.**val-saint-lambert.com

Delvaux
www.delvaux.com

ENTERTAINMENT IN BELGIUM

Magazines on sale in Brussels

In an understated manner, Belgium has a thriving cultural life, showcasing top-quality international and regional performers in all fields. The country has produced major talent, particularly in modern dance, film and in the contemporary arts scene. On a more communal level, town squares and parks host a variety of concerts, usually during summer, for the benefit of local citizens. It is also for their entertainment that most Belgian bars encourage musicians, while clubs and dance halls provide venues for more interactive fun. Among more traditional attractions are the many vibrant carnivals, whose colourful pageants involve all levels of the society.

LISTINGS

Free listings for all forms of entertainment are available at the tourist offices, or in shops, hotels and bars. The English-language weekly, *The Bulletin* (*see p88*), carries information about major cultural events all over Belgium. Likewise, leading newspapers (*see p329*) also carry event listings.

There are several useful websites, notably xPats, **Net Events** and **Visit Belgium**, site of the Belgian tourist office in USA and Canada. Cinema listings can be found online at **Cinebel** and **Cinenews**. Jazz details are available at **Jazz in Belgium**, while rock and pop concert information is given at the **Music in Belgium** site. Club and disco listings can be found at Noctis and **Dance Vibes**.

OPERA

Belgium has four major opera houses – in Antwerp, Brussels, Ghent and Liège. The Vlaamse Opera House in Ghent (*see p135*) and La Monnaie in Brussels (*see p88*) are both sumptuously elegant in the traditional 18th-century style. Ghent and Antwerp mount performances by the well-known Flemish company, **De Vlaamse Opera**, while Liège is the home of the **Opéra Royal de Wallonie**. Operas also take place in the main theatres of Charleroi, Mons and Namur.

BALLET AND DANCE

Contemporary dance is strong in Belgium and has had a huge international impact. Among its leaders is Anna Teresa de Keersmaeker and her Rosas company (*see p88*). **Charleroi/Danses** is the company of the Centre Chorégraphique de la Communauté Française Wallonie-Bruxelles. Directed by Michèle Anne de Mey and others, it performs at Les Écuries in Charleroi, and at La Raffinerie in Brussels. The world-renowned **Royal Ballet of Flanders** is established in Antwerp, but performs across Belgium and internationally. Dance performances feature in most theatres and concert venues around the country.

CLASSICAL MUSIC

Very high standards of music are maintained by Belgium's leading music schools, such as the **Conservatoire Royal de Musique** in Brussels and the **Conservatoire Royal de Liège**. The capital has several important concert halls (*see p88*), but all major cities have their equivalents. One to look out for is the extremely modern **Concertgebouw** in Bruges. The Salle Philharmonique de Liège, former concert hall of the Conservatoire, is now operated by the **Philharmonic Orchestra of Liège**. Concerts are also held at the splendid Art Deco **Le Forum**. Classical and other types of music are performed at both **Koningin Elisabethzaal** and the modern

A spirited performance of the popular classical *Swan Lake* ballet by the Royal Ballet of Flanders

Jazz troupe jamming on stage during a jazz festival outside Brussels

multipurpose **deSingel** in Antwerp. Likewise, it is featured at key venues in smaller cities such as the **Palais des Beaux Arts** in Charleroi.

The biggest music event in Belgium is the **Festival of Flanders** (June–December). Classical concerts, plus ballet and opera, are performed in historic houses, churches and halls. The **Festival de Wallonie** (June–October) is the southern equivalent of this event.

ROCK, POP AND WORLD MUSIC

Belgium is in the middle of the European tour map for top international artistes, rock, pop and world music bands. Fans cross borders to take advantage of cheap tickets and better venues. The biggest concerts take place in Brussels *(see pp88–9)* or at the **Lotto Arena** (Sportspaleis) in Antwerp and some at local venues such as Hasselt's **Muziekodroom**.

Belgium's summer outdoor rock festivals also attract great international attention. They frontline with the current top international acts, and, cost-wise, are considered a bargain. The best known is **Rock Werchter**, which takes place close to Leuven in early July. The mid-July **Dour Festival**, near Mons, is making a name for its techno-oriented fare. In June, **Couleur Café** brings the best of African and South American music to the heart of Brussels. **Pukkelpop** takes place in Hasselt in late August and attracts impressive line-ups. Bruges holds the respected but low-key Cactusfestival *(see p33)* as well as **Klinkers**, a low-cost series of concerts held in July and August. Fans of contemporary French singer-songwriters attend the **Francofolies de Spa** in July.

JAZZ

Belgium's lively jazz scene features home-grown talent playing in European, New Orleans, contemporary and fusion styles. The great jazz guitarist Django Reinhardt (1910–53) was born here, and so was Toots Thielemans (b.1922), hailed as the world's best jazz harmonica player.

In Antwerp, the wonderful Art Deco **Buster** hosts jazz and jam sessions, while the **Jazzcafé Hopper** and **De Muze**, an easy-going place with live jazz every night, are also excellent. Antwerp's highly respected biennial festival, the **Jazz Middelheim**, has attracted top international names since 1969. Equally star-studded is the annual country-wide **Skoda Jazz Festival**, from October to December. Brussels holds an annual Jazz Marathon *(see p88)*. In Ghent, a must-visit is the Art Nouveau **Damberd Jazz Café**, which has live music on Tuesdays. The folksy **Hotsy Totsy** café is also popular. Bruges's **De Werf** is an eagerly attended jazz venue.

CINEMA

The film industry in Belgium is quite active, with noted directors whose works win international attention and awards. These include Jaco van Dormael (*Toto the Hero*, 1991; *The Eighth Day*, 1996), Rémy Belvaux (*Man Bites Dog*, 1992), Alain Berliner (*Ma Vie en Rose*, 1997), Luc and Jean-Pierre Dardenne (*Rosetta*, 1999), Dominique Deruddere (*Everybody's Famous!*, 2000), Nic Balthazar (*BenX*, 2007) and Gérard Corbiau (*Farinelli*, 1999). Actors Jean-Claude Van Damme and Audrey Hepburn were born in Brussels.

Most international films shown are, of course, usually in their original versions. If neither dubbed nor subtitled, they are listed as VO (*version originale*) or OV (*originele versie*). "VO st-bil" or "OV Fr/NL ot" indicate a subtitled version. There are cinemas of all kinds, from small enterprises to huge multiplexes. Belgium also hosts small, specialist film festivals, with the Flanders Film Festival *(see p34)* in Ghent being the best known.

THEATRE

There are plenty of fine theatres in Belgium, with most plays staged in either French or Dutch. Many theatres feature mixed programmes of theatre, dance and music. The **Bruges Stadsschouwburg** hosts a blend of theatre, dance and concerts, while the **Antwerp Stadsschouwburg** is dominated by musicals. The **Bourla Schouwburg**, also in Antwerp, maintains a fine programme of plays performed mainly by its Toneelhuis repertory company. Antwerp's multipurpose concert hall deSingel also runs a highly respected theatre programme. Other noted theatres include **Théâtre Royal de Mons** and **Théâtre de Namur**. The capital also has many venues of note for theatre *(see p89)*.

Bright lights and energetic crowds at the Pukkelpop rock festival in Hasselt

MIXED ARTS AND MUSIC FESTIVALS

The **Europalia** festival is a biennial, countrywide event, focussing on a specific theme, usually the culture of a chosen foreign partner-country. Lasting four months, it presents an ambitious programme of fine music, cinema, dance, theatre and literary events. Belgium's most warm-spirited annual festival is De Gentse Feesten *(see p32)*, a centuries-old celebration where performers, buskers, rock groups and jazz bands compete for the attention of a lively crowd. The Fêtes de Wallonie *(see p34)* is an equally eclectic mix.

PARADES AND LOCAL FESTIVALS

Pageants and parades fill the streets of towns and cities across Belgium throughout the year. There are several famous carnival parades marking Lent, most notably at Binche and Stavelot, as well as costumed religious processions *(see pp32–5)* at Bruges, Mechelen, Tournai, Dendermonde, Mons, Veurne and a number of other cities across the country, each with its own distinctive flavour. Belgian towns also have local fairs – sometimes called *kermesse* or *kermis*. These are generally celebrated with a parade, a fun fair and several assorted musical events.

Antwerp's energetic nightlife at the upbeat Petrol Club

CASINOS

There are several casinos in Belgium, where visitors can play roulette, blackjack, stud poker, slot machines and so on. The most famous are the **Casino Knokke** and the **Casino Oostende**, but there are others at Namur, Blankenberge and Middelkerke. Associated originally with spa towns, Flemish casinos still carry the name Kursaal (Cure Hall). Spa itself has **Casino de Spa**, while the capital city has **Grand Casino Brussels**. Most establishments have a relaxed atmosphere with a smart-casual dress code. Many also welcome guests who arrive simply to relax at the bar in the early hours.

CLUBS AND DISCOS

Antwerp has an international reputation for its spirited club-life. Clubbers from across the country flock to the **Café d'Anvers**, a former church located in Antwerp's red light district, that was turned into a house club in 1991. **Petrol Club** blends hip-hop, electro and rock on its big nights on Fridays and Saturdays. **Red and Blue** is a famous gay club in the city. The Latin-American oriented **Café Local** is also worth a visit. Ghent's most famous nightspot is **Culture Club**. Lier has a reputation for nightlife that far exceeds the town's size, attracting club-bers from countries across the borders and the Netherlands in particular. Its most famous clubs are **Illusion** and **La Rocca**. Bruges has a lively but mercurial clubbing scene – it is best to ask at the tourist office or at a youth hostel for the current popular spots. There are many other clubs and discos, with listings on the Noctis site *(see p89)*.

Colourful costumes at a traditional festival parade in Brussels's Grand Place

DIRECTORY

LISTINGS

Cinebel
www.cinebel.be

Cinenews
www.cinenews.be

Dance Vibes
www.dancevibes.be

Jazz in Belgium
www.jazzinbelgium.com

Music in Belgium
www.musicinbelgium.net

Net Events
www.netevents.be

Visit Belgium
www.visitbelgium.com

OPERA HOUSES

De Vlaamse Opera
Van Ertbornstraat 8,
Antwerp.
Tel (03) 2021011.
Schouwburgstraat 3,
Ghent. *Tel (03) 2681011.*
www.vlaamseopera.be

**Opéra Royal
de Wallonie**
Rue des Dominicains 1,
Liège. *Tel (04) 2214722.*
www.operaliege.be

BALLET AND DANCE

Charleroi/Danses
Les Ecuries, Blvd Pierre
Mayence 65c, Charleroi.
Tel (071) 311212.
www.charleroi-danses.be

**Royal Ballet
of Flanders**
Kattendijkdok-Westkaai
16, Antwerp.
Tel (03) 2343438.
www.flandersballet.be

CLASSICAL MUSIC

Concertgebouw
Het Zand 34, Bruges.
Tel (070) 223302 (tickets).
www.concertgebouw.be

**Conservatoire Royal
de Liège**
www.crlg.be

**Conservatoire Royal
de Musique**
Rue de la Régence 30,
BRU. *Tel (02) 5110427.*
www.conservatoire.be

deSingel
Desguinlei 25, Antwerp.
Tel (03) 2482828.
www.desingel.be

Festival de Wallonie
Rue de l'Armée Grouchy
20, Namur. *Tel (081)*
733781. www.
festivaldewallonie.be

Festival of Flanders
Vlasmarkt 4, Tongeren.
Tel (012) 235719.
www.festival.be

**Koningin
Elisabethzaal**
Koningin Astridplein 26,
Antwerp. *Tel 0900*
00311. www.fccc.be

Le Forum
Rue Pont d'Avroy 14,
Liège. *Tel (04) 2231818.*

Palais des Beaux Arts
Place du Manège 1,
Charleroi. *Tel (071)*
311212. www.charleroi-
culture.be

**Philharmonic
Orchestra of Liège**
Salle Philharmonique,
Boulevard Piercot 25,
Liège. *Tel (04) 2200000.*
www.opl.be

JAZZ

Buster
Kaasrui 1, Antwerp.
Tel (03) 2325153.
www.busterpodium.be

Damberd Jazz Café
Korenmarkt 19, Ghent.
Tel (09) 3295337.
www.damberd.be

De Muze
Melkmarkt 15, Antwerp.
Tel (03) 2260126.

De Werf
Werfstraat 108, Bruges.
Tel (050) 330529.
www.dewerf.be

Hotsy Totsy
Hoogstraat 1, Ghent.
Tel (09) 2242012.
www.hotsytotsy.be

Jazz Middelheim
www.jazzmiddelheim.be

Jazzcafé Hopper
Leopold de Waelstraat 2.
Antwerp.
Tel (03) 2484933.
www.cafehopper.be

Skoda Jazz Festival
www.skodajazz.be

ROCK, POP AND WORLD MUSIC

Couleur Café
www.couleurcafe.be

Dour Festival
www.dourfestival.be

Francofolies de Spa
Rue Rogier 2b, Spa.
Tel (087) 776381.
www.francofolies.be

Klinkers
www.klinkers-brugge.be

Lotto Arena
Schijnpoortweg 119,
Antwerp.
Tel (03) 4006000.
www.lottoarena.be

Muziekodroom
Bootstraat 9, Hasselt.
Tel (011) 231313.
www.muziekodroom.be

Pukkelpop
www.pukkelpop.be

Rock Werchter
www.rockwerchter.be

THEATRES

**Antwerp
Stadsschouwburg**
Theaterplein 1, Antwerp.
Tel 0900 69900.
www.stadsschouwburg
antwerpen.be

Bourla Schouwburg
Komedieplaats 18,
Antwerp.
Tel (03) 2248844.
www.toneelhuis.be

**Bruges
Stadsschouwburg**
Vlamingstraat 29, Bruges.
Tel (050) 443060. www.
cultuurcentrumbrugge.be

Théâtre de Namur
Place du Théâtre 2, Namur.
Tel (081) 256161.
www.theatredenamur.be

**Théâtre Royal
de Mons**
Grand Place 1, Mons.
Tel (065) 395939.
www.mons.be

MIXED ARTS AND MUSIC FESTIVALS

Europalia
Galerie Ravenstein 4, 1000
BRU. www.europalia.be

CASINOS

Casino de Spa
Rue Royale 4, Spa.
Tel (087) 772052.
www.casinodespa.be

Casino Knokke
Zeedijk-Albertstrand 509,
Knokke-Heist.
Tel (050) 630500.
www.casinoknokke.be

Casino Oostende
Oosthelling 12, Oostende.
Tel (059) 705111.
www.cko.be

**Grand Casino
Brussels**
Rue Duquesnoy 14,
1000 BRU. *Tel (02)*
2896868. www.
grandcasinobrussels.be

CLUBS AND DISCOS

Café d'Anvers
Verversrui 15, Antwerp.
Tel (03) 2263870.
www.cafe-d-anvers.com

Café Local
Walsekaai 25, Antwerp.
Tel (003) 2385004.
www.cafelocal.be

Culture Club
Afrikalaan 174, Ghent.
Tel (09) 2330946.
www.cultureclub.be

Illusion
Mechelsesteenweg 382,
Lier. *Tel (015) 310377.*
www.illusionxl.be

La Rocca
Antwerpsesteenweg 384,
Lier. *Tel (03) 4891767.*
www.larocca.be

Petrol Club
D'Herbouvillekaai 25,
Antwerp.
Tel (03) 2264963.
www.petrolclub.be

Red and Blue
Lange Schipperskapel 11,
Antwerp.
www.redandblue.be

SHOPPING AND ENTERTAINMENT IN LUXEMBOURG

Nowhere is the prosperity of Luxembourg more evident than in the elegant shopping streets of the Luxembourg City's Old Town. This is echoed on a minor scale in all major towns, where even the bakers, butchers and pharmacies have a refined and cultured quality. Luxembourg

Dynamic act at a music festival

City also has an entertainment agenda that matches its rank as an important capital of the European Union. It draws international audiences from Belgium, France and Germany. A number of other towns have also developed reputations for consistently mounting music and arts festivals of impressive stature.

Twice-weekly vegetable market at Place Guillaume II, Luxembourg City

OPENING HOURS

Shops are open on Monday afternoons, and from 8am to noon and 2 to 6pm between Tuesday and Saturday. Many shops in larger towns stay open during lunch. Most are closed on Sunday.

WHERE TO SHOP

In Luxembourg City, the main shopping streets are in the pedestrianized area around the Place d'Armes and Place Guillaume II. These have stylish boutiques selling luxury goods, international fashions and accessories, as well as souvenirs and crafts. For more moderate prices, the streets near the railway station are a good hunting ground. The **Auchan** shopping centre in Kirchberg is a flagship branch of the Europe-wide supermarket chain, and a good place to buy general provisions. There are massive shopping centres dotted around the country, such as the **Centre Commercial Belle Étoile** at Bertrange.

WINE

Luxembourg wine is available throughout the country, but it is worth visiting its place of origin, the Moselle valley (*see p248*). Poll-Fabaire, specialist in sparkling wine, has showrooms and a shop at **Caves Vinicoles de Wormeldange**. The largest private wine producer is **Bernard-Massard** at Grevenmacher, whose labels include Château de Schengen, Clos des Rochers and Cuvée de l'Ecusson. The stylish **Cep d'Or** is a family-run winery known for its Gewürztraminer and Chardonnay.

CHOCOLATE

The famous 1863-established chocolate maker **Namur**, is headquartered in Luxembourg City. It also specializes in ice cream, pâtisserie and sweets.

MARKETS

The best-known flea market takes place at the capital's Place d'Armes every second and fourth Saturday. Place Guillaume II has a vegetable market on Wednesday and Saturday. Bright Christmas markets spring up in town squares between 6 December and Christmas Eve.

ENTERTAINMENT LISTINGS

The Luxembourg City Tourist Office publishes reliable sets of listings, such as **Agendalux**, which has both printed and web versions. Listings can be found at the website of **Luxembourgticket.lu**.

CLASSICAL MUSIC, DANCE AND THEATRE

The beautiful **Philharmonie Luxembourg**, completed in 2005, offers classical music concerts, chamber music as well as more popular fare. The **Grand Théâtre de la Ville de Luxembourg** is the main venue for touring companies performing opera, ballet and dance. It also mounts theatre productions. The **Luxembourg Festival** of music, opera, theatre and dance in October and November is a joint venture by Philharmonie Luxembourg and the Grand Théâtre de la Ville de Luxembourg. **Théâtre National du Luxembourg** runs plays that often involve actors of international standing. An eclectic mix of performances and exhibitions is shown at the **Centre Culturel de Rencontre Abbaye de Neumünster**. Since 1975, Echternach has held an **International Festival of Music** over May and June, with classical music and jazz, staged at Église St-Pierre-et-St-Paul and the Trifolion auditorium. The **Open-air Festival of Theatre and Music** at Wiltz (weekends

A performance from the Open-air Festival of Theatre and Music, Wiltz

in July) presents a rich and varied programme of music, opera and dance.

CONTEMPORARY MUSIC

The main venue for rock and pop in the country is **Rockhal** in Esch-sur-Alzette. Its two-hall complex hosts major international acts. Smaller concerts are held in the capital at **Den Atelier**. The biggest rock festival is the one-day **Rock-A-Field**, held near Roeser, on the last Sunday in June. Its frontline billing has become increasingly impressive over the years. Luxembourg City has music festivals running over much of the year. **Printemps Musical-Festival de Luxembourg** presents a broad mix, from jazz to world music. **Summer in the City** (mid-June to mid-September) offers free open-air jazz and blues concerts. This

Crowds gathered for the open-air Summer in the City festival

includes **Rock um Knuedler** (first Sunday of July), a free rock concert at Place Guillaume II and Place Clairfontaine. The **Blues 'n Jazz Rallye** occurs in mid-July in pubs and on open-air stages in the Grund and Clausen.

CINEMA

Films are usually shown in their original language with subtitles. Luxembourg City

has two multi-screen cinemas showing the latest international offerings – **Ciné Utopia** and **Utopolis**. Film buffs should look out for the programme of arthouse and classic movies presented by **Cinématèque de la Ville de Luxembourg**.

CLUBS AND DISCOS

The capital has an active nightlife, especially the area around the station and the adjacent suburb of Hollerich. However, popular venues are mercurial and seem to close just as soon as they get established. The three-storey **Byblos** offers weekend disco and DJs, and prides itself on its sedate vibe. A mellow venue, popular with the student crowd, is **Melusina**. It has different spaces offering a variety of grooves, and a reasonably priced restaurant as well.

DIRECTORY

WHERE TO SHOP

Auchan
Rue Alphonse Weicker, 5
Luxembourg City. *Tel 437 743-1*. **www**.auchan.lu

Centre Commercial Belle Étoile
Route d'Arlon, Bertrange.
Tel 310231-1.
www.belle-etoile.lu

WINE

Bernard-Massard
Route du Vin, 8,
Grevenmacher.
Tel 750545-1.
www.bernard-massard.lu

Caves Vinicoles de Wormeldange
Route de Vin 115,
Wormeldange.
Tel 768211.
www.vinsmoselle.lu

Cep d'Or
Route du Vin 15,
Hëttermillen. *Tel 768383*.
www.cepdor.lu

CHOCOLATE

Namur
Rue des Capucins 27,
Luxembourg City. *Tel 223 408*. **www**.namur.lu

ENTERTAINMENT LISTINGS

Agendalux
www.agendalux.lu

Luxembourgticket.lu
Tel 470895-1. **www**.luxembourgticket.lu

CLASSICAL MUSIC, DANCE AND THEATRE

Centre Culturel de Rencontre Abbaye de Neumünster
Rue Münster 28,
Luxembourg City. *Tel 262 052-1*. **www**.ccrn.lu

Grand Théâtre de la Ville de Luxembourg
Rond-point Schuman 1,
Luxembourg City.
Tel 47963900.
www.theater-vdl.lu

International Festival of Music
Echternach. *Tel 728347*.
www.echternach festival.lu

Luxembourg Festival
Luxembourg City. **www**.luxembourgfestival.lu

Open-air Festival of Theatre and Music
Tel 958145. **www**.festivalwiltz.lu

Philharmonie Luxembourg
Place de l'Europe 1,
Luxembourg City.
Tel 26322632. **www**.philharmonie.lu

Théâtre National du Luxembourg
Route de Longwy 194,
Luxembourg City. *Tel 470 8951*. **www**.tnl.lu

CONTEMPORARY MUSIC

Blues 'n Jazz Rallye
www.bluesjazzrallye.lu

Den Atelier
Rue de Hollerich, 54,
Luxembourg-City. *Tel 495 485-1*. **www**.atelier.lu

Printemps Musical-Festival de Luxembourg
www.printempsmusical.lu

Rock-A-Field
Roeser. **www**.atelier.lu

Rockhal
Esch-sur-Alzette. *Tel 245 551*. **www**.rockhal.lu

Rock um Knuedler
www.rockumknuedler.lu

Summer in the City
www.summerinthecity.lu

CINEMA

Cinématèque de la Ville de Luxembourg
Place du Théâtre 17,
Luxembourg City.
Tel 291259. **www**.cinematheque.lu

Ciné Utopia
Ave de la Faïencerie 16,
Luxembourg City. *Tel 224 611*. **www**.utopolis.lu

Utopolis
Avenue JF Kennedy 45,
Luxembourg City. *Tel 429 511-1*. **www**.utopolis.lu

CLUBS AND DISCOS

Byblos
Rue du Fort Niepperg 58,
Luxembourg City.
Tel 24873321.
www.byblos.lu

Melusina
Rue de la Tour Jacob 145,
Clausen, Luxembourg City.
Tel 435922. **www**.melusina.lu

SPORTING AND ACTIVITY HOLIDAYS

Belgium and Luxembourg are well known for periodically producing a flurry of exceptional sporting talent, such as the cyclist Eddy Merckx or the tennis players Justine Henin and Kim Clijsters. There is a constant level of activity in all fields of sport, especially soccer, water sports, cycling, golf, horse riding and judo. Visitors are always welcome to join in.

Sand yacht at De Panne

Popular holiday activities are cycling, walking, kayaking and windsurfing, as these take full advantage of the hills, rivers, lakes and coastline. Both countries have promoted this by creating an extensive network of paths for the exclusive use of cyclists, walkers and riders, with links to accommodation. Here is a chance not only to get healthy, but also have a holiday.

Cyclists dressed for the part in Belgium

CYCLING

As a convenient mode of transport, a leisure pursuit and a major professional sport, cycling is big in Belgium. Consequently, there is no shortage of specialist shops, bike-hire companies or cycle routes. The flat landscape in much of Flanders is ideally suited to touring by bicycle. The Ardennes in Wallonia and Luxembourg present more of a challenge, with specialist circuits for mountainbikes.

A number of long-distance cycling routes cross this region. In Flanders, **LF Routes** (Landelijk Fietsplatform routes) take cycle-friendly paths between strategic destinations. The **RAVel** network consists of five routes that criss-cross Wallonia, and are reserved for bicycles, other non-motorized vehicles and pedestrians. The roads tend to follow disused railway- and tram-lines and canal towpaths. The longest, RAVel 1, goes east to west via Tournai, Mons, Namur and Liège, while RAVel 2 runs north

to south via Namur and Dinant. **Rando Vélo** provides information about long-distance cycling routes. Another useful reference is the cycling promoter, **Pro Vélo**. Luxembourg's equivalent of the RAVel network – **Fédération du Sport Cycliste Luxembourgeois** – has built some 575 km (355 miles) of dedicated cycle paths, and plans to double that length.

HIKING AND RAMBLING

Belgium and Luxembourg offer some of northern Europe's most rewarding walks. The region is crossed by several of the marked transnational **Les Sentiers de Grande Randonnée** (Long-distance Paths). One of these is the GR 5, which links the Netherlands to the Mediterranean via Liège and Luxembourg. Another, the GR AE (Ardennes–Eifel) includes the Semois valley *(see pp228–9)*. GR 56 crosses the Hautes Fagnes *(see p223)*; GR 57 follows the valley of River Ourthe past Durbuy, Hotton and La Roche-en-Ardenne *(see p226)* into Luxembourg; GR 129 links the rivers Scheldt and Meuse; and GR 12 joins Paris to Amsterdam via Brussels. The RAVel routes in Wallonia are also open to walkers. There are many other circular paths, for instance, around Bouillon *(see p230)*, Rochefort *(see p211)* and Echternach *(see p251)*: maps are available at the local tourist offices.

There are also marked paths for short walks in woodland areas such as Nationaal Park Hoge Kempen *(see p168)*, Averbode Bos *(see p162)* and Forêt de Soignes *(see p165)*.

Luxembourg has a dense network of paths, totalling to over 5,000 km (3,100 miles) in length. Many begin at a point accessible by train or car. The popular Müllerthal Trail in Little Switzerland *(see p250)* has 100 km (62 miles) of interlinked paths.

MARATHONS

The biggest race in Belgium is **20 km de Bruxelles**, a half-marathon run by some 25,000 participants in May. In the same month, Luxembourg has a full marathon. Known as **The Night Run**, it begins at 6pm and may continue past midnight. This event is coupled with a half-marathon.

Grand Duke Henri of Luxembourg in the Luxembourg City marathon

Canoeists at the launch of a voyage on the River Ambléve, near Coo

SWIMMING

There are plenty of public swimming pools in Belgium and Luxembourg. In many of these, both men and women are expected to wear bathing caps, usually available at the pool. Lifeguards oversee swimming areas at the coast and hoist flags to indicate swimming conditions: a red flag means bathing is forbidden, a yellow flag calls for extra caution and a green flag means safe conditions. Various lakes also have swimming beaches, such as at the Lacs de l'Eau d'Heure *(see p191)*.

FISHING

There is fishing of all kinds: on the coast, in rivers, lakes and canals. A permit is needed for inland fishing. Details of this are available from the **Service de la Pêche** at the Ministry of the Wallon Region and the **Fédération Sportive des Pêcheurs Francophone de Belgique**. In Luxembourg, permits are issued by local authorities or District Commissariats, with details at tourist offices.

KAYAKING AND CANOEING

The best-known locations for kayaking and canoeing are on Amblève *(see p225)*, Semois *(see p228–9)*, Lesse *(see p211)* and Ourthe *(see p226)*. All of these have centres offering equipment and guides. The **Nederlandstalig Kano Verbond**, the **Fédération Francophone de Canoë et Kayak** and the **Fédération Luxembourgeoise de Canoë-Kayak** offer information for novices and experts.

WATERSKIING

The lakes and broad rivers of Belgium have numerous waterskiing centres. These include the lakes of Barrage de l'Eau d'Heure and the River Meuse *(see p206)* near Wépion and Profondeville. A good source of information is the **Fédération Francophone du Ski Nautique Belge**. Its parallel in Luxembourg, for waterskiing on the Moselle *(see p249)* and various lakes is the **Union Luxembourgeoise de Ski Nautique**.

WINDSURFING

The brisk breezes of the coast provide excellent conditions for windsurfing. De Panne, Nieuwpoort, Oostende, De Haan, Zeebrugge and Knokke-Heist *(see pp120–21)* are all noted windsurfing centres, with surf shops where equipment can be bought or hired. On beaches shared with swimmers, there are separate windsurfing areas demarcated. Windsurfing is practised on some recreational lakes *(see p191)* as well. Kite-surfing is also popular on the coast.

SAILING

Coastal sailing focusses on the main ports and marinas at Nieuwpoort, Oostende, Blankenberge and Zeebrugge. There is dinghy sailing on some of the larger lakes. Sailing federations such as **Fédération Francophone du Yachting Belge (FFYB)** and **Vlaamse Vereniging voor Watersport** provide useful information. Luxembourg likewise has a number of opportunities for sailing, overseen by the **Fédération Luxembourgeoise de Voile**.

SAND YACHTING

At low tide, the hard surface of the sand beaches along Belgium's coast provide the perfect conditions for sand yachts – wheeled vehicles with sails. This amusement is centuries old; the great Bruges-born mathematician Simon Stevin (1548–1620), had a 26-person sand yacht with two sails. The modern version was invented in the late 19th century near De Panne, the main centre for the sport. Novices must take a training course, for example, at the **Royal Sand Yacht Club**, to obtain a permit for recreational sand yachting.

PROFESSIONAL CYCLING

Belgium ranks among the world's top professional cycling nations. It produced probably the greatest cyclist to date: Eddy Merckx (b.1945), five times winner of the Tour de France and winner of over 140 other titles. Other great names include Rik Van Looy (b.1933) and Roger de Vlaeminck (b.1947). Belgium hosts several of the most important world cycling events, including two of the five one-day classics called the Monuments. Of these, the Ronde van Vlaanderen *(see p32)* includes the notorious cobbled climb, the Mur de Grammont, while the Liège–Bastogne–Liège takes place in the Ardennes. First held in 1882, the latter is the oldest of the Monuments. Other key events include the Flèche Wallonne in April, and the four-day Tour of Belgium in late May–early June. Zesdaagse Vlaanderen-Gent, the 6-day European speed cycling race, is held in late November.

A cyclist speeds to victory

Horse riding through the undulating landscape at Oostduinkerke

GOLF

There are several excellent golf courses in Belgium, such as the **Royal Zoute Club** in Knokke. For Wallonia, these are listed by the **Association Francophone de Golf Belge**. The governing body of the sport is the **Royal Belgian Golf Federation**. Luxembourg has six major golf courses, including **Golf-Club Grand-Ducal**, 7 km (4 miles) from the capital city. Information is available from the **Fédération Luxembourgeoise de Golf**.

TENNIS

Belgium's two great tennis stars, Justine Henin and Kim Clijsters, have made this game particularly popular, and there are now numerous outdoor and indoor courts throughout the country. The top-ranking Proximus Diamond Games, an international ladies tournament, takes place in Antwerp in February. The umbrella organizations for tennis in Belgium and Luxembourg are the **Fédération Royale Belge de Tennis** and the **Fédération Luxembourgeoise de Tennis** respectively.

ROCK-CLIMBING

The rivers of the Ardennes have carved out some dramatic gorges, with the result that rock-climbing and mountaineering (*alpinisme* in French) present rewarding challenges. The best sites are in the valleys of the rivers Meuse and Ourthe: the **Club Alpin Belge** provides information. Potholing, another hill pursuit, is overseen by the **Union Belge de Spéléologie**. In Luxembourg, a permit must be obtained from the Ministry of Environment to climb in the best-known area – Müllerthal, near Berdorf *(see p250)*.

HORSE RIDING AND HORSE RACING

There is plenty of opportunity for riding in both these countries, with stables scattered all over the region. Many rural B&Bs provide riding facilities, and some can even stable their guests' horses. There is a good network of accommodation linked by routes for riders. This is run by **L'Association Wallonne de Tourisme Equestre**. Other important riding associations are the **Fédération Belge des Sports Equestres**, **Fédération Francophone d'Equitation** and **Fédération Luxembourgeoise de Sports Equestres**.

Horse racing takes place at Oostende – the **Hippodrome Wellington** hosts the Grand Prix Prince Rose in July. The Great Flanders Steeple Chase takes place at Waregem in August. The **Hippodrome de Wallonie** at Mons is also a key racing venue. The **Jockey Club de Belgique** has details.

RAILBIKES

Old Western comedy films feature wheeled handcars moved by pumping a pivoted double handle. Visitors can now do the same with pedal-powered railbikes (*draisines* in French) on some disused railway lines. These family-sized **Railbikes of the Molignée** can be rented near Maredsous *(see p206)*, for circuits of up to 14 km (8 miles). Railbikes are also available at Tessenderlo, near Diest *(see p162–3)*.

SKIING

When winter coats the higher parts of the Ardennes with snow, Belgians reach for their skis. There are several centres geared up for this sport. Some have lifts for downhill skiing, but cross-country skiing is the primary pursuit. The main ski areas are in the east and south: around Spa, in the Cantons de l'Est and in the Hautes Fagnes. Tobogganing, snow-shoeing and skidoo-ing are popular at Bastogne, Martelange, Bouillon and St-Hubert. In Luxembourg, cross-country skiing is found in the north, at places such as Weiswampach, Asselborn and Hosingen. **Ardenne Tourisme** has a website with information on snow conditions.

ICE-SKATING

During very cold winters, the canals and ponds freeze over, and become ideal for skating. In December, towns such as Brussels, Antwerp and Bruges, create ice rinks in their central squares as part of their Christmas market attractions. Skaters can also go to indoor rinks year-round, for example at Namur, Charleroi or Liège.

MOTOR RACING

Formula 1 Grand Prix motor racing takes place at the circuit in **Spa-Francorchamps** *(see p224)*. This is considered by many aficionados to be one of the most challenging tracks. The race is held over a weekend in early September.

FOOTBALL

In Belgium, football is followed with passion. The main clubs are **Anderlecht**, **Club Brugge** and **Standard de Liège**, all of which regularly feature in the upper echelons of European championship competitions. The Diables Rouges (or Rode Duivels), Belgium's national team, has an honourable World Cup record, even if it has not yet captured the top prize. The national stadium is the **Stade Roi Baudouin** at Heysel, in northern Brussels.

DIRECTORY

CYCLING

Fédération du Sport Cycliste Luxembourgeois
Route d'Arlon 3, Strassen. *Tel* 292317. www.fscl.lu

LF Routes
www.routeyou.com

Pro Vélo
Tel (02) 5027355.
www.provelo.be

Rando Vélo
www.randovelo.org

RAVel
http://ravel.wallonie.be

HIKING AND RAMBLING

Les Sentiers de Grande Randonnée
www.grsentiers.org

MARATHONS

20 km de Bruxelles
www.20km.be

The Night Run
www.ing-europe-marathon.lu

FISHING

Fédération Sportive des Pêcheurs Francophone de Belgique
Tel (081) 413491.
www.pecheurbelge.be

Service de la Pêche
Ave Gouverneur Bovesse 100, Jambes. *Tel* (081) 335900. www.belgium. be/fr/environment/ biodiversitie_et_nature

KAYAKING AND CANOEING

Fédération Francophone de Canoë et Kayak
www.ffckayak.com

Fédération Luxembourgeoise de Canoë-Kayak
www.flck.lu

Nederlandstalig Kano Verbond
www.nkv.be

WATERSKIING

Fédération Francophone du Ski Nautique Belge
www.skinautique.be

Union Luxembourgeoise de Ski Nautique
www.lwwf.eu.

SAILING

Fédération Francophone du Yachting Belge
Ave du Parc d'Armée 90, Jambes. *Tel* (081) 304979. www.ffyb.be

Fédération Luxembourgeoise de Voile
www.flv.lu

Vlaamse Vereniging voor Watersport
Beatrijslaan 25, Antwerp. *Tel* (03) 2196967. www.vvw.be

SAND-YACHTING

Royal Sand Yacht Club
Dynastielaan 20, De Panne. *Tel* (058) 420808. www.rsyc.be

GOLF

Association Franco-phone de Golf Belge
Tel (02) 6790220.
www.afgolf.be

Fédération Luxembourgeoise de Golf
Domaine de Belenhaff, Junglinster. *Tel* 26782383. www.flgolf.lu

Gold-Club Grand-Ducal
Route de Trèves 1, Senningerberg. *Tel* 340 090. www.gcgd.lu

Royal Belgian Golf Federation
Chausée de la Hulpe 110, BRU. *Tel* (02) 6722389. www.golfbelgium.be

Royal Zoute Club
Caddiespad 14, 8300 Knokke. *Tel* (050) 601 227. www.zoute.be

TENNIS

Fédération Luxembourgeoise de Tennis
Blvd Hubert Clement, Esch-sur-Alzette. *Tel* 574 4701. www.flt.lu

Fédération Royale Belge de Tennis
Galerie de la Porte Louise 203/3, 1050 BRU. *Tel* (02) 5480304. www.kbtb.be

ROCK-CLIMBING

Club Alpin Belge
129, Ave Albert I, Namur. *Tel* (081) 234320. www.clubalpin.be

Union Belge de Spéléologie
Ave Arthur Procès 5, Namur. *Tel* (081) 230009. www.speleo.be

HORSE RIDING AND HORSE RACING

Fédération Belge des Sports Equestres
Tel (02) 4785056.
www.equibel.be

Fédération Francophone d'Equitation
Tel (071) 815052.
www.ffe.be

Fédération Luxembourgeoise de Sports Equestres
Tel 484999.
www.flse.lu

Hippodrome de Wallonie
www.hippodromede wallonie.be

Hippodrome Wellington
Koningin Astridlaan. *Tel* (04) 75784879.

L'Association Wallonne de Tourism Equestre
Tel (071) 818292.
www.awte.be

Jockey Club de Belgique
Tel (02) 6727248.
www.jockey-club.be

RAILBIKES

Railbikes of the Molignée
116 Rue de la Molignée, Warnant. *Tel* (082) 699 079. www.molignee.be

SKIING

Ardenne Tourisme
Tel (084) 411981.
www.infoski.be

MOTOR RACING

Spa-Francorchamps
www.spa-francor champs.be

FOOTBALL

Anderlecht
Tel (02) 5294067.
www.rsca.be

Club Brugge
Tel (050) 402135.
www.clubbrugge.be

Stade Roi Baudouin
Ave du Marathon 135, BRU. *Tel* (02) 4743940.

Standard de Liège
Tel (04) 2299898.
www.standard.be

Belgium and Luxembourg for Children

Bears at the Réserve d'Animaux Sauvages

A great deal of family-oriented socializing and entertainment occurs in both countries. Museums, amusement parks and galleries are organized with families or school parties in mind. There are also a variety of activities such as rides on historic trains and trips on canal boats. Visitors will therefore find it easy to keep children amused in towns and cities. The countryside has its draws in the form of ancient caves and awe-inspiring fortresses. To add to these experiences are the ever-present treats of Belgian chips and waffles.

Thrilling swings and rides at the Walibi theme park near Wavre

THEME PARKS

Visiting theme parks seems to be an integral part of childhood in Belgium, and there are parks to suit people of all ages. Some, notably the **Plopsaland** parks, are specifically aimed at the younger crowd. There are branches at De Panne and Coo, and an indoor Plopsaland at Hasselt. Bobbejaanland *(see p156)*, near Turnhout, is a traditional theme park, packed with thrills-and-spills rides. But the most famous Belgian theme park is Walibi *(see p198)*, near Wavre, to the southeast of Brussels. With its broad variety of rides, from roundabouts to state-of-the-art roller coasters and live entertainment shows, Walibi caters to children of all ages. Attached to it is the swimming complex (pools, shoots, tubes) called Aquilibi. There is a similar swimming complex at Océade, part of the Bruparck complex *(see p84)* on the northern outskirts of Brussels. Bruparck also includes a number of other attractions such as Mini-Europe and a huge cinema complex.

Close at hand is the Atomium *(see p84)*, always fascinating to children. The Bellewaerde Park *(see p124)*, near Ieper, combines a collection of zoo animals with theme park rides. The **Boudewijn Seapark**, near Bruges, has a dolphinarium and performing seal lions, as well as a roller coaster, pirate ship and other rides.

ZOOS AND AQUARIUMS

Shoehorned into a small urban space near the Centraal Station and Diamond District, Belgium's famous **Antwerp Zoo** contains a variety of animals and prides itself on its captive breeding programme and conservation work. The zoo also operates the much larger Planckendael Animal Park *(see p157)* near Mechelen. Parc Paradisio *(see p185)* in Hainaut is very child-friendly. Réserve d'Animaux Sauvages at Han-sur-Lesse *(see p211)* is a safari park with large north European animals such as bears, lynx and bison. The **Monde Sauvage Safari** on the River Amblève *(see p225)* has a more Africa-oriented safari.

Bouillon's castle *(see pp232–3)* has a famous falconry show. Knokke-Heist's Vlindertuin *(see p120)* is a delightful indoor tropical garden with thousands of butterflies. There are two sealife aquariums on the coast: the Noordseeaquarium *(see p122)* at Oostende and the **National Sealife Marine Park** at Blankenberge, which also has a **Serpentarium**. Liège's well respected Aquarium *(see p218)* is operated by the university's Institute of Zoology.

MUSEUMS AND GALLERIES

Many museums and galleries produce printed documentation to make their exhibits more interesting for children, including lists for treasure hunts. Audioguides also help bring the exhibits alive – at the Musée des Instruments de Musique *(see p65)* in Brussels, visitors can listen to the instruments. Demonstrations and costumed characters at the Bokrijk Openluchtmuseum *(see p167)* make this fine collection of historic rural buildings seem almost lived in.

Museums specifically aimed at children include the toy museums, Musée du Jouet *(see p74)* and Speelgoedmuseum *(see p157)*. The Centre Belge de la Bande Dessinée *(see p62)* appeals more to aficionados of the history of the comicstrip form. There are several interactive science museums such as **Scientastic**, where children can experience optical illusions and other tricks of physics. The Parc d'Attractions Scientifiques *(see p189)* offers a host of introductory exhibits on science and technology.

A string puppet of Pinocchio at Mechelen's Speelgoedmuseum

An old steam powered train at Fond-des-Gras

STEAM TRAINS AND TRAM RIDES

Railway engines and tracks have been preserved in many places in Luxembourg and Belgium, and visitors can now enjoy gentle rides into quiet corners of the countryside and into the past. Maldegem's Stoomcentrum (see p137) runs historic steam and diesel trains. Likewise, Mariembourg is the starting point for train trips on the Chemin de Fer des Trois Vallées (see p210). Visitors can also head off down the tracks under their own steam with a railbike (see p314). The Musée du Transport Urbain Bruxellois (see p85) has rides in a historic tram complete with a hooter-blowing conductor, all the way to Tervuren and the Musée Royale de l'Afrique Centrale, which children also enjoy. The industrial museum of Fond-de-Gras (see p248), in southern Luxembourg, operates steam trains along normal-gauge and narrow-gauge rails.

CANAL BOATS

Bruges and Ghent are great places in which to take children on a canal boat trip. This offers a completely different view of the cities, as visitors glide gently along in the company of ducks and moorhens, passing under bridges and encountering new aromas. The ever-changing scenery is captivating, for adults and children alike.

CASTLES AND WAR

Setting alive the imagination with tales of sieges and derring-do are the region's many castles (see p30–31). Bouillon is the most impressive medieval castle, while Beersel (see p164), Jehay (see p220) and Lavaux-Ste-Anne (see p211) could be the backdrops for fairytales. With its thick walls, turrets and crenellations, Gravensteen (see p134) in Ghent also looks the part; it even has an exhibition of instruments of torture. Children will also enjoy tunnelling around the casemates of Luxembourg City. On a more sombre note, older children may find the museum of the former concentration camp at Fort Breendonk (see p156) impressively chilling. Equally, many older children are moved and amazed by the museums, monuments and exhibits marking World War I (see pp126–7), especially the museum called In Flanders Fields at Ieper (see pp124).

BELFRIES AND TOWERS

Offering the chance to see towns and cities from a new angle, Belgium's many belfries are more than just historic monuments. Narrow spiral staircases climb to the parapet, from where there are fine, and sometimes scary, views over the rooftops and of the ant-like activities below. Visitors may hear the carillon tinkle out a tune, or be deafened by the colossal racket of a big bell as the clock strikes the hour.

CAVES

The Ardennes region is riddled with caves, which fascinate children. The most famous of these, at Han-sur-Lesse (see p211), can be explored on foot and by boat. There are many others, each with their

DIRECTORY

THEME PARKS

Boudewijn Seapark
A. De Baeckestraat 12, Bruges.
Tel (050) 383838.
www.boudewijnseapark.be

Plopsaland
De Pannelaan 68.
Tel (058) 420202.
Plopsa Coo 4, 4970 Coo-Stavelot.
Tel (080) 684265.
www.plopsa.be

ZOOS AND AQUARIUMS

Antwerp Zoo
Kongingin Astridplein 26,
Antwerp. *Tel (03) 2024540.*
www.zooantwerpen.be

Monde Sauvage Safari
Fange de Deigné 3, Aywaille.
Tel (04) 3609070. www.
mondesauvage.be

National Sealife Marine Park
Koning Albert I Laan 116,
Blankenberge. *Tel (050) 424300.*
www.sealifeeurope.com

Serpentarium
Zeedijk 147, Blankenberge.
Tel (050) 423162.
www.serpentarium.be

MUSEUMS AND GALLERIES

Scientastic Museum
Bourse Metro Station, Level -1,
Boulevard Anspach, 1000 BRU.
Tel (02) 7321336.
www.scientastic.be

own magical landscapes of glittering stalactites and still pools (see pp208–209).

CHIPS AND WAFFLES

In Belgium, deep-fried food is the basis of traditional snacks. The outdoor *frietkoten* offer cornets of crispy, double-fried chips with some mayonnaise to dunk them into. There are also sweetened waffles from streetside vendors – the traditional snack of fairs and festivals and of summer holidays on the coast. This is the kind of cultural treat that children the world over really relish.

SURVIVAL GUIDE

PRACTICAL INFORMATION

Belgium and Luxembourg are well organized countries, whose people like to see the practicalities of life properly managed in a transparent and efficient manner. Tourism is a major industry in both nations and is actively promoted by the authorities. As a result, tourist offices, both abroad and within the countries, have a wealth of information, much of

Belgium's tourist information sign

which is accessible on the Internet. Travel hubs and most towns also have visitor centres. If things go wrong, these centres have helpful, English-speaking people to help sort out problems. However, it is always best to learn a few basic phrases or to take a phrasebook along. In Wallonia, most information is given in French, while in Flanders it is provided in Dutch.

The glittering Christmas market in Brussels's Grand Place

WHEN TO GO

Both countries can be visited year-round. However, in summer (June–August) there is a better chance of sunshine and warm weather, and towns lay on a host of festivities and outdoor concerts. Summer is also the height of the tourist season, so all museums, galleries and attractions are open to the fullest schedules. From October to March, many of the smaller museums, and the less frequented churches and historic houses, open only at weekends, or may close completely. December has its Christmas markets (see p35) while February and March have carnivals (see pp32–33).

WHAT TO PACK

Where clothing is concerned, visitors need to think in terms of layers. The average temperatures are 20°C (68°F) in summer and 5°C (41°F) in

winter, but the weather is always unpredictable – it is easy to adjust to this by just adding or subtracting a fleece or a cardigan. It is also best to be prepared for wet weather.

Despite Belgium's reputation for cutting-edge fashion, most people dress in a practical, down-to-earth kind of way. Smart-casual would be the dress code for better restaurants and even business meetings and formal occasions. A pair of sturdy walking shoes

is recommended to deal with the cobbled streets. Also essential are adaptor plugs for electrical appliances and mosquito repellent for places with open canals, such as Bruges.

TOURIST INFORMATION

The Belgian authorities, and individual towns and cities, are working hard to promote their country as a holiday destination. They produce copious amounts of promotional

Smart-casual wear and sturdy shoes, the norm in Belgium and Luxembourg

◁ Narrow brick houses fencing a quiet cobbled alley in Bruges

Helpful advice from the Tourist Office in Ghent

material, published both in printed brochures and on the Internet. The degree to which such information is available in English depends to a large extent on how much holiday traffic is expected.

Flanders and Wallonia have separate tourist agencies – **Tourism Flanders** and **Belgian Tourist Office**. Abroad, they often have separate offices. Both deal with Brussels, although Brussels also has its own agency. The best place to begin looking for information is the Internet. Virtually all towns in Belgium have dedicated websites in the format www.townname. be and these generally have links to their tourist offices. Again, almost all towns with any kind of attraction will have a tourist office, often located in the main square, if not in the town hall itself. Most offices and visitor centres have English-speaking staff. They can provide hotel listings and may even offer to make bookings on a visitor's behalf.

The **Luxembourg Tourist Office** also produces a wealth of visitor information. The Grand Duchy has tourist offices in most locations, which generally follow the format www.townname.lu on the Internet.

VISAS AND PASSPORTS

Visitors from countries of the European Union can travel freely to Luxembourg and Belgium provided they have a valid passport or identity card. Passport-holders from the USA, Canada, Australia, New Zealand and Japan do not require a visa for visits of up to 90 days. However, regulations may change, so

it advisable to check before departure. It is a legal require-ment in Belgium to carry identification at all times.

EMBASSIES AND CONSULATES

Belgium has embassies in most capital cities of the world. Queries about visas and other formalities can be addressed to these centres before departure from the home country, although much of this information is available on their official websites. Luxembourg has embassies or consulates in most major coun-tries. Likewise, most nations, including the **UK**, the **USA**, **Canada**, **Australia** and **New Zealand** have embassies in Brussels and Luxembourg.

CUSTOMS

Visitors from EU countries travelling to and from Belgium and Luxembourg face almost no restrictions on the

quantities of alcohol and tobacco they can carry with them, provided that this is for their personal use. Duty-free goods are available only to those travelling to countries outside the EU (such as Canada and the USA), and local restrictions apply regarding how much visitors can bring into their country of destination.

TRAVELLING WITH CHILDREN

Belgium and Luxembourg are both family-oriented nations, and children are widely welcomed – provided that they are reasonably well behaved. Restaurants and hotels are accommodating: Belgian children are taken to restaurants from an early age, and soon adopt the gas-tronomic expertise of their parents. There are numerous concessions for families, such as reduced-price museum entrance tickets and free public transport for children under the age of six (if accompanied by an adult). Apart from this, there are plenty of attractions and activities to keep children entertained (*see pp316–17*). It is also easy for parents to get carried away with the variety of beautiful clothes and toys available from the numerous specialist shops in both countries.

Families at the Plopsaland theme park on the Western Flanders coast

Parking spaces for disabled travellers in front of the Palais Royal, Brussels

FACILITIES FOR DISABLED TRAVELLERS

Belgium is full of historic buildings, steps, kerbs, narrow doors and cobbled streets, but little has been done to the physical environment to accommodate people with reduced mobility. The good news is the Belgians are remarkably willing to assist people with disabilities of any kind. Although improvements are being made all the time, facilities for disabled people in hotels, restaurants and public places are far from uniform, so it is wise never to make assumptions about access, and to phone ahead. Local tourist offices can also advise disabled travellers. Various websites provide more detailed information and help, notably those of the **Infopunt Toegankelijk Reizen** (Accessible Travel Info Point) in Flanders, and **Able Travel**. Tourist offices also recommend the services of the **Belgian Red Cross**. **Brussels For All** has web-based information for travellers with reduced mobility. For those travelling in Luxembourg, **Info-Handicap** is the best resource – but its webpages are, at present, in French and German only.

LANGUAGE

Belgium has two main languages – French (which is spoken in Wallonia in southern Belgium, and in Brussels) and Dutch, which is used in Flanders in northern Belgium (*see pp129*). In addition, German is the third offical language, used in the Cantons de l'Est. English is widely spoken within the tourist industry, especially in the main holiday-destination cities such as Brussels, Ghent, Bruges and Antwerp. Note that Belgium is not, in practice, a bilingual country. Many Flemish do not speak French, and even more French-speaking Belgians do not speak Dutch. In Flanders, it is generally unwise to communicate in French in the first instance. Visitors who do not speak Dutch are better off trying English – French should be used only as a last resort.

The national language of Luxembourg is Lëtzebuergesch (*see p236*). However, French and German are both official

languages and frequently used across the country. English is also widely spoken.

TIME DIFFERENCE

Belgium and Luxembourg are on Central European Time (CET), which is GMT + 1 (one hour ahead of Greenwich Mean Time). Both nations operate the same daylight saving time over winter, which means that they move their clocks one hour forward in spring (last Sunday in March), and one hour back in autumn (last Sunday in October).

WEIGHTS AND MEASURES

Metric to Imperial
1 kilometre (km) = 0.62 miles
1 metre (m) = 3.28 feet (ft)
1 centimetre (cm) = 0.39 inches (in)
1 litre (l) = 1.76 British pints or 2.11 US pints
1 kilogram (kg) = 2.2 pounds (lb)
1 gram (g) = 0.03 ounces (oz)
1°C = 33.8°F
From degrees Celsius to degrees Farenheit, multiply by 1.8 and add 32.

ELECTRICITY

The electrical current in both countries is 220 volts AC, and standard European plugs with two round pins are used. British electrical equipment, which runs on 230 volts, operates fine on 220 volts, but requires adaptors for the standard three-pin British plug. These are best bought

Signboard at the Zwin displaying information in Dutch and French

Specialist equipment on display at the *jenever* museum in Hasselt

in the UK or at the airport before arrival, as they are hard to find in Belgium. American equipment, which runs on 120 volts, requires a voltage converter or transformer, although some equipment, such as electric razors, may run on both.

OPENING HOURS

Most shops and businesses in Belgium are open Mondays to Saturdays between 10am and 6pm or 7pm, with some shops closing for an hour at lunch time. The supermarkets are usually open between 9am and 8pm. Opening hours in Luxembourg are similar. However, shops there tend to be open between 8am and noon, and again between 2pm and 6pm, and many are closed on Monday mornings.

MUSEUMS AND GALLERIES

The Belgians are often avid collectors, and up and down the country there are numerous small private museums – on bicycles, military insignia, beer labels and so forth – that are essentially extensions of private hobbies. There is also a passion for the more established museums, instilled at an early age through school visits – in fact, in 2008, the Flemish introduced a scheme whereby young people under the age of 26 could visit 23 of the leading museums of Flanders and Brussels for just one euro. Public investment is

Ticket information at Oostende aquarium

considerable, with major new museums and galleries being built to the highest standards of presentation and old ones being modernized.

Many museums are closely focussed on local traditions and products – hops in Poperinge *(see p125)*, *jenever* gin in Hasselt *(see p166)* and slate in Bertrix *(see p230)*. Visitors will find that labels are often in one language only (either French or Dutch), but newer museums may have foreign-language audioguides. Almost all have admission charges, and special deals are sometimes available from the city tourist offices that allow visits to many of the museums for a single, much-reduced price. Opening hours vary, but broadly, most public museums, in both Belgium and Luxembourg, are open between 10am and 5pm, with the majority being closed on Mondays.

TIPPING

Tipping is not very common in either Luxembourg or Belgium. A service charge is included in restaurant prices, but customers can leave a small extra tip if service has been particularly good. The service is also included in taxi fares, although rounding up the fare by up to 10 per cent is customary. Ushers who show visitors to their seats in some cinemas will expect a tip of about 50 cents per spectator.

DIRECTORY

TOURIST INFORMATION

Belgian Tourist Office: Brussels-Wallonia
www.belgiumtheplaceto.be
www.belgium-tourism.be
http://diplomatie.belgium.be

Luxembourg Tourist Office
www.luxembourg.co.uk
www.luxembourg.com
www.visitluxembourg.com
www.ont.lu

Tourism Flanders
www.visitflanders.com

EMBASSIES

Australia
Rue Guimard 6-8, 1040 BRU.
Tel (02) 2860500.
www.austemb.be

Canada
Avenue de Tervuren 2, 1040 BRU.
Tel (02) 7410611.
www.international.gc.ca/
missions/belgium-belgique/index

UK
Rue d'Arlon 85, 1040 BRU.
Tel (02) 2876211.
www.ukinbelgium.fco.gov.uk/en

USA
Boulevard du Régent 27, 1000 BRU. *Tel (02) 5082111.*
www.belgium.usembassy.gov

New Zealand
Level 7, 9-31 Avenue des Nerviens, 1040 BRU.
Tel (02) 5121040.
www.nzembassy.com

FACILITIES FOR DISABLED TRAVELLERS

Able Travel
www.able-travel.com

Belgian Red Cross
Rue de Stalle 96, 1180 BRU.
Tel (02) 3713111.
www.redcross.be
Motstraat 40, Mechelen.
Tel (015) 443322.
www.rodekruis.be

Brussels For All
www.brusselvoorallen.be

Info-Handicap
www.info-handicap.lu
www.welcome.lu

Infopunt Toegankelijk Reizen
www.accessinfo.be

Personal Security and Health

Belgium and Luxembourg are relatively safe places for visitors and citizens alike. Politeness, honesty and respect for others are cherished and normal levels of vigilance should suffice. As in any well organized society that broadly looks after its citizens, there is a good network of services to deal with unexpected crises. Those unfortunate enough to fall ill will find that the health service in particular is extremely well run, with first-class hospitals and readily available facilities.

CRIME

Belgium and Luxembourg suffer no more from crime than any other European nation. That said, Brussels recently recorded the highest rates for burglary in Europe and Luxembourg City, by contrast, recorded the lowest. In the cities, visitors need to be alert to pickpockets and bag-snatchers, especially on public transport. Some hotels have reported that smartly-dressed pickpockets have been infiltrating their premises by pretending to be clients, then targeting guests in lifts and other communal spaces. Outside the larger cities, crime is generally not a problem, but it is wise always to be on the alert.

LAW ENFORCEMENT

Belgium has two integrated levels of police. Major crimes and motorway offences are handled by the **Federal Police**. However, visitors are more likely to encounter the Local Police, who are responsible for law and order in their area. Visitors in the capital can also get in touch with the **Brussels Central Police Station**. In Luxembourg, the main law enforcement agency is the **Grand Ducal Police**. Victims of theft will need to go to a police station and acquire the necessary paperwork to claim insurance. Police stations in major cities will have someone who speaks English.

A Belgian police officer

SAFETY GUIDELINES

Precautions to take in Luxembourg and Belgium are similar to those taken in any city in the Western world. Busy, crowded places, such as stations, public transport, major tourist attractions and markets, are the haunts of opportunist thieves and pickpockets. When parking a car, the doors need to be properly locked and bags or possessions that might be construed as potentially valuable be hidden away. When out sightseeing or shopping on foot in the bigger towns and cities, and when sitting in busy cafés or restaurants, bags and wallets should be firmly secured at all times. On public transport and in crowded places, women should wear handbags with the strap across the shoulder and the clasp facing the body. In hotels, rooms and suitcases need to be locked and it is best to avoid leaving cash or valuables lying around. Rooms often come with a safe; if not, there should be one at reception. It is advisable always to keep two separate sets of money and credit cards in case one set gets lost. Avoid lonely and questionable areas after dark.

LOST PROPERTY

The chances of retrieving property are minimal if it was lost in the street. However, Belgians are essentially honest and believe strongly in the inviolable rights of ownership to personal possessions. As a result, property left behind or lost in a restaurant, museum or shop can usually be retrieved. The public transport authorities operate lost-and-found services. For insurance purposes, travellers need to get in touch with the local police station and lodge a report.

TRAVEL AND HEALTH INSURANCE

Under reciprocal agreements, travellers to Belgium and Luxembourg coming from EU countries are entitled to the same subsidized healthcare that local nationals receive, provided they are in possession of an **EHIC** (European Health Insurance Card). British citizens can apply for an EHIC using forms available at post offices or online. Before receiving treatment, EU citizens should make it clear that they have state insurance, or they may end up with a large bill. Patients will usually be asked to pay first and then seek reimbursement from the authorities at home – so it is essential to retain all receipts. While generous, state healthcare subsidies do not cover all problems (such as dental treatment or repatriation) or costs, so it is

Crowded market typical of town squares such as Place d'Armes, Luxembourg

A typical pharmacy store in Belgium, doubling as a herbalist

worth taking out full travel insurance, which covers additional risks such as theft or lost property and travel cancellation. Travellers from outside the EU are strongly advised to take out full travel insurance, with medical cover – a serious accident involving hospitalization and repatriation by special air transport can cost tens of thousands of euros.

DOCTORS, HOSPITALS AND PHARMACIES

Belgium and Luxembourg have efficient health services funded by a mixture of state subsidies and national and private insurance. Hospitals are plentiful, modern and well run, and the quality of treatment is generally very good. Guests taken ill at a hotel will be provided details of local doctors by the staff. Whether or not a person has insurance, doctors will expect to settle the bill on the spot, and in cash. Pharmacists are well trained and run their businesses with clinical efficiency. For minor ailments, they should be the first port of call. Pharmacies are generally open Mondays to Fridays from 9am to 6pm, and every district operates a rota system for late-night, weekend and national holiday cover. All pharmacies also display information about where to find the nearest 24-hour chemist.

EMERGENCIES

Police, **Ambulance and Fire Services** in Belgium and Luxembourg have dedicated nationwide phone numbers.

Visitors can also make use of local knowledge in an emergency as people are quick to step forward and help. Those staying at a hotel can ask staff at the reception for assistance.

PUBLIC TOILETS

In general, most places with tourist footfall have adequate provision for public toilets. Many of these facilities are meticulously maintained by attendants, who charge a rate for usage. Where no rate is shown, people are expected to leave between 25 and 50 cents. If caught short, it is possible to use the toilet of a bar or café, but one would be expected to return the favour by buying a drink or coffee.

SMOKING

In both countries, smoking is officially forbidden in confined public places and on public transport. It is also prohibited in restaurants and large cafés (unless they have a dedicated smoking area, or food represents less than one-third of their business and they have special permission). Smoking may be tolerated in smaller bars. In Luxembourg, a smoking ban comes into force from noon to 2pm and 7 to 9pm in cafés where meals are served.

MOSQUITOES

In Belgium, mosquitoes can be a problem on warm summer nights. The canals of Bruges and the polders of the north are favoured breeding areas and visitors to these places will need suitable repellants.

BEER STRENGTH

Belgian beer is very good, but also very strong – Trappist and Abbey beers regularly contain 6.5–9.5 per cent alcohol by volume (abv). The beer is usually drunk slowly and in moderate quantities. Drinkers who are used to a beer-strength of 3.5–4 per cent abv will really notice the difference, and may run into trouble if they heedlessly apply their normal quantities of intake to Belgian beer.

Bottles of Belgian beer with labels signalling the alchohol content

Banking and Currency

As befits their status at the heart of the European Union, both geographically and administratively, Belgium and Luxembourg have trustworthy and efficient banking systems, dedicated to businesses as well as individuals. The currency used by both countries, as well as by most of the older member-states of the European Union, is the euro. Cash is easily available through Automated Teller Machines (ATMs) and banks, and most of the essential transactions can be conducted through major credit cards.

Debit and credit cards, accepted at major stores and most hotels

ATMs, available in most towns and cities across the two countries

BANKS

Banking hours in Belgium and Luxembourg are generally 9am to 4pm from Monday to Friday. In Belgium, some banks might close for lunch between noon and 2pm. A few branches operate until 4:30pm or 5pm on Fridays, and may open on Saturday mornings. Most banks are happy to serve non-clients, and often offer very competitive exchange rates. They are also able to cash travellers' cheques and exchange foreign currency. To do this, the signatory's passport or some other form of photographic identification will be required. All transactions, especially money transfers, are liable to banking fees, and it is best to check the rates in advance.

ATM SERVICES

Most bank branches have 24-hour cashpoint facilities. Visitors will find that there is often a machine in the lobby used by members of the bank, while a second ATM on the wall outside is available to everyone. ATMs accept a wide range of cards, including those belonging to Maestro and Cirrus. It is advisable to check with the home bank or card-provider whether a card is acceptable abroad. Usually, there is no transaction fee at the ATM itself, but the bank or card-provider at home may have set the exchange rate and will charge a fee.

FOREIGN EXCHANGE BUREAUS

Visitors who are unable to change money at a bank or use a cashpoint machine to obtain euros, may be forced to rely on foreign exchange bureaus (*bureaux de change* in French; *wisselkantoren* in Dutch). These can be found in all cities and travel hubs that regularly receive foreign visitors. They have much longer opening hours than banks, but will often charge a commission of 3–4 per cent, on top of which they may not have as competitive exchange rates. It is worth comparing prices between different bureaus to ensure a good deal.

CREDIT AND CHARGE CARDS

MasterCard and **Visa** cards are widely accepted across the region; more reluctance may be shown towards **Diners Club** and **American Express**. Most hotels accept credit cards to secure reservations, and likewise for payment at the end of a stay. Small hotels and bed-and-breakfast accommodation may take only cash. The mode of payment needs to be established before the stay. Again, restaurants are usually happy to take payment by credit card, but it is best to check before ordering if this is not clear, and there is insufficient cash to cover a meal.

DIRECTORY

CREDIT AND CHARGE CARDS

American Express
Tel (02) 6762121.
www.americanexpress.be

Diners Club
Tel (02) 6265024.
www.dinersclub.be

MasterCard
Tel 0800 15096.
www.mastercard.com/be

Visa
Tel 0800 18397
(in Belgium: (070) 344 344).
www.visaeurope.com

Foreign exchange bureau at the Brussels Midi railway station

CURRENCY

The euro replaced the Belgian franc and Luxembourg franc at the beginning of 2002, and, in contrast to some Euro-zone nations, there are few regrets and little nostalgia for the old currencies. The euro currency is a blessing for travellers moving across Euro-zone nations. It is also easy to handle – with notes in denominations from €5 upwards, shoppers are not unduly burdened with excessive notes or change. Those unaccustomed to the euro will discover that 1-, 2- and 5- cent coins (in French, *centimes*) are of little practical value and tend to accumulate. At the other end of the scale, €500 notes are just too valuable for many enterprises as they are subject to counterfeiting; many refuse to take €500 notes at all.

Bank Notes

Euro bank notes have seven denominations. The €5 note (grey in colour) is the smallest, followed by the €10 note (pink), €20 note (blue), €50 note (orange), €100 note (green), €200 note (yellow) and €500 note (purple). All notes show the stars of the European Union.

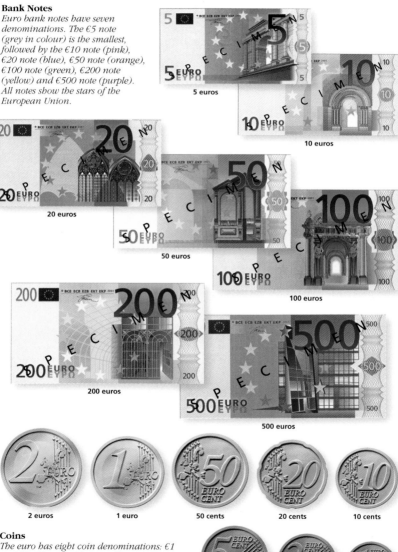

5 euros

10 euros

20 euros

50 euros

100 euros

200 euros

500 euros

2 euros

1 euro

50 cents

20 cents

10 cents

Coins

The euro has eight coin denominations: €1 and €2; 50 cents, 20 cents, 10 cents, 5 cents, 2 cents and 1 cent. The €2 and €1 coins are both silver and golden in colour. The 50-, 20- and 10-cent coins are golden. The 5-, 2- and 1-cent coins are bronze.

5 cents

2 cents

1 cent

Communications and Media

**Post box sign,
Luxembourg**

Belgium and Luxembourg have excellent communications links. Both countries are also areas of rapid change: mobile telephones are replacing landlines and hence telephone boxes; email is undermining the postal service; and the Internet is making inroads into newspaper journalism and broadcasting. However, both nations have a conservative streak that battles to maintain traditional services, but they are also keen to grab a front seat in the communications revolution. As a result, both the old and the new media are generally well provided for.

USING A PUBLIC TELEPHONE

2 Insert the telephone card, arrow side up, in the direction that the arrow is pointing.

3 The display will show how many units are stored on the card and then tell you to dial.

4 Key in the phone number and wait to be connected.

5 If you want to make another call, do not replace the receiver; simply press the follow-on call button.

1 Lift receiver and wait for a dialling tone.

6 When you have finished the call, replace the receiver. The card will emerge from the slot and can be removed.

7 If the card runs out in mid-call, it will re-emerge; remove it and insert another.

Belgacom calling card

DIALLING CODES

- In Belgium and Luxembourg, there is no distinction between a long-distance call and a local call. The former area codes in Belgium have been incorporated into local numbers and must be dialled even when making a call from within the same area.
- To make a direct call from abroad, dial 00, then the country code (Belgium 32, Luxembourg 352).
- For international directory enquiries and operator-assistance in French, dial 1204, or in Flemish, 1304.
- For domestic directory enquiries in Flemish, dial 1313.
- For domestic directory enquiries in French, dial 1212.
- For domestic directory enquiries in German, dial 1407.
- For domestic directory enquiries in English, dial 1405.
- For directory enquiries and international operator assistance in Luxembourg, dial 11817 or 11816.

TELEPHONES

Mobile phone networks cover the region effectively. Note, however, that the ability of a visitor to use a mobile phone depends on the network, and, before travelling, it is a good idea to check with the provider that full roaming services are available to – and how much they cost to use. Hotels generally charge premium rates to use their landline phones for international calls. Public payphones in Belgium are run by the former state operator Belgacom. Public phone booths are still plentiful, but the service information can often be difficult to understand; those in doubt can use the operator services. A few payphones still accept coins, but most take Belgacom phonecards. Both €5 and €10 cards are sold at newsagents, post offices and train stations. A similar system operates in Luxembourg.

POSTAL SERVICES

Post offices in Belgium are open Monday to Friday from 8:30 or 9am to 4 or 5pm. Some stay open late on Fridays, and are open on Saturday mornings. In Luxembourg, opening hours are from 8am to noon and again from 1:30 to 5pm. Post offices are the place to buy stamps, send registered mail and post parcels. Blue "A Prior" stickers are needed for international mail. Stamps of the most common denominations are available at some

The easily recognizable red post box, on a pavement in Belgium

The entrance to a post office, with signs in French and Dutch

newsagents, tobacconists, postcard shops and hotels. Mail boxes, often still bearing the Thurn and Taxis post-horn, are red in Belgium, while in Luxembourg, they are painted yellow.

NEWSPAPERS AND MAGAZINES

Newspapers as well as magazines in the English language are available in most of the main cities in Belgium and Luxembourg. Brussels has its own excellent weekly listings guide called *Brussels Unlimited*. The monthly *Bulletin* magazine carries articles covering the rest of Belgium. Belgian press is split along the language-divide. The main French-language papers in this area are *Le Soir*, *La Libre Belgique* and *La Dernière Heure* (strong on sports coverage). The main Flemish and Dutch papers are *De Standaard*, *Het Laatste Nieuws* and *De Morgen*. The *Grenz-Echo* serves the German-speaking community in the east of the country. In Luxembourg, there are the *Luxemburger Wort* and *Tageblatt*.

TELEVISION

Belgium has two primary broadcasting worlds: French and Dutch. Both have their own state-funded arms. The French-language one is the

Newspaper stand

Radio Télévision Belge de la langue Française (RTBF), while the Flemish-language version is the Vlaamse Radio-en Televisieomroep (VRT). Luxembourg is the base for the far-reaching Radio-Télé-Luxembourg (RTL), a descendant of the original Radio Luxembourg which was founded in 1933.

Visitors to Belgium and Luxembourg may barely become aware of such national distinctions however, because most hotel televisions are supplied by cable, with dozens of channels that come not only from local sources, but also, in a variety of languages, from the neighbouring countries, including France, the UK, Germany and the Netherlands.

INTERNET SERVICES

Belgium and Luxembourg have kept ahead of the game with the Internet, and the network, efficiency and availability of connections are improving all the time. Most major hotels, and even many smaller ones have Wi-Fi. Sometimes guests have to pay for time-limited usage, but often it is provided as part of the hotel service, accessed by codes supplied by the hotel reception. If an Internet link is essential, visitors can ask for it while making the hotel booking. Some bars and cafés also have Wi-Fi. **Belgacom** has a (subscription) hotspot system for Wi-Fi Internet users on the move in Belgium; **Luxembourg City** has a free one. Many towns and cities also have dedicated Internet cafés, but coverage is patchy. The Internet is being increasingly used in the travel industry for booking and ticketing flights and ferry crossings, for researching and booking hotels, and for finding out about holiday destinations. This world of electronic communications is bound to expand even further in future.

People at a free Internet-access computer station

TRAVEL INFORMATION

Belgium and Luxembourg both have abundant and excellent connections by air, rail and road. Brussels in particular, as the capital of the European Union, is the beneficiary of increasingly tight competition between the airlines, although, as a business-oriented destination, the city is not generally the target of bargain-basement flights. High-speed trains, such as

Eurostar logo

Thalys and Eurostar, provide a comfortable and convenient mode of transport, and are the popular alternative to air travel. Travellers from Britain can use the Channel Tunnel to bring their car with them. Motorways criss-cross the region as part of a pan-European network – there are no motorway tolls in either Belgium or Luxembourg, so the main cost of driving is simply the petrol.

An aeroplane from the fleet of the Belgian carrier, Brussels Airlines

ARRIVING BY AIR

The **Brussels Airport**, serving international flights, is located at Zaventem 14 km (9 miles) northeast of the city centre. Most Belgians, including taxi drivers, refer to it as Zaventem. The local international carrier, **Brussels Airlines**, connects many cities in the USA, Europe and around the world. Other major carriers using Zaventem include **Air Canada**, **American Airlines**, **British Airways**, **Lufthansa** and **Delta**. However, travellers from North America may find it cheaper to fly to another European city (for instance, London) and take an onward connection. **CityJet**, the Flemish airline, flies out of London City Airport to Antwerp. Among the budget airlines, **flybe** has connections to Brussels from Manchester and Southampton. Ryanair's Brussels South Airport is in fact **Charleroi Airport**, 55 km (34 miles) southeast of Brussels; **Ryanair** services run from Glasgow, Manchester, Dublin and Shannon. **Antwerp Airport** 6 km (4 miles) from the centre of Antwerp, is linked to

London and is served by VLM. Luxembourg's international airport, **Findel**, lies 6 km (4 miles) east of Luxembourg City and is served by British Airways, as well as VLM Airlines (from London City Airport and Manchester). **Luxair**, the national carrier, flies to various points in Europe and North Africa. The nearest Ryanair destinations are Charleroi, or Frankfurt in Germany, 200 km (125 miles) east of Luxembourg City.

AIRPORT FACILITIES

Zaventem has the full range of facilities expected of an international airport. Arriving passengers will also find ATMs, foreign exchange booths and coin- and card-operated payphones. There are efficient and economic rail connections into Brussels every 20 minutes, running through each of the three main train stations (Gare du Nord, Gare Centrale and Gare du Midi) in turn. The Airport Line bus service connects the airport to Schuman Metro station and th Quartier Léopold station in

the EU district. Taxis can take longer in heavy traffic, and cost up to ten times as much as the train or bus. Charleroi Airport has a bus link to Brussels Midi, and, alternatively, a bus link to the Charleroi-Sud railway station for onward journeys by rail.

Luxembourg's airport offers similar facilities, and a bus service shuttles passengers into the centre of the city.

ARRIVING BY TRAIN

Brussels lies at the heart of Europe's high-speed train networks, connected to London by the **Eurostar** service and to Paris, Amsterdam and Cologne by the Thalys network.

With top speeds of 300 kph (186 mph), these trains offer a viable alternative to air travel, especially given that the stations are located close to city centres and rail travel involves fewer check-in formalities. Eurostar trains leave from St Pancras, London, and take 1 hour 51 minutes to reach Brussels Midi, passing through the Channel Tunnel between Folkestone and Calais (France). It is also possible to join the Eurostar in Kent – at Ebbsfleet or Ashford. Tickets to Brussels are valid to any other Belgian

The sleek high-speed Thalys train, pulling into a Brussels station

Ferry near the coast of Western Flanders

station. To reach Luxembourg City from London, visitors can go by Eurostar to Brussels, then change to **Luxembourg Railways**: the London–Brussels ticket is valid up to Arlon in southeast Belgium.

Luxembourg City's station is located just south of the city centre. Tickets to all European destinations can be booked via **RailEurope** and **Railbookers**.

ARRIVING BY SEA

Belgium can be reached from the UK by ferries. There are frequent cross-Channel ferries to the closest ports: Dover to Calais, served by **P&O Ferries** and Dover to Dunkirk served by **Norfolkline**. There are also longer crossings to ports in Belgium itself: Ramsgate to Oostende, served by **TransEuropa Ferries** and overnight crossings to Zeebrugge from Rosyth/Edinburgh by Norfolkline and from Hull by P&O Ferries. These are geared to passengers travelling with cars. Individual foot passengers will need to make arrangements for getting to and from the ferry ports.

ARRIVING BY CAR

Car drivers from Britain can cross the Channel by ferry to Oostende and Zeebrugge in Belgium, but shorter ferry crossings reach French ports (Calais and Dunkirk) close to the Belgian border. Motorway links from these ports into Belgium are fast: Brussels is about 2 hours and Bruges only 1¼ hours from Calais. The alternative is the Channel Tunnel via the Eurotunnel. Cars and passengers are transported in drive-on, drive-off railway carriages between Folkestone and Calais. Tickets tend to cost a lot less if booked well in advance.

Luxembourg City is 415 km (258 miles) from Calais, via Lille and Namur, with motorways that link over the entire distance. Visitors from Europe can cross freely into both countries, as they are signatories of the Schengen Agreement – there are normally no customs formalities at the land borders.

ARRIVING BY BUS

Eurolines, a group of coach companies forming Europe's largest coach network, operates daily bus services from London to Brussels, and to Ghent, Liège and Antwerp. There are no direct links from London to Luxembourg.

DIRECTORY

ARRIVING BY AIR

Air Canada
Tel (070) 220100.
www.aircanada.com

Antwerp Airport
Tel (03) 2856500.
www.antwerpairport.be

American Airlines
Tel (02) 7119969.
www.aa.com

British Airways
Tel (02) 7173217.
www.britishairways.com

Brussels Airlines
Tel (02) 7232345.
www.brusselsairlines.com

Brussels Airport
Tel (02) 7537753.
www.brusselsairport.be

Charleroi Airport
Tel (071) 251211.
www.charleroi-airport.com

CityJet
Tel (0871) 6665050 (UK).
Tel (032) 878080.
www.cityjet.com

Delta
Tel (02) 7119799.
www.delta.com

Findel
Tel (+352) 24640.
www.luxairport.lu

flybe
Tel (0871) 7002000 (UK).
www.flybe.com

Lufthansa
Tel (0871) 9459747 (UK),
(070) 353030 (Belgium).
www.lufthansa.com

Luxair
Tel (352) 24564242.
www.luxair.lu

Ryanair
Tel (0871) 2460000 (UK).
www.ryanair.com

ARRIVING BY TRAIN

Eurostar
Tel (08432) 186 186.
www.eurostar.com

Luxembourg Railways
Tel (352) 24892489.
www.cfl.lu

Railbookers
Tel (02) 03 327 0800.
www.railbookers.com

RailEurope
Tel (08448) 484064.
www.raileurope.co.uk

ARRIVING BY SEA

Norfolkline
Tel (0844) 8475042 (UK).
www.norfolkline.com

P&O Ferries
Tel (08716) 645645 (UK).
www.poferries.com

TransEuropa Ferries
Tel (059) 340260.
www.transeuropaferries.com

ARRIVING BY CAR

Eurotunnel
Tel (08448) 797379 (UK).
www.eurotunnel.com

ARRIVING BY BUS

Eurolines
Tel (08717) 818181 (UK).
www.eurolines.com

Getting Around Belgium and Luxembourg

Both Belgium and Luxembourg have very effective and reasonably priced public transport, with rail and bus services reaching just about every place of interest. In Belgium, the rail system is the most extensive, complemented by the bus services; in Luxembourg, the rail system is more limited, but a comprehensive bus network fills the gaps. Railways are run with great efficiency and with the kind of pride that produces ticket-collectors who can help passengers in three languages. However, driving is the easiest way to see the countries at leisure.

BY CAR

Traffic jams can be a problem in the big cities, but beyond them, driving becomes much less enervating. The motorways are fast, well maintained, well lit at night and toll-free. Signposting is generally good, but the tendency of many municipal authorities to make their town-centres traffic-free can produce labyrinthine one-way systems that are only comprehensible to those with local knowledge. Breakdowns in Belgium are handled by one of three motoring organizations – **Touring Club de Belgique**, **Royal Automobile Club de Belgique** and **Vlaamse Automobilistenbond** (in Flanders). Luxembourg has the **Automobile Club de Luxembourg**. Major rental agencies, including **Avis**, **Budget**, **Europcar** and **Hertz**, operate in both countries. Vehicles can be rented by anyone who is at least 21 years of age (in some cases 23 or 25), has a year's driving experience and a credit card. It is usually cheaper to book a car before leaving home.

Before starting out, it is advisable to get a full breakdown insurance cover, including damage excess; this can be very expensive if bought when picking up the car.

RULES OF THE ROAD

Traffic in Luxembourg and Belgium drives on the right. Speed limits are 50 kph (30 mph) in built-up areas, 120 kph (75 mph) on motorways and dual-carriageways, and 90 kph (55 mph) on other national roads. A full licence

Cars and taxis threading their way through the main streets of Brussels

from the EU, US, Canada, Australia, New Zealand or South Africa is acceptable, as is an International Driving Licence. The licence must be carried while driving. It is also essential to have at least third-party insurance, and better to have comprehensive insurance (Green Card). Visitors are expected to carry a first-aid kit and a warning triangle: national stickers must be displayed. Drivers of UK cars need to make sure that their headlights are adjusted for driving on the right. Safety belts are obligatory and children under 12 are not allowed to sit in the front if there are other

seats available. Drink-driving is illegal and is heavily penalized. Mobile phones are not permitted while driving, but the use of "hands free" equipment is allowed. In places with tram networks, visitors need to keep a sharp lookout for trams, and always give way to them.

Most roads in Belgium are clearly marked to give priority to the main road, but where junctions are not so marked, drivers coming from the right (and turning to the right) may pull onto the main road without stopping. This is most often seen in city side streets.

PARKING

In many towns, it is possible to park right in the city centre, sometimes in the central square itself, although signs may ban this on market days. There are usually plenty of paying carparks close by. Street parking often requires paying at a coin-operated metre. In many towns, especially in Flanders, street-parking is free, but time-limited: a clock-like cardboard parking disk (available at a newsagent) is placed on the dashboard, showing time of arrival. Blue signs with a rather obscure clock image indicate where this rule is in force, but many do not actually show the length of time allowed for parking. This may vary from 30 minutes to 2 hours – it is best to ask to be sure.

BY TRAIN

Belgian National Railways are run by the Société Nationale des Chemins de Fer Belges (**SNCB**), known in Dutch as the Nationale Maatschappij

A taxi parked by the curb in Luxembourg City

A Luxembourg sightseeing bus carrying visitors on a tour of the city

der Belgische Spoorwegen (**NMBS**). Fares are calculated by distance. Children under six travel free, with a maximum of four children allowed per adult; those aged between six and eleven receive a 50 per cent discount. Several other special tariffs are available, including discounts for adults under 26, and seniors over 65; weekend tickets and day returns may be cheaper by as much as 40 per cent. Rail passes are offered, such as the Railpass, which allows ten trips within Belgium over one year, and the Benelux Pass, which provides unlimited travel on any five days within one month of purchase, on trains in Belgium, Luxembourg and the Netherlands.

In Luxembourg, the primary line runs north–south, from Liège to Luxembourg City, via Clervaux. Day-tickets covering the entire train and public bus network can be bought at a very reasonable price.

BY BUS

Buses come into their own in the remote areas of Belgium and in city suburbs. Buses in Flanders are run by **De Lijn**. In remoter areas individual passengers can telephone De Lijn's Belbus system, for a small bus to take them on an unscheduled route between regular De Lijn stops. De Lijn also operates trams, including the Kusttram, which runs along the Belgian coast. Buses are run by Transport En Commun (**TEC**) in Wallonia. **Luxembourg** buses cover an extensive network of routes. Fares are based on distance and tickets are bought from the driver.

BY RIVER AND CANAL

Boat cruises of varying length operate on the Scheldt, Leie, Meuse and Moselle rivers, as well as on a network of canals. Belgium has more than 2,000 km (1,243 miles) of navigable waterways, used by commercial traffic as well as for pleasure. Cruise details are available from tourist offices in Bruges, Ghent, Dinant, Liège, Namur, Antwerp and Luxembourg.

BY BICYCLE

Belgium and Luxembourg are keen cycling nations and equipment can be rented in most towns for a reasonable price. Cycle hire shops and the tourist offices can also advise on the best routes to follow, such as the RAVel network of dedicated cycle routes *(see p312)*. In Belgium, cyclists are encouraged to use trains, at minimal extra cost. Under the Train and Bike scheme (Train et Vélo in French and Trein en Fiets in Dutch), travellers can rent bicycles from some railway stations as part of the price of a return ticket.

In Luxembourg, bicycles can be conveyed free on trains, if space is available.

SPECIALIST TOURS

To see the best of both countries without inconvenience, a coach tour is a good option. Numerous companies offer tours of the main cities. Others organize thematic tours, focussing on Belgian architecture, battlefields (Waterloo, World War I or II), birdwatching, food, beer or chocolate. Guided tour operators also run day-trips from

the cities themselves; for instance, it is possible to visit the World War I battle sites from Bruges. Details are available at the tourist offices.

Getting around the Cities

Metro station street sign

Civic pride is woven into the fabric of all municipalities in Luxembourg and Belgium, and good public access is high on the agenda. The cities and towns have grown organically as places where people live, work and play, and most still have the human scale that reflects their medieval origins. This means that walking remains one of the best ways to get around the town centres. There are also good means of public transport, or reasonably-priced, centrally-located car parks for those who drive.

Pedestrianized street in the Old Town centre of Luxembourg City

WALKING

Town planners have generally shown great consideration for pedestrians, with broad pavements and plenty of street crossings. Traffic is meant to stop for walkers at zebra-crossings, but this may not always happen. Some crossings also have traffic signals, and drivers will follow them, not a pedestrian's wish to cross: it is best to wait for the green man to light up. Sturdy walking shoes are needed to cope with the many cobbled streets in Belgium.

BUSES

City buses are run by the same companies as provincial buses: De Lijn in Flanders and TEC in Wallonia. The exception is Brussels, where all public transport (buses, trams, and metro) are operated by the Société des Transports Intercommunaux de Bruxelles (**STIB**, or MIVB in Dutch). All bus stops should be treated as request stops, and drivers

need to be signalled to when a person wants to board. In Luxembourg City, buses are the main form of public transport, centring upon Place E Hamilius in the Old Town, and linking with the train station

Some cities, notably Bruges, Brussels and Luxembourg City, offer sightseeing tours by bus, with recorded commentaries. In both nations, this is a hop-off, hop-on service, and tickets are valid for 24 hours.

TRAMS

In addition to bus services, Brussels, Ghent and Antwerp have trams. Running on dedicated lines that are usually (although not always) free of road traffic, they have the advantage of following a reliable published schedule, and move swiftly through the city streets even at rush hour. Maps of the network and ticket offices make planning a journey fairly easy. As with buses, all stops are request stops; equally, the bell-button must be pressed for disembarking.

METRO

The city of Brussels has a Metro (underground) system, which provides quick transport around the centre and to the suburbs in all directions. Stations are marked by signs with a blue "M" on a white background. Scheduled services run from 6am to midnight (with shorter hours at weekends or on public holidays). Brussels and Antwerp both also have a system called PreMetro, where the tram network travels through extensive underground tunnels in the city centre.

TICKETS AND MAPS

In cities with trams or a metro system as well as buses, tickets are normally valid for a continuous onward journey, with changes, regardless of the means of conveyance. In Brussels, STIB tickets for bus, tram and metro can be bought from ticket offices and newsagents. More economical multi-journey cards, or one-day cards, are also available. Elsewhere, bus and tram tickets for individual journeys are bought from the driver. The onboard machine can be used to validate a ticket at the start of a journey, and at each subsequent change. Larger towns and cities publish maps of the bus, tram and metro routes, which are available for free at ticket and tourist offices.

TAXIS

All major towns have taxi services. Cabs are ordinary saloon cars with illuminated taxi signs on the roof. They

City tram moving down Rue Royale towards the Brussels city centre

Cyclists on the seafront promenade at De Panne, on the Belgian coast

cannot be hailed from the pavement – travellers will have to find one of the taxi-ranks, which are usually found in strategic locations such as outside railway stations or close to the central square. It is also possible to phone for a taxi – a tourist office or hotel can supply the relevant numbers. Taxi drivers do not necessarily have a detailed and precise knowledge of their city, so it helps to come armed with full information about the destination. The price of a journey always includes service, despite which it is quite normal to round up the total fare.

BICYCLES

Some towns and cities are good for cycling in, others less so. Thousands of students pedal around Ghent, for instance, and the old streets of central Bruges have relatively light and slow-moving traffic. Brussels is a rather more challenging proposition, with congested, busy, cobbled streets filled with parked cars, trams and frustrated drivers. That said, there are plenty of people who do cycle in Brussels, and who take advantage of recommended cycle routes. Tourist offices and cycle-hire shops can also provide information on routes. In Brussels, bicycles can be taken on the metro except at rush-hour.

CANAL BOATS

The city best known for its canals is Bruges – this is why it is sometimes referred to (misleadingly) as the Venice of the North. From March to November (and at weekends in winter), tour boats leave from various points in the city centre, and make tours of varying length around the extensive canal network – a delightful way to see the city from a quite different perspective. One useful tip is to take an umbrella if it has been raining, as the bridges drip. Ghent also has canals, although rather less extensive than those of Bruges. They again show the city in a new and agreeably tranquil light.

HORSE-DRAWN CARRIAGES

Visitors can step back in time in Brussels, Bruges, Ghent and Antwerp with a ride in an open horse-drawn carriage. In Brussels, the carriages make short trips from Rue Charles Buls, which is close to the Grand Place, during the summer months. In other cities, the season lasts between spring and autumn. Tours in Bruges start from the Markt or the Burg; in Ghent, they start from St-Baafsplein, and in Antwerp from the Grote Markt. Bruges also has the Paardentram, a horse-drawn tram available for group hire.

Carriage-rides may seem to be an expensive indulgence, but they are also an unforgettable experience.

The Paardentram making its way though the Burg in Bruges

FRENCH/DUTCH PLACE NAMES

One of the most confusing aspects of travel in Belgium is the variation between French and Dutch spellings of town names. On road signs in Brussels, both names are given, while in Flanders only the Dutch and in Wallonia only the French are shown. The following list gives main towns:

French	Dutch	French	Dutch
Anvers	Antwerpen	Malines	Mechelen
Ath	Aat	Mons	Bergen
Bruges	Brugge	Namur	Namen
Bruxelles	Brussel	Ostende	Oostende
Courtrai	Kortrijk	St-Trond	St-Truiden
Gand	Gent	Tongrès	Tongeren
Liège	Luik	Tournai	Doornik
Louvain	Leuven	Ypres	Ieper

General Index

346 ACKNOWLEDGMENTS

Acknowledgments

Dorling Kindersley would like to thank the many people whose help and assistance contributed to the preparation of this book.

Main Contributor
Antony Mason is the author of 70 books on travel, art, geography and history, including DK Top 10 Travel Guide to Brussels, Bruges, Antwerp and Ghent, Cadogan Guide to Brussels and Cadogan Guide to Bruges. He has taught writing at Goldsmiths College, University of London, as a Fellow of the Royal Literary Fund. His long-standing admiration for Belgium dates from 1975.

Additional Contributors Zoë Hewetson, Philip Lee, Zoë Ross, Sarah Wolff, Timothy Wright, Julia Zyrianova, Emma Jones, Leigh Phillips

Fact Checker Dan Colwell

Proofreader Swati Meherishi

Indexer Cyber Media Services Ltd

Design and Editorial
Publisher Douglas Amrine
List Manager Vivien Antwi
Managing Art Editor Jane Ewart
Project Editor Alastair Laing
Project Designer Kate Leonard, Shahid Mahmood
Senior Cartographic Editor Casper Morris
Managing Art Editor (jackets) Karen Constanti
Jacket Design Tessa Bindloss
Senior DTP Designer Jason Little
Picture Researcher Ellen Root
Production Controller Rita Sinha

Editorial Assistance Fay Franklin

Additional Picture Research Rhiannon Furbear

DK Picture Library Romaine Werblow

Additional Photography Stuti Tiwari Bhatia, Gerard Brown, Demetrio Carrasco, Anthony Cassidy, Jeoff Davis, Paul Kenward, Mathew Kurien, David Murray, Ian O'Leary, Alessandra Santarelli, Jules Selmes, Tony Souter

Additional Illustrations Gary Cross, Richard Draper, Paul Guest, Robbie Polley, Kevin Robinson

Revisions Team
Claire Baranowski, Caroline Elliker, Amy Harrison, Shikha Kulkarni, Sonal Modha, Catherine Palmi, Preeti Singh, Dora Whitaker, Lesley Williamson

Special Assistance
Dorling Kindersley would like to thank the following: Rym Neffoussi at the Belgian Tourist Office; Serge Moes at the Luxembourg Tourist Office, London; Jean-Claude Conter and Gelz Pit at the Luxembourg National Tourist Office, Luxembourg; Mia Prce at the Musées Royaux des Beaux-Arts de Belgique; Anita Rampall at Tourism Flanders-Brussels, UK

Photography Permission
Dorling Kindersley would like to thank the following for their assistance and kind permission to photograph at their establishments:
Abbaye de Maredsous; Abbaye de Stavelot; Attre Château; Basilica St-Hubert; Bokrijk Openluchtmuseum; Brüsel comic-book store; Brussels Tourism Office; Castle of Jehay; Cathédrale Notre Dame; Cathédrale St-Paul; Centraal Station, Antwerp; Château de Modave; Château des Princes de Chimay; Château-Fort de Bouillon; Comme Chez Soi; Design Museum Gent; Église Ste-Catherine; Église St-Jacques; Église St-Quentin Euro Space Centre, Transinne; Gaasbeek Castle; Grimbergen Abbey Church; Groot Vleeshuis; Grottes de Hotton; Grottes de Lorette; Grottes de Neptune; Hôpital Notre Dame à la Rose; Hotel Eurostars Sablon; Hotel Metropole; Le Falstaff; Le Méridien Hotel, Brussels; Maison de la Metallurgie et de l'Industrie; Memorial Breendonk; Musée d'Ansembourg; Musée de Cire; Musée de l'Art Wallon; Musée de la Bataille des Ardennes; Musée du Circuit de Spa Francorchamps; Musée du Folklore; Musée Groesbeek de Croix; Musée Horta; Musée Provincial des Arts Anciens du Namurois; Musée Royal de l'Armée et d'Histoire Militaire; Musée Tchantchès; Nationaal Jenevermuseum; Noordseeaquarium; Parc du Cinquantenaire; Plantin-Moretus Museum; Rochefort; Rubenshuis; St Christopher's Church, Charleroi; Stadhuis, Antwerp; Stadhuis, Ghent; World War I Museum.

Picture Credits
Key- a - above; b - below/bottom; c - centre; f - far; l - left; r - right; t - top.

Every effort has been made to trace the copyright holders, and we apologize in advance for any unintentional omissions. We would be pleased to add appropriate acknowledgments in any subsequent editions of this publication.

Works of art have been reproduced with the kind permission of the following copyright holders:
Le Journal de Spirou © Dupuis, 1938-2008 24tr; © Lucky Comics 2008 24br; © Moulinsart SA 24tl, 24bc; © Marvano – Dargaud Benelux (Daragud-Lombard s.a.) 2007 25c; Casterman 25 br; © Standaard Uitgeverij 25bl; © IMPS SA 25bc; © DACS, London 2009 80tl; The Domain of Arnheim, 1962, oil on canvas, 146 x 114 cm © Charly Herscovici, with his kind authorization – c/o SABAM-ADAGP, 2009 70bl; Musée Horta © 2009 arch. Victor Horta, SOFAM Belgium 80tl.

The publisher would like to thank the following for their kind permission to reproduce their photographs:
4CORNERS IMAGES: Cozzi Guido 238bl; SIME/Gräfenhain Günter 2-3, 100cl, 140, 158-159/Schmid Reinhard 223cla. MAARTEN VANDEN ABEELE: 88bl. AKG-IMAGES: 26-27c, 37bc, 40tc, 40bl, 44tr, 46bc, 47bc, 47br, 120tc; Collection Schloß Ambras./Erich Lessing 236cb; Kunsthistorisches Museum/Erich Lessing 282tr; Joseph Martin 114ca; Musées Royaux d'Art et d'Histoire. 45crb; Private Collection 282tl. ALAMY: A & J Visage 20clb; Alan King Engraving 235c; Albaimages/Ronald Weir 20cb; Per Andersen 134cl, 160cl; Arco Images/De Meester, J. 213b/Delpho M. 21clb; Arterra Picture Library/Clément Philippe 119bl; Authors Image/ Nicolas Rung 35cra; Sigitas Baltramaitis 20cl; David A. Barnes 193b; Pat Behnke 149tc, 279tl; Bildarchiv Monheim GmbH/Paul M. R. Maeyaert 160bc; BL Images Ltd 55t; David Boag 21fbr; Tibor Bognar 28bl; Jacky Chapman 123crb; Choups 4br, 17tr; CW Images 281cla; David Noble Photography 174-175c; Hasan Doganturk 58tr; Vick Fisher 1c; Foto 28 118br; Fotolincs 20br; Liz Garnett 32bl; D Gee 322tl; Andrew Harrington 21tc; Brian Harris 32cr; Hemis.fr/ Borgese Maurizio 18br/Rieger Bertrand 119t; Peter Horree 39c, 73t, 117bc, 175crb; 280cra, 281br; Imagebroker 326tr/ Michael Krabs 21bc; ImageState/Martin Ruegner 21cb/ Pictor International 50cl, 172cl; INSADCO Photography/ Martin Bobrovsky 278cla; INTERFOTO/Fine Arts 163br; INTERFOTO/Pressebildagentur 236bc; Eric James 134br; Jon Arnold Images Ltd 29tl; JTB Photo Communications, Inc. 320c; Oliver Knight 91cra; Lebrecht Music and Arts Photo Library 40bc; Lordprice Collection 196br; Magestate Media Partners Limited - Impact Photos/Laurent Grandadam 90tr; Mary Evans Picture Library 41bl; Bruce McGowan 38bl; Melba Photo Agency 30bl; Nature Picture Library/Bernard Castelein 20tl, 20fbr, 21cr, 21bl; NRT-Travel 126ca; Witry Pascal 21cl; Pictorial Press Ltd 63br; Picture Contact/Jochem Wijnands 314t; PjrFoto/Studio 43bl; Robert Estall photo agency/Malcolm Aird 38bc; David Robertson 250br; Rough Guides 166br; David Russell 326bl; Stephen Frink Collection/Masa Ushioda 21tr; Stephen Roberts Photography 19t; 280clb; Mark Sunderland 91tl; The London Art Archive/Borch, Gerard ter 42clb/Eyck, Jan van 102tr/Jordaeans, Jacob 103br/Memling, Hans 102bl/Weyden, Roger 102cl/Wouters, Rik 152bl/ Delacroix, Eugene 39tr; The Print Collector 9c, 45bc, 114bl, 153cra; TNT Magazine 125tl; Travelshots.com 10cla; Rohan Van Twest 279cb; Martyn Vickery 126cl; Wild Places Photography/Chris Howes 31crb, 329br; Wilmar Photography 174clb, 178bl, 209bl; Peter M. Wilson 54cl. ANTWERP TOURISM AND CONVENTION: Dave Van Laere 148cl; CH BASTIN & J EVRARD: 165tr. BIERES DE

CHIMAY S.A: 282cr. BRUSSELS AIRLINES: 330cla CORBIS: Atlantide Phototravel 212; Dave Bartruff 25cb; Tibor Bognar 190br; Jon Hicks 146clb; Olivier Polet 53b, 303cla; Schlegelmilch 34cla; Stapleton Collection 85crb; Sygma/ Reuter Raymond 312br/Sophie Bassouls 24cl; Zefa/ Eberhard Streichan 47crb.DAS FOTOARCHIV: 324c.DE MUNT LA MONNAIE: 45tr. RUDY DENOYETTE: 136cla. DIAMOND LAND: 19c. BART VAN DIJK: 135tr. DUNCAN BAIRD PUBLISHERS: Alan Williams 147tr, 283br. DURBUY ADVENTURE: 261tl. EUROSTAR: 330tc. FLANDERS FIELDS MUSEUM: 124br; FLPA: Imagebroker/Anton Luhr 20fbl. PAUL GARLAND: 208cla. GETTY IMAGES: AFP 19br/ Stringer 119cr/Staff/Jean-Loup Gautreau 23cb; DEA/G. Sosio/De Agostini Picture Library 175bl; Popperfoto/Haynes Archive 252bl; Hulton Archive 43bc, 44cl/Stringer 39br; Keystone 47tl; Staff/Pascal Le Segretain 237br; Stone/ Richard Elliott 34br; The Bridgeman Art Library/English Scho 36. PHOTOS CITY OF GHENT –TOURIST OFFICE: 321tl; GROTTES DE REMOUCHAMPS: 209cra. HOTEL BLOOM 257br; HOTEL LES NUITS: 258br; HOTEL METROPOLE: 90clb. MICHAEL HURT: 98-99. INSTITUT ROYAL DU PATRIMOINE ARTISTIQUE: 26tr, 61tc. ISTOCK-PHOTO.COM: Jeroen Peys 228cl; Duncan Walker 37br. KASTEEL BEAUVOORDE: 124c. JOS L. KNAEPEN: 307tl. KONINKLIJK MUSEUM VOOR SCHONE KUNSTEN: 153tc. LANDCOMMANDERIJ ALDEN BIESEN: 142b. LONELY PLANET IMAGES: Glenn van der Knijff 48-49; Martin Moos 149c; Wayne Walton 228bl. LUKAS - ART IN FLANDERS VZW: Musea Brugge/Groeninge Museum 115tl. LUXEMBOURG NATIONAL TOURIST OFFICE: 5t, 11br, 15b, 17bl, 239tr, 242cla, 243cr, 243br, 244cla, 244br, 245tl, 245br, 248br, 249br, 253tc, 310tc, 310cla, 310br, 311tc. MAAGDENHUISMUSEUM: KIK/IRPA, Brussels 148bl. RAF MAES: 307br. MAPPA MUNDO: 90-91c. MARY EVANS PICTURE LIBRARY: 49c, 103bl, 237t, 255c, 319c. ANTONY MASON: 136tr. CLAUDE MATHON: 101cra, 328c, 328cb. MUSEUM DHONDT-DHAENENS: Kris Martin 136br. MUSEE DE L'ART WALLON DE LA VILLE DE LIEGE: Legs M. Aristide Cralle (1884) 45tl. MUSEE EN PLEIN AIR DU SART-TILMAN: Rik Wouters (1882-1916), La Vierge folle ou La Joie de Vivre, 1912. Photo Jean Housen 219cl; MUSEES ROYAUX DES BEAUX-ARTS BELGIQUE: 70cl, 70bl, 71crb, 73b; Photo Cussac 22cl, 44-45c, 68cb, 69clb, 69crb, 71cra, 72tr; Photo Speltdoorn 22br, 23c, 26cl, 69cra, 71tl; 72bl, 103tl; NATIONAAL PARK HOGE KEMPEN: 143tr. NATUREPL. COM: Bernard Castelein 21fbl; Philippe Clement 20bl. BJÖRN OLIEVIER:33c. PETROLCLUB Tom Van Ghent 308tr. PHOTOLIBRARY Age fotostock/Charles Bowman 277tl/ Javier Larrea 181tl/Kevin Galvin 318-319/P Narayan 113tr/ Nils-Johan Norenlind 51tl/Werner Otto 234-235; Corbis 172br, 200-201; Hemis/Rieger Bertrand 105b, 173bl/Renault Philippe 128-129; Image Source 18tl; Imagestate/Brian Lawrence 104/The Print Collector 99c, 171c; Japan Travel Bureau 177b; John Warburton-Lee Photography/Amar Grover 78; Mauritius/Josephine Clasen 254-255, 303bl; Photononstop/Bernard Foubert 192/Yvan Travert 52; Dan Porges 20tr; RESO/Diaphor La Phototheque 141b, 170-171; The Bridgeman Art Library 8-9; Tips Italia/Charles Mahaux 16bc/Alberto Nardi 31tr, 232br/Christina Jansen 183cr. PHOTOSHOT: World Pictures 16t, 33br. ROBBIE POOLEY: 110bc, 114tr. PRIVATE COLLECTION: 37c, 38crb, 44bl, 44br, 115cr, 205cb. ALAIN RIVIERE: 282br. ROBERT HARDING PICTURE LIBRARY: Roger Somvi 32tc. ROYAL BALLET OF FLANDERS: J. Persson/Wim Vanlessen en ensemble 306b. NEIL SETCHFIELD: 26tl, 86br. STAD BRUGGE STEDELIJKE MUSEA: Groeningemuseum 58tl, 115ca; Gruithuis 112tr, 112br. STOOMCENTRUM MALDEGEM: 137br. THE BRIDGEMAN ART LIBRARY: Christie's Images, London: Peter Paul Rubens (1557-1640) Self Portrait 23tl; The

Lacemakers of Ghent, 1913 (oil on canvas), Silbert, Max (b.1871)/Private Collection 27tr; Dawn, Brussels, c.1725-1730 (lace), Flemish School, (18th century)/Musee Crozatier, Le Puy-en-Velay/Giraudon 27br; Portrait of Philip The Good, Duke of Burgundy, and his third wife Isabel of Portugal, 1430 (oil on board), Flemish School, (15th cent.)/ Museum voor Schone Kunsten, Ghent, Giraudon/The Bridgeman Art Library 39bc; The Battle of Pavia, 24 February 1525 (tapestry) (detail 156716), Orley, Bernard van (c.1488-1541)/Museo e Gallerie Nazionale di Capodimonte, Naples/The Bridgeman Art Library 40crb; Ommeganck in Brussels on 31st May 1615: detail of the Triumph of Isabella of Spain (1566-1633) 1615 (detail 69871) (oil on canvas), Alsloot, Denys van (1570-1628)/ Victoria & Albert Museum, London/The Bridgeman Art Library 41t; Philip II (1527-98) Crowned by Victory, 1628 (oil on canvas), Rubens, Peter Paul (1577-1640)/Prado, Madrid, Giraudon/The Bridgeman Art Library 41cb; The Raising of the Cross (panel), Rubens, Peter Paul (1577-1640) (attr. to)/Musee Bonnat, Bayonne/The Bridgeman Art Library 41bc; Louis XIV (1638-1715) of France in the costume of The Sun King in the ballet 'La Nuit' c.1665 (litho), French School, (19th century)/Private Collection/Roger-Viollet, Paris/The Bridgeman Art Library 42br; Interior of a Forge near Huy, engraved by Jean-Baptiste Jobard (1792-1861) (tinted litho), Howen, Anton de (1774-1848) (after)/ Science Museum, London/The Bridgeman Art Library 46clb; Adoration of the Magi, 1624 (oil on panel), Rubens, Peter Paul (1577-1640)/Koninklijk Museum voor Schone Kunsten, Antwerp/Giraudon/The Bridgeman Art Library 103cr; Madonna and Child with Canon Joris van der Paele, 1436 (oil on panel), Eyck, Jan van (c.1390-1441)/ Groeningemuseum, Bruges/The Bridgeman Art Library 102-103c, 114bc; Flemish citizens fighting on foot batter the well armoured and mounted French Knights at the Battle of the Golden Spurs near Courtrai in 1302, c.1900 (colour litho), Bombled, Louis (1862-1927)/Private Collection/Archives Charmet/The Bridgeman Art Library 125br; Pieta, c.1629 (oil on canvas) (detail 179424), Dyck, Sir Anthony van (1599-1641)/Koninklijk Museum voor Schone Kunsten, Antwerp/Giraudon/The Bridgeman Art Library 153crb; Congress of Vienna, 9th June 1815 (engraving), Anon./Museo del Risorgimento, Brescia/Roger-Viollet, Paris/The Bridgeman Art Library 237clb. THE GRANGER COLLECTION, NEW YORK: 43crb, 43tc. MARKO TJEMMES: 207tc, 229ca. TOERISME VLAANDEREN: M. Decleer 121t; D. de Kievith 107t. TOURISME CHARLEROI: Gina Santin 187tr. TOURISME NAMUR: OTN/Cederik Leeuw 203tl. TOURIST OFFICE VILLE DE TOURNAI: 11tc, 26bl, 182bc. TRAVEL-IMAGES.COM: A. Umidova 225cra. ROGER VIOLLET: 42t. VLAAMSE OPERA: 135cl. PHOTO WESTTOER: David Samyn 118bl; WWW.DENDERMONDE. BE: 139br. WWW.HEUVELLAND.BE: VVV Heuvelland 127cr, 127bc. WWW.TRUSSEL.COM: Steve Trussel 219br.

All other images © Dorling Kindersley. For further information see: www.dkimages.com

Cover Picture Credits

FRONT: PHOTOLIBRARY: De Agostini Editore/W Buss. BACK: ALAMY IMAGES: nobleIMAGES cla; AWL IMAGES: Neil Farrin tl; DORLING KINDERSLEY: Demetrio Carrasco bl; PHOTOLIBRARY: imagebroker.net/Christian Handl clb. Spine: PHOTOLIBRARY: De Agostini Editore/W Buss t.

Front Endpaper: 4CORNERS IMAGES: SIME/Gräfenhain Günter tr; CORBIS: Atlantide Phototravel bc; PHOTOLIBRARY: Age fotostock/Werner Otto fcr, Imagestate Brian Lawrence fcl, Photononstop/Bernard Foubert ftr/ Yvan Travert bl.

Phrase Book

Tips for Pronouncing Dutch

The Dutch language is pronounced in largely the
same way as English, although many vowels,
particularly double vowels, are pronounced as long
sounds. *J* is the equivalent of the English *y*, while
v is pronounced *f*, and *w* is *v*.

In an Emergency

Help!	**Help!**	help
Stop!	**Stop!**	stop
Call a doctor!	**Haal een dokter!**	haal uhn **dok**-tur
Call the police!	**Roep de politie!**	roop duh poe **leet**-see
Call the fire brigade!	**Roep de brandweer!**	roop duh **brahnt**-vheer
Where is the nearest telephone?	**Waar ist de dichtsbijzijnde telefoon?**	vhaar iss duh **dikst**-baiy-zaiyn-duh-tay-luh-**foan**
Where is the nearest hospital?	**Waar ist het dichtsbijzijnde ziekenhuis?**	vhaar iss het **dikst**-baiy-zaiyn-duh **zee**-kuh-hows

Communication Essentials

Yes	**Ja**	yaa
No	**Nee**	nay
Please	**Alstublieft**	ahls-tew-**bleeft**
Thank you	**Dank u**	dhank-ew
Excuse me	**Pardon**	pahr-**don**
Hello	**Goed dag**	ghoot dahgh
Goodbye	**Tot ziens**	tot zins
Good night	**Slaap lekker**	slap **lek**-kah
morning	**Morgen**	**mor**-ghugh
afternoon	**Middag**	**mid**-dahgh
evening	**Avond**	**av**-vohnd
yesterday	**Gisteren**	**ghis**-tern
today	**Vandaag**	**van**-daagh
tomorrow	**Morgen**	**mor**-ghugh
here	**Hier**	heer
there	**Daar**	daar
What?	**Wat?**	vhat
When?	**Wanneer?**	vhan-**eer**
Why?	**Waarom?**	vhaar-**om**
Where?	**Waar?**	vhaar
How?	**Hoe?**	hoo

Useful Phrases

How are you?	**Hoe gaat het ermee?**	hoo ghaat het er-**may**
Very well, thank you	**Heel goed, dank u**	hayl ghoot, dhank ew
How do you do?	**Hoe maakt u het?**	hoo maakt ew het
See you soon	**Tot ziens**	tot zeens
That's fine	**Prima**	**pree**-mah
Where is/are...?	**Waar is/zijn...?**	vhaar iss/zayn
How far is it to...?	**Hoe ver is het naar...?**	hoo vehr iss het nar
How do I get to...?	**Hoe kom ik naar...?**	hoo kom ik nar
Do you speak English?	**Spreekt u engels?**	spraykt uw **eng**-uhls
I don't understand	**Ik snap het niet**	ik snahp het neet
Could you speak slowly?	**Kunt u langzamer praten?**	kuhnt ew **lahng**-zarmer-praat-tuh
I'm sorry	**Sorry**	sorry

Useful Words

big	**groot**	ghroat
small	**klein**	klaiyn
hot	**warm**	vharm
cold	**koud**	khowt
good	**goed**	ghoot
bad	**slecht**	slekht
enough	**genoeg**	ghuh-**noohkh**
well	**goed**	ghoot

open	**open**	open
closed	**gesloten**	ghuh-**slow**-tuh
left	**links**	links
right	**rechts**	rekhts
straight on	**rechtdoor**	rehkht dohr
near	**dichtbij**	dikht baiy
far	**ver weg**	vehr vhekh
up	**omhoog**	om-**hoakh**
down	**naar beneden**	naar buh **nay**-duh
early	**vroeg**	vrookh
late	**laat**	laat
entrance	**ingang**	**in**-ghang
exit	**uitgang**	**ouht**-ghang
toilet	**wc**	vhay-say
occupied	**bezet**	buh-**zett**
free (vacant)	**vrij**	vraiy
free (no charge)	**gratis**	**ghraah**-tiss

Making a Telephone Call

I'd like to place a long-distance telephone call	**Ik wil graag interlokaal telefoneren**	ik vhil ghraakh **inter**-loh-kaal tay-luh-foh-**neh**-ruh
I'd like to call collect	**Ik wil "collect call" bellen**	ik vhil "collect call" **bel**-luh
I will try again later	**Ik probeer het later nog wel eens**	ik pro-**beer** het laater nokh vhel ayns
Can I leave a message?	**Kunt u een boodschap doorgeven?**	kuhnt ew uhn **boat**-skhahp **dohr**-ghay-vuh
Could you speak up a little please?	**Wilt u wat harder praten?**	vhilt ew vhat **hahr**-der **praat**-ew
Local call	**Lokaal gesprek**	low-**kaahl** ghuh-**sprek**

Shopping

How much does this cost?	**Hoeveel kost dit?**	hoo-**vayl** kost dit
I would like...	**Ik wil graag...**	ik vhil ghraakh
Do you have...?	**Heeft u...?**	hayft ew
I'm just looking	**Ik kijk alleen even**	ik kaiyk alleyn ay-vuh
Do you take credit cards?	**Neemt u krediet-kaarten aan?**	naymt ew kray-deet kaart-en aan
Do you take travellers' cheques?	**Neemt u reischeques aan?**	naymt ew **raiys**-sheks aan
What time do you open? you close?	**Hoe laat gaat u open? u dicht?**	hoo laat ghaat ew opuh ew dikht
This one	**Deze**	**day**-zuh
That one	**Die**	dee
expensive	**duur**	dewr
cheap	**goedkoop**	ghoot-**koap**
size	**maat**	maat
white	**wit**	vhit
black	**zwart**	zvhahrt
red	**rood**	roat
yellow	**geel**	ghayl
green	**groen**	ghroon
blue	**blauw**	blah-ew

Types of Shops

antique shop	**antiekwinkel**	ahn-**teek**-vhin-kul
bakery	**bakkerij**	**bah**-ker-aiy
bookshop	**boekwinkel**	**book**-vhin-kul
butcher	**slagerij**	slaakh-er-aiy
cake shop	**banketbakkerij**	bahnk-**et**-bahk-er-aiy
chemist	**apotheek**	ah-poe-**taiyk**
department store	**warenhuis**	**vhaah**-uh-houws
newsagent	**krantenwinkel**	**krahn**-tuh-vhin-kul
post office	**postkantoor**	**pohst**-kahn-tor
supermarket	**supermarkt**	**sew**-per-mahrkt
travel agent	**reisburo**	**raiys**-bew-roa

Sightseeing

art gallery	**gallerie**	ghaller-ee
bus station	**busstation**	**buhs**-stah-shown
bus ticket	**ticket/biljet**	tik-et/bil-yet

closed on public holidays	op feestdagen gesloten	op fayst-daa-ghuh ghuh-slow-tuh
garden	tuin	touwn
railway station	station	stah-shown
return ticket	heen en terug	hayn-uhn-trug
single journey	enkele reis	eng-kuh-luh raiys
tourist information	dienst voor toerisme	deenst vor tor-is-muh

Staying in a Hotel

Do you have a vacant room?	Zijn er nog kamers vrij?	zaiyn er nokh kaa-mers vray
double room with double bed	een twees persoons-kamer met een twee persoonsbed	uhn tvhay per-soans-ka-mer met uhn tvhay per-soans beht
twin room	een kamer met twee bedden	uhn kaa-mer met tvhay beh-tuh
single room	eenpersoons-kamer	ayn-per-soans kaa-mer
room with a bath/shower	kaamer met bad/ douche	kaa-mer met baht/doosh
I have a reservation	Ik heb gereserveerd	ik hehp ghuh-ray-sehr-veert

Eating Out

Have you got a table?	Is er een tafel vrij?	iss ehr uhn tah-fuhl vraiy
I would like to reserve a table	Ik wil een tafel reserveren	ik vhil uhn tah-fel ray sehr-veer-uh
The bill, please	Mag ik afrekenen	muhk ik ahf-ray-kuh-nuh
I am a vegetarian	Ik ben vegetariër	ik ben fay-ghuh-taahr-ee-er
waitress/waiter	serveerster/ober	sehr-veer-ster/oh-ber
menu	de kaart	duh kaart
wine list	de wijnkaart	duh vhaiyn-kart
glass	het glass	het ghlahss
bottle	de fles	duh fless
knife	het mes	het mess
fork	de vork	duh fork
spoon	de lepel	duh lay-pul
breakfast	het ontbijt	het ont-baiyt
lunch	de lunch	duh lernsh
dinner	het avondeten	het av-vond-ay-tuh
main course	het hoofdgerecht	het hoaft-ghuh-rekht
starter, first course	het voorgerecht	het vhor-ghuh-rekht
dessert	het nagerecht	het naa-ghuh-rekht
dish of the day	het dagschotel	het dahg-skhoa-tel
bar	het cafe	het kaa-fay
café	het eetcafe	het ayt-kaa-fay
rare	rood	roat
medium	half doorbakken	hahlf door-bah-kuh
well done	gaar	gaar

Numbers

1	een	ayn
2	twee	tvhay
3	drie	dree
4	vier	feer
5	vijf	faiyf
6	zes	zess
7	zeven	zay-vuh
8	acht	ahkht
9	negen	nay-guh
10	tien	teen
11	elf	elf
12	twaalf	tvhaalf
13	dertien	dehr-teen
14	veertien	feer-teen
15	vijftien	faiyf-teen
16	zestien	zess-teen
17	zeventien	zayvuh-teen
18	achtien	ahkh-teen
19	negentien	nay-ghuh-teen
20	twintig	tvhin-tukh
21	eenentwintig	aynuh-tvhin-tukh
30	dertig	dehr-tukh
40	veertig	feer-tukh

50	vijftig	faiyf-tukh
60	zestig	zess-tukh
70	zeventig	zay-vuh-tukh
80	tachtig	tahkh-tukh
90	negentig	nay-guh-tukh
100	honderd	hohn-durt
1000	duizend	douw-zuhnt
1,000,000	miljoen	mill-yoon

Time

one minute	een minuut	uhn meen-ewt
one hour	een uur	uhn ewr
half an hour	een half uur	een hahlf uhr
half past one	half twee	hahlf twee
a day	een dag	uhn dahgh
a week	een week	uhn vhayk
a month	een maand	uhn maant
a year	een jaar	uhn jaar
Monday	maandag	maan-dahgh
Tuesday	dinsdag	dins-dahgh
Wednesday	woensdag	vhoons-dahgh
Thursday	donderdag	donder-dahgh
Friday	vrijdag	vraiy-dahgh
Saturday	zaterdag	zaater-dahgh
Sunday	zondag	zon-dahgh

Food and Drink

asparagus	asperges	as-puhj
bass	zeebars	see-buhr
beef	rundvlees	ruhnt-flayss
beer	bier	beeh
Brussels sprouts	spruitjes	spruhr-tyuhs
chicken	kip	kip
coffee	koffie	coffee
duck	eend	aynt
fish	vis	fiss
fresh orange juice	verse jus	vehr-suh zjhew
fruit	fruit/vruchten	vroot/vrooh-tuh
garlic	knoflook	knoff-loak
green beans	princesbonen	prins-ess-buh-nun
haricot beans	snijbonen	snee-buh-nun
herring	haring	haa-ring
hot chocolate	chocola	sho-koh-laa
lamb	lamsvlees	lahms-flayss
meat	vlees	flayss
mineral water	mineraalwater	meener-aahl-vhaater
monkfish	lotte/zeeduivel	lot/seeduhvul
oyster	oester	ouhs-tuh
pancake	pannekoek	pah-nuh-kook
pheasant	fazant	fay-zanh
pike	snoek	snook
pork	varkensvlees	vahr-kuhns-flayss
potatoes	aardappels	aard-uppuhls
prawn	garnaal	gar-nall
salmon	zalm	sahlm
sea bream	dorade/zeebrasem	doh-rard/zay-brah-sum
skate	rog	rog
spinach	spinazie	spin-a-jee
tea	thee	tay
trout	forel	foh-ruhl
truffle	truffel	truh-fuhl
tuna	tonijn	toe-naiyn
veal	kalfsvlees	karfs-flayss
venison	ree (bok)	ray (bok)
vegetables	groenten	ghroon-tuh
waffle	wafel	vaff-uhl
water	water	vhaa-ter
wine	wijn	vhaiyn

Tips for Pronouncing French

The Walloons and other French-speaking Belgians may display a throaty, deep accent noticeably different from French spoken in France. The vocabulary, however, is mostly the same as that used in France, with a few notable exceptions, such as the use of *septante* (instead of *soixante-dix*) for seventy.

Consonants at the end of words are mostly silent and not pronounced. *Ch* is pronounced *sh*; *th* is *t*; *w* is *v*; and *r* is rolled gutturally. *Ç* is pronounced *s*.

In an Emergency

Help!	**Au secours!**	oh sek**oor**
Stop!	**Arrêtez!**	aret-**ay**
Call a doctor!	**Appelez un médecin**	apuh-**lay**un meds**añ**
Call the police!	**Appelez la police**	apuh-**lay** lah pol-**ees**
Call the fire brigade!	**Appelez les pompiers**	apuh-lay leh poñ-**peeyay**
Where is the nearest telephone?	**Où est le téléphone le plus proche**	oo ay luh tehleh**fon** luh ploo **prosh**
nearest hospital?	**l'hôpital le plus proche**	oo ay l'opeetal luh ploo **prosh**
nearest police station?	**commissariat de police le plus proche**	oo ay luh **kom**-ee-sah-ree-**ah** deh pol-**ees** luh ploo **prosh**

Communication Essentials

Yes	**Oui**	wee
No	**Non**	noñ
Please	**S'il vous plait**	seel voo **play**
Thank you	**Merci**	mer-**see**
Excuse me	**Excusez-moi**	exkoo-**zay** mwah
Hello	**Bonjour**	boñzhoor
Goodbye	**Au revoir**	oh ruh-**vwar**
Good night	**Bonne nuit**	boñ-**nwee**
morning	**Le matin**	matañ
afternoon	**L'après-midi**	l'apreh-**meedee**
evening	**Le soir**	swah
yesterday	**Hier**	ee**yehr**
today	**Aujourd'hui**	oh-zhoor-**dwee**
tomorrow	**Demain**	duh**mañ**
here	**Ici**	ee-**see**
there	**Là-bas**	lah bah
What?	**Quel/quelle?**	kel, kel
When?	**Quand?**	koñ
Why?	**Pourquoi?**	poor-**kwah**
Where?	**Où?**	oo
How?	**Comment?**	kom-**moñ**
Now	**Maintenant**	maynt-**noñ**
Later	**Plus tard**	ploo-**tar**

Useful Phrases

How are you?	**Comment allez vous?**	kom-moñ tal**ay voo**
Very well, thank you	**Très bien, merci**	treh byañ, mer-**see**
How do you do?	**Comment ça va?**	kom-moñ sah **vah**
See you soon	**A bientôt**	byañ-toh
That's fine	**Ça va bien**	Sah vah byañ
Where is/are...?	**Où est/sont...?**	ooh ay/soñ
How far is it to...?	**Combien de kilomètres d'ici à...?**	kom-**byañ** duh keelo-**metr** d'ee-**see** ah
Which way to...?	**Quelle est la direction pour...?**	kel ay lah **dee**-rek-**syoñ** poor
Do you speak English?	**Parlez-vous anglais?**	par-lay voo oñg-**lay**
I don't understand	**Je ne comprends pas**	zhuh nuh kom-**proñ** pah
Could you speak slowly?	**Pouvez-vous parler plus lentement?**	Poo-vay voo par-lay ploos **loñ**tuh-moñ
I'm sorry	**Excusez-moi**	exkoo-**zay** mwah

Useful Words

big	**grand**	groñ
small	**petit**	puh-**tee**
hot	**chaud**	show
cold	**froid**	frwah
good	**bon**	boñ
bad	**mauvais**	moh-**veh**
enough	**assez**	as**say**
well	**bien**	byañ
open	**ouvert**	oo-**ver**
closed	**fermé**	fer-**meh**
left	**gauche**	gohsh
right	**droite**	drawht
straight on	**tout droit**	too drwah
near	**près**	preh
far	**loin**	lwañ
up	**en haut**	oñ **oh**
down	**en bas**	oñ**bah**
early	**tôt**	toh
late	**tard**	tar
entrance	**l'entrée**	l'on-**tray**
exit	**la sortie**	sor-**tee**
toilet	**toilette**	twah-let
occupied	**occupé**	o-koo-**pay**
free (vacant)	**libre**	leebr
free (no charge)	**gratuit**	grah-**twee**

Making a Telephone Call

I would like to place a long-distance telephone call	**Je voudrais faire un interurbain**	zhuh voo-**dreh** faire uñ añter-oorbañ
I would like to call collect	**Je voudrais faire un communication PCV**	zhuh voo-**dreh** faire oon kom-oonikah-**syoñ** peh-seh-veh
I will try again later	**Je vais essayer plus tard**	zhuh vay ess-ay-eh ploo tar
Can I leave a message?	**Est-ce que je peux laisser un message?**	es-**keh** zhuh puh les-**say** uñ meh-**sazh**
Hold on	**Ne quittez pas, s'il vous plait**	nuh kee-**tay** pah seel voo **play**
Could you speak up a little please?	**Pouvez-vous parler un peu plus fort?**	poo-vay voo par-**lay** uñ puh ploo for
Local call	**Communication local**	komoonikah-**syoñ** low-kal

Shopping

How much does this cost?	**C'est combien?**	say kom-**byañ**
I would like....	**Je voudrais**	zhuh voo-**dray**
Do you have...?	**Est-ce que vous avez...**	es-**kuh** voo zav**ay**
I'm just looking	**Je regarde seulement**	zhuh ruh**gar** suhl-**moñ**
Do you take credit cards?	**Est-ce que vous acceptez les cartes de crédit?**	es-**kuh** voo zaksept-**ay** leh kart duh kreh-**dee**
Do you take travellers' cheques?	**Est-ce que vous acceptez les chèques de voyage?**	es-**kuh** voo zak-sept-**ay** lay shek duh vwa**yazh**
What time do you open? you close?	**À quelle heure vous êtes ouvert vous êtes fermé**	ah kel urr voo zet oo-**ver** fer-**may**
This one	**Celui-ci**	suhl-wee **see**
That one	**Celui-là**	suhl-wee **lah**
expensive	**cher**	shehr
cheap	**pas cher, bon marché**	pah shehr, boñ mar-shay
size, clothes	**la taille**	tye
colour	**couleur**	kool-**urr**
white	**blanc**	bloñ
black	**noir**	nwahr
red	**rouge**	roozh
yellow	**jaune**	zhownh
green	**vert**	vehr
blue	**bleu**	bluh
orange	**orange**	oroñzh

pink	rose	roz
brown	brun	broñ
purple	violet	vee-oh-lay
grey	gris	gree

Types of Shops

antiques shop	le magasin d'antiquités	maga-zañ d'oñteekee-tay
bakery	la boulangerie	booloñ-zhuree
bank	la banque	boñk
bookshop	la librairie	lee-brehree
butcher	la boucherie	boo-shehree
cake shop	la pâtisserie	patee-sree
cheese shop	la fromagerie	fromazh-ree
chocolate shop	le chocolatier	shok-oh-lah-tyeh
chip stand	la friterie	free-tuh-ree
chemist	la pharmacie	farmah-see
delicatessen	la charcuterie	shah-koo-tuh-ree
department store	le grand magasin	groñ maga-zañ
fishmonger	la poissonerie	pwasson-ree
gift shop	le magasin de cadeaux	maga-zañ duh kadoh
greengrocer	le marchand des légumes	mar-shoñ duh lay-goom
grocery	l'alimentation	alee-moñta-syoñ
hairdresser	le coiffeur	kwafuhr
market	le marché	marsh ay
newsagent	le magasin de journaux	maga-zañ duh zhoor-no
post office	le bureau de poste	boo-roh duh pohst
supermarket	le supermarché	soo-pehr-marshay
travel agent	l'agence de voyage	l'azhons duh vwayazh

Sightseeing

abbey	l'abbaye	labey-ee
airport	l'aeroport	layr-por
art gallery	la galérie d'art	galer-ree dart
bus station	la gare routière	gahr roo-tee-yehr
bus ticket	billet	bee-yay
cathedral	la cathédrale	katay-dral
church	l'église	laygleez
closed on public holidays	fermeture jour ferié	fehrmeh-tur zhoor fehree-ay
garden	le jardin	zhah-dañ
library	la bibliothèque	beebleeo-tek
museum	le musée	moo-zay
railway station	la gare	gahr
tourist office	les informations	layz uñ-for-mah-syoñ
town hall	l'hôtel de ville	lohtel duh vil
train	le train	luh trañ

Staying in a Hotel

Do you have a vacant room?	est-ce que vous avez une chambre?	es-kuh voo zavay oon shambr
double room with a double bed	la chambre à deux personnes avec un grand lit	la shambr uh duh per-son uh-vek uñ groñ lee
twin room	la chambre à deux lits	la shambr ah duh lee
single room	la chambre à une personne	la shambr ah oon pehr-son
room with a bath	la chambre avec salle de bain	la shambr ah-vek sal duh bañ
shower	une douche	oon doosh
key	clef	clay
I have a reservation	J'ai fait une réservation	zhay fay oon ray-zehrva-syoñ

Eating Out

Have you got a table?	Avez vous une table libre?	avay-voo oon tahbl leebr
I would like to reserve a table	Je voudrais réserver une table	zhuh voo-dray rayzehr-vay oon tahbl
The bill, please	L'addition, s'il vous plait	l'adee-syoñ-seel voo play

I am a vegetarian	Je suis végétarien	zhuh swee vezhay-tehryañ
menu	le menu	men-oo
fixed-price menu	le menu à prix fixe	men-oo ah pree feeks
cover charge	le couvert	koo-vehr
wine list	la carte des vins	kart-deh vañ
glass	le verre	vehr
bottle	la bouteille	boo-tay
knife	le couteau	koo-toh
fork	la fourchette	for-shet
spoon	la cuillère	kwee-yehr
breakfast	le petit déjeuner	puh-tee day-zhuh-nay
lunch	le déjeuner	day-zhuh-nay
dinner	le dîner	dee-nay
main course	le grand plat	groñ plah
first course	l'hors d'oeuvres	or duhvr
dessert	le dessert	duh-zehrt
dish of the day	le plat du jour	plah doo joor
drinks	boissons	bwa-ssoñ
bar	le bar	bah
wine bar	le bar à vin	bar ah-vañ
café	le café	ka-fay
rare	saignant	say-nyoñ
medium	à point	ah pwañ
well done	bien cuit	byañ kwee

Numbers

0	zero	zeh-roh
1	un/une	uñ, oon
2	deux	duh
3	trois	trwah
4	quatre	katr
5	cinq	sañk
6	six	sees
7	sept	set
8	huit	weet
9	neuf	nerf
10	dix	dees
11	onze	oñz
12	douze	dooz
13	treize	trehz
14	quatorze	katorz
15	quinze	kañz
16	seize	sehz
17	dix-sept	dees-set
18	dix-huit	dees-zweet
19	dix-neuf	dees-znerf
20	vingt	vañ
21	vingt-et-un	vañ tay uhn
30	trente	tront
40	quarante	karoñt
50	cinquante	sañkoñt
60	soixante	swahsoñt
70	soixante-dix	swahsoñt dees
	septante	septoñt
80	quatre-vingt	katr-vañ
90	quatre-vingt-dix/ nonante	katr vañ dees nonañt
95	quatre-vingt-quinze	katr vañ-kañz
100	cent	soñ
1000	mille	meel
1,000,000	million	miyoñ

Time

What is the time?	Quelle heure est-il?	kel uhr ay-teel
one minute	une minute	oon mee-noot
one hour	une heure	oon uhr
half an hour	une demi-heure	oon duh-mee uhr
half past one	une heure et demi	oon uhr ay duh-mee
a day	un jour	uhn zhuhr
a week	une semaine	oon suh-mehn
a month	un mois	uhn mwah
a year	une année	oon annay
Monday	lundi	luñ-dee
Tuesday	mardi	mah-dee
Wednesday	mercredi	mehrkruh-dee
Thursday	jeudi	zhuh-dee
Friday	vendredi	voñdruh-dee

Saturday	**samedi**	sam-**dee**	mustard	**moutarde**	moo-**tard**
Sunday	**dimanche**	dee-**moñsh**	orange juice	**jus d'orange**	zhoo doh-ronj
			oyster	**huitre**	weetr

Food and Drink

			pancake	**crêpe**	crayp
asparagus	**asperges**	ahs-pehrj	pepper	**poivre**	pwayr
bass	**bar/loup de mer**	bah/loo duh mare	pheasant	**faisant**	feh-zoñ
beef	**boeuf**	buhf	pike	**brochet**	brosh-ay
beer	**une bière**	byahr	pork	**porc**	por
Brussels sprouts	**choux de**	shoo duh	potatoes	**pommes de terre**	pom-duh **tehr**
	bruxelles	broocksell	prawn	**crevette**	kreh-vet
bread	**pain**	pan	red wine	**vin rouge**	vañ **roozh**
butter	**buerre**	burr	salmon	**saumon**	soh-moñ
chicken	**poulet**	poo-**lay**	salt	**sel**	sel
chocolate	**chocolat**	shok-oh-lah	sausage	**saucisse**	soh-**sees**
cheese	**fromage**	from-**azh**	scallop	**coquille**	kok-eel sañ jak
coffee	**café**	kah-**fay**		**Saint-Jacques**	
draft beer	**bière à la**	byahr ah lah	sea bream	**dorade/daurade**	doh-rad
	pression	pres-**syoñ**	shellfish	**crustacés**	**kroos**-ta-**say**
duck	**canard**	kan-**ar**	skate	**raie**	ray
fish	**poisson**	pwah-**ssoñ**	soup	**potage**	poh-**tahz**
fruit	**fruits**	frwee	spinach	**épinard**	aypeenar
garlic	**ail**	eye	steak	**bifteck**	beef-**tek**
green beans	**haricots verts**	arrykoh vehr	tea	**thé**	tay
ham	**jambon**	zhañ-**boñ**	trout	**truite**	trweet
haricot beans	**haricots**	arrykoh	truffle	**truffe**	troof
herring	**hareng**	ah-**roñ**	tuna	**thon**	toñ
hot chocolate	**chocolat chaud**	shok-oh-lah shoh	veal	**veau**	voh
house wine	**vin maison**	vañ may-sañ	venison	**cerf/chevreuil**	sairf/shev-
lamb	**agneau**	ah**yoh**			rui
lemonade	**limonade**	lee-moh-nad	vegetables	**légumes**	lay-**goom**
lobster	**homard**	oh-ma	waffle	**gauffre**	gohfr
meat	**viande**	vee-**yand**	water	**l'eau**	l'oh
mineral water	**l'eau minérale**	l'oh meenay-ral	white coffee	**café au lait**	kah-**fay** oh lay
monkfish	**lotte**	lot	white wine	**vin blanc**	vañ **bloñ**
			wine	**vin**	vañ

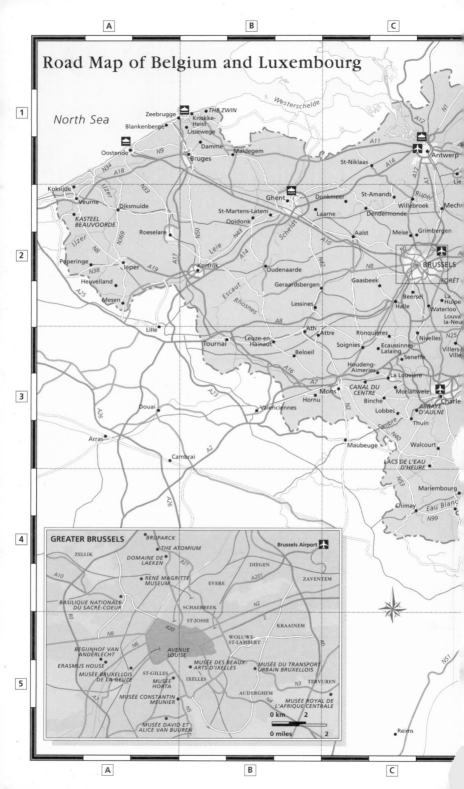